India,
Bharat
and
Pakistan

India, Bharat
and
Pakistan

THE CONSTITUTIONAL
JOURNEY OF A
SANDWICHED CIVILISATION

J. SAI DEEPAK

BLOOMSBURY
NEW DELHI • LONDON • OXFORD • NEW YORK • SYDNEY

BLOOMSBURY INDIA
Bloomsbury Publishing India Pvt. Ltd
Second Floor, LSC Building No. 4, DDA Complex,
Pocket C – 6 & 7, Vasant Kunj,
New Delhi 110070

BLOOMSBURY, BLOOMSBURY INDIA and the Diana logo are
trademarks of Bloomsbury Publishing Plc

First published in India 2022
This edition published 2022

ISBN: HB: 978-93-54353-01-7, eBook: 978-93-54354-52-6
2 4 6 8 10 9 7 5 3 1

Printed and bound in India by Thomson Press India Ltd

To find out more about our authors and books, visit
www.bloomsbury.com and sign up for our newsletters

For Amma, Appa, Akshara and Prasad

ब्रह्म वा इदमग्र आसीदेकमेव तदेकं सन्न व्यभवत्। तच्छ्रेयोरूपमत्यसृजत क्षत्रं यान्येतानि
देवत्रा क्षत्राणीन्द्रो वरुण: सोमो रुद्र: पर्जन्यो यमो मृत्युरीशान इति। तस्मात्क्षत्रात्परं नास्ति।
तस्माद्ब्रह्मण: क्षत्रियमधस्तादुपास्ते राजसूये क्षत्र एव तद्यशो दधाति सैषा क्षत्रस्य योनिर्यद्ब्रह्म।
तस्माद्यद्यपि राजा परमतां गच्छति ब्रह्मैवान्तत उपनिश्रयति स्वां योनिं य उ एनं हिनस्ति स्वां
स योनिमृच्छति स पापीयान्भवति यथा श्रेयांसं हिंसित्वा।

—बृहदारण्यकोपनिषत् 1-4-11॥

– bṛhadāraṇyakopaniṣat 1-4-11

In the beginning (before creation) this (the whole cosmos) was all indeed Bramhan, the one and only. Being the only one, He could not scaffold (the cosmos). He created, further, an excellent form, kṣatriyahood-those kṣatriyas (rulers) among the gods: Indra, Varuṇa, Soma, Rudra, Parjanya, Yama, Mṛtyu and Īśāna. Therefore, there is none higher than kṣatriyahood. Hence the brāmhaṇa upholds the kṣatriya from a lower position in the rājasūya sacrifice. He imparts that glory to the kṣatriya. The brāmhaṇa is the source of the kṣatriya. Therefore, although the king attains supremacy (in the sacrifice), at the end of it he resorts to the brāmhaṇa, his source. He who destroys the brāmhaṇa strikes at his own source. He becomes more wicked, as one is by destroying the enlightened.

स नैव व्यभवत्स विशमसृजत यान्येतानि देवजातानि गणश आख्यायन्ते वसवो रुद्रा आदित्या
विश्वेदेवामरुत इति।

—बृहदारण्यकोपनिषत् 1-4-12॥

– bṛhadāraṇyakopaniṣat 1-4-12

Yet Bramhan could not scaffold (the cosmos). He further created vaiśyas, which are called gaṇaśa, the species of gods who are designated in groups. The eight Vasus, eleven Rudras, twelve Ādityas, thirteen Viśvedevas, and forty-nine Maruts.

स नैव व्यभवत्स शौद्रं वर्णममृजत पूषणमियं वै पूषेयं हीदं सर्वं पुष्यति यदिदं किञ्च।

– बृहदारण्यकोपनिषत् 1-4-13॥

– bṛhadāraṇyakopaniṣat 1–4–13

Yet Bramhan could not scaffold (the cosmos). He further created śūdra varṇa – Pūṣan. This earth is Pūṣan. For it nourishes all this that exists.

स नैव व्यभवत्तच्छ्रेयोरूपमत्यसृजत धर्मं तदेतत्क्षत्रस्य क्षत्रं यद्धर्मस्तस्माद्धर्मात्परं नास्ति।

– बृहदारण्यकोपनिषत् 1-4-14॥

– bṛhadāraṇyakopaniṣat 1–4–14

Yet Bramhan could not scaffold (the cosmos, as he was doubtful about controlling the ferocious kṣatra). He further created Dharma. This Dharma is the controller of kṣatra. Hence, there is nothing greater than Dharma.

Contents

Acknowledgements

Ever since the release of the pre-orders for my first book, *India That Is Bharat: Coloniality, Civilisation, Constitution*, the first book of the Bharat Trilogy, on 7 July 2021, I have been constantly amazed and humbled by the reception it has received from readers in Bharat as well as abroad, who have ensured that the book remains a bestseller till date. This is not a thinly veiled attempt at self-congratulation but a genuine expression of gratitude to all the readers. The book has been embraced with extraordinary warmth and consumed in the manner it was intended to be—slowly, critically, meditatively, individually and collectively. That the readers did not let my archaic, rigid and formal style of writing (akin to legal drafting) come in the way of consumption of the ideas and contents of the book is to their credit and a testament to their faith in and patience with me. Interestingly, my decision to include extracts from sources has been received well by the readers. The subsequent dissemination of the book's ideas and contents through reviews, podcasts, group reading sessions and book club discussions has contributed more layers to the book, liminal and subliminal, which was my hope. To all of them, I have only this to say—Dhanyavadam. As for those who offered their valuable and critical feedback, from the content to the style of writing, thank you for believing that I am capable of doing better. I have attempted to incorporate as many changes as possible while writing this book. Lastly, to those who were unhappy for ideological and other reasons that a work such as this was even conceived of, produced, published and well-received— thank you for vocally expressing yourself and inadvertently enhancing the reach of the book, apart from reinforcing my faith that I have been put on the right path by the devatas.

Coming to this book, *India, Bharat and Pakistan: The Constitutional Journey of a Sandwiched Civilisation*, the process of writing it while balancing my professional schedule as an arguing counsel has come at the expense of time with my family—my parents, wife, brother and three dogs. I am grateful to them once again for being accepting of my unavailability with patience and understanding, and for silently giving me the confidence that they have my back. At a time when the institution of family is constantly under challenge, I have nothing but profuse gratitude for the continued survival of this institution and to the culture of Bharat, which has always placed a premium on it as an integral part of the dharmic way of life. I am also grateful to my relatives and friends who were patient with my prolonged silences and belated responses. To my juniors, Advocates Avinash Kumar Sharma, Abhishek Avadhani and Pranav Krishna, once again a huge thanks is owed for helping me meet my professional commitments during the day with their diligent preparation, which allowed me to attend to my writing schedule at night.

As for the final shape this book has taken, without giving too much away, all I can say is that if the first book was more conceptual and, therefore, a tad bit academic, this one is as real as it gets, even if I say so myself. As with the first book, the process of writing this one too has taught me a lot, but most importantly, it has added a greater sense of immediacy and urgency to the message underlying the trilogy—that the study of history, especially in the context of Bharat, is not and can never be a leisurely and detached academic pursuit for conscious Bharatiyas, given the existential civilisational challenges Bharat is faced with from within and outside.

Critically, I gratefully attribute the alteration of the book's originally intended scope, *after* I began writing it late last year, to an epiphany. When I shared the altered timeline and scope with my research assistants Shaktiki Sharma and Vanya Agarwal, they wholeheartedly supported it since they saw merit in it and were excited at the prospect of panoramically piecing the book together using as many sources as possible. That this alteration also resulted in heavy demands on them would be an understatement. Had it not been for their stellar support, eye for detail, uncomplaining disposition and unshakeable faith in my vision for the Bharat Trilogy, I would not have been able to see this book through within a reasonable timeframe, given my burgeoning professional commitments.

Thanks are specially owed to Praveen Tiwari and others from Bloomsbury India for burning the midnight oil to ensure that this book is released with minimal delay and without a smidgeon of compromise on the quality of the final product. In particular, Praveen's faith in my decision to alter the scope of this book and his availability for discussions at any time of the day or the week gave me the freedom I needed to do justice to the research material my team and I had collected. Kripa Raman and C. Sai Priya must be acknowledged for their fantastic editorial contributions. I must also place on record my appreciation for their efforts to understand the overall structure and flow of the book to do justice to their mandate without interfering with my vision or style of narration. I thank Syed Dilshad Ali for brilliantly executing my idea for the cover design, which had the benefit of additional inputs from Shaktiki, Akshara, JSK, Avinash and Ashish Dhar.

I am grateful to Shri Venugopalan Sankaran, Professor of Sanskrit at Sri Chandrasekharendra Saraswathi Viswa Mahavidyalaya, Kanchipuram, Tamil Nadu, for identifying the appropriate verses from the Vedas, and stotras dedicated to Devi Ma (the Divine Mother) to start and end the book with. I thank Shri Dattaraj Deshpande, Rig Veda Ghanapaati; Ami Ganatra, author; and Uma Devi Bhavaraju, Sanskrit scholar, for their translations of the Vedic verses and Devi stotras. For the final translations which have been used in the book, I thank Shri Srinivas Jammalamadaka, Assistant Professor at School of Shastric Learning, Kavikulaguru Kalidas Sanskrit University, Ramtek, Maharashtra.

Finally, I thank the devatas (in particular Durga Ma), Jagadguru Adi Shankara Bhagavatpada and the Mahaperiyavar of Kanchi Kamakoti Peetham, Jagadguru Shri Chandrashekharendra Saraswathi Mahaswamigal, for this learning opportunity and pray that they bless this sacred land, Bharat, and its dharmic civilisation with shakti (energy), vriddhi (growth) and subhiksham (abundance).

Introduction

The first book of the Bharat Trilogy, *India That Is Bharat: Coloniality, Civilisation, Constitution*, was structured in a manner so as to help Bharatiyas comprehend the construct of European coloniality so that the existence of that state of mind which afflicts the Bharatiya or Indic civilisational consciousness, to the present day, is both identified and acknowledged. To that end, based on primary sources and the work of non-Bharatiya and Bharatiya scholars, the book undertook a focused examination of the religious and racial undergirding of European coloniality and its impact the world over, Bharat being no exception, save for the degree and manner of this impact. In addition to European coloniality, the book introduced the construct of Middle Eastern coloniality and broadly summarised the ways in which it was both similar to and differed from its European counterpart. The rationale behind this was to bring to the fore the fact that unlike the Americas, Bharat has experienced two successive waves of colonisation, in particular settler colonisation, namely Middle Eastern and European, both of which have shaped its contemporary consciousness in their own distinct ways, albeit to the detriment of its indigeneity. In that context, I had taken the position that while seeking to rediscover Bharat's indigenous consciousness and reinscribe it on to its present and future, it is imperative to acknowledge the continuing existence and influence of *both* forms of expansionist colonialities whose ontology, epistemology and theology (OET)-driven animus towards Bharat's indigeneity is a matter of irrefutable and documented fact.

One of the central objectives of the first book, evident from its subtitle, was to present the birth of contemporary constitutionalism in Bharat as a continuum of the religious, social, political and economic structures established by the European coloniser in Bharat so that the politico-theological framework within which these structures operated became clear to the reader. The framework included the use of international law through application of the 'Standard of Civilisation' as the legal prerequisite for admission of countries to the international comity of 'nations'. It was demonstrated that the reshaping of Bharat into a Constitution-driven 'nation state' was not an isolated product of developments within Bharat as much as it was of Europe's (read the West's) remodelling of the world along European/Western lines. To make this case, British parliamentary debates, the circumstances leading to the establishment of the League of Nations, and the Montford Report on Indian constitutional reforms—which led to the enactment of the first British-made Constitution for Bharat, namely the Government of India Act of 1919—were delved into in some detail.

Having thus set the tone by providing a conceptual lens/framework for a more specific assessment of the impact of coloniality on the development of constitutional thought, this book, the second in the trilogy, was originally intended to take the discussion forward by examining the critical period between 1919 and 1951. This would have covered within its ambit (a) the enactment of the second British-made Constitution for Bharat, namely the Government of India Act of 1935, (b) international developments leading to the Second World War, which led to the founding of the United Nations in 1945, (c) the Partition of Bharat and the consequent creation of Pakistan, (d) the framing of the Constitution of 1950, and (e) the events leading to the first amendment to the 1950 Constitution under the stewardship of the first prime minister, Jawaharlal Nehru, aided by the first law minister, Dr B.R. Ambedkar.

However, after perusing the literature and consulting with the research team, I concluded that in order to better understand the cogitations of the Constituent Assembly between 1946 and 1950, it was imperative to panoramically view the all-important period between 1905 and 1924, which witnessed a partnership of convenience between European and Middle Eastern colonialities. Therefore, not only is it important to assess the Constitution for the impact of European coloniality, it is equally imperative to examine it for the influence of Middle Eastern coloniality. This entails a discussion on (a) the Partition of Bengal on religious lines in 1905 and its subsequent reunification in 1911, (b) the emergence of two factions within the Indian National Congress, namely the Moderates/Liberals and the Extremists/Nationalists, following the Partition of Bengal, (c) the rise of Muslim political separatism and the consequent birth of the All-India Muslim League in December 1906, (d) the constitutional entrenchment of the Two-Nation Theory through the introduction of separate electorates for Muslims through the Minto–Morley Reforms of 1909, (e) the outbreak of the First World War in 1914 and the rise of the Khilafat Movement in defence of the Ottoman Caliphate, (f) the Jallianwalla Bagh Massacre, (g) the enactment of the Government of India Act of 1919 based on the Montford Report on Constitutional Reforms, (h) the launch of the Khilafat Agitation in 1919 and the Non-Cooperation Movement in 1920 to redress the Jallianwalla Bagh Massacre and the issue of the Khilafat, (i) the outbreak of riots from 1921 to 1924, including the Moplah Outrage of 1921 in the Malabar, and (j) the end of the Khilafat Agitation in 1924, to name a few.

Critically, I realised that while the Partition of Bengal in 1905 was indeed a concrete step in the general direction of the creation of Pakistan, an analysis of the Pakistan Movement in its entirety would be incomplete without reference to the rise of pan-Islamic movements in Bharat in the eighteenth and nineteenth centuries in the aftermath of the decline of the Mughal empire following the death of Aurangzeb in 1707. This is because these movements sowed the seeds of Pakistan well before Syed Ahmed Khan or Muhammad Iqbal or Muhammad Ali Jinnah showed up on the scene. In other words, it is my case that the idea of Pakistan was born much earlier through these movements but was only given a name and effect to between 1905 and 1947.

Naturally, each of these events had varying degrees of influence on issues linked to consciousness that arose for constitutional cogitation between 1925 and 1950, such as the very identity of Bharat, the characterisation of the future Bharatiya state, the purpose and framework of the Constitution, citizenship, the discourse surrounding fundamental rights, the definition and treatment of religious minorities, and the like. Therefore, unless the period between 1905 and 1924 is made sense of, with a necessary and detailed prelude that discusses the genesis of pan-Islamic movements of the 1700s and the 1800s in the Bharatiya subcontinent, the assessment of the combined impact of European and Middle Eastern colonialities, if any, on the framing of the Constitution of 1950 would be truncated and historically uninformed.

In light of this, I have consciously redrawn the core timeline of this book to the period between 1905 and 1924 set against the backdrop of pan-Islamic movements starting from the 1740s. Consequently, in the third book of the trilogy, I will examine the combined impact of European and Middle Eastern colonialities on the evolution of constitutional thought between 1925 and 1950. While this decision of mine significantly alters the originally intended scope of this book and the next, the theme and intention remain the same as the first book, which is reflected in the title of this book, namely *India, Bharat and Pakistan: The Constitutional Journey of a Sandwiched Civilisation.* The other important objective of this book is to help the reader draw parallels between the challenges faced by the Indic civilisation during the tumultuous period of 1905–1924 on the one hand, and present-day Bharat on the other. It is my position, based on my reading, that the very same attitudes which ultimately led to the Partition of Bharat in 1947 are still alive and kicking, albeit under sanitised labels.

One of the reasons for adopting the above approach to a decolonial revisitation of the Constitution is to drive home the point that it is a document which must be understood against the backdrop of history. Yet another objective is to reinforce my position that 'Supreme' deliberations on constitutional morality, which are rooted in politico-theological frameworks that have no love lost for Indic indigeneity, are devoid of a sense of history and end up preserving constitutionalism at the expense of the civilisation. Conventional constitutional scholarship merely looks for the intent of the framers of the Constitution by sifting through the debates of the Constituent Assembly, but rarely looks for causal factors in history, particularly coloniality, which expressly birthed such intent or shaped it unconsciously. It is for this reason that before plunging headlong into the deliberations of the Constituent Assembly, I thought it necessary to first analyse the national and international developments preceding them. I hope this decision of mine aids the reader in connecting the dots between these developments, and the worldview and intent of the framers of the Constitution as distilled from the proceedings of the Constituent Assembly—a subject that shall be delved into in the third book of this trilogy.

As in the case of the first book, while it is not possible to cover every development, an attempt has been made to cover those which, evidence suggests, had or ought to have had a significant bearing upon the shaping of political thought which eventually translated into legislative action of far-reaching consequence or contributed to the evolution of contemporary constitutional thought in Bharat. Given the nature of this exercise and its end goal, which is that this book may serve as the bridge between the first and the third books, in the interest of fluidity and organisation of thought and discussion, the division of this book is based on broad timelines. Accordingly, the first section covers the period from 1740 to 1898, the second section the period from 1899 to 1909 and the final section from 1910 to 1924. A bit of back and forth between the sections is to be expected. However, in light of the feedback received to the first book from readers, I have attempted to keep the language simple, sentence construction short and the narration lucid without altering my core style of presentation. Also, drawing a lesson from decolonial thought, I have used the word 'contemporary' as a substitute for 'modern' wherever possible and applicable so as to avoid the colonial baggage that comes with the use of the latter.

While I do hope that this book proves to be a worthy sequel to the first, the larger goal remains unaltered: to exhort Bharatiyas to take history and its study seriously, especially in the context of the Constitution, so that the misplaced sense of religiosity towards the document is replaced with a sense of proportion, perspective and purpose. As always, I leave it to the reader and posterity to determine if I have succeeded in my endeavour in the service of the Bharatiya civilisation.

Section 1
1740–1898

The Seeds of Pakistan

Jama Masjid in Delhi built by Shah Jahan, from *Illustrated Handbooks of Art History of All Ages: Architecture, Classic and Early Christian* (London, 1888) by Roger Smith and John Slater

In Chapter 6 of my first book, *India That Is Bharat*, I introduced the concept of Middle Eastern coloniality and briefly touched upon its concrete manifestation in the history of Bharat, namely the birth of the idea of Pakistan. I took the view that the creation of Pakistan must be seen as part of Middle Eastern coloniality's long, troubled and continuing encounter/interaction with the Indic civilisation. The violent creation of Pakistan has been the subject of tomes of literature. So, to avoid being redundant, I intend to view it through the prism of Middle Eastern coloniality to examine its impact on the shaping of Bharat, especially its legal and constitutional infrastructure.

In popular discourse, the Partition of Bengal in 1905 on religious lines by the British is credited with sowing the seeds of the idea of Pakistan. This has created the false impression of communal harmony having existed between

Hindus and Muslims prior to the employment of the so-called divide and rule policy by the British in 1905. While British motivations behind the Partition of Bengal and their subsequent hand in nurturing the idea of Pakistan must and will be examined in some detail, an exclusive focus on British machinations creates the erroneous notion of Hindus and Muslims being equal victims of British rule, drawing attention away from express attempts to restore Islamic rule over Bharat. It bears noting that an Anglocentric approach, which gives Middle Eastern coloniality a free pass in the context of Bharat's Partition, is largely a product of the postcolonial school; this, therefore, reinforces the need for a *decolonial* approach to Bharat's history to prevent the sugar-coating of facts with generous dollops of postcolonial secularisation.

To understand the larger backdrop against which the pan-Islamic movements of the 1800s—such as the lesser-known Faraizi Movement (which was largely limited to Eastern Bengal) and the better-known Wahhabi Movement (which started in Delhi and spread to different parts of Bharat)—were set, we must travel further back in time. A clear understanding of the origins, nature, inspiration and aims of both the movements and their successors is called for in order to grasp the full extent of the psychology and pathology of Middle Eastern coloniality. I have consciously chosen to write about these movements since their profound impact on the revival of Middle Eastern coloniality's quest to regain control over Bharat is rarely mentioned, let alone discussed, in contemporary discourse, out of a misplaced sense of political correctness, aka 'Indian secularism'. This is despite the Indian Wahhabi Movement's manifest and critical contribution to the laying of a fertile ground for Islamism not just in undivided Bharat but also in the larger Indian subcontinent, the impact of which is still being felt in one way or another. Perhaps there is discomfiture in certain 'secular' quarters in recognising the fact that the Wahhabi mindset had and continues to have a strong Indian base.

In the absence of this big picture, the Bharatiya mind, which is currently buried deep under three layers of coloniality—European, Middle Eastern and Nehruvian Marxist/postcolonial—will continue to consume popular, comforting and infantile fictions. One such fiction is the existence of a 'Ganga–Jamuni tehzeeb', the much-touted composite cultural creature that is the supposed product of a syncretic relationship between Hinduism and Islam, creating the so-called unique Indian Islam. To precisely overcome these perception barriers so that facts finally have a chance to breathe and shape the truth, I will touch upon the circumstances which led to the rise of pan-Islamic movements in Bharat. While there is a larger and troubled history of Islam in Bharat which warrants examination, I have chosen to focus on the most proximal cause of the rise of such movements—the decline of the Mughal empire—which had a direct bearing on the Partition of Bharat, so as to assess the latter's impact, if any, on the making of independent Bharat's Constitution.

The other reason for choosing this period of history is that the age of monarchies and dynasties was gradually drawing to a close and the world was being reshaped on European/Western lines. Middle Eastern coloniality too had to grudgingly adapt to these changed circumstances, which translated to a greater involvement of the Muslim masses (the Ajlafs and Arzals, typically of Indian ancestry) in politics, which was hitherto the primary or perhaps even the exclusive preserve of the Muslim nobility and religious elites (the Ashrafs, who claimed non-Indian ancestry). For the purposes of this discussion, I have drawn primarily from the works of R.C. Majumdar, W.W. Hunter, H.V. Seshadri, Qeyamuddin Ahmad, Muin-ud-Din Ahmad Khan, Girish Chandra Pandey, Maulana Syed Abul Hasan Ali Nadwi, Barbara Metcalf and other authors on the subject, including researchers and academics of Pakistani origin, such as Ayesha Jalal, Sana Haroon and Yusuf Abbasi.

The Fall of the Mughal Empire and the Rise of Pan-Islamic Movements in Bharat

The disintegration of the Mughal empire, which began under Aurangzeb, largely due to his disastrous campaign in the Deccan ('the graveyard of the Mughal empire') against the Marathas and his murderous crusade against the Sikh gurus, was expedited after his death, thereby loosening the grip of Islam over Bharat significantly. The clearest sign of the terminal decline of the Mughal empire was its Balkanisation through the establishment of the Asaf Jahi dynasty in the Deccan (also known as the Nizam ul-Mulk of Hyderabad) in 1713, the Awadh dynasty under Nawab Sadat Ali Khan (Burhan ul-Mulk) in 1723 and the Bengal dynasty under Nawab Aliwardi Khan in 1740.[1] To add to it, Nadir Shah's sack of Delhi in 1739 had rendered the Mughal empire hollow and exposed its own decrepitude.[2] In less than 200 years of Babur's victory in the First Battle of Panipat in 1526, Mughal influence was largely limited to Delhi as a result of the growing power of the Marathas, the Jats, the Sikhs and the English. The Battles of Plassey (1757) and Buxar (1764), in particular, established the English as an aspiring contender for religio-political supremacy over Bharat. It was around then that the Ottoman empire too saw a general decline, with its inability to keep pace with the Habsburg and Russian empires becoming more evident.

The simultaneous decline of two avowedly Islamic empires was a cause for concern among Muslim intellectuals of the time. This churn threw up two individuals of consequence—Muhammad ibn Abd al-Wahhab (1703–1792) in central Arabia and Shah Waliullah Dehlawi (1703–1762) in Bharat, both of whom attributed the decline of their respective Muslim empires to the corrosion of their religio-social foundations.[3] Therefore, according to them, Islam was due for a 'Reformation', which meant going back to its 'pristine form' without the heresies and the deviances that had crept into its practice by virtue of its contact with the infidels. Where Christian Reformation meant going back to the basics by undoing the Catholic Church's monopoly over the 'true faith', Islamic Reformation meant recreating Islam, also 'the true faith', as it existed during the Islamic Prophet's life and time.

According to Qeyamuddin Ahmad, Wahhabis are not essentially different from the rest of the Muslims. However, they place greater emphasis on the following aspects, and here I quote Ahmad:[4]

1. *Monotheism:* God is self-existent and the Creator of all other beings. He is unequalled in his attributes. Spiritual eminence and salvation consist in strict adherence to the commands of God as given in the Quran and laid down in the *Shariat* and not in developing mystical feelings of communion and mingling in His feeling.

2. *Ijtehad:* The Wahhabis admit the right of 'interpretation' as given to the Muslims and stress the desirability of exercising this right. They hold that the followers of the four great Imams have, in effect, given up this right. Abdul Wahab wrote several treatises on the subject criticising the advocates of slavish imitation.

The opening of volume two of William Jones's copy of *al-Fatāwā al-'Ālamgīriyyah*, which has signatures/stamps of its previous owners dating back to 1782

3. *Intercession:* The Wahhabis do not believe in the theory of intercession or prayer on another's behalf, by intermediaries that might be of saintly eminence and hence supposedly nearer to God. Passive belief in the principles of Islam is decidedly insufficient.

4. *Innovation:* The Wahhabis condemn and oppose many of the existing religious and social practices for which there is no precedent or justification in the Shariat. Prominent among these are tomb worship, exaggerated veneration of *Pirs*, excessive dowries in marriages, the general show of pomp on festive occasions such as circumcision and *Milad* (celebration of the Islamic Prophet's birthday) and prohibition of widow-remarriages.

When these four salient features are read together, especially in view of the prohibition on innovation, it becomes clear that the room for ijtehad is limited since it permits only the Quran and the Hadith, as opposed to later legal treatises on Islam, to be treated as authorities so that life in contemporary times may be lived as close as possible to the lives of the earliest followers of Islam. This, as stated earlier, is to preserve the 'purity' of an Islamic life.

Wahhab's ideas influenced later Islamic movements in Bharat founded by religious leaders who had travelled to Arabia during Wahhab's lifetime or had been exposed to his teachings during their Haj pilgrimage. However, Dehlawi may be treated as the more direct progenitor of Islamic revivalism in the Bharatiya subcontinent and—incorrectly, or perhaps for the sake of convenience—this revivalism has been dubbed as Indian Wahhabism. While Wahhab's movement was named after him and his followers were called Wahhabis, the movement started by Dehlawi, which was more systematically established by his spiritual successor, Syed Ahmad Shahid Barelvi, was called the Tariqa-i-Muhammadiyyah, or the Path of Muhammad, and its followers were initially called Muhammadis. However, the latter movement too was branded 'Wahhabi' later on, in view of its similarities with the more prominent Middle Eastern variant.[5]

Some scholars have attributed the similarities between Wahhab's and Dehlawi's views to the fact that both were exposed to the works of the thirteenth-century Sunni Islamic scholar Ibn Taymiyyah as part of their education on the Hadith in Medina around the same period.[6,7] In fact, Wahhab and Dehlawi may have been contemporary students of Hadith in Medina, which could explain the similarities in their hard-line positions.[8,9] Among Taymiyyah's primary contributions to Islamic jurisprudence was his pronouncement that jihad could be waged against Muslim rulers too if they did not live as true Muslims and by the Shariat. This fatwa was issued

in the context of fighting Muslim Mongol rulers when the Muslims of the
Levant were unsure if jihad was permitted in Islam against co-religionists.[10]
Taymiyyah's views themselves were mostly drawn from the wider Hanbali
Movement in Baghdad and Syria, which started in the ninth century. This
movement insisted on literal acceptance of the Hadith, avoidance of theology,
repression of popular Sufi practices and intense criticism of corrupt (read
'un-Islamic') Muslim states.[11] Therefore, it could be said that Wahhab and
Dehlawi were proponents of Taymiyyah's Hanbalist views, which makes
Wahhabism a misnomer, and Taymiyyism or Hanbalism the more accurate
term. However, since the literature on the subject refers to the movement
as Wahhabism, and in view of its more recognised association with
Wahhab, I too shall do the same in the interest of literary consistency and
recall value.

Coming to Islamic revivalism in the Bharatiya subcontinent, Dehlawi
stands out as much for his antecedents as he does for his investment in and
contribution to the cause, which, as we shall see, influenced Muslim thought
in the subcontinent for generations to come. This includes successor 'reform'
Sunni movements such as the Ahl-i-Hadith, Ahl-i-Quran, Deobandi, Barelvi,
Nadwah, Aligarh, Tablighi[12,13,14] and Pakistan Movement.[15] Dehlawi was the
son of Shah Abdul Rahim, one of the founders of Madrasah-i-Rahimiyah
in Delhi[16] and a prominent Islamic scholar who was part of the committee
appointed by Aurangzeb to compile the *Fatawa-e-Alamgiri*. This compilation
remains the go-to commentary till date on the Shariat for Sunni Muslims of
the Bharatiya subcontinent.[17]

Dehlawi was trained by his father in Islamic studies before he (Dehlawi)
left for Arabia in 1730 for his higher education. After his return to Delhi in
1732, he wrote prolifically in Persian and Arabic, and engaged in spreading
his knowledge of Islam. In the words of Saiyid Athar Abbas Rizvi, the
following was Dehlawi's conception of Islam:[18]

> The reason which prompted Allah to create the Islamic community originally
> was, according to Shah, mainly a political one. Allah wished that no religion
> superior to Islam should exist on earth and that Islamic law including those
> regarding different forms of punishment, should be adhered to wherever
> people lived a communal life. In this regard, he stated that the chief reason for
> fixing the blood-money for killing an infidel at half that of killing a Muslim was
> necessary in order to firmly establish the superiority of the latter; moreover,
> the slaughter of infidels, diminished evil amongst Muslims.

In his work *Tafhimat-i Ilahiyya*, addressing Muslim rulers of his time,
Dehlawi's fervent exhortation to them on their duty to preserve Islamic
purity in a multi-religious society was as follows:[19]

Oh Kings! Mala'a'la' urges you to draw your swords and not put them back in their sheaths again until Allah has separated the Muslims from the polytheists and the rebellious Kafirs and the sinners are made absolutely feeble and helpless.

It is no wonder then that Dehlawi, as part of his teachings, exhorted Muslims of the subcontinent *not* to integrate into society, since contact with Hindus would contaminate their Islamic purity. He urged them to see themselves as part of the global *ummah*. To this end, although he himself was a *sanad*-holding Sunni Sufi of the Naqshbandiyah Order, Dehlawi wanted Muslims of this part of the world to rid themselves of *bida'a*, i.e. Hindu-influenced Sufi practices and mores which tended to be retained by converts to Islam from the Hindu fold.[20] In other words, only that version of Sufism which was rooted in the Quran and the Hadith was the 'right' one since it was consistent with Islam; non-Islamic and external influences were treated as un-Islamic. Here, Islamic refers to Sunni Islam, as Dehlawi had no love lost for the influence of Shias either on the Muslim identity.

He mandated that Muslims of the subcontinent follow the customs and mores of the early Arab Muslims since they were the immediate followers of the Islamic Prophet. These were his views on the subject:[21]

I hail from a foreign country. My forebears came to India as emigrants. I am proud of my Arab origin and my knowledge of Arabic, for both of these bring a person close to 'the sayyid (master) of the Ancients and the Moderns', 'the most excellent of the prophets sent by God' and 'the pride of the whole creation'. In gratitude for this great favour I ought to conform to the habits and customs of the early Arabs and the Prophet himself as much as I can, and to abstain from the customs of the Turks ('ajam') and the habits of the Indians.

Clearly, birth in Bharat alone does not make someone Bharatiya, since more than race or ethnicity, it is the consciousness of being Bharatiya that matters. As long as the consciousness refuses to embrace the Indic element, it remains alien, notwithstanding claims of accrual of nativity by birth. Dehlawi's commitment to Middle Eastern consciousness is clear from his will, in which he called upon his heirs to give up the customs of pre-Islamic Arabs and the *hunud*, which, of course, was a reference to Hindus.[22]

According to Ishtiaq Husain Qureshi, a Pakistani writer and Pakistani nationalist, Dehlawi desired Muslims of the subcontinent to keep alive their relations with the rest of the Muslim world '*so that the spring of their inspiration and ideals might ever remain located in Islam and tradition of world community developed by it*'.[23] To ensure that they learnt the Quran before they were 'contaminated' by the polytheistic practices and idolatrous beliefs of

their Hindu ancestors and neighbours, Dehlawi translated the Quran into
Persian. The Quran had hitherto been available only in Arabic and hence
required greater dependence on the *ulema*.[24] By translating it into Persian,
Dehlawi made the teachings of the Quran more accessible, in particular to
the children of commoners, converts and soldiers, because Persian was the
official language of the Mughal empire.[25]

On the political front, Dehlawi was of the view that Muslims all over the
world *needed* a central leadership in the form of a caliphate which would
serve two purposes—the first to provide permanent spiritual and temporal
guidance and the second to keep Muslim rulers under some form of unified
umbrella command.[26] He was of the view that there were two caliphates, the
outward and the inward, the former being the preserve of the state and the
latter being the preserve of the ulema. He held that the corruption of the
latter ultimately manifested as corruption in the former, and that it fell upon
the ulema to set the Islamic house in order so as to preserve the unity of the
community. Given that both Islam and Christianity belong to the family of
Abrahamic faiths, it is hardly surprising that the doctrine of two caliphates
is similar, if not identical, to the Theory of Two Kingdoms, Spiritual and
Temporal, which formed the basis of the Protestant Reformation, as discussed
in Chapter 4 of my first book.

Dehlawi's legacy includes a systematic and comprehensive exposition on
the concept, doctrine and necessity of jihad, for which he continues to be
looked up to widely.[27] According to Dehlawi, it was the doctrine of jihad
that made Islam the most perfect of all revealed religions, for it had enabled
the Islamic Prophet to conquer territories where Islam, the only true path,
could be practised.[28] Therefore, jihad was the cornerstone of sociopolitical
equilibrium in the Islamic worldview. If one were to go further back in
time, it would become apparent that apart from adopting Taymiyyah's
views, Dehlawi also took forward the work of Syed Ahmad Sirhindi, also
known as *Mujaddid-i-alf-i-sani* ('reviver' of Islam in the first millennium),
a contemporary of Akbar. Sirhindi strongly espoused the cause of Islamic
Reformation and revivalism by seeking to re-establish Islam in Bharat in its
most pristine form through strict adherence to the Shariat and by purging
it of its heresies such as Sufi mysticism and its attendant un-Islamic beliefs
and practices.[29] In short, Sirhindi wanted a state which was Islamic in both
letter and spirit. To this end, he sought imposition of poll tax on Hindus
and exhorted Muslims to subordinate non-Muslims, especially polytheistic
and idolatrous Hindus, instead of integrating with them.[30] He was against
veneration of saints, celebration of festivals and anything else which reeked
of Hinduness.

Sirhindi effectively represented the Sunni consensus against religious and cultural syncretism at all levels. However, what separated Sirhindi from Dehlawi was the times they lived in. Sirhindi lived under Akbar when the Mughal empire was at the peak of its power. The religious elites could not afford to take on the powerful emperor to put an end to his flirtations with Sufi mysticism, which came at the expense of adherence to the two pillars of Islam, namely the Quran and the Hadith. After further 'degeneration' of Islam was witnessed under Jahangir and Shah Jahan, Aurangzeb ushered in a 'purer' Islamic regime when he took over in 1659. Given his rigid adherence to pure Islam, which translated to bigotry and brutality towards non-Muslims, by and large the ulema did not feel the need for Islamic revivalism during his rule of close to half a century. The codification of the Shariat by way of the *Fatawa-e-Alamgiri* under the stewardship of Aurangzeb further cemented his position as an Islamic icon and role model worthy of emulation ('*Wali*').

In stark contrast, Dehlawi, who took forward the views and work of Sirhindi, was witness to the unstoppable crumbling and bleeding of the Islamic edifice in Bharat as represented by the Mughal empire. As someone who considered Mahmud of Ghazni as Islam's greatest ruler for having launched and sustained the first real conquest of northern Bharat,[31] Dehlawi could not bear to watch the Mughal 'empire' under the licentious and un-Islamic Ahmad Shah Bahadur (1725–1775) survive only at the mercy of the Marathas. Here is a sample of his Islamic proposals to the Mughal dynast Ahmad Shah Bahadur, which went unheeded, much to Dehlawi's angst:[32]

> Strict orders must be issued in all Islamic towns forbidding religious ceremonies publicly practised by the Infidels (such as Holi and ritual bathing in the Ganges). On the tenth of Muharram Shiis should not be allowed to go beyond the bounds of moderation and in the bazaars and streets neither should they be rude nor repeat stupid things (that is, recite tabarra or condemn the first three successors of Muhammad).

Notice how Shias, for whom Dehlawi had no love lost, could celebrate their festivals in public but in moderation, whereas Hindus had no right whatsoever to celebrate their festivals in public. However, since Ahmad Shah Bahadur had no time to attend to matters of the state, given his colourful pursuits, Dehlawi followed in the footsteps of Ibn Taymiyyah and concluded that this un-Islamic ruler had to be deposed to give effect to his larger vision, namely restoration of Islam's dominance the world over, starting with Bharat.[33] This led to fervent appeals by Dehlawi to other Muslim rulers of his time in the subcontinent, such as the Nizam in the Deccan, Najib-ud-Daula (a Rohilla Yousafzai Afghan) and Ahmad Shah Abdali (a Popalzai Pashtun) to restore the supremacy of Islam in Bharat.[34] Here is an extract from his letter to the Nizam:[35]

> It has become clear to my mind that the kingdom of heaven has predestined that kafirs should be reduced to a state of humiliation and treated with utter contempt. Should that repository of majesty and dauntless courage (Nizam al-Mulk) gird his loins and direct his attention to such a task he can conquer the world. Thus the faith will become more popular and his own power strengthened; a little effort would be profoundly rewarded. Should he make no effort, they (the Marathas) would inevitably [be] weakened and annihilated through celestial calamities and in such an event he would gain no credit ... As I have learnt this unequivocally (from the divine) I spontaneously write to draw your attention to the great opportunity I laid before you. You should therefore no[t] be negligent in fighting jihad.

However, the Nizam's subsequent treaty in 1738 with the Marathas which secured for the latter the whole of Malwa from the Mughal emperor disheartened Dehlawi.[36] After Nadir Shah's sack of Delhi in 1739–1740, Dehlawi was pushed to concentrate his energies on Abdali. In one of his earliest letters to Abdali in 1757, Dehlawi expressed great satisfaction at the former's destruction of Mathura but was equally disappointed with the sack of Delhi.[37] On the eve of Abdali's expected campaign in late 1759 against the Marathas after the latter captured power from Delhi to Attock, Dehlawi once more wrote to Abdali at length. This time, he invited Abdali to invade Bharat to check the resurgent Hindu power represented by the Marathas and the Jats.[38] In fact, he gave Abdali a detailed description of the respective strengths and weaknesses of both the Marathas and the Jats.[39] The following are a few extracts from Dehlawi's letter to Abdali:[40]

> We beseech you (Durrani) in the name of the Prophet to fight a jihad against the infidels of this region. This would entitle you to great rewards from God the Most High and your name would be included in the list of those who fought jihad for His sake. As far as worldly gains are concerned, incalculable booty would fall in the hands of Islamic ghazis and the Muslims would be liberated from their bonds. The invasion of Nadir Shah who destroyed the Muslims left the Marathas and Jats secure and prosperous. This resulted in the infidels regaining their strength and in the reduction of Muslim leaders of Delhi to mere puppets.

While inviting Abdali to invade Bharat, Dehlawi was careful to request the protection of Muslims, Sunni and Shia, from the invading army:[41]

> When the conquering army arrives in an area with a mixed Muslim–Hindu population, the imperial guards should transfer the Muslims from their villages to the towns and at the same time care for their property. Financial assistance

should be given by governments to the deprived and the poor as well as the Sayyids and the ulama. Their generosity would them become famous [sic] with prompt prayers for their victories. Each town would eagerly await the arrival of the Islamic army ('that paragon of bounty'). Moreover, wherever there was even the slightest fear of a Muslim defeat, the Islamic army should be there to disperse infidels to all corners of the earth. Jihad should be their first priority, thereby ensuring the security of every Muslim.

The above extracts speak volumes of the saintly legacy of Dehlawi. To ensure against a repeat sacking of Delhi by Abdali, Dehlawi implored Najib-ud-Daula to protect the Muslims of Delhi upon entry of the invading Afghan army.[42] Of course, none of these entreaties were paid heed to by either Abdali or Najib, and Delhi was sacked once more after Abdali's victory at Panipat with the help of Najib. Also, much to Dehlawi's disappointment, Abdali returned to Afghanistan after the battle, while Najib ruled Delhi as the Mughal empire's regent from 1761 until his death in 1770.[43] In 1762, Dehlawi passed away a broken man. Although Panipat brought to a halt the Peshwa-led growth of the Maratha empire in the north-west of Bharat, Abdali himself suffered huge losses and sued for peace with the Marathas after the battle.[44] The Marathas remained the pre-eminent power in Bharat until their defeat at the hands of the British East India Company in the Third Anglo-Maratha War of 1818.

After Dehlawi's death, his son Shah Abdul Aziz Dehlawi (1746–1824) took up the mantle. In 1803, after the Battle of Delhi between the British and the Marathas, the British gained control over Delhi, which led to the Fatawa-e-Azizi being issued by Shah Abdul Aziz.[45,46] The fatwa declared all of Bharat Dar al-Harb, or House of War, in control of the infidels.[47] However, the fatwa's position in relation to Muslim attitudes towards the British seemed ambivalent, for it took note of the fact that although Christian rule extended from Calcutta to Delhi, the religious affairs of Muslims were largely left untouched. Therefore, while some members of the Muslim community interpreted the fatwa as a pragmatic approach to the changed political realities, others interpreted it as a call to jihad. According to Ayesha Jalal, Shah Abdul Aziz's pragmatism may have been a consequence of the fact that the British returned the lands belonging to his family.[48]

While there was confusion among the Muslim community in northern Bharat owing to the Fatawa-e-Azizi's equivocation, or perceived equivocation, around this period, other parts of the country saw the rise of pan-Islamic movements that shared the goal of restoration of Islamic supremacy over Bharat. In his seminal work *History of the Freedom Movement in India*, historian R.C. Majumdar discusses various armed movements in

Bengal against the British that were inspired by religion, such as the Sanyasi Rebellion and the Faraizi Movement.[49] Of these, the latter is of relevance to the discussion at hand because it marked the revival of Islamism in Bengal less than a century before the province's partition in 1905 on religious lines.

The Faraizi Movement was founded by Haji Shariatullah, a resident of Faridpur, then in Eastern Bengal and now in Bangladesh.[50] Shariatullah (1781–1840) went to Arabia at the age of eighteen to perform the Haj and returned to Bharat twenty years later.[51] Around 1820, he started a reformist movement among the Muslims of Eastern Bengal along the same lines as the Wahhabi Movement in Arabia. While Majumdar caveats that there is no evidence to suggest that Shariatullah was directly influenced by the teachings of Wahhab, we may safely make this presumption based on the fact that the former's period of stay in Arabia overlapped with the period when the Wahhabi Movement thrived thanks to the patronage of the Saud dynasty. Also, it is not possible to dismiss the similarities in beliefs and attitudes of Wahhab and Shariatullah as mere coincidence. According to Ayesha Jalal, Shariatullah, like Dehlawi, was an admirer of Arab culture, so much so that he ordered his followers to eat grasshoppers since they resembled the locusts eaten by his Arab co-religionists.[52]

Similar to Shah Abdul Aziz's response to the British takeover of Delhi, Shariatullah declared Bengal under British rule as Dar al-Harb,[53] which is conveniently interpreted by a few contemporary scholars as purely an expression of anti-colonial resistance or patriotic rebellion, in the same way Tipu Sultan's wars with the British are now portrayed. However, such a portrayal would be not only incorrect but also incomplete since it deliberately ignores the place and the role of the Faraizi and similar movements within the larger canvas of the long-term project to restore Islamic reign over Bharat.[54] The goal of the Faraizi Movement may also be discerned from the atrocities meted out by Shariatullah and his faithful against Hindus, which predictably included the breaking of idols of Hindu deities, destruction of Hindu temples and the slaughter of cows.[55]

After Shariatullah, his son Muhsinuddin Ahmad (aka Dudhu Mian) took this campaign forward in a much more systematic fashion until his death in 1860. Dudhu Mian established his headquarters in Bahadurpur (Bengal) and divided Eastern Bengal into circles called *halqahs*, appointing a deputy (Khalifa) in each halqah to bring more Muslims under his influence, to collect contributions and to convert Hindus to Islam.[56] He rallied the peasants (predominantly Muslim) against the landlords (largely Hindu) and the British. The Faraizi Movement lost steam when Mian was arrested in

1857 as a precautionary measure and kept in Alipore Jail, from where he was released in 1859, rearrested and finally released in 1860, shortly before his death. Predictably, the Faraizi Movement has also been characterised by contemporary scholars as a 'peasant rebellion' aimed at 'oppressive landlords', which is not surprising given that the very same template has been used to portray the Moplah Riots, as we shall see later. However, in light of their integral religious character and their stated goal, which was never hidden or glossed over by the dramatis personae themselves, the more realistic way of looking at such movements is that the banner of Islam was used to unite people with the intention of 'reclaiming' what was seen as Muslim territory held by the usurpers, namely the British and the Hindus.

What is critical to note is the merger of the Faraizi Movement in Bengal and Dehlawi's school of thought, which is attested to by the renowned historian Dr Tara J. Chand in his book *History of Freedom Movement in India*. Dr Chand states that the Faraizi Movement was strengthened by the '*appearance and collaboration of the followers of Syed Ahmad Shahid, a disciple of the School of Waliullah of Delhi, and the leader of Mujahids in Bengal*'.[57] This is a reference to Saiyid Ahmad of Raebareli, better known as Syed Ahmad Shahid or Syed Ahmad Barelvi (1786–1831), who is credited with laying the foundations for a pan-India Wahhabi network in a systematic manner. Qeyamuddin Ahmad, whose work on the Wahhabi Movement in Bharat is considered an authority, also observed that the Faraizi Movement should not be understood as an isolated phase but must be '*studied in the wider background of the general Wahhabi Movement*' in Bharat.[58] According to Qeyamuddin, the Faraizi Movement ultimately merged with the Wahhabi Movement under Barelvi's disciple Mir Nisar Ali, aka Titu Mir (1782–1831),[59] who aided the spread of Wahhabism in Eastern Bengal and is most well known for leading the Barasat Rising of 1831. Pertinently, it is parts of Eastern Bengal that later became East Pakistan in 1947 and Bangladesh in 1971.

The Wahhabi Movement under Barelvi must be understood along three broad timelines—the first from the 1820s until Barelvi's death in Balakot in 1831, the second from 1831 to 1858, and the third from 1858 to 1902. While there exists a fair degree of scholarship on the movement, which readers may peruse on their own, my specific objective is to draw attention to the long memory (both territorial and temporal) of Middle Eastern coloniality as reflected by the Wahhabi Movement, its modus operandi and the fact that this mindset still thrives, albeit under different names, thanks to its OET-driven memory, organisation and persistence.

Syed Ahmad Shahid 'Barelvi' (1786–1831)

Born in 1786 in Raebareli, Barelvi was the thirty-sixth direct descendant of Hasan, the son of Ali (who was the cousin and son-in-law of the Islamic Prophet),[60,61] according to scholars. Barelvi came under the tutelage of Dehlawi's son, Shah Abdul Aziz Dehlawi, in 1806, who, in turn, sent Barelvi to his brother Shah Abdul Qadir Dehlawi for training in Islamic studies.[62] He was also initiated into the Qadiriyya, Naqshbandiyya and Mujaddidiyya Sufi Orders by Shah Abdul Aziz himself.[63] After attaining the status of Khalifa, Barelvi returned to Raebareli in 1808, married and lived there for two years.[64] He was back in Delhi in 1811 when Shah Abdul Aziz encouraged him to start his career as a preacher and mercenary under another well-known mercenary of the time, the Nawab of Tonk, Amir Khan Pindari,[65] under whom Barelvi spent close to seven years and developed a reputation as a camp sage after the preaching he undertook.[66] However, the rising power of both the Sikhs under Maharaja Ranjit Singh and the English made it difficult for Barelvi to continue earning his livelihood as a mercenary.[67] Disapproving of the Nawab entering into peace negotiations with the British, he quit his employ and returned to Delhi in 1817.

This time, members of the Dehlawi family, such as Maulana Abdul Hai and Maulana Muhammad Ismail, also known as Shah Ismail Dehlawi (grandson of Waliullah and nephew of Shah Abdul Aziz), were taken in by his personality, his vision and his direct approach to dealing with the decline of Muslim state power. Accordingly, they pledged allegiance to him and urged him to resume preaching with the blessings of Shah Abdul Aziz.[68] Abdul Hai and Shah Ismail Dehlawi would later compile Barelvi's lectures as *Sirat-i-Mustaqeem,* and become his close companions in his Movement until their deaths in 1828 and 1831 respectively.[69] Seeing that his own family members, including his grandson and future successor Shah Muhammad Ishaq Dehlawi (1778–1846), rejected his more pragmatic vision,[70] Shah Abdul Aziz had to anoint Barelvi as the spiritual successor to his father's vision of restoring Tariqa-i-Muhammadiyyah in Bharat and its status as Dar al-Islam, knowing full well that Barelvi's preferred means was a physical or armed jihad.[71,72,73]

Building on Dehlawi's teachings, Barelvi extended the concept of bida'a to include those accretions to Islam which were the consequence of association with Shiites as well as all non-Muslims, whom he referred to as '*Mushrikiyn*'. He asked Muslims to '*follow the example of Muhammad of Arabia and relinquish all the customs of India, Iran and Rome*'.[74] Although Barelvi largely rejected Sufi accretions to Islam, he retained one—the Sufi tradition of *bay'at/baiát,*

A portrait of the scene of the death of Islamic scholar and military leader
Sayyid Ahmad Shahid at the hands of the Sikh Khalsa during the Battle of Balakot

or the pledge of the student and seeker of enlightenment at the hand of a teacher and spiritual guide.[75] This was originally a tradition followed in private. However, using this tradition widely and publicly, Barelvi initiated followers to his movement, a practice that would become a signature part of the Movement even after his death. His preaching, which started in Delhi around 1818, took him to Muzaffarnagar, Saharanpur, Deoband, Gangoh, Nanautah, Rampur, Bareilly, Shahjahanpur, his home town Raebareli, Allahabad (now Prayagraj), Benares (now Varanasi), Kanpur, Sultanpur and Lucknow, among other places.[76,77] In Lucknow, Barelvi met Maulvi Wilayat Ali of the Sadiqpur family of Azimabad (now Patna).[78] Wilayat Ali and his younger brother Enayat Ali (the 'Ali Brothers', not to be confused with the Ali Brothers of the Khilafat Movement) would later go on to spearhead the Wahhabi Movement after Barelvi's death in the Battle of Balakot in May 1831.

Barelvi's preaching tours gave him an insight into the lifestyle of the Muslim ruling elite, whom he saw as un-Islamic.[79] This shaped his decision to invest in the Muslim masses for the cause of jihad. Fortunately for him, his vehement call for practice of Islam in its purest form and for complete abandonment of Indian accretions which had arisen as a product of Muslims' interactions with the infidels (namely the Hindus) found significant traction among Rohilla Muslims, who flocked to him in vast numbers.[80] This was not surprising, considering that Najib-ud-Daula too was a Rohilla Pathan and the Third Battle of Panipat had taken place barely sixty years earlier. In case there existed an 'Indian version' of Islam and if there indeed was a Ganga–Jamuni tehzeeb, it was looked down upon and rejected by influential members of the Muslim community since the syncretism was largely the product of the Hindu ancestry of the converts. This means that what passes off as syncretism was and remains significantly the product of a nouveau convert unable to let go of his Hindu roots, which cannot be construed as Islam having acquired a distinct Bharatiya flavour or as revealing its malleability upon contact with Bharat. In any case, this 'syncretic culture' was given up by the masses, or at least by a significant number of them, at the first call to return to Islam 1.0, the *din*, the 'true religion'. So much for 'Indian Islam'.

Coming back to Barelvi, upon his return to Raebareli after his preaching tours, the growing clout of the Sikhs in Punjab and the diminishing power of the Muslims in the region occupied him a great deal and he began emphasising the need for large-scale militarisation of the Muslim community, which he led by example by bearing arms on his person.[81] In July 1821, he undertook the Haj pilgrimage, and on his way to Mecca visited Calcutta via Azimabad (Patna from now on).[82] By this time, the growing numbers at Barelvi's disposal necessitated a system of organisation and also gave him the luxury of implementing his Dehlawite vision. With the support of the Ali Brothers of the Sadiqpur family, Barelvi created a vast and organised network of carefully chosen stationary and roving preachers through the establishment of a permanent centre at Patna.[83] There, Barelvi appointed four Khalifs and a high priest—the aforementioned Ali Brothers, Maulvi Marhamat Ali, Maulvi Furhat Hussain and Shah Muhammad Hussain, respectively.[84] These Khalifs were sent to different parts of Bharat, in particular to Bombay, Madras, Hyderabad, Bihar and Bengal to spread Barelvi's message and to attract more Muslims to his cause.[85]

From Patna, Barelvi travelled to Calcutta in September 1821, which was a turning point in the history of the Wahhabi Movement and of Islam in Bengal a little under a century before its partition on religious lines in 1905. Barelvi's arrival renewed religious fervour among the Muslims of Bengal, including the descendants of Tipu Sultan (whose family had great relations with Barelvi's ancestors),[86] and elsewhere, who saw him as the prophesied Imam Mahdi and were drawn to him. While Shariatullah's Faraizi Movement had already created conditions conducive for a rousing reception for Barelvi in Bengal, the appearance of Barelvi in Bengal had a multiplier effect, which continued long after the deaths of Barelvi, Shariatullah and Shariatullah's son Dudhu Mian.

From Calcutta, Barelvi left for Mecca and performed the Haj in 1822. After performing the Haj a second time,[87] he returned to Raebareli in April 1824, where he stayed until 1826.[88] During this period, once again the diminishing power of the Muslims in Punjab, including the Pathans, under Maharaja Ranjit Singh troubled him, for it had implications for the survival of Muslim power in Afghanistan and Bharat.[89] To address this, Barelvi followed in Dehlawi's footsteps and urged the Nizam of Hyderabad, Prince Kamran of Herat, Amir Nasrullah of Bukhara and various Pathan tribes in the North-West Frontier (NWF) to 'liberate' Bharat from the hands of the British and Hindu infidels.[90,91]

Of these, only the Pathan tribes in the NWF responded enthusiastically to Barelvi's call for jihad to re-establish Islam as the dominant power in Bharat, and Mubariz ud-Daula, brother of the Nizam of Hyderabad Nasir ud-Daula, became his ardent follower.[92,93] In addition to the Pashtun tribesmen, thanks to the efforts of Bengali Muslim scholars such as Maulana Abdul Hakim of Chittagong, Sufi Noor Mohammed of Meer Sarai and Maulana Imamuddin of Noakhali, who were influenced by Barelvi during his visit to Bengal, thousands of Bengali Muslim youth too would travel all the way to the NWF to participate in the jihad later declared by Barelvi against the Sikhs.[94] This response of the common Muslim convinced Barelvi that the solution lay in investing in the Muslim community at large, namely the Ajlafs and Arzals. Clearly, Sirhindi's call for Islamic Reformation and revivalism during Akbar's era, which was taken forward by Dehlawi and Shah Abdul Aziz after Aurangzeb's death, was driven into the heart of the Muslim society in Bharat and in the larger Indian subcontinent by Barelvi.

In view of the promised cooperation by the Afghan tribes in the NWF, coupled with the fact that other Muslim countries were closer to this region,[95] Barelvi left Raebareli in January 1826 for the NWF. However, before his departure, he is said to have visited the Patna centre once more to put in place a permanent arrangement for supply of men, money and material for the proposed jihad against the Sikhs.[96] In this regard, two of the Khalifs, namely the Ali Brothers, showed huge potential for organisation. They established a number of subordinate branches in Bengal, Bombay, Bihar and the Deccan, which were assigned to their respective local missionaries. The missionaries, in turn, were responsible for *zakat* collection from their respective branches, which was sent to the NWF via Patna. As we shall see later, the organisation and its network created by the Ali Brothers would long survive the deaths of Barelvi and the brothers themselves.

Coming back to Barelvi, in late 1826, he reached Ghazni and camped at the mausoleum of Mahmud Ghaznavi, the plunderer of Somnath.[97] That Barelvi who lived in the eighteenth–nineteenth centuries felt a kinship with Mahmud of Ghazni who lived eight centuries before him should come as

no surprise since it demonstrates the ability of Middle Eastern coloniality to
see common cause for Islam, regardless of region, ethnicity or nationality.
Further, Barelvi's ancestor, Shaikh-ul-Islam Syed Qutubuddin Muhammad
al-Madani, had arrived in Bharat via Ghazni with a group of mujahidin,
which may explain Barelvi's affinity for the region.[98] From Ghazni, Barelvi
made his way to Kabul and finally to Nowshera, which became the base of his
operations.[99] He then proceeded to issue a formal summons, a fatwa calling
for jihad, to Muslims all over the plains of northern Bharat where he had
followers thanks to his preaching tours. Here is an extract from the English
translation of the fatwa:[100]

> The Sikh nation have long held sway in Lahore and other places. Their
> oppressions have exceeded all bounds. Thousands of Muhammadans have
> they unjustly killed, and on thousands they have heaped disgrace. No longer
> do they allow the Call to the Prayer from the mosques, and the killing of cows
> they have prohibited. When at last their insulting tyranny could no more be
> endured, Hazrat Sayyid Ahmad (May his fortunes and blessings ever abide!),
> having for his single object the protection of the Faith, took with him a few
> Musalmans, and, going in the direction of Cabul and Peshawar, succeeded in
> rousing Musalmans from their deep slumber of indifference, and nerving their
> courage for action. Praise be to God, some thousands of believers became
> ready at his call to tread the path of God's service; and on the 21st December
> 1826, the Jihad against the Infidel Sikhs begins.

Thus began a series of bloody battles, starting with the Battle of Akora
between the Wahhabis under Syed Shahid Ahmad Barelvi and the Sikhs under
Maharaja Ranjit Singh, which would go on until the annexation of Punjab by
the British in 1847—i.e., even after Ranjit Singh's death in 1839 and after
Barelvi's death in 1831 at the Battle of Balakot. Interestingly, in 1827, Barelvi
wanted to 'liberate' Kashmir from the Sikhs, which was, however, foiled
by the legendary Sikh commander Hari Singh Nalwa.[101] It was during this
period that Barelvi came in touch with Syed Omar Shah and Syed Akbar
Shah of Sittana in the NWF, who were the descendants of Qambar Ali of
Tirmiz, known for having accompanied Babur to Bharat.[102] Thanks to the
unwavering support of the Syed brothers and their successors, Sittana would
go on to become the most important centre for the Wahhabis in the NWF.

By June 1830, the mujahidin under Barelvi made significant progress,
despite frequent setbacks, and had Peshawar under their control.[103] A de
facto Wahhabi state had come into existence, with an army of close to one
lakh soldiers committed to the cause of jihad.[104] Naturally, this was a matter
of concern for Maharaja Ranjit Singh, who brought to bear his diplomatic
skills by driving a wedge between the Pathan and non-Pathan Muslims in

Barelvi's army.[105] This culminated in a bloodbath between the two factions, which Barelvi himself barely escaped. The feud was partially contributed to by Barelvi's own attempts at 'reforming' the Pathans by demanding that they give up their customs.[106,107] This internal rivalry weakened Barelvi's position significantly. Finally, on 6 May 1831, at the Battle of Balakot, with Prince Sher Singh leading the Sikhs, Barelvi was beheaded and Shah Ismail Dehlawi too was killed.[108]

Readers may note that it is against this backdrop that Balakot in the NWF, now known as the Khyber Pakhtunkhwa Province in present-day Pakistan, continues to be relevant to Bharat and the subcontinent at large, since its role in indoctrinating and training jihadis remains unchanged. Here are the opening lines from Ayesha Jalal's book *Partisans of Allah: Jihad in South Asia*:[109]

> Balakot is in many ways the epicenter of jihad in South Asia. Blanketed by green, terraced fields and thick, dark forests, this beautiful town is situated about eighteen miles from the city of Mansehra in the North West Frontier Province (NWFP) of Pakistan. Situated on the banks of the river Kunhar, it serves as a gateway to the picturesque Kaghan Valley, which is bounded on the east and the south by Kashmir. It is also a point of entry into the history of jihad, struggle in the way of Allah, in the subcontinent. It was here that Sayyid Ahmad of Rai Bareilly (1786–1831) and Shah Ismail (1779–1831), quintessential Islamic warriors in South Asian Muslim consciousness, fell in battle against the Sikhs on 6 May 1831.

This passage also underscores the historical significance of the surgical airstrikes undertaken by the Indian Air Force in Balakot in 2019 in response to the Pulwama suicide bombing. That the seeds for this terror network were sown by Barelvi in the 1800s needs to be pointed out, given the present-day tendency to look at certain incidents in isolation instead of identifying the existence of a thought continuum. Interestingly, the followers of Barelvi have not forgotten their history, whereas those who were the object of hatred of Barelvi and his mujahidin seem to suffer from a short memory. Ultimately, history tends to reward those with a long collective memory.

Growth of the Wahhabi Movement after Barelvi (1831–1858)

After the death of an influential icon and figurehead such as Barelvi, one would have expected the Wahhabi Movement to wither away. However, the genius behind Barelvi's vision was the *permanent* organisational network he put in place with the help of the Ali Brothers from Patna who took over the reins of the Movement after his death. It is important to clarify that

Barelvi's death did not end the relevance of the NWF to Bharat or to the Movement. On the contrary, the NWF's role as the hammer was cemented further, owing to the fact that Syed Akbar Shah of Sittana offered refuge to the remaining mujahidin[110] who were helmed by Barelvi's successor, Sheikh Muhammad Phulti.[111] Sittana and Patna had become the two focii of the Wahhabi Movement. While the former provided a base for launching jihad, the latter provided the organisational base for coordination and supply of ideologically indoctrinated men, capital and material resources, which ensured continuity, notwithstanding the death of a figurehead. In a sense, a Raktabīja (one whose every drop of blood is seed in itself) had been created, especially given that the larger Muslim society, in particular the masses, had been made stakeholders in the Movement through religious, economic and physical participation. For several years after Barelvi's death, it was a practice in Muslim families, especially in northern Bharat, to either earmark a portion of their earnings as their contribution towards jihad or to send their men to participate in the war at least for a few months.[112] This is not so different from the present-day trend of individuals from certain communities being sent to fight for the ISIS.

After Barelvi's death in 1831, the Movement and its operations were reorganised and given a fresh lease of life by the Ali Brothers.[113] As stated

The child maharaja of Lahore Duleep Singh enters his palace in Lahore from the Parade Ground accompanied by an escort of British troops commanded by Brigadier Cureton following the First Anglo-Sikh War (1845–1846)

earlier, Wilayat Ali (the elder of them) and Enayat Ali were responsible for spreading its base in Bihar, Bengal, Bombay and the Deccan, and ensured its continuity at least until 1915. The contribution of the brothers was so significant that Patna became to the Movement what Delhi was under Waliullah.[114] While Wilayat Ali focused his energies on Bombay and the South, Enayat Ali invested heavily in the NWF and Eastern Bengal, which would strengthen Muslim separatism in Bengal and lead to its partition on religious lines in 1905, as we shall see later. Wilayat assumed charge of reorganisation of the Movement and the younger brother exhorted members of his community to avoid all forms of interaction and transaction with the *kafirs*, including the state apparatus set up by the British.[115] The core idea was to make Muslim society independent of the Hindus (including and especially the Sikhs) and the British in every manner. The local masjid became the centre of Muslim life, where disputes between members of the community were resolved. In this regard, in Eastern Bengal, Enayat certainly benefited from the fertile ground created by the earlier Faraizi Movement, which had a lot in common with the Wahhabi Movement.

The Ali Brothers also evolved a mechanism for grooming the next generation. At the Patna centre, students who showed an aptitude for Islamic studies were educated in it, whereas those inclined more towards action were given only basic training in Islam and sent to the NWF to take part in the war against the infidels, namely the 'Hindu Sikhs' and the English.[116] Apart from the permanent centre in Patna, the Movement also depended on roving preachers to convey its message to the masses in different parts of Bharat as well as for collection of funds, which would be pooled in at the Patna centre. For transmission to the NWF, a series of halting places were established, manned by highly trustworthy members, thereby making the passage safe for the men and the money. Further, to protect the secrecy of the Movement, written communication was avoided as much as possible. Instead, the organisation relied on the implicit understanding among its members who were deeply committed to the cause. Where written communication became necessary, codes using numbers, names and events from Islamic history were used for communication.[117]

Having thus laid a strong foundation for all aspects of the Movement, the Ali Brothers stepped up the ante after the death of Maharaja Ranjit Singh in 1839,[118] when the British were occupied with the Afghans until 1842. In the general anarchy that prevailed in the lead-up to and after the defeat of the Sikh empire in the First Anglo-Sikh War of 1845–46, which also resulted in the Dogras taking charge of Kashmir under the Treaty of Amritsar, the Wahhabis under Enayat Ali and Syed Akbar Shah of Sittana made it difficult for both the Sikhs and the Dogras to hold on to their respective territories.[119] In fact, in 1843, Enayat Ali was sent from Bengal to the NWF by Wilayat since the latter believed that the time was ripe to recapture territories lost to the Sikhs in 1831.[120] Accordingly, between December 1845 and September 1846, Balakot and twenty-two other forts were captured by the Wahhabis under Enayat Ali from the Sikhs.[121] Shortly thereafter, in September 1846, Wilayat Ali left Patna and joined his younger brother in the NWF, underscoring their belief that the stage was set for a decisive showdown with the English. By this time, the English had taken over most of Punjab and the de facto Wahhabi state was helmed by Enayat as its Emir, with Wilayat acting as the head of the Wahhabi community.[122]

The Wahhabi campaign against the British started with the Battle of Doob Pass soon after Wilayat's arrival at the NWF, which proved to be disastrous for the Wahhabis.[123] The battle resulted in the surrender of the Ali Brothers and their subsequent transfer to Patna in late 1847 with surety bonds of Rs 10,000 each, being furnished on condition that they would not leave the city for the next four years.[124,125] However, by September 1849, Wilayat was back in the NWF, and by November 1850, Enayat joined him, and both reached Sittana in January 1851.[126,127] Except for Furhat Hussain, their younger brother who was left in charge of the organisation in Patna, the rest of the Sadiqpur family too joined the brothers in the NWF.[128] This also underscores the fact that until early 1851, except for knowledge of the figureheads of the Wahhabi Movement, the British Government was still unaware as to the true extent of the organisation and spread of the Wahhabi network under the stewardship of the Patna centre.

At this juncture, it may be relevant to point out that a few scholars like Babu Rajendra Prasad (in his work *India Divided*) have expressed reservations about the British government's supposed ignorance of the network until 1852.[129] Citing Syed Ahmed Khan, Rajendra Prasad was of the view that the British government was aware of the Wahhabi network but chose to ignore it since the ire of the Wahhabis was directed at the Sikh empire up until the defeat of the latter at the hands of the British. Therefore, according to Prasad, the British government conveniently looked the other way until the Wahhabi problem became its own problem, and then suddenly 'discovered' the existence of the network. Rajendra Prasad believed this to be the British 'divide and rule' policy in action. While this might be true to an extent, Prasad's sympathetic view of the Wahhabis could be characterised as more expedient rather than factual for the following reasons.

First, from the preface of the book *India Divided*, which was originally published in January 1946, it is clear that it was written in the backdrop of

Congress's efforts to placate the leaders of the Pakistan Movement. This explains the premise of the book, namely the claim of the existence of a Hindu–Muslim syncretic culture prior to the arrival of the British and their wily games. That this is the book's objective is also evident from Prasad's tendency to focus excessively on British machinations without accepting the truth of pan-Islamic movements, and their widespread acceptance within the Muslim community. Critically, nowhere does Prasad attempt to examine Barelvi's stated goal to re-establish Bharat as Dar al-Islam based on Dehlawi's vision of Tariqa-i-Muhammadiyyah. After all, Dehlawi's vision was necessitated more by the rising power of the Marathas and Jats, and not of the British, and by the 'contamination' of Islam through contact with Hindus.

Second, if the British indeed wished to feign ignorance of the network only as long as it tormented the Sikhs, that would be illogical, as the Sikhs were a spent force for all practical purposes following Maharaja Ranjit Singh's death in 1839, or at least by 1846. Prasad does not explain British inaction against the Wahhabis between 1839 and 1846 or even thereafter until the network's existence came to light in 1852.

Third, Prasad fails to acknowledge that surely the British could not have been under the misconceived notion that a network which was being nurtured *within* British Indian territory would pose a threat solely to the Sikhs and never turn on it. After all, in Bengal, Patna and other parts of the country, local Wahhabis did indeed create trouble for the British, the Baraset and Patna uprisings being clear cases in point. Such being the case, if the British were indeed aware of the nexus between the network and such uprisings, nothing explains their inaction. Finally, even latter-day authors like Qeyamuddin Ahmad were of the view that until 1852 the British were either unaware of the existence of a countrywide network of a single organisation or did not take it seriously despite local authorities bringing it to their notice. Pertinently, Qeyamuddin, who was clearly sympathetic to the Wahhabi cause and who could have blamed the vilification of the Wahhabis on British opportunism, states as follows in his book:[130]

It has already been shown that ever since 1839, and more particularly since 1852 local officers from such far-flung places as Hazara, Patna, and Rajshahi had been drawing the attention of the Provincial Governments as well as the Government of India to the existence of 'a remarkable nest of emigrants from Hindustan' on the Frontier as also to their 'treasonable activities' inside the country. The apprehensions of the local authorities were not fully shared by the higher authorities. However, it is worth noting that the Lieutenant Governor of Bengal himself had recorded a Minute, dated 26th August 1852,

observing that 'a correspondence exists between Patna and the fanatics in
Sittana and Swat ...' and that '... it was expedient to watch the conduct and
proceedings of the parties implicated.' To hold in face of all this, that nothing
was alleged against the Wahabis is curious indeed. The fact is that the higher
authorities exhibited, in the beginning, a peculiarly shortsighted attitude of
complacency in regard to the Wahabi activities. The inexorable logic of facts
as also the hard knocks taken by the English forces in the Ambeyla Campaign
opened the eyes of these 'august authorities', at a later stage, to the true extent
of the danger.

In light of this passage, I must disagree with Rajendra Prasad and the
secularised school of thought he represents, as I tend to agree with the view
that until 1852 the Wahhabis managed to operate successfully under the
radar to a very large extent. In 1852, a 'treasonable correspondence' from the
Wahhabis to the British troops, specifically to the 4th Native Infantry stationed
in Rawalpindi, was seized by the British authorities.[131] The correspondence
revealed the existence of an organisation which could supply men and arms
all the way from Bengal to the NWF. Around the same time, in August 1852,
the magistrate of Patna reported an alarming rise in the number of Wahhabis
in the city. The British government gradually realised the magnitude of the
problem on its hands, and by autumn 1852, Lord Dalhousie recorded two
important minutes on the subject, the first of which directed a close watch on
the internal organisation of the Movement, and the second a proposal for a
war in the NWF.[132] Following this, in 1853, a number of Muslim soldiers in
the British Indian Army were convicted of treason.

Interestingly, by this time the Ali Brothers had developed differences of
opinion on the means of achieving their objective and the timing of it.[133]
Wilayat was of the view that the English were more powerful and organised
than the Sikhs and must not be confronted without adequate preparation,
which Enayat disagreed with. Eventually, Enayat yielded to his elder brother
and moved to Mangalthana, returning to take charge only after Wilayat's
death at the age of sixty-four in November 1852. With his more cautious
sibling out of the way, Enayat went about implementing his vision, only to
realise over the course of the next half a decade that his brother's assessment
had been correct. Enayat passed away a broken man in Chinglai in March
1858.[134]

The period between Wilayat's passing and Enayat's passing covers two
important milestones—the first the initiation of a series of campaigns by the
Wahhabis against the British under the leadership of Enayat, and the second
the Sepoy Mutiny of 1857. As regards the first, Enayat's premature and
ill-prepared campaigns against the British awakened them to the extent of the

Wahhabi resolve and network all over British India. As regards the second, there have been attempts by a few scholars to give the impression that the Wahhabis supported the Sepoy Mutiny by harassing the British in the NWF during the Mutiny, which may not be entirely factually accurate.

It is true that the events of 1857 allowed Enayat Ali the opportunity to harass the British, but he and the rest of the Wahhabis were clear that their goals were not the same as those of the mutineers of Meerut or Delhi. On this, R.C. Majumdar categorically states that it is not surprising that the Wahhabis as a body practically kept aloof from the Mutiny of 1857. He underscores the fact that while the Wahhabis did attack the British before and after the Mutiny, they stayed out *during* the most eventful period of the Mutiny, thereby demonstrating the non-alignment of goals between the Wahhabis and the mutineers. Given that the Wahhabis were vastly more organised compared with the mutineers, the latter would have benefited from the former *if* their end goals had been the same. According to Majumdar:[135]

> The only satisfactory explanation seems to be that the Wahhabis favoured a purely Islamic movement and did not like to co-operate with the Hindus. This view is supported by the conduct of a number of individual Wahhabis who joined mutineers at Delhi. They (Wahhabis) printed and published a Proclamation, inviting all Mahomedans to arm and fight for their religion. A futwa was also published, declaring that it was the duty of all Mahomedans to make religious war, and that otherwise their families and children would be destroyed and ruined.

Clearly, the aloofness of the Wahhabis during 1857 was consistent with their central and stated belief that Bharat was Dar al-Harb as long as it was ruled by non-Muslims, and the British and the Hindus/Sikhs were both infidels in their eyes. Therefore, any attacks by the Wahhabis on the English during 1857, if any, must be seen as strategic furtherance of *their* stated goals by taking advantage of the Mutiny, and not as an expression of solidarity or identity of purpose with the mutineers. Further, Qeyamuddin points out that while Enayat Ali used the Mutiny to his advantage by increasing the pressure on the British in the NWF, the rest of the organisation and its vast network within British Indian territories lay low to avoid being exposed.[136]

On the claim that Wahhabis must be seen as having waged the first war of independence against the British, the following were Majumdar's views:[137]

> The uninterrupted steady flow of men and money from the eastern part of India, across its whole breadth to the NWFP, at a time when the British authorities were vigilant in their watch against the Wahhabi activities, indicates a highly developed organization to which there is no parallel in the history of the revolutionary movement against the British during the nineteenth century.

To the Wahhabis belongs the credit for the first organized attempt on a large scale to drive out the English after they had established their paramountcy in India. The Wahhabis are regarded by some as having waged the first national War of Independence of India against the British. But it has certainly no claim to be called national in the sense in which we understand the term today. For it was a struggle for freedom, of the Muslims, and by the Muslims. The basis of the movement was religious rather than political, and its inspiration came from communal and not patriotic sentiments. It may be called the first war of independence in India, but not of India—independence of Muslims in India, but not of the people of India. For as shown above, the Wahhabis fought for the establishment of dar-ul-Islam i.e. restoring the Muslim sovereignty in India, not for setting up a Government in which all Indians would be treated as free citizens. The object of the founder, as mentioned above, was to liberate India from the English as well as other infidels. No wonder, the Hindus, as a body, kept themselves severely aloof from the long-drawn struggle.

Clearly, the communal nature of the Wahhabi Movement and its strategic considerations explain its aloofness from the Mutiny. However, this did not translate to its own success against the British, since, as stated earlier, Enayat Ali's zealous impulsiveness resulted in a series of defeats, so much so that the Wahhabis starved for food and survived on roots and leaves. Enayat himself died in March 1858 after a bout of starvation-induced illness. With this, the career of the Ali Brothers came to an end and the Wahhabi Movement once again found itself in want of leadership. Interestingly, while Majumdar is of the clear view that the Wahhabi Movement was primarily communal in nature, and not national, Qeyamuddin Ahmad says this in the context of Enayat Ali's death:[138]

> Thus ended the career, under conditions of acute distress, of one who, having dedicated himself to the noble cause of freeing his country from foreign thraldom, had left behind a happy and affluent home. The least we owe to his memory is to acknowledge his position in the history of the achievement of our country's freedom.

In light of the origins, motivations and the history of the Wahhabi Movement, I tend to agree with Majumdar and not with Qeyamuddin Ahmad, on the communal nature of the Movement. It must be fairly obvious to any reasonable person by now that the history of the Wahhabi Movement does not lend itself to the kind of wishful secularisation that Ahmad resorts to, despite his own detailing of the express religious motivations of the founder of the Movement and his central stated goal—to bring back 'pure' Islam in all its pristine glory and to re-establish the rule of Islam over Bharat as envisaged by Shah Waliullah Dehlawi. This tendency to secularise history by branding documented facts as 'communal' has operated to the detriment of Indic consciousness and can be seen in present-day narratives as well.

Exposure of the Wahhabi Network and the Law of Sedition (1858–1902)

After the death of Enayat Ali, the leadership devolved upon a group of three—Ikramullah, Nurullah and Mir Taqi. Ikramullah died soon after in battle, while the other two held the reins. Once the dust of the Sepoy Mutiny had settled and the British were able to divert their attention away from Delhi, they decided to deal with the Wahhabi threat on the Frontier. Here, the numbers prove the seriousness with which the British addressed the Wahhabi problem. Until 1857, the British undertook sixteen expeditions, and a total of 33,000 regular troops had been sent to the NWF. By 1863, twenty expeditions were undertaken and about 60,000 regular troops were sent to the NWF, excluding the irregular auxiliaries and police.[139] In addition to this, the Sepoy Mutiny and the British clampdown on any and all activity suspected as treasonable affected the regular and smooth supply of men and material from Patna to the NWF without detection by the British.

A major campaign by the British against the Wahhabis was launched in 1858 under Sidney Cotton, who attacked them with 5,000 men, and with

An illustration of Thomas Babington Macaulay from *The Life and Letters of Lord Macaulay* (New York, 1876) by George Otto Trevelyan

success.[140] The Wahhabis were driven away from Sittana and the area was handed back to the local tribes, the Jaduns and the Usmanzais, on condition that they would not let the Wahhabis use their territory for any anti-British activity. However, the Wahhabis regrouped in 1861 and launched raids from Malka, which was thirty-five miles from Sittana.[141] During this period, after Nurullah's death, Maqsud Ali was the head of the Wahhabis until his death in 1862. After that, Wilayat's son, Abdullah Ali, took charge of the group while the Patna centre was headed by Alhamdullah. Abdullah Ali would go on to head the Movement until 1901.

By July 1863, the Wahhabis regained Sittana, and by September of that year a formal declaration of jihad was issued once again, calling on all Muslims to join the war against the English infidels.[142] The British realised that a war with the Wahhabis was now unavoidable. In October 1863, under the stewardship of General Neville Chamberlain, the British launched what has since come to be known as the Ambeyla campaign, which proved to be a near disaster since the British underestimated the Wahhabis, both in terms of their numbers and resolve. Taking a cue from the tactics of Maharaja Ranjit Singh, it was only through diplomacy and inducements that the British were able to buy off some of the tribes, which left the Wahhabis isolated and easier to deal with. After the defeat of the Wahhabis, the British burnt down the Malka settlement. The British themselves suffered close to 1,000 casualties while the Wahhabis and the tribes lost close to 3,000.[143]

As a consequence of the Ambeyla campaign, the Punjab government was forced to declare that the Wahhabis represented a permanent source of danger to British rule in India.[144] In fact, the crackdown on the organisation within British Indian territory, which was aided by serendipity too (as we shall see shortly), began a few months before the launch of the Ambeyla campaign and was spurred on by the bitter lessons from the campaign. Apart from launching more punitive expeditions on the Frontier, between 1863 and 1883 a number of Wahhabi leaders were arrested and prosecuted for, among other things, waging war against the Queen under Section 121 of the Indian Penal Code as it existed then.[145] By 1870, which is the year most scholars treat as the end of the Wahhabi Movement, it lacked the same vigour, with most of its top leadership being arrested, convicted and sent off to the Andamans. Among the most popular trials that took place were the Ambala Trial of 1864 and the Patna Trial of 1865. The former, in particular, is a textbook case of serendipity and makes for an interesting read.

In May 1863, a Pathan police sergeant at Panipat, Ghuzzan Khan, came across a group of Muslims who appeared to be from Bengal and were moving up the Grand Trunk Road.[146,147] Upon being questioned, they confirmed that they were indeed from Bengal and were on their way to the Frontier to take part in the jihad against the British government and invited the sergeant to join them too. The sergeant promptly arrested them; however, they were later acquitted on the grounds that they were bona fide travellers. Offended by their acquittal, Khan sent his son to the Frontier, undercover, to learn everything about the Wahhabi state. The son learnt of the existence of a vast network of Wahhabis all over the country and informed his father, who passed on the information to the Punjab government. This triggered an investigation by the government, which resulted in the organisation's existence, its modus operandi and its Patna connection coming to light,[148] leading to the Patna Trial of 1865,[149] which, in turn, led to the Malda Trial of September 1870 and the Rajmahal Trial of October 1870.[150] In September 1871, Justice Norman, the Chief Justice of Bengal who had presided over the appeal proceedings of the Patna Trial, was mortally wounded in the court premises in Calcutta by a Muslim assassin.[151] Four months later, in February 1872, the Viceroy, Lord Mayo, was fatally stabbed by an Afghan, Sher Ali, in the Andamans.[152]

It is critical to understand that while arrests, trials and convictions of several individuals connected with the Movement went on until 1883, the British were not able to fully dismantle the structure put in place by the Ali Brothers in the 1830s; this was due to the mainstreaming of the Wahhabi mindset and their methods of operating under the radar.[153] As for the Wahhabi presence on the Frontier, they continued to support the hill tribes in their battles against the British, according to Qeyamuddin Ahmad. After Abdullah Ali's death in 1901,[154] his brother Abdul Karim took over the reins and merged the activities of the centre with local politics.[155] He remained the Emir of the Wahhabis until 1915, and after his passing Abdullah Ali's grandson Nimatullah assumed charge.[156]

For the purposes of the discussion at hand on the pathology and psychology of Middle Eastern coloniality which significantly influenced Bharat's journey, the brief look at the Wahhabi Movement undertaken here should suffice since it has showcased the ability of Middle Eastern coloniality to resuscitate itself and operate in obscurity. In view of this, it would be a mistake to treat military defeats, imprisonment or even deaths of leaders as signalling the end of movements such as the Wahhabi. Barelvi's foresight of investing in the community by making its members stakeholders through participation had effectively ensured a constant source of replenishment and rejuvenation. Hence, my earlier comparison of his creation with Raktabīja from the Hindu puranas.

While I am not sure if such a mentality can be tackled solely by means of remedies which operate in the realm of law, it may be of interest to note that the provision relating to sedition was inserted in the Indian Penal Code through an amendment in 1870 primarily to deal with the Wahhabi threat. While sedition was provided for as Section 113 in the draft Penal Code prepared by the First Law Commission under T.B. Macaulay, for some unaccountable reason sedition was omitted when the Penal Code was enacted in 1860. Finally, it was inserted as Section 124A in the Penal Code by way of an amendment which came into force on 25 November 1870. Until then, Section 121 of the Code, which penalised waging war against the Queen, had been invoked against Wahhabi leaders and anyone else who was involved in any act of attempting to overthrow the British government. If there already existed a provision under which the Wahhabis were being prosecuted, what was the need for a separate provision such as Section 124A?

It appears that the introduction of the provision was necessitated by the fact that the existing provisions of the Indian Penal Code at that time did not deter seditious acts that did not amount to waging war against the Queen. In other words, the British government wanted to penalise seditious preaching, fundraising and recruitment activities by the Wahhabis. This is reflected in the views of E.C. Bayley, then Secretary to the Home Department, Government of India, who felt that the law needed amendment to deal with these 'agents of sedition', namely the Wahhabis.[157] This is corroborated by the English jurist James Fitzjames Stephen, who introduced the 1870 amendment to insert Section 124A in the Indian Penal Code before the Imperial Legislative Council. The following are the relevant extracts from his submissions, made in the third person, before the Council in support of the amendment:[158]

> Finally, he (James Stephen) wished to observe that if anyone thought that there was absolutely no occasion for any law of this kind, he ought to look back to incidents which happened not many weeks ago. *A man was convicted and sentenced to transportation for life, substantially for committing the very offence at which this section was directed: it was preaching a Jehad or holy war against Christians in India.* He (James Stephen) had carefully read the evidence and supposing it to be true, it proved that this person was in the habit, for weeks and months and years, of going from village to village and preaching in every place he came to, that it was a sacred religious duty to make war against the Government of India. Is that to be permitted, or is it not? If anyone really meant to say that it was no crime to go into villages and tell the people that a rebellion against the Government was a sacred duty, he could not argue with such a person. But if such conduct was admitted to be a crime, he would ask any person who objected to the proposed section to frame a better one. *Besides*

the man to whom he had referred, there were eight other men under commitment at Patna, who were charged with very similar offences.

Having referred to this matter of the Wahhabi conspiracy, he had just one more remark to make on the subject. We had all seen, in the newspapers published both in England and in India, accounts of disaffection created by that conspiracy represented in a very formidable manner. It was his belief, however, that although the matter was one which ought not to escape the attention of the Government, and which certainly had been shown to exist, yet it was the easiest thing in the world to exaggerate its importance and extent. He had read with great pain—and he was very glad to have an opportunity of disavowing and denying—an imputation made by some papers against the general loyalty of the Muhammadan population of India. These imputations were most unfounded and unjust, and he believed that the only class of persons who deserved them were one of those sects of fanatics who were to be found in every creed. Fanaticism was by no means peculiar to the Muhammadan religion. No one who had seen or read much of the world in which we lived, could find it in his heart to speak with disrespect of any of the great religions which had gained affections of the mankind; and he would not say one word against a religion which had preached, with unequalled efficiency, the great cardinal doctrine that lay at the root of all creeds. But it was a common misfortune of all [c]reeds that in every religion there were those who would carry their theories to extreme results, to an extent inconsistent with peace and good order. His Lordship knew better than most of us, that there was no class of people in the world who had greater public virtues of every kind than the Roman Catholics, and there were no better men and women in private life. But there was a way of looking at the Roman Catholic creed which had been adopted by some persons, and which was inconsistent with real allegiance to the civil Government. And the same might be said with regard to the Protestant religion, although it had been the very life of many European nations, and especially of our own. There had been Protestant fanatics who had been fully as dangerous as Roman Catholics. We had had those who believed that the Pope ought to be able to depose Kings, and we had also had those who preached that there was no King but Jesus, and that they, and they alone, were his representatives. There were some who entertained the opinion that peace between the Muhammadan population and their Christian rulers, however just, was a thing impossible, and that it was a religious duty to make war under such circumstances. He could only say on this subject, that if people would declare war against mankind, they must take the consequences.

It was not with regard to them that he wished to speak. He wished to speak more particularly of the degree in which that doctrine had been rejected by the great body of the Muhammadans. He could not of course enter upon technical questions as to the provisions of the Muhammadan law, but he wished to state as publicly as possible that the Government of this country had no suspicions of the Muhammadan community as such, and knew how to distinguish between the rash opinions of a small and obscure sect, and the sentiments of the vast Muhammadan population, as expressed in the papers he had before him on the subject. He had several letters, but he would only read one: it was the opinion of a large number of Maulavis upon the question of the lawfulness of a Jehad in British India, which he would read to the Council:

'The Mussulmans here are protected by Christians, and there is no Jehad in a country where protection is afforded, as the absence of protection and liberty between Mussulmans and infidels is essential in a religious war, and that condition does not exist here. *Besides, it is necessary that there should be a probability of victory to Mussulmans and a glory to the Islam. If there be no such probability the Jehad is unlawful.*'

The concluding sentences of the futwa were to the effect that, if a Christian were oppressive and did not afford protection, a Jehad would be lawful if there was a probability of success. Upon this he need say nothing more than that it was much like the common European opinion, that when a Government is very bad, the question whether rebellion is justifiable is mainly a question of prudence. In the present case this question did not arise. The substance of the first part of the futwa was that a Jehad was unlawful against a Government which afforded, and by people who had accepted, protection. Whether this opinion was really contained in the Koran and the traditions, was not for him to say; but this he would say most emphatically, that the common good sense and common good feeling of the whole human race would justify it. [Emphases added]

While James Stephen was more understated in his views about the true intention behind the introduction of Section 124A, the subsequent debates on sedition that took place in relation to its further amendment in 1898 were much more forthcoming. On 18 February 1898, Alexander Mackenzie, Lieutenant Governor of Bengal, had the following to say before the Imperial Legislative Council in the context of amendments being proposed to Section 124A:[159]

It is difficult to say anything now when following 17 other speakers in a debate like this, but I am unwilling to give a silent vote in favour of this Bill, both on account of its intrinsic importance and because there has been so much misapprehension as to its true scope and import, especially in Bengal, where the outcry against it has been particularly noisy, almost at times hysterical, the result, it may be feared, in some cases, of a specially guilty conscience. Much of that misapprehension ought to be removed by the speeches to-day of the Hon'ble Legal Member and other Members of this Council, but I feel it to be my duty to express clearly the view that I take of the measure. Sir Fitzjames

Stephen in 1870 explained how by an extraordinary oversight it came to be omitted from the Code as originally passed. He showed that sections dealing with sedition had been drafted both by the original Code Commission and by Sir Barnes Peacock, and that the section drafted by Sir Barnes Peacock, the weight of whose authority will always be acknowledged, was not only more severe than the section prepared by the Code Commission, but more severe than the measure which he then invited the Council to pass. Under Sir Barnes Peacock's section not only were such feelings of disaffection banned as were likely to induce the people to resist the authority of Government, but such feelings as were likely to lead them to disobey that authority, and the mere omission to do what you were told to do was disobedience. *To any one who remembers the conditions of 1870, and who carefully reads Sir F. Stephen's speeches, it will be manifest that what the Government had in its mind at that time was the Wahhabi conspiracy and the open preaching of jehad or religious war against the Government. Sir F. Stephen framed his proposals to meet that exigency, and his purpose was to bring the Code more or less into harmony with the law of England as he then read it.* He admitted, however, that the law of England, though similar to the proposed section, was in reality far more severe ... [Emphasis added]

The intent behind the introduction of Section 124A was once again reiterated on 5 March 1913 by Chakravarti Vijayaraghavachariar before the Imperial Legislative Council.[160] At this stage, I will not delve into the cogitations undertaken in the Constituent Assembly of 1946 in relation to Section 124A, but suffice it to say that the framers of the Constitution were of the considered view that although Section 124A must be retained, its enforcement must be consistent with contemporary jurisprudence, which had enhanced the burden on the state to prove sedition.[161]

Returning to the discussion at hand, did the enactment of Section 124A in 1870 stamp out the Wahhabi network and its activities fully? Qeyamuddin Ahmad points out that even a full decade after the introduction of Section 124A, the Wahhabis continued to operate in Bhopal, Rangoon, Bihar and other places using the same template laid down by the Ali Brothers, namely through gathering of recruits, collection of funds and incitement of those within the state apparatus to revolt against the infidel state.[162] In any case, an organisation can be wiped out, and perhaps even a movement can be cracked down on so long as it operates under the same banner. But how does one deal with a pervasive ideology or a mindset, especially one capable of assuming different names and shapes to achieve the same goal? This brings us to the primary ideological spawns of the Wahhabi Movement, namely the Ahl-i-Hadith, Deobandi, Barelvi, Nadwah and Aligarh Movements.

The Ahl-i-Hadith, Deobandi, Barelvi, Nadwah and Aligarh Movements

By the 1850s, especially in the aftermath of the Rebellion of 1857, the British establishment was constantly on the lookout for traitorous and treasonous conduct. Upon the existence of the Wahhabi network coming to light between 1852 and 1863, the trials involving Wahhabis, starting with the Ambala Trial of 1863, drew a lot of public attention. This had two paradoxical and almost simultaneous consequences—first, the Wahhabis and their cause attracted more sympathisers from the Muslim community, and second, the word Wahhabi had become synonymous with 'disloyal Muslim subject', which could result in legal prosecution. Therefore, even those that agreed with the cause of the Wahhabis or were followers already, consciously avoided embracing that specific label and instead founded their own respective movements and organisations, all or most of which treated Shah Waliullah Dehlawi as their *rahnuma*, or ideological guide. In his book, *British Paramountcy and Indian Renaissance*, R.C. Majumdar states: '*... the reform movement initiated by Saiyid Ahmad Barelvi and his pupils gained fresh strength after the Mutiny and manifested itself in different garbs.*'[163]

The modus operandi of these successor movements and their objectives may be garnered from the actions of Shah Muhammad Ishaq Dehlawi, the

A mosque of Darul Uloom Deoband, 1928

grandson of Shah Abdul Aziz who took over the affairs of the Dehlawi seminary, Madrasah-i-Rahimiyah, after Aziz's passing. Much before the rise of the Khilafat sentiment and the Khilafat Movement in the run-up to the First World War, Shah Muhammad Ishaq Dehlawi attempted to establish contact with the Sultan of Turkey to advocate for a larger struggle for Muslim freedom. He set up a committee under Maulana Mamluk Ali Nanautawi which arrived at the conclusion that, given the changed political realities, impotent armed struggle must be given up in favour of Islamic education and that the time had come for the readjustment of political goals and methods. In the book *Muslim Politics and Leadership in South Asia, 1876–92*, Muhammad Yusuf Abbasi writes:[164]

> In view of changed political circumstances, it was felt that the time had come to bring about a readjustment of political goals and methods. So they sought to train an elite that would keep alive the spirit of Islam and love of freedom among the Muslim community. These aims it was thought, could be achieved by establishing a dynamic system of religious education and immunizing the Muslim mind against the taint of Western culture. They shifted the centre of their activities from Delhi to Mecca. This change of scene also marked a change of approach. In fact, Mamluk Ali was responsible for 'putting the collective movement of Imam Wali Ullah on the new path'.

Also, in order to deal with the 'changed political circumstances', these successor movements strategically avoided naming Syed Ahmad Barelvi, and instead identified with his spiritual and ideological predecessor, namely Dehlawi. Not that avoiding Barelvi and identifying Dehlawi as their guide showed them in better light, since Dehlawi's animus towards Hindus was well documented. It is against this backdrop that the founding and strategy of the successor movements must be contextualised, since they were clearly rooted in Dehlawite thought.

Further, such spin-off movements would reiterate their commitment to the two pillars of Islam, the Quran and the Hadith, and espouse the discarding of so-called syncretic (read Hindu) accretions and un-Islamic variants of Sufism, thereby once again exposing the apocryphal and tenuous nature of the Ganga–Jamuni tehzeeb and 'Indian Islam'. Some of these movements would go on to establish madrassas to institutionalise the teachings of Dehlawi, albeit without using the Wahhabi label or actively waging armed jihad.

Others, realising the futility of taking on the might of the British empire openly, would go to the extent of attempting to prove their credentials as loyal subjects of the British who did not see a conflict between the practice of Islam and their status as British subjects, as long as the former was left untouched. A few others, the so-called modern and Westernised Muslims, would go a step further to establish institutions which blended Islamic education with English education so that Muslims did not lag behind the Hindus in access to positions of power under the British. The Ahl-i-Hadith, Deobandi, Barelvi, Nadwah and Aligarh Movements broadly fell into these baskets.

While there were (and are) internal and nuanced differences among these Sunni reformist movements on several issues, including on the meaning of jihad and in their attitudes towards the British, what is relevant to the discussion at hand is that they were largely in agreement with Dehlawi with respect to the need for removal of Sufi excesses (the Barelvi Movement being an exception) and Shia/Hindu influences from the practice of Islam and the long-term goal of restoration of Islamic sovereignty over Bharat. Only the form and means of achieving these objectives had changed in adaptation to the contemporary realities and to avoid their being nipped in the bud. The following were the leading individuals with direct or indirect relationships with the Dehlawi school of thought, who went on to found their own movements and institutions/organisations:

1. Maulana Syed Mohammed Nazir Hussain Muhaddith Dehlavi (1805– 1902): Founded the Ahl-i-Hadith Movement along with Nawab Sidiq Hasan Khan Bhopali (1832–1890); was a student of the Sadiqpur Madrasah in Patna and the Dehlawi school under Shah Muhammad Ishaq Dehlawi.[165]

2. Maulana Muhammad Qasim Nanautawi (1833–1879) and Maulana Rashid Ahmed Gangohi (1826–1905): Founded the Deobandi Movement; were mentored by Maulana Mamluk Ali Nanautawi and Haji Imdadullah, the latter of whom was closely associated with the Dehlawi family and the Mujahidin Movement. Nanautawi and Gangohi, who hailed from the eponymous towns which Barelvi had visited as part of his preaching tour, established the seminary in Deoband which was modelled after Dehlawi's Madrasah-i-Rahimiyah.[166]

3. Ahmad Raza Khan (1856–1921): Founder of the Barelvi Movement; traced his intellectual lineage to Dehlawi but considered Shah Abdul Aziz as the renewer of Islam of the thirteenth-century Hijri (Muslim calendar).[167]

4. The founders of Nadwatul Ulama in Lucknow looked up to Dehlawi.

5. Syed Ahmed Khan (1817–1898): Founder of the Aligarh Movement and one of the earliest proponents of the Two-Nation Theory; was a student of the Dehlawi school.[168]

Given that there exists a fair degree of standalone literature on these movements, which readers can peruse on their own, in this chapter I will outline the movements only to the extent of demonstrating my premise:

namely that the Shah Waliullah Dehlawi school of Hanbalist/Taymiyyist/ Wahhabi thought was taken forward by them; and its corollary—that there existed the thought continuum of Middle Eastern coloniality. In later chapters, I will touch upon these movements when a reference to them becomes relevant, especially in the context of the Khilafat Movement.

The Ahl-i-Hadith Movement

The Ahl-i-Hadith Movement was founded by Maulana Syed Mohammed Nazir Hussain Muhaddith Dehlavi and Nawab Sidiq Hasan Khan Bhopali when it cleaved into a distinct group in 1864 from the Tariqa-i-Muhammadiyyah/Wahhabi Movement and established separate mosques, madrasas and seminaries. As mentioned earlier, Syed Nazir Hussain spent his formative years at the Patna centre of the Ali Brothers, where he had the opportunity to see Barelvi and his followers in person during the heyday of the Wahhabi Movement.[169] Subsequently, he became a disciple of Shah Muhammad Ishaq Dehlawi, who helmed Madrasah-i-Rahimiyah after Shah Abdul Aziz's passing. According to the scholar Bashir Ahmad Khan, after the Mutiny of 1857, it became clear to Syed Nazir Hussain that physical jihad against the British was suicidal,[170] and so the Ahl-i-Hadith Movement was founded to avoid their being equated with the Wahhabis. In fact, in 1887, the editor of the movement's mouthpiece, *Ishaat-u-Sunnat,* Sayyid Muhammad Husain Batalvi, made a formal request to the British government to treat the Movement as being distinct from that of the Wahhabis and to not use the term Wahhabi when referring to adherents of Ahl-i-Hadith.[171]

It must be clarified that the Movement did not reject the doctrine of jihad but was merely being pragmatic about its chances of success in waging a physical jihad against the British.[172] This is corroborated by Ayesha Jalal as well in her book *Partisans of Allah: Jihad in South Asia*. Critically, the goal of this Movement too was to revive Islam in consonance with Dehlawi's teachings. In fact, the followers of this Movement claimed to be the 'true successors' of Dehlawi's Reformist Movement[173] and frequently issued fatwas branding their co-religionists as kafirs, pitting them against other movements/groups, in particular the Deobandis. Their vehement opposition to shrine-based Islam, veneration of pirs/Muslim saints and Sufi practices meant they were at loggerheads with another major Movement, the Barelvi.[174] In a short span of time, the Ahl-i-Hadith rose to become one of the most popular theological seminaries in northern India. As of 2005, it had over 400 madrasas in Pakistan,[175] which are frequently linked to terror groups such as the Lashkar-e-Tayyiba. According to scholars, it was this organisation that introduced the pro-Wahhabi doctrine in the Kashmiri jihadi crucible.[176] The

Ahl-i-Hadith Movement also produced the Ahl-i-Quran Movement, whose founder, Maulvi Abdullah Chakralawi, went a step ahead and rejected even the authenticity of the Hadith, since, according to him, the Quran was the sole authority in Islam.

The Deobandi Movement

For a comprehensive history of the Deobandi Movement from the horse's mouth, readers may refer to the two-volume tome titled *History of the Dar al-Ulum, Deoband* authored by Sayyid Mahboob Rizvi and published by the institution itself in 1980.[177] The other book on the subject is by Barbara Metcalf, *Islamic Revival in British India: Deoband, 1860–1900*. In addition to these, Sana Haroon's detailed articles on the rise of the Deobandi Movement, especially in the context of the NWF, are both informative and insightful.[178]

In the very first chapter of his book dedicated to the life and contribution of Shah Waliullah Dehlawi, Sayyid Mahboob Rizvi claims that the science of Hadith, which was brought to India by Dehlawi from Hejaz, was saved by Deoband and nurtured for the benefit of all of Asia. In setting out the 'chain of credentials of the great savants of Dar al-Ulum', he names Dehlawi as the fount, followed by Shah Abdul Aziz, Shah Muhammad Ishaq and others, leading to the founders of Deoband, namely Maulana Muhammad Qasim Nanautawi and Maulana Rashid Ahmed Gangohi. As stated earlier, both the founders were educated at Dehlawi's school.

According to Sana Haroon, as 'true claimants' to Dehlawi's mantle, the Deobandis primarily drew their curriculum from Sirhindi and Dehlawi,[179] which naturally meant that un-Islamic Sufi mysticism and Shia/Hindu influences were actively rejected, and the centrality of the Quran and the Hadith reinforced. By 1879, the Dar al-Ulum (DAU) was second only to the Al Azhar seminary in Cairo in terms of its standing in the Islamic world. Apart from attracting scores of students from all over the country, the Deoband seminary became the point of convergence for generations of Pashtuns from the NWF, which was not surprising given the region's pivotal role in the Wahhabi Movement. In fact, the seminary became actively involved in the politics of the NWFP, with the period between 1914 and 1919 marking a point of inflection when the Khilafat Movement was raging, thanks to the break-up of the Ottoman empire in the First World War. The then vice chancellor of the seminary, Maulana Mahmudul Hasan, went to the extent of inviting the Ottoman empire to attack British India on the north-west frontier, which landed him in jail along with 200 of his followers.[180]

In 1919, the political wing of DAU, the Jamiat Ulema-e-Hind (JUH), was established. The JUH saw itself as the representative of Muslims of the subcontinent.[181] The DAU played an active role in seeking a separate electorate for Muslims, non-interference of the state in the religious affairs of Muslims and legal space for customary adjudication of disputes under Islamic law. By 1924, the JUH had a strong presence in Peshawar, which resulted in establishment of the Jamiat Ulema-e-Sarhad (JUS) for the NWFP.[182] Gradually, allegations began to be hurled by the Deobandi ulema against Hindu shopkeepers in Nowshera that they had misbehaved with Muslim women.[183] Hindus were declared enemies of Islam and Muslims, and were socially and economically boycotted. By 1936, Hindu girls were being abducted, forcibly converted to Islam and married off to Muslim men.[184] By 1945, the JUH was further split into JUH and Jamiat Ulema-e-Islam Pakistan (JUI-P), which supported the Muslim League's call for creation of Pakistan.[185] The JUI-P had within its ranks the leading lights of the Pakistan Movement, such as Shabbir Ahmad Usmani, who was one of the founding members of Jamia Millia Islamia in Delhi.

In the 1980s, well after the creation of Pakistan, the JUI-P split into the JUI-F under Maulana Fazal-ur-Rahman and the JUI-S under Maulana Samiul Haq.[186] Ayesha Jalal notes in her book that it was in Samiul Haq's seminary, the Dar-ul-Ulum Haqqania, that future leaders of the Taliban such as Mullah Omar were educated.[187] The Deobandis received a significant degree of state support in Pakistan, with power being shared with another major Sunni group, the Barelvis, who were politically represented by the Jamiat Ulema-e-Pakistan (JUP). Effectively, Pakistan became a Barelvi-Deobandi state, with the former enjoying support in the Punjab province and the latter enjoying support in the NWFP and Baluchistan. But the golden age of the Deobandis, according to Ayesha Jalal, truly arrived with the rise of the Taliban in 1979, which gradually moved towards a Deobandi–Wahhabi alliance with the arrival of Osama bin Laden.[188] Predictably, on the Kashmir front, Deobandis contributed through the creation of the terror group Harkat-ul-Ansar.[189]

In addition to the above list of 'achievements', several prominent Deobandis went on to establish their own movements. For instance, in the late 1920s, Maulana Mohammad Ilyas (1885–1944), a Deobandi educated under Rashid Ahmed Gangohi and who came from a family devoted to Shah Waliullah Dehlawi, founded the Tablighi Jamaat.[190] In fact, Ilyas's ancestors had pledged allegiance (*baiát*) to Syed Ahmad Barelvi. The Tablighi Jamaat's primary focus was to spread Islamic religious practices among the Meos of Mewat (present-day Haryana) and to attract Muslims from all walks of life.[191] It believed in taking Islam out of the confines of the seminary and into society.

The other prominent individual educated by the Deobandi ulema but who would later go on to have troubled relations with the Deobandis was Sayyid Abul Ala Mawdudi,[192] who founded the Jamaat-e-Islami Party in 1941.[193] Between 1924 and 1927, his views on the role of jihad in Islam and in the setting up of an Islamic state were widely read. According to Mawdudi, jihad was central to Islam because Islam's stated objective was to '*alter the social order of the whole world and rebuild it in conformity with its own tenets and ideals*'.[194] He believed, therefore, that for the welfare of humanity, Muslims had an obligation to destroy all states and governments that were opposed to the ideology of Islam. This was the essence of jihad, according to him. Further, to him, dance, music and art were remnants of *jahilliya*[195] (the age of ignorance and darkness), a term used in Islam to refer to the pre-Islamic pagan state of Arabia. He deemed Taymiyyah, Sirhindi and Dehlawi as icons worthy of emulation since the first lived in an age of Mongol tyranny, the second resisted Akbar's gravitation towards polytheistic Sufism, and the third produced the most comprehensive criticism of Sufi and Hindu influences on Islam. Mawdudi praised Barelvi and Shah Ismail Dehlawi for implementing Dehlawi's views on the ground. According to Ayesha Jalal, Muhammad Iqbal was so impressed by Mawdudi's views that he wanted to collaborate with him on reform of Islamic law.[196]

Mawdudi, a distant relative of Syed Ahmed Khan (founder of the Aligarh Movement), initially opposed the Partition of India on the grounds that it would divide the Muslims of the subcontinent. However, after the partition, he moved to Pakistan and created the Jamaat-e-Islami Pakistan, with the original entity remaining in Bharat. He rose to prominence in Pakistan in 1953 on the strength of his opposition to Ahmadis/Ahmadiyyas, whom he wanted legally classified as a non-Muslim minority.[197] The other high point of his career was his support of the Taliban against Soviet invasion and his support of Zia-ul-Haq's policy of turning Pakistan into a strictly Sharia-compliant state.[198]

Clearly, with over 30,000 seminaries the world over, the Deobandi Movement is among the most influential of the movements that drew inspiration from Dehlawi.[199] To quote R.C. Majumdar:[200]

> The foundation of the Dar-al-Ulum at Deoband in A.D. 1866, which has continued to attract students not only from different parts of India but from the neighbouring Muslim countries also, was the greatest achievement of the Wahabi school of thought in India.'

The Barelvi Movement

The Barelvi Movement, which arose in response and opposition to both the Ahl-i-Hadith and Deobandi Movements, was founded in the 1870s by Ahmad Raza Khan. Raza Khan stridently opposed the other two movements on their negation of veneration of saints or pirs, and shrine-based Islam. The Barelvis embrace both aspects, despite tracing their intellectual lineage to Dehlawi, but agree with the other two movements on the need to check alien influences, namely Shia and Hindu.[201] According to Ayesha Jalal, Raza Khan is reported to have said that if a Muslim were presented the choice of offering water to a thirsty infidel or to a dog, he should offer it to the latter.[202] He rejected the use of armed jihad against the British since the religious freedoms of Muslims remained unaffected under them. Given that Raza Khan himself was a Rohilla Pathan, the Barelvi Movement attracted the Pathans of Rohilkhand heavily, and also followers from the rural parts of the United Provinces and Punjab.[203] The Barelvis too make the claim that they alone are the true followers of the Islamic Prophet's path, the Sunnat, and therefore are true Sunnis. As stated earlier, the Barelvis have a major presence in Pakistan's Punjab province, and have a significant presence in Bharat as well.

The Nadwatul Ulama Movement

The Nadwatul Ulama was founded as a council in 1893 by a group of ulema and Muslim officials in the employ of the British, who wanted the different Muslim sects and movements to rise above their sectarian differences and secure state power for Muslims of the subcontinent. This group's focus was on producing Muslims who drew pride from traditional Islamic learning and not from being Westernised.[204] To this end, they founded the Darul Uloom Nadwatul Ulama in 1898, where the focus was on mastery of Arabic and a deep study of the Quran.[205] However, according to Barbara Metcalf, English was not abhorred, since the founder of the seminary, Muhammad Ali Mungeri, was of the view that if Islam had to win converts from the West, especially America, it was imperative for the faithful to learn English. He argued that, after all, Turkish and Persian too were languages of the infidels at one point, until the conversion of the people who spoke them, after which their languages came to be associated with Islam.[206] The focus of the school was 'defence of Islam' from the West and from Hindu resurgence.[207] Over the years, the institution resembled the Deoband in its curriculum and emphasis.[208]

Apart from the reformist movements discussed so far, which had some connection, whether direct or intellectual, with the Dehlawi school of thought, the other movement which arose in the 1870s is the Ahmadiyya Movement, founded by Mirza Ghulam Ahmad (1835–1908). This Movement had its origins in Qadian, Punjab. It too believed that there was an urgent need for reform and that Muslims must return to the basic tenets of Islam. However, what distinguished Mirza Ghulam Ahmad's position is the belief that, akin to the Islamic Prophet, he too was the recipient of divine communication and was himself a prophet.[209,210] To make matters worse, Ghulam Ahmad believed that he was divinely ordained to spread the word that British rule must be accepted by Muslims[211] and that jihad was completely prohibited.[212] Naturally, such declarations did not endear him to other movements. However, notwithstanding his messianic claims, he too had no love lost for Hindus and frequently launched vitriolic attacks against them.[213] Clearly, the common out-group which was the object of unreserved hatred of each of these movements was always the Hindus.

Coming back to the Dehlawite movements, from the Ahl-i-Hadith to the Nadwatul Ulama, there was a gradual movement from puritanism to some room for accommodation of Western education alongside traditional Islamic education. With the Aligarh Movement, we will see a greater emphasis on combining Western and Islamic education. This did not in any manner amount to dilution of the core objectives—of Islamic reform and restoration of Islamic state power in the Bharatiya subcontinent and outside. In this regard, Barbara Metcalf's summary of the Ahl-i-Hadith, Deobandi and Barelvi Movements and their broad areas of intersection and departure is worth reading, since it largely applies to all the Islamic movements of the time and underscores the central point that these new sects merely represented new strategies to reinforce old patterns:[214]

> The three main groups of Sunni 'ulama thought of themselves as rivals, both intellectually and socially. Each represented a different stance within the faith, emphasizing different branches of learning, adhering to different jurisprudential positions, and striking different balances between a primary role as mediator and one as instructor in religious responsibility for the believer himself. Overall, the Deobandi and Ahl-i Hadis, who rejected customary practices and parochial cults, appealed to the more urban and educated, whereas Barelvi support was largely among the rural and less well educated. Moreover, each group of 'ulama was distinguished not only by an intellectual position but by shared roots in a specific geographic area, by membership in a qaum of the north Indian ashraf, and in two cases by ties of Sufi brotherhood.
>
> In fact, however, all these groups were concerned with the Law and with devotion to the Prophet; and all expressed their beliefs in a self-conscious

oppositional style. Although all offered a characteristic set of teachings, the 'ulama of each group were many things to many men. Villagers near Deoband regarded its 'ulama simply as good and holy men—as suggested by the death of one of Rashid Ahmad's most devoted disciples, oblivious of reformist concerns but dedicated to a holy man, during sama' at Ajmer. There were, similarly, not only simple villagers among the supporters of the Barelwis, but government servants as well. Institutionally, too, the edges between the groups tended to blur. All were popularly based and all came to share the modern institutional forms that the Deobandis pioneered. Formal educational institutions, annual conferences, and deputations for proselytization were standard by the beginning of this century. The groups perceived themselves, however, as radically different from each other, and the resulting competition among them provided the motive for what was in fact their common work of religious revitalization and redefinition.

In the first part to this trilogy, I had made the point that the Christian Reformation led to multiple perspectives within the Christian world, but insofar as the individual and collective Christian attitude towards non-Christians, in particular towards the 'pagans', was concerned, it was invariably one of benevolent condescension and competitive evangelism to harvest souls for their respective denominations. Based on the history of the Islamic reformist movements, which started at least with Sirhindi in Bharat, a similar conclusion can be drawn with respect to their attitude towards Indic consciousness. Therefore, reformist movements, whether in Christianity or Islam, did not mellow their antipathy for idol-worshipping or nature-worshipping indigenous communities. On the contrary, reform translated to calls for greater 'purity' and greater Christian (European/Western)/Islamic (Middle Eastern) consciousness, which inevitably translated to purer and more determined hatred, with scriptural and clerical sanction, for those outside the fold.

What is also critical to note is that these pan-Islamic movements arose *after* significant loss of Muslim state power, which points to the fundamental ability of the Middle Eastern consciousness to generate such movements by drawing from within its society. Some may be tempted to interpret such movements and their calls for greater 'purity' in the Muslim identity as a move towards eventual self-destruction of radicalism. However, that would be wishful thinking, because the net effect of these movements in the Bharatiya subcontinent, notwithstanding their internal rivalries, has been heightened Islamic consciousness. In this part of the world, this rejuvenation of Middle Eastern coloniality has necessarily come at the expense of Indic consciousness. While we may not want to treat this as a zero-sum game, the unfortunate reality as a *matter of fact* is that the shared antipathy of these movements for Indic consciousness could not have been pronounced in clearer terms, and has tangibly resulted in the Balkanisation of Bharat, both before and *after* 1947. Hence, my point that enhancement of the Middle Eastern consciousness has translated to the loss of Indic civilisational space.

Some Thoughts on the Ideology of Pan-Islamic Movements in the Subcontinent

Earlier in this chapter, I had raised this question—how does one deal with an ideology or a mindset of the type under discussion, especially if it is capable of assuming different names and shapes to achieve the same goal? In my current limited and tentative view, perhaps the answer lies in adopting a three-pronged approach. First, Indic consciousness must revive its own ability to produce society-based institutions and individuals who can constantly and uncompromisingly advance the Indic civilisational cause and space. It is this ability which preserved Indic consciousness during the two waves of colonisation, and it is this ability that has been dulled and stifled under the third wave of colonisation, namely under the Nehruvian Marxist/postcolonial establishment which allies with both European and Middle Eastern colonialities, to the detriment of Indic consciousness. It is also pertinent to note that the diversity and vehement disagreements among the various pan-Islamic movements have not come in the way of their 'unity' against aliens to the Muslim fold. On the contrary, such diversity contributed to the reawakening and spread of Middle Eastern consciousness, which ultimately led to the vivisection and mutilation of Bharat. This is a lesson for those who believe that 'Hindu unity' requires the sacrifice of sampradayic/ denominational identities and diversity. While internal consensus is important for cohesion in a community, identification of the out-group too plays a huge role in clarifying its priorities and developing an understanding of the challenges it is faced with. Unfortunately, this fundamental aspect of human psychology seems to be lost on certain proponents of 'Hindu unity', who may lack the courage and the conviction to call out the predatory and expansionist tendencies of both European and Middle Eastern consciousness.

Second, the importance and criticality of Indic-oriented state power must not be undermined, since that gives the society the means to implement and amplify civilisational goals, both within and outside, *provided* the reins of thought and consciousness remain in the hands of society. And third, creating a civilisational safe space in the immediate neighbourhood of Bharat through the creation of a Greater Bharat is imperative so that *pax Indica* becomes a reality, at least in the subcontinent, *before* we aspire for the more arduous and ambitious 'Vishwaguru' status. After all, those who cannot set their own house in order and secure their immediate neighbourhood would be building castles in the air if they were to aspire to provide thought leadership to the rest of the world.

With these thoughts, and in light of the history of pan-Islamic thought initiated by Sirhindi, taken forward by Dehlawi and actioned by Barelvi, and which inspired multiple movements, each claiming to trace its intellectual lineage from either or all the aforementioned triumvirate, I will now proceed to discuss perhaps the most well-known and the most impactful of these movements from the standpoint of the creation of Pakistan—the Aligarh Movement, founded by 'Sir' Syed Ahmed Khan, widely considered the architect of the Two-Nation Theory.

Syed Ahmed Khan, the Aligarh Movement and the Two-Nation Theory

Tomb of Syed Ahmed Khan, founder of Aligarh Muslim University,
inside Aligarh Muslim University

In the previous chapter, citing Barbara Metcalf's book, I had pointed out that Syed Ahmed Khan, the founder of the Aligarh Movement, was a product of Dehlawi's seminary Madrasah-i-Rahimiyah at the time of its helmsmanship by Shah Muhammad Ishaq Dehlawi and his brother Yaqub.[1] Therefore, at the very least, this much can be said with confidence—that Syed Ahmed Khan had been exposed to the thoughts and worldview of Dehlawi and his successors. In light of this, a few pertinent questions arise, which must be cogently answered. First, is there any basis to suggest that exposure to Dehlawi's worldview also meant that Syed Ahmed Khan agreed with the same? If yes, how does one reconcile his subscription to Dehlawi's views and his introduction of a markedly greater proportion of Western education than in other Islamic institutions as part of the curriculum for Muslim youth in the institution he founded? Is it possible to conclude, on the basis of his formulation of the Two-Nation Theory, that it was but a restatement and repackaging of Dehlawi's views in a 'modern' idiom through the prism of the nation-state prevalent during his own life and times? After all, European or Western political thought was quite well entrenched by then, as demonstrated in the first book of this trilogy. In this chapter, I will attempt to address these questions with evidence and draw reasonable inferences as far as possible.

Based on the history of the evolution of pan-Islamic movements in the Bharatiya subcontinent, this much is clear: those movements that started in the immediate aftermath of the loss of Muslim state power in the eighteenth and early nineteenth centuries were more reactionary and visibly anti-colonial, since the British, along with Hindus/Sikhs, were seen as usurpers of Muslim-ruled territory or Dar al-Islam. Their first response was to launch physical jihad against the Sikh empire, and thereafter against the British establishment, as exemplified by the Wahhabis under Syed Ahmad Barelvi and the Ali Brothers. Their course of action was, in fact, consistent with the teachings of Islam, which mandate jihad from within to restore the status of a territory to Dar al-Islam or require emigration (*hijrat*) to a Dar al-Islam so that the practice of Islam is not interfered with and jihad may be launched from the outside with the support of Muslim states.

The second response was to return to traditional centres of Islamic learning and convergence to 'reform' Islam and prepare it for reclamation of state power as and when the atmospherics were conducive. The inability of the Wahhabis to militarily dislodge the British convinced the proponents of this school of thought that this course of action was the more pragmatic one. This was a conscious decision taken to deal with the changed realities, as evident from the decision of the committee formed by Shah Muhammad Ishaq Dehlawi under the stewardship of Maulana Mamluk Ali Nanautawi.

However, even this school of thought witnessed a gradual change. The first wave of conservative movements, such as the Ahl-i-Hadith, the Ahl-i-Quran, Deoband and Barelvi Movements, focused more on traditional Islamic learning, defining a 'true Muslim' and observing political quietude by remaining aloof towards the colonial power structure, and rejecting Western education. This is attested to by both Barbara Metcalf and Ayesha Jalal in their respective books.[2] This rectitude had direct consequences—a significant cross-section of Hindus learnt English and became part of the colonial infrastructure, either because it gave them an opportunity to play a role in the process of governing their country while retaining their Indic consciousness, or because they were taken in by European coloniality. On the other hand, a significant cross-section of Muslims refused to learn English and 'lagged behind', but retained their Middle Eastern consciousness. Perhaps this could be the subject of a case study for those interested in understanding the relationship between language, semantics, education and consciousness.

As time went by, some members of the Muslim community realised that the policy of self-imposed isolationism and sectarian rivalry operated to the detriment of their community since it resulted in cession of political space to Hindus, which hurt the Muslim collective memory as the 'former rulers of Hindustan'.[3] Therefore, the community gradually opened itself to Western education, starting with significant regional efforts by the Muslim leaders of Bengal in the 1850s and 1860s. This was, of course, in response to the increased political awareness and consciousness of the Hindus of Bengal, who had embraced English education early on and had become part of the colonial power structure—something that had been hitherto either not possible or not easy under the Muslim establishment. In this sense, Bengali Hindus were perhaps ahead of the rest of the country in pressing into service their political awareness, one which eventually gave birth to 'Indian nationalism'. The Muslims of Bengal too, therefore, aspired to become part of the colonial infrastructure. This meant that well before the crystallisation of the Two-Nation Theory by Syed Ahmed Khan, both Hindus and Muslims typically established distinct community-specific institutions in the realms of education, culture and politics, which underscores the tenuous and synthetic nature of the so-called syncretic culture.

Among the earliest 'modern' Muslim organizations to be established by the Muslims of Bengal was the Muhammadan Association in Calcutta in 1856, followed by the Mohammedan Literary Society in 1863 by Nawab Abdul Latif, a Sunni, who would go on to support the efforts of Syed Ahmed Khan, and the Central National Mohammedan Association founded in Calcutta by Syed Ameer Ali, a Shia, in 1877, who would play a huge role in the founding of the Muslim League and beyond.[4] Of these, Nawab Abdul Latif not only initiated efforts to foster understanding between the Muslims in Bengal and the British establishment, but also worked towards containment of the Wahhabi influence in East Bengal to placate the British.[5] He invited influential Sunni ulema, such as Maulvi Karamat Ali Jaunpuri, to declare that India was not Dar al-Harb under the Christian British government. Interestingly, Maulvi Jaunpuri was a disciple of Syed Ahmad Barelvi, who had worked towards spreading the message of Wahhabism/Tariqa-i-Muhammadiyyah in Bengal, albeit through non-violent means.[6] To support his British loyalist position further, Nawab Abdul Latif cited British support to the Ottoman empire in the Crimean War against the Russian empire, the cordial relations between the British and Ottoman Egypt, and the dependence of the Emir of Afghanistan on the British. He even obtained a fatwa from the Mufti of Mecca that Bharat was Dar al-Islam under the British and had 5,000 copies of the fatwa distributed among Muslims in Bengal through the Mohammedan Literary Society. In 1877, for his promotion of English education among Muslims, he was bestowed the title of 'Khan Bahadur' by the British.[7]

In the United Provinces, North-Western and Punjab provinces, the Aligarh Movement, which began in the 1860s, and the Nadwatul Ulama Movement of the 1890s, took upon themselves the responsibility of imparting Islamic and Western education to Muslim youth—each, of course, in varying proportions. The Aligarh Movement and its institutions were deemed too Western and British loyalist by many within the Muslim community, despite the Movement's contributions to the creation of a 'national' Muslim identity. In fact, some of its founding members, such as Shibli Nomani, later moved to the Darul Uloom Nadwatul Ulama, citing the Aligarh establishment's pro-Western tendencies, which were reflected in its educational model. The Deobandis, in particular, shared this grievance against the Aligarh model. With a view to tip the balance and increase the Islamic quotient in the education of Muslim youth, institutions such as the Darul Uloom Nadwatul Ulama and the Jamia Millia Islamia were later established in 1898 and 1920, respectively.

Despite all the criticism levelled against it by Muslims from different backgrounds for their own reasons, the fact remains that the Aligarh Movement was the first 'national' Muslim movement to embrace 'modernity' and institutionally combine it with Islamic or Islam-oriented education. In this sense, the impact of the Movement was wider compared with the efforts of the Muslim leaders of Bengal, although the latter were the pioneers in combining Islam with English education. Critically, Syed Ahmed Khan, although a self-confessed Wahhabi, established institutions catering to both Sunnis and Shias, as we shall see, which made possible the creation of a 'national' Muslim identity beyond sectarian divides. This is because the Aligarh model was a consequence of the founder's realisation or belief that this was to be the way of the future. In other words, Syed Ahmed Khan believed that if the goals of the Dehlawite vision had to be realised, an Islamic environment was needed, where Islamic learning could be combined with Western education to produce individuals who could navigate the colonial state and the 'modern' world to reclaim Muslim state power. Clearly, it was a pragmatic decision to operate within the European paradigm, but with the clear objective of pushing the goals articulated by Shah Waliullah Dehlawi. In this sense, it was a postcolonial approach of subverting the Western paradigm by using the Western framework itself to meet Islamic ends. This is what distinguished the Aligarh Movement from its predecessor or even other contemporary movements. Additionally, since it contributed to the creation of Pakistan through Syed Ahmed Khan's exposition of the Two-Nation Theory, to say that Dehlawi's goal was achieved, at least in part, would not be incorrect, since according to Dehlawi the whole of the Bharatiya subcontinent belonged to Islam. No wonder Jinnah called Aligarh 'the Muslim arsenal of India', so much so that in 1939 he named Aligarh Muslim University as one of the primary beneficiaries in his will.[8]

It is important to understand that while Syed Ahmed Khan was the progenitor of the Aligarh Movement, it also attracted several individuals who would build on the Two-Nation Theory, either as part of the Movement or through the founding of their own institutions and political parties. Therefore, this Movement needs to be dealt with in some detail, especially in view of the fact that the Partition of Bengal in 1905 on religious lines and the founding of the All-India Muslim League in 1906 were temporally proximate to the Aligarh Movement and, in many ways, were effects of the Movement itself. That apart, as pointed out earlier, the Aligarh Movement also contributed to the Khilafat and Pakistan Movement. Therefore, for the sake of continuity in the narrative, in this chapter I will limit the discussion on the Aligarh Movement primarily to Syed Ahmed Khan and his formulation of the Two-Nation Theory. The contribution of the Movement subsequent to Khan's death in 1898 will be discussed, wherever necessary, in the next two sections as part of the larger backdrop of the tectonic events that took place between 1899 and 1924.

Origins and Early Influences

In *Islamic Revival in British India: Deoband, 1860–1900*, Barbara Metcalf traces the lineage and moorings of Syed Ahmed Khan: born in 1817, he came from a family that had strong ties to the Naqshbandi Order of Sufis. We might recall that Dehlawi too belonged to the same Order, despite his hard-line positions against Sufi mysticism and its dilution of the position of the Quran and Hadith in the practice of Islam. Metcalf unambiguously states the following on Dehlawi's impact on Syed Ahmed Khan's worldview:[9]

> Sayyid Ahmad's family, especially on his mother's side, had deep ties to the line of the Naqshbandi Mujaddidi that was represented in Delhi by Shah Ghulam 'Ali (d. 1824). This line had been known for its commitment to sobriety in the Sufi path. Ghulam 'Ali was considered even more strict than Shah 'Abdu'l-'Aziz in opposing customary practices; he, however, did not share 'Abdu'l-'Aziz's concern with reaching beyond the spiritual elite. *Sayyid*

Ahmad was clearly influenced by the moral and spiritual vitality of both lines and by the popular concerns of the Waliyu'llahi line, as well. [Emphasis added]

According to Aziz Ahmad:[10]

He [Syed Ahmad] received some schooling in the Naqshbandi Khanaqh of Shah Ghulam Ali, which conformed to religious orthodoxy as much as his second school, run by the disciples of Shah 'Abd al-'Aziz, where the reformist near-Wahhabi tradition of Shah Wali Allah flourished. Sayyid Ahmad Khan's maternal relatives were disciples of Shah 'Abd al 'Aziz, and his own mother was a devout and learned lady.

Aziz Ahmad confirms that it was in Dehlawi's seminary that 'Sayyid Ahmad Khan imbibed the principles, which were already being preached by Shah Isma'il and others, of purifying Indian Islam from practices borrowed from other religions'.[11] Therefore, the impact of the Dehlawite worldview on Syed Ahmed Khan is undeniable. In *The Life and Work of Syed Ahmad Khan*, G.F.I. Graham, who considered Khan his close friend and even translated his books from Urdu to English, wrote that Khan's paternal and maternal ancestors were 'men of mark' under the Mughal dynasty (not 'empire').[12] Khan's father, Syed Ahmed Takki, who was a close friend of the then Mughal 'Emperor' Akbar II, was offered prime ministership, which he declined. After Takki's death in 1836, the then (and last) Mughal 'Emperor' Bahadur Shah Zafar bestowed upon Syed Ahmed Khan the titles of his grandfather

Sir Syed Ahmed Khan in Punjab (1890): from *Sir Syed Album* by Khaliq Ahmad Nizami

and additional titles. No wonder Barbara Metcalf makes it abundantly clear that Syed Ahmed Khan was 'acutely sensitive' to the loss of Mughal power and was keen on restoring the pride of the Muslim ruling class and nobility, a vision consistent with Dehlawi's.[13]

In 1837, Khan entered British service in the criminal department at the sub-judge's office in Delhi.[14,15] In 1847, while still in the employ of the British, in his first book *Asarus Sanadid*, he was all praise for the jihad undertaken by Shah Ismail Dehlawi and Syed Shahid Barelvi. He hailed Shah Ismail Dehlawi as 'the Extirpator of Heresy' (*Qami'al-Bid'at*) and extolled the jihad of the Wahhabis under him against the Sikh empire as follows:[16]

> The worshippers of God have not till today relinquished his cause. Every year the mujahids (holy warriors) go from different native places for the jihad, and the merit of this good work will forever reach his soul.

Prior to the Mutiny of 1857, this so-called modern Islamic reformer subscribed to traditional Islamic positions even in matters of science, as evidenced by his monograph of 1850 titled *Qaul-i-matin dar ibtal-i harakat-i zamin* ('Firm Assertion with Regard to the False Motion of the Earth'), wherein he denied the earth's rotation.[17] Given his family's proximity to the Mughal dynasty, his training in the Dehlawite school of thought and his unambiguous Quranic views on matters of science, it is not possible to believe that the Two-Nation Theory was an aberration from Khan's central worldview. On the contrary, it was entirely consistent with it, as we shall see, and any statement made by Khan to the contrary at any point in his life must, in fact, be seen as his pragmatism at work, which made no difference to the Dehlawite end goal. This pragmatism is evident from the fact that when the Wahhabis started directing their jihad towards the British after the latter's annexation of Punjab, Khan could no longer afford to be as open in his adulation of the Wahhabis. Therefore, he redacted the above extracted paragraph from the very same book in 1854.[18]

Rebellion, 'Reformation' and Reincarnation

It was only *after* the Mutiny of 1857, when Syed Ahmed Khan realised that Muslims could not compete with the British owing to the latter's superior organisation and technological prowess, that he adopted a more realistic position. Pertinently, he lost a few family members to the British response to the Mutiny,[19] pointing to a significant degree of personal investment in the causes he espoused thereafter. It was between 1857 and 1870 that Khan's role as the 'modern' defender of Islam was shaped better, which manifested broadly in three ways—defence of the Muslim community; defence of

Islam; and the mainstreaming of English/Western education in the Muslim community through an Anglo-Islamic model.

On the subject of defending the Muslim community from the ire of the British, Syed Ahmed Khan felt that Muslims were being unfairly singled out for their participation in the Mutiny, so much so that he even contemplated moving to Egypt. Both Ayesha Jalal in her book *Partisans of Allah: Jihad in South Asia*,[20] and M.S. Jain in his comprehensive monograph titled *The Aligarh Movement, Its Origin and Development (1858–1906)*[21] say as much, while Metcalf claims that he contemplated moving to Hejaz in Arabia following in the footsteps of his teacher Shah Muhammad Ishaq Dehlawi.[22] However, he chose to stay on, and through his writings, such as *Causes of the Indian Revolt* (which was originally published in Urdu in 1858 as *Asbab-i-Baghawat*) and *The Loyal Muhammadans of India* (1860), he sought to build a defence for Muslims in Bharat by advancing two specific positions— that Muslim participation in the Mutiny was not religious but political, arising out of British attitudes and policies, specifically non-admission of natives in the Legislative Council;[23] that Hindus and Muslims alike feared imposition of Christianity by the British establishment, and that the majority of Muslims in Bharat were otherwise loyal to the British despite British excesses.

Syed Ahmed Khan (*bottom-centre*), his sons, Syed Mahmood (*standing, 3rd from left*) and Syed Hamid (*standing, far left*), and others

On the first count, he was factually incorrect, in light of the express call for jihad and restoration of Mughal rule given by the Muslim mutineers. The following is an extract on the subject from Yusuf Abbasi's book:[24]

> Maulvi Inayat Ali preached jihad to some of the Indian troops. Maulana Fazal-i-Haq Khairabadi was one of the ulema who drafted the fatwa declaring the struggle of 1857 to be a jihad. Military leaders like Bakht Khan considered it imperative to give a religious and legal basis to the struggle against the British. Consequently, a meeting of the prominent ulema was convened in Delhi, and they issued a fatwa calling upon every Muslim to stand up in arms against the British. Henceforth, religious, political and military leadership was centred in Delhi, which assumed its old symbolic character in the Muslim national sentiment. *The cry of jihad rang out all over the Subcontinent, and the Muslim people from Delhi to Madras were stirred to action by the lofty sentiment of this call.* Not surprising therefore to find the green robed Mujahids of Bareilly rushing at the English guns and bayonets with cries of 'Din Din Bismillah' or to witness them fighting to the last on the ramparts of Delhi. The ulema were no idle scholars excelling in the art of religious disputation but men cast in a heroic mould, who set a shining example in courage as well as learning. The saga of valour and martyrdom, of exile and imprisonment, of trials and tribulation, inscribed in the blood and suffering of ulema like Ahmad Ullah, Imdad Ullah, Abdul Jalil, Liaqat Ali, Kafi, Pir Ali, Ghulam Hussain and others, during the eventful year of the uprising and after, shall ever remain a source of inspiration for freedom fighters. However, the heroic resistance of the ulema ended in a defeat which shattered their political leadership. [Emphasis added]

In light of these facts, it is not possible to contend that Muslim participation in the Mutiny was purely political. Importantly, even Syed Ahmed Khan did not refute the fact that calls for jihad were indeed issued at the time—his sole disagreement was that the calls were without Islamic basis, and hence invalid. He argued against the use of jihad under colonial rule, but *not against* jihad itself, since according to him, Muslims of the subcontinent had no right to wage war against the British as long as their religious freedoms were not interfered with.[25] The following were Khan's views on the subject; here he simultaneously made the point that jihad against the British was unjustified whereas the Wahhabi jihad against the Sikhs was justified:[26]

> There are, again, no grounds for supposing that the Mohammedans had for a long time been conspiring or plotting a simultaneous rise or a religious crusade against the professors of a different faith. The English Government does not interfere with the Mohammedans in the practice of their religion. For this sole reason it is impossible that the idea of religious crusade should have been entertained. Thirty-five years ago a celebrated Moulvie, Muhammad Ismael by name, preached a religious crusade in Hindustan, and called upon all men to

aid him in carrying it out. But on that occasion, he distinctly stated that natives of Hindustan, subject to the British Government, could not conscientiously take part in a religious war within the limits of Hindustan. Accordingly, while thousands of Jehadees congregated in every district of Hindustan, there was no sort of disturbance raised within British territory. Going northwards, these men crossed the Panjab frontier, and waged war in those parts of the country. And even if we should imitate the know-nothings in the various districts and call the late disturbance a religious war, it is very certain that no preparations were made for it before the 10th of May 1857.

The 'Moulvie, Muhammad Ismael' referred to in the above extract from *Causes of the Indian Revolt* was a reference to Shah Ismail Dehlawi, whom Khan had celebrated in 1847 as the 'Extirpator of Heresy'. Khan's position was glaringly inconsistent, since in the very same book he cited interference with the religion of the natives as one of the primary causes of the Mutiny, which provides us material basis to conclude that the Muslim mutineers had indeed launched a jihad to protect their religious freedom in accordance with the tenets of Islam. In fact, on the subject of the proselytising push by the Christian colonial establishment triggering the Mutiny, which I dealt with in detail in my first book, I agree with Khan. The following is an extract on Christian colonial conduct from Khan's book *Causes of the Indian Revolt*, which, unfortunately, still resonates with current evangelical realities in Bharat:[27]

Interference in Matters of Religion – There is not the smallest doubt that all men, whether ignorant or well-informed, whether high or low, felt a firm conviction that the English Government was bent on interfering with their religion, and with their old-established customs. They believed that Government intended to force the Christian religion and foreign customs upon Hindu and Mussulman alike. This was the chief among the secondary causes of the rebellion. It was believed by every one that Government was slowly but surely developing its plans. Every step, it was thought, was being taken with the most extreme caution. Hence it is that men said that Government does not speak of proselytising Mohammedans summarily and by force; but it will throw off the veil as it feels itself stronger, and will act with greater decision.

Events, as I shall presently show, increased and strengthened this conviction. Men never thought that our Government would openly compel them to change their religion. The idea was, that indirect steps would be taken, such as doing away with the study of Arabic and Sanskrit, and reducing the people to ignorance and poverty. In this way, it was supposed, the people would be deprived of a knowledge of the principles of their own faith, and their attention turned to books containing the principles of the Christian creed. *It was supposed that Government would then work on the cupidity and poverty of its subjects, and, on condition of their abjuring their faith, offer them employment in its own service.*

In the year 1837, the year of the great drought, the step which was taken of rearing orphans in the principles of the Christian faith, was looked upon throughout the North-West Provinces as an example of the schemes of Government. *It was supposed that when Government had similarly brought all Hindustanees to a pitch of ignorance and poverty, it would convert them to its own creed.* The Hindustanees used, as I have said, to feel an increasing dismay at the annexation of each successive country by the Honourable East India Company. But I assert without fear of contradiction that this feeling arose solely from the belief in their minds, that as the power of Government increased, and there no longer remained foreign enemies to fight against, or internal troubles to quell, it would turn its attention inwards, and carry out a more systematic interference with their creed and religious observances.

In the first days of British rule in Hindustan, there used to be less talk than at present on the subject of religion. Discussion on this point has been increasing day by day, and has now reached its climax. I do not say that Government has interfered in these matters; but it has been the general opinion that all that was done was according to the instructions and hints of Government, and was by no means displeasing to it. It has been commonly believed that Government appointed missionaries and maintained them at its own cost. It has been supposed that Government, and the officers of Government throughout the country, were in the habit of giving large sums of money to these missionaries, with the intention of covering their expenses, enabling them to distribute books, and in every way aiding them. *Many covenanted officers and many military men have been in the habit of talking to their subordinates about religion; some of them would bid their servants come to their houses and listen to the preaching of missionaries, and thus it happened that in the course of time no man felt sure that his creed would last even his own lifetime.*

The missionaries, moreover, introduced a new system of preaching. *They took to printing and circulating controversial tracts, in the shape of questions and answers. Men of a different faith were spoken of in those tracts in a most offensive and irritating way.* In Hindustan these things have always been managed very differently. Every man in this country preaches and explains his views in his own mosque or his own house. If any one wishes to listen to him, he can go to the mosque or house and hear what he has to say. *But the missionaries' plan was exactly the opposite. They used to attend places of public resort—markets, for instance, and fairs, where men of different creeds were collected together—and used to begin preaching there. It was only from fear of the authorities that no one bade them be off about their business. In some districts the missionaries were actually attended by policemen from the station. And then the missionaries did not confine themselves to explaining the doctrines of their own books. In violent and unmeasured language they attacked the followers and the holy places of other creeds, annoying and insulting beyond expression the feelings of those who listened to them.* In this way, too, the seeds of discontent were sown deep in the hearts of the people.

Then missionary schools were started in which the principles of the Christian faith were taught. Men said it was by the order of Government. In some districts covenanted officers of high position and of great influence used to visit the schools and encourage the people to attend them; examinations were held in books which taught the tenets of the Christian religion. Lads who attended the schools used to be asked such questions as the following, 'Who is your God?' 'Who is your Redeemer?' and these questions they were obliged to answer agreeably to the Christian belief—prizes being given accordingly. This again added to the prevailing ill-will. *But it may be said with some justice, 'If the people were not satisfied with this course of education, why did they let their children go to the schools.' The fact is, that we have here no question of like or dislike. On the contrary, we must account for this by the painfully degraded and ignorant state of the people. They believed that if their children were entered at the schools, they might have employment given them by Government, and be enabled to find some means of subsistence. Hence they put up with a state of affairs in reality disagreeable enough to them. But it must not be thought that they ever liked those schools.*

When the village schools were established, the general belief was that they were instituted solely with the view of teaching the doctrines of Jesus. The pergunnah visitors and deputy inspectors who used to go from village to village and town to town advising the people to enter their children at these schools, got the nickname of native clergymen. When the pergunnah visitor or deputy inspector entered any village, the people used to say that the native clergyman had come. Their sole idea was, that these were Christian schools, established with the view of converting them. Well-informed men, although they did not credit this, saw nevertheless that in these schools nothing but Urdu was taught. They were afraid that boys while reading only Urdu would forget the tenets of their own faith, and that they would thus drift into Christianity. They believed, also, that Government wished such books as bore upon the doctrines of the former religions of Hindustan to fall into entire disuse. This was to be done with the view of ensuring the spread of Christianity. In many of the eastern districts of Hindustan where these schools were established, boys were entered at them by compulsion, and by compulsion only. It was currently reported that all this was in pursuance of the orders of Government.

There was at the same time a great deal of talk in Hindustan about female education. Men believed it to be the wish of Government that girls should attend and be taught at these schools, and leave off the habit of sitting veiled. Anything more obnoxious than this to the feelings of the Hindustanees cannot be conceived. In some districts the practice was actually introduced. The pergunnah visitors and deputy inspectors hoped, by enforcing the attendance of girls, to gain credit with their superior. In every way, therefore, right or wrong, they tried to carry out their object. Here, then, was another cause of discontent among the people, through which they became confirmed in error. [Emphases added]

Given such a detailed and specific enumeration of religious grievances by Syed Ahmed Khan himself against the colonial establishment's proselytising conduct, his argument that there was no legal basis in Islam for the call of jihad given by the Mutineers was incongruent. In this regard, Ayesha Jalal too is unequivocal that Syed Ahmed Khan did not reject the concept of jihad; on the contrary, his efforts were directed at *protecting* its doctrinal legitimacy by distancing the failure of the Mutiny of his co-religionists from the concept of jihad since, according to Khan, the Mutineers did not live up to the lofty Islamic requirements of jihad.[28] To sound convincing in his criticism of Muslim Mutineers and simultaneous defense of jihad as a religious doctrine, Khan also ran down the maulvis and maulanas who called for jihad as 'pseudo-Maulvis' and the Mughal dynast Bahadur Shah Zafar himself as an 'imbecile king' for having paid heed to them.[29] Apart from the above tenuous defence, given his own role in holding Bijnor for the British during the Mutiny when he was a sub-judge under the British, Syed Ahmed Khan marshalled his personal conduct as proof of the loyalty of Muslims towards the British.[30] On his efforts to protect the British during the Mutiny, his friend G.F.I. Graham wrote as follows:[31]

> During the anxious weeks that the English ladies, gentleman and children remained in Bijnore, Syed Ahmed Khan did all that man could do to render their stay safe, and was ultimately the means of saving the whole party. As Sir John Strachey, late Lieutenant-Governor of the North-West Provinces, said of him in a speech at Allygurh, on the 11th December 1880: 'No man ever gave nobler proofs of conspicuous courage and loyalty to the British Government than were given by him in 1857: no language that I could use would be worthy of the devotion he showed.'

On his part, Syed Ahmed Khan declared that insofar as the Mutiny was concerned, *'the parties really guilty may have been Ramdin and Matadin!'*, which was, of course, a reference to Hindus.[32,33] He went so far as to say that Mohammedans would never harm Christians since both had shared religious beliefs and were People of the Book. Here is a relevant extract from his work *The Loyal Mohammedans of India*, where Khan repeatedly appealed to Muslim–Christian brotherhood:[34]

> Now the season of dire extremity to which I allude is that which befell the Mohammedans in 1857–58. *There was no atrocity committed then of which the blame was not imputed to the Mohammedans, although the parties really guilty*

may have been Ramdin and Matadin. An oriental poet has well said: 'There is no misfortune sent from heaven which, ere it descended to earth, did not seek for its resting-place the dwellings of Mohammedans!'

Long and anxiously have I pondered upon the events which marked the terrible crisis that has passed over this country; and I am free to confess that the facts which have come to my knowledge, and which I firmly believe to be true, have been a source of genuine comfort to my soul, inducing, as they do, the proud conviction that the rumours defamatory of the Mohammedans that have got abroad from the four quarters of the world are utterly without foundation. Some of the acts of the horrible drama have already been exposed; but as day by day all the particulars are gradually brought to light, then, when the naked truth stands revealed then will this one glorious fact stand out in prominent relief, that if in Hindustan there was one class of people above another who, from the principles of their religion, from habits and associations, and from kindred disposition, were fast bound with Christians, in their dread hour of trial and danger, in the bonds of amity and friendship, those people were the Mohammedans; and then will be effectually silenced the tongue of slander, now so loud in their condemnation.

I am an attentive reader of the newspapers, and I have also read the various works that have been written upon the mutiny and rebellion, and in all do I find the most bitter denunciations against the Mohammedans, who are freely represented as being everything that is vile, treacherous, and contemptible. There was no prickly thorn in those awful times respecting which it was not said that it was planted by a Mohammedan! There was no fiery whirlwind that was not raised by a Mohammedan! And yet what are the facts? The very opposite, indeed, of what the mistaken popular opinion would show them to be; for I really do not see that any class besides the Mohammedans displayed so much single-minded and earnest devotion to the interests of Government, or so willingly sacrificed reputation and status, life and prosperity, in its cause. It is an easy thing to make empty profession of loyalty and service, and to write an occasional bulletin of news, false or true; but it is to the Mohammedans that the credit belongs of having stood the stanch [sic] and unshaken friends of the Government amidst that fearful tornado that devastated the country, and shook the empire to its centre; and who were ever ready, heart and hand, to render their aid to the utmost extremity, or cheerfully to perish in the attempt, regardless of home and kindred, of life and its enjoyments.

Be it known, however, that I certainly am no advocate of those Mohammedans who behaved undutifully, and joined in the rebellion; on the contrary, I hold their conduct in utter abhorrence, as being in the highest degree criminal, and wholly inexcusable. *At that momentous crisis it was imperatively their duty—a duty enjoined by the precepts of our religion—to identify themselves heartily with the Christians and to espouse their cause, seeing that they have, like ourselves, been favoured with a revelation from heaven, and believe in the prophets, and hold sacred the word of God in His holy book, which is also an object of faith with us ... Verily, such unworthy Mohammedans have well deserved the righteous indignation of all right-thinking men;* but at the same time, I must deprecate that wholesale denunciation against Mohammedans as a race, in which the newspapers are wont to indulge, and which stains the pages of those who have written upon the events of 1857. [Emphases added]

Here, Khan proves himself to be the forerunner of the Pakistani mindset, which creates the bad cop, plays the good cop and takes the West for a ride to continue the pursuit of its anti-Hindu/anti-Bharat agenda. Had the Mutiny succeeded, Syed Ahmed Khan would probably have hailed it as proof of success of jihad and credited the Hand of Providence. Since it did not succeed, the concept of jihad had to be protected from the blemish of failure and the Muslim community absolved of participation in the Mutiny by pointing fingers exclusively at 'Ramdin and Matadin' as well as at the British for triggering the Mutiny through their policies.

Clearly, as stated earlier, Khan's case of 'Muslim loyalty' towards the British empire was the convenient product of the Muslim inability to compete with the British on the battlefield, which proved the futility of armed jihad against them. Critically, it also underscored the fact that Muslims could not afford to stay aloof from the colonial establishment either, since that would allow a Hindu takeover. To address the latter, Khan took it upon himself to act as the interlocutor between Muslims in Bharat and the colonial Christian establishment by encouraging inter-community dining and comparative study of the Quran and the Bible to demonstrate that they, as the People of the Book, were not that far apart.[35] His objective, of course, was to convey the message that in view of the shared Abrahamic antecedents of Christianity and Islam and their similarities, Muslims and the British could establish a 'mutually beneficial alliance'.[36] I leave it to the reader to infer who this Holy and mutually beneficial alliance was meant to be aimed at.

While encouraging greater interaction between Muslims and the British, Khan also employed the Christian polemic framework to respond to Christian criticism of Islam, an effort in which he was not alone. There were others, such as Syed Ameer Ali, Shibli Nomani, and Maulvi Chiragh Ali. Chiragh Ali, who worked for the Nizam of Hyderabad and after whom a prominent lane in Hyderabad is still named, saw a mentor in Syed Ahmed Khan. The cause for the defence of Islam was served on a platter to the community and to these individuals when William Muir's four-volume treatise, titled *Life of Mahomet,* was published between 1856 and 1861. This treatise critiqued and criticised Islam through examination of its fundamentals and history. On this, Ayesha Jalal writes:[37]

There was enough ammunition here for a million Muslim mutinies. Muir's work was seen as a threat to the faith of the younger generation of Western-educated Muslims. The first to retaliate with a verbal jihad was Sayyid Ahmad Khan, taking heart in the Prophet's saying that the ink of the scholar is weightier than the blood of the martyr. Locating himself within the Islamic tradition, he borrowed the polemical methods of Christian apologists.

Syed Ahmed Khan's retaliation—or 'verbal *jihad*', as Jalal calls it—took the form of twelve essays in Urdu titled *Khutbat-i-Ahmadiya,* which were translated largely by his son Syed Mahmud and published in English in 1870 as *A Series of Essays on the Life of Mohammed and Subjects Subsidiary Thereto.* And Syed Ameer Ali wrote *A Critical Examination of the Life and Teachings of Mohammed.* In my view, this incident was a textbook case of two Abrahamic colonialities, namely the European and the Middle Eastern, attempting to demonstrate their respective moral superiorities and their claims to 'civilisation', 'enlightenment', 'liberty', 'truth', and all that is 'pure' and 'rational' under the sun. On the one hand, Christian writers employed the colonial orientalist framework to a significant extent while their Muslim counterparts employed the postcolonial framework, but on the other hand, neither was interested in acknowledging the scripture-sanctioned treatment meted out to non-Christian and non-Muslim societies and cultures in the name of their respective 'true faiths'.

Syed Ahmed Khan's response to Muir's criticism of Islam and the Islamic Prophet required him to 'rationalise' several Quranic miraculous claims and, in the process, depart to a significant extent from the literal interpretation of the Quran as propounded by Dehlawi. In other words, similar to his Hindu contemporaries, Khan felt the need to prove that his religion too was rational, scientific, 'modern' and, therefore, relevant. This experience would go on to shape his approach to the West as well as to Islam. The tendency to reform the Muslim community was driven partly by subconscious coloniality—to bring his community 'at par' with the West—and partly by Dehlawite reformist thoughts. The former would lead to the setting up of institutions that combined Islam and Western thinking, while the latter would drive efforts for restoration of Islam's purity and its sovereignty over Bharat.

Aligarh

Syed Ahmed Khan founded the Translation Society in Ghazipur in January 1864, which was shifted to Aligarh in April that year and renamed Scientific Society of Aligarh under the auspices of the Aligarh Institute. According to some scholars, in establishing the Society Khan was inspired by Nawab Abdul Latif's Mohammedan Literary Society during his visit to Calcutta.[38] Khan's

Raja of Mahmudabad with leaders of the Aligarh Movement.
(*Left to right, sitting*): Nawab Viqar-ul-Mulk, Raja of Mahmudabad and
Sahabzada Aftab Ahmad Khan. (*Left to right, standing*): Miya(n) Sadiq Ali Khan,
Sir Ziauddin Ahmad, Shaikh Habibullah (1 January 1930).

project was received warmly by the British, as evidenced from the fact that a
land grant was made for the Society's establishment.[39] The objectives of the
Scientific Society were twofold—to encourage greater interaction between
Englishmen and Muslim intelligentsia, and to translate Western works,
especially in the realm of the sciences and the arts, into Urdu. Although this
initiative was not successful in creating a wide impact, it certainly seemed to
have left Khan deeply in awe of Europeans and their scientific progress, and
also *sympathetic* to their disdain for Indians. His subsequent trip to England
in 1869 for the admission of his younger son Syed Mahmud to Cambridge
deepened his awe of that country and the West in general, and exacerbated
his contempt for Indians.[40] This was revealed in his letters published in the
Aligarh Institute Gazette,[41] an extract from which is reproduced here:

> We in Hindoostan look upon the English as possessing evil disposition ...
> saying that they look upon Hindoostanees as animals, or beasts, and consider
> them low to a degree ... They do not understand us; and, moreover, I say in
> truth that we are so. I say without exaggeration and in all sincerity, that all
> Hindoostanees from the highest to the lowest, the richest and the poorest, the
> merchants and the labourers, the best educated and the most ignorant—*we*

are, in comparison with the breeding and affability of the English, as dirty, unclean
wild beasts in the presence of beautiful and worthy men ... I know my countrymen
will take this as hard thing from me. [Emphasis added]

Counterintuitively, Khan's trip to England may have strengthened his
position, which broadly mirrored Dehlawi's, that the reason for the decline
of Muslim society was its deviation from the Quran by placing primary
reliance on the pronouncements of various schools of Islamic law instead
of applying one's own rational faculties to the text to keep pace with the
times. In calling for greater reliance on the Quran and selective reliance on
the Hadith, Khan's position was closer to the views of the Ahl-i-Hadith and
the Ahl-i-Quran Movement;[42] however, the difference in approach between
these Movements and Khan was that while these Movements were more
insular and isolationist, Khan was of the view that Islam, if practised in its
pristine form, was not at loggerheads with scientific temper and progress but
was, in fact, welcoming of it. According to Syed Ahmed Khan, complete
reform of Muslim life in Bharat, starting with religious beliefs and practices,
was necessary in order for the Muslims to take their 'rightful' place in Bharat
as well as to take on the challenge of the West. Thanks to these views, Khan,
according to Metcalf, was seen by his contemporaries as a 'Westernized'
Islamic reformer with Wahhabi convictions, i.e., the goals were generally
Islamic and specifically Wahhabi/Dehlawi, while the means of achieving the
same were a combination of Islamic and Western.[43] In this sense, Khan was
a more 'refined', anglicised and Westernised version of Syed Shahid Barelvi,
since he too pursued Dehlawi's vision, but in a manner acceptable to the times
he lived in, namely, through the pen and institution building, i.e., intellectual
and institutional jihad, as opposed to Barelvi's overt and armed version.

Interestingly, Khan's Wahhabi beliefs, or at least his agreement with
Wahhabism, came to the fore in 1872 when he responded to William Hunter's
book *The Indian Musalmans,* which examined the Wahhabi Movement.
Similar to his defence of the Muslim community in the aftermath of the
Mutiny of 1857 without undermining the concept of jihad, Khan's defence
again supported Wahhabi beliefs but took the position that the entire Muslim
community could not be accused of being complicit with the Wahhabi
Movement and its jihad against the British.[44] Here, it is pertinent to recollect
that in his first book in 1847, which was written in Urdu, he had not only
hailed the Wahhabis for their jihad but had also himself acknowledged that
'*every year the mujahids (holy warriors) go from different native places for the*
jihad' against the Sikhs in the NWF. Clearly, facts and positions are diluted
in their journey from Urdu to English, a phenomenon that Dr Arun Shourie
described in his work on the destruction of Hindu temples by Islamic invaders

when he noticed the progressive dilution of facts as they traversed a path from Arabic to English through Urdu.[45]

Coming back to Syed Ahmed Khan, his Westernised Wahhabi reformist impulses led to the establishment of two traditional madrasas—one in Moradabad and the other in Ghazipur—where he intended to implement his reformist vision as well as offset the criticism that he diluted traditional Quranic learning. In 1870, he founded a journal, *Tahzib-ul-Akhlaq,* or the Muhammadan Social Reformer, to demonstrate through his writings that Islam, reform and progress were not mutually exclusive.[46] Khan was supported in his views by his *man Friday* Maulvi Samiullah Khan, the Nawabs Muhsin'ul-Mulk and Vaqar'ul-Mulk (the future founders of the All-India Muslim League), the scholar Dr Nazir Ahmad and the poet Altaf Hussain Hali. Gradually, the founding of these institutions and subsequent ones came to be known as the Aligarh Movement since Aligarh was chosen as its base. According to M.S. Jain, it was during his trip to England that Syed Ahmed Khan chose Aligarh as the epicentre of his Movement, owing to the Muslim-majority composition of the neighbouring districts and the strong presence there of a Muslim feudal aristocracy. That apart, since the name Aligarh contained 'Ali', which held a special significance for the Islamic Prophet, the choice seemed apt to Syed Ahmed Khan.[47]

Naturally, the Movement attracted the former ruling Muslim elite in and around Aligarh and the young scions of Muslim aristocracy from across the Bharatiya subcontinent. However, it was vehemently opposed for its Westernised approach to Islam as well as for Khan's British loyalist interpretation of jihad by several of his contemporaries, like Haji Ali Baksh Badauni and Haji Imdadul Ali. The former went so far as to obtain a fatwa of *kufr* (means against the tenets of Islam) from Hejaz against Khan in 1873.[48] As a consequence of such opposition, when Khan floated the proposal for a Mohammedan college, which would have, among other things, English as its medium of instruction alongside traditional Islamic learning under ulema whose curriculum he would *not* interfere with, the budgetary target of Rs 10 lakh that Khan had set for himself could not be met.[49] However, with the encouragement of Samiullah Khan and the support of powerful Muslim aristocrats such as Salar Jung, who at that time was the prime minister of the Nizam of Hyderabad, Syed Ahmed Khan founded the Muhammadan Anglo-Oriental College as a primary school on 24 May 1875. Interestingly, William Muir, with whom Khan had sparred on the subject of Islam, visited the college in October 1875 and addressed its students.[50] Similarly, W.W. Hunter visited the institution in 1882 as part of the Commission on Indian Education and held its first session in the college.[51] Both these visits represented significant milestones in the changed attitudes of the British and Muslims towards each other, for which Syed Ahmed Khan's efforts, along with those of others such as Nawab Abdul Latif and Syed Ameer Ali, must be credited.

In keeping with his position that Muslims must overcome their sectarian divides in order to forge a 'national identity' and reclaim their 'rightful place', Sunnis and Shias were allowed to formulate their own religious curricula in the college. Accordingly, Maulvi Chiragh Ali from Hyderabad and Maulvi Samiullah Khan were appointed secretaries of their respective Shia and Sunni education committees.[52] In 1876, Syed Ahmed Khan retired from government service to devote all his time and energy to the college, whose foundation stone was laid by the Viceroy of the time, Lord Lytton, on 8 January 1877.[53] The reason that the British establishment viewed Khan's initiatives and the Aligarh College with favour was that it was keen on countering the growing political awareness of the Hindus who, as stated earlier, had been exposed to English education for at least five decades since its introduction in 1817, i.e., even before Macaulay's Education Policy of 1835. According to R.C. Majumdar:[54]

> The British, like all imperial powers, instinctively followed the policy of divide and rule in governing India. They could not be possibly unaware of the fact that while the Muslims resented the establishment of British political authority, the Hindus welcomed it, and so at the beginning they unduly favoured the Hindus. But after two generations of the Hindus had imbibed Western ideas through English education, they showed signs of political development which was regarded by the Government as anti-British and almost revolutionary. So they eagerly seized the opportunity, offered by Syed Ahmad, of enlisting the support of the great but politically undeveloped Muslim community, and holding it as a counterpoise to the progressive Hindu community. Henceforth the British Government steadily followed the policy of clogging or putting a brake on one wheel of the car of India's political evolution, so that its progress may be slowed down, even if not altogether stopped.

British support to the Aligarh establishment is evident from the fact that several Englishmen contributed to the construction of the college, which was equally reciprocated by the college, which hired a good number of Englishmen among its faculty, including as principals. In particular, according to Majumdar, Theodore Beck, the first principal of Aligarh College, contributed heavily to the stoking of both Muslim nationalism and anti-Hindu bias in the minds of his students. Beck gave up a career in England and dedicated his life to the faithful service of Muslims in Bharat, who regarded him as their 'faithful friend'.[55] Apart from vilifying Bengali Hindus, he stoked the fear that a Hindu-majority parliamentary democracy would be a disaster for Muslims since Hindus 'would be the absolute masters as no Muhammadan ever was'. In the 1889 session of the Indian National Congress at Bombay, when Charles Bradlaugh (a member of the British House of Commons) promised to introduce the Indian Councils Amendment Bill (also known as the Home Rule Bill) in the House of Commons, Beck prepared a petition to oppose the Bill on behalf of Muslims. He proceeded to Delhi with a few of his students and obtained the signatures of 20,000 Muslims to oppose the Home Rule Bill by misleading the signatories to believe that it was a petition against a ban on cow slaughter proposed by the Hindus.[56]

In 1893, under Beck's encouragement, a few Muslim intellectuals established the Muhammadan Anglo-Oriental Defence Association of Upper India for the purpose of advocating the Muslim cause before the British establishment. Beck, as the secretary of the Association, held the following views on the Congress demand for introduction of democracy in India:[57]

> The objective of the Congress is to transfer the political control of the country from the British to the Hindus. It demands the repeal of the Arms Act, reduction of military expenditure, and the consequential weakening of the frontier defences. *Musalmans can have no sympathy with these demands. It is imperative for the Muslims and the British to unite with a view to fighting these agitators and prevent the introduction of democratic form of government, unsuited as it is to the needs and genius of the country. We therefore, advocate loyalty to the Government and Anglo-Muslim collaboration.* [Emphasis added]

His stoking of anti-Hindu sentiments is evident from the speech delivered by him in 1895 in London, which was summarised by the *Aligarh College Magazine* as follows:[58]

1. A friendship between the British people and the Muslims was possible, but not between Muslims and followers of other religions; for example, the followers of Shivaji and those of Guru Govind Singh would never agree with the Muslims in accepting Aurangzeb as their hero;
2. Muslims would never accept a system of government in which the Hindu majority would rule over them; the Muslims of Kashmir who were living under the yoke of Brahmin officers envied the good fortune of the Muslims who were living happily under the British rule;
3. Indians themselves did not like a democratic system; they preferred monarchy;
4. Muslim behaviour during and after the Revolt (of 1857) had warned the community against agitational politics of Hindus, and they were now wisely acting on the advice of Sir Syed—it was the advice of loyalty to the British;
5. Muslims were opposed to the holding of the competitive examinations in India, for they knew that this step would mean the replacement of many impartial British officers by anti-Muslim Hindus.

After Beck's death in 1899, his anti-Hindu legacy was taken forward by his successor Theodore Morrison, who remained the principal until 1905. There is no doubt that a divide and rule policy was at work behind British support to the Aligarh College. However, to hold Beck responsible for Syed Ahmed Khan's views would be to ignore Khan's own moorings and leanings, which were consistently reflected both in his writings and speeches much before Beck. It would be naïve and factually incorrect to overlook the Dehlawite motivations of Khan. In other words, the Aligarh Movement and its institutions represented the 'mutually beneficial alliance' proposed by Khan, much to the detriment of the Indic civilisational consciousness and space. Critically, Khan was clear that the purpose of the college was not to merely churn out loyal and competent employees for the British establishment but also to provide a space for Muslim solidarity and regeneration, with its graduates serving as 'modern' ambassadors of the cause. In 1876, Khan told his students:[59]

> There is no god but Allah, this is the cornerstone of our faith, and only by believing in it we are a nation. If you excel in other fields but do not believe in it, then we shall cease to be a nation. We would have nothing to do with you, even if you shine like stars in the firmament.

While pledging loyalty to the British, his vision was restoration of the former position of the Muhammadan 'nation' ('qaum') through a 'peaceful revolution', i.e., by becoming part of and thereafter taking over the colonial power structure.[60] To this end, 'Muhammadan' was consciously included in the name of the college, to primarily attract Muslims, and funds were refused from Hindus who wanted the college established in Allahabad instead of Aligarh.[61] While the Aligarh College did succeed significantly in creating the 'national' Muslim identity, i.e., a Muslim identity which overcame sectarian, regional and linguistic divides, its very strengths became its weaknesses. The institution's marked Western slant, its insistence on a sense of loyalty to the British Crown and the presence of English staff, including principals, contributed to the belief that the atmosphere of the school encouraged students only from the Muslim aristocracy and not the lower strata of Muslim society. To make matters worse, in a speech delivered in Lucknow in 1887, Syed Ahmed Khan dismissed the idea of the 'lower classes' climbing up the ladder to rule over the 'nobility'.[62] So much for Islamic egalitarianism and brotherhood. These aspects of the institution led to some of its leading lights moving away from it to other institutions committed to traditional Islamic learning. For instance, as stated earlier, in 1894, Shibli Nomani moved to the Nadwatul Ulama since he did not believe in accepting the colonial state and engaging with it.[63] He sought an Islamic state which was governed by Shariat, and Aligarh, according to him, was not moving in that direction. Despite these criticisms and setbacks, under the stewardship of Syed Ahmed Khan, the Aligarh Movement and its institutions did play a hugely impactful role in the fostering of Muslim nationalism, which was its founding objective.

The Two-Nation Theory

Contrary to what some would have us believe, this much is clear from the journey of Syed Ahmed Khan, that the Two-Nation Theory was not the product of a sudden disillusionment with the Hindu-majority Indian National Congress, which was founded in 1885. It was present all along, as reflected in Khan's own earliest writings in 1847, in which he openly expressed support for the Wahhabis. Even in his book *Causes of the Indian Revolt*, which was originally published in Urdu in 1858, he referred to Hindus and Muslims as 'two antagonistic races' when highlighting the British folly of bringing them together in a single unit, thereby endangering the British position. Here is a relevant extract from Graham's book, where he quotes Khan from the latter's book:[64]

> The English army system in India has always been faulty, and one great fault was the paucity of English troops. When Nadir Shah conquered Khorassan, and became master of the two kingdoms of Persia and Afghanistan, he invariably kept the two armies at equal strength. The one consisted, or rather was composed, of Persians and Kuzul Bashies, and the other was composed of Afghans. When the Persian army attempted to rise, the Afghan army was at hand to quell the rebellion, and vice versa. The English did not follow this precedent in India. The sepoy army was no doubt faithful in its day and served the Government well, but how could Government feel certain that it would never act contrary to its orders. What measures had Government taken for quelling at once on the spot any emeute in that vast army, such as that which happened last year?
>
> *Government certainly did put the two antagonistic races into the same regiment, but constant intercourse had done its work, and the two races in regiment had almost become one. It is but natural and to be expected, that a feeling of friendship and brotherhood must spring up between the men of a regiment, constantly brought together as they are. They consider themselves as one body; and thus it was that the difference which exists between Hindus and Mohammedans had, in these regiments, been almost entirely smoothed away.*
>
> If a portion of the regiment engaged in anything, all the rest joined. *If separate regiments of Hindus and separate regiments of Mohammedans had been raised, this feeling of brotherhood could not have arisen, and, in my opinion, the Mohammedan regiments would not have refused to receive the new cartridges.* [Emphases added]

A mass meeting of Muslims held in Dacca on 4 September 1906 in favour of the Partition of Bengal. The photo was published in *The Sphere* on 27 October 1906.

Not only did Khan subscribe to the view that the communities were two different and *antagonistic* races/nations, he also wanted the British to keep them apart in order to preserve the latter's control over Bharat. Again, in 1867, when a debate arose as to whether Hindi or Urdu should be used in the vernacular universities being set up, and for administrative purposes—which snowballed into the Urdu Movement—Khan was reported to have told the Commissioner of Benares that Hindus and Muslims were 'two nations' and even spoke of the separate political evolution of Muslims.[65] In fact, deposing before the Commission on Indian Education helmed by W.W. Hunter, Khan is reported to have passionately argued that '*Urdu was the language of gentry and of people of high social standing, whereas Hindi was to be the vulgar*'.[66] Khan was of the view that the replacement of Urdu by Hindi would reinforce the loss of Muslim authority over Bharat, which led him to advocate Urdu as a symbol of Muslim heritage. He was supported in this position by Muslims across the board, including his opponents from within the Muslim community, leading to the founding of organisations such as the Urdu Defence Association and the Anjuman Taraqqi-i-Urdu.[67] This was yet another clear manifestation of the Two-Nation Theory, which would significantly contribute towards the crystallisation of 'Pakistan' once the cause was adopted by the All-India Muslim League.

According to M.S. Jain, the Two-Nation Theory also manifested itself in the second-class treatment of Hindu students in the Aligarh College, which was justified by the college administration on the grounds that:[68]

1. Hindu–Muslim unity was a farce;
2. the college was primarily meant to attract Muslims;
3. Hindus had no basis to expect education from the Muhammadan College or equal treatment, and those that were admitted were being accommodated owing to the help received from Hindus for the founding of the college.

I must clarify that in my view it makes very little sense to vilify either Syed Ahmed Khan or the institutions he founded for their views on non-Muslims and their treatment of them. Since the stated object of founding such institutions was uplift of a particular community and restoration of its former status as 'rulers of Hindustan', the blame must be laid at the door of those Hindus who wallowed in notions of unity—to such an extent that they were open to their children being educated in such institutions. Clearly, Western education had not dulled the conviction or clarity of purpose of Middle Eastern consciousness, while the same cannot be said of the Indic consciousness, which refused to (and still refuses to) accept realities for what they were (and are).

Even according to Majumdar, the Two-Nation Theory formed the 'solid basis' of the Aligarh Movement. He believed that the very conception of the Movement was communal in nature, and that while it regenerated the Muslim community politically and socially, it *'widened the political cleavage between the Hindus and Muslims, and created a distinct Muslim unit in Indian politics'.*[69] Majumdar identified the following four fundamental principles of the Movement, which formed the very basis of the Two-Nation Theory in my opinion:[70]

1. Hindus and Muslims form two separate political entities with separate outlooks and conflicting interests;
2. The grant of representative institutions based on democratic principles and appointment to high offices by open competitive examination in India would be detrimental to the interests of the Muslims, as they would be subject to Hindu domination, which is far worse than British rule;
3. Muslims should regard the paramountcy of the British as the chief safeguard of their interests, and keep themselves aloof from political agitation against the government;
4. As Muslim interests are quite safe in the hands of the British, they should confine their attention to cultural development, and avoid politics except insofar as necessary to counterbalance the mischief of Hindu political agitators.

Majumdar supported his identification of these guiding principles of the Aligarh Movement by citing specific instances revealing Syed Ahmed Khan's opposition to treatment of Hindus and Muslims as a single nation. For instance, in 1883, Khan expressed detailed and vehement opposition to the introduction of representative institutions on the basis of simple elections since he felt that *'the larger community would totally override the interest of the smaller community'.*[71] In other words, the dangers of a 'Hindu majoritarian democracy', of which we hear so often these days, were being aired by Syed Ahmed Khan in his time. Evidently, his issue was not with democracy but with a *Hindu-majority* democracy, since his Dehlawite worldview could not tolerate the spectre of Muslims living in a Bharat where Hindus wielded power. Ironically, as seen earlier, Khan was comfortable taking the position that Bharat was Dar al-Islam or at least Dar al-Aman under the British so long as Muslim religious freedom was not interfered with, but the very same concession was not to be extended to the Hindus. This is because he believed that Muslims and Christians had shared religious beliefs being People of the Book or Ahl al-Kitāb, unlike with Hindus. Also, how could the former 'rulers' live under the former *kafir dhimmis?* In my view, this is at the heart of present-day Bharat's so-called majority–minority debate which, unfortunately, cannot be pointed out without inviting all sorts of pejorative labels. So long as Hindus continue to be a majority in Bharat, it is inevitable that Syed Ahmed Khan's Two-Nation Theory will be pushed under the garb of opposition to 'Hindu majoritarianism' and 'minority oppression'. As pointed out in the first book, this is a textbook case of Middle Eastern consciousness riding on the coattails of European coloniality by pushing its own agenda under the garb of 'protection of minorities in a Hindu-majority State'.

It is important to note that the above-mentioned views of Syed Ahmed Khan on larger–smaller and majority–minority communities were expressed two years *before* the Indian National Congress was established in 1885. Also, since these views were in line with his previous position on the need to restore Muslim rule in Bharat, the founding of the Congress only gave him *additional* reason to build further on his Two-Nation Theory. Here are a few extracts from his speech vehemently opposing the Congress and expressly hinting at the possibility of revival of physical jihad if Muslims of the subcontinent were expected to live under a Hindu-majority government helmed by the Congress:[72]

In a country like India where homogeneity does not exist in any one of these fields (nationality, religion, ways of living, customs, mores, culture, and historical traditions), the introduction of representative government cannot produce any beneficial results; it can only result in interfering with the peace and prosperity of the land ... The aims and objects of the Indian National Congress are based upon an ignorance of history and present-day realities; they do not take into consideration that India is inhabited by different nationalities; ... I consider the experiment which the Indian National Congress wants to make fraught with dangers and suffering for all the nationalities of India, specially for the Muslims. *The Muslims are in a minority, but they are a highly united, minority. At least traditionally they are prone to take the sword in hand when the majority oppresses them. If this happens, it will bring about disasters greater than the ones which came in the wake of the happenings of 1857. The Congress cannot rationally prove its claim to represent the opinions, ideals, and aspirations of the Muslims.* [Emphasis added]

In 1886, in response to the founding of the Congress, Syed Ahmed Khan founded the Annual Muslim/Mohammedan Educational Conference, meetings of which would be held annually in difference places to coincide with the Congress's annual sessions. The objective of the Conference was to cover '*the whole of upper India with a network of societies, committees and individuals, all working harmoniously in the great cause, so that a big evil may be dealt with by a strong remedy and by the vigorous work of one generation the tide of misfortune may be turned and the Mohamedan Nation may be set moving on the tide of progress abreast of all the other Nations of India*'.[73] In order to demonstrate that I am not reading more into his views than warranted, here are a few more instances where Khan articulated his Two-Nation Theory with clarity, truly leaving nothing to the imagination. In November 1887, he wrote in the *Pioneer* that the parliamentary form of government was '*unsuited to a country containing two or more nations tending to oppress the numerically weaker*'.[74]

On the eve of the Congress annual session in Madras, on 18 December 1887, Khan addressed his co-religionists in Lucknow at an event organized by the Mohammedan Educational Conference. Here are a few relevant extracts from his speech which showcase his Dehlawite worldview and whose tone and tenor find resonance in the speeches of a few present-day leaders who subscribe to Khan's worldview:[75]

> GENTLEMEN,—I am not given to speaking on politics, and I do not recollect having ever previously given a political lecture. My attention has always been directed towards the education of my brother Mahomedans, for from education I anticipate much benefit for my people, for Hindustan, and for the Government. But at the present time circumstances have arisen which make it necessary for me, I think, to tell my brother Musalmans clearly what my opinions are. The object, gentlemen, of this lecture is to explain the attitude which the Mahomedan community ought to adopt with regard to the political movements of the time. I am not going to give a philosophical discourse, nor to speak of those abstract questions on political economy which would require many lectures fully to deal with; but I am simply going to express my opinions in a plain and straightforward manner, leaving it to everyone who hears me to agree with me or differ from me. The reason why I stand here to address you today is because there has grown up in India a political agitation, and it is necessary to determine what action should be taken by the Mahomedan community with regard to it. Although my own thoughts and desires are towards my own community, yet I shall discuss whether or not this agitation is useful for the country and for the other nations who live in it. If it be useful, we must follow it; but if dangerous for the country or our nation, we must hold aloof.

... There is now another great duty of Government. That is, that in whatever country Government establishes its dominion, that dominion should be made strong, firm, and secure. I believe that if any of my friends were made Viceroy; he would be as loyal to Her Majesty the Queen-Empress of India as is our present Viceroy, Lord Dufferin. And his first duty would be to see that the Empire of Her Majesty were made so firm that no enemy, external, or internal, could shake it. (Cheers.) If it were my fortune to be Viceroy; I speak from my heart when I say I would not be equally, but more, anxious to see the rule of the Queen placed on a firm basis. (Cheers.) *It is a first principle of Empire that it is the supreme duty of everyone, whether Hindustani or Englishman, in whose power it rests, to do what he can to strengthen the Government of Her Majesty the Queen.* The second duty of Government is to preserve peace, to give personal freedom, to protect life and property; to punish criminals, and to decide civil disputes. Now, everyone will admit that Government completely fulfills its duty in this respect.

... Leave this a moment, and consider what are the conditions which make the introduction into a country of competitive examinations expedient, and then see whether our own country is ready for it or not. This is no difficult question of political economy. Everyone can understand that the first condition for the introduction of competitive examination into a country is that all people in that country, from the highest to the lowest, should belong to one nation. In such a country no particular difficulties are likely to arise. The second case is that of a country in which there are two nationalities which have become so united as to be practically one nation. England and Scotland are a case in point. In the past many wars were waged between those countries, and many acts of bravery were done on both sides; but those times have gone, and they are now like one nation. But this is not the case with our country, which is peopled with different nations. Consider the Hindus alone. The Hindus of our Province, the Bengalis of the East, and the Mahrattas of the Deccan, do not form one nation. If in your opinion the peoples of India do form one nation, then no doubt competitive examination may be introduced; but if this be not so, then competitive examination is not suited to the country. The third case is that of a country in which there are different nationalities which are on an equal footing as regards the competition, whether they take advantage of it or not. Now, I ask you, have Mahomedans attained to such a position as regards higher English education, which is necessary for higher appointments, as to put them on a level with Hindus or not? Most certainly not. Now I take Mahomedans and the Hindus of our Province together, and ask whether they are able to compete with the Bengalis or not? Most certainly not. When this is the case, how can competitive examination be introduced into our country? (Cheers.)

Think for a moment what would be the result if all appointments were given by competitive examination. *Over all races, not only over Mahomedans but over*

Rajas of high position and the brave Rajputs who have not forgotten the swords of their ancestors, would be placed as ruler a Bengali who at sight of a table knife would crawl under his chair. (Uproarious cheers and laughter.) There would remain no part of the country in which we should see at the tables of justice and authority any face except those of Bengalis. I am delighted to see the Bengalis making progress, but the question is—What would be the result on the administration of the country? Do you think that the Rajput and the fiery Pathan, who are not afraid of being hanged or of encountering the swords of the police or the bayonets of the army, could remain in peace under the Bengalis? (Cheers.) This would be the outcome of the proposal if accepted. Therefore if any of you—men of good position, Raïses, men of the middle classes, men of noble family to whom God has given sentiments of honour—*if you accept that the country should groan under the yoke of Bengali rule and its people lick the Bengali shoes, then, in the name of God! jump into the train, sit down, and be off to Madras, be off to Madras! (Loud cheers and laughter.)* But if you think that the prosperity and honour of the country would be ruined, then, brothers, sit in your houses, inform Government of your circumstances, and bring your wants to its notice in a calm and courteous manner.

The second demand of the National Congress is that the people should elect a section of the Viceroy's Council. They want to copy the English House of Lords and the House of Commons. The elected members are to be like members of the House of Commons; the appointed members like the House of Lords. Now, let us suppose the Viceroy's Council [to be] made in this manner. *And let us suppose first of all that we have universal suffrage, as in America, and that everybody, chamars and all, have votes. And first suppose that all the Mahomedan electors vote for a Mahomedan member, and all Hindu electors for a Hindu member; and now count how many votes the Mahomedan members have and how many the Hindu. It is certain the Hindu members will have four times as many, because their population is four times as numerous. Therefore we can prove by mathematics that there will be four votes for the Hindu to every one vote for the Mahomedan. And now how can the Mahomedan guard his interests? It would be like a game of dice in which one man had four dice, and the other only one.*

In the second place, suppose that the electorate be limited. Some method of qualification must be made; for example, that people with a certain income shall be electors. Now, I ask you, O Mahomedans! Weep at your condition! Have you such wealth that you can compete with the Hindus? Most certainly not. Suppose, for example, that an income of Rs. 5,000 a year be fixed on, how many Mahomedans will there be? Which party will have the larger number of votes? I put aside the case that by a rare stroke of luck a blessing comes through the roof, and some Mahomedan is elected. In the normal case no single Mahomedan will secure a seat in the Viceroy's Council. *The whole Council will consist of Babu So-and-so Mitter, Babu So-and-So Ghose, and*

Babu So-and-so Chuckerbutty. (*Laughter.*) Again, what will be the result for the Hindus of our Province, though their condition be better than that of the Mahomedans? What will be the result for those Rajputs, the swords of whose ancestors are still wet with blood? And what will be the result for the peace of the country? Is there any hope that we and our brave brothers the Rajputs can endure it in silence?

Now, we will suppose a third kind of election. Suppose a rule to be made that a suitable number of Mahomedans and a suitable number of Hindus are to be chosen. I am aghast when I think on what grounds this number is likely to be determined. Of necessity, proportion to total population will be taken. So there will be one number for us to every four for the Hindus. No other condition can be laid down. Then they will have four votes and we shall have one.

Now, I will make a fourth supposition. Leaving aside the question as to the suitability of members with regard to population, let us suppose that a rule is laid down that half the members are to be Mahomedan and half Hindus, and that the Mahomedans and Hindus are each to elect their own men. Now, I ask you to pardon me for saying something which I say with a sore heart. In the whole nation there is no person who is equal to the Hindus in fitness for the work. I have worked in the Council for four years, and I have always known well that there can be no man more incompetent or worse fitted for the post than myself. ('No, No!') And show me the man who, when elected, will leave his business and undertake the expense of living in Calcutta and Simla, leaving alone the trouble of the journeys. Tell me who there is of our nation in the Punjab, Oudh, and North-Western Provinces who will leave his business, incur these expenses, and attend the Viceroy's Council for the sake of his countrymen. When this is the condition of your nation, is it expedient for you to take part in this business, on the absurd supposition that the demands of the Congress would, if granted, be beneficial for the country? Spurn such foolish notions. It is certainly not expedient to adopt this cry—Chalo Madras! Chalo Madras!—without thinking of the consequences.

... Everybody knows well that the agitation of the Bengalis is not the agitation of the whole of India. But suppose it were the agitation of the whole of India, and that every nation had taken part in it, do you suppose the Government is so weak that it would not suppress it, but must needs be itself overwhelmed? Have you not seen what took place in the Mutiny? It was a time of great difficulty. The army had revolted; some budmashes had joined it; and Government wrongly believed that the people at large were taking part in the rebellion. I am the man who attacked this wrong notion, and while Government was hanging its officials [actually, 'while the Government officials were hanging people'], I printed a pamphlet ['The Causes of the Indian Revolt'], and told Government that it was entirely false to suppose that the people at large were rebellious. But in spite of all these difficulties, what harm could this rebellion do to Government? Before the [reinforcing] English troops had landed she had regained her authority from shore to shore. Hence, what benefit is expected from all this for the country, and what revolution in the Government can we produce? The only results can be to produce a useless uproar, to raise suspicions in Government, and to bring back again that time which we experienced thirty or thirty-one years ago. This is on the supposition that by all of us coming together we could do something; but if you take the agitation as it is, what could it accomplish? The case of Ireland is held up as an example. I will not discuss the question whether that agitation is right or wrong. I will only point out that there are at this moment in Ireland thousands of men ready to give up their lives at the point of the sword. Men of high position who sympathise with that movement fear neither the prison nor the bayonets of the police. Will you kindly point out to me ten men among our agitators who will consent to stand face to face with the bayonets? When this is the case, then what sort of an uproar is this, and is it of such a nature that we ought to join it? ...

... We ought to consider carefully our own circumstances and the circumstances of Government. If Government entertains unfavourable sentiments towards our community, then I say with the utmost force that these sentiments are entirely wrong. At the same time if we are just, we must admit that such sentiments would be by no means unnatural. I repeat it. If Government entertains these bad sentiments, it is a sign of incompetence and folly. But I say this: we ought to consider whether Government can entertain such thoughts or not. Has she any excuse for such suspicions, or not? I reply that she certainly has. Think for a moment who you are. What is this nation of ours? We are those who ruled India for six or seven hundred years. (Cheers.) From our hands the country was taken by Government into its own. Is it not natural then for Government to entertain such thoughts? Is Government so foolish as to suppose that in seventy years we have forgotten all our grandeur and our empire? Although, should Government entertain such notions, she is certainly wrong; yet we must remember she has ample excuse. *We do not live on fish, nor are we afraid of using a knife and fork lest we should cut our fingers. (Cheers.) Our nation is of the blood of those who made not only Arabia, but Asia and Europe, to tremble. It is our nation which conquered with its sword the whole of India, although its peoples were all of one religion. (Cheers.)* I say again that if Government entertains suspicions of us, it is wrong. But do her the justice and admit that there is a reasonable ground for such suspicions. Can a wise ruler forget what the state of things was so short a time ago? He can never forget it. If then the Mahomedans also join these monstrous and unreasonable schemes, which are impossible of fulfilment, and which are disastrous for the country and for our nation, what will be the result? If Government be wise and Lord Dufferin be a capable Viceroy, then he will realise that a Mahomedan agitation is not the same as a Bengali agitation, and he will be bound to apply an adequate remedy. If I were Viceroy; and my nation took part in this affair, I would first of all drop down on them, and make them feel their mistake.

... Our course of action should be such as to convince Government of the wrongness of her suspicions regarding us, if she entertain any. We should cultivate mutual affection. What we want, we should ask for as friends. And if any ill-will exist[s], it should be cleansed away. I am glad that some Pathans of the N.-W. P. [North-West Provinces] and Oudh are here today, and I hope some Hindu Rajputs are also present. My friend Yusuf Shah of the Punjab sits here, and he knows well the mood of mind of the people of the Punjab, of the Sikhs and Musalmans. Suppose that this agitation that has arisen in Bengal—and I imagine that no danger can spring from it there—suppose that this agitation extends to these Provinces, to the Rajputs and Pathans of Peshawar, do you think it will confine itself to writing with the pen—giz, giz, giz, giz, giz [the scratching of a pen]—and to mere talking—buk, buk, buk, buk [babbling]? It will then be necessary for Government to send its army and show by bayonets what the proper remedy for this agitation is. I believe that when Government sees the Mahomedans and other brave races taking part in this stupid agitation, it will be necessary for Government to pass a new law and to fill the jails. O my brothers! Children of my heart! This is your relationship to Government: you should conduct yourself in a straightforward and calm manner; not come together to make a noise and a hubbub like a flock of crows. (Cheers and laughter.)

Another very laughable idea is this. Stress is laid on these suggestions: that the Arms Act be repealed, that Indian Volunteers be enlisted, and that army schools be established in India. But do you know what nation is proposing them? If such proposals had come from Mahomedans or from our Rajput brothers, whose ancestors always wore the sword, which although it is taken from their belts yet still remains in their hearts—if they had made such proposals there would have been some sense in it. But what nation makes these demands? I agree with them in this, and consider that Government has committed two very great mistakes. One is not to trust the Hindustanis and [not] to allow them to become volunteers. A second error of Government of the greatest magnitude is this: that it does not give appointments in the army to those brave people whose ancestors did not use the pen to write with; no, but a different kind of pen—(cheers)—nor did they use black ink, but the ink they dipped their pens in was red, red ink which flows from the bodies of men. (Cheers.) *O brothers! I have fought Government in the harshest language about these points. The time is, however, coming when my brothers, Pathans, Syeds, Hashimi, and Koreishi, whose blood smells of the blood of Abraham, will appear in glittering uniform as Colonels and Majors in the army.* But we must wait for that time. Government will most certainly attend to it; provided you do not give rise to suspicions of disloyalty. O brothers! Government, too, is under some difficulties as regards this last charge I have brought against her. Until she can trust us as she can her white soldiers, she cannot do it. But we ought to give proof that whatever we were in former days, that time has gone; and that now we are as well-disposed to her as the Highlanders of Scotland. And then we should claim this from Government.

I will suppose for a moment that you have conquered a part of Europe, and have become its rulers. I ask whether you would equally trust the men of that country. This was a mere supposition. I come now to a real example. When you conquered India, what did you yourself do? For how many centuries was there no Hindu in the army list? But when the time of the Moghal family came and mutual trust was established, the Hindus were given very high appointments. Think how many years old is the British rule. How long ago was the Mutiny? And tell me how many years ago Government suffered such grievous troubles, though they arose from the ignorant and not from the gentlemen? Also call to mind that in the Madras Presidency, Government has given permission to the people to enlist as volunteers. I say, too, that this concession was premature; but it is a proof that when trust is established, Government will have no objection to make you also volunteers. And when we shall be qualified, we shall acquire those positions with which our forefathers were honoured. Government has advanced one step. She has also shown a desire to admit us to the civil appointments in the Empire. (Cheers.)

In the time of Lord Ripon I happened to be a member of the Council. Lord Ripon had a very good heart and kind disposition, and every qualification for a Governor. But unfortunately his hand was weak. His ideas were Radical. At that time the Local Board and Municipality Bills were brought forward, and the intention of them was that everybody should be appointed by election. Gentlemen, I am not a Conservative, I am a great Liberal. But to forget the prosperity of one's nation is not a sign of wisdom. The only person who was opposed to the system of election was myself. If I am not bragging too much, I may, I think, say that it was on account of my speech that Lord Ripon changed his opinion and made one-third of the members appointed and two-thirds elected. Now just consider the result of election. In no town are Hindus and Mahomedans equal. Can the Mahomedans suppress the Hindus and become the masters of our 'Self-Government'? In Calcutta an old, bearded Mahomedan of noble family met me and said that a terrible calamity had befallen them. In his town there were eighteen elected members, not one of whom was a Mahomedan; all were Hindus. Now he wanted Government to appoint some Mahomedan; and he hoped Government would appoint himself. This is the state of things in all cities. In Aligarh also, were there not a special rule, it would be impossible for any Mahomedan, except my friend Maulvi Mahomed Yusuf, to be elected; and at last he too would have to rely on being appointed by Government. Then how can we walk along a road for which neither we nor the country is prepared?

I am now tired and have no further strength left. I can say no more. But in conclusion, I have one thing to say, lest my friends should say that I have not told them what is of advantage for our nation and for the country; and by what thing we may attain prosperity. My age is above seventy. Although I cannot live to see my nation attain to such a position as my heart longs for it, yet my friends who are present in this meeting will certainly see the nation attain such honour, prosperity and high rank, if they attend to my advice. But my friends, do not liken me to that dyer who, only possessing mango-coloured dye, said mango-coloured dye was the only one he liked. I assure you that the only thing which can raise you to a high rank is high education. *Until our nation can give birth to a highly-educated people, it will remain degraded; it will be below others, and will not attain such honour as I desire for it. These precepts I have given you from the bottom of my heart. I do not care if any one calls me a madman or anything else. It was my duty to tell those things which, in my opinion, are necessary for the welfare of my nation, and to cleanse my hands before God the Omnipotent, the Merciful, and the Forgiver of sins.* [Emphases added]

And here are a few extracts from his follow-up speech delivered in Meerut on 16 March 1888, where he continued his diatribe against Bengali Hindus and exhortation to the Muslims to extend loyalty to the British, citing shared Abrahamic beliefs:[76,77]

I think it expedient that I should first of all tell you the reason why I am about to address you on the subject of tonight's discourse. You know, gentlemen, that, from a long time, our friends the Bengalis have shown very warm feeling on political matters. Three years ago they founded a very big assembly, which holds its sittings in various places, and they have given it the name 'National Congress.' We and our nation gave no thought to the matter. And we should be very glad for our friends the Bengalis to be successful, if we were of the opinion that they had by their education and ability made such progress as rendered them fit for the claims they put forward. But although they are superior to us in education, yet we have never admitted that they have reached that level to which they lay claim to have attained. Nevertheless I have never, in any article, or in any speech, or even in conversation in any place, put difficulties or desired to put difficulties in the way of any of their undertakings. It has never been my wish to oppose any people or any nation who wish to make progress, and who have raised themselves up to that rank to which they wish to attain and for which they are qualified. But my friends the Bengalis have made a most unfair and unwarrantable interference with my nation, and therefore it is my duty to show clearly what this unwarrantable interference has been, and to protect my nation from the evils that may arise from it. It is quite wrong to suppose that I have girded up my loins for the purpose of fighting my friends the Bengalis; my object is only to make my nation understand what I consider conducive to its prosperity. It is incumbent on me to show what evils would befall my nation from joining in the opinions of the Bengalis: I have no other purpose in view.

The unfair interference of these people is this—that they have tried to produce a false impression that the Mahomedans of these Provinces agree with their opinions. But we also are inhabitants of this country, and we cannot be ignorant of the real nature of the events that are taking place in our own North-West Provinces and Oudh, however their colour may be painted in newspapers, and whatever aspect they may be made to assume. It is possible that the people of England, who are ignorant of the real facts, may be deceived on seeing their false representations; but we and the people of our country, who know all the circumstances, can never be thus imposed on. Our Mahomedan nation has hitherto sat silent. It was quite indifferent as to what the Babus of Bengal, the Hindus of these Provinces, and the English and Eurasian inhabitants of India, might be doing. But they have now been wrongly tampering with our nation. In some districts they have brought pressure to bear on Mahomedans to make them join the Congress. I am sorry to say that they never said anything to those people who are powerful and are actually Raïses [nobles] and are counted the leaders of the nation; but they brought unfair pressure to bear on such people as could be subjected to their influence.

In some districts they pressed men by the weight of authority, in others they forced them in this way—saying that the business they had at heart could not prosper unless they took part; or they led them to suppose that they could not get bread if they held aloof. They even did not hold back from offering the temptation of money. Where is the man that does not know this? Who does not know who were the three or four Mahomedans of the North-West Provinces who took part with them, and why they took part? The simple truth is they were nothing more than hired men. (Cheers.) Such people they took to Madras, and having got them there, said, 'These are the sons of Nawabs, and these are Raïses of such-and-such districts, and these are such-and-such great Mahomedans,' whilst everybody knows how the men were bought. We know very well the people of our own nation, and that they have been induced to go either by pressure, or by folly, or by love of notoriety, or by poverty. If any Raïs on his own inclination and opinion join them, we do not care a lot. By one man's leaving us our crowd is not diminished. But this telling of lies that their men are landlords and Nawabs of such-and-such places; and their attempt to give a false impression that the Mahomedans have joined them—this is a most unwarrantable interference with our nation. When matters took such a turn, then it was necessary that I should warn my nation of their misrepresentations, in order that others should not fall into the trap; and that I should point out to my nation that the few who went to Madras, went by pressure, or from some temptation, or in order to help their profession, or to gain notoriety; or were bought. (Cheers.) No Raïs from here took part in it.

This was the cause of my giving a speech at Lucknow [in 1887], contrary to my wont, on the evils of the National Congress; and this is the cause also of today's speech. And I want to show this: that except Badruddin Tyabji, who is a gentleman of very high position and for whom I have great respect, no leading Mahomedan took part in it. He did take part, but I think he made a mistake. He has written me two letters, one of which was after the publication of my Lucknow speech. I think that he wants me to point out those things in the Congress which are opposed to the interests of Mahomedans, in order that he may exclude them from the discussion. But in reality the whole affair is bad for Mahomedans. However, let us grant that Badruddin Tyabji's opinion is different from ours; yet it cannot be said that his opinion is the opinion of the whole nation, or that his sympathy with the Congress implies the sympathy of the whole community. My friend there, Mirza Ismail Khan, who has just come from Madras, told me that no Mahomedan Raïs of Madras took part in the Congress. It is said that Prince Humayun Jah joined it. Let us suppose that Humayun Jah, whom I do not know, took part in it; yet our position as a nation will not suffer simply because two men stand aside. No one can say that because these two Raïses took part in it, that therefore the whole nation has joined it. To say that the Mahomedans have joined it is quite wrong, and is a false accusation against our nation. If my Bengali friends had not adopted this wrong course of action, I should have had nothing to do with the National Congress, nor with its members, nor with the wrong aspirations for which they have raised such an uproar. Let the delegates of the National Congress become the stars of heaven, or the sun itself—I am delighted. *But it was necessary and incumbent on me to show the falsity of the impression which, by taking a few Mahomedans with them by pressure or by temptation, they wished to spread, that the whole Mahomedan nation had joined them. (Cheers).*

Gentlemen, what I am about to say is not only useful for my own nation, but also for my Hindu brothers of these Provinces, who from some wrong notions have taken part in this Congress. At last they also will be sorry for it—although perhaps they will never have occasion to be sorry; for it is beyond the region of possibility that the proposals of the Congress should be carried out fully. These wrong notions which have grown up in our Hindu fellow-countrymen, and on account of which they think it expedient to join the Congress, depend upon two things. *The first thing is this: that they think that as both they themselves and the Bengalis are Hindus, they have nothing to fear from the growth of their influence. The second thing is this: that some Hindus—I do not speak of all the Hindus but only of some—think that by joining the Congress and by increasing the power of the Hindus, they will perhaps be able to suppress those Mahomedan religious rites which are opposed to their own, and, by all uniting, annihilate them. But I frankly advise my Hindu friends that if they wish to cherish their religious rites, they can never be successful in this way. If they are to be successful, it can only be by friendship and agreement. The business cannot be done by force; and the greater the enmity and animosity, the greater will be their loss. I will take Aligarh as an example. There Mahomedans and Hindus are in agreement. The Dasehra and Moharrum fell together for three years, and no one knows what took place [that is, things remained quiet]. It is worth notice how, when an agitation was started against cow-killing, the sacrifice of cows increased enormously, and religious animosity grew on both sides, as all who live in India well know. They should understand that those things that can be done by friendship and affection, cannot be done by any pressure or force.*

If these ideas which I have expressed about the Hindus of these provinces be correct, and their condition be similar to that of the Mahomedans, then they ought to continue to cultivate friendship with us. Let those who live in Bengal 'eat up their own heads' [that is, involve themselves in difficulties]. What they want to do, let them do it. What they don't want to do, let them not do it. Neither their disposition nor their general condition resembles that of the people of this country. Then what connection have the people of this country with them? *As regards Bengal, there is, as far as I am aware, in Lower Bengal a much larger proportion of Mahomedans than Bengalis. And if you take the population of the whole of Bengal, nearly half are Mahomedans and something over half are Bengalis. Those Mahomedans are quite unaware of what sort of thing the National Congress is. No Mahomedan Raïs of Bengal took part in it, and the ordinary Bengalis who live in the districts are also as ignorant of it as the Mahomedans. In Bengal the Mahomedan population is so great that if the aspirations of those Bengalis who are making so loud an agitation be fulfilled, it will be extremely difficult for the Bengalis to remain in peace even in Bengal.* These proposals of the Congress are extremely inexpedient for the country, which is inhabited by two different nations—who drink from the same well, breathe the air of the same city, and depend on each other for its life. To create animosity between them is good neither for peace, nor for the country, nor for the town.

After this long preface I wish to explain what method my nation—nay, rather the whole people of this country—ought to pursue in political matters. I will treat in regular sequence of the political questions of India, in order that you may have full opportunity of giving your attention to them. *The first of all is this—In whose hands shall the administration and the Empire of India rest? Now, suppose that all English, and the whole English army, were to leave India, taking with them all their cannon and their splendid weapons and everything, then who would be rulers of India? Is it possible that under these circumstances two nations—the Mahomedans and the Hindus—could sit on the same throne and remain equal in power? Most certainly not. It is necessary that one of them should conquer the other and thrust it down. To hope that both could remain equal is to desire the impossible and the inconceivable. At the same time you must remember that although the number of Mahomedans is less than that of the Hindus, and although they contain far fewer people who have received a high English education, yet they must not be thought insignificant or weak. Probably they would be by themselves enough to maintain their own position. But suppose they were not. Then our Mussalman brothers, the Pathans, would come out as a swarm of locusts from their mountain valleys, and make rivers of blood to flow from their frontier in the north to the extreme end of Bengal. This thing—who, after the departure of the English, would be conquerors—would rest on the will of God. But until one nation had conquered the other and made it obedient, peace could not reign in the land. This conclusion is based on proofs so absolute that no one can deny it.*

Now, suppose that the English are not in India, and that one of the nations of India has conquered the other, whether the Hindus the Mahomedans, or the Mahomedans the Hindus. At once some other nation of Europe, such as the French, the Germans, the Portuguese, or the Russians, will attack India. Their ships of war, covered with iron and loaded with flashing cannon and weapons, will surround her on all sides. At that time who will protect India? Neither Hindus can save nor Mahomedans; neither the Rajputs nor my brave brothers the Pathans. And what will be the result? The result will be this: that foreigners will rule India, because the state of India is such that if foreign Powers attack her, no one has the power to oppose them. From this reasoning it follows of necessity that an empire not of any Indian race, but of foreigners, will be established in India. Now, will you please decide which of the nations of Europe you would like to rule over India? I ask if you would like Germany; whose subjects weep for heavy taxation and the stringency of their military service? Would you like the rule of France? Stop! I fancy you would perhaps like the rule of the Russians, who are very great friends of India and of Mahomedans, and under whom the Hindus will live in great comfort, and who will protect with the tenderest care the wealth and property which they have acquired under English rule? (Laughter.) Everybody knows something or other about these powerful kingdoms of Europe. Everyone will admit that their governments are far worse—nay, beyond comparison worse—than the British Government. It is, therefore, necessary that for the peace of India and for the progress of everything in India, the English Government should remain for many years—in fact forever!

When it is granted that the maintenance of the British Government, and of no other, is necessary for the progress of our country, then I ask whether there is any example in the world of one nation having conquered and ruled over another nation, and that conquered nation claiming it as a right that they should have representative government. The principle of representative government is that it is government by a nation, and that the nation in question rules over its own people and its own land. Can you tell me of any case in the world's history in which any foreign nation, after conquering another and establishing its empire over it, has given representative government to the conquered people? Such a thing has never taken place. It is necessary for those who have conquered us to maintain their Empire on a strong basis. When rulers and ruled are one nation, representative government is possible. For example, in Afghanistan, of which Amir Abdur Rahman Khan is the ruler, where all the people are brother-Afghans, it might be possible. If they want, they can have representative government. But to think that representative government can be established in a country over which a foreign race rules, is utterly vain, nor can a trace of such a state of things be discovered in the history of the world. Therefore to ask that we should be appointed by election to the Legislative Council is opposed to the true principles of government, and no government whatever, whether English or German or French or Russian or Musalman, could accept this principle. The meaning of it is this: 'Abandon the rule of the country and put it in our hands.' Hence, it is in no way expedient that our nation should join in and echo these monstrous proposals.

... How can we possibly claim as a right those things on which the very existence and strength of the Government depends? We most certainly have not the right to put those people in the Council whom we want, and to keep out those whom we don't want; to pass those laws that we want, and to veto those laws that we dislike. If we have the right to elect members for the Legislative Council, there is no reason why we should not have the right to elect members for the Imperial Council. In the Imperial Council thousands of matters of foreign policy and state secrets are discussed. Can you with justice say that we Indians have a right to claim those things? To make an agitation for such things can only bring misfortune on us and on the country. It , pposed to the true principles of government, and is harmful for the peace of the country. The aspirations of our friends the Bengalis have made such progress that they want to scale a height to which it is beyond their powers to attain. But if I am not in error, I believe that the Bengalis have never at any period held sway over a particle of land. They are altogether ignorant of the method by which a foreign race can maintain its rule over other races. Therefore reflect on the doings of your ancestors, and be not unjust to the British Government to whom God has given the rule of India; and look honestly and see what is necessary for it to do, to maintain its empire and its hold on the country. You can appreciate these matters; but they cannot who have never held a country in their hands nor won a victory.

... *Oh! my brother Musalmans! I again remind you that you have ruled nations, and have for centuries held different countries in your grasp. For seven hundred years in India you have had Imperial sway. You know what it is to rule. Be not unjust to that nation which is ruling over you, and think also on this: how upright is her rule. Of such benevolence as the English Government shows to the foreign nations under her, there is no example in the history of the world. See what freedom she has given in her laws, and how careful she is to protect the rights of her subjects.* She has not been backward in promoting the progress of the natives of India and in throwing open to them high appointments. At the commencement of her rule, except clerkships and kaziships [judgeships] there was nothing. The kazis of the pargana, who were called commissioners, decided small civil suits and received very small pay. Up to 1832 or 1833 this state of things lasted.

If my memory is not wrong, it was in the time of Lord William Bentinck that natives of India began to get honourable posts. The positions of Munsif, Subordinate Judge, and Deputy Collector, on respectable pay, were given to natives, and progress has been steadily going on ever since. In the Calcutta High Court a Kashmiri Pandit was first appointed equal to the English Judges. After him Bengalis have been appointed as High Court Judges. At this time there are perhaps three Bengalis in the Calcutta High Court, and in the same way some Hindus in Bombay and Madras. It was your bad fortune that there was for a long time no Mahomedan High Court Judge, but now there is one in the Allahabad High Court. (Cheers.) Native High Court Judges can cancel the decision of English Judges and Collectors. They can ask them for explanations. The subordinate native officers also have full authority in their posts. A Deputy Collector, a Sub-Judge, or a Munsif decides cases according to his opinion, and is independent of the opinion of the Judge or Collector. None of these things have been acquired by fighting or opposition. As far as you have made yourselves worthy of the confidence of Government, to that extent you have received high positions. Make yourselves her friends, and prove to her that your friendship with her is like that of the English and the Scotch. After this what you have to claim, claim—on condition that you are qualified for it.

... About this political controversy, in which my Hindu brothers of this Province—to whom I have given some advice, and who have, I think, joined from some wrong notions—have taken part, I wish to give some advice to my Mahomedan brothers. I do not think the Bengali politics useful for my brother Mussalmans. *Our Hindu brothers of these provinces are leaving us and are joining the Bengalis. Then we ought to unite with that nation with whom we can unite. No Mahomedan can say that the English are not 'People of the Book.' No Mahomedan can deny this: that God has said that no people of other religions can be friends of Mahomedans except the Christians. He who had read the Koran and believes it, he can know that our nation cannot expect friendship and affection from any other people. At this time our nation is in a bad state as regards education and wealth, but God has given us the light of religion, and the Koran is present for our guidance, which has ordained them and us to be friends.*

Now God has made them rulers over us. Therefore we should cultivate friendship with them, and should adopt that method by which their rule may remain permanent and firm in India, and may not pass into the hands of the Bengalis. This is our true friendship with our Christian rulers, and we should not join those people who wish to see us thrown into a ditch. If we join the political movement of the Bengalis our nation will reap loss, for we do not want to become subjects of the Hindus instead of the subjects of the 'People of the Book'. And as far as we can we should remain faithful to the English Government. By this my meaning is not that I am inclined towards their religion. Perhaps no one has written such severe books as I have against their religion, of which I am an enemy. But whatever their religion, God has called men of that religion our friends. We ought—not on account of their religion, but because of the order of God—to be friendly and faithful to them. If our Hindu brothers of these Provinces, and the Bengalis of Bengal, and the Brahmans of Bombay, and the Hindu Madrasis of Madras, wish to separate themselves from us, let them go, and trouble yourself about it not one whit. We can mix with the English in a social way. We can eat with them, they can eat with us. Whatever hope we have of progress is from them. The Bengalis can in no way assist our progress. And when the Koran itself directs us to be friends with them, then there is no reason why we should not be their friends. But it is necessary for us to act as God has said. Besides this, God has made them rulers over us. Our Prophet has said that if God place over you a black negro slave as ruler, you must obey him. See, there is here in the meeting a European, Mr. Beck. He is not black. He is very white. (Laughter.) Then why should we not be obedient and faithful to those white-faced men whom God has put over us, and why should we disobey the order of God?

I do not say that in the British Government all things are good. Nobody can say that there is any Government in the world, or has ever been, in which there is nothing bad, be the Government Mahomedan, Hindu, or Christian. There is now the Sultan of Turkey; who is a Mahomedan Emperor, and of whom we are proud. Even his Mahomedan subjects make complaints of his government. This is the condition of the Khedive of Egypt. Look at the Governments of Europe, and examine the condition of the Government of London itself. Thousands of men complain against Government. There is no Government with which everybody is satisfied.

If we also have some complaints against the English Government, it is no wonderful thing. People are not even grateful to God for His government. I do not tell you to ask nothing from Government. I will myself fight on your behalf for legitimate objects. But ask for such things as they can give you, or such things to which, having due regard to the administration of the country, you can claim a right. If you ask for such things as Government cannot give you, then it is not the fault of Government, but the folly of the askers. But what you ask, do it not in this fashion—that you accuse Government in very action of oppression, abuse the highest officials, use the hardest words you can find for Lord Lytton and Lord Dufferin, call all Englishmen tyrants, and blacken columns on columns of newspapers with these subjects. You can gain nothing this way. God had made them your rulers. This is the will of God. We should be content with the will of God. And in obedience to the will of God, you should remain friendly and faithful to them. Do not do this: bring false accusations against them and give birth to enmity. This is neither wisdom nor in accordance with our holy religion.

Therefore the method we ought to adopt is this: that we should hold ourselves aloof from this political uproar, and reflect on our condition—that we are behindhand in education and are deficient in wealth. Then we should try to improve the education of our nation. Now our condition is this: that the Hindus, if they wish, can ruin us in an hour. The internal trade is entirely in their hands. The external trade is in possession of the English. Let the trade which is with the Hindus remain with them. But try to snatch from their hands the trade in the produce of the country which the English now enjoy and draw profit from. Tell them: 'Take no further trouble. We will ourselves take the leather of our country to England and sell it there. Leave off picking up the bones of our country's animals. We will ourselves collect them and take them to America. Do not fill ships with the corn and cotton of our country. We will fill our own ships and will take it ourselves to Europe!' Never imagine that Government will put difficulties in your way in trade. But the acquisition of all these things depends on education. *When you shall have fully acquired education, and true education shall have made its home in your hearts, then you will know what rights you can legitimately demand of the British Government. And the result of this will be that you will also obtain honourable positions in the Government, and will acquire wealth in the higher ranks of trade. But to make friendship with the Bengalis in their mischievous political proposals, and join in them, can bring only harm. If my nation follow my advice they will draw benefit from trade and education. Otherwise, remember that Government will keep a very sharp eye on you because you are very quarrelsome, very brave, great soldiers, and great fighters.* [Emphases added]

It is pertinent to note that even as of March 1888, i.e., seventeen years before the Partition of Bengal in 1905 by Lord Curzon on religious lines, Syed Ahmed Khan was conscious of the growing Muslim demographic in Bengal and its implications for political assertion by Muslims, which, as we shall see, was a clear sign of things to come. Again, in 1888, when A.O. Hume and Badruddin Tyabji tried to secure Khan's support for the Congress, he retorted thus:[78]

I do not understand what the words 'National Congress' mean. Is it supposed that the different castes and creeds living in India belong to one nation, or can become a nation, and their aims and aspirations be one and the same? I think it is quite impossible, and when it is impossible there can be no such thing as a National Congress, nor can it be of equal benefit to all peoples. You regard the doings of the misnamed National Congress beneficial to India, but I am sorry to say that I regard them as not only injurious to our own community but also to India at large. I object to every Congress in any shape or form whatever which regards India as one nation.

In 1892, about six years before his passing, he expressed the following views:[79]

Some reflection is required to grasp the nature of Muslim nationality. From time immemorial, communities have been held together by ties of common descent or common homeland. The Prophet Muhammad obliterated all territorial and ancestral conventions and laid the foundations of a broad and enduring kinship which comprehends all those who subscribe to the formula of faith ... This tribe divine assimilates all human beings, regardless of colour or place of birth.

We Muslims should hold religion in our right hand and worldly pursuits in the left ... In Islam alone lies our salvation [he told a gathering of Muslim students at Lahore]. I use the word community to include all Muslims. Faith in God and His Prophet and the proper observance of the precepts of the faith are the only bonds that hold us together. You are irrevocably lost to us if you turn your back upon religion. We have no part or lot with transgressors or derelicts, even if they shine like the stars of the firmament. I want you to dive deep into European literature and sciences, but at the same time I expect you to be true to your faith.

The Congress tried its best to court Muslims to participate in the national movement for political autonomy by even offering a compromise on the delicate issue of ban on cow slaughter in its Madras session of 1887. At this session, under the presidentship of Badruddin Tyabji, the Congress decided that questions of social reform that relate to a particular community, especially Muslims, would be decided by leaders of that community alone.[80] While one may be tempted to see this as a sign of statesmanship on the part of the Congress and intransigence on the part of those representing the Muslim community, the fact of the matter is that the Congress had already embarked on the path of compromise by putting civilisational non-negotiables on the line, which served to further embolden the proponents of the Two-Nation Theory. Unsurprisingly, the Congress's offer of a via media too was rejected even by quite a few Muslim delegates of the Congress, which was interpreted by contemporary opinion makers as the direct impact of Syed Ahmed Khan on Muslim attitudes across the board. In the words of Surendranath Banerjea, a Congress stalwart:[81]

The Muhammadan community, under the leadership of Sir Syed Ahmad, had held aloof from the Congress. They were working under the auspices of the Patriotic Association in direct opposition to the national movement. Our critics regarded the National Congress as a Hindu Congress, and the opposition papers described it as such. We were straining every nerve to secure the co-operation of our Muhammadan fellow-countrymen in this great national work. We sometimes paid the fares of Muhammadan delegates and offered them other facilities.

Majumdar cites Gopal Krishna Gokhale, who remarked in one of his letters that '*seventy millions of Muhammadans were more or less hostile to national aspirations*' and that resolutions condemning the Congress were passed by the Muslims of Allahabad, Lucknow, Meerut, Lahore, Madras and several other places:[82]

> *The Mahomedan Observer, The Victoria Paper, The Muslim Herald, The Rafiq-i-Hind* and the *Imperial Paper*—all spoke with one voice against the Indian National Congress. *The Aligarh Institute Gazette*, a powerful Muslim organ of Northern India, never missed the opportunity of reprinting all sorts of views opposed to the Congress ideology from other newspapers and magazines. The Central National Muhammadan Association of Bengal, the Muhammadan Literary Society of Calcutta, the Anjuman-i-Islamia of Madras, the Dindigal Anjuman and the Muhammadan Central Association, Punjab, denounced, in the strongest possible terms, Congress aims and activities. Important Muslim organizations in India refused to send delegates to the Congress when invited to do so.

From the brief history of Syed Ahmed Khan discussed above, it is clear that his formulation of the Two-Nation Theory was indeed the Dehlawite vision at work all along, couched in the European template of a nation-state. The consistency with which Khan advanced the Dehlawite position makes it abundantly evident that his occasional statements about his being a 'Hindu' too were merely rhetoric meant for public consumption before a predominantly non-Muslim audience.[83] However, his core beliefs came to the fore when addressing his 'nation', or his *qaum*, as he called it. By the time of his death in 1898, thanks to his efforts, Muslim Nationalism and the consequent Muslim separatism had been firmly entrenched, while Indic consciousness was still wallowing in misplaced and utopian notions of a Ganga–Jamuni syncretic culture. The journey towards Pakistan had begun even before the founding of the All-India Muslim League (1906), and well before the Khilafat Movement of 1919. Khan's Aligarh Movement was also able to forge a 'national' Muslim identity, which other Dehlawite movements could not. As stated earlier, the contributions of these movements to the solidification of the idea of Pakistan shall be discussed in the next two sections.

However, before proceeding, it is important to discuss another critical aspect. Although Syed Ahmed Khan worked towards the creation of a national Muslim identity informed and driven by his Dehlawite Islamic worldview that divided the world into Muslims and non-Muslims, it appears, based on the available literature, that he was not too keen on the idea of global pan-Islamism that started gaining traction in the 1870s and had become a major subject for Western powers to contend with in the decades that followed. After all, Muslims in Bharat had collected funds for Turkish Relief to support the Ottoman empire in its wars against the Russians in 1877–78 and against the Greeks in 1897.[84] Khan's lack of enthusiasm, and perhaps even opposition, to global pan-Islamism, may have been the consequence of his British loyalism and his belief that it was important for the Muslims in Bharat to have the British on their side to keep the Hindus in check. Clearly, this was an expedient and limited departure from Dehlawite pan-Islamism. This is evident from his own words in one of his letters to his confidantes:[85]

> I am in favour of the consolidation of the British Government, not because of any love or loyalty to the British, but only because I see the welfare of the Indian Muslims in that consolidation. And I feel that they can emerge from the present state of decline only with the help of the British Government.

Interestingly, after his trip to London in 1869–70, which gave him the opportunity to observe other cultures and societies, such as parts of the Ottoman empire, Khan was impressed by the Ottoman Turks and Middle Eastern Muslims who seemed to be at home with both Arabic and French, and occasionally even Latin. This was reflected in his writings in 1872, prior to the establishment of the M.A.O. College in Aligarh, wherein he had recommended the Turko-Western-style uniforms for Muslim students in Bharat:[86]

> Muslim students will have a uniform consisting of a black alpaca, half sleeved chugha and a red Fez cap. All students shall be required to put on a pair of socks and shoes of western style.

When Theodore Beck, the first principal of Aligarh, objected to the introduction of this uniform, Khan's reaction in his speech of 1894 to the students of Aligarh was as follows:[87]

> The apparel which is now yours, that is, a Turkish coat and fez cap and English shoes is an elegant dress. It would be desirable if all your coats were of the same dark colour. In the court of the Turkish sovereign all nobles and attendants also wear shoes and the red fez, and this is the dress we have chosen for you. Even our English Government here has allowed the wearing of boots and shoes in court circles. Only those Englishmen who are short sighted or who are arrogant and lack vision would object to your wearing this dress, because they would like to insult or disgrace Indians.

Khan had even sent a copy of his *Essay on the Life of Mohammed* for the blessings of Ottoman Sultan Abd-al Aziz with the following words:[88]

> That your Imperial and Royal Majesty may long continue to grace, defend and strengthen the throne of the Caliph is, and ever will be the earnest and heart-felt prayer of the humble writer.

It might be of note to recollect that Khan's mentor at Madrasah-i-Rahimiyah, Shah Muhammad Ishaq Dehlawi, had reached out to the Ottoman Sultan to advocate for a global Muslim movement. In contrast, the following was Khan's position in response to the rising chorus for solidarity with the Ottoman empire in view of its growing tensions with Europe and the West:[89]

> ... even taking for granted that the Sultan of Turkey is the Caliph, we say that if he is the Caliph, he is the Caliph only in that country which he governs and for those Mohammedans only who owe him allegiance; he is Caliph only in that country in which he can inflict punishments of death or retaliation and maintain the laws of religion; he is not Caliph in that country over which he does not hold the supreme authority and control; in which he can neither give orders for death or retaliation nor can he maintain the faith nor can he protect its Mohammedan inhabitants ...

> We are not the subjects of Sultan Abdul Hameed Khan nor does he possess any authority over us or over our country. He is no doubt a Mohammedan sovereign and consequently we sympathise with him as Mohammedans— happy for his happiness and grieved at his troubles—but he is not our Caliph either according to Mohammedan law or Mohammedan religion ... It is no doubt true that he is the guardian of the two sacred places; nay he is the guardian of more than two sacred places, i.e., of the Holy Kaaba, Madina and of Jerusalem—the last-named place being sacred alike for the Jews, Christians and the Mohammedans—but this guardianship has nothing to do with his being a Caliph.

When Muslims in India celebrated Turkish victory over Greece, he reacted as follows:[90]

> To call such a victory the victory of Islam is to do no honour to Islam. Victory and defeat are awarded by God to whom He will. When the Turks [with British and French help] defeated Russia in the Crimean War, would it be right to term this a victory of Islam? And when the Turks lost at the hands of the Russians, would it then be proper to [Allah forbid!] ascribe this to a defeat for Islam? It is incorrect to mix up mundane actions and causes with the message of Islam, which has been and will remain victorious ... We should be happy that a Muslim state has achieved victory in its battles and not disaster. But to put this matter in Islamic garb is a sign of excess ... After all, everyone knows that Greece is of little consequence when it comes to fighting the Turks. It would be like a sparrow trying to fight a hawk ... What would need investigation is how the Greeks felt encouraged to confront the Turks so boldly, and here one might consider that behind the scenes some Great Power must have prodded them on with offers of assistance. This speculation receives support from the vituperative speeches and writings of Mr Gladstone and the statements and telegrams of the 'deranged' radicals of London ... But when it came down to the actual war, neither the British government, nor the French or German governments offered concrete support to the Greeks.

However, this conflict between Khan's commitment to his community and his attitudes towards the Ottomans was a product of his pragmatic loyalty to the British. When constrained to choose between loyalty to the British and support for pan-Islamist sentiments, the Muslim community had gradually started veering in favour of the latter according to scholars such as Aziz Ahmad:[91]

> The separatist line taken by Sayyid Ahmad Khan in relation to Hindu–Muslim politics was accepted by the Muslim consensus in India with extensive concessions to his loyalist attitude, but his loyalism was rejected when it came into conflict with pan-Islamic sympathies. A large section of the Urdu press of the 1890s reflects this trend.

This calibrated shift in the attitudes of Muslims in Bharat towards the British empire in favour of pan-Islamism, by July 1897, is best captured by the following extract from Secretary of State for India Lord Hamilton's letter to the Viceroy, Lord Elgin:[92]

> We have, however, a new element of intrigue and commotion introduced into India by the Pan-Islamic Council in Constantinople and the close connection which is being established between the Sultan and Indian Mahomedans.

This shift in attitudes was the result of the influence of an individual who presented the most formidable challenge to Syed Ahmed Khan's leadership of Muslims in Bharat, Syed Jamal al-Din al-Afghani (1838–1897), who, ironically, was not a native of the Indian subcontinent. Some have hailed Afghani as the most influential Muslim thinker of the nineteenth century for his role in the entrenchment of the idea of a global ummah and his consequent contribution to the idea of a khilafat/caliphate at least two decades before the actual birth of the Khilafat Movement in 1919. Therefore, the broad contours of his global pan-Islamic vision, his vision of a caliphate, his influence on the Muslim community in Bharat, and his agreements and disagreements with Syed Ahmed Khan, warrant attention.[93]

Syed Jamal al-Din al-Afghani, Ummah and the Caliphate

The antecedents of Syed Jamal al-Din al-Afghani, also known as Syed Jamaluddin Afghani, are themselves the subject of debate and dispute. Some scholars contend that he was born in Afghanistan, whereas others believe he was born to a Shia family in Asadabad (then in Persia), and that the appellation 'al-Afghani' to his name was a later addition in 1869 to enable reach to a wider Muslim audience without drawing attention to his Shia roots. The latter belief is best represented by Nikki R. Keddie, who authored an authoritative biography of Afghani.[94]

According to Keddie, Afghani was most probably born in November 1838 to a family of Sayyids, i.e., descendants of the Islamic Prophet. While

Afghani's stay in Bharat between late 1879 and late 1882 (which we shall discuss) is fairly known about, less is known of his time in Bharat during his teens between 1854 and 1858, which coincided with the Sepoy Mutiny of 1857.[95] In his paper on Afghani's Indian contacts, Aziz Ahmad dates Afghani's first visit to Bharat to 1854, when, at the age of sixteen, he was sent to Bombay by his teacher Shaykh Murtada Ansari, owing to opposition to his religious views from the Persian ulema.[96] Afghani apparently lived in Bombay for over a year, and in Calcutta for a few months. Both Keddie and

Jamal al-Din al-Afghani (1838–1897)

Ahmad agree that Afghani was witness to the events of 1857, particularly to the treatment meted out to the Mutineers by the British, which may have laid the foundation for his views on the need to resist Western imperialism.

Keddie surmises that during this period Afghani may have also been exposed to the Sufi Orders of Shah Waliullah Dehlawi, including to the latter's views on the need for a caliphate under which Muslims the world over could unite. This may have contributed to Afghani's later formulation of pan-Islamism under a centralized caliphate as an imperative to protect and reclaim 'Muslim lands' through jihad.[97] Keddie also believes that it was during this stay in Bharat that Afghani was exposed to the Western education system established by the British, which would go on to shape his views on the need for the global Muslim community to embrace Western knowledge in order to compete with the West and push back against its imperialism. Akin to Syed Ahmed Khan, Afghani was open to reinterpretation of Islam to make it more compatible with scientific progress. This was perhaps a necessity in order to reconcile Islam with science, as also an attempt to encourage Muslims to not shun Western education while remaining rooted in Islam.

According to Sharif al-Mujahid, an Indian-born journalist who moved to Pakistan after the partition and wrote a detailed thesis on Afghani in 1954, Afghani's worldview was based on the central assumption that Islam was universally valid for 'for all peoples, all times and all cultural conditions'.[98] This reinforces my point that both Middle Eastern consciousness and European consciousness demonstrate a shared belief in their respective universal and exclusive validities, which informs their respective colonialities and drives their expansionism. No wonder neither consciousness nor coloniality can co-exist with other systems which differ from theirs; and this also explains their innate tendency to proselytise/convert through any means possible, violent or 'peaceful'. Since the end goal is treated as being divinely sanctioned and ordained, the morality of the means employed to achieve it is secondary or irrelevant. Afghani believed that one of the essential prerequisites of Islam was to purge the minds of the people of all false beliefs and superstitions, which included idolatry and incarceration or suffering of a divine being, which was a reference to the Christian belief that Jesus's death was for the good of all humanity. Not so surprisingly, like all other Islamic reformist movements discussed thus far, Afghani too believed that regeneration of Muslim society everywhere, especially in colonised parts of the world, lay in returning to Islam as 'preached by the Prophet and his immediate followers', in modern/Western education, and in a unified leadership.[99] His beliefs' resonance with the Dehlawite template, as customised and modified by Syed Ahmed Khan, could not have been clearer, with the primary difference being the scale and focus of their respective efforts. As we shall see, while Khan's vision and preoccupation was limited to Muslims of the Bharatiya subcontinent, Afghani's was broader, towards the global ummah. To this extent, it could even be argued that Afghani was closer than Syed Ahmed Khan to Dehlawi in his views on the need for Muslims in Bharat to rethink themselves as part of the global ummah. It is against this backdrop that Afghani's life and his criticism of Syed Ahmed Khan must be understood.

Following his stay in Bharat from 1854 to 1858, Afghani travelled to Mecca, to Shiite shrine cities in Iran and Iraq, and to Istanbul between 1858 and 1866 until his arrival in Afghanistan in October 1866, where he was received and employed by the Amir of Afghanistan, Mohammed Azam Khan.[100] This stint lasted for a period of two years until his expulsion by the next Amir, Sher Ali Khan, in December 1868. This was owing to the fact that he worked on building an anti-colonial base with some help from the Russian empire, much to the concern of the British.[101] In December 1868, he left for Bombay, and from there reached Istanbul via Cairo in 1869.[102] His stay in Bharat lasted barely a month, during which British authorities were careful enough to not let him meet with other Muslim opinion makers.[103] He was then shipped to Cairo, where he stayed for over a month, interacting with students of the Al Azhar University, including one in particular, Muhammad Abduh, who would go on to become his most popular disciple.

His subsequent move to Istanbul in 1869 was inspired by the fact that the epicentre of the Islamic world was the Ottoman empire under Sultan Abdul Aziz.[104] This meant that Istanbul was better suited for the implementation of Afghani's ideas given the position of the Ottoman empire in the Muslim world which enabled wider dissemination.[105] Also, since the Ottoman empire seemed much more open to the idea of learning from the West in the realm of scientific progress, it fit Afghani's expectations of a 'modern Islam', which he envisioned could rise to the challenge of the West. Istanbul met his expectations when he was made a member of the Council of Education, which was tasked with the mandate of 'modernising' the prevalent education system as part of the larger Tanzimat reforms which was a wider reformist movement in the Ottoman empire. However, unfortunately for Afghani, in a speech he delivered in late 1870 at the Dar ul-Funun, an institution of higher education in Istanbul, he compared prophethood with the role of philosophers and called both the 'noblest of crafts' to make the point that philosophers filled the social requirement of learned men in every age in the absence of prophets/imams. While this was not intended to derogate either prophethood in general or the prophethood of the Islamic Prophet Muhammad, this comparison resulted in Afghani's expulsion from Istanbul under pressure from Ottoman ulema, who were already searching for reasons to oppose the Tanzimat reforms. They labelled his position heretic for having compared the role of fallible philosophers with the infallibility of the Islamic Prophet.[106]

After his expulsion from Istanbul, Afghani went back to Cairo in mid-1871, where he lived for eight years until his expulsion in 1879 by Egypt.[107] At this juncture, it is important to understand that after its defeat at the hands of the Ottomans in 1517, the Mamluk Sultanate-ruled Egypt, which was the earlier Islamic Caliphate, became an Ottoman Province.[108] This defeat also led to the transfer of the mantle of Islamic Caliphate from Egypt to the Ottoman empire, which, as we shall see, would have a huge bearing during the Khilafat Movement of 1919–1924. By 1805, under Muhammad Ali Pasha as the Khedive or Viceroy of the Ottoman empire, Egypt had become a Khedivate or a Viceregal Province of the empire. At the time of Afghani's arrival in Egypt in 1871, trouble was brewing in Khedivate Egypt due to opposition from Egyptian society to European control, primarily British and French, over the then Khedive Ismail. It was during this period that Afghani delivered a series of lectures on a variety of subjects, but what is of relevance was his exhortation to young followers to free Egyptian society from Western domination. Given the conduct of the West in Egypt, which resulted in pushing the country deep into debt, Afghani's call for resistance to Western domination, but not necessarily to Western ideas and education, and for the deposition of Khedive Ismail, found traction. This elevated him to the status of a political figure and popular orator.[109] After Khedive Ismail

was replaced by Tawfiq as the new Khedive of Egypt through the efforts
of the British and the French, Tawfiq expelled Afghani in August 1879 at
the behest of his colonial benefactors. This was because Afghani's speeches
and activities, along with those of the Egyptian Nationalist Movement under
'Young Egyptians' led by Ahmed Urabi (also known as Arabi Pasha), were
directed at the new Khedive's benefactors.[110]

This time, Afghani once again travelled to Bharat, specifically to the
Nizam-ruled princely state of Hyderabad and later to Calcutta, where he lived
until 1882.[111] Given his track record in Afghanistan and Egypt, the British
government kept a close watch on his activities. In Hyderabad, Afghani came
in contact with a number of followers of Syed Ahmed Khan.[112] As mentioned
earlier, Syed Ahmed Khan's position as the pre-eminent representative of
Muslims in Bharat and as the proponent of the Two-Nation Theory was
fairly well established by this time. Given Khan's repeated calls for embrace
of Western education by Muslims, one would have expected Afghani to
throw his weight behind Syed Ahmed Khan and his views. However, in 1881,
Afghani published a scathing criticism of Syed Ahmed Khan's views in his
tome *The Refutation of the Materialists*, where he criticised Khan's approach
to Islam as well as his British loyalism.[113] Afghani's critique of Khan's
approach to the Quran and the Hadith was a consequence of multiple factors.
Apart from his own beliefs, Afghani had a personal incentive—in light of the
allegation of heresy which was levelled at him by the Ottoman ulema—to
cleanse his reputation by defending a traditional approach to Islam.[114]

As regards his opposition to Khan's British loyalist leanings, Afghani saw
the British as '*a dragon which had swallowed twenty million people*' and, having
drunk up the waters of the Ganges and the Indus, was '*still unsatiated and
ready to devour the rest of the world and to consume the waters of the Nile and the
Oxus*'.[115] Clearly, this was based on his first-hand experience with the British
in Bharat, Afghanistan and Egypt. To defeat the West, and to protect Islam
and 'Muslim lands', Afghani strongly believed that a concerted effort on the
part of the ummah under a caliphate was the only way forward. Since Syed
Ahmed Khan stood in the way of integration of Muslims in Bharat with the
ummah and in the creation of a caliphate/khilafat, he saw Khan as his primary
adversary in Bharat.[116] His push for pan-Islamism was also partly encouraged
by the rising tide of pan-Islamism in Istanbul under Sultan Abdul Aziz, his
successor Sultan Abdul Hamid, and Ottoman thought leaders such as Namik
Kemal. In fact, during the reign of Sultan Abdul Aziz, the *khutba* (Friday
sermon) was read in mosques in Bharat in his name, which emphatically
underscores the fact that the Khilafat sentiment was not the sudden product of
the 1920s.[117]

From Hyderabad, Afghani arrived in Calcutta in early 1882 and met with Nawab Abdul Latif, in whom he found a British loyalist in the same mould as Syed Ahmed Khan. His opinion of Syed Ameer Ali was no different.[118] Disappointed with these 'moderate reformers' and their pro-British leanings, Afghani spent his time in Calcutta interacting with students who were passionately anti-colonial and also delivered a lecture at Albert Hall.[119] However, as tensions grew in Egypt due to the Arabi Pasha Movement, the British authorities in Bharat tightened their surveillance on Afghani, given his past association with Pasha's Movement which had resulted in his expulsion from Egypt. Finally, in November 1882, Afghani left for Paris to continue his anti-colonial activities and pan-Islamic messaging through his Arabic newspaper *Al-Urwa al Wuthqa* (the Indissoluble Link) along with his disciple Muhammad Abduh.[120]

From 1883 until his death in 1897, Afghani invested his energies in vain to get Russia to declare war on the British and involved himself in the politics of Persia. However, the two most significant events of this period which are of relevance to Bharat are Afghani's pan-Islamic appeal/petition in 1885 to the Ottoman Sultan Abdul Hamid, and his recognition of the latter as the Caliph of all Muslims. Ironically, Sultan Abdul Hamid later kept Afghani in confinement in Istanbul until his death in 1897. Certain excerpts from Afghani's appeal are of consequence, which are provided here:[121]

> To the Firm Pillar of the Kingdom and the People and the Impregnable Fortress of the Eternal Lofty Government, the Glory of the Ottoman Race and Soul of the Body of All the Muslims, the Pivot of the State and the Glorious One:
>
> I respectfully submit:
>
> Although some of the people of Istanbul have wronged this unfortunate one and followed the path of oppression, nevertheless from the millat I have not seen oppression and I have not experienced the bitterness of tyranny from Islam. And since I am counted a part of the millat and a piece of that ummat, if a calamity befalls them or the thorn of humiliation pricks their foot, there is no doubt that I will be steadfast in self-sacrifice, and will choose my death over such a life of humiliation. Consequently, when I looked at the state of the lofty Ottoman Government in this age, and when I considered the condition of the Islamic nation (millati-islamiyyeh) it rent the shirt of my patience and I was overcome by fearful thoughts and visions from every side. Like a fearfully obsessed man day and night, from beginning to end, I have thought of this affair and have made the means of reform and salvation of this millat my profession and incantation. In order to find a means of delivery from these terrible difficulties I have studied the condition of former peoples and states (milal va duval, pl. of millat va daulat) and the cause of their ascent

and decline and their rising and setting, and I have considered the great deeds that have emanated from individual men which are worthy of strong wonder and awe—Until my attention fell in passing on the life of Abu Muslim of Khurasanian stock, who with high purpose and skill extirpated, root and branch, a government like the government of the Bani Umayya, at the peak of power and the height of fortune, and who scraped their proud face into the dust of baseness. And also at the time of the ranging of my thoughts in this field, the life of Peter the Hermit passed before my perception: The zeal of that indigent hermit and the resolution of that poor monk; how he took a cross on his back and traversed deserts and mountains and entered city after city of the Franks, and in every kingdom raised the cry: 'On to battle'; so that he became the cause of the Crusades and the kindler of those horrendous events. The flame of emulation was lit in my heart, and the devotion and skill of the Khorasanian made life and ease forbidden (haram) for me. I knew that to consider deeds difficult is nothing but meanness of spirit and baseness and vileness of nature, and that every difficult thing is simple to possessors of resolution and every trouble is accepted by those with zeal. And since that magnificent pivot of the state (i.e., the addressee) is known in all climes for complete resolution, and is praised on all tongues of the people of the cities and has chosen love of the nation (hubb-i millat) and has seen his honour in the perpetuation of this holy people (ummat-i muqaddaseh); therefore I will with full freedom express my thoughts to Your Excellency, without regard for the fact that I am an unknown and insignificant person, and Your Excellency is a famous Amir; since the sages of the world on questions of service to the millat and love for the government and ummat pay no attention to rank but always keep their eyes on the goals, from wherever it may come and from whomever it may be.

And these thoughts are:

FIRST: Since the Muslims of India, with their great numbers are mostly holders of property and wealth, and are extremely firm in Islam and are devoted in the defense of the faith and the millat, despite the frailty of their bodies; and although these rich men always boast of their equity and liberality and are happy to give, especially in support of the faith, and wish for praise and fame in the path of religion and the protection of the faith, and seek glory; nevertheless they have slept the sleep of neglect and reposed on the bed of ignorance; and they have not understood the benefits of unity and harmony and they do not perceive the harm of division and discord. Therefore, this humble one (i.e., I) desires for the love of the community (Arabic, hubban fi'l milla) to proceed to that kingdom and to meet with all the novvabs and princes and 'ulama' and grandees of that land and explain to them one by one the results which are manifested from unity and solidarity in the whole world and the injuries which have appeared from division and disunity; and to caress their ears with the mystery of the hadith, 'the faithful are brothers'; and to express inspiring and prudent words and to attract the friendship and cooperation of the learned and the eloquent; and to breathe into them the new spirit of love of nationality [ruh-i jadid-i hubb-i milliyyat—an indication that Afghani recognized the novelty of this spirit] and to rend the curtain of their neglect; to explain to them the place of the sunni Sultanate in the world of Islam; and to reveal and make manifest to this group the fact that the perpetuation of religion depends on the perpetuation of this government. And in all the mosques of the famous cities I shall light a flame in their inner hearth by means of appealing sermons and hadiths of the Best of the Prophets, and I shall altogether burn out their patience and long-suffering. And I shall dispatch some of the eloquent 'ulam' among them to some of the distant cities and I shall call all the Muslims of India to contribute money, and I shall not follow another road but this, without encroaching upon the policy of the English Government or speaking a word against them. Indeed I shall lay the foundation of my case on the intentions of the Russians [against the Muslims] and will speak eloquently on this subject. And there is no doubt that the English nation (ta'ifeh) will be made happy by this wise movement, which will be the cause of the repulsion of the Indians from the Russians; and it is possible that the English, when they recognize that this movement is in harmony with their policy, they too will encourage them [the Indians] to contribute financially, and will become a true partner in this affair. When the movement takes place in India it will have several advantages: first, I have no doubt that incalculable financial aid will be forthcoming; second, strong friendship and cooperation, perhaps Unity of all Islam (ittihad-i tamm-i islamiyyeh) will come about among the Muslims; third, when the Unity of all the Muslims becomes understood by the English nation of course they will always maintain a firm policy [in support of] the Ottoman Government; fourth, a fine point which is not hidden from those of perception. [? Implying a revivified and expanded Muslim empire under the Sultan?]

SECOND: I wish after the completion of the Indian affair to go to Afghanistan and invite the people of that land, who like a wild lion have no fear of bloodshed and do not admit hesitation in war, especially religious war, to a religious struggle and a national endeavour [*muharibeh-yi diniyyeh va mujahideh-yi milliyyeh*—an interesting indication of the admixture of secular and religious 'nationalism' in Afghani; the secular word for war is modified by 'religious' while the 'holy war' word is defined as 'national', though at this time *milliyeh* could still also have a religious meaning, and both meanings were probably intermixed in Afghani.] I shall emphasize Russia's aims and convey with an eloquent tongue that if, God forbid, a calamity befalls the Ottoman Government, neither will permanence remain to Mecca nor majesty to Medina, and not even the name of Islam or a rite of the faith will survive. And that afterwards they will neither hear the voice of the mu'azzin nor see the Qur'an reader. They will be as low as the Jews of Bokhara, and like sheep without masters a prey to the rapacious wolf. I shall strike the call, 'Arise to battle,' and raise the sound, 'O, sacrifice for Islam.' And I shall send the good eloquent 'ulama' to all the people, to the valleys and the mountains, and I shall sponsor alliances with the princes and nobles and warriors and khans. And in all religious sermons I shall make clear the advantages of zeal and ardour and will make a general call to the milli war to all, young and old, weak and strong. And I will send some of the experienced, informed, and wise 'ulama' secretly to Kokand and Bokhara to explain conditions for the people of those lands, and make them await the time and the hour and the arrival of the end of the period [*muntaẓir-i vaqt va sa'at va hulul-i muddat*—the exact terminology used to herald the advent of the *mahdi*].

And after finishing the call in Afghanistan I will go to Baluchistan with the greatest speed and call the people of that land, who are continually employed in brigandage and raiding and plunder, to [join] the general war, with religious exhortation and the lure of worldly profit, and will bring to bear on them the old tricks of diplomacy. And I will send out some of the Afghan 'ulama' in those lands to the [various] districts and regions. And from there I will head to the Turkomans—those unfortunates who were always known for bravery and daring, and celebrated in all tongues for bloodshed and rebelliousness, but recently have worn the hat of shame on their head and the shirt of disgrace on their breast, and thrown their fame of so many years to the wind, and submit to the subjection of the commands of Russia—and I will call them to revenge and incite the pride of their Turkish race [*jinsiyat-i turkiyyeh*—another modern thought?] and carry the banner of Unity of Islam (ittihad-i islamiyyeh) on my shoulder into those regions also, and call to religious war, and as usual not overlook any stratagem or ruse, and plant the seed of ardour and zeal within them, always working with the wisest 'ulama'. And I shall send missionaries of sharp tongue to Kashgar and Yarkand to call the believers of those lands to the unity of the people of the faith. And it is obvious that, when the people begin to fight, the amirs perforce will enter the field without delay. Since I know the customs and temperament of those people and have insight into their nature and habits, I have no doubt that all the Muslims will attack the Russians enthusiastically. They will conquer the Russians on that side, and even altogether destroy them. And no one can deny the immediate advantages of such an event, and its far-reaching benefit, which is the unity of Islam and the union of the community (ittihad-i islamiyyeh va ittifaq-i ummat). And along with this when the people of Afghanistan, who are really the wall and buttress of India, attack Russia, the English will inevitably and forcibly devote their whole efforts to the fight, and will be mired up to their necks and give up the thoughts of domination. [There is an ambiguity, probably deliberate, as to whether the Russians, the English or, by implication, both, will be so distracted by this fight as to give up attempts at domination of the Muslims and Ottomans.]

And if someone should object to this plan, saying: The people of Kokand and Bokhara and Shahr-i Sabz and the Turkomans, are they not the very ones who did not bring the ardour to resist the Russians, and who did not carry honour from the field, and who chose a dishonourable life over an honourable death, and committed that kind of dishonour, therefore what benefit can come from asking their aid; I say that those wars which occurred were entirely for the sake of tyrannical amirs or oppressive governors; and when does a man give his life for the sensual pleasures of this kind of amir and governor, and why should he place the foot of firmness and manliness into the field. But if they fight for the defense of religion and the preservation of the faith they would either have a crown of martyrdom on their heads or the robe of honour on their breast. For in that time everyone for the sake of his beloved object alone will seek to step into the battlefield and seek battle for the glory of religion. And after explaining the plan I respectfully submit that this humble one in no way wishes either a dirham or a dinar from the government. Rather I will arise to this dangerous cause for the love of Islam. Yes—After getting financial aid in India it occurs to this humble one that I would like some medals for the Afghan, Baluch, and Turkoman amirs. The commission of such an important, weighty affair without permission and authorization from the government would be considered a presumption and an unacceptable act. Also, since those lands are extremely far from the centre of politics, and their people are cut off from news of the world and of the Ottoman Government at this time, if I carry out this work without authorization perhaps the amirs of those lands will not like it, and from the seeking of unity discord will arise. Therefore I beg that this letter be passed before your perceptive eyes and its suggestions be weighed one by one by the eyes of your unerring mind, without regard for the fact that the writer is a low and insignificant man, who has no high rank and who has not achieved exalted office; because to that fortunate one (i.e., you) it is apparent that in every age great deeds of this sort issue from a man like me, wandering and with rough garments, knowing cold and heat, bitter and sweet, and having traversed many mountains and deserts and experienced the ways of men. For the men of position are apprehensive about their station, and the owners of wealth and possessions fear for their wealth and property, and possessors of luxury have not been able to endure hardship. Therefore, if this supplication is accepted by the firm judgment and discriminating mind of that lord of wisdom and intelligence, invest me with a letter of authorization and fortify this humble one with a clear permit, so that with the utmost speed, before time is lost, I may set to work, and in this arena may sacrifice my life for the sake of the millat. And if for the purpose of receiving instructions it should be necessary for this humble one to come to Istanbul, I am wholly submissive to the order.

The rest is the command of that lord of commands (i.e., the addressee). [Emphasis added]

The reference to the Muslims in Bharat being part of Afghani's grand pan-Islamic vision is of consequence, since he could not have counted on their support unless he had sensed it during his stay in Bharat. Pertinently, this was not a one-off impulsive communication to the Sultan, since Afghani followed this up with a similar communication in 1892, thereby demonstrating his commitment to pan-Islamism.[122] Further, despite a British ban on Afghani's newspaper *Al-Urwa al Wuthqa*[123] which limited its circulation in Bharat, his writings were well known here especially in prominent Islamic institutions. Critically, according to Aziz Ahmad, the foundational ideas that contained the seeds of the pan-Islamic Khilafat Movement were to be found in Afghani's articles, and managed to reach Shibli Nomani in Nadwatul Ulama and Deoband's Maulana Mahmud al-Hasan.[124] Since both of them found his views in sync with theirs, they became ardent proponents of Afghani and his views on pan-Islamism.[125] As stated in the previous chapter, Maulana Hasan would co-found the Jamiat Ulema-e-Hind in 1919 as part of the Khilafat Movement.

Apart from Shibli Nomani and Maulana Hasan, the other prominent individual who would later be influenced by and would fully subscribe to Afghani's pan-Islamism was Maulana Abul Kalam Azad, who would go on to play a key role in the Khilafat Movement. Ayesha Jalal, in fact, attributes the entrenchment of Afghani's ideas on pan-Islamism and jihad as an instrument against the West among Muslims in Bharat to Maulana Azad, who brought to bear his erudition in and understanding of Islam to refine and build on Afghani's ideas.[126] At the end of the Khilafat Movement, Azad would join the Indian National Congress and also become independent Bharat's first education minister.

While I will discuss Azad's contribution to pan-Islamism and the Khilafat Movement in the third section, it is important to understand that Afghani's views as conveyed through his writings in his newspaper, significantly influenced Muslims in Bharat and encouraged them to look past national identities, ignoring Syed Ahmed Khan's British loyalist position. At this juncture, it must also be noted that during his stay in Bharat, although Afghani did speak of the need for Hindu–Muslim unity to oppose the British, his larger message of pan-Islamism, return to 'pure' Islam and repeated calls for establishment of a caliphate/khilafat, went against his claimed belief in Hindu–Muslim unity. This is evident from his later writings in Paris, which were summarised by Aziz Ahmad as follows:[127]

> *He (Afghani) regarded it as the religious duty of Muslims to reconquer any territory taken away from them by others, and if this was not possible, then to migrate from what had become as a result of alien conquest Dar al-Harb, to some other land in the Dar al-Islam. Resistance to non-Muslim aggression and reconquest was the duty not merely of the Muslims of the particular region involved, but of all*

Muslims. The tragedy of the Dar al-Islam, in his view, was that it was being conquered by others in detail without any concerted resistance. Similarly, the cause of the decline of Islam was that it was no longer politically integrated and all-embracing; it had become reduced to religious dogmas without the necessary moving principle to enliven it. *The 'ulama' of various lands had lost mutual contact; the common people of one Muslim country knew even less about those of another ...*

The solution which al-Afghani proposed was that the 'ulama' of Islam should build up their regional centres in various lands, and guide the commoners by ijtihad based on the Qur'an and the Hadith; these regional centres should be affiliated to a universal centre based at one of the holy places, where representatives of the various centres could meet in an effort towards a unified ijtihad, in order to revitalise the Umma and prepare it to meet external challenges ...

Now, if the history of Islam was a single historical process, it followed that the threat to the independence of one Muslim country was a threat to all. Al-Afghani therefore deplored the division of Dar al-Islam into petty states, leading decadent lives, ruled by petty rulers propped on their thrones by the strategy or rivalry of European Powers, and seeking aid from them to keep their own people in bondage.

Along with the search for a universal Muslim centre for the ijtihad of the 'ulama' of Islam, al-Afghani was even more actively occupied in the search for a political centre, a universal Muslim Khilafat. [Emphases added]

In light of these views, Hindu–Muslim unity and pan-Islamism could not realistically hope to survive together, as we shall see from the rise and fall of the Khilafat Movement.

By the second half of the 1890s, thanks to the position already enjoyed as the Khalifa by the Ottoman Sultan among Sunni Muslims in Bharat, coupled with Britain's growing tussles with the Ottoman empire in different parts of the world, and wider dissemination of Afghani's pan-Islamic views in Bharat by the ulema, the shift in Muslim attitudes here from the British loyalist position advocated by the likes of Syed Ahmed Khan to Afghani's pan-Islamism had gradually begun. No wonder that in July 1897, as stated earlier, the Secretary of State for India reported to the Viceroy with alarm the growing proximity between Muslims in Bharat and the Ottoman Sultan.

What is also important to note is that Afghani's pan-Islamic ideas and vision of reclaiming 'Muslim lands' had laid out the template not just for the Khilafat Movement, but also for the Pakistan Movement, since, essentially, Pakistan was meant to be the Dar al-Islam, to which Muslims in Bharat could emigrate by performing hijrat. Pakistan would serve as the new homeland from where jihad could be launched against Dar al-Harb, i.e., Bharat, to 'restore' its status to Dar al-Islam. This has parallels with the rationale of

Syed Ahmad Barelvi's hijrat to the NWF to wage jihad against the Sikhs (and later the British), thereby demonstrating the thought continuum between Shah Waliullah Dehlawi, Syed Ahmad Barelvi and Syed Jamal al-Din al-Afghani. The combined effect of Syed Ahmed Khan and Afghani was the simultaneous growth of Muslim nationalism and pan-Islamism, and reconciliation between the two, which did not bode well for Bharat, as we shall see in the next two sections.

Section 2
1899–1909

The Partition of Bengal
(1899–1905)

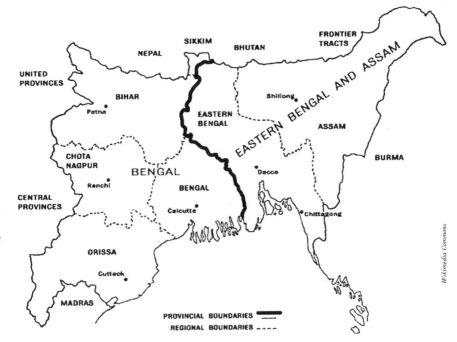

Image showing the Partition of Bengal into the Province of Bengal and the Province of Eastern Bengal and Assam in 1905

It can be said with sufficient basis, given the discussions in the previous section, that by 1898 the sagging fortunes of Middle Eastern coloniality/consciousness in Bharat after the loss of Muslim state power in the first half of the eighteenth century had been resuscitated by a slew of ulema-driven Dehlawite movements which had Delhi, Patna, Deoband, Bareilly, Aligarh, Lucknow, Mewat and Qadian as their centres. This did not mean that the influence of these movements was limited to these centres; on the contrary, they had mosques, seminaries and madrasas spread all over the subcontinent, proving that the ulema enjoyed the support of a wide cross-section of the Muslim community. Further, thanks to the efforts of Syed Ahmed Khan and Syed Jamal al-Din al-Afghani, Muslim nationalism and pan-Islamism had firmly taken root in Muslim society in Bharat. Strictly speaking, while Khan and Afghani may have seen each other as competitors for the hearts and minds of Muslim society in the Bharatiya subcontinent, these two schools of thought were not mutually exclusive but in fact complemented each other, as we shall see. From a practical perspective, it was possible for Afghani's caliphal vision and Khan's vision of revival of Muslim political fortunes in Bharat to not just coexist under a federal green flag, but also collaborate to achieve their respective global and local goals. After all, given that Middle Eastern consciousness was the common fount of both streams of thought, they were united in their shared antipathy for the Indic civilisational consciousness, which always put things in perspective whenever one tried to survive at the expense of the other or prevail over the other.

While Syed Ahmed Khan and Afghani had a pan-India impact, as stated earlier, the part of the country that produced its own influential Muslim leaders well before the others was Bengal, which had Nawab Abdul Latif and Syed Ameer Ali leading the charge. As we saw, even prior to their arrival, a fertile ground for Islamic revivalism in Bengal had been created by the Faraizi Movement of Haji Shariatullah and his son, along with the later efforts of Enayat Ali, Titu Mir and Maulvi Karamat Ali Jaunpuri, who worked extensively in Bengal (specifically in Muslim-dominated Eastern Bengal) to attract greater numbers to the Wahhabi cause. To be fair, as stated in the previous chapter, Nawab Abdul Latif had worked towards reducing Wahhabi influence in Bengal to minimise the distance between the British establishment and Muslims; he even enlisted the support of Maulvi Karamat Ali to encourage the Muslims of Bengal to take up Western education.[1] However, the reality was that the sustained investment of at least two generations of Faraizis and Wahhabis was too well entrenched in the Muslim society of Bengal; Karamat Ali himself had spent thirty-eight years in Bengal spreading Syed Ahmad Barelvi's teachings.[2]

The other milestone that led to the deepening of Islamic consciousness in Bengal was the census of 1872, since it raised questions regarding the ethnic antecedents of the Muslim population in the province.[3] This ethnocentric approach to colonised populations was consistent with the British establishment's coloniality, of which race consciousness was an integral part. Some Englishmen were of the view that the large number of Muslims in Bengal was attributable to conversion of the 'dregs of the Hindu Community' who had 'embraced Islam as a shortcut to social promotion' to escape the rigidity of the 'caste system'.[4] What is both interesting and critical to note is that prior to the arrival of the European coloniser, Muslim historians and chroniclers did not feel the need to cite the 'caste system' as the reason for conversion of

Hindus to Islam. These explanations were invented by the British to lay the ground for evangelical activity in Bharat, and were subsequently adopted by the Muslim intelligentsia to explain the 'voluntary' conversion of scores to Islam from the Hindu fold. This reinforces the point I had made in Chapter 6 of my first book, that the sanitised templates provided by the European colonial establishment proved useful for the Muslim intelligentsia, who were only too happy to embrace these colonial versions of Bharatiya history to sanitise *their* history of conversion and to draw attention away from the actual means employed to secure converts. Equally, there were other commentators such as Dr James Wise, who wrote in 1883 as follows:[5]

> The farther we advance in our knowledge of the early history of Bengal the more certain is it, that previous to the eighteenth century the Hindu inhabitants of Bengal far exceeded the Muhammadan in numbers. The enthusiastic soldiers, who, in the thirteenth and fourteenth centuries, spread the faith of Islam among the timid races of Bengal, made forcible conversions by the sword, and, penetrating the dense forests of the Eastern frontier, planted the crescent in the villages of Silhet. Such appear to be the main reasons for concluding that the Bengal Muhammadan of the present day is a converted Hindu, and not a scion of any Mughal or Pathan stock.

Naturally, this did not go down well with the Muslim nobility who were proud of their non-Bharatiya, or claimed non-Bharatiya, origins. In his book on the roots of Muslim separatism in Bengal, Amalendu De points out that Khondkar Fuzli Rubee, the Dewan of the Nawab of Murshidabad, wrote a book titled *Haqiqat-i-Musalman-i-Bangala* with the intention of proving the foreign origin of upper-class Muslims in Bengal.[6] Rubee highlighted the differences between the Bengali spoken by Muslims and Hindus, and also drew a line that distinguished the Muslim nobility from the Muslim 'masses' who were invariably drawn from the Hindu fold.[7] Clearly, the Ashraf-versus-Ajlaf-and-Arzal distinction within the Muslim community was not limited to any particular region in Bharat. The divide was so pronounced that the Ajlaf were referred to by such derogatory terms as *kamina*, meaning wretch, or *razil* (a corruption of *rizal*), meaning worthless.[8] The Arzal Muslims, or 'the lowest of all', were forbidden from entering mosques or using public burial grounds.[9] In fact, according to the 1911 census, Muslim society in Bengal alone consisted of *eighty different castes*.[10] Given the ethno-religious nature of this divide, it needs to be asked why this manifestly birth-based, race-driven divide within the Muslim community does not receive the kind of generous and round-the-clock attention that is showered on the 'Hindu caste system', which is not even based on ethnicity. Further, the prevalence of such a divide in Muslim society also begs the question as to what benefits accrued to the so-called 'dregs of the Hindu community' by such conversion to Islam, if it only resulted in greater social stratification and inequality in a supposedly egalitarian faith. This suggests that the stratification of Muslims along the lines of their Arab and non-Arab origins in the subcontinent has nothing to do with Hinduism 'infecting' Islam with caste, as is repeatedly alleged, but is, in fact, inherent to the Islamic faith and worldview. No wonder the leading lights of Islamic reformist movements such as Dehlawi underscored their non-Bharatiya origins and exhorted the Hindu converts to follow the Islam of the early Arab converts.

Coming back to the 1872 census, it was revealed that the population of Hindus and Muslims in Bengal was 1.81 crore and 1.76 crore, respectively.[11] By 1891, Hindus were slightly over 1.8 crore, against 1.95 crore Muslims.[12] Districts such as Bogra, Rajshahi, Noakhali, Chittagong, Pabna, Backergunge, Tipperah and Mymensingh had become Muslim-majority districts, with Muslims comprising more than 60 per cent of the population, and in some cases close to 80 per cent.[13] According to Amalendu De, this demographic change was accompanied by heightened Islamic consciousness and greater assertiveness on the part of the Muslim community as well as its leaders such as Nawab Abdul Lateef and Syed Ameer Ali.[14] However, given their British loyalist positions on the same lines as Syed Ahmed Khan, these leaders stood in the way of Muslim separatism translating into an anti-British position. What changed this state of affairs was the arrival of Syed Jamal al-Din al-Afghani in Calcutta in 1882. According to Amalendu De, during his visit, Afghani's pan-Islamism and anti-colonial position influenced the Muslim elite of Calcutta, such as Pandit Reazuddin Ahmed Mashahdi, so much so that Mashahdi authored a book on Afghani's life in 1889, titled *Samaj o Samskarak*, which was banned by the British.[15] As observed in the previous chapter, Afghani's pan-Islamism bolstered the anti-colonial sentiment among Muslims in the subcontinent, which was a departure from the British loyalist positions of Syed Ahmed Khan, Nawab Abdul Latif and Syed Ameer Ali. Since no credible attempt was made by influential Muslim leaders to reconcile the anti-colonial pan-Islamic strain of thought with the need to coexist with Hindus, says De, this naturally led to the solidification of Muslim separatism.[16]

To my mind, even this is wishful apologia, because De's analysis fails to take into account the innate anti-indigenous/anti-Indic pathology of Islamic reformist movements such as the Faraizi and Wahhabi Movement, which had deeply entrenched the separatist nature of the Muslim identity in Bengal and other parts of the country long before Afghani's arrival. This separatist nature, it could be contended, is consistent with the central tenets of Middle

Eastern consciousness. Therefore, agreeing with De's analysis, which pins the blame for Muslim separatism primarily on Afghani's pan-Islamism, would amount to blithely and wilfully ignoring the long history of Islamic puritanism and consequent separatism in Bharat. When coupled with an altered and favourable demographic balance, such puritanism was bound to have adverse implications for Indic consciousness and its adherents. After all, instances of religious harmony and acceptance of Indic/Dharmic belief systems and practices when state power vested in Muslims or the demographic balance tilted in their favour have been rare, if at all, in Bharat's history.

Further, in view of the altered demographic balance, Muslim assertiveness and separatism also manifested in the community's attitudes towards education. For instance, even while leaders such as Abdul Latif and Ameer Ali encouraged the Muslim community to take up Western education, they did not call for abandonment of Islamic learning, since they understood the latter's importance in keeping alive Islamic consciousness, distinctiveness and separatism.[17] This is because a strong traditional Islamic support base from the masses strengthened the bargaining position of the Muslim elites with the colonial establishment, and presented the community as a formidable ally of the British against the Hindus. To avoid secularisation of the Muslim mind, Muslim leaders of Bengal preferred establishment of separate institutions for the community that combined Islamic and English education. In this regard, scholar Nilanjana Paul's dissertation, titled 'Muslim Education and Communal Conflict in Colonial Bengal: British Policies and Muslim Responses from 1854 to 1947', sheds light on the relationship between Muslim attitudes to colonial educational policies and its impact on Muslim separatism in Bengal.[18]

Paul holds that apart from the Muslim insistence on formulation of Muslim-specific education policies, the British government too, on its part, created specific incentives for more members of the Muslim community to pursue English education. Such incentives included provision of grants-in-aid to create English and vernacular schools and appointment of Muslim teachers in English schools in Muslim-majority districts.[19] And yet, none of these initiatives bore fruit. Consequently, in 1882, to undertake a more systematic analysis of the reasons behind the failure of these initiatives, and the general state of 'education' in India, the Viceroy of the time, Lord Ripon, appointed the Indian Education Commission under W.W. Hunter, also known as the Hunter Commission of 1882. Here are a few relevant extracts from the conclusions and recommendations of the report of the Hunter Commission, which shed light on the status of adoption of English education by the Muslim community at the time and the underlying causes of the same:[20]

556. Reasons alleged by the Muhammadans for holding aloof from the Education offered in Government Schools—What the causes were which deterred the Muhammadans from such cultivation was debated even among themselves. While some held that the absence of instruction in the tenets of their faith, and still more the injurious effects of English education in creating a disbelief in religion, were the main obstacles, others, though a small minority, were of opinion that religion had little to do with the question. Some contended that the system of education prevailing in Government schools and colleges corrupted the morals and manners of the pupils, and that for this reason the better classes would not subject their sons to dangerous contact. The small proportion of Muhammadan teachers in Government institutions; the unwillingness of Government educational officers to accept the counsel and co-operation of Muhammadans; numerous minor faults in the Departmental system; the comparatively small progress in real learning made by the pupils in Government schools; the practice among the well-to-do Muhammadans of educating their children at home; the indolence and improvidence too common among them; their hereditary love of the profession of arms; the absence of friendly intercourse between Muhammadans and Englishmen; the unwillingness felt by the better born to associate with those lower in the social scale; the poverty nearly general among Muhammadans; the coldness of Government towards the race; the use in Government schools of books whose tone was hostile or scornful towards the Muhammadan religion;—these and a variety of other causes have been put forward at different times by members of the Muhammadan community to account for the scant appreciation which an English education has received at their hands. All such causes may have combined towards a general result, *but a candid Muhammadan would probably admit that the most powerful factors are to be found in pride of race, a memory of bygone superiority, religious fears, and a not unnatural attachment to the learning of Islam.* But whatever the causes, the fact remained; though the enquiries made in 1871–73 went to prove that except in the matter of the higher education there had been a tendency to exaggerate the backwardness of the Muhammadans.

580. Conclusions and Recommendations of the Commission—In the foregoing pages, we have preferred to reproduce the statements made with regard to the condition of the Muhammadans in the several Provinces, rather than to attempt generalisations of our own. The wide differences in the circumstances of the Musalmans in the three Presidencies render such an attempt hazardous. *But apart from the social and historical conditions of the Muhammadan community in India, there are causes of a strictly educational character which heavily weight it in the race of life. The teaching of the mosque must precede the lessons of the school. The one object of a young Hindu is to obtain an education which will fit him for an official or a professional career. But before the young Muhammadan is allowed to turn his thoughts to secular instruction, he must commonly pass some years in*

going through a course of sacred learning. The Muhammadan boy, therefore, enters school later than the Hindu. In the second place, he very often leaves school at an earlier age. The Muhammadan parent belonging to the better classes is usually poorer than the Hindu parent in a corresponding social position. He cannot afford to give his son so complete an education. In the third place, irrespectively of his worldly means, the Muhammadan parent often chooses for his son while at school an education which will secure for him an honoured place among the learned of his own community, rather than one which will command a success in the modern professions or in official life. [Emphases added]

The above extracts need to be read and reread carefully, *not* from the perspective of understanding how Muslims 'lagged behind' by staying away from English education, but to infer and assess the impact of abandonment of Indic knowledge systems by a sizeable cross-section of *Hindus* to fit in the colonial structure. Of course, this is not to deny the revival of Hindu consciousness, thanks to movements under giants and icons such as Sri Ramakrishna Paramahamsa, Swami Vivekananda and others in the second half of the nineteenth century, and later efforts by stalwarts such as Mahamana Pandit Madan Mohan Malaviya, who founded the Banaras Hindu University in 1916. However, the significant extent of colonialisation and consequent Christianisation/secularisation of the Indic consciousness and its movement away from its Dharmic roots are undeniable. This must be primarily attributed to the mainstreaming of English education by the colonial establishment coupled with the *reciprocal* adoption of English education and simultaneous abandonment of indigenous knowledge structures and systems by the Hindu elites. While one does not subscribe to isolationism, indigeneity/indigenous thought is best transmitted through an indigenous education; therefore, relegating indigenous thought in education to secondary status significantly paved the way for replacement of the Indic civilisational consciousness with colonial consciousness or a dual consciousnes which was skewed in favour of the colonial quotient.

In contrast, the religio-linguistic awareness of the Muslim community in Bengal of the same period was evident from the reluctance of the community to being taught even in Bengali, since Urdu was the preferred medium of education, given its association with Islam.[21] Even when Bengali was accommodated to educate Muslims from the lower strata, Muslim leaders like Nawab Abdul Latif insisted that Bengali be 'purified' by the use of Arabic and Persian words and be freed from the influence of the 'Sanskritism of learned Hindoos'.[22] Once again, this highlights the association between language and faith, which is sometimes dismissed in contemporary discussions from the lofty heights of secular cosmopolitanism. On the subject of the impact of Muslim education on Muslim consciousness and English education on Hindu consciousness in colonial Bengal, yet another work worth reading is *Muhammadan Education in Bengal,* published in 1900 and written for the All-India Mohammedan Educational Conference founded by Syed Ahmed Khan. In this work, the author, Abdul Karim, who was an assistant inspector of schools in Bengal and a Fellow of the Calcutta University, observed as follows:[23]

> Justice had all along been administered in India in the language of the conquerors. From the beginning of their rule, Persian was the official language of the Musalman rulers. The Hindus readily learnt Persian and some of them even became teachers thereof. The English continued the use of Persian in courts so as to make as little change at first as possible. But in due course Persian gave way to the Indian Vernaculars and English as the Court languages of British India.

> Our utilitarian fellow-countrymen, the Hindus, quick to perceive the immense advantage which a knowledge of English literature and science would give them, early devoted themselves to western studies ...

> Whilst the Hindus were thus showing readiness, zeal and generosity towards the spread of English education in India, far different were the feelings of the Musalmans, whose attitude towards English education was anything but friendly. When it was proposed to appropriate the whole of Government Educational grants to English education, there was a petition against it from the Musalmans of Calcutta, signed by about 8000 persons, including all the learned and respectable Muhammadan gentlemen of this city. They regarded the introduction of English as a step towards conversion to Christianity. This hostile attitude of the Musalmans towards English education stands in strong contrast to the attitude of the Hindu community, and accounts for the vast disparity in English education between the two communities, which still subsists.

> ... Had oriental learning found a place in the curriculum of English schools and colleges, as at present, most probably there would not have been misapprehension. But unfortunately it was decided that the object of the British Government was to be 'the promotion of European literature and Science among the natives of India, and that all the funds appropriated for the purpose of education would be best employed on English education alone'. *The exclusive study of a foreign language and the total neglect of the classical and vernacular languages of the people not unnaturally created suspicion, the result of which, as will be shown later on, has proved detrimental to the interests of my co-religionists.* The advocates of English education have overshot their mark, when Lord Macaulay, as their mouth-piece, declared, with his characteristic facility for exaggeration, that 'a single shelf of a good European library was worth the whole native literature of India and Arabia ...'

Arabic, Persian and Sanskrit, held by the people in great reverence as the only source of wisdom, were in consequence of such teachings looked upon with unconcealed contempt by those who were receiving English education. Moreover, the effect produced by the exclusive study of English was far from satisfactory. The first generation of Indian students of English literature, who learnt English along with their classical languages, consisted of sound, substantial and self-made men with definite religious views and high character. The next generation, the first fruits of exclusive education in a foreign language, consisted of men of a different type. The students of Shakespeare and Milton could scarcely spell their names in their own mother-tongue. Not being grounded in their ancestral theology and traditions, these men were infected with scepticism; and the morals of educated Bengalis suffered in consequence. Indeed the Hindu society of the time presented the appearance of chaos. The orthodoxy of Hindus was seriously affected and their national characteristics were also, to some extent, affected. Some of the most intelligent English scholars of the time did not hesitate to embrace Christianity. All these circumstances, viz. the exclusive study of English with a total disregard of oriental learning, the lowering of morals, and the effect on manners due to the exclusively secular education imparted through a foreign language, and the conversion to Christianity of some of the students, rightly or wrongly attributed thereto, could not but alarm a religious people like Musalmans. Consequently, they, for the most part, kept aloof from English education. [Emphases added]

This extract clearly captures the point that there exists an undeniable relationship between language, education and consciousness. Further, while embrace of English education may have hastened the process of Hindu elites becoming part of the colonial infrastructure, the absence of an indigenous foundation to offset the impact of colonial education resulted in significant loss of indigeneity on all fronts, including political thought. On the other hand, the decision of the Muslim community to stay away from English education (as reflected in the position of the early Dehlawite movements), or to adopt a hybrid model, such as the Aligarh model, which provided an Islamic environment for Anglo-Islamic education, enabled retention of the Middle Eastern consciousness by the Muslim elites while equipping them to engage with the colonial establishment. Not surprisingly, it is equally true that the disparity in the socio-economic status of the Hindus and Muslims of that period must be attributed to their respective decisions to either embrace or stay aloof from English education. In view of this, the standard narrative of later postcolonial/Marxist scholars to give the impression that the Hindus *deliberately* kept Muslims behind or deprived them of opportunities is baseless, since both communities had to bear or enjoy the consequences of their respective trajectories in relation to English education—from the perspectives of access to employment opportunities, presence in the state infrastructure, and retention of their consciousness/indigeneity.

What is interesting and ironic is that, as we shall see, exposure to English education allowed Hindu leaders of the time to use European political thought to merely demand greater participation in governance of Bharat without seeking to secede from the empire, while the decision of the Muslim leaders to embrace an Anglo-Islamic model of education went hand in hand with Muslim separatism and their pragmatic British loyalist position to keep Hindus in check. From a decolonial perspective, these nuances are important to bear in mind when one attempts to make sense of Bharat's 'Independence movement' and the evolution of contemporary political and constitutional thought. In other words, the critical question is, in the process of securing political freedom through *internalisation* of European education and worldview, did Hindus compromise on their Dharmic/Indic consciousness, including in their political and constitutional outlook? Similarly, notwithstanding Pakistan's current state of affairs, did the creation of Pakistan reflect the success of the Muslim community's ability to combine traditional Islamic learning with English education to achieve the Dehlawite goal, even if in part? *These* are the questions that are central, not just to this book but also to the next one, in which I shall discuss the Partition of Bharat and the framing of independent 'India-that-is-Bharat's' Constitution. The other question that needs to be asked is, if English education had begun the process of alienation of Hindus from their native consciousness at least from the 1850s, when the society still had indigenous institutions to offer, could it not be said that the current state of the Hindu mind reflects a much more advanced stage of cultural/psychological colonisation and hence alienation from its Indic roots? As a corollary, does this also explain the contemporary tendency to label anyone attached to or associated with 'traditional' Indic institutions as 'orthodox', 'Brahminical' and 'anti-modern'? I leave it to the reader to ponder these questions.

Coming back to the Partition of Bengal, while the facts and factors discussed so far help us understand the reasons for the existence and sustenance of Muslim separatism in Bengal in the 1890s, it is also important to know the geographical extent of the Bengal Province to understand the Partition of Bengal from an administrative perspective. Prior to 1874, the province comprised Bengal proper, Bihar, Orissa (now Odisha), the entire United Provinces, including Delhi, parts of the Central Provinces, Chota Nagpur and Assam.[24] It was the Orissa famine of 1866 that led to the realisation on the part of the British establishment that Bengal was too large a province to manage, which started a churn for reorganisation of the provinces.[25] In January 1868, Secretary of State for India Stafford Henry Northcote suggested cleaving Assam and Orissa from Bengal, citing the massive size of the province, on account of which its outlying territories were suffering from paucity of administrative attention.[26] Accordingly, in 1874, the province was reorganised by making Assam and the Bengali-speaking districts of Sylhet, Cachar and Goalpara a separate province under a Chief Commissioner who reported directly to the Governor General in Council. Despite this, the province comprising Bengal proper, Bihar, Orissa and Chota Nagpur remained mammoth, of 1.89 lakh square miles in size and a population of close to 7.9 crore.[27]

In 1892, the transfer of Chittagong Division and Lushai Hills to Assam was considered, and again in 1896 the transfer of Chittagong and the districts of Dacca and Mymensingh to Assam was proposed. However, finally, only Lushai Hills was transferred to Assam in 1897.[28] What must be noted is that Eastern Bengal and the adjoining parts of Assam were predominantly Muslim, which meant that if Eastern Bengal and Assam were combined, the resulting province would have a Muslim-majority population—that is, in the population of 3.1 crore, the proportion of Muslims would be 59 per cent.[29] In view of the British loyalist positions of the Muslim leaders of that period, this would have had the effect of weakening the rise of Bengali Hindu-led 'Indian nationalism' (the true nature of which we will examine in the next chapter) and strengthening the hands of the Dehlawite movements. In a nutshell, to understand the events that led to the Partition of Bengal in 1905, one must consider (a) the prior existence of Islamic consciousness, and Islamic revivalism through the Faraizi and Wahhabi Movement, (b) the consequent Muslim separatism, (c) the favourable Muslim demographics in Bengal by 1891, (d) the existence of a vocal and influential Bengali Muslim intelligentsia represented by Nawab Abdul Latif and Syed Ameer Ali, among others, (e) the British need to find a counterweight to Bengali Hindu-led 'Indian nationalism', and (f) the administrative-cum-economic considerations. These factors distinguished Bengal from other Muslim-majority provinces such as Punjab. After all, according to the 1901 census, Muslims constituted 49.6 per cent of Punjab's population, Hindus 41.3 per cent and Sikhs 8.6 per cent.[30] Also, as we shall see, Muslim-majority Punjab was partitioned in November 1901 and the North-West Frontier Province was created, which too was Muslim majority. And yet, it was the Partition of Bengal that proved to be more instrumental in providing an impetus to Muslim political separatism, which may be attributed to the six non-exhaustive factors identified above.

In the midst of this religious, political, demographic and administrative landscape in Bengal and the rest of Bharat, George Nathaniel Curzon, better known as Lord Curzon, arrived in Bharat in 1898,[31] a year after Afghani's death and the year Syed Ahmed Khan passed away. In January 1899, Curzon was made the Viceroy. As Viceroy, among his 'accomplishments' was the proposal to build the Victoria Memorial Hall in Calcutta (which began in 1906 and was completed in 1921) to demonstrate his reverence and affection for Queen Victoria, who passed away on 23 January 1901.[32] His other achievement was the holding of the Delhi Durbar in 1903 to celebrate the succession of Edward VII as the 'Emperor of India', represented at this event by the Duke of Connaught, Prince Arthur.[33] These were proof of Curzon's love of the spotlight and show of imperial power. On the administrative front, Curzon's attitude is perhaps best captured in the words of Peter Hardy, according to whom Curzon saw Bharat as a *'dominion of packages rather than a dominion of men'*.[34] In 1901, Curzon is reported to have said: *'As long as we rule India, we are the greatest power in the world. If we lose it, we shall straightway drop to a third-rate power.'*[35]

These tendencies of showmanship on Curzon's part and the treatment of Bharat as a resource/territory which needed to be run efficiently under the racially superior guidance of English administrators were reflected in the centralising nature of the administrative policies promulgated by him from 1899 onwards. For instance, he abolished dual control over the Frontier areas and made a case for creation of a separate North-West Frontier Province out of Punjab, which came into existence in November 1901.[36] Perhaps this decision was justified in the context of the Frontier areas given the need to secure the borders of British Indian territory. However, his centralising streak was evident from his irritation at the independence of the governors of the Madras and Bombay Presidencies. In his words:[37]

> Decentralisation is all very well, but it appears to me in the case of Bombay and Madras to have been carried to a point in which the Supreme Government is nowhere, and in which the petty kings of those dominions are even unconscious that responsibility attaches to anyone but themselves.

To address this, he proposed demotion of the status of Bombay and Madras to mirror that of Bengal and Punjab, a suggestion that was not acceptable to the Secretary of State for India and the Cabinet in England. In matters of bureaucracy, Curzon was driven by the belief that Indians, as a race, lacked the ability to govern themselves with honesty, and therefore needed able English administrators to educate them on good governance. Henry Cotton's views on Curzon's centralising initiatives across the board were as follows:[38]

> Lord Curzon had weakened and discouraged the beneficent schemes of local self-government which Lord Ripon introduced and did so much to foster; he had officialised the universities, and as far as possible the whole system of popular education; he had substituted a system of nomination to government service in place of competitive examinations; *and had announced a practical*

declaration of race disqualification for the higher public offices. The end in view was to officialise the administration by every means in his power, and this sinister aim was known to be underlying the project which raised such universal and bitter opposition—the Partition of Bengal. [Emphasis added]

Under Curzon, the stated policy of the British establishment in Bharat was that *'the bureaucracy knows what is for the good of the people'*.[39] I leave it to the readers to ask themselves whether this belief is still prevalent in the present-day bureaucracy of *independent* Bharat. Curzon then went on to introduce a slew of legislative measures which made him hugely unpopular among the educated and politically conscious cross-sections of the Bharatiya population. For instance, the Official Secrets Act of 1904 pushed the envelope beyond what was provided under the 1898 and 1899 Acts by bringing within its ambit even *criticism* of government that was *likely* to bring the government into suspicion or contempt. These and other such legislations, that stifled legitimate political expression as well as local self-government, alienated Curzon from the intelligentsia and the masses alike. But what broke the proverbial camel's back was the Partition of Bengal, which bolstered the 'national movement', both peaceful and armed, for the first time in a major way after the Mutiny of 1857.

Before I proceed to discuss the specifics of the Partition of Bengal, it is important to state my own position based on the literature. Although Curzon's move to Partition Bengal had his imperial personality written all over it, it would be factually incorrect to assume that heightened Islamic consciousness in Bengal and outside of Bengal—and the prospect of securing a Muslim-majority province in the seat of British power in Bharat—had no role, or only a negligible part, to play in it. It must be appreciated that around this period, Syed Ahmed Khan's death in 1898 had created a huge vacuum in Muslim society, which felt the need for an organisation that could represent its interests and demands before the British establishment and contain the growth of Congress-led 'nationalism'. Co-travellers of Syed Ahmed Khan's Aligarh Movement, such as Mohsin ul-Mulk and Viqar-ul-Mulk, pointed out to the Muslim community that there were only two choices available to them—either to join the Congress, or to establish their own organisation.[40] Between the two choices, the former was 'tantamount to suicide', according to these leaders, and the existing institutions, including the ones in Aligarh, were deemed inadequate to safeguard and advance the interests of the community in the political realm.

These views were shared by other Muslim leaders too, which finally led to a meeting of the leading lights of the Muslim community in Lucknow in October 1901 under the stewardship of Syed Sharfuddin, who would later become a judge of the Calcutta High Court. Citing the need for greater representation of Muslims in government services as well as in the central and provincial legislatures, Viqar-ul-Mulk presented a scheme for establishment of a political organisation that would secure the interests of Muslims. The following was resolved at the said meeting:[41]

1. The Muslims of India should form an organisation which should act in respect of their social and political needs and interests;
2. It is necessary for the Muslims to keep away from the Congress for the following reasons: the two main objectives of the Congress—representative government and recruitment to government services through competitive examinations—are manifestly inimical to Muslim interests.

Despite the initial sluggishness, this scheme seemed to gain traction in the Muslim community in early 1902. By 1903, the *Aligarh Institute Gazette* started mobilising large-scale support for the scheme by taking the unequivocal position that the Muslims of the subcontinent were a single and separate nation from the Hindus owing to their religious identity, and that there was a need to organise and consolidate the members of the community. Between July 1903 and March 1904, quite a few political organizations for Muslims were set up in Saharanpur and Aligarh in the United Provinces, and in Murshidabad in Bengal, which led to calls for establishment of a central political organisation to avoid creation of multiple splinter groups.[42] These facts demonstrate that circumstances were ripe for the crystallisation of Muslim political separatism and for the creation of a base from which this vision of a separate Muslim political organisation and representation could be given concrete effect. In appreciating the events leading to the Partition of Bengal and its subsequent implications for 'Indian nationalism' and Muslim separatism, this backdrop must be borne in mind each time we are tempted to place the blame entirely, solely and comfortably on the divide and rule policy of the British. In other words, colonial attempts to drive a wedge between Hindus and Muslims and the independent existence of Muslim separatism are *not* mutually destructive facts. In fact, at best, colonial policies can be blamed for *taking advantage of a pre-existing religious, civilisational and political divide, but not for creating one.*

Coming back to Curzon, after carving out the NWFP from Punjab and having failed to pare down the powers of the governors of Bombay and Madras, he turned his attention to Bengal. While most literature cites 1903 as the year when he mooted the proposal to Partition Bengal, his letter of 30 April 1902 to Secretary of State for India George Hamilton said this:[43]

I am not sure that this will not be a proper occasion on which to examine into the larger question of the boundaries of Governments, or some of them, in general. Bengal is unquestionably large a charge for any single man. Ought

Chittagong to continue to belong to it, or ought we to give Assam an outlet to the sea? Is Orissa governed from Calcutta? Ought Ganjam to be given?

Fortunately for Curzon, he was not alone in holding the view that the provinces required reorganisation. After the transfer of Lushai Hills to Assam in 1897, in February 1901 Andrew Fraser, then Chief Commissioner of the Central Provinces, proposed adding Sambalpur to Orissa. This communication, along with the suggestion to place Berar under the Central Provinces, reached Curzon's office only in May 1902, which drew his ire at the delay caused by what he called 'departmentalism'.[44] Given the number of such suggestions, Curzon confessed to A. Godley of the India Office that his ambition was to '*fix provincial boundaries for the next generation*'.[45] Since the Viceroy himself was predisposed to a general reorganisation of provinces, in early 1903 Andrew Fraser, now Lieutenant Governor of Bengal, revived his earlier proposal of 1897 to transfer the Chittagong Division and the districts of Dacca and Mymensingh to Assam.[46] This received the support of the Chief Commissioner of Assam, J.B. Fuller, who was keen on justifying construction of the Assam–Bengal Railway, which in turn depended on diversion of greater traffic to Chittagong port and away from Calcutta port.[47] The development of the tea, oil and coal industries of Assam with a port of its own in Chittagong further provided economic justification for the reorganisation of Bengal.[48]

It could be argued that it was in view of these stated administrative and economic exigencies that in June 1903 Curzon drew up a detailed minute on the redrawing of territories in Bharat, which was not limited to Bengal. The second part of this minute dealt with Bengal.[49] According to the proposal, in order to give greater attention to the outlying areas of Bengal and to expand the jurisdiction of Assam so that it may have a coast, Bengal would be divided, with Chittagong, Dacca and Mymensingh being added to Assam. Further, apart from seeking to unite the scattered Oriya-speaking population in a single territory, Chota Nagpur was proposed to be added to the Central Provinces.[50] Critically, in his minute dated 1 June 1903 on the proposed redistribution of territories, Curzon spoke his mind thus:[51]

> The argument of the Lieutenant Governor of Bengal Sir A. Frazer attaches the utmost weight which cannot be absent from our consideration. He has represented to me that the advantage of severing these Eastern districts of Bengal which are a hotbed of the purely Bengali movement unfriendly if not seditious in character and dominating the whole tone of Bengal administration will immeasurably outweigh any possible drawbacks.

While ostensibly administrative and economic reasons were offered as justifications for the Partition of Bengal, clearly one of the central considerations was to break the momentum of the 'nationalist movement' in Bengal. Further, it is also impossible to ignore the division of the Bharatiya identity on linguistic lines by the colonial establishment, which was perhaps the forerunner for the reorganisation of States on a linguistic basis in 1956 in *independent* Nehruvian India.

In December 1903, the entire proposal for the Partition of Bengal was conveyed in letters written by the secretary to the Government of India, H.H. Risley, to the governments of those territories that would be affected by it, capturing the administrative and economic reasons for the proposed redistribution of territories.[52] Upon publication for public consumption in January 1904,[53] the proposals immediately drew vehement and vociferous opposition from Bengalis (in particular Hindus), from professionals such as lawyers, and from trade bodies such as the Bengal Chamber of Commerce, which represented European traders.[54] Each of these stakeholders stood to lose a lot—the tilting of the demographic balance in favour of Muslims in the proposed Province of Eastern Bengal and Assam, the loss of professional opportunities owing to the establishment of a court in Dacca, which would adversely affect the fortunes of the powerful Calcutta lawyers, and, of course, the division of a large existing market and creation of a new set of bureaucratic hurdles for European traders. According to A.C. Mazumdar, who served as president of the Indian National Congress at the time of the signing of the Lucknow Pact in 1916, the opposition to the proposal to partition Bengal was 'simply unprecedented in the history of public agitation in this country' in its '... magnitude, volume and intensity'.[55]

Between December 1903 and October 1905, over 2,000 public meetings were held in opposition to the proposal. The Indian National Congress opposed it in its annual sessions of 1903 and 1904, which were held in Madras and Bombay, respectively.[56] While it is true that prominent Muslim voices such as Nawab Salimullah of Dacca initially opposed the partition as a 'beastly arrangement', their opposition gradually turned into support.[57] In fact, it quickly led to the founding of the Muslim League in 1906 in Dacca, with Nawab Salimullah as one of its founders, as we shall see. Apart from the prospect of rallying Muslims of Eastern Bengal and Assam under his leadership in the proposed Muslim-majority province, the other incentive that influenced the Nawab's decision to support the partition was the advancement of a low-interest loan by the British to the tune of 100,000 sterling pounds to stave off a personal bankruptcy.[58] Other than Nawab Salimullah, Nawab Syed Ali Chowdhury of Mymensingh also supported the partition, and Nawab Abdul Latif advised his co-religionists to avoid attending any meetings organised by Hindus opposing the partition.[59]

The so-called change in Muslim attitudes to the Partition of Bengal may be only partly attributed to the hard-sell by Curzon of the advantages of the partition to the Muslims of Bengal, which is corroborated by scholars such as Peter Hardy.[60] As Viceroy, since Curzon had spent close to five years in Bharat by 1903, he was presumably aware of the existence of Muslim separatism in Bengal and other parts of the country, and knew how the creation of a Muslim-majority province was bound to strengthen separatist tendencies. That he was aware of these foreseeable consequences and was still keen on propping up a counterweight to Congress-led 'nationalism' is evident from his letter dated 17 February 1904 to Secretary of State for India John Brodrick, which reveals that the so-called administrative reasons which were offered as justification for the proposed partition were not entirely true:[61]

> The Bengalis, who like to think of themselves a nation, and who dream of a future when the English will have been turned out and a Bengali Babu will be installed in Government House, Calcutta, of course bitterly resent any disruption that will be likely to interfere with the realisation of this dream. If we are weak enough to yield to their clamour now, we shall not be able to dismember or reduce Bengal again; and you will be cementing and solidifying, on the eastern flanks of India, a force already formidable and certain to be a source of increasing trouble in future.

This letter was written on the eve of his address to a predominantly Muslim audience on 18 February 1904 in Dacca as part of the tour he undertook[62] to assess public reaction to the proposed partition.[63] In his address, he expressly wooed the Muslims of Eastern Bengal and Assam by harkening back to the golden age of Muslim glory in Bharat as follows:[64]

> Let me put before you for a moment another aspect of the case. Much use has been made in this controversy of history, and of all that it is supposed to teach. I also in a small way am a student of history: and if it has taught me anything of these parts, the lesson has been that under the present system of administration, Dacca, which was once the capital of Bengal, has steadily declined in numbers and influence, and that not until the jute trade was introduced some thirty years ago did it begin to revive. In 1800 Dacca was a city of 200,000 people. In 1870 it had sunk to 69,000. Since then it has risen, owing to the circumstances that I have mentioned, to 90,000 in the last census; but whereas the increase was 10,000 between 1870 and 1880, it has only been 11,000 in the ensuing 20 years. Will anyone here pretend that, even after this advance, Dacca is anything but a shadow of its former self? Is it not notorious that for years it has been lamenting its downfall, as compared with the past?
>
> *When then a proposal is put forward which would make Dacca the centre, and possibly the capital, of a new and self-sufficing administration, which must give to the people of these districts, by reason of their numerical strength and their superior*

culture, the preponderating voice in the province so created, which would invest the Mahomedans in Eastern Bengal with a unity which they have not enjoyed since the days of the old Musulman Viceroys and Kings, which must develop local interests and trade to a degree that is impossible so long as you remain, to use your own words, the appanage of another administration, and which would go far to revive the traditions which the historical students assure us once attached to the Kingdom of Eastern Bengal—can it be that the people of these districts are to be advised by their leaders to sacrifice all these great and incontestable advantages, from fear of being tied on to the tail of the humble and backward Assam? [Emphasis added]

That Curzon's views and strategy were shared by others in the colonial establishment is evident from H.H. Risley's letter dated 13 September 1904 on behalf of Government of India, which contained the details of the partition. In the letter, Risley clearly stated that Dacca would be the capital of the proposed new province and that the interests of Muslims of the province would take precedence.[65] This is corroborated by R.C. Majumdar, who extracted the following contents of the letter:[66]

> The boundary suggested would bring within the Eastern Province the bulk of the characteristic Muhamadans of Bengal who form 78 per cent of the population in Rajshahi, 50 per cent, in Dinajpur, and 48 per cent, in Malda. Not only would it give Dacca a central position in relation to the rest of the new Province, but it would tend, in course of time, to confer on that city the special character of provincial capital, when Muhamadan interests would be strongly represented, if not predominant.

After his tour of Eastern Bengal, where he interacted predominantly with Muslim audiences, in a letter dated 2 February 1905 addressed to Brodrick, Curzon revealed his understanding of the importance of Calcutta for the nationalist movement:[67]

> Calcutta is the centre from which the Congress party is manipulated throughout the whole of Bengal, and indeed the whole of India. Its best wirepullers and its most frothy orators all reside there. The perfection of their machinery, and the tyranny which it enables them to exercise, are truly remarkable. They dominate public opinion in Calcutta; they affect the High Court; they frighten the Local Government and they are sometimes not without serious influence upon the Government of India. The whole of their activity is directed to creating an agency so powerful that they may one day be able to force a weak Government to give them what they desire.

Henry Cotton, a civil servant at that time, had the following to say on Curzon's proposal:[68]

> The object of the measure was to shatter the unity and to disintegrate the feelings of solidarity which are established in the province. It was no administrative reason that lay at the root of this scheme. It was part and parcel

of Lord Curzon's policy to enfeeble the growing power and to destroy the political tendencies of a patriotic spirit.

Based on these facts, it is evident that Curzon understood the demographic, religious and political implications of creating a Muslim-majority Eastern Bengal and Assam, and that the originally stated administrative and economic reasons for the partition *did not* present the complete picture. Clearly, one of Curzon's stated intentions was to nip the nascent Bengali Hindu-led 'nationalist movement' in the bud by using Muslims of Eastern Bengal and Assam as a counterweight. Even if the proposal was originally mooted to address only administrative and economic considerations, perhaps Curzon was quick to realise its potential political benefits, such as breaking the momentum of 'Indian nationalism', the epicentre of which was Bengal. Ironically, Curzon's actions provided *direct* impetus to the movement *and* also resulted in giving concrete political expression to Muslim separatism. After all, the pro-Muslim pitch by Curzon was the precise opportunity leaders of the Muslim community in Bengal and elsewhere of that period were looking for to dislodge Hindus from the colonial power structure. Here are R.C. Majumdar's views on the subject:[69]

> Lord Curzon undertook a tour in East Bengal ostensibly with the object of ascertaining public opinion, but really to overawe it. He was soon convinced of the strength and solidarity of public opposition to any scheme for partitioning Bengal. This evidently confirmed his views about the strength of Bengali nationalism and the danger it spelt to British rule in India. He therefore decided to remove this danger, before it was too late, by effectively destroying the solidarity of the Bengalis. He now conceived the much more comprehensive plan of dividing the Bengali speaking area into two separate Provinces. Towards the end of the year 1903 Lord Curzon's Government proposed to separate the whole of Chittagong Division and the Districts of Dacca and Mymensingh from Bengal, and to incorporate them with Assam. In East Bengal, the Muslims, politically less advanced and more loyal to the British than the Hindus, would be in a majority, while in Bengal, the Bengalis would form a minority by the inclusion of Bihar and Orissa. Thus the Bengalis would be divided from their kith and kin; the Bengali Hindus, hated and dreaded by Curzon for their advanced political ideas, would form a minority in both Provinces; and a thin wedge would be driven between the Hindus and Muslims of Bengal. It was undoubtedly a master-plan to destroy the nascent nationalism in Bengal.

The following is an extract from A.C. Mazumdar's book, first published in 1915, wherein he corroborates Curzon's employment of the divide and rule policy and the gradual but unequivocal reciprocation of the Muslims of Eastern Bengal to Curzon's overtures to woo them:[70]

Fully resolved to crush this new spirit by dividing the people against themselves, Lord Curzon proceeded to East Bengal and there at large meetings of Mahomedans, specially convened for the purpose, explained to them that his object in partitioning Bengal was not only to relieve the Bengal administration, but also to create a Mahomedan province, where Islam would be predominant and its followers would be in ascendancy, and that with this view he had decided to include the two remaining districts of the Dacca Division in his scheme. *The Mussalmans of East Bengal headed by Nawab Salimullah of Dacca saw their opportunity and took the bait. Henceforth the Mahomedans of Eastern Bengal deserted the national cause and gradually began to secede from the anti-partition agitation.* [Emphasis added]

To be fair, Mazumdar did point out that the Nawab's own brother and a few other Muslim leaders did not agree with his decision; but that said, the undeniable fact remains that the prospect of creating a Muslim-majority province with preferential treatment for Muslims dangled by Curzon was accepted by the majority of Muslims of Eastern Bengal and Assam. This is why I reiterate, that to blame the outcome solely on the divide and rule policy of the British is to wishfuly and wilfully ignore uncomfortable and 'unsecular' facts. The British policy succeeded only because there were serious, pre-existing and irreconcilable religious, cultural, linguistic and civilisational fissures, which eventually enabled the Partition of Bengal. If Ganga–Jamuni tehzeeb truly mattered or had an existence worth writing about, it should have risen to the occasion at this juncture, which it did not.

Also, thanks to the efforts of Muslim leaders like Syed Ahmed Khan, Nawab Abdul Latif and Syed Ameer Ali at least since the late 1850s and the early 1860s, by 1903 a new generation of Muslim leaders who could compete with English-speaking Hindus and demand their share in the colonial political space had come into existence. Their position to assert themselves was perhaps *better* than that of the Hindus on account of the institutions created by the Dehlawite movements, which provided the strong traditional Islamic mass base needed to support and complement the efforts of English-speaking Muslims. Simply put, there was a clear identity of goals among the two classes of Muslims, which provided both the intelligentsia and the masses needed to reclaim state power in accordance with the vision of Dehlawi and Syed Ahmed Khan. To add to this, since the British saw an ally in Muslims to keep Bengali Hindu-led nationalism in check, Syed Ahmed Khan's stated vision of a 'mutually beneficial alliance' between the British (Christians) and Muslims was beginning to take shape. That the combined province of Eastern Bengal and Assam was the reward for the pro-British loyalism of Muslims was a position echoed even by later Muslim scholars. For instance, in his book *Muslim Struggle for Freedom in Bengal (1757–1947)*, Muin-ud-Din Ahmad Khan had the following to say on the Partition of Bengal:[71]

> The formation of Eastern Bengal and Assam into a Lieutenant-Governor's province with headquarters at Dacca, brought to the Muslim population the promise of social and economic emancipation. In the first place, the city of Dacca, which was the site of decaying Muslim civilisation, was still under dominant Muslim influence where the Muslims had a greater chance of success than in Calcutta. Secondly, in the new province the Muslim population greatly outnumbered all other communities. Thirdly, it relieved them considerably from competing with the more advanced Hindus of Calcutta. *The partition was, therefore, hailed by the Muslims who acclaimed it as the fruit of loyalism.* [Emphasis added]

Interestingly, apart from candidly admitting to the convenient loyalism of Muslims of this period to the British, Muin-ud-Din Ahmad Khan employed the tried-and-tested Marxist template of sidelining religious causes and focused exclusively on the economic inequality between Hindus and Muslims to justify Muslim separatism. Conveniently, he chose not to mention the self-imposed and religious nature of the Muslim decision to not embrace English education. This once again demonstrates the cosy relationship between Marxism and Middle Eastern coloniality, wherein the former's template of class struggle was and continues to be employed to justify Muslim separatism just as is done for justifying the Moplah Riots of 1921. It may be of consequence to note that this template continues to be pressed into service to justify and defend the genocide and forced exodus of Kashmiri Hindus from the Valley in the 1990s.

Returning to Curzon, having secured the support of Muslim leaders of Bengal for the partition, he sent his revised scheme to Secretary of State for India John Brodrick on 2 February 1905 for his approval. This was received by the latter on 18 February 1905. Despite encountering widespread opposition from Bengali Hindus, far from revisiting the scheme of the partition, Curzon's revised scheme was even more drastic than the original. Instead of a few portions of Eastern Bengal being added to Assam as originally proposed, the revised scheme expanded it to include the districts of both Eastern and northern Bengal with Assam, which would form the new province of 'Eastern Bengal and Assam'. This new province, with an area of 106,540 square miles, would have Dacca as its capital, and a demographic composition of 18 million Muslims and 12 million Hindus.[72] The rest of Bengal was left with an area of 141,580 square miles, with 42 million Hindus and 9 million Muslims.[73] Here are the extracts from the proceedings of the House of Commons dated 5 June 1905, which record the fact that Curzon's revised scheme for the Partition of Bengal was under consideration by John Brodrick:[74]

MR. HERBERT ROBERTS (Denbighshire, W.) I beg to ask the Secretary of State for India whether he has received any proposals from the Government of India for partitioning the province of Bengal; and, if so, whether he will state what decision has been arrived at upon the subject.

THE SECRETARY OF STATE FOR INDIA (Mr. BRODRICK,) Surrey, Guildford The proposals of the Government of India for the reconstruction of the provinces of Bengal and Assam have been received and are under consideration. A decision will be communicated to India very shortly.

Shortly thereafter, in the same month, the scheme was approved with a few modifications, which was informed by Brodrick to the House of Commons on 4 July 1905 as follows:[75]

MR. HERBERT ROBERTS (Denbighshire, W.)

To ask the Secretary of State for India whether he is aware that an influentially-signed petition opposing the contemplated partition of Bengal is under submission from the inhabitants of Eastern Bengal; and whether he will postpone passing Orders on the proposals of the Government until this memorial has been considered.

(Answered by Mr. Secretary Brodrick.) The proposals of the Government of India on this subject reached me on the 18th of February, and I have already communicated to them the decision of the Secretary of State in Council accepting their proposals.

The revised scheme for partition was adopted through a Government Resolution dated 19 July 1905, which announced that the partition would come into effect from 16 October 1905.[76] Upon publication of the Resolution in the press on 20 July 1905,[77] public agitation increased in volume and intensity, which was taken note of even by the House of Commons on 1 August 1905 as follows:[78]

Mr. HERBERT ROBERTS (Denbighshire, W.)

I beg to ask the Secretary of State for India whether he has received and considered a memorial, signed by 60,000 of the inhabitants of Eastern Bengal, protesting against the proposals of the Government of India in reference to the partition of Bengal; whether the Papers upon this subject which are to be laid before Parliament have arrived; and whether he will name a date upon which they will be in the hands of Members of the House.

MR. BRODRICK

The memorial to which the hon. Member refers was received by me yesterday, and will be duly considered, but the hon. Member will realise that the scheme of the Government of India was not decided upon without the fullest deliberation; The Government of India have framed a resolution on the subject of the reconstitution of the provinces of Bengal and Assam which I expect to receive from India in a few days, and which I hope to lay before Parliament before the end of the session; but I cannot at the present time name the precise date on which it will be laid on the Table.

MR. HERBERT ROBERTS

When will the Papers be in our hands?

BRODRICK

I am afraid I cannot say.

It was this agitation that gave birth to the Swadeshi and Boycott Movements on 7 August 1905 at the Town Hall of Calcutta under leaders such as Surendranath Banerjea and Babu Ananth Bandhu Guha. The Boycott pledge drafted by Banerjea was as follows:[79]

I hereby pledge myself to abstain from the purchase of all English made goods for at least a year from this date, so help me God.

Processions chanting 'Bande Mataram' were taken out, and this further strengthened Muslim separatism, given the slogan's association with Bankim Chandra Chatterji's novel *Anandamath* and Hindu deities such as Devi Durga.[80] The British cracked down on the agitation by banning the chanting of 'Bande Mataram', and the following discussion took place on 8 August 1905 in the House of Commons:[81]

MR. HERBERT ROBERTS

I beg to ask the Secretary of State for India whether, in regard to the decision arrived at as to the partition of Bengal, he will state the line of demarcation and the territories actually to be transferred to Assam; whether he will state what is the form of administration and the name of the new province and when the new system of government will come into operation; what is the estimate of the cost connected with the creation of the new system of government and the increased annual charge to be incurred in the maintenance of the administration; whether an inquiry will be held with a view of ascertaining the feeling of the large populations affected by the change of administration; and whether, in view of the opposition of the inhabitants affected, he will suspend the operation of the Orders passed until further consideration has been given to their representations.

MR. BRODRICK

The territories to be transferred from Bengal to the new province consist of the districts of the Chittagong and Dacca Divisions, those of the Rajshahi Division except Darjeeling, and the district of Malda. The line of demarcation will follow the present boundaries of those districts. The new province, which will be a Lieutenant-Governorship, will be called 'Eastern Bengal and Assam.' The new system will come into operation as soon as the necessary arrangements can be completed, but I am not able at present to mention the date. The increased annual charge is estimated by the Government of India at rather more than ten lakhs of rupees, and the initial cost of buildings at Dacca at ten lakhs; there will probably be other expenses, of which no estimate can at present be given. The question has been under the consideration of the Government of India for more than two years, and has been the subject of a number of memorials and meetings. The Viceroy has personally visited some of the districts affected, and has replied in a series of speeches to the points raised, and is fully aware of the opposition to be encountered. I have laid on the Table the Resolution of the Government of India describing these changes, and a perusal of it will, I think, make it clear that no good could result from further inquiry.

MR. HERBERT ROBERTS

Has the right hon. Gentleman received information as to a large number of influential meetings which have been held in Bengal in order to protest against this Order?

MR. BRODRICK

Yes, Sir, I have had a number of resolutions forwarded to me which have been passed at a large number of meetings. I am aware that there is great anxiety about this question. I hope the publication of the Resolution may have some effect in allaying that anxiety, and I have no doubt the Viceroy will do what he can to make the change palatable to the population concerned.

MR. HERBERT ROBERTS

I beg to ask the Secretary of State for India whether, in accordance with the precedent followed in the case of the formation of the North-West Frontier Province, he will include in the Papers to be laid in reference to the partition of Bengal, in addition to the Resolution of the Government of India, the whole of the correspondence between the Viceroy and the Secretary of State upon the subject; and whether these Papers will be in the hands of Members before the rising of the House on Friday next.

MR. BRODRICK

Every case in which it is proposed to present Papers to Parliament is necessarily considered on its own merits. I hope that the Papers which on this occasion it is possible to publish may be in the hands of Members this evening. No time has been lost, so far as I am concerned, in laying them, as the Resolution only arrived yesterday.

Again, on 9 August[82] and 10 August[83] 1905, the House of Commons received petitions from Bengal and London for withdrawal of the Order of

Partition. The massive opposition to the partition was reported even in a few London-based newspapers. Here is an extract from one such report:[84]

> Very little is known in this country concerning the scheme for the partitioning of Bengal as to which our Calcutta correspondent addresses us ... In India the announcement seems to have come as a complete surprise ... It cannot be good statesmanship to launch these new provinces in a condition of seething discontent, or to alienate a third of our fellow-subjects in India ... We are convinced that Mr. Brodrick would greatly add to the service which he has already done to India if he could call a halt in this matter of the Partition.

Importantly, the opposition to the partition was not limited to Bengal, but became a nationwide movement through the Swadeshi and Boycott Movements. However, Curzon was not one to be deterred in the least and proceeded to give effect to the partition on the appointed date of 16 October 1905. The people of Bengal observed the day as one of national mourning.[85] In view of his growing unpopularity, Curzon was then advised to leave India, and so he left for England in November 1905 without even the customary farewell in Calcutta.[86] While the British chose to treat partition as a 'settled fact', the agitation continued, led by Surendranath Banerjea and Bipin Chandra Pal in Bengal.[87] The Indian National Congress once again denounced the partition and endorsed the Swadeshi and Boycott Movements in its annual session of December 1905 in Benares.[88] In fact, right until the reunification of Bengal in 1911, the Indian National Congress would continue to denounce the partition and demand reunification.

In the next chapter, the period following the Partition of Bengal in October 1905 until the Minto–Morley Reforms of 1909 shall be examined in some detail. This period covers the following major developments which chart the thought continuum of Middle Eastern consciousness/coloniality and its combined impact, along with that of European coloniality, on constitutional thought in Bharat:

1. Bengali Hindus continued to oppose the partition which led to the spread of the Swadeshi and Boycott Movements to the rest of Bharat. However, the aftermath of the partition also revealed fissures within the Indian National Congress, which was split between the Moderates/Liberals and the Extremists/Nationalists. This split had an impact on the national movement as well as on Bharatiya constitutional thought;

2. Muslims of Eastern Bengal and Assam supported the Partition of Bengal. Eventually, under the leadership of Nawab Salimullah and others, with Dacca as its base, Muslim separatism in Bengal and Islamic movements in the rest of the country, such as the Aligarh Movement, culminated in the founding of the All-India Muslim League in December 1906; and

3. Thanks to the efforts of Muslim leaders through the Simla Deputation of October 1906, the concept of communal representation through separate electorates on the basis of religion was introduced in the Indian Councils Act of 1909 as part of the Minto–Morley Reforms.

The Story of Moderate Nationalism, Muslim Nationalism and Electoral Separatism (1905–1909)

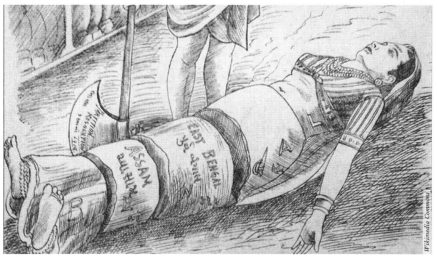

'Vandalism', a cartoon from the magazine *Hindi Punch*, 1906

The purpose of the first three chapters was to capture the trajectory of Middle Eastern consciousness from the decline of the Mughal empire, post the death of Aurangzeb in 1707, to the Partition of Bengal in 1905. The core objective was to showcase the ability of Middle Eastern consciousness to preserve its collective memory, perpetuate its worldview, and demonstrate its tenacity in clawing its way back into the power structure even under the British colonial establishment. This discussion was critical, for it sets the tone for assessment of the constitutional developments following the Partition of Bengal by charting the course of two layers of history that influenced each other:

1. The first layer deals with the imposition of colonial constitutionalism in Bharat. Its origins, politico-theological foundations, objectives and journey until the enactment of the Government of India Act of 1919 were discussed in the first book. This book, from here on, will build on

the broad foundations laid out in the first book and specifically examine the evolution of constitutional thought within the Indian National Congress. This includes a look at the fissures that were forming within the Congress, namely the divide between the Moderates/Liberals and Extremists/Nationalists, which came to the fore after the Partition of Bengal. Divergent views began to surface on issues such as the meaning of nationalism and the goals of the national movement in relation to the British establishment, the means adopted to secure their respective goals, and the nature of Bharatiya constitutionalism (a brief examination of the origins of the Congress and its relationship with the colonial establishment will be unavoidable as part of this discussion).

2. The second layer deals with the birth of the All-India Muslim League in December 1906 and its rise, which marked the next step in Middle Eastern coloniality's efforts to reclaim state power in Bharat. The League's establishment, its religio-political goals, its disagreements with the Congress and its pragmatic alliance with the British, all had a tangible and direct bearing on Bharat's constitutional journey. Specifically, it directly contributed to the entrenchment of religio-political separatism in Bharat's body politic and polity, the effects of which continue to be felt till date.

Accordingly, these two layers will henceforth be examined to understand the evolution of contemporary constitutionalism. To this end, this chapter will discuss the period between 1905 and 1909, with digressions to the periods before wherever necessary. In a way, this chapter serves as a critical bridge between the first and the present volumes of the Bharat Trilogy.

Reactions to the Partition of Bengal

After the Partition of Bengal, Curzon was succeeded as the Viceroy by Lord Minto in November 1905, while John Morley was appointed as the Secretary of State for India. The tenure of the Minto–Morley pair witnessed the rejuvenation of the so-called unarmed national movement (not necessarily anti-colonial), represented for the most part by the Indian National Congress, along with the rise of armed revolutionary movements and the further rise of Muslim separatism. The Partition of Bengal was by no means a 'settled fact', especially to those who could not accept the vivisection of a culture and a sacred geography that meant more to them than just an 'administrative province'. However, the uncomfortable reality was that this was a sentiment largely prevalent among Bengali Hindus, with only a smattering of support from a small section of Muslims for the anti-partition agitation. The

Citizens of Dacca waiting along Islampur Road to welcome J.B. Fuller, the first Lieutenant Governor of the new Province of Eastern Bengal and Assam, on 16 October 1905

majority of the Muslim population of Bengal and Assam was firmly behind pro-partition Muslim leaders such as Nawab Salimullah and his co-religionist associates such as Nawab Syed Ali Chowdhury.

Despite the open alliance between the British and most of the Muslim organisations in Bengal and Assam, the Bengali Hindu-led opposition to the partition continued, both on the armed and unarmed fronts, spurring the so-called national movement even outside Bengal. On the armed front, this period saw the rise of at least fourteen revolutionary and underground societies, such as the lesser-known Atmonnati Samiti, which was established in 1897, and the well-known Anushilan Samiti, established around 1902. The former ultimately merged with the latter in 1902.[1] The Samitis, whose presence extended into the old and new provinces of Bengal,[2] produced Revolutionaries like Aurobindo Ghosh, his brother Barindra Ghosh, Bhupendranath Datta, Khudiram Bose, Prafulla Chaki and Jatindra Nath Mukherjee (also known as Bagha Jatin). Interestingly, Bhupendranath Datta was the brother of Narendranath Datta, whom the world knows better as the cyclonic Swami Vivekananda.

This period also witnessed the growth of revolutionary organs such as *Yugantar, Bande Mataram* and *Sandhya*, in which Revolutionaries such as Barindra Ghosh called for the destruction of British rule in Bharat. Here is an example of one such exhortation:[3]

Will the Bengali worshippers of Shakti shrink from the shedding of blood?
The number of Englishmen in this country is not above one lakh and a half,

and what is the number of English Officials in each district? If you are firm in your resolution you can in a single day bring British rule to an end. Lay down your life, but first take a life. The worship of the Goddess will not be consummated if you sacrifice your lives at the shrine of independence without shedding blood.

According to R.C. Majumdar, the Anushilan Samiti's presence was not limited to Bengal, but extended to Assam, Bihar, Punjab, the United Provinces, the Central Provinces and Bombay.[4] Among the most prominent incidents associated with the Anushilan Samiti was the Alipore bomb case,[5] which resulted in the conviction, imprisonment and/or exile of its leading members such as Aurobindo Ghosh, which we shall discuss more later.

These revolutionary societies, whose members were initiated with the teachings of the Bhagavad Gita, Swami Vivekananda and Bankim Chandra's *Anandamath*, added to the woes of the British establishment, which was already alarmed at the scale and intensity of the challenge to its position in Bharat stemming from the unarmed Swadeshi and Boycott Movements. Due to the efforts of leaders like Bipin Chandra Pal, for at least two years starting from August 1905, these unarmed movements resulted in a drastic, countrywide reduction in the import of goods from Britain and an increased impetus to home-grown industries.[6] The extent of public participation in these movements can be gauged from the fact that even religious institutions turned active stakeholders. For instance, the chief purohit of the Kamakhya temple in Assam appealed to the other purohits in the temple and to the grocers and sweetmeat sellers around the temple not to deal in foreign goods.[7]

The spirit of these movements also spilled over into college and school campuses, so much so that district magistrates had to issue stern circulars to the heads of educational institutions directing them to rein in their students, failing which they would lose their grants-in-aid and affiliation with universities.[8] The crackdown on the anti-partition agitation intensified when delegates of the Anti-Partition Bengal Provincial Conference, who included Surendranath Banerjea, were manhandled in full public glare in April 1906 in Barisal.[9] Revolutionaries even considered assassinating the Lieutenant Governor of Eastern Bengal and Assam, J.B. Fuller, to retaliate against the sexual exploitation and abuse of women by soldiers, presumably with Fuller's approval. However, this plot was shelved at the intervention of Banerjea.[10]

The heightened political awareness and anti-colonial sentiment of the post-partition period also revealed fissures within the Indian National Congress. For instance, a rift that had been brewing for a while between the so-called Moderates and Extremists within the Congress surfaced clearly in the Benares annual session held in December 1905.[11] The rift was based on their positions in relation to colonial rule and their respective visions for Bharat. The former faction was led by Mohandas Karamchand Gandhi's political mentor Gopal Krishna Gokhale and the 'Grand Old Man of Indian Nationalism' Dadabhai Naoroji, while the Extremist/Nationalist faction was headed by the 'Lal–Bal–Pal' trio, namely Lala Lajpat Rai, Bal Gangadhara Tilak and Bipin Chandra Pal.

The influence of coloniality on political thought in 1905 should be evident from the fact that those who sought a colonial form of self-government within the British empire through 'peaceful, gradual and constitutional methods' were called 'Moderates/Liberals', whereas those who wanted to maintain pressure on the colonial establishment through the Swadeshi and Boycott Movements in order to achieve autonomy/independence from the British were branded 'Extremists/Nationalists'.[12,13] The fundamental belief of the Moderates/Liberals was that Bharat's destiny was tied to British fortunes and that the future progress of the country was possible *only under the British,* since in their view Bharatiyas lacked both the capacity as well as the unity to build their own independent future. The following is an extract from Gokhale's views on the subject, in his own words:[14]

Only mad men outside lunatic asylums could think or talk of independence.

Some have gone so far as to talk of independence as an object of practical pursuit. We owe to the best interests of the country to resist the propaganda with all our resources. It means the sure destruction, or at any rate, the definite postponement of all these opportunities for slow but peaceful progress which are at present within our reach. There is no alternative to British rule, not only for now but for a long time to come and any attempts made to disturb it, directly or indirectly, are bound to recoil on our own heads.

The position of the Extremists/Nationalists is best captured by Bipin Chandra Pal in his book *The Soul of India:*[15]

The reawakening of national consciousness and aspirations in India in our own time has revived the ancient idealism of the Sakti cult: and Durga, Kalee, Jagadhatree, Bhawanee, and all the other great forms used by the Hindu sakti-worshippers, have received a new meaning. All these old and traditional gods and goddesses who had lost their hold on the modern mind, have been re-installed with a new historic and nationalist interpretation in the mind and soul of India ... Hundreds of thousands of our people have commenced to hail their motherland to-day as Durga, Kalee, Jagadhatree, Bhawani. These are no longer mythological conceptions or legendary persons or even poetic symbols. They are different manifestations of the Mother. This Mother is the spirit of India. This geographical habitat of ours is only the outer body of the Mother. Behind this physical and geographical body, there is a Being, a Personality—the Personality of the Mother.

Clearly, the Liberal and Nationalist factions of the Congress differed both in their goals and in their opinions on the means to achieve them. It could be said that the Liberal faction was more colonial in its approach, reflected by its tying of Bharat's fortunes to those of the coloniser and its policy of 'petition and persuasion' with the British; whereas the views of the Nationalists and the nature of their nationalism were significantly inspired by civilisational ideals and their confidence in the ability of Bharatiyas to chart their own destiny. However, as we shall see, these factions were not watertight compartments and the position of individuals would vary with time and circumstance, thereby making labels such as Moderate and Extremist transient.

In his doctoral thesis of 1964, Daniel Argov has brilliantly summarised the differences between the Moderates/Liberals and the Extremists/Nationalists as follows:[16]

> Both the moderates and the extremists came from the middle class, both were reacting towards British rule, and both voiced Indian grievances. The moderates claimed social equality and a share in the British Government of India on the grounds that they were British subjects; the extremists demanded social equality and political emancipation as their birthright. The moderates appealed to Englishmen in England and placed their reliance on English history and English political ideas; the extremists drew sustenance from India's heritage and appealed to Indians by invoking religious patriotism. The moderates emphasised the need for political apprenticeship under the providential guidance of British rule; the extremists rejected the idea of England's providential mission in India as an illusion. They disparaged the constitutional agitation of the moderates as 'Mendicancy', and their stress on apprenticeship as an acceptance of ceaseless political servitude. Instead, they called for self-reliance and self-apprenticeship through Swadeshi, Boycott and Passive-Resistance. In contrast, the moderates stressed that their constitutional agitation was practical statesmanship, that emotional idealism was fraught with peril, that rashness was not courage, that British rule would not come to an end because of Boycott, and above all that the removal of British rule would result in chaos and anarchy.

> The moderates reconciled loyalty to England with Indian patriotism, believing that the two were necessarily compatible and complementary. For the extremists, Indian patriotism and loyalty to British rule were two diametrically conflicting entities. The moderates tenaciously sought gradual reform and could see no half-way-house between order and revolution. The extremists held that revolution was but rapid evolution, and that peace and order under British rule amounted to national stagnation. The moderates used English political ideas as their weapons for arguments and petitions. The extremists bolstered up India's past and advocated militant struggle, not debate ...

Thus the differences between the moderates and the extremists were not confined to different methods of agitation, but were fundamental differences in aim and methods.

In hindsight, this rift within the Congress could be interpreted as a tussle between a significantly colonialised school of thought, represented by the Liberals, and at least a partly decolonial/indigenous school, represented by the Nationalists. This suggests that despite significant colonialisation of the Hindu elites of this period through decades of Western education and exposure to Western political thought, civilisational indigeneity still survived to a significant extent, thanks to Dharmic stalwarts such as Sri Ramakrishna Paramahamsa and Swami Vivekananda, to name a few. Not surprisingly, the Moderates/Liberals had the ear of the British establishment, which conveniently chose to treat them as the sole representatives of Bharat. The Extremists/Nationalists were marginalised as a fringe, unreasonable and impractical minority, both by the Moderates as well as by the British. The fact that this was no accident, but the product of a conscious decision taken by the British establishment even in the early days under Curzon's rule, can be distilled from the following extract, taken from a letter dated 20 September 1899 written to Curzon by the then Secretary of State for India, George Francis Hamilton:[17]

> I think the real danger to our rule in India, not now but say 50 years hence, is the gradual adoption and extension of Western ideas of agitation and organization, and, if we could break the educated Hindu party into two sections holding widely different views, we should, by such division, strengthen our position against the subtle and continuous attack which the spread of education must make upon our present system of Government.

Although these words once again demonstrate the motive underlying the Partition of Bengal, which was to destabilise the growing solidarity of the Bengalis, the critical question that needs to be asked is whether the divide within the Congress in its attitudes towards the British had a deeper history which might be traceable to the very origins of the Congress and the role of the British in its founding.

The Colonial Origins of the Indian National Congress and Its 'Moderate Nationalism' (1876–1885)

There are two competing schools of thought on the genesis of the Indian National Congress. According to the first, the Indian National Congress was the organic and inevitable product of and societal reaction to the excesses of the British Raj, coupled with decades of exposure among Bharatiyas to Western

education and Western political ideas. However, according to the second
school of thought, the founding of the Congress itself was attributed to the
'safety valve theory'—i.e., the Congress was set up with British benediction
to provide a government-friendly platform for the ventilation, containment
and management of public angst towards the colonial establishment so as to
prevent or at least stall a repeat of the Mutiny of 1857. The truth, however,
may be a combination of both schools of thought.

To understand the facts better, I have drawn from sources such as *The
History of the Indian National Congress* by B. Pattabhi Sitaramayya, *A History
of the Indian National Congress* by S.R. Mehrotra, *India and the Commonwealth*
by S.R. Mehrotra, *Indian National Evolution* by A.C. Mazumdar, *History of
the Freedom Movement in India* by R.C. Majumdar, the Proceedings of the
First Indian National Congress which was held in Bombay from 28 to 30
December 1885, and several scholarly articles on the subject. On the history
of the rift between the Moderates and the Extremists within the Congress, I
have placed significant reliance on a doctoral thesis of 1964 by Daniel Argov,
which I found to be both detailed and insightful.

In what may be indicative of the colonial consciousness of the Indian
National Congress, A.C. Mazumdar, himself a member of the Congress,
said the following in 1915 in the introductory chapter of his book on Indian
political evolution:[18]

First session of the Indian National Congress, Bombay, 28–31 December 1885.
A.O. Hume, the founder of the Indian National Congress, is shown in the middle (*third row
from the front*). To his right is Dadabhai Naoroji; to his left, in sequence, are
W.C. Bannerjee, Pherozeshah Mehta and Gopal Krishna Gokhale.

The Indian National Congress marks an important epoch in the history of British Rule in India. *Apart from the questions of reforms with which it is immediately concerned, it is engaged in a much wider and nobler task for which it has already laid a fairly solid foundation—the task of Nation-building in India after the model of modern Europe. Coming in contact with Western people and Western culture the Indian mind could not fail to expand in the direction of Western ideas and Western institutions* ... A barbarous race may become extinct; but two civilized people coming in close contact are in spite of all their differences and conservatism bound to coalesce and act and react upon each other. The superior may dominate the inferior; but cannot transform it altogether: while the latter, however vigorously it may struggle to maintain its peculiar identity, is bound gradually and even unconsciously to imbibe and assimilate, either for the better or the worse, some of the properties of the former. *The Indian National Congress and the evolution which is slowly working its way through almost every phase of Indian life, are the natural and visible manifestation of such a contact.* [Emphases added]

The agenda of 'reform', the acceptance that the task before the Congress was to recast Bharat in a 'modern' European mould, and the aspirational tone used for Western ideas and institutions unmistakably reflect the entrenchment of colonial consciousness in the DNA of the Indian National Congress. This is further supported by Mazumdar's primer in the very same book on the genesis of the political movement in India, which contains a glowing tribute to Raja Rammohan Roy as the 'progenitor of modern India' and the 'greatest champion' of Western education in Bharat.[19] Here is the relevant extract:

Raja Ram Mohan Roy, the recognized progenitor of modern India, was the first apostle of a political creed based upon constitutional agitation in this country ... It was not until the fifties of the last century that with the dawning light of Western Education, of which the pioneer Indian Reformer was perhaps the greatest champion of his time, the public mind began to expand and political ideas and activities began to manifest themselves in one form or another in different parts of the country.

The significance of this reverential tone used for Roy by a senior member of the Congress and a chronicler of its history indicates a meeting of minds between the Congress and Roy on Bharat's past and its vision of the future. In this regard, one of Roy's letters (from which I included an extract in Chapter 9 of my first book), dated 11 December 1823, to the then Governor General William Pitt is worth recollecting. In that letter—using language that would befit a present-day Marxist—Roy derided Sanskrit and indigenous knowledge systems, and implored the colonial master to shine the light of Western education on the heathen native. This was in stark contrast to the consistent efforts of the Muslim community to preserve Islamic learning, *even* when it was at loggerheads with scientific facts such as the rotation of the earth or its heliocentric position. Even in the anglicised Aligarh model of Syed Ahmed Khan, Western education was imparted in an Islamic environment, with equal emphasis on traditional Islamic education and the freedom to learn languages most associated with Islam, namely Arabic, Persian and Urdu.

The difference between the Hindu elite's and Muslim elite's attitudes to Western education and to their respective traditional knowledge systems could not have been starker—'Hindoo reformers' like Raja Rammohan Roy and his ideological successors contributed to the gradual but steady alienation of the Hindu community from its roots by replacing indigenous education with Western education; on the other hand, the leading lights of Islamic reformist movements, including anglicised ones like that of Syed Ahmed Khan, placed greater or at least equal emphasis on Islamic and Western education. The Muslim community's commitment to Islamic learning was evident from the fact that Syed Ahmed Khan's Aligarh model was deemed too British-loyalist by the community, which led to the establishment of Darul Uloom Nadwatul Ulama and Jamia Millia Islamia. In a nutshell, after the advent of the British coloniser, 'reform' to the Hindus meant moving *away* from their roots, whereas Islamic reformist movements sought to move *closer* to the practice of early Islam.

Further, to Muslim thought leaders, Western education was but a means to navigate the colonial establishment and ultimately restore Muslim state power, whereas 'Hindoo social reformers' seemed visibly eager to assimilate and integrate into the colonial society from the political, economic, cultural and religious perspectives. The stark differences in consciousness, goals, priorities and methods between the Hindu elite and Muslim elite of this period may explain the current state of proud deracination of the former's successors and the unabashed rootedness of the latter's successors. I leave it to the readers to decide if Roy's Hindu reform agenda has strengthened Hindu indigeneity and consciousness compared with Khan's Aligarh model, which strengthened Middle Eastern consciousness and ultimately paved the way for the creation of Pakistan.

Coming back to the events that led to the founding of the Indian National Congress, Mazumdar points out that from the early 1850s, as a consequence of exposure to Western education, there was a sizeable English-educated class from Calcutta, Bombay, Madras and Delhi which sought employment in the colonial establishment, only to find that there were barriers, either owing to paucity of vacancies or ethno-religious glass ceilings. Naturally, this class was constrained to find employment independent of the government, in fields such as law, education and journalism, which contributed to the stirring of political and public life in Bharat.[20] This gradual increase in size of a politically aware English-speaking class led to the founding of associations such as the British Indian Association in Bengal and the Bombay Association in the Bombay Presidency; Dadabhai Naoroji was instrumental in the founding of the latter.[21] Pertinently, as early as in 1852, the British Indian Association raised the issue of a representative government in its petition to the British Parliament.[22] Again, in July 1867, W.C. Bannerjee, who would later become the first president of the Indian National Congress in 1885, sought a representative and responsible Government of India. In the south, which was relatively late to catch up with Bengal and Bombay in this regard, the establishment of *The Hindu* in 1878 marked the stirrings of political activity. What is important to note is that the establishment of such organisations since the early 1850s—i.e., even before the Mutiny of 1857— indicates a degree of interest in Western political ideas which were introduced by the British. This gradually but steadily veered towards vocalisation of an interest to participate in the process of lawmaking and governance *as part* of the colonial administrative structure.

To add to this, the continued treatment of Bharat as a mere resource or a port of revenue by the colonial establishment only contributed to the growing murmur among English-educated Indians for political participation. Fortunately for this class of Indians, from the late 1840s they had the support of the 'friends of India' in Britain, as Mazumdar calls them. Such 'friends', who were critical of the manner in which the British governed India, included John Bright. Here's a sample expression of Christian colonial sympathy for India by this friend of India, John Bright, in 1853:[23]

> There never was a more docile people, never a more tractable nation. The opportunity is present, and the power is not wanting. Let us abandon the policy of aggression and confine ourselves to a territory ten times the size of France, with a population four times as numerous as that of the United Kingdom. Surely, that is enough to satisfy the most gluttonous appetite for glory and supremacy. *Educate the people of India, govern them wisely, and gradually the distinctions of caste will disappear, and they will look upon us rather as benefactors than as conquerors. And if we desire to see Christianity, in some form professed in that country, we shall sooner attain our object by setting the example of high-toned Christian morality, than by any other means we can employ.* [Emphasis added]

The Christian condescension and Christian evangelical goal of this 'friend of India' could not have been clearer, notwithstanding his expression of sympathy and the sane counsel to the British Parliament. We might ask ourselves what an 'unfriendly voice' would have sounded like in its evangelical and colonial objectives if this was what passed for a sane and

India-friendly voice in the British establishment at the peak of the empire's powers. That A.C. Mazumdar in 1915 deemed it fit to treat John Bright as an early friend of India only underscores my point about the entrenchment of colonial consciousness in the very fibre of the Indian National Congress.

Despite the presence of such 'friendly' voices, the colonial establishment, as pointed out in Chapter 10 of my first book, was reluctant to enable representative participation by Indians in the legislative process, especially following the Mutiny of 1857. In lieu of such participation, the 'natives' were given the opportunity to become part of the British establishment in Bharat through inclusion in the Civil Service, which was specifically provided for in Section 32 of the Government of India Act of 1858. Subsequently, nominal legislative participation was introduced for the first time through the Indian Councils Act of 1861, wherein the Governor General/Viceroy could nominate Indians as additional members to his Council and Indians could hold non-official positions for a tenure of two years. Section 10 of the 1861 Act reads as follows:

> Section 10: Additional Members to Be Summoned for the Purpose of Making Laws and Regulations—For the better exercise of the power of making laws and regulations vested in the Governor general in council, the governor general shall nominate, in addition to the Ordinary and extraordinary members above mentioned, and to such lieutenant governor in the case aforesaid, such persons, as to him may seem expedient to be members of Council for the purpose of making laws and regulations only; and such persons shall not be entitled to sit or vote at any meeting of council, except at meetings held for such purpose:

> Provided that not less than one half of the persons so nominated shall be nonofficial Persons, that is persons who, at the date of such nomination, shall not be in the Civil or military service of the crown in India, and that the seat in council of any nonofficial Member accepting office under the crown in India shall be vacated on such acceptance.

Under Section 29 of the Act, such additional members could be nominated by the Governors of the Madras and Bombay Presidencies too, for their respective councils. However, Section 14 of the Act clarified that vacancy in any such non-official additional position would make *no difference* to the validity of introduction or enactment of any legislation. Extracted below is the provision:

> Section 14: No Law to Be Invalid by Reason of Number of Non-Official Members Being Incomplete—No law or regulation made by the Governor General in Council in accordance with the provisions of this Act shall be deemed invalid by reason only that the proportion of nonofficial additional members hereby provided was not complete at the date of its introduction to the Council or its enactment.

Clearly, the inclusion of Indians in the Council, and that too by *nomination* by the Governor General as non-official additional members, was but a half-hearted attempt at involving the 'native' in the legislative process. There was no significant change in this situation under the Indian Councils Act of 1874, which continued to reflect the British belief that Indians were unfit, or at least not yet ready, for representative institutions. Naturally, 'educated', rather, Western-educated English-speaking Indian elites (mostly Hindus) felt that the British assessment of their fitness for representative institutions did injustice to their Western education and exposure to Western political thought. In addition to this, there were genuine grievances against the manner in which the Crown ran Bharat through its appointees, with negligible native participation in law and policymaking.

For instance, under Governor General Lord Lytton, the period between 1876 and 1880 witnessed a flurry of disastrous policy decisions, such as an exorbitant salt tax, recurring British-induced famines in several parts of Bharat, which wiped out millions of people, the subsequent appalling management of these man-made disasters, the enactment of the Vernacular Press Act of 1877, which repressed the non-English press on the ground that it was seditious, the passing of the Arms Act and the disastrous campaigns against the Afghans in 1878. All these only added to the list of grievances against the establishment.[24] What exacerbated the already tense situation was the expensive Durbar of 1877, which was held to proclaim Queen Victoria as the Empress of India at a time when millions of Indians were dying from British-induced famines.[25]

It is no wonder then that this period saw the founding of the Indian Association in Kolkata in July 1876 by Surendranath Banerjea and Ananda Mohan Bose.[26] By 1877, Banerjea and Bose used their platform to galvanise Bengal against the British prime minister's decision to reduce the maximum age limit for the Indian Civil Service, which would have the effect of excluding a vast number of Indians from the bureaucracy.[27] In addition, Banerjea demanded the conduct of simultaneous examinations in England and Bharat for recruitment to the Civil Service. It must be pointed out that Banerjea, who has been hailed as the 'first all-India nationalist leader' and has been called 'Rashtraguru', was an officer of the 1869 batch of the Indian Civil Service until 1874, when he was dismissed on grounds of carelessness in the discharge of his duties.[28] With his career prospects ruined, Banerjea decided to plunge into public life, which led to his founding of the Indian Association two years later.

According to scholars, his pride in his 'Kulin Brahmin' heritage competed with his anglophilia, so much so that he has been described as the textbook embodiment of Macaulay's prediction of what English-educated Indians would ultimately become as a result of Western influence: '*Indians in blood and colour but English in taste, in opinions, in morals, and in intellect.*'[29] This dual consciousness would characterise most Indian leaders of this period, and they generally saw no conflict between the two identities. Critically, this duality characterised Banerjea's early agitation through the Indian Association against the colonial establishment, since the essence of the agitation was parity for Indians with English citizens of the British empire. As we shall see, strikingly similar expectations would underpin the founding of the Indian National Congress.

It is around this period under Lord Lytton's tumultuous tenure as the Governor General that a member of the Civil Service, Allan Octavian Hume, the future architect of the Indian National Congress, started receiving police reports from across the country documenting growing discontent with the government. This, he feared, could lead to an uprising comparable to or perhaps worse than the Mutiny of 1857. Palme Dutt, a journalist of Marxist persuasion, wrote in his best-known work, *India Today and Tomorrow*, citing Hume, that the latter was in receipt of several volumes of police reports that warned of rising disaffection towards the British government and of the rapid spread of underground activities.[30] Tracing the genesis of the Indian National Congress in his work *History of the Freedom Movement in India*, R.C. Majumdar too attested to this fact as follows:[31]

> But whatever may be the genesis, the credit of organizing the Indian National Congress undoubtedly belongs to a large extent to Allan Octavian Hume, a retired member of the Indian Civil Service, and son of the founder of the Radical Party in England. There is no doubt that he was inspired by a genuine sympathy for the interest and welfare of India, and it by no means, detracts from the merit of this noble-minded Englishman that in setting up a political organization like the Congress, he could not possibly be, and was certainly not, inspired by the same national sentiment and patriotic yearning for freedom of India which characterized the advanced political thinkers of Bengal and other parts of India. The reasons which induced him to conceive the idea of a political organization like the Indian National Congress were of an entirely different character. He was deeply impressed by the general discontent in India threatening imminent danger to the Government. 'From well-wishers in different parts of the country he received warnings of the danger to the Government, and to the future welfare of India, from the economic sufferings of the masses, and the alienation of the intellectuals'. A memorandum preserved among the papers of Hume, describes in detail, how, about fifteen months before the end of Lord Lytton's administration, he (Hume) got very definite information about the seething discontent among

the masses from religious devotees held in highest veneration by the people. They approached him 'because they feared the ominous unrest throughout the country which pervaded even the lowest strata of the population, would lead to some terrible outbreak, destructive to India's future, unless men like him, who have access to the Government, could do something to remove the general feeling of despair and thus avert a catastrophe'.

The evidence which convinced Hume of 'the imminent danger of a terrible outbreak' 'was contained in seven large volumes shown to him. These contained a vast number of communications from over thirty thousand different reporters from different parts of India. These seemed to indicate that even men of the lowest classes all over the country were determined to do something and that something meant violence'.

... Hume 'now became convinced that some definite action was called for to counteract the growing unrest'.

In the above extract, Majumdar relied extensively on William Wedderburn's authoritative biography of Hume. Here are a few relevant extracts from the biography itself:[32]

Towards the close of Lord Lytton's viceroyalty, that is, about 1878 and 1879, Mr. Hume became convinced that some definite action was called for to counteract the growing unrest. From well-wishers in different parts of the country he received warnings of the danger to the Government, and to the future welfare of India, from the economic sufferings of the masses, and the alienation of the intellectuals. But happily the arrival of Lord Ripon revived hope among the people, and produced a lull; and Mr. Hume postponed definite organization until, by his retirement from the service, he should be free to act, and able to take advantage of the growing improvement in the popular feeling produced by Lord Ripon's benign presence.

As Wedderburn says, fortunately for Hume, Lytton's successor, Lord Ripon, who was Viceroy from 1880 to 1884, realized that the situation required urgent redressal if the British government were to enjoy any semblance of confidence among the natives. Among the measures he took in consultation with Hume, one was to cultivate those 'elements' which Ripon deemed essential for the shaping of public opinion, namely an English-educated class of Indians who had expectations and aspirations.[33] Ripon's strategy was to ensure that these expectations and aspirations did not turn into disaffection and enmity towards the British establishment and lead to the incitement of the masses. Therefore, he chose to acknowledge the existence of this English-educated class by actively engaging with them, and '... *by timely foresight, take steps to supply the legitimate outlets for those aspirations and to satisfy those ambitions consistent with the maintenance of [British] authority*'.[34] This sentiment was captured in Ripon's correspondence in 1883 to Lord Kimberley, who was the Secretary of State for Colonies from 1880 to 1882. This correspondence was written two years before the founding of the Indian National Congress in December 1885.

Accordingly, under the advice of Hume, Ripon began engaging with English-educated Indians, apart from implementing reforms in local self-government.[35] Even after Hume's retirement from the Civil Service in 1882, he retained his proximity to Ripon, owing to his ability to act as a conduit between the Governor General and the 'educated' Indian leadership of Bombay and Bengal.[36] In March 1883, Hume began giving effect to his idea of a political organisation that could act as a single all-India body of educated Indians who could put forth their ideas and grievances to the government on moral, social and political issues. To this end, he issued a circular to the graduates of the Calcutta University urging them to come forward to work for the progress of India. Whether individuals from different parts of the country responded organically to this call or were hand-picked is unclear; however, Hume's call was answered by individuals from different parts of the country, leading to the founding of the Indian Political Union.[37] While the idea of a conference for this Union, to be held in Poona, was being mulled over, a Preliminary Report was issued to the members of the Union containing the suggestions and conclusions of 'the most eminent and earnest politicians' of the British empire. Among the first things the Report stated was as follows:[38]

> ... the Union, so far as it has been constituted, appears to be absolutely unanimous in insisting that unswerving loyalty to the British Crown, shall be the key note of the institution. The Union is prepared when necessary to oppose, by all constitutional methods, all authorities, high or low, here or in England, whose acts or omissions are opposed to those principles of the government of India laid down from time to time by the British Parliament, and endorsed by the British Sovereign, but it holds the continued affiliation of India to Great Britain, at any rate for a period far exceeding the range of any practical political forecast, to be absolutely essential to the interests of our own National Development.

If at all there was any doubt as to Hume's intentions behind the founding of the Union and its successor organisation, the Indian National Congress, this extract should put it to rest. Not only does it prove that members of the Union were expected to conform to the principles laid down by the British Parliament, they were also expected to swear allegiance to the Crown for all time to come. For all practical purposes, this was a fiat or a firman demanding fealty to the British empire, and on this there was *no room* for negotiation. In effect, Hume's proposal spoke of cultivating 'moderate nationalism' as a counterweight to extremist nationalism or revolutionary nationalism by building an alliance with 'loyalist moderates'.[39] The following was the role envisaged for the Indian Political Union by Hume:[40]

A safety-valve for the escape of great and growing forces, generated by our own action, was urgently needed and no more efficacious safety-valve than our Congress movement could possibly be devised.

Unfortunately for Hume, despite Ripon's policy of rapprochement with and cultivation of the English-educated class of Indians, the opposition to the Ilbert Bill of 1883 by Britons signalled to the Indian elites that they would never be considered at par with the British/European subjects of the Crown, owing to the latter's perceived religious and racial superiority. The Ilbert Bill, officially known as the 'Bill to amend the Code of Criminal Procedure, 1882, so far as it relates to the exercise of jurisdiction over European British subjects', as the name suggests, was meant to empower magistrates and sessions judges of Indian origin to preside over criminal matters in which the accused were Europeans.[41]

Named after C.P. Ilbert, a member of the Indian Legislative Council, the Bill was opposed bitterly by Britons living in England as well as in Bharat, their dissent primarily attributable to their sense of ethno-religious supremacy. According to Daniel Argov, the principle of equality, regardless of race, which underlay the Ilbert Bill, was resented by Englishmen.[42] Here are a few samples of English reactions to the Ilbert Bill, distilled from Argov's thesis, which underscore the Christian colonial consciousness that was deeply entrenched in the British establishment, despite more than 120 years having passed since the Battle of Plassey and two years to go for the founding of the Indian National Congress. Not so shockingly, English tea planters in Assam opposed the Ilbert Bill since they believed that an English judge would be more sympathetic to their occasional manhandling of the 'niggers' who were their 'coolies', whereas an Indian judge might find them guilty of assault.[43]

Deputy Commissioner of Sylhet H.L. Johnson's views embodied the religion-inspired, race-driven supremacism of European colonialism when he said:[44]

When an Englishman says he will not he tried by a Bengali, he has history, science, even the apostle Paul on his side. His assertion of his race superiority is specially justified by the fact that the Bengali belongs to a race he has conquered.

The views of the commissioner of the Burdwan Division on the Bill, which also reflected the apprehensions of the English establishment about the growing political awareness of the Indian English-speaking class, were as follows:[45]

There has been growing up of late years a class of natives who though numerically few, have become by their extravagant pretentions and excessive self-conceit, by their unreasonable and unsatisfied longing for power, and by their morbid discontent and disloyalty, a serious danger to the stability of our rule in India. It is we who have created these men, and we have now to fear lest as the poet writes 'we perish by the people we have made'.

Some saw the Ilbert Bill as a curtain raiser for grant of self-government to India and opposed it on the ground that a self-governing India '*would prove an abortive parliamentary democracy which would run into chaos and become subjected to military dictatorship*'.[46] Others warned that English capital and enterprise would leave Bharat if the Ilbert Bill and the policy of racial equality it stood for were implemented. The deep-rooted conviction of the English community and the strength of their resolve were evident from the fact that they set up the Anglo-Indian and European Defence Association, which organized several protest meetings against the Bill in Bombay, Madras and Calcutta.[47]

Given such virulent opposition, a much-watered-down version of the Bill was finally passed in January 1884, under which an accused would have the right to demand that at least 50 per cent of the jury trying him be European. To add to the heightened tension caused by the agitation surrounding the Ilbert Bill, Surendranath Banerjea was held guilty of contempt of court and sentenced to tw   ~ths' imprisonment for his comments on the conduct of the Chief Justice of Calcutta High Court, Justice Norris, who had ordered that an idol of a Hindu deity be brought to the court for identification.[48] Apart from his imprisonment, what added to the gravity of the incident was the fact that Justice Norris had opposed the Ilbert Bill prominently and vehemently.[49] This incident only contributed to enhancing the political profile of Banerjea and led to an important development that would directly affect the course of Indian national life.

Having been reminded of their position in the eyes of their British coloniser, the English-educated Indian class realised that they would need to embrace the path of organisation and agitation. Under the leadership of Surendranath Banerjea's Indian Association, the Indian National Conference was held in Calcutta in December 1883.[50] Among the key demands of the Conference was introduction of representative assemblies, which meant going beyond the nominal representation under the existing Indian Councils Act. In the run-up to and during the Conference, Banerjea was particular about steering clear of any revolutionary tendency and insisted on the practice of moderation through adherence to constitutional agitation, a policy that would shape the Indian National Congress in the years ahead.[51] Banerjea's ultimate goal was to unite the middle and upper classes to secure the same self-governing status as other colonies under the Crown, to the benefit of India and the glory of England.[52] Banerjea made his case for self-government and *perpetual* union with England in the following words:[53]

> It is not severance that we are looking forward to, but unification, permanent embodiment as an integral part of that great Empire which has given the rest of the world the models of free institution.

While there were still no calls for complete independence from the British, Ripon took note of this development and wrote to Kimberley as follows in April 1884 before the end of his tenure as Viceroy/Governor General of India:[54]

> You may rely upon it that there are few Indian questions of greater importance in the present day than those which relate to the mode in which we are to deal with the growing body of Natives educated by ourselves in Western learning and Western ideas.

In early 1885, realising that there was a churn under way, which if not contained and managed could loosen the British empire's hold over Bharat, Hume worked towards organising the maiden conference of the Indian Political Union to compete with Banerjea's Indian National Conference. Accordingly, in May 1885 Hume met Lord Dufferin in Simla, where he presented his plan to hold the first Indian National Congress of the Indian Political Union.[55] It appears that Dufferin, who had taken over from Ripon as the Governor General in December 1884, gave his approval to Hume's plan, with the caveat that the plan and its implementation should not be traced back to him (Dufferin) as long as he was in India.[56,57] Here is a relevant extract from Wedderburn's biography of Hume on the interaction between Hume and Dufferin on the Political Union and the first Congress:[58]

> But here it must be noted that, although the Congress movement has always been looked on with undisguised hostility by that section of officials who are in permanent antagonism to the educated and independent classes, *this disfavour has not, as a rule, extended to the higher authorities.* This was especially the case at the outset. Indeed, in initiating the national movement, Mr. Hume took counsel with the Viceroy, Lord Dufferin; and whereas he was himself disposed to begin his reform propaganda on the social side, it was apparently by Lord Dufferin's advice that he took up the work of political organization, as the matter first to be dealt with. Lord Dufferin seems to have told him that as head of the Government he had found the greatest difficulty in ascertaining the real wishes of the people; and that, for purposes of administration, it would be a public benefit if there existed some responsible organization, through which the Government might be kept informed regarding the best Indian public opinion. He further observed that, owing to the wide differences

in caste, race, and religion, social reform in India required local treatment, rather than the guidance of a national organization. These kindly counsels were received with grateful appreciation by all concerned. Indeed so cordial were the relations, that Lord Dufferin was approached with a view to the first Congress being held under the presidency of Lord Reay, then Governor of Bombay. Lord Dufferin welcomed the proposal, as showing the desire of the Congress to work in complete harmony with the Government, but he considered that many difficulties would be involved if a high official presided over such an assembly. *The idea was therefore abandoned, but none the less the first Congress was opened with the friendly sympathy of the highest authorities.* [Emphases added]

Notwithstanding Dufferin's cautious approach to Hume's proposal and his decision to maintain an official distance from it for reasons of pragmatism, the fact remains that Hume's intentions behind setting up the Indian Political Union were to minimise and mellow the opposition to the British empire, which had the blessing of the Viceroy. On Dufferin's role and on Hume's objective behind establishing the Union/Congress, R.C. Majumdar had the following to say:[59]

It is very likely that Dufferin's share in the whole project has been misunderstood. Some have gone to the extent of suspecting the veracity of this account or rejecting it as untrue. Howsoever that may be, there seems to be no doubt whatsoever that the Congress was really designed by Hume to arrest the progress of a revolutionary outbreak. Wedderburn clearly states this in his biography of Hume: 'The ill-starred measures of reaction, combined with Russian methods of Police repression, brought India under Lord Lytton within measurable distance of a revolutionary outbreak, and it was only in time that Mr. Hume and his Indian advisers were inspired to intervene.'

This passage leaves no doubt as to the real motive which inspired Hume to set up the Congress organization with the advice and blessings of the Viceroy, Lord Dufferin. So far as its political objectives were concerned, it was not intended to subserve the object of securing representative Government for India such as inspired the National Conference in Calcutta, nor was it actuated by the more moderate desire of training Indians in Parliamentary form of Government, as has so often been claimed. *It was solely designed to hold back the Indian intelligentsia from joining an apprehended general outbreak against the British.* [Emphasis added]

As to why leading Indian political leaders joined the Congress under Hume, R.C. Majumdar writes:[60]

There was probably another consideration which weighed with those who responded to the clarion call of Hume. The Government, they rightly thought, would not look with kindly eyes upon any political organization of the Indians, demanding substantial reforms in the administration. But if the leading part were taken by an Englishman, who once held a high office, the hostility of the official class would be considerably neutralized. The great Indian political leader Gokhale gave expression to this view when he said that 'if the founder of the Congress had not been a great Englishman and a distinguished ex-official, such was the distrust of political agitation in those days that the authorities would have at once found some way or the other of suppressing the movement.' This feeling also probably influenced, to a large extent, the organizers of the National Conference in Calcutta to merge it in the Indian National Congress.

In any event, there is no doubt that once Hume set the ball rolling, it gathered a momentum beyond expectation. Hume himself generously referred in his public speeches to the help he received from Indian leaders. The Congress movement, he said, was the outcome 'of the labours of a body of cultured men mostly born natives of India. It appears that he met and discussed his plans with good many a leader of Bombay such as Badruddin Tyabji, Dadabhai Naoroji, Pherozshah Mehta and K.T. Telang. But he did not consult Surendranath Banerjea. According to B.C. Pal, Hume had a personal dislike for Surendranath, partly for his dismissal from Government service and partly for his advanced political views. The Government of the day did not like the political advance made in Bengal and Surendranath was definitely in their blacklist. These considerations might have also dissuaded the other more moderate Indian leaders of those days from associating themselves with the 'extremist' Surendranath. No other Indian leader had done so much to foster the idea of an all-India political organization such as the Congress was intended to be. Yet he does not seem to have been taken into confidence by Hume along with others named above. There can be hardly any doubt that Surendranath was deliberately kept out of this organization at its initial stage. This fact as well as the selection of W.C. Bannerjee as the President of the First Congress gives a fair idea of the political outlook of the founders of the Congress. Mr. Bannerjee lived the life of an Englishman and not only kept himself aloof from, but also ridiculed all sorts of political agitation. He was not even a member of the Indian Association, the premier political organization of Bengal.

While all this may explain the attitude of the sponsors of the Congress towards Surendranath, it is not easy to explain why the National Conference silently merged itself with the Congress.

Yet another author who agreed with the safety valve theory on the origins of the Congress is S.R. Mehrotra, who wrote in his book *India and the Commonwealth*:[61]

The spread of English education and of Western ideas of liberty, equality and nationality provided the motive force. It was encouraged by the growth of

self-government in the Colonies and the national movements in Europe—
the unification of Italy and Germany, and, more especially, the Home Rule
agitation in Ireland. Economic and social discontent, racial bitterness, and
cultural revivalism, all played an important part.

*The Congress, however, did not begin as an organization in opposition to British
rule. It owed its origin largely to the initiative of a retired British civil servant, Allan
Octavian Hume; it was blessed by the Viceroy of the day, Lord Dufferin. Hume
had the sympathy and wisdom to understand that 'the broadcast dissemination of
Western education and Western ideas of liberty, the rights of subjects, public spirit
and patriotism' had let loose forces in India which needed control and direction into
channels through which they might 'flow, not to ravage and destroy but to fertilize
and regenerate'. The Congress was to serve the purpose of 'a safety-valve', an 'overt
and constitutional channel' for the discharge of the Indian ferment. Its fundamental
objectives were laid down to be the promotion of Indian nationality, the social,
moral and political advancement of the Indian people, and 'the consolidation of
the union between England and India, by securing the modification of such of its
conditions as may be unjust or injurious'.*

*Unswerving loyalty to the British Crown was to be 'the keynote of the institution'.
'The continued affiliation of India to Great Britain, at any rate for a period, far
exceeding the range of any practical forecast,' was considered 'to be absolutely
essential to the interests of our own National Development'. The Congress was
to work not to supplant the British Government in India, but to supplement it.
It was to acknowledge frankly and gratefully the many blessings of British rule
and to seek their extension.* Real grievances were to be voiced and reasonable
concessions demanded in a loyal and temperate manner. The people of India
were to be educated into 'a genuine parliamentary frame of mind' and the
virtues of united, patient, constitutional agitation. The authorities in India
and England were to be acquainted with the needs and aspirations of their
Indian fellow-subjects. Official acts and omissions were to be subjected to fair
criticism. Suggestions and modifications were to be offered in order to make
the British administration in India more beneficent. The Congress was to
insist that British policy in India be guided by the noble spirit which inspired
the Act of 1833 and the Queen's proclamation of 1858. *It was to demand that
the rights and privileges of British citizenship be gradually extended to Indians.*
[Emphases added]

It can be said with sufficient basis from the literature cited above that the
creation of the Indian National Congress did indeed have a British/colonial
hand in it, whose intention was to prevent an outbreak of extremist or
revolutionary nationalism through the cultivation of 'moderate nationalism'.
On what constitutes moderate nationalism, Sanjay Seth's elaboration of it is
educative. Here are his views on the 'moderate' nature of the nationalism
that underpinned the founding of the Congress:[62]

Most accounts of Indian nationalism include, or begin with, the last two or three decades of the nineteenth century. They do so despite the fact that in the pre-Congress era, as in the early years of the Indian National Congress (INC), the goal of Indian nationalists fell well short of full national independence, and the methods they employed in pursuit of their goals included neither mass mobilization nor the extra-constitutionalist methods that were later to be characteristic of the Congress. Why this should qualify as part of the story of Indian nationalism at all is, therefore, itself a question. Part of the answer is simply that for many historical accounts the history of Indian nationalism is synonymous with the history of the Indian National Congress, and therefore all activities associated with the Congress form part of the history of nationalism. This is either taken to be so self-evident as to require no argumentation, or else the equation is justified by the claim that the Congress was the first body organized on an all-India scale, and that sought to speak for Indians, rather than (as with earlier organizations) Bengalis, landholders, Hindus, or Muslims, or their caste brethren.

For histories for which nationalism in India is the vehicle for the arrival of the modern—and there are many such—the early period of the Congress belongs to the history of nationalism because, even if it was rather half-heartedly nationalist, it was nonetheless part of the story of the modern. This is particularly, though not exclusively, true of Marxist and left-liberal accounts. Thus in the communist R. Palme Dutt's influential book of 1940, *India To-Day*, for the early Indian bourgeoisie that provided the leadership of the early Congress, 'The main enemy was not British rule as such, but the backwardness of the people, the lack of modern development of the country, the strength of the forces of obscurantism and ignorance'; and thus despite the limitations of their nationalism, 'they represented at that time the most progressive force in Indian society.'

For the same reason, the 'patriotic princes' and suchlike, those who were also critical of the British administration of India but who came to be seen as part of the pre-modern past that nationalism was to sweep away, do not generally find an honourable place in such narratives. Therefore, either because they were part of the Congress, or because they were part of the story of the emergence of the modern in India, the early leaders of the Congress find a place—often as the beginning of nationalism—in most accounts of Indian nationalism. However, the description of the various activities directed at securing political and economic reform in the period 1870–1905 as 'nationalist' is frequently qualified; usually, this is designated as the period of 'moderate nationalism.'

The term 'moderate' is used in one of three ways. It can signify the historians' adoption of a term commonly used at the time. Rendered in uppercase, 'Moderate' serves to distinguish and contrast this nationalism from its 'Extremist' competitor and critic. A second use of the term occurs where what

is being stressed is the ambiguous or two-sided nature of the phenomenon—
that it was nationalist but in a very qualified fashion, because its demands were
modest and were accompanied by loyalty to crown and empire. Almost all
uses of the phrase 'moderate nationalism' fall into this category, although they
may fall into the other categories as well. A third use is one that incorporates
the second, but where additionally this 'ambiguity' is seen as a 'lack,' as
incompleteness. Since 'lack' is a relative term implying a contrasting notion
of plenitude, and incompleteness is measured against completion, this occurs
when moderate nationalism has been inserted into a narrative that has a
conception of a fuller, more complete nationalism as its culminating point.
Here, very frequently, all three meanings or uses of the term are invoked:
moderate nationalism is contrasted to extremist nationalism, a contrast that
highlights the ambiguous or qualified nature of this nationalism; and this
ambiguity is interpreted as a lack, an incompleteness that is later overcome.

On the subject of Congress's moderate nationalism, Daniel Argov too had
similar views as Sanjay Seth, and they are as follows:[63]

> The present tendency to depict the early history of the Indian National
> Congress as 'The History of the Freedom Movement' ignores the fact that
> the moderate leaders of the Congress constantly harped on the theme of
> securing the permanence of British rule in India. For Banerjea, Swaraj meant
> self-restraint; while Sinha and Gokhale said, on different occasions, that if the
> British were to leave India, Indians would call them back before they reached
> Aden.

That the Congress's founding spirit was one of textbook 'moderate
nationalism' is, therefore, fairly evident from Hume's intentions. Clearly, the
goal of the Indian National Congress at the time of its founding was to secure
Western education, Western-style development and Western democracy by
operating under the Crown, rather than *freedom from* the empire in all senses.
Whether the leaders of the Congress were using Hume for their collective
goals or whether Hume was using them for his colonial goals hinged on
the vision for Bharat envisaged by the Moderate/Liberal leaders of the
Congress and their subsequent rift with the Extremists/Nationalists. After
all, as mentioned earlier, the Extremists' demand for complete independence
from the British was met with derision from the Moderates. In light of this,
the critical question, and perhaps the only one that matters, is this: which of
the two factions prevailed, and did it have a bearing on Bharat's indigenous
consciousness and the framing of 'independent' Bharat's Constitution?
Or is the Constitution the product of both influences, namely colonial *and*
indigenous/decolonial? If yes, which is predominant?

Coming back to the First Indian National Congress, to draw attention
away from Surendranath Banerjea's second Indian National Conference,

which was to be held from 25 to 27 December 1885, Hume scheduled the first Indian National Congress of the Indian Political Union to be held from 28 to 30 December 1885. According to A.C. Mazumdar, before December 1885, K.T. Telang of the Union wrote extensively to Banerjea on the goals of the latter's first Indian National Conference held in 1883, which indicates a certain degree of interest in the latter's platform.[64] Further, W.C. Bannerjee of the Indian National Congress invited Surendranath to attend the Congress. However, the latter could not accept the invitation for the following reason, which he stated in his autobiography:[65]

> While we were having our National Conference in Calcutta, the Indian National Congress, conceived on the same lines and having the same programme, was holding its first sittings at Bombay ... Mr. W.C. Bannerjee, who presided over the Bombay Congress, invited me to attend it. I told him that it was too late to suspend the Conference, and that as I had a large share in its organization it would not be possible for me to leave Calcutta and attend the Bombay Congress.

Bipin Chandra Pal, however, refuted the above version and attributed Banerjea's absence at the First Indian National Congress to the fact that Hume and other leaders of the Congress found Banerjea 'extremist' in his views, primarily because of the latter's dismissal from the Civil Service and his imprisonment for contempt of court.[66] Notwithstanding this, the fact remains that the thought process and the broad goals of Banerjea's Indian National Conference and Hume's Indian National Congress were not too different. This is evident from Banerjea's own words; he felt that the National Conference and the Indian National Congress had the same agenda, which ultimately led to collaboration between the two from 1886. In any case, owing to the support of the moderate leaders of the Indian Political Union and Hume's support, the Indian National Congress, which was finally held in Bombay instead of Poona,[67] ended up drawing more attention than Banerjea's National Conference, which was held in Calcutta.[68]

The proceedings of the First Indian National Congress make for critical reading because they reflect the 'moderate nationalism' which shaped the Congress's formative years. Here are a few extracts from the proceedings of the First Congress, which shed light on its thought process:[69]

Origin and Composition of the Congress

In March 1885 it was decided to hold a meeting of the Representatives from all parts of India at the then coming Christmas. Poona was considered the most central and therefore suitable place, and the following circular was issued.

'A Conference of the Indian National Union will be held at Poona from the 25th to the 31st December 1885.

The Conference will be composed of Delegates—(1) *leading politicians well acquainted with English language*—from all parts of the Bengal, Bombay and Madras Presidencies.

The direct objects of the Conference will be—(1) to enable all the most earnest labourers in the cause of national progress to become personally known to each other; (2) to discuss and decide upon the political operations to be undertaken during the ensuing year.

Indirectly this conference will form the germ of a Native Parliament and, if properly conducted, will constitute in a few years an unanswerable reply to the assertion that India is still wholly unfit for any form of representative institutions. The first Conference will decide whether the next shall be again held at Poona, or whether following the precedent of the British Association, the Conferences, shall be held year by year at different important centres.' [Emphases added]

The timing of the Conference around Christmas, the linguistic prerequisite expected of delegates (English) and the goal of proving to the British coloniser that Bharat was fit for representative institutions in the Western mould speak volumes of the nature of the Congress's 'moderate nationalism'. Today, when people wonder as to why 'independent' Bharat's Constitution of 1950 was written in English and continues to be interpreted in English, perhaps they must look back at the linguistic prerequisite of the First Indian National Congress to find an answer. Pertinently, in his maiden speech as the first president of the Congress, W.C. Bannerjee made it a point to underscore his loyalty to the British government and acknowledged the 'benefits' accrued to India on account of British rule. Here is a relevant extract from the proceedings of the Conference:[70]

[Bannerjee said] Much had been done by Great Britain for the benefit of India, and the whole country was grateful to her for it. She had given them order, she had given them railways, and above all she had given them the inestimable blessing of Western education. But a great deal still remained to be done. The more progress the people made in education and material prosperity, the greater, would be the insight into political matters and the keener their desire for political advancement. He [Bannerjee] thought that their desire to be governed according to the ideas of Government prevalent in Europe was in no way incompatible with their thorough loyalty to the British Government. All that they desired was that the basis of the Government should be widened and the people should have their proper and legitimate share in it. The discussions that would take place in this Congress would, he believed, be as advantageous to the ruling authorities as he was sure it would be to the people at large.

Telegrams of sympathy with the objects of the Congress were then read from the British Indian Association, from the Provincial Conference recently held at

Calcutta, from a Public Meeting held in Assam under the Presidency [of] *the Hon'ble Ananda Mohan Bose.* [Emphasis added]

Apart from the founding spirit of the Congress, a cordial interaction between the Indian National Conference and the Indian National Congress has also been alluded to in this extract, which may explain their subsequent collaboration in 1886–1887. In addition to the speech made by W.C. Bannerjee, the speeches of various other participants also clearly showcase colonial consciousness in the realm of national politics and the consequent 'moderate nationalism' of the Congress. Here is what the chairman of the Congress, G. Subramania Iyer from Madras, had to say, which is more or less reflective of the tone and tenor of the other delegates, including Dadabhai Naoroji:[71]

> The proposition which I have been asked to move relates to a subject of utmost importance to the country; it relates to a periodical enquiry into the material and moral progress of our people by the Imperial Parliament, the final arbiters of our destiny. By a merciful dispensation of Providence, India, which was for centuries the victim of external aggression and plunder, of internecine wars and general confusion, has been brought under the dominion of the great English power. Gentlemen, I need not tell you how that event introduced a great change in the destiny of her people, how the inestimable good that has flown from it has been appreciated by them, how profoundly grateful they feel for it. The rule of Great Britain has given India peace and security, and on the whole, has been better in its results and direction than any former rule. At home that rule is directed by forces which the whole history of the world shows, are the most conducive to high material and moral prosperity. It has for ages developed and fostered individual liberty and social freedom which have made the English people what they are at present—the most prosperous, the most pushing and the most enlightened nation in the world, enjoying sovereignty over nearly one-seventh of the globe with control over millions of diverse races and creeds ... From today forward we can with greater propriety than heretofore speak of an Indian nation, of national opinion and national aspirations. Gentlemen, to what do we owe this marvellous change over the people? Do we not owe it to that spirit of justice and generosity, to that spirit of progressiveness, so remarkable in the English political character? Well then, it is our duty to watch jealously, so that the contact of that influence with the Government of this country is regular and constant and does not suffer prolonged intermission. It is a matter of the deepest concern to us that affairs of our country should be periodically, if not continuously, brought to the notice of the Parliament and people of England, and be subjected to the healthy influences of a free and open enquiry conducted by the best of English politicians.

In light of this gushing praise for the British empire by the founders of the Indian National Congress, would it be unreasonable to conclude that its very creation was steeped in coloniality? Perhaps not. As for the resolutions that followed this sanguine expression of eternal gratitude to the British empire, they primarily revolved around the need for greater elected representation in Legislative Councils, and therefore reforms to the Indian Councils Act. The other expectation that was aired was for greater British parliamentary oversight over capricious and whimsical bureaucratic action. The resolutions did *not* call for and were *not* in relation to the demand for independence. And here's how the First Congress concluded on 30 December 1885:[72]

> Mr. Hume, after acknowledging the honour done to him, said that as the giving of cheers had been entered on he must be allowed to propose, on the principle of better late than never, the giving of cheers, and that not only three, but three times three, and if possible thrice that, for one the latchet of whose shoes he was unworthy to loose, one to whom they were all dear, to whom they were all as children—need he say Her Most Gracious Majesty, the Queen-Empress.
>
> The rest of the speaker's remarks were lost in the storm of applause that instantly burst out and the asked for cheers were given over and over again with a vehemence and enthusiasm rarely equalled.
>
> The Congress was then dissolved.

At this juncture, lest I should be misunderstood as running down all the contributions of the founders of the Indian National Congress in my decolonial quest, I should clarify something: It could well be argued that coloniality was not just a product of conditioning but was also a pragmatic necessity to survive under the colonial administration. It could also be argued that the intention of the founders of the Indian National Congress was to incrementally reclaim state power through constant demand for greater elected representation in the administration of the country as well as greater participation in its bureaucracy. However, such a contention needs to be tested against the statements and conduct of the Moderates vis-a-vis the so-called Extremists who demanded greater autonomy/independence. As seen earlier, and as we shall see again, the former faction of the Congress, which represented the founding spirit of the organisation, dismissed the latter's aspirations of autonomy/freedom from the British as 'lunacy', which would come at the expense of all the opportunity and promise of growth represented by tying Bharat's destiny with that of the British empire/ Commonwealth.

After the first Congress session of 1885, there was greater interaction between Banerjea's Indian Association, which conducted the Indian National Conference, and Hume's Indian National Congress. In fact, the second session of the Indian National Congress, which was held in Calcutta in December 1886, was organised with the cordial cooperation of the Indian Association.[73] The reason for including Banerjea in the second session was that the Congress could not afford to exclude him in Bengal, where he occupied centre stage. In any case, by this time Hume's reservations about Surendranath Banerjea's political views perhaps stood addressed, since Banerjea's political ideas were already in line with Hume's version of moderate and British loyalist nationalism. Scholars such as R.C. Majumdar have treated the collaboration between the Indian Association and the Indian National Congress as a merger of the two platforms. However, while there was no formal merger, the Association assumed the role of a provincial arm of the Congress in Bengal. In other words, the Congress played a pan-India role whereas the Association took the lead in Bengal.[74]

It was around this period in 1886, readers may recollect, that Syed Ahmed Khan founded the Mohammedan Educational Conference in response to the establishment of the Congress and insisted on communal representation in Legislative Councils. By 1888, the Mohammedan Educational Conference was in active and complete opposition to the Congress, since Syed Ahmed Khan saw Congress as both Bengali supremacist and Hindu supremacist, whereas the Congress saw itself as the representative of all Indians.[75]

Having discussed the colonial origins of the Indian National Congress, it becomes important to understand in brief the journey of its brand of moderate nationalism in order to better appreciate the rift between the Moderates/ Liberals and the Extremists/Nationalists in 1905, post the Partition of Bengal.

Growth of 'Extremist Nationalism' within the Indian National Congress (1885–1905)

From 1885 until 1904, quite a few annual sessions of the Congress were presided over by Englishmen such as George Yule, Hume's biographer William Wedderburn, Alfred Webb and Henry Cotton, who preserved Hume's vision of moderate nationalism, all under the benign oversight of the British empire.[76] As for the Indian leaders of the Congress, on the one hand they paid lip service to Bharatiya heritage, while on the other their approach to the issues of the day was entirely influenced by Western political values. This was evident from Naoroji's speech at the second session of the Congress in Calcutta in 1886, in which he declared that only British rule, and no Hindu rule in the past, had made it possible for Indians to speak as 'one nation'.[77] Apart from asserting the fact that members of the Congress were 'loyal to the backbone' to the British government, Naoroji credited English education for bringing Indians out of the darkness of Asiatic despotism and into the light of the English civilisation.[78] All that the Congress expected was that Britain introduce in Bharat the very same representative institutions that were taken for granted in England. Simply put, the call for self-government was primarily a call for treatment of Indians at par with British citizens in England. Importantly, the Congress did not ask for universal adult franchise; instead, it wanted both educational and financial prerequisites to be mandated for exercise of the right of franchise. This would effectively exclude most Indians who were not English-educated, those that Banerjea referred to as *'people unfit to exercise the franchise—the ignorant peasantry of the country'*.[79] [Emphases added]

Despite its elitism, the Congress wanted to be recognised as the sole, or at least the primary, representative of all Indians. But Syed Ahmed Khan saw Congress as a Hindu supremacist organisation which did not represent and could not claim to represent Muslims. One might recollect Khan's speech in Lucknow in December 1887 on the eve of the Madras session of the Congress; he declared that only those Muslims who wanted to live under Hindu rule should attend the Congress session. To offset this criticism and to prove its 'secular' credentials, the Congress elected Badruddin Tyabji as its president

Lala Lajpat Rai of Punjab, Bal Gangadhara Tilak of Bombay and Bipin Chandra Pal of Bengal—the triumvirate were popularly known as Lal–Bal–Pal.

for the Madras session. While Syed Ahmed Khan was crystal clear about his priorities, which was to reclaim state power for Muslims, or at the very least ally with the British to check the advance of what he saw as 'the Hindu Congress', the degree to which the Congress was willing to genuflect to and accommodate Muslims is evident from the following statement of Banerjea:[80]

> We were straining every nerve to secure the co-operation of our Mohamedan fellow countrymen ... we sometimes paid the fares of Mohamedan delegates and offered them other facilities.

I leave it to the readers to ask themselves if anything has changed between 1887 and the present. According to Argov:[81]

> Banerjea argued before a Muslim meeting in Dacca that even Sir Syed Ahmad Khan described India as a bride whose two eyes represented the Hindu and Muslim communities. Banerjea claimed that throughout the period of Muslim rule in India, Hindus and Muslims had lived as brothers who worked jointly for the advancement of the interests of their common country. He denied that the programme of the Congress sought to secure the higher appointments in the Indian Civil Service exclusively for the Hindus, and attempted to refute the view that the Hindus would dominate the proposed reformed Legislative Councils. Assuring his Muslim listeners that they stood to gain from the Congress, Banerjea challenged them by arguing that if the Congress had any shortcomings they should better join it instead of criticising it from the outside.

Until the fifth session of the Congress, which was held in Bombay in 1889, despite almost the same resolutions being passed in every session, neither the British government in India nor the British Parliament paid heed to them.[82] S.R. Mehrotra called the Congress of this period a 'dignified debating society' that would meet every year at Christmas to pass a slew of resolutions, only to meet the following year and repeat the same exercise.[83] Despite this pliant and moderate brand of nationalism, the Congress had no dearth of detractors in the colonial establishment. For instance, the Congress's demand for self-government was dismissed as baseless by John Strachey, who declared that self-government was reserved for 'nations' and India by no yardstick qualified as one, given its diversity and lack of either racial, cultural or linguistic unity.[84] Readers may recollect from my first book that such dismissals of Bharat as a single political unit resulted in the production of copious literature by Bharatiya scholars, who set out to demonstrate the fundamental cultural unity of Bharat as a civilisation.

It is in the above context that the Congress's Bombay session of 1889 must be understood. At this session, which was presided over by William Wedderburn, a Member of the British House of Commons, Charles

Bradlaugh, was present. Owing to his interest in India, he was called 'Member for India'. Bradlaugh had prepared a Bill, the Indian Councils Amendment Bill (which would later be called the Home Rule Bill), in accordance with the Congress's demand for expansion of the Legislative Councils as well as to introduce an elective component to demonstrate Bharat's readiness for elected representative institutions.[85] Although the Bill was introduced in the British Parliament in February 1890 and a deputation from the Congress was sent to England to advocate its position, the Bill could not be taken up for deliberation. The following year, Bradlaugh died. Notwithstanding the failure of the Home Rule Bill, it would set the tone for the amendment to the Indian Councils Act in 1892, as we shall see.

What is also pertinent to note is that a Muslim delegate of the Congress demanded an equal number of Muslims and Hindus in the Legislative Councils, and the majority of Muslim delegates voted against the Bill.[86] For all its claims of representing both Hindus and Muslims, the fact was that the Congress of this period was unable to contain the influence of Syed Ahmed Khan's views, even on its own Muslim members. Clearly, electoral/political separatism was not an overnight phenomenon of 1909 under the Minto–Morley pair or of the 1930s; it was very much a reality even in the 1880s. Each of these facts must be borne in mind to understand the nature and pace of developments that led to the communal Partition of Bengal in October 1905 and the birth of the All-India Muslim League in December 1906.

Between the Congress deputation of 1890 to England and the enactment of the Indian Councils Act of 1892, there was widespread criticism of the role and purpose of the Congress since it had failed to achieve anything of consequence for the Indian people except to prove to the British that it was not a seditious organisation and that its loyalty to the empire remained unimpeachable. By the time of its seventh session in 1891, which was held in Nagpur, Hume had resigned from his position as the general secretary of the Congress and was keen to return to England.[87] At the 1891 session, once again, the Congress reiterated its demand for provision of elected representatives in the Councils Act. Finally, in 1892, under Viceroy Lansdowne, the number of non-official additional members in Legislative Councils was increased, but direct election of representatives to the Councils was still not provided for.[88] Instead, the nominated members would be selected from those elected by municipal and district boards, universities, chambers of commerce and landholders' associations.[89] This revealed the futility of the Congress deputation to England. To add to this, in 1893, when the British Parliament passed a resolution agreeing to hold simultaneous examinations in England and India for the Civil Service, the Secretary of State for India and the

Government of India intervened and overruled the resolution.[90] This shook the Congress out of its belief that it could influence the British government in India by making its case before the British Parliament. The Madras session of the Congress of 1894 was held in the backdrop of this disappointment, and yet leaders such as Banerjea continued to express their deep conviction in the need to preserve loyal connections with the British in the following words:[91]

> We have everything to lose, nothing to gain by the severance of our connection with England. We owe whatever position or prestige we have acquired to our English education and culture. If you were to leave the country our English education and culture would be at a discount. We are not particularly anxious to commit political suicide.

Again, in March 1895, Banerjea expressed the following views in a private meeting:[92]

> I am not credited with being particularly loyal to the British connection. It is an obloquy which has haunted me through life. I am loyal because I am patriotic, because I feel in my heart of hearts that with the continuance and indeed the permanence of British rule in India are bound up the best prospects of Indian advancement.

Even when a British speaker at the 1894 session expressed the hope that the Congress would secure Home Rule for India, Banerjea corrected him to clarify that the goal of the Congress was *not* Home Rule 'but a transformation of India into an organic part within a federated British Empire'.[93] Fortunately for Bharat, despite this brand of 'moderate nationalism' or 'British loyalist nationalism' being the dominant position of and within the Congress, by the late 1880s and the early 1890s, the alternative dissenting position, namely the Extremist/Nationalist position, had begun to rear its head through Bipin Chandra Pal, Lala Lajpat Rai and Bal Gangadhara Tilak. In addition to this firebrand triumvirate, in 1893, Aurobindo Ghosh published a series of articles heavily criticising the Congress for its myopic and British loyalist position.[94] By 1899, the fact that the Congress was an anglicised organisation which had no intentions of demanding complete independence was a widely shared sentiment.

While Aurobindo Ghosh drew heavily from Hindu philosophy to make a case for nationalism and complete independence from the British, Lala Lajpat Rai reflected his Arya Samaji leanings when he criticised the Congress's attempts to placate or accommodate the sentiments of Syed Ahmed Khan's followers in order to present itself as the sole voice of all Indians. Rai believed that such attempts were not only an exercise in futility but were also detrimental and dangerous to Hindu interests in the long run.[95] He felt that the Congress ought to have channelled its energies in fostering

Hindu national unity instead of pursuing the mirage of representing both Hindus and Muslims.[96] Similarly, in 1895 Tilak argued that the Congress should not attempt to Westernise Hindu society in the name of 'reforms' under the influence of the British, and that it must, instead, focus on forging Hindu unity.[97] Interestingly, it is believed that the Constitution of India Bill of 1895 was the brainchild of Tilak, although the actual details of the Bill's authorship remain unclear.[98] This Bill, which has also been referred to as the Home Rule Bill or Swaraj Bill, contained 110 provisions and was based on the principle of self-government. Although this Bill too preserved ties with the British and, in fact, vested sovereign power over Bharat in Britain, it marked a significant departure from the Congress's incremental approach, which was primarily fixated with administrative reforms.

Broadly speaking, Rai, Pal, Tilak and Ghosh represented the first wave of non-moderate nationalism which rejected the servility of the Congress's oxymoronic moderate nationalism. I call it 'non-moderate nationalism' and not simply 'nationalism', because the initial focus of some members of this group too was self-government within the British empire and not complete independence. The fundamental positions of this group, as identified by R.C. Majumdar, were as follows:[99]

1. Belief in the greatness of Bharat's civilisation which, it felt, ought to be the basis of its future;
2. Vehement disagreement with the Congress's methods, which it labelled 'mendicancy';
3. Goal of Swaraj or self-government, and not piecemeal administrative reforms;
4. Belief that the Congress was an organisation of anglicised elites that had failed to strike a chord with the masses, and therefore there was an urgent need to awaken the political consciousness of the masses.

We shall see later that the call for Swaraj by the 'Extremists', which was initially interpreted as self-government, would make way for a call for complete independence, whereas the 'Moderates' would move from mere elective representation in Legislative Councils to self-government. In this sense, the Extremists/Nationalists were successful in and responsible for pushing the envelope.

Coming back to the beginnings of non-moderate nationalism, by 1897, Tilak's writings in his papers *Kesari* and *Maratha* and his speeches during the Ganapati and Shivaji festivals had assumed revolutionary tones. The British treated his writings as having inspired the Chapekar brothers (Damodar, Balkrishna and Vasudeo) who assassinated the British Plague Commissioner

W.C. Rand and his military escort Lieutenant Ayerst on 22 June 1897 for the former's insensitive handling of the outbreak of bubonic plague of 1896–1897 in Poona.[100] Tilak was charged with sedition and incitement to murder, and sentenced to eighteen months' imprisonment. While he emerged a hero from prison, the Congress felt that Tilak's methods had undermined its commitment to constitutional and peaceful agitation. This needs to be understood well, as when people accuse Mohandas Karamchand Gandhi of inducing a pacifist spirit in the Indian National Movement, they fail to note that 'constitutional and non-violent methods' were the *chosen* template of the Congress even *before* Gandhi showed up on the national scene. In fact, to distance the Congress from Tilak's views, Sankaran Nair, the president of the thirteenth session of the Congress held in 1897 in Amravati, underscored again the peaceful, British loyalist DNA of the Congress in the following words:[101]

> From our earliest school days, the great English writers have been our classics; Englishmen have been our professors in Colleges; English history is taught us in our schools; the books we generally read are English books which describe in detail all the forms of English life; week after week English newspapers, journals and magazines pour into India. We in fact now live the life of the English ...

Therefore, he concluded, it was only natural that English political ideas animated the thinking of the Congress and its aspirations of a permanent bond with the English. In the process of reiterating the Congress's loyalty to British rule, Nair unintentionally summarised the story of European coloniality and its impact on Indic consciousness. After Nair, Banerjea also condemned violent methods and underscored the Congress's commitment to peace, orderly government and 'constitutionalism':[102]

> We, men of the Congress, are the friends of peace and orderly Government. We denounce violence; we condemn violent methods; for we believe in our heart of hearts that order is the first condition of political progress ... We, the men of the Congress true to ourselves, remain firm in our allegiance to those principles which gave birth to the Congress movement. Now as of old, we raise aloft the banner of constitutionalism on which are engraved in characters of light the words 'devotion to the British Crown and the sacred interests of our country'. Now as of old we wish for the permanence of the British rule.

Predictably, apart from the above reiterations of loyalty, both the moderate establishment of the Congress and the 'liberal Hindus' of the period, represented by the likes of Justice Mahadev Govind Ranade, sneered at 'old orthodox beliefs and practices' represented by the community-driven Ganapati and Shivaji festivals organized by Tilak, and also felt that they were harmful for 'Hindu–Muslim unity'.[103] In a nutshell, Tilak was accused of communalism for attempting to forge Hindu unity through community celebrations that broke caste and economic barriers. His attempts at preventing cow slaughter only added to the communal labels being slapped on him.[104]

By 1899, when the fifteenth session of the Congress was held in Lucknow and Lord Curzon had arrived in Bharat as the Viceroy, members of the Congress were openly calling its annual event a three-day 'Christmas tamasha'.[105] However, the rift between the Moderates and the Extremists had reached a point where the Congress's primary agenda at the Lucknow session was to put together an internal constitution to rein in the Extremists. Banerjea attacked them in his speech:[106]

> We are the friends of Reform because we are enemies of Revolution. We have made our choice, let our enemies make theirs. Do they wish to belong to our camp or do they wish to belong to the camp of revolutionists? There is no intermediary step between Reform and Revolution. Therefore, you must enlist yourselves under the banner of Reform or you must take your place behind the standard of Revolt.

Ironically, barely two months before the Lucknow session, the Moderate camp of the Congress proved the Extremists right when they displayed what Lord Curzon called 'a most exemplary and gratifying loyalty' by expressing their displeasure at the non-inclusion of Indian troops in the South African War of 1899.[107] In other words, according to the Moderates, the absence of native troops in the War demonstrated the continued distrust of Indians by the British, which undermined the Congress's loyalty to the empire. Naturally, leaders of the Nationalist group, such as Lala Lajpat Rai, found such expressions of cloying loyalism embarrassing and detrimental to Bharatiya interests. Before the Calcutta session of 1901, Rai wrote a series of stinging articles criticising the Congress's goals, methods, its anglicised elitism, its inability to connect with the masses and its incapacity to ideate on practical issues such as the economic and industrial advancement of Bharat, which could enable its political empowerment.[108]

In the November 1901 issue of *Kayastha Samachar*, Rai was scathing in his attack of the Congress's untenable claim of representing Hindus and Muslims when they did not even represent all strands of Hindu opinion.[109] He categorically advocated for creation of a Hindu political or semi-political Congress or Conference, since, according to him, any attempt to treat Hindus, Muslims, Christians and Parsis as a single nation was futile and detrimental to the goal of strengthening Hindus as a religious nationality. Rai did not mince words in saying that Hindu interests must not be diluted in order to accommodate Muslims and Christians. Critically, in his article titled 'A Study of Hindu Nationalism', he made a strong case for Hindu nationalism on the basis of Hindu religious unity and rejected the Congress's contention that all strands of Indian nationalism were the exclusive products of Western influence.[110] Clearly, this was a relatively indigenous and significantly decolonial position, considering the overarching coloniality of Rai's period, which was reflected in the founding spirit of the Congress. In this sense, it is true that the Two-Nation Theory, although propounded by Syed Ahmed Khan, *did* find acceptance even among leaders such as Rai, who saw facts for what they were instead of wallowing in the wishful thinking of the Moderates. To this extent, it would not be incorrect to submit that Syed Ahmed Khan and Rai were more accepting of the reality, however uncomfortable or politically incorrect, than the Moderate leaders of the Congress.

Thanks to such yawning differences in their positions, effectively, by the 1901 Calcutta session of the Congress, the stage was set for the deepening of fissures between the Moderates and Extremists, which would only worsen after the Partition of Bengal under Curzon in 1905 and lead to a clear split at the Surat session in 1907. The only interesting aspect of the Calcutta session of 1901 was the appearance of Mohandas Karamchand Gandhi, who sought the Congress's support to fight the racial discrimination suffered by Indians in South Africa.[111,112]

The gradual change in the Moderate position under pressure from the Nationalists, however, was evident at the 1902 session in Ahmedabad, where, for the first time, Banerjea suggested in his presidential speech that Indians must use indigenous goods as far as possible since the British government did not protect Indian industries through imposition of tariffs on foreign goods.[113] This was a predecessor to the Swadeshi Movement of 1905, which Banerjea would launch in Calcutta after the formal announcement of the proposal to partition Bengal. But for the Nationalist pushback against the Congress's undying loyalism to the British, such a suggestion probably would not have been made by Banerjea, one of the leading lights of the Moderate faction. Of course, in the very same speech Banerjea branded the Nationalists as 'pessimists' for their lack of faith in the Congress's constitutional methods and the 'fairness' of the British government.[114]

For all their attempts to snub the voice of the Nationalists within the Congress, the Moderate leaders realised that the Congress's methods and their non-effectiveness were beginning to push society into the arms of the Nationalists and Revolutionaries. As we saw earlier, revolutionary and secret societies had sprung up in different parts of the country by 1902 under the leadership of Aurobindo Ghosh and his associates, who looked up to Bal

Gangadhara Tilak for thought leadership. To make matters worse for the Moderate Congress, Curzon's brand of brash imperialism, his racist approach to intake of Indians in the bureaucracy, greater concentration of powers in the hands of bureaucracy, the proposal to construct the Victoria Memorial Hall at great expense, the holding of the Delhi Durbar in 1903 at a time of famine, the passing of the Official Secrets Act and the stifling of whatever little progress had been made in local self-government, only vindicated the criticism by the Extremists of the starry-eyed approach of the Moderates to the English establishment.

That the Moderates had realised the ineffectiveness of their chosen constitutional methods became evident at the nineteenth session of the Congress held in 1903 in Madras. What was noteworthy about this session was the open criticism of the Congress's own autocratic way of functioning in the presidential speech of Lal Mohan Ghosh. He underscored the stark inconsistency between the Congress's demand for greater democracy from the British government and its own autocracy within.[115] Once again, the session ended with a reiteration of the Congress's past demands for greater inclusion of Indians in the Civil Service and for separation of executive and judicial functions. In addition, new resolutions were passed against racial discrimination in South Africa and the Official Secrets Act.

The twentieth session of the Congress was held in December 1904 in Bombay, by which time Curzon's proposal to partition Bengal had been announced in December 1903–January 1904. Given the impact the proposed partition would have on the national movement, one would have expected the proposal to occupy the entirety of the attention of the 1904 session. However, the Moderates were more interested in preserving the legitimacy of their vision as well as their leadership. Therefore, in order to secure a stamp of validation from the White Man, Henry Cotton was invited to preside over the session, and he, predictably, praised the exalted leadership of the Moderates and summarised the goal of the Congress as follows:[116]

> The ideal of an Indian patriot is the establishment of a federation of free and separate states, the United States of India, placed on a fraternal footing with the self-governing Colonies, each with its own local autonomy, cemented together under the aegis of Great Britain.

This was the first time the Congress had spelt out in clear terms that self-government *within* the British empire was its goal, which only underscored the impact of the Nationalists on widening the horizons of the Congress. That said, the immediate issue of the Partition of Bengal received marginal attention, for that would have required the Congress to question the intentions of the British government at the highest levels. Instead, the focus remained on Curzon's racial and racist approach to recruitment in the Civil Service, best captured in his own words:[117]

> ... the highest ranks of civil employment in India must as a general rule be held by Englishmen for the reason that they possess partly by heredity, partly by upbringing, and partly by education, the habits of mind and the vigour of character which are essential for the task; and that the rule of India being a British rule and every other rule being in the circumstances of the case impossible, the tone and standard should be set by those who have created and are responsible for it.

Having been reminded of their place in the colonial pecking order once more, diehard loyalists in the Congress experienced what one would call jilted disillusionment. However, they once again chose to plead their case in England, for which Gokhale and Rai were selected. The selection of Rai reflected an attempt at reconciliation with the Nationalists. Another attempt in this direction was the drafting of a new constitution for the Congress, in which Rai took part. In London, however, Rai pressed for Home Rule, much to Henry Cotton's displeasure, as he had expected Rai to toe the Moderate line.[118] Upon his return to Bharat, Rai realistically concluded that Bharatiyas must put faith in their own efforts to secure Home Rule. He went a step further and questioned the effectiveness of constitutional agitation to achieve this goal, which put him in the crosshairs of the British government.[119] Fortunately for Rai, Curzon's Partition of Bengal in October 1905 supplied the Nationalists in the Congress with the perfect opportunity to call out the mendicancy of the Moderates, both in their vision and their methods.

Having discussed the colonial origins of the Congress and the history of the split between the Moderates/Liberals and the Extremists/Nationalists up to October 1905, we will now resume the discussion of the period between 1905 and 1909, which witnessed a clear division within the Congress, the birth of the All-India Muslim League and the constitutional accommodation of Muslim separatism through the Minto–Morley Reforms of 1909.

A Divided Congress, the Simla Deputation, the All-India Muslim League and the Minto–Morley Reforms (1905–1909)

As discussed in the beginning of this chapter, after the Partition of Bengal in October 1905, Lord Minto succeeded Curzon as the Viceroy in November, and John Morley was appointed Secretary of State for India. In the wake of the Partition of Bengal, Minto had inherited a volatile Bharat from Curzon and a Congress which was increasingly being pushed away from its moderate nationalism by the Extremists/Nationalists. The general impact of the Nationalist group on the Congress's style of functioning, and specifically on

The founding members of the All-India Muslim League at the *baradari* of Shah Bagh in Dacca on 30 December 1906

the anti-partition agitation, can be gauged from the fact that before leaving Bharat in October 1905, Curzon wrote to then Secretary of State for India, John Brodrick, as follows:[120]

> ... the agitation is now being conducted by methods of open terrorism and violence. It has been converted ... into a purely political movement organized by a small disloyal faction.

Naturally, when the Congress met for its twenty-first annual session at Benares in December 1905—as always, after Christmas—all was not well within the organisation and sparks were expected to fly between the Liberal and Nationalist camps. When the Subjects Committee of the Congress proposed to pass a resolution welcoming the visiting Prince of Wales, Gokhale and Banerjea insisted on passing the resolution whereas Rai opposed it, saying that in view of the Partition of Bengal, there was no need to create a facade of loyalty and normalcy.[121] However, the resolution was passed by the majority of the Subjects Committee, which led to Tilak and Rai warning that they would openly oppose the passage of the resolution in the assembly. This led to a verbal spat between Tilak and Rai on one side and veteran Moderates on the other, until Gokhale intervened. At his request, Tilak and Rai agreed to abstain from the passing of the resolution. As the president of the Benares session, reiterating the goal set for the Congress by Henry Cotton in the 1904 session, Gokhale said:[122]

> The goal of the Congress is that India should be governed in the interests of the Indians themselves, and that in the course of time a form of Government should be attained in this country similar to what exists in the self-governing Colonies of the British Empire.

In appreciating this re-emphasising of the goal of self-government by Gokhale, it is important to bear in mind that there seemed to be a shift in the position of the Moderates, which was being driven by their fear of losing ground to the Extremists. That said, while Gokhale supported the Swadeshi Movement, he was still not enthusiastic about the Boycott Movement, since he felt it would reflect a vindictive tendency towards the British, which was 'out of question'.[123] Interestingly, Pandit Madan Mohan Malaviya too leaned in favour of Gokhale's position and dissuaded the spread of Boycott to provinces other than Bengal. Rai, of course, was in support of an all-India Boycott Movement against British goods.[124] The differences in the aims and methods of the two camps are best reflected in the language of the resolutions passed in the 1905 session. From a reading of the following extract of the resolution seeking reunification of Bengal, I leave it to the reader to decide whether the accusation of mendicancy against the Moderates levelled by the Extremists had any merit:[125]

> That this Congress records its emphatic protest against the Partition of Bengal in the face of the strongest opposition on the part of the people of the province. That having regard to the intense dissatisfaction felt by the entire Bengali Community at the dismemberment of their province and their manifest disinclination to accept the partition as an accomplished fact, this Congress appeals to the Government of India and the Secretary of State to reverse or modify the arrangements made, in such a manner as to conciliate public opinion and allay the excitement and unrest present among all classes of the people. That this Congress recommends the adoption of some arrangement which would be consistent with administrative efficiency and would place the entire Bengali community under one undivided administration.

Here is an extract of another resolution, which captures the Moderate reluctance to support the Boycott Movement:[126]

> That this Congress records its earnest and emphatic protest against the repressive measures which have been adopted by the authorities in Bengal after the people there had been compelled to resort to the boycott of foreign goods as a last protest and perhaps the only constitutional and effective means left to them of drawing the attention of the British public to the action of the Government of India in persisting in their determination to partition Bengal in utter disregard of the universal prayers and protest of the people.

Despite this half-hearted defence of the Boycott Movement by the Congress, the fact is that the pressure of the Extremists on the Moderates to show results was growing, forcing even Moderate leaders like Banerjea to publicly support the Boycott Movement in their speeches. However, the primary drivers of this Movement were Bipin Chandra Pal and Aurobindo

Ghosh. At this point, Bengali Hindus, under leaders like Pal and Ghosh, sustained the anti-partition agitation, despite the repressive measures of the colonial establishment and the restrained and heavily caveated support of the Moderates in the Congress. They had also to deal with the pro-partition agitation of the Muslim community of Eastern Bengal and Assam under leaders such as Nawab Salimullah.

In the immediate aftermath of the partition, the Provincial Mohammedan Political Union was founded, with Nawab Salimullah as its chief patron,[127] along with associates from Eastern Bengal, such as Muhammad Yousuf of Rajshahi, Nawab Syed Ali Chowdhury of Comilla and Fazlul Haque of Barisal. These leaders exhorted members of their community to stay away from the anti-partition protests and urged them to stay loyal to the British government against the Hindus.[128] Some may be tempted to treat Muslim attitudes towards the Swadeshi and Boycott Movements as a reaction to factors such as the Hindu nationalism of Rai and Tilak, in particular celebration of the Ganapati and Shivaji festivals, the use of 'Bande Mataram' from Bankim Chandra's *Anandamath* to protest against the Partition of Bengal, the activities of the Arya Samaj, the anti-cow slaughter movement and the Hindi–Urdu/Devanagari–Persian controversy. However, in doing so they would be necessarily turning a blind eye to the thought continuum of Middle Eastern coloniality and its in-built Two-Nation Theory, which became even more pronounced after the loss of Muslim state power in the first half of the eighteenth century.

Critically, after the Partition of Bengal, the new Muslim-majority province of Eastern Bengal and Assam became the centre for consolidation of Muslim interests and the point of convergence of Muslim organisations from across the country. This was further helped by the fact that the British establishment in the new province under Lieutenant Governor J.B. Fuller, previously the Chief Commissioner of Assam, wore its pro-Muslim bias on its sleeve, adding to its brutal repression of the anti-partition agitation. Fuller also favoured Muslims in appointments to government posts; he issued a circular dated 25 May 1906 laying down that a fixed proportion of government posts should be reserved for Muslims, and until that proportion was reached no qualified Muslim candidate should be rejected in favour of a Hindu candidate, even if the latter was *better* qualified.[129] This pro-Muslim bias was made further evident when Fuller compared himself with Shaista Khan, a Mughal governor who was appointed to Bengal under Aurangzeb. Comparing the Hindu and Muslim populations of the province, he caustically remarked that he had two wives, one Muslim and the other Hindu, and that he was pushed into the arms of the former owing to the rudeness of the latter.[130] Such conduct and statements vindicated Hindu apprehensions of living in a Muslim-majority province under a partisan British establishment.

Further, this was all the encouragement Muslim separatists at the time needed, and what followed was in many ways a dress rehearsal for the ghastly genocide of Bengali Hindus in 1946–47. No sooner had the Partition of Bengal materialised than the ulema resumed their incendiary preaching about how the flag of Islam had been revived in Bharat through the partition. Public proclamations were made by the ulema to the effect that the British administration was on the side of Muslims, that courts of law had been suspended for a period of three months, and that no penal consequence would visit them if they attacked Hindus or looted their business or abducted Hindu widows.[131] Predictably, riots, which have been called among the 'worst possible', broke out in Eastern Bengal in Comilla, Jamalpur and Mymensingh.[132] The American journalist Henry W. Nevinson, who was visiting Bharat around that time, wrote:[133]

> ... temples were desecrated, images broken, shops plundered, and many Hindu widows carried off. Some of the towns were deserted, the Hindu population took refuge in any 'pukka' house (i.e., house with brick or stone walls), women spent nights hidden in tanks, the crime known as 'group rape' increased, and throughout the country districts there reigned a general terror, which still prevailed at the time of my visit.

Rightly, in view of these riots and other tactless decisions by Fuller, such as withdrawal of recognition given to a few educational institutions for their participation in the anti-partition agitation, members of the public and the press demanded his resignation. Under pressure from both Minto and Morley, Fuller resigned in August 1906,[134] which was seen by Muslims of Eastern Bengal and Assam as the British establishment succumbing to pressure from Hindus. The disappointment and resentment of the Muslim community in and outside Bengal is best captured in a letter written by Mohsin ul-Mulk in August 1906 to the then principal of Aligarh College, William A.J. Archbold. Quoting Nawab Syed Ali Chowdhury of Comilla in the letter, Mohsin ul-Mulk wrote:[135]

> Up till now the Mohammedans of Bengal have been careless. They have now begun to feel the consequences of their carelessness. If only the Mohammedans of Bengal, instead of following the government, had agitated like the Hindus and had enlisted the sympathies of the Mohammedans of the whole of India, and raised their voice up to the Parliament, they would never see these unfortunate consequences. The resignation of Sir Bamfylde Fuller has produced an unrest throughout the Mohammedans in the whole of Bengal, and their aspirations for higher education and increased rank and responsibility being subsided.

Looking at it from one point of view, the Government has taught a good lesson to the Mohammedans by accepting Sir Bamfylde's resignation. It has served to awaken them after a sleep of carelessness. We shall now have to proceed on the same lines as the Hindus, not only in India, but in England.

Effectively, this meant that both the Congress and Muslim leaders were keen to have the ear of Minto for their respective interests. Unlike Curzon, Minto was open to meeting a deputation from the Congress, provided the deputation had 'influential members', by which he meant those whose loyalty towards the British was above question, namely the Moderates.[136] He felt that since the Congress could not be ignored in Indian political life, it was best to develop friendly relations with Moderate leaders such as Gokhale and Banerjea. Morley, on the other hand, was not as trusting of the Congress and suggested to Minto that he go slow on acceding to the Congress's request for a meeting. However, both Minto and Morley agreed on the dangers of importing English political institutions into India since, according to them, India was not ready and would not be ready in their life and time.[137]

But both acknowledged that in view of the growing impatience within the Congress and the hold of the Extremist faction over the Indian youth, preventing or stalling extension of the 'spirit' of English political institutions to India would drive more youth into the arms of the Extremists.[138] This was Minto's assessment, based on the apprehensions expressed by Gokhale.[139] This was because by mid-1906, while the Moderates had moved from demands for mere administrative reforms to self-government within the British empire at par with other self-governing colonies, the Extremists had moved from demands for self-government to demands for 'absolute national autonomy', which was interpreted as freedom from British rule. The Extremists were inspired by the defeat of Russia at the hands of Japan, which had dented the European sense of racial superiority. Consequently, the Extremists had no faith in what they called the mendicancy of the Moderates.[140] The Moderates were described by some sections of the Congress in the following words:[141]

> English-educated Indians have become slaves to the feringhis and say we must live with them as partners. The management of the Congress must he wrested from the hands of the demi-feringhis.

It seemed to observers that the Congress was headed for a split in the upcoming Calcutta session of December 1906, as was evident from the consolidation of the Moderate and Extremist factions.[142] Expectedly, this did not bode well for the English establishment, which relied on the Moderates to 'manage' Indian angst and expectations. Therefore, as before, it was decided by the Minto–Morley duo that in order to defuse the situation, the British government in India had to be seen as initiating political reforms on its own without buckling under Congress pressure, specifically under Extremist pressure.[143] Accordingly, in July 1906, in his budget speech in the House of Commons, Morley announced the following:[144]

> I do not say that I agree with all that the Congress desires; but speaking broadly of what I conceive to be at the bottom of the Congress, I do not see why any one who takes a cool and steady view of Indian Government should be frightened ... Then there is the extension of the representative element in the Legislative Council—not the Executive Council, but the Legislative. I am glad to say that the Governor General is about to appoint a small Committee from his Executive Council to consider what reforms in this direction can be expediently carried forward.

This announcement in July 1906, coupled with the riots of 1906 which was followed by the resignation of Fuller in August 1906 under pressure from the Bengali Hindus, effectively set in motion a series of events which led to the constitutional crystallisation of the Two-Nation Theory. As we shall see, the period from 1904 to 1906 was a defining one for the proponents of the Two-Nation Theory, much before the Lahore Resolution of 23 March 1940, when Pakistan's flesh-and-blood character was etched out. No sooner had Morley announced Minto's decision to appoint a committee to look into legislative reforms than alarm bells started ringing in the minds of Muslim leaders, since introduction of the elective component on a wider scale than before would mean being outnumbered by Hindus in the Legislative Councils. After all, this was Syed Ahmed Khan's primary reason for opposing the very introduction of parliamentary democracy in Bharat—state power would return to the hands of Hindus after the age of the Maratha and the Sikh empires, which was unacceptable to the Dehlawite worldview or, more accurately, to the Middle Eastern consciousness.

Muslim leaders from across the country urged Mohsin ul-Mulk of the Aligarh establishment to take up the issue with the Viceroy. In early August 1906, he wrote as follows to the then principal of Aligarh College, W.A.J. Archbold, who was in Simla for the summer:[145]

> You must have read and thought over Mr. John Morley's speech on the Indian Budget ... I have got several letters drawing attention particularly to the new proposal of 'elected representatives' in the Legislative Councils. They say that the existing rules confer no rights on Mohammedans, and no Mohammedans get into the Councils by election; every now and then Government nominates a stray Mohammedan or two by kindness, not, however, on the ground of his ability, but of his position, who is neither fit to discharge his duties in the Council, nor is he considered a true representative of his community. If the new rules now to be drawn up introduce 'election' on a more extended scale,

the Mohammedans will hardly get a seat, while Hindus will carry off the palm by the dint of their majority, and no Mohammedan will get into the Councils by election.

It has been proposed that a memorial be submitted to His Excellency the Viceroy to draw the attention of Government to a consideration of the rights of Mohammedans.

I feel it is a very important matter, and if we remain silent, I am afraid, people will leave us to go their own way and act up to their own personal opinions.

Will you therefore inform me if it would be advisable to submit a memorial from the Mohammedans to the Viceroy, and to request His Excellency's permission for a deputation to wait on His Excellency to submit the views of Mohammedans on the matter?

Apart from revealing the true concerns of Muslim leaders, this extract also showcases the role played by the English principals of the Aligarh College— they acted as messengers between the Aligarh establishment and the British government. Having thus written to Archbold, Mohsin ul-Mulk requested other Muslim leaders to commence work on the memorial/representation to be submitted to the Viceroy. In the meantime, Archbold sent Mohsin ul-Mulk's letter to Minto, who, in turn, shared it with Morley. By 10 August 1906, Archbold had heard from Dunlop Smith, the private secretary to Minto, that the Viceroy had agreed to receive the Muslim deputation to hear its views. Archbold, accordingly, informed Mohsin ul-Mulk and even offered to help with the drafting of the memorial. The following were his suggestions on how the memorial to Minto must be framed:[146]

The formal letter should be sent with the signatures of some representatives Musalmans. The deputation should consist of the representatives of all provinces. The third point to be considered is the text of the address. I would here suggest that we begin with a solemn expression of loyalty. The Government decision to take a step in the direction of self-government should be appreciated. But our apprehension should be expressed that the principle of election, if introduced, would prove detrimental to the interest of Muslim minority. It should respectfully be suggested that nomination or representation by religion be introduced to meet Muslim opinion. We should also say that in a country like India, due weight must be given to the views of Zemindars.

Personally, I think it will be wise of the Muslims to support nomination, as the time of experiment with elections has not yet come. In elections it will be very difficult for Muslims to secure their due share. But in all these views, I must be in the background. They must come from you ... I can prepare for you the draft of the address or revise it. If it is prepared in Bombay, I can go through it, as you are aware, I know how to phrase these things in proper language.

Please remember that if we want to organize a powerful movement in the short time at our disposal, we must expedite matters.

The deep and critical role played by the Aligarh establishment, including its principals, in aiding (not creating) Muslim separatism and its application in the electoral context is crystal clear from the above extract. On 14 August 1906—i.e., forty-one years before the founding of Pakistan—Archbold sent another letter to Mohsin ul-Mulk attaching a draft of the memorial to be submitted to Minto by the Muslim deputation.[147] Two days later, on 16 August, in accordance with Morley's prior announcement in the House of Commons, Minto appointed a committee of his Executive Council to deliberate on the amendments to be made to the Indian Councils Act, specifically on increased representation of both princes and other native members on the Viceroy's Legislative Council as well as increased native representation in local governments.[148] Around this time, the anti-partition agitation was still raging, forcing Minto to comment that perhaps the agitation was not entirely politically motivated by Bengali Hindu leaders and had a certain degree of genuineness to it. He did also note that the Muslims of Eastern Bengal in particular seemed happy with the partition.[149] Interestingly, even at the height of the anti-partition agitation, the Moderate leaders of the Congress and the British establishment at the highest level enjoyed a comfortable relationship. This is discerned from the fact that Minto summoned Gokhale for a personal meeting to ask him to suspend the anti-partition agitation in view of the impending visit of the Prince and Princess of Wales to India. It appears that neither party was unhappy with the quality and outcome of the meeting.[150]

On 18 August 1906, in his reply to Archbold's letter of 14 August 1906, Mohsin ul-Mulk confirmed receiving a draft of the memorial to be submitted to Minto. Critically, he informed Archbold of the growing sentiment among Muslims for a full-time political organisation which could advance their interests before the British government. This was an expression of the organisational inadequacy of the Mohammedan Educational Conference established by Syed Ahmed Khan, because although it wielded significant influence over Muslims, it was seen more as a social institution for Muslim solidarity than as a full-fledged political body. This yearning, which led to the establishment of the All-India Muslim League within a few months of this correspondence, is captured in Mohsin's letter to Archbold:[151]

The Mohammedans have generally begun to think of organizing a political association and forming themselves into political agitators. Although it is impossible for Mohammedans, on account of their lack of ability and union and want of funds, to attain any success like Hindus, and they are likely to lose rather than gain by such a course, it is yet, impossible for anybody to stop them. The Mohammedans of Eastern Bengal have received a severe shock. I have got a letter from Nawab Syed Ali Chowdhury of Dacca which gives utterance to the extremely sorrowful feeling prevailing there.

These people generally say that the policy of Sir Syed and mine has done no good to Mohammedans. They say that Government has proved by its actions that without agitation there is no hope for any community and that if we can do nothing for them we must not hope to get any help for the College; in short Mohammedans generally will desert us because the policy of the College is detrimental to their interests.

My dear Archbold, nobody can say that the present state of Mohammedan feeling is without justification. The Liberal Government is at the bottom of it, and is responsible for it ... Is it right for the Government to allow an important section of the Indian population, which has always supported and even depended on Government to safeguard its interests, to be disappointed and get up a spirit of agitation like the Hindus? I only hope that the Government of India will do something to subside the growing Mohammedan feeling and remedy their hopelessness.

This extract shows that there was a significant meeting of interests, albeit for different reasons, between the British government and the Muslim leadership in Bharat. Both were deeply troubled and disturbed by the growing national movement for greater political autonomy, which was directly caused by the pressure exerted by the Extremist/Nationalist group within the Congress on the Moderates. No wonder both were trying to defuse and contain this development in their own ways—the British by offering legislative reforms as an olive branch, and the Muslims by agitating for the right to remain under the British *because* they did not want to be under a Hindu-majority democracy.

Shortly after the above-mentioned exchange between Archbold and Mohsin ul-Mulk, a draft memorial for Minto on behalf of Muslim leaders was prepared by Mohsin ul-Mulk, along with Imad ul-Mulk Syed Hussain Bilgrami, the private secretary to the Nizam of Hyderabad. The memorial was finalised at a meeting of Muslim leaders held in Lucknow on 15–16 September 1906.[152] Critically, apart from finalising the memorial, the setting up of an all-India Muslim organisation was discussed, and it was decided that the upcoming All-India Mohammedan Educational Conference at Dacca in December would be used to lay the foundation for such an organisation and also to draw up its constitution.[153] In fact, at this meeting in Lucknow, the name 'Muslim League' was proposed by Barrister Mian Mohamed Shafi and unanimously adopted. It was decided that the issue of its organisation would be taken up after the Simla Deputation.

On 1 October 1906, a deputation of thirty-five Muslim representatives headed by the Aga Khan was received by Minto in Simla, which would thenceforth be known as the Simla Deputation, which would alter the course of Bharatiya history. Six other representatives, including Nawab Salimullah of Dacca, were also supposed to be part of the Deputation but were held back due to illness and other reasons. The originally intended forty-one Muslim representatives had members from Bombay, Punjab, Lahore, Patna, Mymensingh, Calcutta, Madras, Sindh, the Central Provinces, Oudh (Awadh), the United Provinces, Hyderabad, Dacca, Surat and Hazara. Clearly, the forerunners of the Pakistan Movement were not limited to any particular part of Bharat, as is often claimed and projected.[154] The memorial submitted by the Simla Deputation must be read for its categorical assertion of the distinct nature of 'the Muslim Nation' ('qaum' as Syed Ahmed Khan called it), which formed the basis of the demand for separate and special treatment of Muslims. On a related note, I would strongly recommend for reading all three volumes of 'Foundations of Pakistan', *All India Muslim League Documents*, which contain most of the critical documents that capture the birth of Pakistan, from the memorial submitted by the Simla Deputation to Minto on 1 October 1906 to the proceedings of the All-India Muslim League of June 1947.

Interestingly, the 1906 memorial of the Simla Deputation was in many ways similar to an earlier memorial submitted on behalf of the Central National Mohammedan Association by Syed Ameer Ali to Lord Ripon on 6 February 1882, in the backdrop of the Hunter Report on Indian education. Pertinently, Syed Ameer Ali was a member of the Simla Deputation. It is no wonder that Dr Muhammad Yousuf Abbasi, citing the similarities between the 1882 and 1906 memorials, commented:[155]

> The Simla Deputation was not a prelude to separate Muslim representation, as is commonly supposed, but a climax of a political process which had begun to unfold during the momentous eighties of the 19th Century.

To showcase the continuum between the 1882 and 1906 memorials, I will extract portions from Ameer Ali's article titled *A Cry from the Indian Muslims*, published in August 1882 in *The Nineteenth Century* (which elaborated on his memorial to Ripon),[156] and the 1906 memorial. Here are a few pertinent extracts from Ameer Ali's article:

> The over-sensitiveness of the Indian Government and its subordinate officers to outside criticism has the tendency to discourage, among the intellectual and educated classes of India, the frank expression of political feelings, even when their publication is likely to prove of value to the Government itself. An honest criticism is often construed into a hostile attack; and outspoken comments on

the policy of the Government, however legitimate in their character, are not unfrequently supposed to imply disloyalty. In Bengal, however, the Hindu community is enabled, by the wealth and education of its representative members, to ignore to some extent this liability to disfavour, and to express its views on important questions affects its own interest with sufficient candour and emphasis to reach the ears of the governing classes. The Muslims possess neither the wealth nor the education of the Hindus; and in consequence, have generally failed to attract the attention of the authorities to their grievances.

I propose in this paper to point out what are the requirements and legitimate expectations of the Muslims of India, and to suggest in what way the benevolent intentions of Her Majesty's Government, for the amelioration of this large class of her subjects, may be best carried out. Unless effective measures of reform are adopted, and that without delay, the unsatisfactory condition of the Muslims threatens to become a source of anxiety and danger to British administration in India ... That a homogenous people like the Muslims of India, numbering fifty millions and having a common language and religion, should be discontented with the position they now occupy, is a matter for the serious consideration of the administrators of Indian policy.

... The present Lieutenant-Governor of Bengal, whose term of office, unfortunately for this province, is fast drawing to a close, has personally done much to improve the prospects of the Muslims. And within the last twenty years the Muslims themselves have made the most strenuous exertions to qualify themselves for competition with the Hindus under English rule. The fact, however, remains that with every avenue to public employment already jealously blocked by an antagonistic and versatile race, it is almost impossible for a Muslim candidate to obtain a footing in any Government office. In every walk of life, in every matter, whether it concerns the disposal of a post or the dispensing of state hospitality, the Hindu has obtained an influence which he will not willingly share with another. I make these remarks without the smallest animus against the Hindus, amongst whom I reckon many friends; but a sense of duty compels me to point out the disadvantageous circumstances under which the Muslims are found to labour. The independent professions form no exception to the rule, and are, for the most part, the monopoly of the Hindus. Forty years ago, the Muslim pleaders of the old Sadar Diwani Adalat formed by their wealth as well as by their number a most influential body of citizens. In 1881, out of a hundred or more pleaders practising in the High Court of Calcutta, only two are Muslims. Out of ninety-seven attorneys, only one is a Muslim. Excluding the higher medical officers who hold gazetted appointments, there are in Bengal about 200 assistant surgeons. Out of these, if my information be not incorrect, only four are Muslims. It is difficult to believe that the Government of Lord Ripon can be oblivious of the gravity of the danger involved in a continuance of this unfortunate situation.

I have thus far endeavoured to state briefly, without exaggeration and without bias, the chief grievances of the Muslims of India. I now propose to offer a few practical suggestions, from a Muslim standpoint, for the solution of the great Muslim problem. The unsatisfactory condition of the Muslims has already forced itself on the attention of Government. It is necessary, therefore, that the views of the Muslims themselves, as to the remedial measures essential for their well-being, should be plainly and publicly stated. The time for mere sentimental expressions of sympathy and infructuous minutes and resolutions, leading to nothing, has gone by. Effectual measures are needed; Words alone have no practical result. Government has for some time past expressed its sympathy for the Muslims, and the present Government is notably animated with a sincere desire to redress their wrongs and grievances. The Viceroy's reply to a recent address of the National Muhammadan Association lays special stress upon his desire to deal with all her Majesty's subjects on a footing of equality. Inspite of all this, the condition of the Muslims, instead of improving, has within the last decade become worse. This, no doubt, arises from the fact that the same desire to deal equitably with the Muslims is not shared by the officers who really hold the threads of government in their hands.

The first and foremost condition necessary for the prosperity of the Muslims is that the balance of state patronage between them and the Hindus should be restored. This however, cannot be achieved unless the officers with whom rest the actual distribution and dispensation of it lend their zealous support to the efforts of Government. Under the Treaty of 1765 the Muslims are fairly entitled to ask for greater consideration at the hands of the British than latterly been shown to them, though perhaps it would be unreasonable of them to expect any such preponderating influence under the English Government as they possessed under their own sovereigns. But this is not, as Dr. Hunter in eloquent terms has pointed out, their petition and their complaint. 'It is not that they have ceased to retain the entire state patronage, but that they are gradually being excluded from it altogether. It is not that they must now take an equal chance with the Hindus in the race of life, but that, at least in Bengal, they have ceased to have a chance at all.' Under their own government the Muslims possessed several avenues to wealth and power. The army and police were officered by them; the administration of justice and the collection of the Imperial revenues were largely monopolised by Muslims. The department of education was exclusively in their hands. Long before the great Hindu Chancellor, Todar Mal, had introduced Persian into the subordinate departments, the Hindus had begun to learn the language of their masters with as much zeal as they now learn the English. Even towards the close of their empire, the Muslims represented the intellectual power of the land. Their system of education was 'infinitely superior to any other system of education then existing in India.' It was a reflex of the system which had been in vogue at Cordova and Baghdad, and which had enabled their ancestors to hold aloft the torch of knowledge, while all around them was lost in darkness. Their polish and their civilisation were by no means inferior to that of the Western nations, and their intellectual supremacy was as undisputed as their material power.

Dr. Hunter remarks that 'during the first seventy-five years of our rule, we continued to make use of this (the Muslim system of education) as a means for producing officers to carry out our administration. But meanwhile we had introduced a scheme of public instruction of our own; and as soon as it trained up a generation of men on the new plan, we flung aside the old Muslim system, and the Muslim youth found every avenue of public life closed in their faces.' 'Had the Muslims been wise,' continues Dr. Hunter, 'they would have perceived the change and accepted their fate.' But they were not wise; they felt secure in a fool's paradise, and thus, when the old system was suddenly abolished, they either could not divest themselves of the traditions of their nobler days, or could not accustom themselves easily to the new order of things. They soon found themselves supplanted by men who had been specially trained according to the new method. The Muslims have simply been 'crowded off', to use an expressive Americanism, from the public service and the independent professions. The entire government of the country, so far as it affects the natives of India, is virtually in the hands of the Hindus. Their influence is all-powerful in every department of State, and that influence is almost invariably exercised to exclude the Muslims, whom they regard as aliens, from their proper and legitimate share in official preferment. ... will not be contended by the warmest advocate of the Hindu, that he is intellectually superior to, or possesses more stamina than the Muslim. The truth is, that for the last fifty years the Muslims have been, and still are, most grievously handicapped.

The time has arrived when Government should insist upon all its officers giving loyal effect to the order recently passed, for the more extended employment of the Muslims in the service of the State. In the gazetted appointments also the present disproportion between Hindus and Muslims should be removed. Appointments to the subordinate judicial service are made, I understand, on the recommendation of the High Court, but for some reason the claims of the Muslims to a fair share of the patronage of the High Court have, for some years past, been so overlooked, that at the present moment the disproportion between Hindus and Muslims is probably greater in the subordinate judicial than in any other branch of the public service. The judicial service of the future must, from the necessity of things, be largely officered by the natives of India. Stamina and strength of character are as much needed in these offices as versatility and finesse. Few can doubt that a larger introduction of the Muslim element into the judicial service will add strength to the administration of the country.

It may seem strange to English readers that I lay so much stress upon State employment as the keystone of Muslim prosperity. It will be said, not without reason, that this inordinate dependence upon extraneous support betrays a weakness in the national character. It must not be forgotten, however, that a race of conquerors, who not more than a hundred years ago possessed a monopoly of power and wealth, has not yet developed commercial and trading instincts. Half a century's degradation has deadened all spirits of enterprise among the Muslims, and the absence of capital is another stumbling-block in their path to commercial success.

In the next place, I would suggest the withdrawal of the order substituting the Nagri character for the Persian in the Bihar courts. The change was not wanted for the well-being of the people, and appears to have been made upon insufficient data. It has irritated and alarmed the Muslims without satisfying the Hindus. The greater part of the Hindus in the province of Bihar are, in their manners, their customs, and their modes [of] amusement, Muslims. Their polish and their culture are derived from the Muslims. They pride themselves upon speaking pure Urdu. It may be said, without much fear of contradiction, that the change in question has proved vexatious to all the educated classes in Bihar.

In a nutshell, Ameer Ali proceeded to recount how the advent of the British had resulted in loss of wealth, position and power for Muslims in India. He underscored the benefits accrued to Hindus as a consequence of their English education through better representation in government jobs, including in the judiciary. Ameer Ali also aired his grievance with respect to the replacement of the Urdu script with Devanagari in 1872, which he saw as an onslaught on Urdu by the British establishment. Critically, he treated Hindus and Muslims as two distinct races, reflecting his belief in Syed Ahmed Khan's Two-Nation Theory. The memorial of the Simla Deputation in October 1906 was on similar lines. Here are a few sample extracts that portended what was to come:[57]

May it please Your Excellency,—Availing ourselves of the permission accorded to us, we, the undersigned nobles, jagirdars, talukdars, lawyers, zemindars, merchants and others, representing a large body of Mohammedan subjects of His Majesty the King Emperor in different parts of India, beg most respectfully to approach Your Excellency with the following address for your favourable consideration ...

1. ...

2. ...

3. One of the most important characteristics of British policy in India is the increasing deference that has, so far as possible, been paid from the first to the views and wishes of the people of the country in matters affecting their interests, with due regard always to the diversity of race and religion, which forms such an important feature of all Indian problems.

4. Beginning with the confidential and unobtrusive method of consulting influential members of important communities in different parts of the country, this principle was gradually extended by the recognition of the right of recognized political or commercial organisations to communicate to the authorities their criticisms and views on measures of public importance; and, finally, by the nomination and election of direct representatives of the people in Municipalities, District Boards, and—above all—in the Legislative Chambers of the country. This last element is, we understand, about to be dealt with by the Committee appointed by Your Excellency, with the view of giving it further extension; and it is with reference mainly to our claim to a fair share in such extended representation and some other matters of importance affecting the interests of our community that we have ventured to approach Your Excellency on the present occasion.

5. The Mohammedans of India number, according to the census taken in the year 1901, over sixty-two millions, or between one-fifth and one-fourth of the total population of His Majesty's Indian dominions; and if a reduction be made for the uncivilised portions of the community enumerated under the heads of animists and other minor religions, as well as for those classes who are ordinarily classified as Hindus, but, properly speaking, are not Hindus at all, the proportion of Mohammedans to the Hindu majority becomes much larger. We therefore desire to submit that under any system of representation, extended or limited, a community in itself more numerous than the entire population of any first class European power, except Russia, may justly lay claim to adequate recognition as an important factor in the State. We venture, indeed, with Your Excellency's permission, to go a step further, and urge that the position accorded to the Mohammedan community in any kind or representation, direct or indirect, and in all other ways, affecting their status and influence, should be commensurate not merely with their numerical strength, but also with their political importance, and the value of the contribution which they make to the defence of the Empire; and we also hope that Your Excellency will, in this connection, be pleased to give due consideration to the position which they occupied in India a little more than a hundred years ago, and of which the traditions have naturally not faded from their minds.

6. The Mohammedans of India have always placed implicit reliance on the sense of justice and love of fair dealing that have characterised their rulers, and have, in consequence, abstained from pressing their claims by methods that might prove at all embarrassing; but earnestly as we desire that the Mohammedans of India should not in the future depart from that excellent and time-honoured tradition, recent events have stirred up feelings, especially among the younger generation of Mohammedans, which might in certain circumstances and under certain contingencies, easily pass beyond the control of temperate counsel and sober guidance.

7. We, therefore, pray that the representations we herewith venture to submit, after a careful consideration of the views and wishes of a large number of our co-religionists in all parts of India, may be favoured with Your Excellency's earnest attention.

8. We hope Your Excellency will pardon our stating at the outset that representative institution of the European type are new to the Indian people. Many of the most thoughtful members of our community, in fact, consider that the greatest care, forethought, and caution will be necessary if they are to be successfully adapted to the social, religious, and political conditions obtaining in India; and that, in the absence of such care and caution, their adoption is likely, among other evils, to place our national interests at the mercy of an unsympathetic majority.

    Since, however, our rulers have, in pursuance of the immemorial instincts and traditions, found it expedient to give these institutions an increasingly important place in the government of the country, we Mohammedans cannot any longer, in justice to our own national interests, hold aloof from participating in the conditions to which their policy has given rise. While, therefore, we are bound to acknowledge with gratitude that such representation as the Mohammedans of India have hitherto enjoyed has been due to a sense of justice and fairness on the part of Your Excellency and your illustrious predecessors in office, and the Heads of Local Governments by whom the Mohammedan members of the Legislative Chambers have, almost without exception, been nominated, we cannot help observing that the representation thus accorded to us has necessarily been inadequate to our requirements, and has not always carried with it the approval of those whom the nominees were selected to represent. This state of things was probably, under existing circumstances unavoidable; for while on the one hand, the number of nominations reserved to the Viceroy and Local Governments has necessarily been strictly limited, the selection, on the other hand, of really representative men has, in the absence of any reliable method of ascertaining the direction of popular choice, been far from easy. As for the results of election, it is most unlikely that the name of any Mohammedan candidate will be submitted for the approval of Government by the electoral bodies as now constituted, unless he is in sympathy with the majority in all matters of importance. Nor can we, in fairness find fault with the desire of our non-Moslim fellow-subjects to take full advantage of their strength and vote only for members of their own community, or for persons who, if not Hindus, are expected to vote with the Hindu majority, on whose good-will they have to depend for their future re-election.

    It is true that we have many and important interests in common with our Hindu fellow-countrymen, and it will always be a matter of the utmost satisfaction to us to see these interests safeguarded by the presence, in our

Legislative Chambers, of able supporters of these interests irrespective of their nationality. Still it cannot be denied that we Mohammedans are a distinct community with additional interests of our own, which are not shared by other communities, and these have hitherto suffered from the fact that they have not been adequately represented. Even in the provinces in which the Mohammedans constitute a distinct majority of the population, they have too often been treated as though they were inappreciably small political factors that might, without unfairness, be neglected. This has been the case, to some extent, in the Punjab; but in a more marked degree in Sind and in Eastern Bengal.

9. Before formulating our views with regard to the election of representatives, we beg to observe that the political importance of a community to a considerable extent gains strength or suffers detriment, according to the position that the members of that community occupy in the service of the State. If, as is unfortunately the case with the Mohammedans, they are not adequately represented in this manner, they lose in the prestige and influence which are justly their due. We, therefore, pray that Government will be graciously pleased to provide that, both in the gazetted and the subordinate and ministerial services in all Indian provinces, a due proportion of Mohammedans shall always find place. Orders of like import have, at times, been issued by Local Governments in some provinces, but have not unfortunately, in all cases, been strictly observed, on the ground that qualified Mohammedans were not forthcoming. This allegation, however well-founded it may have been at one time, is, we submit, no longer tenable now; and wherever the will to employ them is not wanting, the supply of qualified Mohammedans has increased, a tendency is unfortunately perceptible to reject them on the ground of relatively superior qualifications having to be given precedence. This introduces something like the competitive element in its worst form, and we may be permitted to draw Your Excellency's attention to the political significance of the monopoly of all official influence by one class. We may also point out in this connection that the efforts of Mohammedan educationists have, from the very outset of the educational movement among them, been strenuously directed towards the development of character, and this, we venture to think, is of greater importance than mere mental alertness in the making of a good public servant.

10. We venture to submit that the generality of Mohammedans in all parts of India feel aggrieved that Mohammedan Judges are not more frequently appointed to the High Courts and Chief Courts of Judicature. Since the creation of these Courts, only three Mohammedan lawyers have held these honourable appointments, all of whom have full justified their elevation to the Bench. At the present moment there is not a single Mohammedan Judge sitting on the Bench of any of these Courts, while there are three

Hindu Judges in the Calcutta High Court, where the proportion of Mohammedans in the population is very large; and two in the Chief Court of the Punjab, where the Mohammedans form the majority of the population. It is not therefore an extravagant request on our part that a Mohammedan should be given a seat on the Bench of each of the High Courts and Chief Courts. Qualified Mohammedan lawyers eligible for these appointments can always be found, if not in one province then in another. We beg permission further to submit that the presence on the Bench of these Courts of a Judge, learned in Mohammedan law, will be a source of considerable strength to the administration of justice.

11. As Municipal and District Boards have to deal with important local interests, affecting to a great extent the health, comfort, educational needs, and even the religious concerns of the inhabitants, we shall, we hope, be pardoned if we solicit, for a moment, Your Excellency's attention to the position of Mohammedans thereon before passing to higher concerns. These institutions form, as it were, the initial rungs in the ladder of self-government, and it is here that the principle of representation is brought home intimately to the intelligence of the people. Yet the position of Mohammedans on these Boards is not at present regulated by any guiding principle capable of general application, and practice varies in different localities. The Aligarh Municipality, for example, is divided into six wards, and each ward returns one Hindu and one Mohammedan Commissioner; and the same principle we understand, is adopted in a number of Municipalities in the Punjab and elsewhere, but in a good many places the Moham...   -payers are not adequately represented. We would, therefore, respectfully suggest that local authority should, in every case, be required to declare the number of Hindus and Mohammedans entitled to seats on Municipal and District Boards, such proportion to be determined in accordance with the numerical strength, social status, influence, and special requirements of either community. Once their relative proportion is authoritatively determined, we would suggest that either community should be allowed severally to return their own representatives, as in the practice in many towns in the Punjab.

12. We now also suggest that the senates and syndicates of Indian Universities might be similarly dealt with: that is to say, there should so far as possible, be an authoritative declaration of the proportion in which Mohammedans are entitled to be represented in either body.

13. We now proceed to the consideration of the question of our representation in the Legislative Chambers of the country. Beginning with the Provincial Councils, we would most respectfully suggest that, as in the case of Municipalities and District Boards, the proportion of Mohammedan representatives entitled to a seat should be determined and declared with due regard to the important considerations which we have ventured

to point out in paragraph 5 of this address; and that the important Mohammedan landowners, lawyers, merchants, and representatives of other important interests, the Mohammedan members of District Boards and Municipalities, and the Mohammedan graduates of Universities, of a certain standing, say 5 years, should be formed into electoral college, and be authorised, in accordance with such rules of procedures as Your Excellency's Government may be pleased to prescribe in that behalf, to return the number of members that may be declared to be eligible.

14. With regard to the Imperial Legislative Council, whereon the due representation of Mohammedan interests is a matter of vital importance, we crave leave to suggest:

    (a) That, in the cadre of the Council, the proportion of Mohammedan representatives should not be determined on the basis of the numerical strength of the community, and that, in any case, the Mohammedan representatives should never be an ineffective minority.

    (b) That, as far as possible, appointment by election should be given preference over nomination.

    (c) That, for purposes of choosing Mohammedan members, Mohammedan landowners, lawyers, merchants, and representatives of other important interests of a status to be subsequently determined by Your Excellency's Government, Mohammedan members of the Provincial Councils and Mohammedan Fellows of Universities should be invested with electoral powers to be exercised in accordance with such procedure as may be prescribed by Your Excellency's Government in that behalf.

15. An impression has lately been gaining ground that one or more Indian Members may be appointed on the Executive Council of the Viceroy. In the event of such appointments being made, we beg the claims of Mohammedans in that connection may not be overlooked. More than one Mohammedan, we venture to say, will be found in the country fit to serve with distinction in that august chamber.

16. We beg to approach Your Excellency on a subject which most closely affects our national welfare. We are convinced that our aspirations as a community and our future progress are largely dependent on the foundation of a Mohammedan University, which will be the centre of our religious and intellectual life. We therefore most respectfully pray that Your Excellency will take steps to help us in an undertaking in which our community is so deeply interested.

17. In conclusion, we beg to assure Your Excellency that, in assisting the Mohammedan subjects of His Majesty, at this stage in the development of Indian affairs, in the directions indicated in the present address, Your Excellency will be strengthening the basis of their unswerving loyalty to

the Throne and laying the foundation of their political advancement and national prosperity, and Your Excellency's name will be remembered with gratitude by their posterity for generations to come; and we feel confident that Your Excellency will be gracious enough to give due consideration to our prayers.

Upon receipt of the memorial, Minto replied to it by assuring the members of the Deputation of British appreciation of Muslim loyalty and promised them the protection of Muslim interests. He also agreed with the principle of communal representation proposed by the Deputation in its memorial. Extracted below are the relevant portions of Minto's reply:[158]

But, Gentlemen, you go on to tell me that sincere as your belief is in the justice and fair dealing of your rulers and unwilling as you are to embarrass them at the present moment, you cannot but be aware that 'recent events' have stirred up feelings amongst the younger generation of Mohammedans which might 'pass beyond the control of temperate counsel and sober guidance'. Now I have no intention of entering into any discussion upon the affairs of Eastern Bengal and Assam, yet I hope that, without offence to anyone, I may thank the Mohammedan community of the new provinces for the moderation and self-restraint they have shown under conditions which were new to them, and as to which there has been inevitably much misunderstanding, and that I may at the same time sympathize with all that is sincere in Bengali sentiment. But above all, what I would ask you to believe is that the course the Viceroy and the Government of India have pursued in connection with the affairs of the new Province, the future of which is now assured, has been dictated solely by a regard for what has appeared best for its present and future populations as a whole, irrespective of race or creed; and that the Mohammedan community of Eastern Bengal and Assam can rely as firmly as ever on British justice and fair-play for the appreciation of its loyalty and the safeguarding of its interests.

You have addressed me, Gentlemen, at a time when the political atmosphere is full of change. We all feel it. It would be foolish to attempt to deny its existence. Hopes and ambitions new to India are making themselves felt. We cannot ignore them. We should be wrong to wish to do so. But to what is all this unrest due? Not to the discontent of misgoverned millions, I defy anyone honestly to assert that; not to any uprising of a disaffected people; it is due to that educational growth in which only a very small portion of the population has as yet shared, of which British rule first sowed the seed, and the fruits of which British rule is now doing its best to foster and to direct. There may be many tares in the harvest we are now reaping; the Western grain which we have sown may not be entirely suitable to the requirements of the people of India, but the educational harvest will increase as years go on, and the healthiness of the nourishment it gives will depend on the careful administration and distribution of its products.

You need not ask my pardon, Gentlemen, for telling me that 'representative institutions of the European type are entirely new to the people of India', or that their introduction here requires the most earnest thought and care. I should be very far from welcoming all the political machinery of the Western world amongst the hereditary instincts and traditions of Eastern races. Western breadth of thought, the teachings of Western civilisation, the freedom of British individuality can do much for the people of India. But I recognise with you that they must not carry with them an impracticable insistence on the acceptance of political methods.

And now, Gentlemen, I come to your own position in respect to the political future—the position of the Mohammedan community for whom you speak.

You will, I feel sure, recognise that it is impossible for me to follow you through any detailed consideration of the conditions and the share that community has a right to claim in the administration of public affairs. I can at present only deal with generalities. The points which you have raised are before the Committee which, as you know, I have lately appointed to consider the question of representation, and I will take care that your address is submitted to them. But at the same time I hope I may be able to reply to the general tenor of your remarks without in any way forestalling the Committee's report.

The pitch of your address, as I understand it, is a claim that, in any system of representation, whether it affects a Municipality, a District Board, or a Legislative Council, in which it is proposed to introduce or increase an electoral organisation, the Mohammedan community should be represented as a community. You point out that in many cases electoral bodies as now constituted cannot be expected to return a Mohammedan candidate, and that, if by chance they did so, it could only be at the sacrifice of such a candidate's views to those of a majority opposed to his own community, whom he would in no way represent, and you justly claim that your position should be estimated not merely on your numerical strength, but in respect to the political importance of your community and the service it has rendered to the Empire. I am entirely in accord with you. Please do not misunderstand me; I make no attempt to indicate by what means the representation of communities can be obtained, but I am as firmly convinced as I believe you to be, that any electoral representation in India would be doomed to mischievous failure which aimed at granting a personal enfranchisement regardless of the beliefs and traditions of the communities composing the population of this continent. The great mass of the people of India have no knowledge of representative institutions, I agree with you, Gentlemen, that the initial rungs in the ladder of self-government are to be found in the Municipal and District Boards, and that it is in that direction that we must look for the gradual political education of the people. In the meantime I can only say to you that the Mohammedan community may rest assured that their political rights and interests as a community will be safeguarded in any administrative reorganisation with which I am concerned, and that you and the people of India may rely upon the British Raj to respect, as it has been its pride to do, the religious beliefs and the national traditions of the myriads composing the population of His Majesty's Indian Empire.

From a reading of the memorial of the Simla Deputation and Minto's reply, it becomes evident that Muslim separatism/the Two-Nation Theory had been spelt out in the clearest of terms possible and that its validity had been accepted by the British government in India at the highest levels. Not only was it here to stay, it had also entered legal and constitutional thought in a manner that could no longer be ignored. It bears noting and reiterating that while Archbold did help to put together the memorial for the Deputation, the fact of the matter was that Muslim separatism and its political aspirations were *not* his making; he was merely instrumental in enabling its articulation on behalf of its proponents.[159] That this helped the divide and rule policy of the British as well does not take away from the fact that the sentiment had roots which *preceded* the advent of the British. In light of this, the Congress's subsequent denunciation of the Deputation as the handiwork of the British, of which Archbold was supposedly the orchestrator, was baseless, and resulted from its inability to accept the independent reality of Muslim separatism. M.S. Jain, who has written extensively on the Aligarh Movement and its contribution to the Pakistan Movement, had the following to say on the Deputation and its antecedents:[160]

Therefore, both the factors—the desire of the Muslims to have a separate political existence and the willingness of the British government to accept them as stooges—were responsible for the deputation of 1906. The British were willing to take the Muhammadans into their fold, since they felt the necessity of a pawn on the chess-board of Indian politics. But we must remember that Muslims in India had been holding out the prospect of being used as anti-national forces since 1870. The Muslims' desire to get their special claims recognized in the coming constitutional reforms in India, to carve out a separate political existence for themselves, to get their historical role in India recognized by the British government, and their 'insatiable' hunger of not remaining content with the share which would fall to their lot on the basis of population and educational advancement and ability were responsible for the Simla deputation of 1906. Minto's biographer clearly says that the Muslim leaders decided 'to seek an interview with the Viceroy and state their grievances.' And if we bear in mind the memorandum drafted by the Muhammadan Defence Association enumerating the Muhammadan demands in 1896, we would find that there was no material difference between the demands of 1896 and 1906.

The question of the Simla deputation having been a 'Command Performance', initiated at the manipulations of the British Indian government, needs a careful examination. There have been writers, both contemporary as well as later, who have believed in or challenged the theory of British manipulation of this deputation. The private papers of Lord Minto throw a flood of light on the whole question, and now it may be safely asserted that the British government had no hand in the whole scheme of the Simla deputation except that it agreed to welcome and receive it.

Clearly, there was a continuity of thought between Ameer Ali's memorial of 1882, the Muhammadan Defence Association's memorial of 1896 and the Simla Deputation's memorial of 1906. It could, therefore, be said that the facts and circumstances that led to the Partition of Bengal and the deliberate creation of a Muslim-majority province indicate conducive atmospherics for a sympathetic hearing of the long-pending Muslim demands by the British. The effect of this sympathetic hearing and the British assurances of appreciation for loyalty was that the members of the Deputation quickly went about discussing the subject of the 'Muslim League'. Within days of the Deputation, the Aga Khan, who had led the Deputation, suggested it convert itself into a permanent Mohammedan Committee that would see through the work initiated by the Deputation.[161]

The other effect of the assurances of the Viceroy to the Simla Deputation was that the Muhammadan Defence Association of Calcutta encouraged members of the Muslim community to celebrate 16 October, the date of the Partition of Bengal, as a day of rejoicing while the Hindus mourned. To express solidarity with the Muslim organisations of Bengal, similar appeals were made by organisations in Assam, such as Anjuman-i-Islamia of Silchar and the provincial Muhammadan Association of Eastern Bengal and Assam. The official position of these organisations was that '*any kind of agitation against the Government is against the canons of Islam*'.[162] By November 1906, Syed Ameer Ali, who had been advocating the need for a Muslim political party ever since he founded the Central National Mohammedan Association, wrote an article saying that while the Hindus had powerful institutions to safeguard their rights and privileges, Muslims had none.[163] In the very same month, Nawab Salimullah, who could not participate in the Simla Deputation, floated a ten-point proposal for an All-India Muslim Confederacy. This contained the most proximal seed for the All-India Muslim League. Here are the relevant extracts from Salimullah's proposal:[164]

1. This day being the birthday of His Majesty our most gracious King Emperor, I think it an auspicious occasion for me to-day to place before my Mohammedan brethren my views on the project of our Muslim All-India Confederacy.

2. Owing to my inability to attend the All-India Mohammedan Deputation to His Excellency the Viceroy at Simla, I penned a few notes for the information of my brother delegates on the advisability of forming a Central Mohammedan Association for all India, which could bring into touch the aims and aspirations of our community throughout the country.

3. These notes were, I learnt, discussed at an informal meeting of those present at Simla and it was proposed, without coming to any definite resolution, that the matter should be finally settled at the All-India Mohammedan Educational Conference at Dacca during the Christmas week next December, and in the meantime the scheme, as drafted, may be submitted for discussions to all our various Mohammedan associations and societies, as well as to those pre-eminent amongst our co-religionists, for their collective and individual opinion and advice.

7. The Necessity of a Central Association: To the majority of my countrymen, I believe, the necessity of a central association is fully established; the key-note of it was struck by our All-India Deputation to the Viceroy where in the address we have stated as follows: Still it cannot be denied that we Mohammedans are a distinct community with additional interests of our own, which are not shared by the other communities, and these have suffered from the fact that they have not been adequately represented.

And it is hardly possible that these additional interests, peculiarly our own, can be safeguarded and protected unless there is a central authority to which the Government can look for aid and advice, and it would not be out of place to quote here the remarks of the *Times of India*. In its article on the Mohammedan Deputation to the Viceroy it states, 'it may be hoped that one result of the unity of feelings thus aroused amongst Muslims will be that they will be able to express, from time to time, as occasion requires, the views of the community which is in many respects distinct, with, as the Memorial said, additional interests of its own which are not shared by any other community.' The *Times of India* foreshadows what is really being felt by thoughtful members of our community: that the authorities are getting bewildered owing to the multiplicity of Muslim associations now coming into existence, and our young men, in various parts of the country, assuming to speak on behalf of the whole Muslim community of India, and on many occasions, which I need not here mention, in direct opposition and conflict to each other. I am aware of several instances wherein untold mischief has occurred through irresponsible Mohammedan gentlemen, and associations sprung up and were created by some (who really at heart have no regard for our community) for the sole purpose of establishing their own political importance, addressing Government and the public, without anyone to question their right to do so ... Of course Government cannot refuse to receive any representation from any corporate body or individual, however distinguished or undistinguished they or he may be, yet such representation fails to carry weight owing to the authorities not knowing how far the views contained therein are consonant with the views of the Muslim community as a whole. And even when such views are adopted by the authorities, they fail in receiving respectful concurrence from the Muslims in general, as being the views of only some particular associations or individuals, and more or less misleading, thereby causing much harm to the Muslim community as a whole. Hence if there were an All-India association of the kind I propose, Government will be able to refer to it all such representations as may be received by the authorities, to ascertain the views of the community in general before finally passing orders thereon; and there will then be no danger of any party or parties misrepresenting the facts to serve individual interests.

8. The Aims and Objects of the Association: It is absolutely necessary that the aims and objects of the Association should be definitely stated; and although I am sure I shall not receive any hearty support from some of my co-religionists, yet I for one honestly believe that the time has come when, if the Association is to be a force and power for good, it must at the very outset lay down its policy and object and I would do so as follows:

That the sole object and purpose of the Association shall be, whenever possible, to support all measures emanating from the Government and to protect the cause and advancement of the interest of our co-religionists throughout the country.

9. How this is to be done I show below:

Name: A suitable name is one of the greatest desiderata of an institution such as we contemplate, and after a careful consideration of several appellations, I think, The Mohammedan All-India Confederacy would suit us best, as the Association would be the mouth-piece of all the various Muslim institutions, social, religious and political, as well as of the leading men throughout the country, who will have allied themselves together for the one common object of protecting the interests and advancing the cause of their co-religionists.

The Object or Raison d'être:

(a) To controvert the growing influence of the so-called Indian National Congress, which has a tendency to misinterpret and subvert the British Rule in India, or which may lead to that deplorable situation, and

(b) to enable our young men of education, who, for want of such an association, have joined the Congress Camp, to find scope to exercise their fitness and ability for public life.

10. From the trend of the discussion at Simla, there is, I believe, some disinclination to state our object and reason in this bold and blunt manner,

as it will, it is contended, arouse the ire and anger of our Hindu brethren. But I think that time has come when we must no longer mind matters ... we must not stand upon sentiment—it is mere sentiment that is causing such havoc and misery in the present partition of Bengal. And the question that we, the Mohammedans, must honestly discuss and decide is whether the policy now openly declared by those who are termed 'extremists' is one conducive to the maintenance of the British Raj; and if, as we must hold, it is not, we must then consider whether those gentlemen forming the 'Extremist Party' do or do not form part and parcel of the Indian National Congress, and unless the Congress is an open and public assembly, and by a resolution disassociates itself from the views of this party, we Mohammedans cannot countenance or be associated with the Congress. We are sorry, but cannot deny that the so-called Indian National Congress has become a potent voice in the counsels of the country. We must therefore, as true and loyal subjects of the British Raj, do our utmost to controvert and thwart that influence which it has attained, when we find it working for the destruction of all that we hold dear ... There is no doubt that many of our young educated Mohammedans find themselves shoved off the line of official preferment and promotion, unless they join, or at least show sympathy with, the Congress Party. All our Mohammedan newspapers are full of the cry that there is now-a-days not the same dearth of Mohammedan graduates and under-graduates as before, but they are passed over (in fact this was pointedly alluded to in the All-India address to the Viceroy) on the ground that they do not come up 'to the Government standard of efficiency'. The Executive Committee of the Confederacy will be in constant communication with all the local associations, and will watch the career of our promising young men, who will no longer look to the Congress for their advancement in life.

What is most interesting to note in Salimullah's proposal is his expression of concern about the growing clout of the Extremists/Nationalists within the Congress and the threat posed by their views and actions to the stability of British rule in Bharat. Clearly, the colonial establishment needed the Moderates and the Muslims to keep the Extremists in check, and the Muslims needed the Moderates and the British to keep the Extremists in check. In other words, a confident and assertive form of nationalism, as represented by the Extremists, which was based on the civilisational ethos of Bharat, was unacceptable to the Moderates in the Congress, the British establishment and the Muslims. As long as the native consciousness surrenders or abandons or forgets its right to reclaim its civilisational roots, all is well. However, any attempt to revive or retain civilisational memory must necessarily be branded and treated as 'extremism', since it threatens to expose and resist the conduct of expansionist colonialities, both European and Middle Eastern. Is the situation that meets the eye in the present materially different? I leave it to the readers to draw their own conclusions.

The concern expressed by Salimullah on the growing clout of the Extremists is attributable to the fact that by 1906 the popularity of the Extremists/Nationalists had grown so much that the Moderates feared capture of the Congress by them under the leadership of Tilak. To prevent this, the Moderates, through Banerjea, invited the 'Grand Old Man of India', Dadabhai Naoroji, all the way from England to preside over the 1906 session in Calcutta (the twenty-second session of the Congress) in the hope that his seniority, personal influence and stature would deter the Extremists.[165,166] The 1906 session saw the highest attendance since the Bombay session of 1889, and the speeches delivered by Naoroji, Tilak, Pal and Ghosh laid bare their stark and irreconcilable differences. Naoroji reiterated that the Congress's goal was self-government within the British empire, which was the meaning of Swaraj, according to him. He said:[167]

> I say we are British citizens and are entitled to and claim all British citizens' rights ... This birthright to be 'free' or to have freedom is our right from the very beginning of our connection with England when we came under the British flag. When Bombay was acquired as the very first territorial possession, the government of the day in the very first grant of territorial rights to the East India Company [March 24, 1669] declared thus: 'And it is declared that all persons being His Majesty's subjects inhabiting within the said Island and their children and their posterity born within the limits thereof shall be deemed free denizens and natural subjects as if living and born in England.'

The following resolution was passed on self-government:[168]

> 'that the system of Government obtaining in the self-governing British Colonies should be extended to India' and urged the immediate adoption of certain reforms as 'steps leading to it.'

Naturally, the Nationalists ran out of patience owing to the ambiguity imputed to 'Swaraj' by the Moderates. To make matters worse, the Moderates opposed the demand of the Extremists to extend endorsement of the Boycott Movement outside Bengal too, which led to the following feeble resolution on the matter:[169]

> Having regard to the fact that the people of this country have little or no voice in its administration and that their representation to the Government do [sic] not receive due consideration, this Congress is of opinion that the Boycott Movement inaugurated in Bengal by way of protest against the partition of that province, was and is legitimate.

In stark contrast, the following resolution was passed endorsing the Swadeshi Movement:

This Congress accords its most cordial support to the Swadeshi movement and calls upon the people of the country to labour for its success by making earnest and sustained efforts to promote the growth of indigenous industries and to stimulate the production of indigenous articles by giving them preference over imported commodities, even at some sacrifice.

Bipin Chandra Pal, who voiced his displeasure on behalf of the Extremists, clearly disagreed with the soft-pedalling of the Moderates on the question of extending the Boycott to provinces outside Bengal and strongly advocated the use of Boycott as a permanent weapon against the British establishment. Gokhale objected to this and said that those who wished to operate beyond the resolutions of the Congress were welcome to do so without doing it in the name of the Congress. The endeavour to attempt a patch-up between the two factions by inviting Naoroji to preside over the session proved to be an utter failure, with the fissures only deepening in full public glare.[170] Interestingly, there was no significant discussion at the Calcutta session on the Simla Deputation or the Viceroy's communal assurances to the Deputation, which ought to have occupied the attention of the Congress.[171] The delusional attitude of the Moderate-led Congress is evident from the fact that Nawab Salimullah's scheme for an All-India Muslim Confederacy was laughed at. The fact that a mere forty-five of the 1,663 delegates at the Calcutta session were Muslim failed to awaken the Congress to the reality of Muslim political separatism. On the contrary, Naoroji quoted Syed Ahmed Khan and called him a 'nationalist to the bone', in an attempt to court Muslims.[172]

In December 1906, around the same time as the Calcutta session of the Congress, the annual All-India Mohammedan Educational Conference was organised at Dacca on 30 December 1906. It was presided over by Viqar-ul-Mulk, and Nawab Salimullah moved the motion for formation of the All-India Muslim League, which was accepted. The League was formed to achieve the following objects:[173]

1. to promote among the Musalmans of India, feelings of loyalty to the British Government, and to remove any misconception that may arise as to the intention of the Government with regard to any of its measures;
2. to protect and advance the political rights and interests of the Musalmans of India, and to respectfully represent their needs and aspiration to the Government;
3. to prevent the rise, among the Musalmans of India, of any feeling of hostility towards other communities, without prejudice to the other aforementioned objects of the League.

Ironically, despite its stated object of preventing the rise of any feeling of hostility towards other communities, within three months of the founding of the League, riots broke out in Comilla and Jamalpur. R.C. Majumdar attributed these riots to, among other reasons, the infamous *Lal Ishtehaar* or Red Pamphlet, which was circulated in Dacca when the League was founded. The author of the pamphlet was revealed to be one Ibrahim Khan.[174] Here are a few extracts from it:[175]

> The Hindus, by various stratagems, are relieving the Mahomedans of nearly the whole of the money earned by them.
>
> Among the causes of the degradation of Mahomedans is their association with the Hindus.
>
> Among the means to be adopted for the amelioration of Mahomedans, is boycotting Hindus.
>
> Ye Musalmans arise, awake! Do not read in the same schools with Hindus. Do not buy anything from a Hindu shop. Do not touch any article manufactured by Hindu hands. Do not give employment to a Hindu. Do not accept any degrading office under a Hindu. You are ignorant, but if you acquire knowledge you can at once send all Hindus to jehannum (hell). You form the majority of the population of this Province. Among the cultivators also you form majority. It is agriculture that is the source of wealth. The Hindu has no wealth of his own and has made himself rich only by despoiling you or your wealth. If you become sufficiently enlightened, then the Hindus will starve and soon become Mahomedans.
>
> Hindus are very selfish. As the progress of Mahomedans is inimical to the self-aggrandisement of Hindus, the latter will always oppose Mahomedan progress for their selfish ends.
>
> Be united in boycotting Hindus. What dire mischief have they not done to us! They have robbed us of honour and wealth. They have deprived us of our daily bread. And now they are going to deprive us of our very life.

Majumdar had this to say on the riots:[176]

> There were a number of communal riots, the most serious of which were those at Comilla and Jamalpur. The depth of infamy to which the Muslim propaganda descended is best exemplified by the notorious document, known as Lal Ishtahar, or Red Pamphlet, which was the most virulent anti-Hindu proclamation and an open incitement of the Muslims against the Hindus.
>
> The disturbances at Comilla broke out on the 4th of March, 1907, and continued for about 4 days. They synchronized with the visit of Nawab Salimullah of Dacca to Comilla town to put fresh vigour into the anti-Swadeshi agitation. When the Nawab was being taken in a procession through the public streets, there occurred a case of assault on Hindus, and looting of a few Hindu, particularly Hindu Swadeshi, shops. These incidents were a signal for a general outbreak of hooliganism involving assault, looting, destruction of properties

and arson. The most notable feature was the indifference and callousness of the local officials and the police. On the other hand, the Government officials were full of praise for the Muhammadans for their self-restraint. The Comilla riot was followed by various other outbreaks of a similar nature, though of less intensity. Considerable bodies of Muhammadans, armed with lathi, mustered from time to time and molested the Hindus. As a result, there was widespread panic among the Hindu minority population in East Bengal and a growing estrangement and bitterness between the two communities. The most serious disturbance broke out at Jamalpur in the District of Mymensingh. In addition to the troubles in the town started by the Muslims, in the course of which hundreds of Hindus—men and women—had to take shelter in a temple throughout the night, the riot spread to the outside areas. There were indiscriminate looting and molestation of Hindus in a large number of localities. We find the following in the confidential reports of the police: 'The rough and turbulent Mohammedan population of the North-Western thanas, lined between the Jamuna River and the Garo Hills, were instigated by the prevailing excitement to the belief that they had an opportunity of looting with impunity. The accounts which have appeared in the Calcutta Press are exaggerated but it is unfortunately certain that a certain number of villages and huts were the subject of looting and, in some cases, of incendiarism, and further that the greatest panic and alarm prevailed among the respectable classes.

... Another Special Magistrate in the same place, himself a Muslim, observed: 'There was not the least provocation for rioting, the common object of the rioters was evidently to molest the Hindus.' In his judgment on a rioting case, 'Emperor Vs Habil Sircar', the same Magistrate observes as follows: 'The evidence adduced on the side of the prosecution shows that the accused Habil Sircar had read over a notice to a crowd of Musalmans and had told them that the Government and the Nawab Bahadur of Dacca had passed orders to the effect that nobody would be punished for plundering and oppressing the Hindus. Soon after, the image of Kali (Hindu goddess) was broken by the Musalmans and the shops of the Hindu traders were also plundered. In some of the shops fire was set to heaps of papers by the Musalmans for the purpose of searching the shops of the Hindus by the light of the fire. In my opinion the witnesses do not make any false statements in their evidence' etc. Mr. Baraeville, I.C.S., the Sub-Divisional Officer of Jamalpur, says in his report on the Melanda hut riots, 'that some Musalmans proclaimed by beat of drum that the Government had permitted them to loot the Hindus.' In an abduction case against some Muhammadans the same Magistrate remarks 'that these outrages were due to the announcement that the Government had permitted the Mohammedans to marry Hindu widows in Nika form.

Despite the manifest anti-Hindu nature of the riots, which were instigated at the behest of the Muslim leaders of Bengal, in cahoots with the British establishment, the author of *Red Pamphlet*, Ibrahim Khan, was released on a personal bond with a mere warning that criminal proceedings against him would be reinstituted should he publish further copies of the document. The following is an extract from the American journalist Nevinson's book on the brazen partisan conduct of the English establishment:[177]

> And in Eastern Bengal this national inclination is now encouraged by the Government's open resolve to retain the Mohammedan support of the Partition by any means in its power. It was against the Hindus only that all the petty persecution of the officialdom was directed. It was they who were excluded from Government posts; it was Hindu schools from which Government patronage was withdrawn. When Mohammedans rioted, the punitive police ransacked Hindu houses, and companies of little Gurkhas were quartered on Hindu populations. It was the Hindus who in one place were forbidden to sit on the river bank. Of course, the plea was that only the Hindus were opposed to the Government's policy of dividing them from the rest of their race, so that they alone needed suppression.

The Comilla Riots were also discussed in the House of Commons. Here's the extract from the proceedings of 19 March 1907 which sheds light on the role played by Nawab Salimullah and the evasive reply given by Morley:[178]

MR. O'GRADY (Leeds, E.)

I beg to ask the Secretary of State for India whether his attention has been called to a riot that occurred at Comilla, in the new province, between a Mahomedan procession, escorting the Nawab of Dacca to a pro-partition meeting; whether the Mahomedans assaulted the Hindus indiscriminately and looted Hindu shops, many Hindus being injured; whether the Nawab, in justification of the riot, stated that a stone was thrown at him a fortnight previous at the Comilla District Conference; and, if so, what steps have been or will be taken to bring the Nawab and the other offenders to justice, and to prevent pro-partition demonstrations being held in those quarters where the Hindus live and carry on their business.

THE SECRETARY OF STATE FOR INDIA (Mr. Morley,) Montrose Burghs I have received a Report of the disturbance referred to. The Local Government appear to have taken steps to prevent illegal action or rioting, whether by Hindus or Mahomedans, at Comilla.

Here's another extract from the proceedings of 16 April 1907 which shows the one-sided nature of this so-called riot:

MR. O'GRADY (Leeds, E.)

I beg to ask the Secretary of State for India whether his attention has been called to the recent disturbances at Comilla, where a number of Mahomedans entered the bazaar crying that the Nawab of Dacca had ordered them to beat the Hindus and raze the shop of one Gogiram Pal to the ground, and, further, that in general Hindu shops were entered, the occupants assaulted, goods trampled on, and common robbery committed; and whether steps will be taken to institute a public inquiry with a view to recompense being made by the Nawab to the assaulted and robbed.

I beg also to ask the Secretary of State for India whether he is aware that the Hindus at Comilla have lodged complaints at the inaction of the police in the recent riots, in not preventing the looting of shops; and whether, seeing that rioting or disturbance between Mahomedans and Hindus was of rare occurrence prior to the partition of Bengal, steps will be taken to prevent incitement to disorder by the Nawab of Dacca and those responsible for pro-partition demonstrations.

I beg further to ask the Secretary of State for India whether he is aware that serious charges have been made against the district magistrate and the district superintendent of police at Comilla, in that the former justified the recent disturbances as the result of seditious speeches made by speakers from Calcutta, and the latter, in that when informed whilst at his club that a golmal was in progress at the bazaar, did not consider the matter worth his special attention on the spot; and whether, seeing that subsequently the Commissioner telegraphed for reinforcements and 125 military police, and the assistant inspector-general left Dacca and Silchar to quell the disturbance, and in view of the fact that Hindus were beaten, goods destroyed, and robbery committed, he will give instructions for a public inquiry into the whole matter.

THE SECRETARY OF STATE FOR INDIA (MR. JOHN MORLEY,) *Montrose Burghs Perhaps the hon. Member will allow me to answer his three Questions on this subject together. The local Government have submitted a detailed report on the disturbances at* Comilla, and have called for further reports and explanations on some points, pending the receipt of which a final expression of opinion must be reserved. Meanwhile precautions have been taken against a recurrence of the disorders, and all complaints made by individuals are under investigation or settlement in the courts of law. I do not think any action on my part is necessary at present.

MR. O'GRADY

Is the right hon. Gentleman aware that one of the men has already suffered imprisonment?

MR. JOHN MORLEY

Yes, Sir.

The pro-Muslim attitude of the British government and its indifference to loss of Hindu lives could not have been clearer. It is to the credit of Bengali Hindus that neither the riots nor the British government's complicity in the riots diverted attention away from or diluted their anti-partition agitation. While the riots, whose brunt was being borne by Bengali Hindus, were still not fully under control, on 6 June 1907 Morley informed the House of Commons that the Government of India had commenced deliberations on electoral reforms. On 24 August 1907, a tentative shape of the proposed reforms was shared with provincial governments for their inputs. After receipt of their inputs, the revised reforms were presented before the House of Lords on 17 December 1908, subsequent to which the Councils Bill of 1909 was introduced in the British Parliament. After a few amendments, the Bill was passed in May 1909, and the Indian Councils Act of 1909 received royal assent on 25 May 1909.[179]

The Indian Councils Act of 1909 contained eight sections, and they had the effect of amending the Indian Councils Act of 1861 and 1892 and the Government of India Act of 1833. For the purposes of our discussion, what is relevant is the fact that Section 1 of the 1909 Act amended the 1861 and 1892 Acts to the extent of providing for regulations to nominate and elect additional members to Legislative Councils. Also, the number of nominated and elected members was increased. To this extent, on the face of it the elective component in Legislative Councils was increased by the Minto–Morley Reforms. However, the most important provision of the 1909 Act was Section 6, which read as follows:

> *The Governor General in Council shall, subject to the approval of the Secretary of State in Council, make regulations* as to the conditions under which and manner in which persons resident in India may be nominated or elected as members of the Legislative Councils of the Governor General, Governors, and Lieutenant-Governors, and as to the qualifications for being, and for being nominated or elected, a member of any such council, and as to any other matter for which regulations are authorized to be made under this Act, and also as to the manner in which those regulations are to be carried into effect. *Regulations under this section shall not be subject to alteration or amendment by the Legislative Council of the Governor General.* [Emphases added]

Effectively, this provision concentrated the power to frame regulations for nomination and election of Council members entirely in the hands of two individuals, namely the Governor General and the Secretary of State. Even the Legislative Council of the Governor General, i.e., the Imperial Legislative Council, had no say in it. In other words, while an elective component was indeed introduced, the process of nomination and election and the eligibility criteria for the same were entirely in the hands of two individuals. Students of law would understand that this effectively meant complete delegation of a so-called 'democratic' or 'representative' process to executive control, with no supervision even by the Legislative Council. In standard legal parlance, this was a textbook case of 'excessive delegation' of powers to the executive with no legislative oversight. The regulations enacted under Section 6 were called the East India (Executive and Legislative Councils) Regulations, which came into force in November 1909.

To make matters worse, the provision for communal electorates too was not made in the Act but was left entirely to the regulations, and therefore to the control of the very same individuals at the top. In addition to this, the regulations also laid down eligibility criteria for the electorate, namely who could vote. The net result was that the process was designed to yield outcomes favourable to the British establishment, as opposed to favouring the will of the governed or the electorate. By no stretch of the imagination was this a transparent process for election of representatives.

The opacity and unpredictability of the regulations was further evident from the fact that no single method was identified for nomination or election of Muslim representatives. Instead, the regulations allowed for multiple ways of ensuring class representation of Muslims as a separate electorate. This, according to the British, was consistent with the demands of the Simla Deputation, i.e., Muslim representation would be provided for in each Legislative Council after taking into account their political importance in each province and without being limited by their numerical strength in the overall population of the province. One of the methods formulated to achieve this object was 'rotation', under which the representative of the landholders of the Bombay Presidency was elected in the first, third and subsequent alternate years by the landholders of Sindh, most of whom were Muslims, and in the even-numbered years, the representative was to be elected by the remainder of the electorate. In provinces where Muslims and Hindus were in equal number, the representative of such constituencies would be Muslim and Hindu alternately. If in a given year the Bombay and Punjab seats were held by non-Muslims, two Muslim members would be elected from special Muslim electorates in the United Provinces and in Eastern Bengal and Assam. This is an illustration of but one of the ways in which the regulations and rules under the 1909 Act ensured significant representation of Muslims in Legislative Councils, in accordance with Minto's promise to the Simla Deputation. Simply put, while all other communities were treated as members of the general electorate without any communal stratification, Muslims as a community were treated as a separate electorate. In this manner, the special treatment of Muslims in the electoral calculus of Councils was provided for through the 1909 Act, and Muslim separatism was constitutionally cemented in the political psyche of Bharat.

Given this far-reaching consequence, two strands of parallel developments need to be understood better to make sense of the period between June 1907 and December 1909:

1. The cogitations and developments which took place within the Indian National Congress and the Muslim League during the said period, which contributed to the Indian Councils Act of 1909; and

2. A snapshot of the debates undertaken in the British Parliament and Governor General's Imperial Legislative Council in India between 1907 and 1909 on the Minto–Morley Reforms to understand the thought process of the British establishment behind their introduction.

Accordingly, in the next chapter, I will examine these two developments before I proceed to discuss the developments of the period after 1909.

The Indian Councils Act of 1909: Yet Another Ad Hoc Safety Valve (1907–1909)

Gilbert John Elliot-Murray-Kynynmound (1845–1914), 4th Earl of Minto, popularly known as Lord Minto, was the Viceroy and Governor General of India from 1905 to 1910.

In the previous chapter, I discussed the sequence of events leading up to the enactment of the Indian Councils Act of 1909. In this chapter, I will continue charting the journey of the Congress and the Muslim League between 1907 and 1909, which contributed to the Councils Act. I will also present select legislative debates that took place in England and Bharat on the Minto–Morley Reforms so that the narrative presented thus far finds further support, straight from the horse's mouth.

The Purge of the Nationalists, a Rising League and the Revolutionaries

From January to May 1907, after the disastrous Calcutta Congress session of 1906, the Nationalists, under Tilak, Rai, Pal and Ghosh, actively set out to seek support for their position. Their clear position was that as a colonised people it was foolish on the part of Bharatiyas to expect the British to treat them at par with English citizens. In July 1907, Tilak presented the message of the Nationalists in the following words:[1]

> At present we are clerks and willing instruments of our oppression in the hands of an alien Government. The new party wants you to realise the fact that your future rests entirely in your own hands. If you mean to be free, you can be free; if you do not mean to be free, you will fall and be forever fallen. So many of you need not like arms, but if you have not the power of active resistance, have you not the power of self-denial and self-abstinence in such a way as not to assist this foreign government to rule over you? This is boycott, we shall not have their goods, we shall not give them assistance to collect revenue and to keep the peace. We shall not assist them in fighting beyond the frontiers or outside India with Indian blood and money. We shall not assist them in carrying on the administration of justice. We shall have our own courts and when time comes we shall not pay taxes. Can you do that by your united efforts? If you can, you are free from tomorrow.

Lala Lajpat Rai, 1908

Rai denounced the Moderates' portrayal of Bharat's colonisation as beneficial political apprenticeship under the 'benign tutelage' of the British coloniser. And, in ways which continue to be relevant to the present, Bipin Chandra Pal brilliantly called out the coloniality of the Moderates in the following manner:[2]

> We loved the abstraction we called India but we hated the thing that it actually was. Our patriotism was not composed of our love for our own history, literature, arts and industries, culture and institutions, but as a prototype of England which we wished her to be. The new spirit cured us of an imaginary and abstract patriotism. Love of India means a love for its rivers and mountains, for its paddy fields and its arid sandy lands, its towns and villages and poor people, for its languages, literature, philosophies, religion, culture and civilization.

Both Pal and Aurobindo Ghosh called for 'passive resistance'; while Pal defined it as 'non-aggressive active resistance', the latter saw it as 'lawful abstention from any kind of co-operation with the Government'.[3] This effectively meant that the spirit of the Boycott and Swadeshi Movements would extend to the realms of education, administration, courts of law, police and even the army. The twofold objective of this resistance was to paralyse the colonial establishment and inculcate the spirit of self-reliance in Bharatiyas. To my mind, this was a clear articulation of the principle of non-cooperation at least fifteen years before Gandhi adopted it.

Interestingly, according to Daniel Argov, even within the Nationalist group, views on the actual meaning of self-government were diverse.[4] For instance, Tilak's vision was closer to that of the Moderates, who sought self-government within the British Commonwealth, with the primary difference being the means employed to secure that vision. Rai, Pal and Ghosh, on the other hand, denounced both the methods of the Congress as well as its end goal. Rai was of the view that there could be no possible conciliation between patriotism for Bharat and loyalism to the British empire; Pal wanted an 'autonomous government' which was absolutely free from British control; and Ghosh defined Swaraj as 'a free national Government unhampered even in the least degree by foreign control'. Of all the Nationalists, Aurobindo Ghosh was perhaps the clearest and the most decolonial in his exposition of freedom from the British in the spiritual, cultural and political realms. He was of the view that a revolution was necessary for Bharat to purge itself of 'Western tutelage'.[5]

In addition to these expositions of the Nationalists' ideological positions and their differences with the Moderates, the unrest in the Punjab Province in 1906–1907 provided Lajpat Rai with the opportunity to advance the

Nationalist position and demonstrate the efficacy of the doctrine of passive resistance. The period of 1906–1907 was restive in Punjab owing to certain land- and water-related legislative measures proposed by the British— the most prominent of them being the Punjab Land Colonisation Bill and the Doab Bari Act. In fact, the unrest in this province began in 1900 with the passing of the Punjab Land Alienation Act of 1900, which limited the transfer of landownership by creating a divide between 'agriculturists' and 'non-agriculturists'. The Colonisation Bill provided that property would devolve on the British government if a person died without an heir, while under the Doab Bari Act water rates were increased. The reactions and opposition to these legislations resulted in movements such as the Pagri Sambhal Jatta Movement, which forced the British government to withdraw the Colonisation Bill.[6] Lajpat Rai, along with Bhagat Singh's father Kishan Singh and uncle Ajit Singh, was at the forefront of this agitation, and at one point it was feared that the Sikh units of the British Indian Army would revolt against the government at the behest of Rai. The impact of Rai and Ajit Singh is evident from the fact that Donald Ibbetson, at that time the Lieutenant Governor of Punjab, urged the Central government to recognise the seriousness of the situation and recommended their deportation.[7] Minto acceded to this request for deportation of Rai and Singh and also vetoed the Colonisation Bill to calm frayed tempers in Punjab.[8]

While the deportation of Rai to Burma in May 1907 (he was released in November 1907 under public pressure[9]) did not result in a widespread revolt against the British, it resulted in two different realisations for two different parties—first, Rai's deportation by the British increased his importance in the eyes of the public and therefore caused greater insecurity among the Moderates; and second, the Nationalists too realised that the Moderate policy of petition and persuasion had dulled the revolutionary instincts and appetite of Bharatiyas in general, which needed to be addressed. To counter the growing influence of the Nationalists, Moderate leaders like Gokhale embarked on a tour to stir the masses; Gokhale argued against severance of relationship with the British empire because he believed that there was room within the empire for a self-respecting India to achieve its aspirations with 'minimum disturbance of existing ideas'.[10] For the same reason, he categorically denounced the Nationalist doctrine of passive resistance on the grounds that the policy was impractical, injurious, and would have the effect of altering the foundations of public life. Clearly, Gokhale's position captured the inherent coloniality in the stance of the Moderates and their consequent defence of the status quo in the realms of thought, ideation and action.

To purge the Congress of the Extremists—in particular Tilak—and their influence, the venue of the 1907 session of the Congress was shifted from Nagpur to Surat, which was the home turf of Pherozeshah Mehta, a well-known Moderate.[11] To add to it, Dr Rash Behari Ghosh, another Moderate, was elected as the president of the Surat session, whereas the Extremists wanted to elect Lala Lajpat Rai, who had been released on 15 November 1907.[12] Also, a new constitution was proposed, which, among other things, expected every delegate to get on board with the Moderate vision and means—namely, self-government for Bharat within the British empire at par with other colonies, and constitutional agitation. Naturally, this was a message to the Extremists to either fall in line or leave the Congress.[13] In response, a few days ahead of the Surat session, Aurobindo Ghosh organised a Nationalists Conference on 23 December 1907 in Haripur, on the outskirts of Surat. Both Tilak and Rai presided over the Conference and the delegates were expected to subscribe to the Nationalist vision and means—namely, complete independence and total boycott of the British.[14] The drawing of battle lines between the two camps could not have been clearer.

On the first day of the Surat session, i.e., on 26 December 1907, Pherozeshah Mehta brought over three dozen men armed with sticks to intimidate the Extremists, which was a new low even for the Moderates and the Congress.[15] When Surendranath Banerjea rose to address the assembly and announce the election of Rash Behari Ghosh as the president-elect, he was heckled because the delegates wanted to listen to Rai and Tilak.[16] On the second day of the session, Tilak vocally objected to Rash Behari Ghosh's election as the president, which led to a general pandemonium, and the police had to be called in to tackle the situation.[17] Thus ended the twenty-third session of the Congress in a limbo, whose split had now widened and was out in the open. Following this, the Moderates met in private and immediately issued a notice to the delegates of the Surat session informing them of a 'National Convention' to be held on 28 December 1907. As expected, the Convention was open only to those delegates who envisioned a colonial model of self-government, which was to be achieved strictly through constitutional means.[18] At the Convention, which was attended by 900 of the total 1,600 delegates of the Surat session, a committee was appointed to draw up a new constitution for the Congress. Following the Surat session, 300 delegates of the Nationalist camp too met under the stewardship of Aurobindo Ghosh and reiterated their demands for countrywide Swadeshi and Boycott Movements and autonomous self-government.[19] In February 1908, attacking the ends and the means of the Moderates, Tilak wrote:[20]

The Indian people must adopt the way of resistance to achieve the complete rights of svarajya, and to eliminate all differences between blacks and whites. Nothing will be gained by petitions, pleas, or conciliation. Those who still want to remain moderate may remain so. We do not quarrel over words. But make the definition of moderate so broad that it will even include the determination to be ready to go to jail by intentionally breaking the tyrannical laws of government. When you have the determination to do this, whether it is done moderately or extremely, on that day we will be saved. Otherwise remember that the slavery which is written on your forehead [as your fate] will never end.

The eviction of the Extremists from the Congress gladdened Minto, who believed it was a great triumph for the British government since the Moderates would be more receptive to the government's ideas on reforms in the absence of the Extremists. Not surprisingly, the Moderates too shared the government's sense of relief.[21] To quickly take advantage of this breather and to set the record straight once and for all on the goals and methods of the Congress, the convention committee of the Moderates met in Allahabad in April 1908 and drew up a constitution as well as rules of conduct for members of the Congress. Here is Article 1 of the constitution, which every member of the Congress was expected to commit to in writing:[22]

The Objects of the Indian National Congress are the attainment by the people of India of a system of government similar to that enjoyed by the self-governing Members of the British Empire, and a participation by them in the rights and responsibilities of the Empire on equal terms with those Members. These Objects are to be achieved by constitutional means by bringing about a steady reform of the existing system of administration and by promoting national unity, fostering public spirit and developing and organizing the intellectual, moral, economic and industrial resources of the country.

If the intention was to cement the purge of the Nationalists and close the doors on them, the new constitution achieved its intended objective. Tilak and other Nationalists refused to adhere to Article 1. In the months that followed, the Nationalists accused the Congress of squandering and betraying the people's mandate and compromising Bharat's individuality in order to preserve its position as a subordinate satellite colony under an alien imperial order.[23] By November 1908, Pherozeshah Mehta made it abundantly clear that the Congress would not let the Nationalists back in since the differences between the Moderates and the Nationalists were irreconcilable and also because he believed that the presence of the Nationalists undermined the Congress's loyalty to the British government.[24] Congratulating the Moderates on the purge of the Extremists and for staying true to the Congress's founding objectives, Hume and Wedderburn wrote to the Congress as follows:[25]

> The objects and methods of the Congress set forth in Article One of the constitution, are precisely those with which our movement started when we inaugurated it at the first Bombay Congress in December 1885.

No wonder Daniel Argov remarked that the Congress had proved and fulfilled its function as a 'safety valve'.[26]

Meanwhile, the Muslim League's first session, after its founding on 30 December 1906, was held in Karachi on 29 and 30 December 1907. In the intervening year, the League's primary preoccupation was to oppose the anti-partition agitation in Bengal and push for separate electorates in response to Morley's announcement of June 1907.[27] Apart from assuring the government of its loyalty and expressing gratitude for the manner in which the Simla Deputation was received and assured of the protection of Muslim interests, the League's constitution was settled in the Karachi session. Pertinently, Karachi was chosen because '*Sindh is that pious place in India, where Muhammad Bin Qasim came first, with the torch of religion and the gift of Hadis.*'[28] To add to this, the president of this session, Adamjee Pirbhoy, remarked in his presidential speech:[29]

> If a handful of men under a boy could teach Kalima to the territory of Sindh and promulgate the law of true shariat of God and His Rasul, can seven crores of Mussalmans not make their social and political life pleasant?

In the Aligarh sitting of March 1908, which was a continuation of the Karachi session of 1907, the League—taking a cue from the Congress, which had been advocating its cause both in India and in England—decided to set up a branch in London to present its cause and counteract the Congress's influence there.[30,31] Accordingly, the League founded its London branch on 6 May 1908, which was headed by Syed Ameer Ali. Also, before the second annual session of the League in December 1908, to increase its mass base, the League rapidly set up provincial and district branches in Punjab, Bihar, Western Bengal, Eastern Bengal and Assam, Bombay, Madras, the Central Provinces and the United Provinces.[32]

It is important to note at this juncture that apart from the Congress and the League, the third entity which the British had to contend with was the revolutionary front. Unfortunately for Minto and the Moderates (synonymous with the Congress at this point), as Syed Wasti points out in his brilliant thesis, the removal of the Nationalists from the Congress had, at best, resulted in the cleansing of dissenting voices within the Congress. However, it could not stifle other movements outside the Congress, in particular the revolutionary movements inspired by the vision of the Extremists as well as their dismissal of constitutional methods.[33] Aurobindo Ghosh's direct participation in revolutionary activities provided an impetus to them and also strengthened British suspicions of a nexus between the Extremists and the 'Revolutionaries', who were looked upon as terrorists. Since a detailed look at the revolutionary movements of this period is beyond the scope of this trilogy, those interested may read R.C. Majumdar's *History of the Freedom Movement in India* (Volume 2) and James Campbell Ker's *Political Trouble in India, 1907–1917* to understand the full extent of the revolutionary movements and the threat it posed to the existence of the British establishment in Bharat.[34] Ker was a senior officer in the Home Department under the British Indian Government and worked as personal assistant to the Director of Criminal Intelligence from 1907 to 1913. It may be noted that after the tapering down of the armed side of the Wahhabi Movement, the revolutionary societies established in the early 1900s presented the most potent armed resistance to the British government after the 1857 Mutiny. In addition to drawing from the ideas of the Extremists/Nationalists, as briefly mentioned in the previous chapter, a good number of the revolutionary societies/samitis were inspired by Shakta traditions, the Bhagavad Gita, the teachings of Swami Vivekananda, and European, including Russian, revolutionary movements.

The activities of these societies, which were spread over several parts of Bharat—in particular Bengal, Punjab and Maharashtra—received significant support from Bharatiyas residing abroad such as Shyamji Krishna Varma. In London, Varma founded the Indian Home Rule Society in 1905 as well as India House, a hostel for Bharatiya students.[35] Through his publication, *The Indian Sociologist*, Varma disseminated revolutionary ideas, which were consumed by Bharatiya Revolutionaries in Britain as well as in Bharat. On the other side of the Atlantic, New York served as an important centre of convergence for Bharatiya Revolutionaries.[36] To draw young talent and train them in revolutionary activities, Varma offered scholarships annually to three Bharatiya students to pursue their education abroad. Wasti points out that among the first recipients of this scholarship was Vinayak Damodar Savarkar, then the editor of *Vihari* in Bombay. It was during his stay at India House that Savarkar authored his seminal work, *The Indian War of Independence, 1857*, in response to the fiftieth anniversary celebrations of the quelling of the 1857 Mutiny by the British.[37] The activities of the Revolutionaries were not limited to publishing radical literature but also extended to smuggling of arms and ammunition into Bharat in an organised manner.[38]

The seriousness of the Revolutionaries can be gauged from their attempt to assassinate D.H. Kingsford, the Chief Presidency Magistrate in Calcutta, who was trying cases against nationalist publications like *Yugantar*, *Bande Mataram* and *Sandhya*.[39] However, instead of Kingsford, the bomb attack, which was undertaken by Khudi Ram Bose and Prafulla Chaki, resulted in the mistaken deaths of two English women on 30 April 1908 in Muzaffarpur. It was during the course of the investigation into this case that the existence of a revolutionary safe house in Maniktola Gardens in Calcutta, where bombs were being manufactured, was revealed, leading to the Alipore bomb conspiracy case. As mentioned in the previous chapter, this resulted in the arrest of Aurobindo Ghosh, his brother Barindra Ghosh and others.[40] As the first step in dealing with revolutionary activity, the Press Act was passed on 8 June 1908 to curb the spread of 'seditious literature'.[41] As was expected from the Moderates, both Gokhale and Rash Behari Ghosh termed the enactment inevitable and necessary.[42] Subsequently, on 24 June 1908, Tilak was arrested and charged with sedition for his articles in his publication *Kesari,* wherein he praised the Bengal Revolutionaries for their activities.[43] Tilak was represented by Barrister Muhammad Ali Jinnah in this case; however, he was found guilty by a jury and sentenced to six years' imprisonment in Mandalay, Burma,[44] from where he would be released in 1914. This experience, as we shall see, would result in a significant mellowing and even change of attitude on Tilak's part upon his release, which would show in the form of support for Indian participation in the British war effort in the First World War, apart from his subscription to constitutional agitation. As for the end goal, he would remain staunchly committed to self-government, as we shall see.

In December 1908, on recommendations from the governments of Bengal and of Eastern Bengal and Assam, Minto ordered the arrest and deportation of several Revolutionaries such as Subodh Chandra Mullick, Manoranjan Guha Thakurta, Kristo Kumar Mitra, Sachindra Prasad Bose, Shamsumder Chakravarti, Aswini Kumar Dutt, Satish Chandra Chatterji, Pulin Behari Das and Bupesh Chandra Nag.[45] As a matter of practice, deportation was employed under Regulations of 1818 whenever the government suspected an individual of participation in subversive and seditious activities but did not have enough evidence to substantiate it in a court of law.[46] Shortly after these deportations, samitis such as the Anushilan Samiti were banned under the Indian Criminal Law Amendment Act.[47] There were recommendations for deportation of Aurobindo Ghosh too. However, in view of the unpopularity of the deportation of Lajpat Rai both in Bharat and in England, the government decided against it. In any case, Ghosh and a few of his associates were acquitted in the Alipore case in April 1909, while seventeen others were convicted in 1910 and sentenced to varying degrees of punishment, from transportation for life to rigorous imprisonment.[48] In addition to this, the British bureaucracy resorted to repression in response to revolutionary activities, which only added to the resentment among the people and pushed more youth into the arms of the Extremists and the Revolutionaries.

In fact, even as the Councils Bill was being debated in the British Parliament and in the Imperial Legislative Council in India in 1909, the year witnessed a spate of bomb explosions, assassination attempts and assassinations in Bengal, Maharashtra, London, Ahmedabad and Punjab.[49] The year began with bomb explosions in both Bengals. Outside of the Bengals, in Gwalior and the Deccan, the existence of secret revolutionary societies was discovered in March 1909. They were being run under the stewardship of Ganesh Damodar Savarkar, brother of Vinayak Damodar Savarkar. In July, Madan Lal Dhingra shot dead the aide de camp at the India Office in London, William Curzon Wyllie. In November, there was an attempt on the Viceroy's life in Ahmedabad. In December, the district magistrate trying Ganesh Savarkar was murdered. In January 1910, the deputy superintendent of police, Khan Bahadur Shams-ul-Alam, who was assisting the prosecution in the Alipore case, was murdered.

In light of the above state of affairs, here is a summary of the sequence of events for an understanding of the circumstances and motivations that shaped the Minto–Morley Reforms:[50]

1. Starting from the 1904 Bombay session until the 1907 Surat session, thanks to pressure from the Extremists, the Moderates shifted their goals from mere administrative reforms and increased representation in the bureaucracy, to self-government within the empire, which was to be achieved through constitutional agitation;

2. The Extremists, who were evicted from the Congress in the 1907 Surat session, sought freedom from the empire through passive resistance;

3. At least from 1902, Bharatiya Revolutionaries who were inspired by the Extremists sought freedom from the empire through active and armed resistance, which was only spurred further by the Partition of Bengal in 1905;

4. The Muslim League professed loyalty to the government, in lieu of which it demanded separate electorates in excess of its numerical strength to cushion the blow of living in a Hindu-majority parliamentary system. In short, it sought fulfilment of the charter of demands presented in the Simla Deputation of October 1906; and

5. The British wanted to hold fast to their power by managing as many expectations and interests as possible while dealing firmly with the Extremists and the Revolutionaries. For this, they realised they would

have to strike a balance between giving the Indian educated classes an opportunity to participate in the administration, including in the process of legislation, and retaining actual decision-making powers in British hands.

It is against this backdrop that the crafting of the Indian Councils Act of 1909 must be understood. Before proceeding further, it is important to underscore the fact that while the term 'Minto–Morley Reforms' gives the impression of unanimity of ideas and opinion between Minto and Morley, in reality they had differing views on several important issues. From the handling of Extremists and Revolutionaries, to the nature and scope of native representation in Legislative Councils, and on addressing Muslim expectations of class representation, Minto and Morley often had differing opinions, as revealed by their correspondence.[51]

Morley, as the Secretary of State for India who was directly answerable to the British Parliament, was more interested in preserving British control as well as the optics of liberality in governance. On the other hand, Minto, as the Viceroy/Governor General who was the man on the ground, was interested in preserving the position of the Raj through accommodation of as many Indian interests as possible. He recognised that the way to keep the Extremist and revolutionary voices at bay was through accommodation of Moderate and loyal interests, but without acceding to the demand of self-government. He was of the view that self-government was an 'impossibility' in India and that 'constitutional autocracy' was better suited to Indian conditions. On several occasions, the literature reveals, Minto had to summon his powers of persuasion to convince Morley about some particular course of action, including one to keep the Moderates on their side.[52] Minto's definition of constitutional autocracy is best described in his own words:[53]

> We are ready to accept Indian assistance, to share our administration with Indians, to recognize their natural ambitions, but, for their own sakes, the supreme guidance must be British ...

In keeping with this goal, Minto and Morley agreed that the way forward was to increase native presence in the Legislative Councils of the Viceroy and provincial governments as non-official additional members while retaining the official majority. Minto was also open to increasing native presence in local bodies such as district councils and municipalities. To address such specifics, the appointment of a committee was announced in July 1906 (as mentioned earlier), and in August 1906 a five-member committee was appointed under the chairmanship of A. Arundel.[54] This was prior to the Simla Deputation of 1906. Following the meeting with the Deputation, the issue of

Muslim representation was taken up by the Arundel Committee as part of its deliberations on reforms. Within eleven days of the Simla Deputation, the Committee submitted its report containing its recommendations. Importantly, the members of the Committee were divided on the appointment of an Indian member to the Viceroy's Executive Council.[55] The difference of opinion owed to apprehensions regarding reactions from the Anglo-Indian community, apart from concerns relating to preservation of confidentiality of the Council's decisions by an Indian member. Subsequently, a dispatch was sent by Minto to Morley on the Committee's report.

On 6 June 1907, after deliberations in England based on the report of the Committee, in particular on the issue of an Indian member in the Viceroy's Executive Council, Morley announced in the House of Commons that the Government of India had put together a report on the proposed reforms.[56] However, while he mentioned the appointment of an Indian member to his council, he consciously omitted the issue of an Indian member on the Viceroy's Executive Council. Subsequently, he followed up with his announcement and appointed K.G. Gupta and S.H. Bilgrami to his own council in August 1907.[57] In the very same month, the Government of India issued a letter to provincial governments seeking their inputs on the outlined reform proposals.

Until December 1908, the issue of appointment of an Indian member to the Viceroy's Executive Council remained unresolved. Finally, on 17 December 1908, in the face of much opposition and with the support of Minto, Morley announced to the House of Lords his intention to appoint an Indian member in the event of a vacancy in the Viceroy's Executive Council.[58] However, this presented a dilemma, since the question was whether the member would be a Hindu or a Muslim. Unsurprisingly, Syed Ameer Ali, who headed the London branch of the Muslim League, lobbied for a Muslim member.[59] Morley took the view that the issue would be decided based on merit and not religion. In the end, Advocate General S.P. Sinha was appointed, based on his track record, among other things—one of the other things being his *complexion*. He was chosen over Sir Ashutosh Mukherji because he was '*comparatively white*' and was '*more in touch with European society*', which made his appointment less vulnerable to Anglo-Indian and English resistance. Here's the relevant extract from Wasti's thesis, which attests to this:[60]

> Minto personally liked Dr. A. Mukherji and was insisting on his appointment to his Council. But when Sinha's name was proposed to him, it was impressed upon him that Sinha stood high in public estimation because of his professional skill and ability. *Besides Sinha and his family were more in touch with European society.* Being a barrister, his appointment to the Council would require no legislation, and the upward step from Advocate General would not seem

unnatural. Minto wanted to take the line of least resistance in making this great change. '*Moreover please do not think me terribly narrow! but Sinha is comparatively white, whilst Mukherji is as black as my hat! and opposition in the official world would not be regardless of mere shades of colour,*' *Minto wrote to Morley.* Hence Sinha was appointed on 23 March 1909. [Emphases added]

Muslims were assured of representation in the Viceroy's Executive Council in due course. And accordingly, Sinha's successor was Syed Ali Imam (not to be confused with Syed Ameer Ali) of the Muslim League, who would preside over the 1908 Amritsar session, as we shall see shortly. The next thorny issue before the Minto–Morley pair was the question of Muslim representation and satisfaction of the assurances given to the Simla Deputation by Minto. While the two agreed on the principle of class representation for Muslims, they had divergent views on the manner in which such representation had to be secured. Minto proposed a combination of election and nomination, whereas Morley preferred joint electoral colleges, as captured in his dispatch to Minto dated 27 November 1908.[61] According to Morley's suggestion, representation would be based on the proportion in the overall population and, where necessary, this system would be supplemented by nomination to ensure fair representation of Muslims. This proposal was, naturally, unacceptable to the Muslim League since, according to it, it defeated the very purpose of seeking separate electorates in excess of Muslims' numerical strength in the population. The League accused Morley of being influenced by Hindus to sacrifice the interests of 'minorities'.[62] The Congress, of course, welcomed Morley's suggestion since the proposal struck a balance between Muslim expectations and the Congress's position, while Minto felt that it was contrary to the assurances he had given to the Simla Deputation.[63] Interestingly, Gokhale was of the view that Morley's proposal was not alive to the real divides between Hindus and Muslims.[64] This indicates that even Gokhale tacitly accepted the validity of the Two-Nation Theory.

The December 1908 sessions of the League and the Congress would both be defined significantly by this dispatch from Morley to Minto.[65] This session of the League was its second annual session and was held in Amritsar on 30 and 31 December. Its primary focus was (a) rejection of Morley's modified proposal of electoral colleges, (b) reiteration of the demands of the Simla Deputation, namely provision of separate electorates for Muslims in excess of their numerical strength, and (c) expression of vehement opposition to the continuing anti-partition agitation in Bengal.

This session of the League was also important for the clear-eyed speech delivered on 30 December 1908 by its president, Syed Ali Imam. A barrister by profession, Imam would later become the prime minister of the princely state of Hyderabad under the Nizam, and, as stated earlier, a member of the Viceroy's Council. Interestingly, his younger brother Syed Hasan Imam (also a barrister) was a member of the Congress. Syed Ali Imam's speech, in my view, spelt out the historical foundations of the Two-Nation Theory even better than Syed Ahmed Khan's exposition of it, and is therefore mandatory reading. In fact, this speech is a brilliant illustration of the worldview of Middle Eastern consciousness and its thought continuum over the centuries. While the entire speech is in the Appendix, I have extracted a few portions here which convey the essence of the historical basis for the League's demand for separate electorates for Muslims:[66]

Politically speaking, the Mohammedans of India occupy a unique position. I believe it is without a parallel in the history of the world. Close upon a thousand years ago, the Arab Mohammedan scented the desert air of Sind and found its sand-mounds and date-groves reminding him of Hejaz, of Arabia Felix. Since then wave upon wave of Muslim conquest has rolled over the entire length and breadth of India. In serried ranks, Musalman Royal Houses rose and fell, but Muslim domination of the country remained more or less an unbroken chain, till in comparatively more recent times supremacy hung in the balance between the Marhatta spear and the British bayonet. Islam, in its world-wide career of conquest and conversion, met on Indian soil with a resistance which had little of the admirable military prowess of the Hindus. What Hindu chivalry was powerless to protect, Hindu ethics, Hindu philosophy and Hindu social system had made impregnable. Centuries rolled by but the conqueror and the conquered in point of nationality, character and creed suffered not from their political association. Characteristics of race and religion and political and social ideals of the two presented irreconcilabilities ... In the East, religion enters into the very life of the people. It permeates the fabric of society, supplies the spring of individual action in everyday life, and dominates habits of thought in a measure unknown to the West. The social relations of the Indian Muslim and the Hindu have not yet received the geniality of a common dinner-table nor the sacrament or legal sanction of matrimony. The two communities, from the truly social point of view, are as far-apart today as they were a thousand years ago. Time has not worn out any of the angularities that characterized their social systems when they first came face to face ...

It is clear, therefore, that, apart from ethnic diversity of character, the two communities have nothing in common in their traditional, religious, social and political conceptions. There must be something imperishable in the cherished beliefs of both. Each has so far passionately clung to its own ... Under such conditions the fusion of the two, Hinduism and Islam, could not be predicated. The verdict of history is that, in holding India under subjection for centuries, the Mohammedan held only her body and not her soul. For political ends, for the happiness of the country as a whole and the formation of a flourishing commonwealth, the relation of the two communities was anomalous and out of joint. The keen-sighted statesmanship of the great Akbar saw this and aimed at unification by conciliation, compromise and concession in religious, social and political directions. A long and tolerant reign of about 50 years proved the failure of the experiment. Unification demands absorption and obliteration of the old landmarks of differences and divergences. The imperial reformer at best achieved a friendly understanding with his Hindu subjects, which resulted more from the consciousness of a just liberal government than any acceptance of the ethics of Islam or its religious, social and political principles. The innate difference of creed and character, of race and tradition and of social and political ideas remained ready to spring into active hostility as soon as a favourable opportunity presented itself. Aurangazeb saw, no less than his great-grandfather, the political necessity of unification. He adopted, however, the desperate and hazardous method of religious intolerance and forcible conversion. The experiment failed again. Prejudices and practices of both the communities, sanctified by the observance of ages, defied cohesion. Persuasion and persecution equally proved futile. With the weakening of administrative control, the Musalman found himself isolated. New Hindu powers rose in rebellion round the tottering throne of the Mogul. The strife had all the character of a crusade, and the disruption was but the reflexion of the irreconcilability of Hinduistic with Islamic conceptions.

Having thus elaborated on the Two-Nation Theory, Syed Ali Imam then voiced his disagreement with Hindu nationalism, a Hindu-majority administrative structure, the Congress's flirtations with Swaraj, and, finally, with Morley's modified proposal, to which he objected as under:

Gentlemen, the last Despatch of Lord Morley to His Excellency the Viceroy on the scheme of the Reform of Councils, seems to overlook the principle that representation to minorities must have its origin in a denominational basis from the very start to the finish, from the first voting unit to the elected representative. Without this the Musalmans cannot hope to secure the true protection which their interests demand. Hasty expression to my views on this Despatch, received last week, I hesitate to give; but the principle involved is of vital consequences to our community, and a united expression of our views alone can save us from the perils of imperfection contained in the Despatch. Gentlemen, I again call upon you to unite. It is a solemn and sacred duty you owe to yourself and to your posterity.

Imam's clarity of thought and expression shines through this speech, which must be read over and over again to understand the relevance of these lines to the times we live in.

Coming to the Congress, its session of 1908, which was treated as its twenty-third session in continuation of the tumultuous Surat session, was

held in Madras. This was the first session held after the complete purge of
the Nationalists. The session began with Rash Behari Ghosh's reiteration
of the Congress's commitment to constitutional agitation, its loyalty to the
government and its relief at having gotten rid of the Nationalists. The Congress
also expressed its gratitude to the government for announcing legislative
reforms, including the proposal of electoral colleges with a fixed number of
seats for Muslims.[67] Banerjea declared the reforms as 'the crowning triumph
of constitutional agitation' and hailed Morley as the 'author of Parliament in
India' who had paved the way for colonial self-government.[68] To understand
the bubble in which the Moderates lived, here are the contrasting views
of Gokhale and Minto on the significance of the reforms and the future of
representative government in Bharat. Gokhale said:[69]

> Hitherto we have been engaged in what might be called responsible association
> with the administration. From agitation to responsible association, and from
> responsible association—a long and weary step but the step will have to
> come—to responsible administration.

And here is what Minto said:[70]

> I am no advocate of Representative government for India in the Western sense
> of the term. It could never be akin to the instincts of the many races composing
> the population of the Indian Empire. It would be a Western importation
> unnatured to Eastern tastes.

And this is what Morley, the 'author of Parliament in India', had to say:[71]

> If it could be said that this chapter of reforms led directly or necessarily to
> the establishment of a parliamentary system in India, I for one would have
> nothing to do with it.

From these excerpts it appears that the Moderates inhabited a parallel,
fictitious universe and stubbornly refused to see, let alone acknowledge
or accept, reality for what it was, despite repeated exhortations from the
Nationalists to do so. The Nationalists held that the British coloniser's race
consciousness and his position as the coloniser would never allow him to
treat Bharatiyas as a people capable of governing themselves using Western
institutions or, for that matter, any kind of representative institution. I could
be accused of hindsight bias, but the fact of the matter is that for the most
part, the Extremists/Nationalists, in particular Aurobindo Ghosh, could see
right through the coloniality of the British establishment as well as that of
the Moderates, despite being contemporaries and products of the very same
English education system as the Moderates. Commenting on the cognitive
dissonance of the Moderates and their refusal to see the 'reforms' for what
they truly were and were not, S.R. Mehrotra had this to say:[72]

Strange though it might appear, Indian nationalists welcomed the reforms for the very reason which Morley and Minto had so emphatically and repeatedly disavowed. They interpreted them as an advance towards parliamentary self-government.

The reference to 'Indian nationalists' here was to the Moderates. Commenting on the ad hoc nature of the British policy behind the reforms, Mehrotra said:[73]

> The Morley-Minto reforms were a typical product of that nineteenth-century English liberalism which believed that statesmanship was mainly a question of determining how far popular demands should be conceded, but which seldom bothered to think out the fundamentals of policy, or relate it to a well-defined larger purpose. 'Lacking a clearly distinguishable and steadily developing British policy towards the growth of politics in India,' justly comments Professor C.H. Philips, 'Morley and Minto were driven to devising not so much a coherent plan as a series of expedients to meet the particular and admittedly difficult situation.'

At this juncture, it is important to address a question—if the British establishment was of the view that Western representative institutions were unsuited to Bharat, or rather Bharat was unfit for Western representative institutions, how can one blame them for the introduction of Western institutions in Bharat? There are two tentative responses to this question. First, the European belief that the races of the East were inherently incapable of Western-style democracy [1] therefore constantly needed the benign paternal supervision of the European, led to the policy of gradual conversion of the East at every level, including societal, until the colonised society was ready for mental integration with the West. This is best captured in Morley's own words from October 1908:[74]

> What are we in India for? Surely in order to implant—slowly, prudently, judiciously—those ideas of justice, law, humanity, which are the foundation of our own civilization.

This takes us to the second possible response: ironically for Morley, the Moderates in the Congress *were* the products of this slow, prudent, judicious implantation of Western ideas of justice, law and humanity, which reflected in their craven pleas to be treated at par with the British subjects of the empire. In other words, the difference of opinion between the British government and the Moderates of the Congress was primarily that of timing and the extent of British control over Bharat, but *not* about the very existence of British control. While the British felt that India was not yet ready for self-government at par with other colonies, the Moderates in the Congress were eager to prove that they were indeed worthy of that imperial benediction.

This demonstrates my position, which I stated in the first book, that colonial consciousness or coloniality is a two-way street. There is only so much that one can blame the coloniser for, beyond which the natives (in this case the Moderates) *must* take responsibility for eagerly embracing the colonisers' worldview and for stifling voices of resistance and indigeneity (those branded Extremists/Nationalists at that point in time) from within their own society.

If my criticism of the Congress of this period, in particular of the Moderates, seems too harsh compared with my appreciation for the League's clear-cut approach to reclaim state power for Muslims, here is an illustration of the level to which the Congress had fallen in the pursuit of its warped dual policy of British loyalism and moderate nationalism that would justify my point of view. For the 1908 session, one of the delegates, S. Sankaranarayana, campaigned for replacement of the slogan 'Bande Mataram' with 'Bande Matapitarau', with Bharat being the Mata (Mother) and England being the Pita (Father).[75] In fact, in the pamphlet, England was depicted as the guru or preceptor to Bharat, showering the light of its education and political thought on this land of heathens. Clearly, the difference between Muslim and Congress loyalties to the British was that the former's loyalty was calculated to contain the growth of Hindu power, whereas the latter truly believed that Bharat's fortunes were eternally tied to those of the British and for the better. In any case, given the irrefutable civilisational bond between Hindus and Bharat, the Congress could not have justified its pro-British position by comparing it with Muslim loyalty to the British. That said, the Congress did not see itself as the voice of the Hindus alone; instead, it had grandiose notions of being the sole voice of all Indians, the reality of Two-Nation Theory notwithstanding.

Coming back to the reforms and the question of Muslim representation, after the Amritsar session of the League, a long campaign of protests by Muslims began all over the country and petitions were being sent to Minto. Syed Ameer Ali was active in London and advocated strongly for the Muslim cause. Minto cautioned Morley of Muslim reactions to his proposal of electoral colleges for Muslim representation contained in his dispatch of 27 November 1908; in fact, several members of the British establishment opposed Morley's suggestion, including Minto.[76] On 27 January 1909, a Muslim Deputation led by Syed Ameer Ali and Bilgrami met with Morley to convey the position and apprehensions of Muslims. Morley attempted to assuage their concerns by informing them that his proposal of an electoral college was a mere suggestion and that he did not envisage its practical implementation nor was he attached to his proposal.[77] Ultimately, in responding to the growing opposition to his proposal, and despite the support of a few individuals such as Henry Cotton and Ramsay MacDonald, at the second reading of the Indian Councils Bill on 23 February 1909 in the House of Lords, he was compelled to affirm his commitment to the assurances made to the Simla Deputation by Viceroy Minto. Endorsing Morley's change in position, Minto wrote to him in April 1909:[78]

> Mahomedan electorates are absolutely necessary—if we retreat at all from that view, we shall have an infinitely worse trouble than anything that can arise from Hindu opposition.

This was one occasion when even staunch loyalist Moderates such as Surendranath Banerjea had to express their disapproval of the British.[79] To put the matter to rest, Minto met a select group of Muslims in Simla in April 1909 and explained to them that though the government intended to abide by the assurances given to the earlier Simla Deputation, it was impractical to expect an entirely separate Muslim electorate.[80] Accordingly, three proposals were discussed. The following is a summary of the discussions by Syed Wasti:[81]

> ... first the electoral college scheme; secondly separate electorates conferring exclusive representation, the Muslims not voting in any mixed electorates; and thirdly separate electorates, supplemented to the full extent of their legitimate claims by further representation either through mixed elect ....s, or by nomination where they failed to obtain a fair share of the elective seats. The first one had been dropped, for the second a majority of Muslims were insisting, but the third was the proposal of the Government of India.

Ultimately, Minto stuck to the government's proposal despite the mixed reactions from Muslim leaders.[82] To give effect to the government's proposal, it was decided to leave the question of method to the Rules and Regulations under the 1909 Act instead of casting it in stone in the Act itself. Accordingly, Section 6 of the Act spoke of regulations which would be framed by the Viceroy with the approval of the Secretary of State. To this extent, the League felt that the demands of the Simla Deputation had been met significantly, if not ideally.[83]

As for the Congress, in stark contrast to its sky-high praise of the reforms in the 1908 session, after the publication of the Regulations in November 1909 it realised that the so-called reforms were illusory.[84] While enlarging the Legislative Councils by providing for both nominated and indirectly elected members, the 1909 Act still allowed the government to retain an official majority.[85] Also, on the issue of Muslim representation, the Act deviated from Morley's proposal of electoral colleges and introduced communal electorates through regulations. Finally, as stated in the previous chapter, the arrogation of power in the hands of the Viceroy and the Secretary of State without legislative oversight of the framing of regulations which governed the conduct of elections, including the eligibility criteria for the elected and electorate, meant that the process was entirely at the mercy of the government.

In other words, the net result of the so-called reforms was only that they would allow the natives, in particular the Congress, to criticise the government from within as part of the Legislative Councils, which was hitherto being done from the outside through the resolutions of the Congress.[86] With this 'magnanimity', the British government furthered the process of co-option of the Moderates, the original 'safety valves', as part of the colonial administrative structure. Now that its demands for native presence and participation in the Councils were fulfilled, at least on the face of it, the Congress once again found itself in a jaded position, which reflected in the moribund and predictable nature of its resolutions in the Lahore session of 1909. In fact, the resolutions reveal that the Congress had failed to understand the implications of the Simla Deputation of October 1906 in time to counter Muslim demands, apart from having underestimated the will of the Muslim League to ensure that its demand for separate electorates be granted. Tellingly, for all the Congress's claims of being the sole legitimate representative of both Hindus and Muslims, out of the 243 delegates who attended the 1909 session, only five were Muslim.[87]

Here are a few extracts from the Congress resolutions of 1909, among which is one recognising Mohandas Karamchand Gandhi's efforts to fight discrimination in Transvaal, South Africa:[88]

Resolution No. III: High Appointments

That this Congress thanks the Government of His Imperial Majesty for appointing the Hon'ble S.P. Sinha, as a member of His Excellency the Governor General's Executive Council and the Right Hon'ble Mr. Ameer Ali as a member of the Privy Council.

Resolution No. IV: Council Reform

That this Congress while gratefully appreciating the earnest and arduous endeavours of Lord Morley and Lord Minto in extending to the people of this country a fairly liberal measure of constitutional reforms, as now embodied in the Indian Councils Act of 1909, deems it its duty to place on record its strong sense of disapproval of the creation of separate electorates on the basis of religion, and regrets that the regulations framed under the Act have not been framed in the same liberal spirit in which Lord Morley's despatch of last year was conceived. In particular the Regulations have caused widespread dissatisfaction throughout the country by reason of:

(a) the excessive and unfairly preponderant share of representation given to the followers of one particular religion;

(b) the unjust, invidious, and humiliating distinctions made between Moslem and non-Moslem subjects of His Majesty in the matter of the electorates, the franchise and qualifications of candidates;

(c) the wide, arbitrary and unreasonable disqualifications and restrictions for candidates seeking election to the Councils;

(d) the general distrust of the educated classes that runs through the whole course of the regulations; and

(e) the unsatisfactory composition of the non-official majorities in Provincial Councils rendering them ineffective and unreal for all practical purposes.

And this Congress earnestly urges the Government to so revise the Regulations, as soon as the present elections are over, as to remove these objectionable features, and bring them into harmony with the spirit of the Royal Message and the Secretary of State's despatch of last year.

Resolution No. VIII: Partition of Bengal

This Congress earnestly appeals to the Government of India and the Secretary of State for India, not to treat the question of the Partition of Bengal as incapable of reconsideration, but to take the earliest opportunity to so modify the said Partition as to keep the entire Bengali-speaking community under one and the same administration.

This Congress humbly submits that the rectification of this admitted error will be an act of far-sighted statesmanship. It will restore contentment to the Province of Bengal, give satisfaction to other Provinces, and enhance the prestige of His Majesty's Government throughout the country.

This Congress appoints Messrs. Surendranath Bannerji and Bhupendranath Bose to proceed to England as a deputation, to lay the question of the Partition before the authorities, and the public there.

Resolution No. IX: Transvaal Indians

This Congress expresses its great admiration of the intense patriotism, courage and self-sacrifice of the Indians in the Transvaal—Mohameddan and Hindu, Zoroastrian and Christian—who heroically suffering persecution in the interests of their country are carrying on their peaceful and selfless struggle for elementary civil rights against heavy and overwhelming odds.

This Congress offers its warmest encouragement to Mr. M.K. Gandhi and his brave and faithful associates, and calls upon all Indians, of whatever race or creed, to help them unstintedly with funds; and, in this connection, the Congress begs to convey to Mr. R.J. Tata its high appreciation of the patriotic instincts which have inspired his munificent donation of Rs. 25,000 to his suffering countrymen in South Africa in their hour of need and trial ...

From these resolutions, it is evident that the initial jubilation of the Congress in 1908 over the proposed reforms gave way to disappointment after the 1909 Act was passed. Yet, the Congress did not reconsider its position with respect to the purge from within its ranks of the Extremists of the time, who seemed to understand the true nature of the colonial beast and had no unrealistic expectations of just and fair treatment from it. The Muslim League did not hold a session in 1909, but within three years of its founding it had achieved a major victory on its journey to re-establish Muslim state power in the Bharatiya subcontinent, namely the constitutional entrenchment of the Dehlawite vision and its Two-Nation Theory. This would haunt Bharat until 1947 and beyond, albeit under a different label, namely the so-called majority–minority divide.

The Debates on the Indian Councils Act of 1909

As stated earlier, on 6 June 1907, Morley informed the House of Commons of the Government of India deliberations on the reforms. The following were his words:[89]

> But now I come to my last point. Last autumn the Governor General appointed a Committee of the Executive Council to consider the development of the administrative machinery, and at the end of March last he publicly informed his Legislative Council that he had sent home a despatch to the Secretary of State proposing suggestions for a move in advance. This was not in accordance with instructions from us; it emanated entirely from the Government of India. Now let us consider this. The Viceroy with a liberal—I do not use the word in a Party sense—with a liberal courageous mind entered deliberately on the path of improvement. The public in India were aware of it. They waited, and are now waiting the result with the liveliest interest and curiosity. Meanwhile the riots happened in Rawalpindi, in Lahore. After these riots broke out, what was the course we ought to take? Some in this country lean to the opinion—and it is excusable—that the riots ought to suspend all suggestions and talk of reform. Sir, His Majesty's Government considered this view, and in the end they took, very determinedly, the opposite view. They held that such a withdrawal from a line of policy suggested by the Governor General would, of course, have been construed as a triumph for the party of sedition. They held that, to draw back on account of local and sporadic disturbances, however serious, anxious, and troublesome they might be, would have been a very grave humiliation. To hesitate to make a beginning with our own policy of improving the administrative machinery of the Indian Government would have been taken as a sign of nervousness, trepidation, and fear; and fear, which is always unworthy in any Government, is in the Indian Government, not only unworthy, but extremely dangerous. I hope the House concurs with His Majesty's Government ... The Government of India will now frame what is called a Resolution. That draft Resolution, when framed by them in conformity with the instructions of His Majesty's Government, will

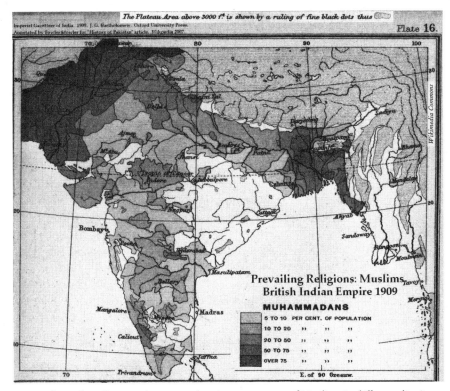

Map of British Indian Empire, 1909, showing percentage of Muslims in different districts, from the *Imperial Gazetteer of India* (Oxford University Press, 1909)

in due course be sent here. We shall consider that draft, and then it will be my duty to present it to this House if legislation is necessary, as it probably will be; and it will be published in India to be discussed there by all those concerned. The proposals I would adumbrate are these. We have given approval to the establishment of an advisory Council of Notables.

On the same day, another member of the House of Commons, Earl Percy, commented on the stark distinction between the positions of the Moderates and the Extremists, on why India was not yet ready for self-government, and how India did not, in his opinion, constitute a 'nation':

Whatever defects there may be in the machinery of administration, it is, at all events, remarkable testimony to the confidence which men of all Parties in this country feel in the handful of men to whom is entrusted the burden of British rule in India that, from first to last, throughout recent events public opinion has refused, and rightly refused, to take an alarmist view of the situation. And, whatever other moral may be drawn from those events, nothing can be more encouraging than the manifestations of loyalty which they have evoked from the leaders of almost every section of native opinion, whether Sikh, Rajput, or Mahomedan. It is obvious that the stories to which the right hon.

Gentleman has alluded came from the same mint as the scandalous accusations which were trumped up a few years ago against the British soldiers engaged in plague operations at Poona; and, while I quite agree that we need not lash ourselves into any unnecessary anger or fury, I do hope the Government of India will devote their utmost efforts to tracing those stories to their source, and will punish their authors as they deserve. I think the right hon. Gentleman has pointed out with unanswerable force the objection there would be to a prosecution in cases of arrest and deportation like those of Lajpat Rai and other ringleaders; but do not the same arguments apply with equal force to the present method of proceeding against seditious language in the native Press? Prosecution is in very many cases precisely what the local newspaper desires; and I cannot help thinking that power ought to be given to the local Governments, if they do not possess it, to suppress a paper after sufficient warning if it persists in disregarding that warning, without any preliminary prosecution at all. With regard to the reorganisation of the sanitary staff in India, I hope that the right hon. Gentleman will consider the desirability of enlisting a certain number of trained native assistants. *Passing to the question of reform I suspect that a good many people will think that the concession of any reforms at the present moment is injudicious because it is almost certain to be very widely described as a concession to agitation.* I do not approach the question from that point of view, partly for the reason which the right hon. Gentleman stated, but partly also because I hold very strongly the view that the demands put forward by the party of reform in India are totally inadmissible, and therefore if I thought the changes contemplated by the right hon. Gentleman were calculated in any degree to further their aims and objects, I should regard them with equal disapproval and hostility whether they were introduced now, or at a later period. Of course, when I say the demands are inadmissible I do not refer to the demand made for a larger employment of natives in the detailed work of administration. That is a natural and laudable aspiration with which everybody must sympathise, and every effort has been made to give effect to it. Already by far the larger number of provincial posts are held by natives, and a considerable number of the higher posts, especially in the judiciary, are in native hands also. *But the demands, even of the moderate section of the Reform Party in Congress,* go much further than that. What they really demand is the establishment, sooner or later, of Parliamentary institutions, and the substitution for autocratic rule of the system of government by majorities. The right hon. Gentleman has said that for as long a time as he can foresee British rule in India must be personal and autocratic. I should be inclined to go still further and say that for all time the attempt to govern by majorities in India must in the nature of things be doomed to failure. It is not that we distrust the loyalty of the Indian people. It is not that they are deficient in education or backward in political training. These defects might be corrected by a gradual concession of responsibility, and have never been admitted to be a barrier to the grant of considerable powers of *self-government* in municipal affairs. The real difficulty, the impossibility, lies in the two facts which are at the root of the *Indian problem,* and which differentiate it from any other. The first is that India is not a homogeneous nationality with common sentiments and aspirations, but a congeries of races animated to a large extent by different and even antagonistic ideals, and only deterred, as we see in Eastern Bengal, by the constant interposition of the Central Power from attempting to force their own ideas on other people by violent means. The second is that in this congeries of races nature has chosen to assign the qualities that make for physical predominance to the races which are neither intellectually the most versatile nor the largest in point of numbers. The result is, as it seems to me, that any attempt to govern India on the principle of government by majorities must mean the government of the strong by the weak, a government which could not exist for a day except by the support of British bayonets, of that very Army which is described by the reformers as the instrument of an alien Power. When we are told that British rule is not popular in India, it may be so. *I do not believe any western Government is exactly popular with an Oriental people,* and I am not sure that they are likely to feel any greater respect for it when it displays so constant a tendency to self-accusation and self-examination, and has such a perfect passion for conducting those operations in public. I daresay our rule is not in the strict sense of the word popular, though I do not believe it that is unpopular; but if you wish to devise a means of making it not merely unpopular, but absolutely abhorrent to the people of India, I can imagine nothing more certain to effect that object than a system under which British authority would be utilised in order to force upon a number of proud and warlike races a Government of intellectuals which they not only hate but despise, and which, so far as those races are concerned, would be no whit less foreign than we are ourselves. If that premise be granted, if Parliamentary institutions are clearly impossible, surely we are deluding ourselves as well as the Indian people if we induce them to believe that the changes adumbrated to-day, or any changes that we can ever introduce, will carry us a single step further in the direction of the real aims of the Congress party. It seems to me to be much better to lay it down at the outset that we start with a wholly different objective, and that however true in the abstract it may be to say, as the Prime Minister said last year—and a most unfortunate observation, I think it was—'that good government is no substitute for self-government,' *so far as India, at all events, is concerned, it is good government and not self-government that we have in view.* And if this be the case, if, in the words of the King's Speech, we can allow nothing which would weaken the strength and unity of the executive power, then it seems to me that any changes that we can introduce into the Councils at home or in India must be framed with the object not of giving these Councils any share in the control of policy, but of making them, if possible, more useful as advisory bodies. [Emphases added]

Yet another member, George Hardy, touched on the aspirations of the Moderates in the Congress, the outrages in Punjab and Bengal, and J.B. Fuller's preferential treatment of Muslims:

> The right hon. Gentleman had shown his friendship to India by the reduction of the salt tax, and by conferring various other advantages. When they listened to the right hon. Gentleman they realised that the people of India would recognise that at last they had a Minister in the House of Commons in whom they might have confidence. In moving the Amendment standing in his name he fully recognised that it was the duty of the Government to maintain law and order in India at all costs. He would not criticise in any way the work of the Government and their efforts to carry out that work. But there was a feeling amongst a large part of our own fellow-countrymen that the recent trouble might have been avoided with a little care and thought, and had perhaps been brought about by methods which were alien to the spirit which Englishmen extended to other races with free institutions. Fears had been expressed to him as to the advisability of moving this Resolution, but it would be an evil day when an Englishman could not be a friend of India without being an enemy of his own country. They had lately received alarming reports of riots, boycotting, and meetings where fierce denunciations of the Viceroy and his policy were indulged in. The native Press has been unfortunately like some of our own newspapers, stirring up the people by appealing to their baser passions. *There had been conflicts between Mahomedans and Hindus.* They also knew that there was never smoke without fire, and the consequence was that he and his friends had brought this Motion forward that afternoon to ask His Majesty's Government to consent to an inquiry by either a Parliamentary Committee or a Royal Commission in India into the causes which had led to this serious unrest. The late Lord Randolph Churchill, supported by Mr. Gladstone, desired that the Government should, like the old East India Company, inquire into the methods of the Government of India every twenty years. The Secretary of State had stated that he would grant such an inquiry, and they were delighted to hear it. What were the causes which had led to this spirit of unrest? *There had been disturbances in Eastern Bengal and in the Punjab. Though those disturbances had occurred at the same time, the reasons for them were entirely different. The original cause which had culminated in the late unhappy episode, had been the failure of the educated classes of Hindus to obtain the slightest recognition by constitutional methods of their demands for reform.* Twenty-two years ago they started their great Annual Congress. Educated Hindus from all parts of India assembled, at great expense and inconvenience, and in a perfect constitutional manner they stated the needs and wants of the Indian people. Sometimes the Congress was presided over by English gentlemen of the highest reputation, and Members of this House. In the Congress the hopes and aspirations of the educated people of India centred. England to them was

the Mecca of freedom. They had studied English institutions and English history; and they believed that if they adopted constitutional methods, the Viceroy would listen sympathetically and use them as a method of finding out the needs of the people. For twenty-two years they met, but their resolutions which were sent to the Viceroy were ignored, and their receipt was only officially acknowledged. Slighted and snubbed they steadily kept in view the true constitutional side, believing that in the end they would succeed. The moderate party, always telling the Congress that the time would come when their demands would be listened to, kept within constitutional limits and trusted that they would eventually attain their end. But hope deferred maketh the heart sick. When the present Government came into power, much was hoped and looked for. The expectations which had arisen from the bold statesmanlike manner in which the Government had dealt with the Transvaal were dashed to the ground, although they felt that the time was ripe, and that at last they would be able to obtain some of the reforms they had been asking for so long. *Then occurred the difficulties which brought about the present trouble. It should be remembered that throughout the Congresses there had always been a small section of members who were extremists, and the danger was that those extremists might persuade the people of India no longer to follow constitutional methods, but to try agitation.* He did not think that there was the slightest fear that when the people of India found that the reforms which he and his friends advocated were going to be granted they would feel they had come from the policy of agitation. We were bound in retaining our hold on India to keep our conscience clean. We were bound, if we were to justify our claim to rule, to give the people of India something more than a slow sort of justice. We were bound to give those people an opportunity of rising to a higher plane of civilisation and comfort than they at present enjoyed. We could not do that unless we listened to their requests. We could not put down by force those who only demanded justice or equality. After all, it had to be remembered that righteousness exalted a nation, and we should do right to the inhabitants of India so that, if at any time we had to fight, we should have a good cause. *The danger was that from the Himalayas to the plains of India, if the people found that they could obtain no redress for their grievances by using constitutional methods they would follow the most advanced leaders. Another great cause of unrest was the partition of Bengal.* It might be a question of sentiment; but sentiment was a great factor in the government of the world. What would the people of Scotland or of Ireland say if their country were to be split in half? The heather would be on fire with a vengeance. The Bengalees felt that in some way or another this partition was a dismemberment of the mother-land; and the result was that ever since it had taken place the unrest had steadily increased. The authorities might drive that unrest under; that could be easily done. But, all human experience taught that a great governing nation should allow constitutional steam to blow off rather than compress political gas. To show the intensity of the feeling of the people over the partition of Bengal, when the day arrived for its accomplishment hundreds of thousands went into mourning. No fires were kindled, no shoes or stockings were worn, and only a loin cloth was wrapped round the body. The constitutional party held over one thousand meetings to protest against the partition. The request was this, and it was made to day—Even if you cannot give us back Bengal, give us some modification of the present position of affairs, so that we may not be a country cut in half. It had been said that the agitators were a microscopic minority, but the House must remember that they appealed to a mighty host. They must recollect that these educated and advanced men who were using constitutional means to secure what they wanted, having been educated and knowing town life, went back to their native villages once a year. They were therefore acquainted with the condition of their people, and realised their needs. Indeed, there were no other people in India who had a greater opportunity of doing so. How much better it would have been if the policy which had been declared that night had been declared five years ago! It would have saved trouble and unrest. They had, he thought, to thank the Secretary for India for his timely and bold action. He would not speak further about *Bengal, where the trouble had arisen from a certain governor publicly declaring in the form of an eastern allegory that he had two wives, and that as his Hindoo wife was sulky, he was determined to pay attention to his Mahomedan spouse.* He also issued circulars instructing his subordinates in making appointments to give preference to Mahomedans, even if better Hindus were available. Taking their cue from their master, the Mahomedan officials openly showed partiality and spoke disrespectfully, and mischief had been done which it would take a generation to put right. [Emphases added]

On the subject of allowing more native members in Legislative Councils and the role played by Nawab Salimullah in inciting riots against Hindus after the Partition of Bengal, James O'Grady commented as under:

They had asked again and again that one or two natives should be admitted to the Viceroy's Executive Council. Some hon. Gentlemen appeared to think that that claim should not be put forward in view of the fact that India was an Empire in which *there were many races, speaking different languages, and holding different religions, and also caste distinctions, it being believed that the natives themselves would object, and that they would prefer Europeans on the Council rather than men who possibly spoke a different language from themselves.* What was lost sight of was the fact that there was a growing national life in India gradually breaking down the barriers of caste and creed, and Indians would not be satisfied until they had representation in the Executive Council. Another matter that he desired to bring before the attention of the House was the unfortunate riots at Commilla. These he attributed to causes having their origin in the colossal blunder of the Viceroy in partitioning Bengal. The

Mahomedans thought that something had been conceded to them, and they construed it as a licence to do as they liked. He had asked Questions on the matter, and he regretted to say that they had not been satisfactorily answered. The Nawab of Dacca went down into the locality, and held pro-partition demonstrations for the purpose apparently of showing his loyalty but, like the player Queen in Hamlet, he protested his loyalty too much; it was said that somebody threw a brick at him. That charge afterwards dwindled down until it was said that only a stone was thrown. He spoke subject to correction by the right hon. Gentleman, but it was reported that the Mahomedans, after the change in the administration, maltreated the Hindu traders, strewed their goods about their shops in the bazaar, and committed acts of common robbery. However that might be, the fact remained that as the result of the partition of Bengal great religious disturbances took place. The gentleman he had named went back to the Viceroy's Council and talked of the reign of King Demos being ended, and had the temerity to use these words—We only appeal to the Government to put down with a firm hand every attempt to sow the seeds of disaffection, and to seduce the people from their faith and belief in your Excellency's Government. Personally he thought that gentleman was the greatest agitator in the whole of the unfortunate disturbance. On the question of the riots alone there was need for inquiry. He came to the most important part of what he had to say, namely, the arrest and the deportation of Lajpat Rai and Ajit Singh. The right hon. Gentleman had gone out of his way to apologise for the circumstances under which the arrest was made. [Emphasis added]

On the quality of Curzon's tenure and the volatile state of affairs that was bequeathed by him to Minto, here is an account of how Donald Smeaton weighed in:

The Motion on the Paper asserted the existence of dissatisfaction in India. He [Smeaton] was aware that there was dissatisfaction, but he differed from the opinion of many of his hon. friends as to its causes. The causes of the present dissatisfaction and unrest lay deeper than had been described by previous speakers. He was sorry to say, but he said it with a full sense of responsibility, that the unrest was largely due to what he was bound to call the maladministration of the late Government of India, the late Viceroy. *The late Viceroy, Lord Curzon, unfortunately did not know, and never learnt, what kind of people he had to govern.* He (Mr. Smeaton) admitted and appreciated the high ideals which, at the outset at least, Lord Curzon had set before himself. But he completely failed throughout, and particularly during the last half of his administration, to understand, and indeed on certain occasions resolutely refused to understand, the particular temperament of the people with whom he had to deal. *There had been a long series of most regrettable incidents during the last two or three years of the late Viceroy's term of office, due largely to his own blundering; but they had had the effect of raising the temper of the people in India to a fever heat, of causing uneasiness and distrust everywhere; so that bitter dissatisfaction had been the heritage bequeathed by Lord Curzon to Lord Minto,* the present Viceroy. That was the reason of the intense feeling of irritation which caused the people of India to view everything done by the Government as wrong. The first incident to which he attached importance was the meretricious show in 1903—that Field of the Cloth of Gold—that Delhi Durbar. That incident shocked the people of India, because at the time 25,000 to 30,000 people were dying every week of plague, and millions of them were only recovering from famine. The National Congress pronounced a severe condemnation of that extraordinary pageant, and its condemnation found an echo in every village. *Several of the Native Princes resented the way in which they were summoned, and the Ameer of Afghanistan (as the right hon. Gentleman had stated) point blank refused.* The Official Secrets Bill and the officialisation of the universities were untimely measures and were quite unnecessary, and irritated the educated classes. The latter was regarded as an attempt to render education more expensive, and to prevent the poorer classes of the people from obtaining it. Then there came the destruction of the representative elective system on the Calcutta Municipality, followed by the invasion of Tibet. The latter event had had a much more far-reaching effect than had ever been understood in this country. There was not a native State in India which did not feel that its position and safety were jeopardised by that invasion. It was an open secret that in consequence of it the Ameer of Afghanistan would not visit India during Lord Curzon's Viceroyalty. Then there were the extraordinary scenes in the Legislative Council. There were recriminatory debates and attempts to stifle independent statements of opinion. *Then followed the refusal of the Viceroy, perhaps on bona fide ground, but it was difficult to say what they were, to receive a deputation of the National Congress. Lord Curzon declined to receive that deputation or to have anything to do with the very temperate and moderate representations of the Congress*—a body which, whatever its other characteristics, could fairly claim to represent millions of the educated and law-abiding and loyal people of India. On what possible ground dared he refuse to listen to a deputation from such a body? Then there was the partition of Bengal, and—what was perhaps the worst sin of all—the speech delivered at the convocation of the University of Calcutta, in which the Viceroy compared most unfavourably the people of the East with the people of the West, and declared that the people of the East were unfit for government, and that the only people who were entitled to govern were the white people from the West. That speech was accompanied by vituperative epithets which deeply offended the people of Bengal, and were rebuked even by the English Press in India. All this culminated in the partition of Bengal. *He [Smeaton] differed from his hon. friends the Members for Nottingham and Walworth in the opinions they had expressed about the partition of Bengal. No doubt it was unfortunate and untimely, but he thought there were grounds for at least a redistribution of territory, and if it had not been for the extraordinary secrecy, if not trickery, with which the measure was consummated he was inclined to think that the partition, or rather the redistribution of the Province of Bengal might have been accomplished without raising the fierce resistance which it had now encountered.* If there had been honest candour, a free interchange of opinion and a frank disavowal of all sinister intentions—had there been all these, and had not the partition been carried out away up in Simla out of reach of the people concerned—had these steps been taken, he believed the partition would now have been effectually accomplished and the province would have settled down contentedly. But those steps were not taken, and the result was to excite combative and fierce resistance which would go on for some time. The right hon. Gentleman the Secretary of State had told them of the reforms which he meant to introduce, and parenthetically he might say that if only the Viceroy had had on his Executive Council at Simla an Indian gentleman when he decided on the drastic measure of deportation his hands would have been greatly strengthened throughout the country. He thought the right hon. Gentleman had been very well advised in those moderate measures of reform which he had adumbrated. The presence of one or two Indian gentlemen of experience on the Council of India in London would be a really valuable acquisition, and would act as a useful tonic to the Administration. As to the Advisory Council, he hoped that the right hon. Gentleman would go still further than he had done and would give to that Council a certain amount of independent authority, subject of course to a veto of the chief executive, and not confine them merely to the function of advising. If that were done he was convinced that there would be a much greater future in store for India than it had experienced in the past. [Emphases added]

On 27 March 1908, as part of the debates in the Governor General's Council in India on the proposed Minto–Morley Reforms, Tikka Sahib Ripudaman Singh, the Maharaja of Nabha, drew attention to the riots in Punjab and the British administration's deliberate policy to look the other way when Hindus and Sikhs were being butchered by members of the majority Muslim community in that province. As discussed earlier in this chapter, there was a general state of unrest in the Punjab Province in 1906–07 owing to a host of agrarian- and land-related legislations passed by the British. Using the pretext of a general revolt against the British establishment, acts of violence were also being committed by members of the Muslim community against Hindus and Sikhs of Punjab. This brutality was part of the larger organised violence being committed against Europeans, Hindus and Sikhs by the Wahhabis since the mid-1800s. This was earlier captured in the debates of 1866–67 in the Imperial Legislative Council on the Murderous Outrages in Panjáb Bill, which was specifically mooted to increase the term of punishment to deal with the fanatics committing such murders. Here are a few extracts from these debates of 1866–67 which shed light on the religious nature of such murders.

On 21 December 1866, the Murderous Outrages in Panjáb Bill was moved by one of the members of the Governor General's Council, J.E.L. Brandreth, who said:[90]

> ... in moving for leave to introduce a Bill for the suppression of murderous outrages in certain districts of the Panjáb, said that the recent murderous attacks, attributable to religious fanaticism, made on Europeans in stations on the Panjáb frontier, which were the main cause of the present Bill being proposed, were doubtless well known to the Council from the newspapers and other sources, and it would not be necessary that he should enter into their details ...

> If there was reasonable ground for expecting that we had heard the last of these outrages, he (Mr. Brandreth) should have been far from recommending any change in the existing law. He did not think that our Codes of law, with all the safeguards which they insisted upon, should be set aside to meet a case of barely possible contingency. But there was no reasonable ground for such a hope. This crime had been too frequent of late to justify such an expectation. Not to take into account the crimes which occurred during the earlier period of our possession of the Panjáb, in one year of which, if he recollected aright, no less than four of these crimes were committed, take the last five years or thereabouts. Within that period, no less than five of these cases of murderous outrages took place. In three of these cases the crime was complete. Three Europeans were murdered by fanatics ...

On 4 January 1867, another member of the Imperial Legislative Council, Summer Maine, supported the Bill as under (reported in third person):[91]

> ... that he entirely approved of the Bill. He believed that the recital in the preamble was certainly true; that in certain districts of the Panjáb, fanatics had frequently murdered and attempted to murder servants of the Queen and other persons whose religion differed from that of the offender, and further that the general law of the country was not adequate to suppress such offences. As regarded [sic] the second category—persons other than servants of the Queen—he might vouch His Excellency the Viceroy authority for the statement that, not only European Christians, but the Hindú traders who resorted to these frontier regions for purposes of business were occasionally the victims of these fanatical assassinations. It was true that the list of victims, even as extended by the letter which Mr. Brendreth had read, was not very large, but still the very reason of its smallness was that the Panjáb authorities on the frontier had found it practically impossible to act on the general law of the country. Whenever one of these assassinations was reported, the

administration officer invariably stated that he had been obliged summarily to execute the culprit, and when the facts were reported, they invariably constituted so strong a case, that the person who had thus gone beyond the law received the approval not only of this Government, but of the Secretary of State ...

Supporting the Bill and also commenting on how Hindu traders too were attacked by the fanatics, the then Viceroy John Lawrence said:[92]

His Excellency The President said that he was very much in favour of this Bill. He considered that its introduction was urgently required in the Panjáb ... *He could fully bear out what his Hon'ble friend Mr. Maine had said, that in former days, when His Excellency was Chief Commissioner of the Panjáb, assaults were continually made on Hindú traders. Some of them were carried away into captivity, from which they were not liberated without payment of heavy ransoms, and in some cases where ransom was refused, they were tortured and put to death. No doubt the love of plunder was often, to a considerable extent, the actuating motive of the criminals in these cases. But fanaticism also operated, and in proof of this he might mention that it was only Hindú traders, and never Muhammadans, that were thus maltreated.* [Emphases added]

This should come as no surprise, given the history of the Wahhabi Movement and the hatred of the Wahhabis for the Sikhs and Hindus.

Coming back to the Maharaja of Nabha's statement on 27 March 1908 on the Minto–Morley Reforms, he had this to say on the communal disturbances in Punjab and British indifference to it:[93]

The culprits who made such a cowardly and mean attack in December last on the life of Mr. Allen (who has since then happily recovered from his injuries) and *those who burnt a certain Sikh Gurdwara in the Punjab not many months ago, are still at large,* and no trace of them is to be found ... I may be permitted to make a few passing remarks about the Gurdwara arson case to which I have just alluded. In that case all the accused were discharged by the trying Magistrate, but there are one or two points in his judgment dated the 5th December 1907, which deserve attention. He says:

'I may state here that my reason for not trying the case myself was, that I had watched the police proceedings from the beginning and had consequently formed opinions as to the bona fides of the prosecution witnesses. I transferred the case to my own Court however on the 2nd November 1907 for reasons "which need not be specified".

'The investigation has proved to me conclusively that the outrage was not the result of local religious antipathies but merely an attempt on the part of some of the Muhammadans of Udharwal to induce the Hindus to come back to the village and look after their property.'

I have taken these extracts of the judgment from the Khalsa Advocate dated the 11th January 1908, a weekly published in Amritsar. Now as regards the first point, the Magistrate ought to have given his reason for transferring the case to his own Court, which he says 'need not be specified'. But the question arises why? He admits himself that before hearing the case, nay even before recording evidence, he had formed his own opinions regarding it, and in these circumstances what else could have been expected from him than what subsequently happened? On the second point I need not say much, because the absurdity of the Magistrate's argument is self-evident. What an extraordinary theory that the outrage was not the result of religions antipathies—a theory which it was the duty of the Magistrate to verify by the facts of the case. A supposition could not and should not have found a place in a judicial record. *The Government encourages the people at the time of plague to evacuate their houses, but in Udharwal, when the poor Hindus went forth, our Muhammadan brethren amused themselves, as the Magistrate practically tells us, by burning their Dharmsala, in order to induce the Hindus to come back to their houses and* look after their property. I sincerely trust that the Government will not allow this matter to rest here, and that we shall hear before long of the arrest and exemplary punishment of the real culprits in that case. [Emphases added]

On the British administration's attempts to impose Urdu through the education system in Punjab, the Maharaja of Nabha had the following to say before the Governor General's Council in India:

In the first place, an attempt should be made to instruct the pupils in reading, writing and arithmetic in their own language, not as it is done now in Urdu, which is a foreign language. The result is that after three or four years' study they hardly understand the meaning of the words they read or repeat. Education to be of any real advantage must be given first in the easiest language to learn; and could there be any language easier to learn than one's mother-tongue? So primary education in the Punjab ought to be given through the Punjabi only, and in the characters peculiar to that language. When the Government has recognised a knowledge of Punjabi as a desideratum for the British military and civil officers, it is very strange indeed that the Educational Department should have forced on the poor Punjabis the necessity to forget their own vernacular for the camp language of the Mughal Emperors which is not a general household language in India. [Emphasis added]

Questioning the rationale and intent behind the proposal to introduce separate electorates exclusively for Muslims, the Maharaja observed:[94]

Coming to the proposals regarding the Imperial Legislative Council, in my humble opinion it would be most unfortunate and undesirable to introduce any racial feeling in this matter or to give any sort of prominence to any particular community. This would cause great heart-burning among other communities. Under paragraph 12 of the Government of India's letter I strongly object to the proposal that in the

Viceroy's Council two members should be elected by the members of a certain community, and that out of four non-officials to be nominated by the Viceroy, two seats at least should be filled by members of the same class. Thus four seats will be the exclusive monopoly of a certain community, while no such provision is made for other communities like Hindus, Parsis, Jains and Sikhs. The reason given by the Government for this proposal is that the Muhammadans form a minority and that their interests must be safeguarded. *Now as far as minority is concerned the Parsis and Sikhs form even a smaller minority numerically than the Muhammadans*, and yet no provision is made for their representation. No other community in India can be found more educated, more enlightened and more advanced than the Parsis. The Sikhs, though still backward in the matter of education, have always proved themselves firm supporters of Government, are not men of words but of deeds, have fought the battles of their King, as well under the burning rays of the sun as on snow-clad mountains, and are always ready to lay down their lives for their beloved Emperor. When no provision is made for other communities, it does not seem at all fair to favour a particular community by giving it special privileges. The same reasons apply to paragraph 17 of the Government of India's letter as to the proposal that a certain number of seats should be exclusively reserved for and filled by members of a particular community in the Provincial Legislative Councils.

The Government of India in paragraph 19 itself admits that as in two of the seven provinces with Legislative Councils the followers of Islam constitute a majority, therefore a certain number of Muhammadans may also be returned to the Imperial Council under sub-head (b) of head D. I apprehend that perhaps they have overlooked the fact that in the same way under sub-head (c) of head D a certain number of Muhammadans are bound to be returned to the Imperial Council. Therefore, if the proposals as they now stand are finally sanctioned, there will be a great preponderance of Muhammadans in the Imperial Council, and perhaps at times this number might be as much as three-fourths of the whole non-official Indian members. Under the present arrangement only two seats will be available, under head E of the circular letter, for nomination by His Excellency the Viceroy for all other communities, a number which is all too small for such a vast country as India. Therefore, I submit that under head D, sub-head (d), and under head E, all six seats should be reserved for nomination by the Viceroy, without any distinction as provided for in the letter. The Government of India in the concluding portion of paragraph 17 itself admits that Indian gentlemen of position sometimes refuse to offer themselves as candidates to an electorate, and at least for this reason, as I have suggested above, the six seats should be reserved for nomination by His Excellency the Viceroy. [Emphases added]

On 17 December 1908, responding to a question on the need for separate electorates for Muslims, the then Under-Secretary of State for India, Thomas Buchanan, said in the House of Commons:[95]

We intend to *secure a representation of the landholding class, the Mahomedans, the planting community in certain provinces,* and there will be a large increase in the number of members elected to the Councils by the municipalities and district boards. In Bengal there are now three members so elected, in the future there will be eight. In the United Provinces the increase will be from four to ten, and in Bombay from three to eight. The numbers on the Viceroy's Legislative Council will also be increased from twenty-four to sixty-two, excluding the Viceroy in both cases. But here we shall maintain a permanent official majority. We shall largely increase, from four to twelve, the elected representatives on the Viceroy's Council from the Provincial Legislative Councils: we shall endeavour to provide special representation of landholders and Mahomedans from various provinces, and we shall increase the representation of chambers of commerce and the Indian commercial community. These are dry figures, which will be more easily understood from the Papers, and with regard to which there are certain details not yet worked out. There are, as hon. Members are aware who have studied the question, difficulties in the method of obtaining representation of communities like the Mahomedans or landholders. We want to minimise nomination as much as possible, and we want to avoid creating special electorates if we can. Anyhow, we have made suggestions to the Government of India to the effect that it might be possible to devise a system of electoral colleges by which in the more advanced provinces the Mahomedans, landholders and other special communities might obtain their representation on the Councils in proportion to their numbers and importance without the creation of special electorates. We have not yet received the views of the Government of India on this subject and its practicability. But hon. Members will clearly see what our aim is. We recognise that there are special communities and interests which should and must get representation on the Councils. They would not obtain it if we were to introduce there our home electoral system. We want to secure it for them in the least invidious way, and the way most acceptable to themselves. [Emphasis added]

While introducing the Councils Bill for a second reading on 23 February 1909 in the House of Lords, Morley, having received heavy opposition to his proposal of electoral colleges for Muslim representation, reaffirmed his commitment to the Simla Deputation as follows:[96]

There is one very important chapter in these regulations which I think now on the Second Reading of the Bill, without waiting for Committee, I ought to say a few words to your Lordships about—I mean the Mahomedans. That is a part of the Bill and scheme which has no doubt attracted a great deal of criticism and excited a great deal of feeling in that very important community. We suggested to the Government of India a certain plan. We did not prescribe it, we did not order it, but we suggested and recommended this plan for their consideration—no more than that. It was the plan of a mixed or composite electoral college, in which Mahomedans and Hindus should pool their votes, so to say. The wording of the recommendation in my Despatch was, as I soon discovered, ambiguous—a grievous defect, of which I make bold to hope I am not very often in public business guilty. But, to the best of my belief, under any construction the plan of Hindus and Mahomedans voting together in a mixed and composite electorate would have secured to the Mahomedan electors, wherever they were so minded, the chance of returning their own representatives in their due proportion. The political idea at the bottom of that recommendation which has found so little favour was that such composite action would bring the two great communities more closely together, and this idea of promoting harmony was held by men of very high Indian authority and experience who were among my advisers at the India Office. *But the Mahomedans protested that the Hindus would elect a pro-Hindu upon it, just as I suppose in a mixed college of say seventy-five Catholics and twenty-five Protestants voting together the Protestants might suspect that the Catholics voting for the Protestant would choose what is called a Romanising Protestant and as little of a Protestant as they could find. Suppose the other way.* In Ireland there is an expression, a 'shoneen' Catholic—that is to say, a Catholic who, though a Catholic, is too friendly with English Conservatism and other influences which the Nationalists dislike. And it might be said, if there were seventy-five Protestants against twenty-five Catholics, that the Protestants when giving a vote in the way of Catholic representation would return 'shoneens.' I am not going to take your Lordships' time up by arguing this to-day. With regard to schemes of proportional representation, as Calvin said of another study, 'excessive study either finds a man mad or makes him so.' At any rate, the Government of India doubted whether our plan would work, and we have abandoned it. I do not think it was a bad plan, but it is no use, if you are making an earnest attempt in good faith at a general pacification, out of parental fondness for a clause interrupting that good process by sitting too tight.

The Mahomedans demand three things. I had the pleasure of receiving a deputation from them and I know very well what is in their minds. They demand the election of their own representatives to these councils in all the stages, just as in Cyprus, where, I think, the Mahomedans vote by themselves. They have nine votes and the non-Mahomedans have three, or the other way about. So in Bohemia, where the Germans vote alone and have their own register. Therefore we are not without a precedent and a parallel for the idea of a separate register. Secondly, they want a number of seats in excess of their numerical strength. Those two demands we are quite ready and intend to meet in full. There is a third demand that, if there is a Hindu on the Viceroy's Executive Council—a subject on which I will venture to say a little to your Lordships before I sit down—there should be two Indian members on the

Viceroy's Council and that one should be a Mahomedan. Well, as I told them and as I now tell your Lordships, I see no chance whatever of meeting their views in that way to any extent at all.

To go back to the point of the registers, some may be shocked at the idea of a religious register at all, of a register framed on the principle of religious belief. We may wish, we do wish—certainly I do—that it were otherwise. We hope that time, with careful and impartial statesmanship, will make things otherwise. Only let us not forget that the difference between Mahomedanism and Hinduism is not a mere difference of articles of religious faith. It is a difference in life, in tradition, in history, in all the social things as well as articles of belief that constitute a community. Do not let us forget what makes it interesting and even exciting. Do not let us forget that, in talking of Hindus and Mahomedans, we are dealing with and brought face to face with vast historic issues, dealing with some of the very mightiest forces that through all the centuries and ages have moulded the fortunes of great States and the destinies of countless millions of mankind. Thoughts of that kind are what give to Indian politics and to Indian work extraordinary fascination, and at the same time impose the weight of no ordinary burden. [Emphases added]

On 29 March 1909, Maneckjee Byramjee Dadabhoy pointed out the serious concerns that would arise with the creation of communal electorates in a multi-religious society such as Bharat in the proceedings of the Governor General's Imperial Legislative Council:[97]

The introduction of the principle of class representation on the basis of the fancied importance of Mahomedans has at once taken away the chief merit of the Scheme, and given umbrage to the great non-Moslem communities of India. My Lord, I am not a Hindu; I am under no personal obligations to the Hindu; I do not hold his brief; I bear no animosity to the Mahomedan. My remarks are grounded only upon my conceptions of the political necessities of the situation. *And I shall be wanting in duty if I do not say that I fail to see the justice and the wisdom of Lord Morley's concessions to Mahomedan demands. Religion is widely apart from politics, and once the religious element is eliminated from the discussion, I do not understand how Hindu interests are opposed to Mahomedan interests in politics.* I shall be glad to know what these so-called Mahomedan interests are. I cannot conceive them. It is a mistake to suppose that the bulk of the Indian Mahomedans are separated from their Hindu congeners by any sharp cleavage of race and tradition. In their present backward state they cannot have better representatives than Hindus. Where there are deserving Mahomedans they have as good a chance as Hindus. In Municipalities, Local Boards, District Boards and the Legislative Councils, Hindus and Mahomedans have so far worked hand in hand and shoulder to shoulder in cordial co-operation; there has never been any complaint on the score of ineffective representation, and never any demand for separate election. Even now Mahomedan opinion is by no means unanimous on the point. Why then should this wholly novel and invidious principle of election be introduced into the Reform Scheme, in supersession of a method which has so far produced excellent results, and in disregard of the fact that ample provision was made in the Scheme for the adequate representation of minorities? And what would be the result? Separate representation in all stages must be productive of considerable heartburning among the different communities who constitute the Indian people, will interfere with administrative efficiency, and what is perhaps the greatest of evils, will accentuate and perpetuate racial differences and prevent for all time to come the formation of one united Indian Nation; in other words, will produce results the opposite of what has been the objective of British Indian statesmanship so long.

My Lord, the question of comparative importance raises important issues and can only be the source of perennial quarrel among the different communities of India. There are communities—the Sikhs, the Rajputs, the Mahrattas who have each as great a record of past services and past greatness as any in India. The Parsis, about whom such flattering things were said in the House of Lords, and the progressive domiciled Anglo-Indian community are likewise important. Once this contentious and invidious method of representation is accepted, how are the conflicting claims of these various communities going to be settled? If Mahomedans are granted separate representation, with what justice, with what fairness, can the privilege be denied to the other great communities? And where is all this to end in a country like India peopled as it is by a congeries of innumerable sects and races? And is this method practicable? Really this is a step well calculated to damp the popular enthusiasm for the Reform Scheme. Add to this elimination of statutory provision for the creation of Provincial Executive Councils with the resultant prevention of the popularisation of Provincial Administration, and I should not be surprised if the popular feeling oscillated back to the point from which it turned to greet with such genuine enthusiasm the Reform Scheme. That would be a disaster. My Lord, the action of the House of Lords is viewed by the people with keen and bitter disappointment, and some of the reasons advanced by noble lords opposing the measure have caused them great distress. My Lord, the people have just cause to resent their wholesale condemnation on the grounds of unfitness and incapability of impartial and dispassionate criticism in spite of their proved capacity and impartiality in difficult and delicate spheres of action. But they have one consolation: They feel they have in Your Excellency a champion of their cause, who will do all in his power to ensure them a bright future. I hope, too, the Provincial Governments will rise equal to the occasion, and by the weight of their favourable opinion facilitate the reinsertion of the deleted clause in the India Councils Bill. The people attach great importance to it, and nothing will satisfy them except its reinsertion. Mahomedan opinion coincides with Hindu opinion in the demand; the voice of the nation is unanimous. What is the danger, my Lord, in having a clause of that kind? It seeks only to vest a certain discretion in this Government which is absolutely necessary in view of the engrossing work of Parliament and its want of leisure to deal with Indian matters with that promptitude which their importance demands. Government may be trusted to use the discretion with care and proper consideration of local conditions and in consultation with the Local Government concerned. Why then the meaningless opposition to a wholesome provision? The Centralisation Commission also recommends the reform. [Emphases added]

Not so surprisingly, Gokhale responded to this question, in principle *agreeing* with the concept of communal electorates, and in particular for Muslims. He suggested only a minor modification to the method proposed by the British government for a supplementary electorate instead of a separate one for Muslims. However, even this middle path was not acceptable to the League. Here is what Gokhale said:[98]

The third question connected with the reforms, round which controversy has raged for some time, is that of Mahomedan representation. As this question is arousing a considerable amount of feeling in the country, I would like to state briefly my own view of the matter. That view is practically the same as that of the Government of India, and I have embodied it in the note which I had the honour to submit to the Secretary of State last September on the subject of constitutional reforms. I think the most reasonable plan is first to throw open a substantial minimum of seats to election on a territorial basis, in which all qualified to vote should take part without distinction of race or creed. And then supplementary elections should be held for minorities which numerically or otherwise are important enough to need special representation, and these should be confined to members of the minorities only. *What minorities in the different Provinces should have special representation and how many seats should be assigned to each minority must depend upon the special circumstances of each Province.* It will not do to be guided in the matter by a strict regard for numbers only; for it may be necessary at times to give special representation to a minority so small as not to be entitled even to a single member on a strict numerical basis. *This was practically the plan advocated by the Government of India in their despatch as I understand it, and now that the idea of joint Electoral Colleges has been abandoned, I earnestly trust that it will be carried out.* The great advantage of this plan is that it provides for composite action by all communities up to a certain point and then it prevents injustice, in practical operation, to minorities by giving them special supplementary electorates of their own. My Lord, it has been urged by some of my countrymen that any special separate treatment of minorities militates against the idea of the union of all communities in public matters. Such union is no doubt the goal towards which we have to strive, but it cannot be denied that it does not exist in the country today and it is no use proceeding as though it existed when in reality it does not. *Not only this, but unless the feeling of soreness in the minds of minorities is removed by special separate supplementary treatment such as is proposed by the Government of India, the advance towards a real union will be retarded rather than promoted.* One thing, however, must here be said. The idea of two water-tight compartments for Hindus and Mahomedans separately will not promote the best interests of the country, and moreover it is really not feasible. For there cannot be only two such compartments, unless all minorities other than Mahomedan are to be joined to the Hindus, in which case the division will practically be Mahomedans and non-Mahomedans. Further, where only one member is to be returned by a whole province, as in the case of land-holders or the non-official members of some of the Provincial Councils, any division of those who are qualified to vote into two or more groups becomes impossible. *The objection has been raised that under the plan of the Government of India, members of minorities will vote in general election as also in their own supplementary election. But the matter must be looked at in a large way and in a practical spirit. The aim is not to secure a scientific accuracy of method but to obtain substantially just and satisfactory results. Let it be remembered that a member more or less for either the Hindus or the Mahomedans does not really much matter.* The existence of the Government is not to depend upon the votes of non-official members, neither are its members to be drawn from those who are in a majority in the Councils. Let it also be remembered that the most important part of the proposed reform of Legislative Councils is the power that will be conferred on members to raise discussions on administrative questions in the Council and for this purpose the exact proportion of members returned by any community is a matter of small importance. My Lord, I respectfully suggest that the Government should take an early opportunity to make a clear and firm declaration on this subject, calculated to allay apprehensions and give reasonable satisfaction to all parties. It is necessary that the new arrangements should be inaugurated with the utmost good-will from all sections of the people. I earnestly appeal to my countrymen—both Hindu and Mahomedan—to exercise special mutual forbearance at this juncture and meet each other half way. We owe this to ourselves and to our country's future; we owe it also to those who are granting us these important measures of reform ...

On my return to India *I noticed attempts made in certain quarters to rouse Mahomedan feeling against the reform scheme, as outlined in Lord Morley's despatch, by representing it as a result of Hindu intrigue in London. And after a time my name was openly mentioned in that connection. As the line I had taken on the Mahomedan question was practically the same as that of the Government of India, I thought—and several of my friends agreed with me in this view—* that the best way to counteract this mischief, which threatened to grow quite serious, was to publish the views which I had laid before the Secretary of State. Before communicating the note to the Press, however, I sent a copy to Sir Herbert Risley, requesting him to include it, if possible, among any fresh papers on reforms that the Government might issue—a request that he at once and very courteously complied with. I took this course because it was thought necessary in the best interests of our public life that no room should be left for the allegations of intrigue against Mahomedans, which were being openly and unscrupulously made. There was no thought of suggesting that it was the note that had influenced the Secretary of State in his decision, and no such suggestion has ever been made by me by word or by whisper. [Emphases added]

On the same day, Nawab Salimullah's speech thanking the government for the reforms was read out on his behalf, extracts from which went as follows:[99]

As regards the representation of my friend Mr. Ali Imam, on behalf of the All-India Moslem League, what has been urged therein has my fullest support; but I need not enlarge on it here inasmuch as Lord Morley has acceded to our main request, both from his seat in the House of Lords and in his reply to the deputation that waited on him under the auspices of my venerable friend Mr. Syed Ameer Ali, and for the expression of his opinion on both these occasions we Muhammadans are most sincerely grateful to His Lordship. My Lord, it indeed wanted a firmness of purpose to have withstood the bitter and violent character of opposition the representation to Your Lordship of Mr. Ali Imam, has met with in this country. But this very violence has made Lord Morley see the necessity of granting us our boon and admitting the validity of the considerations on which he has promised the increased and special electorates for our representation. I need only mention one of these considerations, viz., that it was felt that unless the scheme was substantially modified, it would work most injuriously to the Muhammadans by subjecting their interests to the goodwill of another community; and without the modification asked for, their representation on the enlarged Council would be nominal and worthless.

We Musalmans have sought our shares in the political privileges about to be conceded by these reform proposals, such as would, to use the language of Your Excellency, be commensurate with our number, and with our political and historical importance, and the weight of these and the other considerations advanced in Mr. Ali Imam's representation to Your Excellency, and those advanced by the deputation that waited upon Lord Morley, has not in the least been lessened or reduced by what has been urged at the Town Hall meeting of Wednesday last, while in support of our just claim to special representation I beg to cite the weighty words of Lord Reay, perhaps the most able and single-minded of our latter day Governors. His Lordship in the recent debate in the House of Lords, I see, said: 'He was glad the Secretary of State had yielded to the claims of the Mahomedans for separate representation. It was of the utmost importance that the Mahomedan community should be represented by those in whom they have confidence; and any one who have followed their great world movement—and it must be remembered, they numbered 245 millions—were aware of their determination to defend with intensity their own faith.

The virulence of the Native Press appears to me to have been directed more against our claim to historical and political importance, the Aga Khan and Mr. Ali Imam personally and the Moslem League in particular, than to the merit of our representation; as regards our claim to historical and political importance Your Lordship has graciously admitted the same when receiving our deputation at Simla. As regards the League and my friends, they need no advocate to defend them, as their work is before an intelligent, discerning and impartial public and they are prepared to be judged by it. [Emphases added]

On 1 April 1909, at the second reading of the Indian Councils Bill in the House of Commons, the Under-Secretary of State for India, Thomas Buchanan, spelt out the manner in which the proportion of Muslim representation under the reforms would be calculated:[100]

If you start from our democratic theories of representative government, of course, all such special representation is an anomaly, but we have to deal with the practical problem which is before us—*the best practical solution which is available. And more than that, particularly with regard to the Mahomedans, they have a special and overwhelming claim upon us, namely, the solemn promises, given by those who are entitled with full responsibility to speak for us, that they would get adequate representation to the amount and of a kind they want—a promise given to them by Lord Minto specifically in October, 1906, repeated in a despatch by the Secretary of State in 1907, and again repeated by the Secretary of State to a deputation here and in a speech in another place. From that promise we cannot go back, we ought not to go back, and we will not go back.*

Let me for a moment deal with what has caused a certain amount of misunderstanding. There was a suggestion in a despatch of the Secretary of State for India that it might be possible to secure the representation of the Mahomedan minority, and other minorities of those sections of the community which claimed representation, by some general system of minority representation. The object that we had in view was certainly a good one. We thought we might bring in the whole of these various bodies of men under a general system of representation, particularly the Mahomedans, and if they were so brought in they would occupy undoubtedly a somewhat stronger position in the Legislative Council than they otherwise would have. It was merely a suggestion sent out by us to the Government of India. But the moment it was made it was viewed with the utmost suspicion and distrust by those chiefly concerned, by the Mahomedans, and it found no friends in other quarters in India. The result of that was that it was dropped the moment it got to India.

The consequence of that is this, that that suggestion having been dropped, we have fallen back on the proposals of the Government of India contained in their despatch in this Blue Book, summarised in paragraph 30, with the result that the Mahomedan representation will be obtained in future in different ways in different provinces. In some by a system of Mahomedan electorates specially constructed; in other cases by asking Mahomedan associations to name representatives; in other cases, at any rate, for a time, by nomination. I cannot give the House full particulars as to the various policies in the various provinces; but after having been in telegraphic communication with India, I can say with regard to the United Provinces that we have the assurance from the Lieut.-Governor that he holds to the scheme proposed in the Blue Book in the letter from the Government of the United Provinces, par. 24 of enclosure No. 20. The substance of that is this, that of the four Mahomedans to be placed on the Legislative Council of the United Provinces two will be elected by the Mahomedan electorate and two by the Lieut.-Governor. With regard to Eastern Bengal, the two Mahomedan representatives who are included in the constitution of the new council will be on that council in accordance with the ideas submitted in the big Blue Book from the Government of Eastern Bengal—that is to say, certain Mahomedan representatives of Eastern Bengal will be asked to choose two representatives. The only other province that has advanced a recommendation at the present moment is Madras. They are unable for the time being to devise a scheme of Mahomedan electorates; and have proposed, at any rate at first, to nominate two Mahomedan representatives to that council. [Emphasis added]

On the same day, the prime minister of Britain, Herbert Asquith, cited Gokhale's views in support of the reforms as representative of the view of the 'Indian Reformers' or the Moderates:

... I will come now to consider the criticism on the actual scheme which the Government proposes. The Noble Lord has said that Indian reformers will not be satisfied with the proposals in the Bill. *It is not unimportant to point out the language of Indian reformers. As late as Monday last Mr. Gokhale considered the nature of Indian reform. The language which was used by Mr. Gokhale fairly represents the opinions of Indian reformers. He said he had a perfectly impartial mind in dealing with the question. He eulogised Lord Minto and Lord Minto's attitude with regard to this particular proposal, and he declared that Lord Morley has saved India from being driven into chaos. I do not say that the aspirations of Mr. Gokhale are met by this Bill, or those of his friends, but it is a step which will avert the serious danger which has been confronting us for the last few years.* [Emphasis added]

Asquith further justified the reforms on the grounds that the differences between the Hindu and the Muslim communities were vast, warranting a separate electorate system. The Muslim League and the British government were clearly on the same page with respect to the practical application of the Two-Nation Theory:

The Noble Lord spoke of the position of the Mahomedans. Speaking generally with regard to that, the Noble Lord has stated that my Noble Friend dropped his original proposal in regard to the electoral college—dropped them in deference for objections made to a large extent by the Mahomedans themselves—and that when the Bill comes into law it will be a matter prescribed by regulation in each of the particular provinces as to how they shall elect their representatives. Undoubtedly there will be a separate register for Mahomedans. *To us here in this country at first sight it looks an objectionable thing, because it discriminates between people, segregating them into classes, on the basis of religious creed. I am sure the Noble Lord will not regard that as a formidable objection, because the distinction between Mahomedan and Hindu is not merely religious, but it cuts deep down not only into the traditions and historic past, but into the habits and social customs of the people. Provided that, as we may assume, the regulations adequately safeguard the separate registration of the Mahomedan electorate, I do not think any practical suggestion has yet been made for more completely giving that kind of representation which undoubtedly as a minority they are entitled to demand.* [Emphasis added]

Interestingly, there were other members of the British Parliament who foresaw the consequences of communal electorates. Charles James O'Donnell, responding to the British prime minister's position, said:

... for although the Prime Minister stated there was nothing revolutionary in this measure, yet the proposal with regard to religious discrimination is a revolution of a kind that we will ultimately regret. The Prime Minister also stated that this Bill was an extension and development of the present system. Under the present system of legislative councils some members are appointed by election and some by nomination. At the present time there is no suggestion of religious discrimination. At the present time there are on the Viceroy's councils 16 non-official members. Of these three are Mussulmans, two nominated and one elected. I mention this as showing at the outset that there is no necessity for this system. I am one of those who very, very warmly accepted the measure introduced by the Secretary for State into the House of Lords last December, but since then I hope to show that there has been a very great change indeed. That message was accepted in India as a message of peace and goodwill to all classes, all religions, and all communities. My attitude towards this measure is very much the attitude of several hon. Members towards the late Education Bill. That also was a measure of conciliation which it was hoped would bring together all classes in this country in educational matters, but it contained one bad proviso, and that was contracting out, and on the strength of that anyone who had an interest in education rejected it. Similarly this measure is an admirable measure as a matter of progress towards introducing the people of India into the councils of the Sovereign or of the Viceroy. But it also has one great defect, and that is the religious discrimination.

I do not wish to say one word—it would be impossible and unjust—to say one word unfavourable to the Mussulmans. Their faith is a noble one, and contains some of the very finest ideals of Christianity besides the conception of one great, all-merciful God. But while one may regard the Mussulman community with affection, it is most regrettable that any religion should be brought down into the arena of political controversy. It was mentioned by Lord Morley in another place last December that while he proposed there should be separate Mussulman representation, he disliked religious discrimination. I was prepared to accept that, and the Hindus also in India in a most broad-minded, kindly, and willing manner were also prepared to accept the idea that a certain number of members of the legislative council should be Mussulmans. But there is a difference when you propose to select these members by a strictly sectarian vote. This is an idea that has never existed in India before down to three months ago. Up to that time it was still the proposal that there should be a certain number of Mussulman members, but that they would not be elected by sectarian votes, and it was also recognised, and justly and properly recognised by Mussulmans and Hindus alike down to three months ago, that Mussulmans should be represented in proportion to their number. Clearly and manifestly that was a just idea, but it is now proposed that the Mussulmans should have a preponderance in excess of their proportion of the population. *Three months ago an agitation was started that I extremely regret to obtain for the Mussulmans specially favourable terms, not only a larger number in proportion to the population, but also this special electorate. A deputation waited on the Secretary of State, and was received by him with great courtesy. It was a deputation of Mussulmans. I cannot help remembering that three years ago the Hindus of Bengal, the nobility, the great traders, the loyalists, the landlords of Bengal, desired a deputation from their body to be received by Lord Morley, the Secretary of State for India, to protest against the partition of Bengal. Lord Morley, then in this House, in answer to a question from me, declined to receive that deputation. I must say I feel, and feel strongly, that even then, three years ago, there was religious discrimination in the treatment of Indian questions.*

This great change that has passed over this measure, the special favour to the Mussulmans both in regard to the special electorate and in regard to numbers, I am glad to say, was not acceptable at first to Lord Morley. In his speech in the House of Lords on 23rd February he distinctly said:— To the best of my belief, under my construction, the plan of Hindus and Mussulmans voting together in a mixed and composite electorate would have secured to the Mahomedun electorate, wherever they were no [sic] minded, the chances of returning their own representatives in their due proportion. He went on to say that this idea of promoting harmony was held by men of very high Indian authority and experience who were among my advisers at the India Office. It is most important to recognise this fact, that the advisers Parliament has given to the Secretary of State on the Indian Council advised Lord Morley to have the original arrangement by which the Mussulmans received no special favour but were treated in the same reasonable and proper manner as Hindus were.

Unfortunately the idea of promoting harmony was not the idea of the Government of India. It is a regrettable fact. Lord Morley distinctly said that 'the Government of India doubted whether our plan would work, and we have abandoned it.' Why has it been abandoned? The reason of the abandonment is that the Mussulmans protested that the Mussulmans elected under the ordinary system might be pro-Hindu. I don't suggest that the idea is that these men should be anti-Hindus. It is a charge I should be extremely slow to make against any section of the Government of this country; but none the less the fact remains that because there was a certain fear expressed that the men who were elected would be pro-Hindu, the Government of India protested against it, and the Secretary of State, I greatly regret, abandoned his own wise decision. What would be the effect of anti-Hindu members of the legislative councils? It would be exactly the effect that we know in Ireland of the Orangeman, the man who is not only a good Protestant, but is also an anti-Catholic, and that is an idea which I hope the Government of India on reconsideration will refuse to introduce into India. And this policy is only a continuation of that which created such extreme bitterness in Eastern Bengal. It was only when the Hindus began to appreciate that the result of the partition was that the Mussulmans were put in a specially favourable position that they lost their temper, and broke into that series of violences which I believe the Secretary of State and the Government of India have at last put down. In this matter my sympathies were entirely with Lord Morley. I cannot imagine a Liberal Secretary of State put in a more difficult position than he was in having to deal with the anarchy and crime that broke out in India. I dislike the idea of the bastille and deportation, but, taking it all in all, it is a better system than the cruel way in which anarchy is put down in Russia. It is with the very, very greatest pleasure that I recognise that the nine Bengali gentlemen, though I believe unwisely arrested, have been treated in an admirable manner while under arrest. But why I still more and more object to this system is that in the second page of the Memorandum it is stated that one of the objects of this Bill is the election of a certain proportion of members by popular vote—that is, by the vote of the people—and the proposal is that we should go down to the people of India and spread amongst them these ideas of sectarianism, which now do not exist, and which up to the present have found no part in our system of government. *Let there be Mussulman members. Nobody objects to that. Let them be elected in the ordinary way. If a sufficient number are not elected, there is nomination. Hindus and every man who takes any interest in India would be delighted to see Mussulmans nominated, if not elected. It seems to me, after all, this introduction of religious test is entirely unnecessary.* At the present time the Hindu population of Madras, in a proportion of 90 per cent, to the rest, is represented by a Mahomedan. The same thing has happened in several other provinces. When you find Hindus so willing to return Mussulmans to the legislative council, does it not seem unwise, intensely unwise, to listen to a few gentlemen who assemble here in

London—I might mention that there are practically no names of authority connected with these Mussulmans except one Prince, and he is not an Indian at all; he is a Persian. His ancestors only 80 years ago were driven out by some palace feud or intrigue at Teheran, and came to Bombay. *There is no such thing as a Mussulman nationality. You might as well talk about Baptist nationality.* Anybody who reads the papers, particularly the Indian papers, will see that the Hindus feel themselves being put in a position of inferiority. There is no shadow of a doubt that throughout India at the present time the people will say that the Government, through the instrumentality of this Bill, is favouring the Mussulman. If it were not so, why give them representation larger than their population entitles them to? Why give them a separate electorate? Why not give a separate electorate to the Sikhs and others? *That there is unwise favouritism going on seems certain. I believe it is temporary, and intended to be so, but I am afraid it will have results that will be eminently bad, because the great princes are Hindus, the wealthy and educated classes are Hindu, the vast mass of the people are Hindu. I am sure that the Secretary of State, Lord Morley, has no intention of that description, but you must consider what the effects will be on the Hindus of India. They know what it has been to be under the heel of the Mussulman for centuries, and there is a feeling spreading throughout India that is much to be deplored.* Amongst the Hindus there are some of the finest warlike races of the world. The Sikhs and others have supplied quite three-quarters of our fighting men in the native army of India. Amongst them the idea is spreading that the favourites are their old conquerors. As there have been so many quotations from newspapers, particularly from 'The Times,' I tender one from the 'Westminster Gazette,' which says that—Thoughtful men will feel that separate representation is impossible ... Ton will embitter mutual relations ... *You will poison social life in district and village homes: you will make a hell of India and shake British power to its foundations if you provide the numerous races and creeds with separate representatives and mutually hostile political aspirations.* I venture in conclusion, to appeal to the House to maintain the great tradition, the old policy of this great Empire. Our power has grown up, and will grow stronger on the principles of equality, by the principle of treating all races, all religions, all creeds, with equal justice. I especially turn to the Conservative benches. I believe that we should move cautiously there; slowly and conservatively. I opposed the partition of Bengal because it was the breaking up of one of our great principles in India. That was not only to treat the creeds with justice and propriety, but also to treat nationalities with justice. We broke up a great nationality—the greatest nationality in India. We abandoned in India the Conservative way. Before us to-night there is a still greater principle, and that is the old principle that we should treat all religions with equality. The danger that lies before us—and I cannot exaggerate it—is that we are face to face with a calamitous experiment with the most treasured, the most successful portion of our Administration. I beg right hon. Gentlemen not to awake the fanaticism of the Hindu and of India. [Emphases added]

Justifying the concept of separate electorates on the basis of the Two-Nation Theory, Donald Smeaton remarked:

I was rather disappointed to hear the hon. Members for East Nottingham and Walworth import into their speeches what they called the religious and sectarian differences and discrimination in reference to the proposed special electorate for the Mahomedans. I can claim, I think with all respect, wider knowledge of the populations of India than either of those two hon. Gentlemen. *My knowledge extends to the vast bulk of the Mahomedan populations outside Bengal, and I must challenge the historical accuracy of my hon. Friend when he declares that there is no substantial difference in race or manners or interests between the Mahomedan population and the Hindus. The Mahomedans of Eastern Bengal are, I know, of the very meanest sort of the followers of Islam, and they were comparatively recent converts to Mahomedanism; but when he talks of recent converts he really means the converts of five, six, or seven hundred years ago. That conversion really connotes a difference in race, because during these several hundred years social distinctions have been gradually widening between them and the Hindus, until now they really are not only a different religious sect, differing on every conceivable point of religion, but they have become a different race. In the parts of India which I know well—that is the whole of the northern part of India, in which the fighting Mahomedan races live and flourish—not only are they of a different race and speech, but are of a totally different nature altogether. They will have nothing to do socially or politically or in any other way with the Hindus among whom they live. They are a completely separate community,* and to tell me they are to submit to an election by a numerically superior body of Hindus to what is called a representative council is reducing the whole principle of election to an absurdity. The only solution is that which has finally been adopted by the Secretary of State, namely, to give the Mahomedans a separate representative and a separate electoral register, and enable them to secure for themselves on those councils where their great interests are at stake such a representation as is approved by their co-religionists. [Emphasis added]

Here is another interesting rationale for separate electorates, provided by another member, Joynson Hicks, where he cited Muslim loyalty to the British as one of the reasons:

I should like to say one word on a matter of detail with regard to the Mahomedans. The Member for Nottingham suggested that the Mahomedans and the Hindus were of the same race and almost of the same creed. I cannot concur in that expression of opinion. While the Mahomedan is perfectly willing to be ruled by an Englishman, you find throughout India that he is not willing to be ruled by a Hindu; and if you establish any system you like in the Executive Councils or in the legislative councils, whereby the Hindus get preponderating power, you will turn the whole Mahomedan population against us. To-day the Mahomedans are the most loyal of the population of India; they are devoted to English rule; but if we throw them over and put them under the heel of the Hindus, who have for centuries past been somewhat bitter opponents of their religion and race, you will have the Mahomedans just as disloyal as large sections of the Hindus are, and joining as they have not hitherto done in the seditious movement and the opposition to British rule. I cannot concur in the views which have been expressed on the other side of the House with regard to the nonofficial majority in the legislative councils. That provision is bound to produce intense friction. [Emphasis added]

On the same subject, here is an exchange between different members of the British Parliament bringing out their multiple perspectives on the subject:

MR. REES... Then, coming to the Mahomedans, I must say that here I differ altogether from my hon. Friend the Member for Walworth. I accept the Mahomedan position. I am not going to trouble the House with any reason for my opinion, except that I have been accustomed to the Mahomedans, their ways and their literature, and *I think it would be absurd if the Government were going to treat the Mahomedans as if they were entitled to no representation except that which they are entitled to by mere numbers.* It would be a grave political error, and show ignorance on the subject with which they were dealing. Lord Morley has not taken up that attitude, and he agrees with the late Lord Kimberley, who said the notion that Parliamentary representation could ever be arranged in India was the wildest imagination that the heart of man could conceive. *He further warned us, in dealing with Indian reform, to beware of Hindu opinion, which is Hindu opinion only. I differ here from Lord Kimberley. I think that where you have a question of Hindu versus Mahomedan, Hindu opinion has its value, as indicating what you should avoid. It has its value, but only in that sense.* I also wish to quote an authority on this matter, which must be received on this side of the House with the utmost respect and deference. It is Mr. Gladstone who said:—The danger is that you get representation of cliques, classes and interests. The educated classes, who are a small minority, claim to represent all classes, and they oppose all measures likely to lessen their influence. Those are words which should not be lightly passed over; they should be written up over the doors of all the offices which deal with this subject. Lord MacDonnell, whose opinion we hear with great respect, said the Hindus often would elect Mahomedans to the Council. *I should like to ask Lord MacDonnell if he was in the House how was it that no Mahomedan was ever elected in the United Provinces, which he governed so extremely well himself.*

SIR HENRY COTTON: In March last there was an election for the Legislative Council of the United Provinces. They elected a Hindu, and out of 11 Mahomedan electors 8 voted for the Hindu.

MR. REES: Was the Hindu elected, or the Mahomedan?

SIR HENRY COTTON: The Hindu.

MR. REES: That bears out what I was saying. I said no Mahomedan had ever been elected. My hon Friend confirms what I said.

SIR HENRY COTTON: Two Mahomedans have been elected to the Viceroy's Legislative Council—the Nawab of Pahasu and the Raja of Mahmudabad.

MR. REES: Since when?

SIR HENRY COTTON: Within the last five or six years.

MR. REES: I thought the hon. Gentleman was going to say in the last five or six days. At any rate I should require a little confirmation of that. Lord MacDonnell also made a point which is really immensely important upon this question. He said Bengal was the Province best educated—which is not borne out by the census Commissioners or any other figures I could find—and the most advanced—which I freely admit they are in some respects—and he said 'we want to get this partition undone.' What is at the bottom of the desire to reintroduce clause 3, and get a Governor in Council for Bengal is the desire to get a Governor in Council for a united Bengal. *They want to get the two provinces put together again, so that a Governor in Council may rule over it. I do not hesitate to say that to undo the partition would shake the British Empire in India to its foundations.* I sincerely hope it will never be contemplated, nor can I understand how the hon. Member for Nottingham could possibly suggest that any such measure is desirable or even possible. Had this partition taken place a little before it did, when my hon. Friend was Chief Commissioner of Assam, he would perhaps have become the Lieutenant-Governor of Eastern Bengal and Assam, and I am sure he would have continued to carry out the same in an obedient and efficient manner—the orders of his superior officers—as he did in the lesser appointment which he had the good fortune to hold.

SIR HENRY COTTON: I declined the amalgamation when I was Chief Commissioner.

MR. REES: Do I understand that the hon. Gentleman was offered the Lieutenant-Governorship?

SIR HENRY COTTON: No.

MR. REES: That was my point. *From historical, racial, political, physical, every conceivable reason, the Mahomedans have good grounds to claim that they should have an entirely separate electorate and that they shall have their own men to represent themselves.* I do not believe in representative institutions in India, but if you are to have them, at least let the men have those whom they wish to represent them. It is an absurd thing to say to a Mahomedan you shall have a converted Hindu, who is unrecognisable from the Hindus around you, to be your representative. Nor can I follow the hon. Member for Walworth in his speech, in which he seemed to hold that the difference between *Hindus and Mahomedans was like the difference between a Baptist and a Wesleyan.* Surely the real fact is that the Mahomedan is far nearer to the Christian than to the Hindu.

MR. C.J. O'DONNELL: I must really interrupt. I never mentioned such an argument.

MR. REES: About the Baptist?

MR. O'DONNELL: I never spoke about a Wesleyan.

MR. REES: *My hon. Friend mentioned a Baptist, and I introduced the Wesleyan. I think really they get on very well together. Mahomedans and Hindus do not.* As an administrator who has had to keep the peace, and has had to deal with these subjects, I can assure the hon. Member that they do not get on well together. [Cries of 'Where?'] All over the country. At the time of festivals special police arrangements have to be made to keep them from flying at one another's throats. And even now that this appointment has been made of Mr. Sinha, a gentleman of whom I wish to speak with the utmost respect—and if an appointment of this character is to be made at all he is the right man in the right office—strong objection is taken by Mahomedans. That shows that infinite difficulty surrounds this question. Hindus claim to have won a victory without the help of the Mahomedans. These are positions which certainly come to mind when we are considering the question of Mahomedan representation and the appointment of a member to the Viceroy's Executive Council. Then there are other people who are entitled to special representation, and I must take the opportunity of mentioning specially the representations of the Anglo-Indian Association, Calcutta, and the European and Anglo-Indian Defence Association, Calcutta, which are highly important and representative bodies. I do not think that in all these papers there are many points which are not sufficiently taken into account. Because they do not send people over here to represent their case they do not get the consideration which is obtained by those who call out day after day until they get satisfied. If the Under-Secretary of State's ears are open for a moment I wish to say that these communities should have consideration, and that their case also should be taken into account as well as that of the Mahomedans. The Noble Lord opposite dealt a great deal in his interesting speech with the difference between the proposals of this Bill and those the Government of India finally sent forth, and no doubt there is a far-reaching change in doing away with the official majorities on the provincial councils. I never would have done that, because I believe that if these great provincial councils are beaten or cannot get through their legislation, the prestige of the Government in India no doubt must suffer. At the same time, I do realise that if something is to be done to meet the wishes of the advanced Indians, I do not know of anything more likely to please them at a less cost than this. Because it looks a far greater change than it actually is. As one who has lived in India a great many years I can say that administration is everything, legislation matters very little. So many subjects are excluded from the powers of these bodies (including the Army and Navy I am happy to think). If it is the case that the Secretary of State had set to work to try and please as far as possible the advanced Indians without doing great harm to the British supremacy, I do not think he could have hit upon a better measure than this which I support, and to which, on the whole, no very serious objection has been taken. We come then to the Imperial Legislative Council. I, like the Noble Lord opposite, understand that the changes that have been introduced here would reduce the number of the council by two below that advised by the Government of India. I cannot see any great harm in that.

EARL PERCY: I do not see how the Government are going to carry out the pledge which the Secretary of State gave—namely, to increase the proportion assigned to Mahomedans above that which was originally assigned. The figures in that respect were fixed before.

MR. REES: I presume it would be possible to adjust that by taking two off some other interest, and that some other interest would bear reduction, and I do not see that that is so serious a matter as might be thought. [Emphases added]

Were there any international considerations in the creation of separate electorates for Hindus and Muslims in India? Yes, there were, and this aspect was revealed in the debates of 26 April 1909 in the House of Commons, when the amendments to some of the provisions of the Councils Bill were being deliberated:[101]

The object of moving this Amendment, as hon. Members will see from the Paper, is to ensure the carrying out of a promise which was given to the Mahomedan community two and a half years ago by the Viceroy, a promise which was subsequently reiterated and emphasised by the Secretary of State on the second reading of the Bill. The promise was to the effect that in the event of political privileges being extended to the peoples of India the Mahomedan community would be secured a share in those privileges commensurate not only with their numbers but with their historical and political importance. As to the methods by which it is proposed, or was proposed, to secure those ends, I shall have something to say in a moment, but I should like first of all to associate myself entirely with the Viceroy and the Government of India in their decision to grant to the Mahomedan community a share in those new privileges in excess of their actual numerical strength. *The claim based upon historical reasons I do not think can be ignored. Hon. Members will recollect that it was from a Mahomedan sovereign that the East India Company acquired their rights in three of the richest provinces in India.* It was a Mahomedan sovereign whose paramount influence was recognised by the East India Company, and many of the Hindu Chiefs are very proud of the titles presented to them by Mahomedan kings. The political importance of all this cannot be gainsaid, and in attempting to form a just estimate of the political importance of the Mahomedans we must cast our eyes far beyond the confines of the Indian Empire. We must remember that countries with whose destiny the destinies of our own country as an

Eastern Power are indissolubly woven—Afghanistan, Persia, and Turkey—
are countries peopled by Mahomedans, and are centres of Mahomedan power.
But the influence of Mahomedans does not stop there, for we find that this race
spreads itself over Africa, Central Asia, and some parts of China. Therefore,
upon historical and political grounds alone, Mahomedans have a just claim
to a substantial share in any political privileges which may be granted to the
peoples of India.

But there is a further reason why the Mahomedans should be granted
representation in excess of their actual number, and I think it is one which will
appeal to hon. Members as having greater practical validity than those reasons
which I have already mentioned. The reason I allude to is that there are
millions of people included for statistical purposes among the Hindus, who, as
a matter of fact, are not Hindus at all. If hon. Members can bring themselves
to delve into the monstrous Blue Book presented by the India Office not very
long ago—which, so far as arrangement is concerned, may be justly claimed
to be the triumph of chaos over order—they will find the following memorial
from the Dravidians to the Government of Madras:— *The differences between
the Hindu and the community of the memorialists are so great that it is a deplorable
mistake to regard them as forming a part of the Hindus. There has been existing for
centuries enmity and hatred between their community and that of the Hindus.* That
is only a single example, but I think it shows that it would be absurd to class
these men, who number something like one-sixth of the total population of
Madras, among the Hindus for representation purposes, though I have no
doubt they are classed amongst them by the statistician. *I quite agree that it is a
very difficult thing to arrive at any accurate conclusion as to what the number of this
class may be. One authority estimates them at 50,000,000, while the statisticians
of the India Office estimate them at 88,000,000. That is sufficient to show that it
would be grievously unjust to the Mahomedans to base their amount of representation
upon a purely numerical basis. That being so, and the Government having come to
the conclusion that the Mahomedans ought to be granted representation in excess of
their actual numbers,* it remains to be decided how this change is to be brought
about. Upon that point the Mahomedans themselves had, and still have, very
distinct and definite ideas. They maintain, and I think they very justly
maintain, that this need cannot be supplied unless the Government accept two
main principles, which are as follows: In the first place, the Mahomedans
should be assigned a number of seats on the representative bodies in excess of
their numerical strength, that number in all cases to be fixed by Executive
authority. The second principle is that whenever one of these seats assigned to
the Mahomedans by Executive authority is to be filled by election the electorate
should be composed exclusively of Mahomedans. I understand that the
Government of India and the Government at home have accepted those two
principles. I think the speech of the Viceroy and the speech made on the
second reading by the Secretary of State for India puts that matter absolutely

beyond dispute. May I remind the House of the words used by the Viceroy two and a half years ago in replying to the Mahomedan deputation which waited upon him? He said:—The pith of your address, as I understand it, is a claim that in any system of representation whether it affects a municipality, a district board, or a legislative council, in which it is proposed to introduce or increase an electoral organisation, the Mahomedan community should be represented as a community, and you justly claim that your position should be estimated not merely on your numerical strength, but in respect to the political importance of your community, and the service it has rendered to the Empire. I am entirely in accord with you. That is a pretty definite expression of the Viceroy's opinion, and he was entirely in accord with the Mahomedan deputation when they demanded from him these two principles. The words of the Secretary of State were no less definite, indeed, I think, they were more definite, and I will therefore venture to read to the House the words used by the Secretary of State for India upon the second reading of this Bill in another place. He said:—*The Mahomedans demand three things*. I had the pleasure of receiving a deputation from them, and I know very well what is in their minds. They demand the election of their own representatives to these councils in all the stages just as in Cyprus, where, I think, the Mahomedans vote by themselves ... Secondly they want a number of seats in excess of their numerical strength. Those two demands we are quite ready and intend to meet in full. I do not think even such a master of lucid explanation as the Prime Minister could have improved upon the lucidity of that pledge which was given by the Secretary of State for India in another place. It may be asked why, after those definite pledges, I should have thought it necessary to move my amendment. It is because something like consternation has been created in the minds of Mahomedans here and in India by the speech made in this House last week on the Committee stage of the Bill by the Financial Secretary to the Treasury. He read a telegram as to the methods by which it was proposed to secure elections to these various bodies, and the telegram read as follows: 'The method proposed is simply that in general electorates, such as municipalities, district boards, and members of provincial councils, all sects and classes, including Mahomedans, will vote together.' I ask the particular attention of hon. Members to these words: 'All sects and classes, including Mahomedans, will vote together.' The words appear to me to constitute a direct reversal of the pledge given by the Viceroy. How the Government propose to reconcile their action with their promises passes my comprehension; but that is not all. The hon. Gentleman went on to say, 'By this means some, but not sufficient, representation will be obtained for Mahomedans, and in addition a certain number of seats will be reserved for the Mahomedans, and nobody but the Mahomedans.' That is in force at the present time. What does the Government of India say as to this system? *In a circular of August 24th, 1907, paragraph 16, the Government of India said: 'Under the system of election hitherto in force,*

Hindus largely predominate in all, or almost all, the electorates, with the result that comparatively few Mahomedan members have been elected. These have been supplemented by nomination made by the Government.' But even so, 'the total representation thus effected has not been commensurate with the weight to which the Mahomedan community is entitled.' I should like to ask the Government how, by this mixed electorate, the Mahomedans will secure representation? How do they know? They do not know. They cannot know. If you take the united provinces, in which there is a large and important Mahomedan community approximating to 7,000,000 in number, you will find that under the system hitherto in force no single Mahomedan representative under a mixed electorate has ever found his way to a provincial council. May I take the case of the proposed reconstituted council of the Viceroy as an example? As I understand it from the information at our disposal, there are to be 28 elected members to the reconstituted council. *Five of the memberships are to be reserved for Mahomedans. The remaining 23 seats are to be filled under a mixed electorate. The Government of India tell us that under a mixed electorate Mahomedans will secure 12 per cent of the seats on the legislative council. If the system works as the Government think it will work, the Mahomedans may possibly get seven elected members out of the 28 elected members.* No one would regard that number as an adequate representation for the Mahomedans, still less as an adequate representation if they are promised to have a representation in excess of their numbers. May I add that the leaders of Mahomedan thought would not recognise a representative who is elected by others than Mahomedans. Every Mahomedan would say that every elected person of an electorate not exclusively Mahomedan will not be in the least the sort of man to represent real Mahomedan interests. I have one other thing to say. What Mahomedans say is that as far as every elected Mahomedan is concerned they require an exclusively Mahomedan electorate, as promised by the Viceroy. If they receive that they are quite willing, and are even anxious, to forgo the privilege of voting for the election of every other electoral body. They would be quite content to have their own members and elect their own members to the councils. If an hon. Member thinks that I have put an exaggerated case, or that I have said more than is really in the minds of the Mahomedan leaders, I ask his careful attention to this cable from India, which was received during the past week in reply to a speech of the Financial Secretary of the Treasury. '*The Times' Correspondent at Lucknow cables as follows:—The Mahomedans are indignant at what they conceive to be the violation of the pledges given by Lord Minto and Lord Morley guaranteeing separate electorates. They consider Mr. Hobhouse's statement in the House to mean that the Government accepts Mr. Gokhale's proposals, which would virtually place the Mahomedans absolutely in Hindu hands. Under mixed general electorates Congress Mahomedans will be freely elected to count as genuine Mahomedan representatives. Mahomedans protest against the surrender of their rights at the dictation of political agitators and are demanding separate electorates throughout. I commend these words also to the attention of hon. Members:—Meetings of protest have been arranged everywhere. This telegram was dated April 21st. The second telegram to which I will call attention is from a Mahomedan of great influence amongst his co-religionists in India, a member of the Viceroy's Executive Council and one of the leading Talukdars of Oudh (Rajah of Mahmudabad), and this telegram is as follows:— Protest against supplementary election. Demand separate electorate, otherwise reforms useless. And the third telegram is also from a Mahomedan of influence (Nawab of Dacca), and his telegram reads as follows:—A mass meeting of 6,000 Mahomedans held here under my presidentship, three resolutions passed—the first opposing nomination, the second insisting upon separate election, and the third upon representation in excess of numerical proportion. I think anybody who reads these telegrams, which are the result of the speech of the hon. Gentleman last week, must realise that the Mahomedans throughout India are at present suffering under a sense of grievous wrong and of grievous injustice.* They consider that the pledges which were given to them in the most explicit language by the Viceroy and the Secretary of State are being broken. And may I say this, in conclusion, that I personally have no desire whatsoever to identify myself with one of the great communities of India rather than with another. I have no reasons for espousing the cause of the Mahomedans except this, that I believe, in the first place, that their demands are not only just, but that they are expedient under the present circumstances; I believe, in the second place, that the Government have told them that they intend to meet the two demands to the full; and, thirdly, I espouse their cause on this occasion because I foresee that if the Government of this country follow on a course which is in any way calculated to shake the faith of any great community in India in the inviolability of their pledged word they are going far to undermine the whole fabric of British supremacy in India. I beg to move. [Emphases added]

From these debates and the history of this period discussed in the previous chapter, the following points emerge:

1. The Minto–Morley Reforms were not the exclusive product of the divide and rule policy of the British, but were, in fact, the combined result of Muslim separatism, which was underpinned by the Two-Nation Theory, and the British need to find a counterweight to the growing clout of the Extremists/Nationalists within the Congress by incentivising 'moderation' through accommodative measures;

2. A significant number of British voices at the highest levels saw Muslims as their loyal allies, as a community and religion closer to Christianity and who therefore could not be allowed to live under a Hindu-majority democracy. Muslim leaders were all too happy to live under the British but not as part of a Hindu-majority democracy since, 'having ruled over

the Hindus for 800 years' as claimed by Muslim leaders, they viewed
themselves as superior;

3. The British establishment was conscious of Muslim presence in this part
   of the world, namely Asia, even outside Bharat, which weighed on their
   decision to support communal electorates;

4. Veiled threats issued by Muslim leaders such as Nawab Salimullah also
   pushed the British Government into pledging support for communal
   electorates;

5. Gokhale, who represented the Moderates, was in favour of mixed
   electorates, namely a general electorate coupled with a supplementary
   electorate for Muslims, which too was unacceptable to the Muslim
   community.

In light of all this, and from the detailed discussions undertaken in the
previous chapters, which bring out the inherent separatist tendency of
Middle Eastern consciousness starting from Syed Ahmed Sirhindi under
Mughal emperor Akbar to Syed Ahmed Khan of Aligarh, the Two-Nation
Theory must be accepted as a reality which cannot be wished away. It was as
an actuality much before Jinnah arrived, and remained so until the partition
of Bharat in 1947. No wonder Dr Ambedkar emphasised this in his book
Pakistan or the Partition of India.

I leave it to the reader to decide whether the Two-Nation Theory, long
after the creation of Pakistan, animates Bharat's present or not—albeit under
different labels—by taking into account the state of affairs that meets the eye
from Kashmir to Kerala, and from Gujarat to Bengal and Assam. As for my
personal opinion—*res ipsa loquitor*, i.e., the facts speak for themselves or,
in this case, history speaks for itself. Plus, it is worth bearing in mind that
Pakistan was first a state of mind before it became a reality, and a state of
mind is never limited by geography or time.

Such being the case, would it not be logical to treat the demand for
communal electorates in 1909 as a direct consequence and natural corollary
of the Two-Nation Theory? Would it not be fair to conclude that the
Muslim-majority character of at least two major provinces, namely Punjab
and Bengal, coupled with the arrival of the Aligarh-trained English-educated
Muslims who subscribed to the Dehlawite vision, had set the stage for the
demand for communal electorates? If yes, given the history of the deep
divide that long *preceded* the advent of the British, what alternative other than
communal electorates would have been acceptable to those who subscribed
to the Dehlawite worldview? In my view, the advent of 'modern' democracy,
constitutionalism and the European state apparatus merely provided weak
'safety valves' like communal electorates in the hope of avoiding or stalling

a worse outcome. Ultimately, the events of the partition of 1947 proved the futility of such safety valves, since, after all, they could not withstand the weight of history.

With this, we conclude the discussion of events up to 1909. In the next section, I will undertake an examination of the period between 1910 and 1924 to chart the course of Bharat's civilisational-cum-constitutional evolution through the respective journeys of the Congress, the League and the British government. As we shall see, this period would witness the coming together of Muslim separatism and global pan-Islamism in Bharat, thereby further cementing the road to Pakistan, which in turn would directly impact Bharat's constitutional discourse.

Section 3
1910–1924

Reunification of Bengal, the First World War and the Lucknow Pact: Murmurings of Khilafat (1910–1916)

The Delhi Durbar of 1911

Annulment of the Partition of Bengal and Muslim Displeasure (1910–1911)

The Minto–Morley Reforms and the issue of communal/separate electorates for Muslims, as we saw, were the political subjects of attention from October 1906 until December 1909. In addition to these, there was an uninterrupted anti-partition agitation during this period, which reflected in the resolutions of the Congress and the League at their annual sessions. Readers may recollect that the Congress had passed a resolution in its December 1909 session seeking annulment of the Partition of Bengal. And although the Muslim League did not hold its third annual session in 1909, it had vehemently opposed calls for reunification of Bengal in its 1908 Amritsar session, calling the anti-partition agitation 'mischievous'.[1]

The third session of the League was held in Delhi on 29 and 30 January 1910. At this session, which was held at Sangam Theatre in the city, the

Osman Ali Khan, Asif Jah VII, the Nizam of Hyderabad, paying homage at the Delhi Durbar, 1911. King George V and Queen Mary are seated on the dais.

president of the reception committee of the League, Mohammad Ajmal Khan, after whom a prominent road in Delhi is named, commented as follows on the choice of Delhi for the session:[2]

> Important and distinguished as the present assembly is, no better place could have been selected for it than Delhi, Imperial Delhi, the mention of whose name carries the mind back to a glorious past, whose fascinating life-story has ever captivated the imagination of students of history and whose uniquely favourable position led British Viceroys to hold the two memorable Durbars

of modern days on its historic soil. And it was in the fitness of things that a body (the Muslim League) which took its birth in the city of Jahangir (Jahangirabad or Dacca) should have completed the stage of its infancy in the city of Shahjahan (Shahjahanabad or Delhi).

Expressing gratitude to the British government for the Indian Councils Act of 1909 and also supporting the government's crackdown on the Revolutionaries, Ajmal Khan said:[3]

The period that has elapsed since the last annual meeting of the League held at Amritsar has been crowded with notable events. Indeed, the country is still passing through times at once stirring and epoch-making. The introduction of the Reform Scheme opens a fresh chapter in the history of British rule in Hindustan, and we are now standing on the threshold of a new era in the Indian polity. Great and invaluable concessions have been granted to the people, and British statesmanship, ever characterized by generosity and beneficence, is exerting itself to lead the peoples of this land, step by step, along the path of political progress on Western lines. Real and effective participation of the representatives of the people in the actual work of daily administration is being ensured, and the highest executive and deliberative assemblies of the Empire have been thrown open to the sons of the soil. The Hon'ble Mr. Sinha's nomination to the Viceroy's Executive Council and the Right Hon'ble Syed Ameer Ali's elevation to the Judicial Committee of the Privy Council stand as conspicuous landmarks in last year's history of the British Empire.

In spite, however, of the bestowal of new privileges on the people, the difficulties of government have not altogether disappeared and the atmosphere continues to be surcharged with grave anxiety. The despicable crime of Sir Curzon Wyllie's murder, the more recent assassination of Mr. Jackson, the vile attempt on the Viceroy at Ahmedabad, the nearer-home bomb discovery at Ambala, and the latest atrocity of Mr. Shamsul Alam's murder within the precincts of the Calcutta High Court are a few dark deeds out of a number which, though planned by anarchical propaganda, undoubtedly owe their inspiration to the pestilential teachings of the sedition mongers. Unfortunately for the peace of the country, the forces of disorder and disruption are still at work and the administration has had to strengthen its position, by adopting repressive measures. If, on the one hand, we deplore a resort to strong steps, we cannot, on the other, shut our eyes to the paramount duty of the State to uphold law and preserve order, which is the first essential of all progress. When the spirit of sedition and lawlessness is abroad, when the cult of the bomb is preached and practised, when assassinations have been attempted and committed, and when wildly suicidal schemes of Swaraj are hatched, is it wise or even possible for any government that cares for its own safety and of its subject-races to remain an unconcerned spectator of the game of violence sought to be played by the anarchist and the revolutionist? The responsibility for enforcement of repressive measures must therefore rest with those whose insanity has forced their adoption on the State, and it should be the imperative duty of peaceful citizens to co-operate with the officers of Government in putting out the fire of sedition and anarchy.

Underscoring the fact that Hindu–Muslim solidarity was contingent on the Hindus *not* seeking to supplant British rule, and thanking the Minto–Morley pair profusely once more on behalf of the Muslim community, Ajmal Khan said:[4]

> I am sure I can speak for my co-religionists throughout the Indian continent in declaring emphatically that Mohammedans regard as their brethren all loyal and law-abiding Hindus, whose exertions to advance the welfare of India, if they do not aim to remove the protection of the Union Jack, they are prepared to support and supplement in a broadminded spirit of judicious Catholicism.

> Reverting to the Reform Scheme and the definite recognition therein of the position of the Musalmans, as an integral but distinct part of the Indian population, I must give expression to our feelings of deep satisfaction at the Government having, in the main, carried out the pledges which had been held out to us, though our fate hung in the balance and swayed between hope and fear for a considerable time ...

> I should be guilty of an unpardonable dereliction of duty if I omitted to proclaim what I believe is at this moment uppermost in the minds of you all. We are deeply grateful to the two illustrious statesmen who are now at the helm of Indian affairs and to whose generous appreciation of the Muslim community in India we are indebted for the equitable recognition of our communal rights. In His Excellency Lord Minto we have truly found a benefactor, whose memory our future generations will bless. We are no less thankful to the Right Hon'ble Lord Morley, who has grasped the Indian situation with rare precision and whose attitude towards His Imperial Majesty the Emperor's Muslim subjects has throughout been characterized by justice and sympathy ... Loyalty to his rulers is ingrained in the Muslim's nature and is inculcated by his religion. The Quran expressly lays down that the Musalman and the Christian are nearer each other than the followers of any other two faiths. We also realize that the presence of the British in India is the best guarantee for the preservation of peace and order in the country and for the equitable protection of Muslim interests.

After Ajmal Khan's reception speech welcoming the delegates, the then Imam of the Jama Masjid of Delhi, Maulana Syed Ahmed, recited a few verses from the Quran.[5] After this, the Aga Khan echoed the sentiments of Ajmal Khan and brought up the issue of establishing a Muslim university at Aligarh. In his words, he wanted Aligarh to become a Muslim Oxford.[6] From the words of Ajmal Khan and the Aga Khan, this much is clear—the

Congress, the League and the British were all on the same page, holding that 'disloyal elements' such as the Extremists and the Revolutionaries had no right to exist, and therefore had to be dealt with, with a firm hand. Critically, peace between Hindus and Muslims was contingent on ensuring the stability and permanence of British rule in India. Therefore, while the League saw the British as a strategic necessity to prevent Hindus from reclaiming state power, most of the Hindu elites sought continued ties with the British since they had assimilated the coloniser's worldview and did not foresee a future for a prosperous Bharat which was independent of the European coloniser. The net result was the alienation, marginalisation and subjugation of those Hindu voices that sought spiritual, cultural and political decolonisation—in short, independence at all levels.

By February 1910, as a result of the British government's massive crackdown on the Revolutionaries and the Extremists, the former's movement suffered a setback but would still go on, whereas the latter gradually moved towards moderation in their methods while largely retaining their vision. This change was discernible in the writings of Aurobindo Ghosh and Bipin Chandra Pal and in the activities of Lajpat Rai (Tilak was in prison in Mandalay, Burma, until 1914). After his acquittal in the Alipore case, Ghosh withdrew from all political activity and moved to Pondicherry in April 1910, then a French colony, to escape prosecution by the British government for an article he wrote—an open letter of sorts titled 'To My Countrymen'. In this letter, he maintained his position that Swaraj meant 'absolute autonomy free from foreign control'. However, instead of revolutionary methods, he now advocated passive resistance through the formation of an Indian government in control over internal affairs, with the caveat that this ought to be achieved 'so far as that could be done without disobeying the law or questioning the legal authority of the bureaucratic administration'.[7] Until he left his mortal coil in 1950, he would remain in Pondicherry from where he would shine the light of Bharatiya spirituality.[8]

Bipin Chandra Pal too advocated passive resistance without sounding seditious, perhaps in view of Tilak's imprisonment.[9] As for Rai, he spent the better part of the period between 1908 and 1914 addressing issues within Hindu society through his Arya Samaji lens, and also attacking the Congress's quest for 'Hindu–Muslim unity'.[10] On the latter subject, after the enactment of the Indian Councils Act of 1909 and the coming into force of separate electorates for Muslims, Rai was, as before, scathing in his attack of the Congress for having sacrificed Hindu interests in its quest to become the sole and legitimate representative of both Hindus and Muslims. He urged the Congress to reshape itself as a Hindu party and focus on Hindu unity—as opposed to Indian unity—for he felt that the latter goal was a mirage, given the reality of the Two-Nation Theory and communal electorates.[11] Exhibiting a clear awareness of the nexus between language and consciousness, Rai also exhorted Punjabis to *boycott* Urdu literature and actively promoted the use of Hindi.[12]

Apart from the crackdown on the Extremists and the Revolutionaries, two other important developments would take place in 1910. In May 1910, George V became the Emperor of India, and by November 1910, Minto was succeeded as the Viceroy by Lord Hardinge and Morley was succeeded as the Secretary of State by Lord Crewe. The reason these developments were significant was that George V had visited Bharat as the Prince of Wales in 1905–1906 when the anti-partition agitation was raging, and by the time he returned to England he was convinced that the Partition of Bengal had been a mistake.[13] Therefore, there was hope that as the King-Emperor he would be sympathetic to the cause of reunification of Bengal.

On the exact sequence of events that led to the annulment of the partition, there appears to be some disagreement between the version presented by Hardinge in his own memoir[14] and the narratives presented by later scholars such as Eustis and Zaidi who have written on this specific subject. For the purposes of our discussion, what is relevant is that the convergence of several factors and interests led to the decision to undo the partition, but not in full.

What is commonly attested to by both sources is that despite the crackdown against the Revolutionaries, Bengal was in a state of unrest. Here's what Hardinge claimed to have felt within a few days of his arrival in Calcutta on 21 November 1910:[15]

> During those two days I had long talks with many Indians, and I began to feel that if only the trials for sedition then in progress, could be finished and set aside there might be some hope of peace. Curzon's policy of the partition of Bengal, to which the unrest was chiefly due, was severely criticized on all sides, but in those days I never held out the slightest hope of the reversal of that policy. Still, even in Bengal there was a general feeling that, in view of the decision of the King to hold an Imperial Durbar in India in a year's time, peace was very desirable, and the hope was repeatedly mentioned that it would be the King who would reverse the partition of Bengal, a hope that was realized, although nothing was more improbable at that time.

He also wrote:[16]

> Before I arrived in India I was well aware that the Province of Bengal was seething with sedition, the outcome of the policy of partition. Dacoities and assassinations of police and informers were almost of daily occurrence in Calcutta and its neighbourhood, and it was practically impossible to secure

a conviction by the ordinary process of law. But I hardly realized till I was actually in Calcutta the state of political unrest and terrorism that prevailed, and the number of prosecutions for sedition that had been instituted and that were likely to extend over at least a year. Some of these prosecutions, in fact most of them, presented no likelihood of a successful issue and had been initiated through the shortsightedness of the Lieutenant-Governor, Sir Edward Baker, and his legal advisers. In India, nothing could be worse than prosecutions that failed. They lowered the prestige of the Government and gave encouragement to the lawless. As soon as I had realized the true situation I sent for the Lieutenant-Governor and told him how much I disliked all these unsatisfactory prosecutions just at a moment when I was most anxious for a policy of conciliation in view of the impending visit of the King and Queen within a year's time, and I laid down the rule that no new political prosecution was to be initiated without my personal consent, and that in any case, where there was a doubt as to the sufficiency of evidence to secure a conviction, the prosecution was to be withdrawn.

Within an hour of assuming office as the Viceroy, Hardinge claimed to have become acutely aware of the communal consequence of the partition. He said:[17]

Within an hour of being sworn in as the Viceroy and Governor-General I had an interesting lesson as to the relative value of British and Indian troops for the preservation of order. The Lieutenant-Governor of Bengal, Sir E. Baker, came to see me and informed me that the police were unable to cope with a band of Mahomedans who were looting the bazaars, and asked permission to send two companies of an Indian regiment to restore order. I agreed. An hour later he asked for more troops and I authorized the use of the whole battalion. Later on he telephoned to say that the Indian troops were of no use, whereupon I gave orders for two companies of the Rifle Brigade to proceed to the scene of disturbance, and immediately after their arrival order was completely restored without a shot being fired.

Without dispute, it is evident that Hardinge was occupied with two important things—first, the situation in Bengal, and second, the holding of the Imperial Durbar.

As for the Congress and the League, given the continued state of unrest in Bengal, the issue of its partition would feature in the annual sessions of 1910 of both organisations, albeit with diametrically different takes. Critically, it appears that prior to their respective annual sessions of 1910, an attempt was made by William Wedderburn to build bridges and mend fences between the Congress and the League, which he mentioned in his presidential address at the Allahabad session of the Congress held that December.[18] The Allahabad session was the Congress's twenty-fifth, and while the session is usually glossed over, there were quite a few noteworthy aspects to it.[19] For instance, resolution VII is of interest to students of law since it sought separation of executive and judicial functions, which the Congress had been insisting upon even in the previous years. Notwithstanding the so-called reform of the Legislative Councils under the Minto–Morley Reforms, the separation of powers was yet to come about. Also, while resolution VI extended support to the Swadeshi Movement, there was no reference to the Boycott Movement. Resolution X reiterated the demand for annulment of the Partition of Bengal. Resolution XI deprecated the extension of the principle of communal electorates to municipalities, district boards and other local bodies. Interestingly, this resolution was proposed by Muhammad Ali Jinnah, who was then a member of the Congress, and seconded by two other Muslim delegates, one of whom was Syed Hasan Imam, brother of Syed Ali Imam of the Muslim League.

In his presidential speech at Allahabad, Wedderburn was of the view that the watchwords of the Congress ought to be 'Hope', 'Conciliation' and 'United Effort'. According to him, Hope and Conciliation applied to relations between the government and Indians, and between Europeans and educated Indians; Conciliation applied to Hindus and Muslims, as also to the Moderates and the Extremists (whom Wedderburn called 'impatient idealists'). On the question of Conciliation between Hindus and Muslims, he suggested that the League and the Congress must work together to achieve the goal of self-government within the empire, as also to address their common concern of racial discrimination against Indians in South Africa. As we shall see, the Congress and the League would indeed collaborate for a limited period on the issue of self-government, which would result in the Lucknow Pact and the Congress–League scheme for self-government in 1916.

Wedderburn then attempted to woo the Extremists back to the Congress by citing the Indian Councils Act of 1909 as proof of the 'success' of Moderate methods. As part of his recommendations under United Effort, he remarked that the Partition of Bengal was a mistake which needed to be rectified, but he was at the same time firm that self-reliance under the Swadeshi Movement should not result in India moving away from the British empire. In the latter regard, Wedderburn's views must be read in his own words to understand how 'moderate nationalism' and British paramountcy remained the position of the Congress even as of December 1910:[20]

> In India there is a new-born spirit of self-reliance. That is good: but do not let it degenerate into dislike for the people of other lands. Race prejudice is the palladium of your opponents. Do not let any such feeling hinder you from cultivating brotherhood with friends of freedom all over the world,

and especially in England. It is only by the goodwill of the British people that India can attain what is the best attainable future—the 'United States of India' under the aegis of the British Empire, a step towards the poet's idea of a Federation of the world. In his eager desire for self-government, let not the 'impatient idealist' forget the solid advantages of being a member of the British Empire; the Pax Britannica within India's borders; the protection from foreign aggression by sea and land; the partnership with the freest and most progressive nation of the World. No one supposes that under present conditions India could stand alone. She possesses all the materials for self-government; an ancient civilisation; reverence for authority; an industrious and law-abiding population; abundant intelligence among the ruling classes. But she lacks training and organisation. A period of apprenticeship is necessary; but the period need not be very long; if the leaders of the people set themselves to work together in harmony—hand in hand with the British people, India can most safely take her first steps on the new path of progress. (Cheers)

It is evident that both English and Indian members of the Congress saw India as a protectorate of the British.

Coming to the Muslim League's annual session of December 1910, which was its fourth, it was held in Nagpur from 28 to 30 December. In this session too there was profuse expression of gratitude towards the British Crown, which now adorned George V, and towards Lord Minto for strengthening the political position of Muslims in India. Also, due to Wedderburn's attempts earlier that year to build bridges between the Congress and the League, there were references to the need for Hindu–Muslim unity in the speeches delivered at this session. In this regard, here are a few extracts from the speech delivered by the president of the Nagpur session, Syed Nabiullah, who identified the preconditions for this Hindu–Muslim unity under the head 'Hindu–Mohammedan Relations':[21]

... As we all desire to bring about a rapprochement between the two communities I shall be perfectly frank with my Hindu brethren. I am grieved to say that certain events and incidents have happened within recent years which have given offence to Mohammedans, and caused many searchings of heart among them. At present I will deal with only one such event, namely, the 'worship' of Sivaji. Let it be granted that the world judges men like Sivaji, Robin Hood, Clive, Dalhousie, Napolean, Bismarck, etc., not by the usual standard of morality applicable to ordinary mortals. But what is the inner meaning of these Sivaji celebrations? Do they not convey a serious warning to all concerned? Do they not suggest the revolt of Hinduism against Islam and, by implication, against foreign domination? The apotheosis of Sivaji gives us a foretaste, as it were, of what the poor Mohammedans have to expect under Hindu hegemony. If, then, our feelings are irritated, is it to be wondered at?

I am, however, glad to note that since a certain firebrand had been removed from the scene of his labours, the cult of Sivaji appears to be dying out.

Clearly, the reference in the last line was to Tilak, who organised Shivaji celebrations. It was ironic that for a group that glorified the Mughals and all the Islamic invaders that preceded them, including Mohammed bin Qasim, the Muslim League took offence at Shivaji celebrations. This once again underscores the point made earlier—that Hindu–Muslim unity was contingent on Hindus giving up their heroes and their attempts to overthrow the British yoke, since the former offended the sentiments of Muslims and the latter would result in Muslims living in a Hindu-majority state, even if a democracy. Every time someone is tempted to cite the existence of Hindu–Muslim unity prior to the arrival of the British or thereafter, they must be reminded of the fact that this 'unity' was premised on a unilateral and untenable sacrifice that was expected to be made by Hindus, which was to disavow their religion, roots, language and history. We shall see this expectation coming up again in the context of the Hindi–Urdu debate.

Syed Nabiullah then went on to acknowledge the efforts of Wedderburn in trying to bring the Congress and the League together and spoke of a joint conference to be held by both organisations. In his speech, Nabiullah also repeated the wish that the British government would help in the establishment of a Muslim university at Aligarh, which could be named after George V. This session also saw the League insist that Urdu be treated as the lingua franca of India, instead of giving space to Hindi and other Bharatiya languages. Here's resolution VIII in this regard, which was passed on 30 December 1910:[22]

> The All-India Muslim League deplores the persistent attempts that are being made in various forms to set up what are called Hindi and Punjabi as the vernaculars of the United Provinces and the Punjab respectively, and to displace Urdu from the position so long occupied by it as the lingua franca of India, and having regard to the fact that the preservation of the Urdu language and literature is essential to the general progress of the country, particularly in Northern India, the League hopes and prays that the Government will be pleased to discountenance all such attempts to injure Urdu.

In support of this resolution, one of the delegates, Sheikh Zahur Ahmed, went on to recount the history of Urdu and its origins under the Mughal empire. In the name of Hindu–Muslim unity, evidently Hindus did not even have the right to revert to their native Bharatiya tongues. That the application of Middle Eastern coloniality extended to all aspects of culture, including language, could not have been clearer. With such deep fissures between the communities, which could not agree on heroes, villains, language, notions of sacredness and impurity, or anything else, the talk of 'Hindu–Muslim unity', obviously, was a collaboration of convenience to achieve limited political goals under the supervision of Englishmen such as Wedderburn. Such was the nature and strength of this *unity* that it required the paternalistic presence and oversight of the Christian European coloniser.

Following the Allahabad and Nagpur sessions of the Congress and the League, respectively, in December 1910, as proposed by Wedderburn a Hindu–Muslim conference was held in Allahabad in January 1911. At this conference, Gokhale, Gandhi's political mentor, exhorted the Hindus to display broad-mindedness and not be dismissive of Muslim concerns about Hindu majoritarianism.[23] It should come as no surprise that such pontifications to the Hindu community only served to strengthen the conviction of the Muslim League of the moral righteousness of its exceptionalist demands. Further, Gokhale and the Moderates operated under the hope that since Muslim demands for separate electorates had been granted, the Muslims would now work with the Congress to jointly demand colonial self-government from the British. However, this conference only resulted in demand for greater concessions by the Muslim League; its clear position was that no issue which was detrimental to Muslim interests must be raised, and this included language policy, cow protection, music played in the vicinity of mosques, and so on.[24] Predictably, the Congress's openness to consider these concerns of the League opened the doors for enhanced expectations of accommodation of Muslim demands. Among the thorniest issues was, of course, the continuing agitation demanding reunification of Bengal, which the Muslim League was dead set against.

It is against the above backdrop that the events leading to the annulment of the Partition of Bengal must be appreciated. As mentioned earlier, the decision to reunify Bengal was the product of a convergence of multiple interests. The new Viceroy, Hardinge, needed to bring the Bengal agitation under control and also acquit himself well in the arrangement of the Durbar to better the previous one organised by Curzon in 1903. Further, the British needed to monkey-balance their act to keep the Congress in good humour and to make up to them for the grant of communal electorates; the King, for whom the Durbar was being put together, wanted to grant his Indian subjects a suitable 'boon or concession' to mark his visit;[25] the Congress, which was facing flak from the Extremists and Revolutionaries for settling for the Minto–Morley Reforms and communal electorates, needed to show something to justify its continued loyalty to the British. In hindsight, the natural solution to address each of these interests was to reunify Bengal, which was unacceptable to the Muslim League.

According to Eustis and Zaidi, the suggestion to reunify Bengal as the King's permanent gift to his Indian subjects was offered on 13 December 1910 by Arthur Bigge, the King's private secretary, to Hardinge,[26] and on 16 December 1910, the King himself wrote to Hardinge as follows:[27]

> I hope that you will consult all the best men in India to consider what would be the best way to mark the fact of the first visit of the King-Emperor to India. Why not make two Bengals into a Presidency like Bombay and Madras; this would flatter the Bengalis very much, allay discontent and stop sedition, and would be well worth the extra cost to the country; think this over.

Secretary of State Crewe too remarked as follows on the King's views on the subject:[28]

> More than anything else, he had set his heart upon doing something which would, to some extent, satisfy that section of opinion in India which regarded partition as a mistake. He himself had always disliked the change and he had been supported in this view by many people ...

In fact, the King was keen on making an announcement on these lines at the Durbar and instructed Crewe to work on executing this proposal. However, Hardinge was not optimistic about the reunification of Bengal, and after discussion with members of his Council he felt that such a move would be a blow to 'the loyal section' of the Indian people, who too may resort to sedition and violence to achieve their goals.[29] By 'loyal section of the Indian people' he meant Muslims, who supported the partition and had benefited from it for half a decade. The reference could not have been to the Congress, since it opposed the partition and had reiterated its demand for its rollback in its resolutions since 1905. Given the resistance within Hardinge's own Council to the proposal to undo the partition, he conveyed his reluctance to the proposal to the Secretary of State, Crewe, in the following words in his letter dated 22 February 1911:[30]

> I can well understand that His Majesty would desire to make a striking announcement at the Durbar, ... and I warmly sympathize with his idea of setting right what has been represented to him as a grievance, but I am quite sure that you will agree with me that an announcement of this kind which would alienate the Mahommedan population, and would even arouse the future resentment of a large section of the Bengalis, is not at all what the King or we desire. What India requires above everything at the present moment is peace and quiet. We do not want fireworks or any political concessions designed to produce an effect. India has passed during the last five years through something very like a revolution on small scale, and time is required in order that things may adjust themselves to the new conditions. If all goes well, there is every reason to hope and believe that in a year's time we may be

again in smooth water. It would be the greatest possible mistake to do anything that might disturb the current of events which is now flowing strongly in our favour. And I am quite certain that the last thing His Majesty would wish to do would be to take any step that might embitter afresh feeling in this country.

Crewe agreed with Hardinge that even if the King's proposal had to be given effect, there was no question of restoring the position of Bengal to what it was prior to Curzon's time.[31] In other words, the annulment of the partition was merely meant to calm frayed tempers in Bengal without effecting a complete reversal of the policy. This meant that if push came to shove, the two Bengals would be reunited under a Lieutenant Governor or a Governor in Council, whereas Assam, Bihar and Orissa would have a Chief Commissioner each. Crewe further suggested making Calcutta an Imperial Enclave—i.e., a Union Territory, in today's parlance.[32] Both suggestions met with opposition from members of Hardinge's Council, for administrative reasons as well for protecting the interests of Muslims.[33] Hardinge's letter dated 22 February 1911 to the King conveying this negative consensus seemed to have had the desired impact on the King, who abandoned his proposal to reunite the two Bengals.[34] However, this left the King without a 'boon' to grant his Indian subjects on his visit.

It was at this point that a member of the Viceroy's Council, John Jenkins, who was originally opposed to reversal of the partition, suggested that if at all the government was keen on undoing the partition, it must vacate Calcutta instead of creating an Imperial Enclave there. This was because treating Calcutta as an Imperial Enclave would only make matters worse, given its importance to Bengal from the political, social and economic perspectives.[35] In other words, Jenkins wanted the focus to shift from reunification of Bengal to transfer of the capital from Calcutta to Delhi, presumably to placate Muslim sentiments, given the association of Delhi with the Mughal empire and Muslim state power. Narrating this sequence of events, Hardinge wrote in his memoir:[36]

> The moment has now arrived to give an account of the most important decision that I took during the 5½ years of my Viceroyalty, and which pervaded the whole of that period.

> It was in the month of January 1911, barely two months after my arrival in India, that I received a proposal from Lord Crewe suggesting the possibility of a modification of the partition of Bengal, which had been effected by Lord Curzon, and which had ever since been a festering political sore and the cause of all the anarchical agitation in Bengal. His proposal was intended to satisfy that section of the Indian political community who regarded the partition as a mistake. His idea was to create a Governorship instead of a Lieutenant-

Governorship of Bengal with the capital of the Province at Dacca or elsewhere, to form an Imperial Enclave of Calcutta directly under the Viceroy, and to appoint Commissioners for various divisions, as in Sind. The suggestion was that the rectification of the partition should be announced by the King at the Durbar, His Majesty being strongly in favour of it in principle. Before replying to this proposal I consulted several officials in responsible positions, since having been hardly two months in the country I was not in a position to give a definite opinion of my own, and as all those whom I consulted pointed out very strong objections to it, I declared the scheme to be impracticable, and Crewe thereupon allowed it to drop.

During later months it was brought home to me that if there was to be peace in the two Bengals it was absolutely necessary to do something to remove what was regarded by all Bengalis as an act of flagrant injustice without justification. There was at the same time a feeling of expectancy abroad that something would be done at the time of the Durbar to remove this injustice, and I appreciated the fact that if nothing were done we would have to be prepared for even more serious trouble in the future than in the past in Bengal. Moreover, I realized after six months in Calcutta that the Government of Bengal was practically non existent as far as the maintenance of peace and order was concerned, that it was really the Viceroy who administered the Province and that it was to him and his Council that the Lieutenant-Governor and his officials looked for advice and support. Moreover, the presence of the Legislative Assembly in Calcutta created an undue and inevitable Bengali influence upon the Members, which was detrimental to their legislative impartiality and presented a field for intrigue in which the Bengalis excelled. All these aspects of the situation in Bengal were most unsatisfactory and were a constant source of anxiety to me, for which I did not then see the remedy. It was Sir John Jenkins, the Home Member of my Council, who in a letter to me dated the 17th June 1911 sent me a memorandum which caused my views to materialize into a definite policy. He, as the Member responsible for security in India, held very strong views upon the urgency of the transfer of the Capital from Calcutta to Delhi which he thought 'would be a bold stroke of statesmanship which would give universal satisfaction and mark a new era in the history of India'. With this scheme the reversal of the partition of Bengal was to be associated as well as other changes in the delimitation of the provinces. He urged that these changes should be announced by the King in Durbar at Delhi, and he expressed his opinion that the change would be magical since, in the imagination of the masses of the people, Delhi and Empire have been associated from time immemorial. What Sir John did not fully appreciate was the implacable opposition that would be offered to the scheme by the British commercial community in Calcutta, who resented the change of Calcutta from an Imperial to a Provincial capital, and the loss of prestige due to the withdrawal of the Viceroy, Commander-in-Chief, Government of India, Legislative Assembly and a host of officials to a new capital at Delhi. Otherwise Sir John Jenkins' forecast proved absolutely correct ...

After long discussion with Sir J. Jenkins, with whose views I was quickly in general agreement, I drew up a very secret memorandum which I submitted to the Members of my Council for their opinion. The principal points were: (1) The transfer of the capital from Calcutta to Delhi, (2) The creation of United Bengal into a presidency with a Governor in Council appointed from England. (3) The creation of Behar and Orissa into a Lieutenant-Governorship with a Legislative Council and a capital at Patna, and (4) the restoration of the Chief Commissionership of Assam. All the members of my Council agreed in principle, some of them pointing out objections that might be raised to the scheme, none of which were however in any way vital. I decided therefore to submit the scheme for the consideration of the Secretary of State, giving him not only my own views but those of all and each of the members of my Council. On the 19th July I wrote a long letter to Crewe containing full details of the policy I proposed, placing before him the advantages to be obtained, and the objections that might be raised, but advocating strongly its acceptance as the best and only certain means of securing peace and reconciliation in Bengal, with at the same time a statesmanlike change in the general situation of the Government of India. I urged upon Crewe the necessity for extreme secrecy whether my scheme was accepted or not, and I told him that I felt this need so strongly that I myself made copies of all my letters on the subject, while the notes of the Members of my Council had been privately typewritten.

It was on the 7th August that I received a very satisfactory telegram from Crewe telling me that I had his 'entire support and full authority to proceed'. He agreed that the first announcements as regards Delhi and the Governorship of Bengal must be made at the Durbar and that absolute secrecy should be maintained till then. He asked at the same time that he should receive a formal despatch from my Government which I could send to him personally as a private letter for the sake of secrecy, and which should be prepared with a view to ultimate publication in its entirety.

I had already drafted an official despatch to Crewe setting forth my scheme in elaborate detail. When I understood that it was to be for ultimate publication I revised it, and after certain modifications suggested by Members of my Council, it assumed the form in which it was eventually published as a State paper. It became later the subject of acute controversy in the House of Lords, although history has since entirely vindicated its conclusions.

Lord Crewe confided the substance of my scheme in the first instance to the King in the presence of Sir A. Bigge. H.M. accepted it with great keenness, was very anxious to make the announcement himself at the Durbar, and was very insistent as to the need of complete secrecy. Later Crewe confided it to Lord Morley and Asquith. Both were deeply impressed and favourable, being struck by the adroitness with which the creation of new grievances was avoided while removing old ones. Asquith was greatly struck by the bigness of the idea and considered that its merits and advantages far outweighed any hostile arguments, though he anticipated, like many others, much opposition and grumbling from the Calcutta Europeans. As far as this question was concerned the remaining months before the Durbar were fully occupied in considering the legislative and statutory measures that would be necessary to carry out the new policy all of which had to be done with the greatest care so as to ensure secrecy. The secret was known to only twelve people in India during the six months that preceded the Durbar on December 11 and there was absolutely no leakage at all. On November 3rd I was informed by Crewe that the India Council in London was in favour of the scheme, and it was accepted a few days later by the Cabinet.

Eustis and Zaidi too confirm that John Jenkins was responsible for convincing Hardinge by explaining to him that as long as the partition remained, it would continue to fester, like the situation in Ireland.[37] Importantly, notwithstanding the opposition he expected from Muslims to the annulment of the partition, Hardinge was now convinced that he had to address the issue of partition significantly, if not fully. This shows that the state of unrest created in Bengal, primarily by the Revolutionaries and the Extremists, coupled with the soft agitation by the Congress, was responsible for pushing the British government in this direction. Hardinge also recognised that the grievances of Bengali Hindus were compounded by the creation of separate electorates for Muslims under the Indian Councils Act of 1909, which he acknowledged as follows:[38]

> At first, the opposition to the partition was, in the main, based on sentimental grounds; but since the enlargement of the Legislative Councils, the grievance of the Bengalis, has become real and tangible. In the Legislative Councils of both provinces they find themselves in a minority, being outnumbered in the one by Beharis and Ooryas, and in the other by Mahommedans and Assamese. As matters now stand, the Bengalis can never have in either province that influence to which they consider themselves entitled by reason of their numbers, wealth and education. This is a legitimate grievance which will be all the more keenly felt as time goes on, and the influence of the Legislative Councils upon the conduct of public affairs grows greater, as it is bound to do. Everyone must wish to find some means of appeasement if it is in any way possible to do so.

Effectively, Hardinge saw Jenkins' proposal as a via media which addressed multiple concerns and interests:[39]

1. Although the two Bengals would be reunited, Assam, Bihar and Orissa would be cleaved out and made into separate administrative units.

This would address Bengali sentiments and also reduce the size of the undivided Bengal. The new reunited and redrawn Bengal would be elevated to the status of a Presidency;

2. To placate Muslim sentiments, the Viceroy's Council consciously redrew the territories in a manner so as to ensure that Muslims would remain in a majority in the new Bengal.[40] Further, the transfer of the capital to Delhi would signify shifting the centre of power back to the seat of Muslim/Mughal state power. Also, since Nawab Salimullah was heavily in debt of the British, who had pulled him out of bankruptcy, he was expected to be pliant or at least less troublesome;

3. The provision of separate administrative units on a linguistic basis would impede the creation of a national identity, apart from placating Bihari, Assamese and Oriya sentiments. In other words, the reorganisation of provinces on linguistic lines had a bearing on national unity. Unfortunately, despite this experience, 'independent India' would still go on to reorganise its States on linguistic lines in 1956.

Finally, on 12 December 1911, at the Delhi Durbar, the King-Emperor George V made the following announcements, in this order:[41]

1. The capital of British India was being transferred to Delhi from Calcutta;

2. Bengal had been elevated to a Governorship;

3. Bihar, Orissa and Chota Nagpur would have a Lieutenant Governor; and

4. Assam was back to being under a Chief Commissioner.

Expectedly, the Congress welcomed the decision while the Muslim League declared that Muslims had lost all faith in the British government. Sharp reactions came forth from Bengali Muslim leaders such as Nawab Salimullah and Abdullah Al-Mamun Suhrawardy,[42] the uncle of Huseyn Shaheed Suhrawardy (who would play a key role in the Direct Action Day Riots of August 1946, which earned him the epithet of 'Butcher of Bengal'). Curzon too was unhappy with the reversal of his policy; in February 1912, he criticised, in vain, the Durbar declarations as a breach of faith which led to a trust deficit between Muslims and the British Government.[43] The issue was debated in the British Parliament almost until the end of February 1912, with Curzon leading the charge against the Durbar declarations. He questioned the constitutionality of the declarations made by the King-Emperor, including the secrecy with which they were carried out, and the wisdom behind the decisions.[44] Both Lord Minto and Lord MacDonnell responded to Curzon's criticism, effectively blaming Curzon for the revival of Indian nationalism and for deepening the pre-existing fault lines between Hindus and Muslims.

Eventually, on 22 February 1912, Curzon withdrew his motion challenging the Durbar declarations.[45] In any case, independent of the merits of the response to Curzon's criticism, the Durbar declarations could not have been retracted since, after all, the King-Emperor could not take back the 'boon' he had granted to his Indian subjects.

It must be appreciated that, thanks to the reversal of the Partition of Bengal and the cleaving of Assam from Eastern Bengal in 1911, Assam would become one of the bones of contention between the Congress and the League, and even more so after the partition of 1947. After all, East Pakistan, which largely corresponded to erstwhile Eastern Bengal, saw Assam as an extension of itself. It is no wonder then that infiltration into Assam from East Pakistan started immediately after the partition. After the bifurcation of Pakistan in 1971 and the creation of Bangladesh, the latter would continue to see Assam as unfinished business and entertain notions of a 'Greater Bangladesh' which included Assam. It is in this context that the issue of continued Bangladeshi infiltration to turn Assam into a *lebensraum* must be understood. That said, the issue of Bangladeshi infiltration is no more limited to Assam or the North-East.

Coming back to 1911, in addition to annulment of the Partition of Bengal and transfer of the capital to Delhi, a dispatch dated 25 August 1911 from the Government of India to the Secretary of State was published, wherein it was stated: '*... in the course of time, the just demands of Indians for a larger share in the Government of the country will have to be satisfied, and the question will be how this devolution of power can be conceded without impairing the supreme authority of the Governor General in Council.*' To this end, the British government realised that it gradually had '*to give the Provinces a larger measure of self-government until at last India would consist of a number of administrations, autonomous in all provincial affairs, with the Government of India above them all*'.[46]

Naturally, in the twenty-sixth session of the Congress, which was held in 1911 in Calcutta, it was now the Congress's turn to heap praises on the government and express gratitude for the annulment of the partition and for the dispatch.[47] However, the Secretary of State, Crewe, emphatically clarified in June 1912 that the dispatch was by no means an indication of the grant of self-governing Dominion status to India.[48] The other noteworthy aspect of the 1911 session was Gandhi's representation of racial discrimination in South Africa. Recognising his efforts and those of the Indian community in Transvaal, resolution XXIX was passed which, among other things, urged the British government to protect the dignity and interests of Indians in Transvaal. This time the resolution in relation to Transvaal was much more detailed and specific compared with the earlier resolutions on the subject.

As for the Muslim League, it did not hold a session in 1911; instead, one was held in Calcutta on 3 and 4 March 1912, with Nawab Salimullah as the president of the session, which was the League's fifth. Around the time of this session, trouble had started brewing in the Balkans, in Tripoli and Persia (now Iran), which was a matter of concern to Muslims in Bharat.[49] In particular, the invasion of Ottoman Tripoli by Italy with the support of British and French forces in September 1911 was the first trigger. The bombardment of Arabian ports, which endangered the Muslim holy cities of Mecca and Medina, was a matter of grave concern to Muslims all over the world, with Muslims in Bharat being no exception. This resulted in the Muslim League passing a resolution on 15 October 1911 expressing solidarity with Turkey, demanding British intervention to stop Italy, making an appeal for collection of funds to support Turkey and urging for a complete boycott of Italian goods by Muslims.[50] Following the Italian invasion of Tripoli, the Imam Raza Shrine in Meshed, Persia, was bombarded by Russia, which disturbed a significant cross-section of Muslims in Bharat, in particular the Shias, who shared common ties with Persian Muslims.[51] Once again, Muslims here sought, in vain, the intervention of the British to put pressure on Russia to withdraw from Persia.

The international developments only added to the sense of disillusionment of Muslims with the British at the annulment of the Partition of Bengal, notwithstanding the British attempts to placate them by creating a reunited Muslim-majority Bengal and the transfer of the capital to Delhi. It is against the above backdrop of international and national developments which affected the global ummah that the deliberations at the 1912 session of the League must be understood. Here are a few relevant extracts from the opening speech of Maulvi Badruddin Haider Khan Bahadur, the chairman of the reception committee; they portended the coming of a global Muslim movement and the participation of Muslims from Bharat in it:[52]

> I shall now, with your permission, proceed to review some of the more important events of Muslim interest that have occurred since the last session of our League. *The Muslim community all over the world is passing through very stirring times. Coming events are casting their shadows before them; and the whole Muslim world waits on the tip-toe of expectation to see what the womb of futurity has in store for us.* Of these great events, the Italian raid on the Tripolitan coast at present looms biggest on the international horizon. There can be no manner of doubt that the course of action pursued by Italy in the present case is utterly unjustifiable and wholly uncalled for. I will not swell the literature already existing, and daily growing, upon this unfortunate subject by expressing my personal views in the matter. I will only content myself with saying that I quite fail to see how any internal mismanagement by an autonomous power can

give a rival power the right of territorial acquisition. It stands to reason that if Turkey had failed to guarantee fair treatment to her Italian subjects, Italy might have entered a strong protest against such a breach of international equity. She might even in the last resort have demanded of Turkey the surrender of all Italian subjects and the payment of fair and equitable compensation for any losses incurred by them. But no political reasoning, however sound, and no logic, however subtle, can establish her claim to a right of territorial sovereignty over the whole of Tripoli, just because a microscopic minority of the Tripolitan foreign population was alleged to be labouring under Turkish iniquities. Even granting that there had been—but I wholly deny that there was—such a maladministration, we should still fail to find any justification for the high-handed action on the part of Italy. *It is a matter of great gratification for the Muslim community to find that the cold-blooded atrocities committed by the Italians have elicited strong and unqualified condemnation from almost all great International Powers. It remains to be seen how far these protests will be followed up by more vigorous declarations of policy, sufficiently practical to prevent a possible recurrence of such unfortunate and disreputable instances of international greed. In this connection the British Government in particular has its duties clearly outlined for it by the serious gravity and the magnitude of its own political stake. The British Government has a greater number of Mohammedan subjects than any other single power, European or Asiatic; and it is to the best interests of Britain herself to see that the sentiments and feelings of this vast population are not wantonly outraged. The Muslim community of India, therefore, confidently expects that it will not be long before the British Cabinet will become alive to its serious responsibilities, and, discarding the present halting policy of passive neutrality, will attempt to bring about some sort of reconciliation which may be acceptable to both the contending parties. Action in this matter is urgently called for, and procrastination will only intensify the gravity of the situation.*

The political situation in Persia is also a matter of grave concern to the whole Muslim world. Here, again, we have a superior power trying to bully a weaker constitution, and seeking to establish an utterly iniquitous claim by the primitive and highly objectionable rule of 'might is right'. How far Britain has involved herself inextricably in this mesh of international relations we are not in a position to judge. But rightly or wrongly, the idea has of late been gaining ground that the part taken by Britain in these transactions has not been wholly in consonance with ideas which we entertain of British Justice. I, for one, am hopeful that these misgivings will prove groundless. The British Government, however, owes it to its Muslim subjects to set their mind at rest once and for all by a final declaration of the line of action it means to pursue, if matters come to a head and Russia persists in her irrational and obstinate conduct. The subjects of the British Empire have been taught from their cradles to believe that wherever the interests of British subjects are involved—directly or indirectly—we may rely on the international potency of Pax Britannica to secure fair and equitable treatment. The Muslim community all over the world expects that this conviction will ere long be actualized, and that the British Government, both at home and in India, will take an active part in ensuring political autonomy and territorial integrity to unfortunate Persia. [Emphases added]

This extract makes it clear that by this time the Muslim community in Bharat saw itself as part of the global ummah, as desired by Syed Jamal al-Din al-Afghani, and took active interest in the treatment of Muslims elsewhere and the state of Muslim power outside Bharat. These facts have to be borne in mind to appreciate the events leading to the Khilafat Movement, which will be discussed later in this section.

Maulvi Badruddin's speech was followed by Nawab Salimullah's presidential speech on the transfer of the capital to Delhi and the annulment of the Partition of Bengal. Here are the relevant extracts:[53]

Transfer of the Capital

First, as regards the transfer of the capital from Calcutta to Delhi. We in Eastern Bengal are not much concerned with the effects, immediate or remote, of the transfer of the capital; but none the less we rejoice, because our brethren in the United Provinces and the Punjab will be benefited by the change. *We rejoice, because the high officials who control the destinies of India will naturally now be in close touch with so remarkable a centre of Muslim intellectual activity as Aligarh, such refined seats of Muslim culture as are to be found in the principal cities of the United Provinces, such exemplary types of Muslim manhood as the virile Musalmans of the Punjab. We rejoice with them, and pray to the Almighty Disposer of events that this momentous change of the transfer of the capital to Delhi may be for the good of all classes of the people, and that it may usher in an era of progress for Islam in those parts, which may redound to the glory of our community all over India. May the heart of Islam be resuscitated and vivified even as the historic city of Delhi will come to new life in this restoration to her of her past dignity, and may the ancient glories of Islam be revived a hundredfold under the aegis of British rule, so that our future generations may hold aloft the banner of culture, progress and civilization as our forefathers did, when the mighty flag of the Musalman Emperors floated triumphantly over the walls of Delhi.*

Annulment of Partition

I am now forced to refer to another Durbar announcement which compels me to say some bitter truths, but on which I cannot keep altogether silent, for I am sure my silence would be misunderstood. I am sorry I have got to take the risk of saying things which may perhaps expose me to contumely; but I feel that I cannot let this opportunity pass without an attempt at expressing our real feelings over a matter which weighs so heavily on our hearts—I mean the annulment of the Partition. I hope I will not be misunderstood. I am not one of those who used to look upon the Partition, in itself, as the only panacea for all our evils. The Partition gave us a great opportunity to bestir ourselves, and it awakened in our hearts the throbbings of a new national life which went pulsating through the various sections of our community in Eastern Bengal. I hope, gentlemen, you will believe me when I assure you that the Musalmans of East Bengal supported the Partition, not out of enmity to our Hindu brethren or at the bidding of the Government, but because we felt sure that the new administrative arrangements in East Bengal would afford us ample opportunities for self-improvement. We felt sure that the people of East Bengal, particularly the Musalmans, would be immensely benefited by a sympathetic administration easily accessible to them, and always ready to devote its time and attention exclusively to their welfare. As for ourselves, the Musalmans of East Bengal, we came to realize for the first time in our history that we too had rights and privileges as British subjects, and that it was only necessary for us to put our own shoulders to the wheel to free ourselves from that state of servile dependence on a dominant community in which we had been living before the Partition. How far we took advantage of these opportunities of self-improvement offered to us, it is now needless for me to discuss. This is now an integral part of the history of the East Bengal districts for the six years (1905–1911) during which the Partition remained in force.

Our ill-wishers at once perceived that the Partition would necessarily bring to the fore the long-neglected claims of the Musalmans of East Bengal, and although we never got more than what was justly our due, what little we gained was so much a loss to them. We regretted that this should be so, but it was unavoidable. It was perhaps unavoidable also that the philanthropy of our opponents should not be equal to the occasion, for they saw in the maintenance of the Partition a possibility of the Musalmans of East Bengal regaining a portion of their well-deserved rights as citizens of the British Empire. Those who are forced to give up a portion of their long-enjoyed monopoly, however unjustifiable in nature and origin, will readily understand the feelings of our enemies after the Partition. It was, therefore, only natural that they started a vigorous agitation to have the Partition annulled and to secure a reversion to the old order of things. Over the vehemence of this agitation, the excesses to which some of the agitators could go, and the violent crimes of which they became guilty in giving expression to their pent-up feelings against the Government, I would draw a veil, for they are matters of public notoriety and will soon pass into history. Seditious writings in the press were backed up by revolutionary speeches on the platform, and a band of irresponsible agitators roamed at large over the country to instil into the receptive minds of the youths the deadly poison of anarchical ideas. To give effect to their disloyal feelings against the Government, the agitators organized a boycott of British goods, and under colour of supporting an economic movement, sought to inflame the minds of the ignorant masses against Britain and its people. For some time the whole of Bengal seemed to be in the throes of a violent revolution, and there was hardly any peace in the land. Political murders were followed by political dacoities, and the officials entrusted with the maintenance of law and order were harassed in a way which would have exhausted even the patience of Job.

The reason for all this violent agitation was not far to seek. The agitators themselves alleged that Bengali sentiment had been outraged by placing them under two separate administrations, and that the Government wanted to injure their interests by placing them in a minority. It is a pity that this specious excuse for all this violent agitation and sedition should have been accepted by Government and believed by shrewd politicians like His Highness the Aga Khan. The real cause of the Bengali opposition to the Partition lay far deeper than in the plausible excuse of outraged sentiments, and I do not wish to repeat what I have already said on this point.

The Musalmans naturally refused to join the agitation because it was so violently opposed to their feelings of loyalty, and because it was directed against a measure which had proved of so much benefit to their interests. The agitators strained every nerve to win them over to their side and seduce them from their loyalty, but without success. Those who know the utter helplessness of the Musalmans at the hands of their Bengali landlord, lawyer or creditor, will easily have an idea of the tremendous sacrifices which Musalmans had to make in rallying on the side of law and order. Bitter feelings arose between the two communities—not on account of the Partition, as the Government of India seem to imply in their Despatch, but because the Musalmans refused to join the agitators in their seditious conspiracies against the Government.

Vigorous measures were then adopted by the Government to vindicate its authority, and although they brought about an apparent calm, they inflamed the minds of the agitators more fully against the Government. Gradually, the position of affairs was this—on one side there was the community of agitators with, in many cases, wealth, education and influence to back them, and on the other, there was the loyal community, both of Hindus and Musalmans, who had faced the onslaught of the agitators and incurred their bitter hostility in supporting the Government.

All at once the Government of India decided upon the annulment of Partition, based, as they have said, on broad grounds of administrative expediency, but affected in a way which to the popular mind conveyed the impression of having been exacted by clamour and agitation. The ignorant masses understand nothing about constitutional struggles, and by them the anti-Partition agitation and its apparent successes were regarded as the outcome of a trial of strength between the Bengali politician and the Government. When the Partition was annulled, the popular interpretation was that the Government had been defeated, and the exultant agitators in their hour of triumph did all they could to exaggerate the importance of their victory. The result has been a serious blow to British prestige all over the country, especially in East Bengal. But this is not all. The annulment of the Partition had all the appearance of a ready concession to the clamours of an utterly seditious agitation. It has appeared to put a premium on sedition and disloyalty, and created an impression in the minds of the irresponsible masses that even the Government can be brought down on its knees by a reckless and persistent defiance of constituted authority. Moreover, it has discredited British rule to an extent which is deeply to be regretted. It has hitherto been felt throughout the East that the word of the British Government is its bond, and that, come what may, Government cannot go back on its plighted word. Anything which weakens this belief must irreparably injure British prestige in India and the East in general.

To us, the Musalmans of East Bengal, the annulment means the deprivation of those splendid opportunities at self-improvement which we had secured by the Partition. But it is not the loss of these opportunities merely, heavy as that is, that forms the burden of grief over the annulment of the Partition. It is the manner in which the change has been brought about, without even warning or consulting us, which adds to the poignancy of our grief. I think I may fairly claim that though we should doubtless have urged our views strongly, our subsequent action has shown that we would have felt that Government by consulting us had shown its full confidence in our loyalty. And had there even been a chance of a Mohammedan agitation in East Bengal, the mere fact that the announcement had been made by His Gracious Majesty himself would have sufficed to render it impossible. We preferred to restrain ourselves from the course which might have commended itself on the first impulses of the moment, and did not wish to embarrass Government by agitation against an administrative measure which, however galling to our feelings, has had the impress of the Royal assent and approval. We hope we have succeeded in setting an example of genuine loyalty and willing obedience to the words of our Sovereign which can stand the severest tests. [Emphasis added]

The resolutions passed in this regard were the following:[54]

Annulment of Partition

The All-India Muslim League places on record its deep sense of regret and disappointment at the annulment of the partition of Bengal in utter disregard of Muslim feeling, and trusts that Government will take early steps to safeguard Muslim interests in the Presidency of Bengal.

The Persian Situation

The All-India Muslim League places on record its deep sympathy with the people of Persia, who are connected with the Indian Musalmans by the closest ties of blood, religion and a common culture, in their unmerited sufferings in their noble efforts to save their unfortunate country from Russian encroachments, and while trusting that the British Government is fully alive to the grave consequence likely to result from the dismemberment of Persia, respectfully urges upon the Imperial Government to get Russia to adhere to the spirit of the Anglo-Russian Convention and more effectively ensure the integrity and independent development of the country. [Emphasis added]

The annulment of the Partition of Bengal and the state of global Islam tested the loyalty of Muslims in Bharat towards the British despite the latter's grant of separate electorates to them and transfer of the capital to Delhi. As we shall see, these developments, coupled with the Congress's tendency to accommodate Muslim demands to secure self-government and the outbreak of the First World War, which dismantled the Ottoman empire and undermined its position as the Islamic Caliphate of the time, would lead to heightened Islamic consciousness in Bharat. This consciousness would result in the Khilafat Movement which, in turn, would provide further impetus to Muslim exceptionalism in Bharat. The Congress's willingness to go along with this exceptionalism would be evident from its own resolutions and from the statements and conduct of its leaders.

A Troubled Ummah, the First World War and the Lucknow Pact (1912–1916)

One of the consequences of the annulment of the Partition of Bengal and the Congress's attempts to accommodate the Muslim League's demands was the disillusionment of a certain section of Muslims with the League. They felt that since the government seemed amenable to pressure from the Congress, as demonstrated by the annulment of the partition, it made sense to have Muslim presence in the Congress as well to secure Muslim interests through another route. After all, the Congress was an older organisation than the League, had greater experience of dealing with the British, and had a presence in the Imperial and Provincial Legislative Councils and in London too. Further, since the Congress had gone out of its way to purge the Extremists/Nationalists to prove its loyalty to the British and its 'secular' character to Muslims, it had become more 'Muslim-friendly'. Importantly, while opposing separate electorates, the Congress still had prominent voices such as Gokhale who sympathised with the Muslim demand for separate and equal representation, at par with Hindus, notwithstanding their status as a numerical minority. The Hindu–Muslim Conference organised in Allahabad in 1911 under the supervision of Wedderburn had also signalled the openness of the Congress to stay mum on Hindu concerns that offended Muslim interests. Importantly, by October 1912, the first of the Balkan Wars began, with Bulgaria, Serbia, Greece and Montenegro successfully allying against the Ottoman empire, which resulted in huge loss of territory for the latter.[55] The Muslim League,

'The Boiling Point', a *Punch* cartoon by English cartoonist Leonard Raven-Hill, depicting Britain, France, Germany, Austria-Hungary and Russia sitting on a lid on top of a pot marked 'Balkan Troubles', satirising the situation in the Balkans leading up to the First Balkan War

naturally, condemned the war against the Ottoman empire and objected to the division of its European territories amongst the victorious Balkan states. A Red Crescent Society was established in Calcutta and London to collect funds for Turkey. Each of these domestic and international developments influenced the League's disposition towards the Congress favourably and opened possibilities for collaboration between the two.[56,57]

Before I discuss the Congress session of 1912, it is important to touch upon an incident which reminded the country that the Revolutionaries were still active and kicking. On 23 December 1912, Hardinge survived a bomb attack which killed his attendant and wounded him severely. The bomb attack was executed by Basanta Kumar Biswas and masterminded by Rash Behari Bose. This incident reminded the British establishment of the active presence of Revolutionaries in Bengal and Punjab, the two provinces that saw the maximum revolutionary activity in the country. In what came to be known as the Delhi–Lahore Conspiracy case,[58] Basanta Kumar Biswas and ten others were charged with conspiracy to murder, and the murder of an Indian employee. Out of the ten, five were acquitted, three were sentenced to death, and three, including Basanta, were transported out of the country for life.[59] Rash Behari Bose escaped to Japan in 1915, from where he would continue his work and contribute to the building of the Indian National Army, later known as Azad Hind Fauj, under Subhas Chandra Bose.

The Delhi bomb attack would feature prominently in the 1912 session of the Congress, in addition to the situation in the Balkans. Interestingly, the Congress would hold its annual session in Bankipur, Bihar and the League too would hold its council meeting (not its annual session) at the same place. As stated earlier, to prove its Muslim-friendly credentials, the Congress in the twenty-seventh session of December 1912 expressed its sympathy for and solidarity with Muslims over the plight of the Ottoman empire and the situation in Persia. For all practical purposes, all the right things were said by the right people to satisfy Muslim sentiments, as shall be seen from the extracts of the proceedings of the Congress's Bankipur session. Importantly, Lala Lajpat Rai re-entered the Congress in 1912, now sounding mellow, to the extent that he even condemned the Delhi bomb attack. Given Tilak's experience of imprisonment in Burma after being charged with sedition, perhaps Rai wanted to avoid a similar fate and therefore said what the Moderates and the British wanted to hear. But that Rai had not changed his views despite re-entry into the Congress would soon become apparent.

The chairman of the reception committee of the Bankipur session was Mazhar-ul-Haque. Here are a few extracts from his speech which throw light on the Congress's attempt to woo Muslims and to soften the Muslim League:[60]

> To me it has been a cause of deep and abiding regret that my own co-religionists have not seen their way to join this national assembly. *It is an undeniable fact that Mohamedans as a community have kept themselves aloof and those who have joined have joined in their own individual capacity. Although in spite of this regrettable defection the Congress has got on very well, the Congress ideals have triumphed and most of the items in the Congress propaganda have been accepted*

by the Government (Cheers), yet I believe that we would have got on better if our Muslim brethren had joined, and made common cause with us in the great and noble task of building up a nation. Then we would have moved on with quicker pace. A people counting among themselves seventy millions of souls and some of the very finest intellects and Specimens of manhood, is a factor and a force which cannot and ought not to be lightly ignored. Often have I dreamed of a picture in my mind of three hundred and fifteen millions of human beings with one ideal, one aim, full of determination and enthusiasm marching on the road of peaceful progress to the ultimate realization of their destiny. Such a force would be irresistible anywhere in the world. Perhaps the picture is too idealistic for its ever coming to be true. However, its reverse side where seventy millions of people detach themselves from the main group and march in the opposite direction is too gloomy to be contemplated with equanimity. [Emphasis added]

Under the head 'Europe and Islam', Haque remarked as follows:

The recent treatment of Islam by Europe has turned the scales. The sacrilege committed by the Russian troops on the sacred mausoleum of Imam Moosi Raza at Meshed in Persia exasperated the religious feelings of Muslims throughout the world. Sir Edward Grey, the author of the Anglo-Russian Convention, never raised his little finger to prevent the outrage. Then Italy invaded Tripoli, a country peopled wholly by Muslims of Arab descent and living peacefully under Turkish rule. It was a shameless act of brigandage attended by most inhuman atrocities, but this time Sir Edward Grey, with what I can only call indecent haste, recognized the sovereignty of Italy over a country which still remained to be conquered. *Then came the greatest blow to the prestige of Islam, the invasion of the seat of its Khalifate by the Balkan States. While Turkey was still fighting Italy, she was treacherously attacked on all sides. If the belligerents had fought purely for territory, the war would not have produced any visible effect upon the Musalmans of India. But these Christian States openly preached a crusade against Islam. It was not a war against the Turks but a war to turn Muslims out of Europe, a war between the Asiatics and the Europeans, a war between the Cross and the Crescent. Then the feelings of the Muslim world rose in indignation against the perpetrators of this outrage upon humanity and their religion. It is to be regretted that most of the responsible Ministers of the British Government, including the Prime Minister of England himself, gave vent to their feelings which clearly showed their intolerance of Islam. Mr. Asquith in his Guildhall speech referred to Salonica as the gate through which Christianity had spread in Europe and expressed his pleasure that it was once more in the hand of a Christian Power. There was not a word of regret at the humiliation of England's old ally, Turkey, not a word of sympathy with the Muslim world, but a hope that Constantinople itself might fall and be cleared of the presence of the hated Turk (Cries of 'shame'). Read the speeches of Mr. Lloyd George, Mr. Churchill, Mr. Masterman and Mr. Acland,*

and you will find the same exultant tone at the expulsion of the followers of Islam from Europe. This attitude of the British Ministers deeply offended the sentiments and wounded the religious feelings of seventy millions of Musalman subjects of his Imperial Majesty in India. [Emphasis added]

On the Congress's sympathy for the Muslim cause and Hindu–Muslim relations, Haque said:

But more, much more than this official sympathy, what moved the Muslim community most was the *universal sympathy shown by their Hindu* brethren (Loud cheers) in their dire affliction. It clearly demonstrated the fact that in times of danger and distress the two sister communities of India could still unite (Cheers). The moral and material support that we have received from them has gone straight to our hearts and conquered us. *And in this respect no one has done nobler work than our veteran leader, Mr. Surendranath Banerjea (Loud cheers). You, Sir, day after day, in your paper, have soothed the lacerated feelings of your Muslim brethren, expressed your sincere sympathy with their outraged sentiments and vigorously pleaded their cause. I personally know that the daily comments in the* Bengalee *on the progress of the war, were read by the Muslims of Behar with eagerness and gratitude.* You, Sir, have made a place for yourself in the hearts of your Muslim brethren, a place, permanent, abiding, which can never be shaken by any adverse wind of political controversy (Loud cheers). You and my Hindu brethren have done great work. You have brought the Hindus and Musalmans of India appreciably nearer to each other. It is only a question of time when the two will stand side by side on this our national platform and work shoulder to shoulder for the regeneration of our common motherland (Cheers). *I do not know whether you are aware of the fact, that already a great and powerful party of liberal Musalmans has arisen, whose aims and ideals are the aims and ideals of the Indian National Congress (Hear, hear and cheers). It is their firm determination to work with their Hindu brethren. Your sympathy in their hour of adversity has accelerated the work and strengthened the hands of this party. And this is the party which is bound to lead in future the Muslims of India (Hear, hear).* But I must raise a note of warning. Remember that this grand work of building up a great and powerful nation may be entirely and irretrievably ruined by one single thoughtless word or heedless expression uttered on the public platform or written in the press. The gentlemen of the press, I implore and entreat to be exceedingly careful how they handle any question which has the slightest bearing upon the Hindu–Muslim problem (Hear, Hear). It is no use to have a battle royal over insignificant matters such as the post of a deputy magistrate or a sub-inspector of police (Laughter). The press has great power in doing immense good to the country. It has also the power of doing immense harm. Let its power be utilized for doing good. Some people have the notion that by writing vigorously and strongly on a few appointments or a few nominations of municipal commissioners they are championing the cause of justice. Nothing can be further from the truth. They are simply creating dissension where there should be harmony, they are breeding ill-will where there should be feeling of brotherhood and affection. Let these petty things be left to smaller minds who cannot rise above their level. Let us have highest ideals and try to achieve them (Hear, hear).

To my Hindu brethren I say, treat your Muslim brethren with sympathy and please do not run away with the idea that all Muslims are hopelessly reprobate and there is no hope for their regeneration. Nothing of the kind. Try to understand them by putting yourselves in their position (Hear, hear). I have read of criticisms that the Musalmans of India think more of Turkey and Arabia than they do of India. It is quite true. But have these critics ever tried to understand why this is so? The fact of the matter is that religion is still, as it has ever been in this world, the chief determining factor of the conduct of a man and a nation. And the religion of the Muslims is outside India. Their holy places Mecca and Medina, the Mausoleums of all their Imams, Sahabas and saints, are outside India. It is one of the cardinal tenets of Islam that all Muslims, no matter to what nationality, race or rank of life they may belong, are brothers. In their house of God, there are, no reserved pews or any places of distinction, and the humblest Muslim will not give way to the proudest monarch of the world (Hear, hear). This doctrine is observed not only in theory but in actual practice. So there should be no cavilling at Musalmans looking outside India. As long as one is a Musalman one must look and cannot help looking outside India for one's religious salvation. What I want to impress upon my Hindu brethren is to have a wider outlook, accept facts as facts, and handle the situation with delicacy and toleration. Indeed, I believe that if they thoroughly and sympathetically understood the position, it would be a source of strength rather than of weakness to the cause of Indian nationality.

To my own co-religionists I say, as you are Musalmans you cannot but look beyond India, but do not forget your motherland. India has great claims over all her sons and your neglect of her interests is almost sinful. I invite you, nay I call upon you in the sacred name of your motherland to join this national assembly, which knows no distinction of class or creed, no distinction of Hindu or Musalman (Cheers). I have heard some friends say that the Indian National Congress is a Hindu organization. I deny the charge altogether. I repudiate it entirely. It may be worked by the Hindus; but why? Simply because Musalmans will not come forward and take their proper share (Hear, hear). Its ideals have always been national and never sectarian. If the Muslim community have any grievances against the Congress, I invite them to come here and ventilate them on this our common platform. I prophesy that they will find all their grievances chimerical and imaginary and will go away absolutely converted to the Congress cause. But perchance, if I prove to be a false prophet, then we have a safeguard in our constitution to the effect that if a majority of ¾ths Muslim delegates object to a certain resolution being passed, it shall be dropped. Can there be anything fairer than this safeguard in our constitution?

I know and I am confident that this appeal of mine will not go unheard and unanswered. It has already been heard in my own province. Look around you in this Pandal and you will find many Musalmans of light and leading taking part in our proceeding. Those who are not in the seats reserved for the delegates, are there in the seats allotted to the visitors. Perhaps thinking of the past, they have felt a little delicacy in openly joining us this year (Laughter), but they are now as true Congressmen, as any of us. Only their body is in the gallery there, their heart is with us on the dais here. (Cheers). I have dwelt a little too long on this Hindu–Musalman question and I have no doubt that I have tired you, (Cries of No, no), but I could not help myself. This is my life-work. I wish the two sister communities to understand each other, have tolerance for each other's weaknesses, join hands and work together. To my mind this is one of the greatest works to which an Indian could devote his life. I have spoken freely and fearlessly. If I have offended any one in this Pandal or outside it, I beg his pardon and seek his forgiveness. I could not keep back my honest thoughts from this great gathering of my countrymen. I may have made a mistake, but I felt a call to speak out. [Emphases added]

To these opening remarks by Haque, here's how the president of the Bankipur session, Rao Bahadur Raghunath Narasinha Mudholkar, responded:[61]

I desire to thank you, Mr. Mazharul Haque, for the very kind words which you have spoken of me and of the great Hindu community to which I have the honour to belong (Cheers). Let me assure you that the troubles and the tribulations of Islam have awakened a deep and responsive echo in the heart of the great Hindu community in India (Cheers). We deeply sympathise with Turkey in her misfortunes, with Persia in her troubles and tribulations, with you, my Mahomedan fellow-countrymen, in your sorrow for the misfortunes of Islam. May this feeling of solidarity and growing sympathy between Hindus and Mahomedans increase and deepen to the mutual advantage of both the communities and to the abiding, lasting and permanent benefit of the motherland to which we all belong. That is the hope, the ideal, the aspiration of every Indian, be he a Hindu or a Mahomedan ...

On the Turkish situation, Mudholkar said:

Brother-delegates, before I proceed to touch upon those questions which demand our immediate consideration, I have, on your behalf and of my humble self, to give expression to the profound sorrow and sympathy which the Hindus and all non-Moslem Indians feel for our Moslem brethren in the great misfortune which has overtaken the Khalifate, and the struggle for existence which the Turkish Empire has to carry on against a powerful combination. When the political sky is overcast with dark and threatening clouds, it is not desirable for us, the subjects of a Power which is striving to preserve the strictest neutrality, to enter into the merits of the quarrel between the various belligerent Powers, nor are we in a position to discuss them with adequate knowledge. But as staunch believers in the supremacy of the moral law and upholders of the principle of peaceful evolution, this much I believe is permissible to us to say, that it is possible to satisfy the just and legitimate aspirations of the Christian provinces of the Turkish Empire without destroying the existence or the importance of Turkey or subjecting her to the humiliating condition of powerlessness.

It must be borne in mind that these expressions of solidarity with Muslims over the Balkan situation and the sanctity of the Islamic Caliphate were uttered by the Congress *seven years* before the Khilafat Movement began in 1919. In my view, given the unreserved genuflection to Muslim interests that the Congress had embarked upon from 1910 and even before, in order to become the sole representative of all Indians, its subsequent participation in and active support to the Khilafat Movement under Mohandas Karamchand Gandhi between 1919 and 1924 was in no way out of character. One would have expected the Congress to have learnt its lesson on the reality of the Two-Nation Theory and its consequences for the Indic civilisation at least after the Partition of Bengal in 1905 and the entrenchment of communal electorates in 1909. However, it pursued a diametrically opposite policy, which only served to embolden Middle Eastern consciousness and its innate ethno-religious supremacism and separatist vision. The absence of a pushback to the Congress's approach at the Bankipur session is evident from the fact that Lala Lajpat Rai too was constrained to denounce the 'cult of bomb', referring to the attack on Hardinge, and delivered a speech in Urdu, in stark contrast to his earlier calls for boycott of Urdu literature.[62]

Although the Muslim League did not hold an annual session in view of the Balkan situation,[63] as also due to Syed Ameer Ali's unavailability,[64] it held a council meeting in Bankipur, Bihar, on 31 December 1912, which was presided over by the Aga Khan. What is noteworthy is that Muhammad Ali Jinnah attended this meeting, and so did Mazhar-ul-Haque. The following was the carefully worded four-point resolution passed by the League in the meeting, indicating its priorities—namely, loyalty towards the British and advancement of Muslim interests, *followed* by friendly relations with other communities and colonial self-government for India:[65]

1. To promote and maintain among Indians feelings of loyalty towards the British Crown;
2. To protect and advance the political and other rights and interests of the Indian Musalmans;
3. To promote friendship and union between the Musalmans and other communities of India;

4. *Without detriment to the foregoing objects*, the attainment of a system of self-government *suitable* to India by bringing about, through constitutional means, a steady reform of existing system of administration; by promoting national unity and fostering public spirit among the people of India, and by co-operating with other communities for the said purposes. [Emphasis added]

The fourth point, which was subject to the first three, was a cautious reciprocation of the Congress's eagerness to collaborate with the League to achieve the goal of self-government. Further, by using the phrase 'system of self-government suitable to India' as opposed to 'self-government on colonial lines' or 'colonial self-government', which was the phrase used by the Congress, the League meant that any form of representative self-government that may be introduced in Bharat must recognise the position of Muslims as recognised by the Minto–Morley Reforms of 1909. In short, separate electorates for Muslims would be a prerequisite for any self-government that may be introduced in Bharat.

The sixth session of the League was held in Lucknow on 22–23 March 1913. Jinnah, who attended the Council meeting of December 1912 as a non-member, attended the Lucknow session as a member.[66] Among the notable aspects of this session were:

1. Condemnation by the president of the session, Mian Muhammad Shafi, of the Delhi bomb attack on Hardinge;
2. Passing of a new constitution for the League consistent with its four-point resolution adopted in December 1912, including self-government suitable to India, which meant self-government with due regard to the rights of Muslims;
3. Demand for separation of executive and judicial functions; and
4. Reference to the situation in the Balkans, Tripoli and Persia, along with appeals to the British government for intervention to protect Muslim interests outside India.

The reference to self-government once again in the Lucknow session signalled the League's attempts at reciprocating—much more than at its December 1912 session—the sensitivity the Congress had shown towards Muslims. This, in fact, led to correspondence being exchanged between leaders of the Congress and the League from March to May 1913 to explore the possibility of concrete joint action and a proposal to hold a meeting at Lucknow in September 1913 with representatives of both sides.[67] Although the meeting did not materialise, owing to the Kanpur mosque incident, the League gravitated further towards collaborating with the Congress. The incident was triggered when a portion of the Machhli Bazaar Mosque in

Kanpur, which was used for *wuẕu* or ritual ablutions, was demolished to widen a road under the directions of the then Lieutenant Government of the United Provinces, James Meston.[68] While a temple too was sought to be demolished, Pandit Madan Mohan Malaviya's intervention saved it, whereas the Muslims could not save the portion of the mosque that was demolished, despite petitions by Maulana Muhammad Ali Jauhar, one of the Ali Brothers who would play a leading role in the Khilafat Movement, the other being Shaukat Ali. On 1 July 1913, before the Muslim League could intervene, the portion of the mosque sought to be acquired for road widening was demolished under police protection, which fetched widespread criticism from the Muslim community from all over the country. Also, on 3 August 1913, under the supervision of District Magistrate Tyler, the police fired at Muslim protesters, which resulted in the death of at least twenty-five protesters, which further inflamed Muslim sentiments. Although Hardinge himself visited Kanpur in October 1913 to assuage Muslim sentiments and directed the restoration of the demolished portion of the mosque at government expense,[69] this incident resulted in the Muslim leadership questioning the community's dependence on and loyalty towards the British.

In fact, the period between 1911 and 1913 revealed the existence of three camps within the Muslim community—the Muslim Nationalists (such as Jinnah, Mazhar-ul-Haque and Wazir Hasan), who wanted to work with the Congress to secure Muslim interests and self-government, the pan-Islamists (such as Maulana Abul Kalam Azad, Maulana Muhammad Ali, Shaukat Ali and Saifuddin Kitchlu), who championed collaboration with global Islam and were open to collaboration with the Congress to counter Western imperialism in order to defend the Caliphate, and the conservatives (such as Nawab Salimullah), who were against any rapprochement with the Congress and were staunchly loyal to the British.[70] Interestingly, Mazhar-ul-Haque and Jinnah were members of both the Congress and the League, with Haque having joined the League before Jinnah. Jinnah too would become a member of the League in 1913 whilst retaining his Congress membership.

It must be underscored at the expense of reiteration that securing Muslim interests remained the top priority of all three factions of the Muslim community, their primary difference of opinion being in relation to the means employed to secure the community's interests. This was in stark contrast to the 'secular' approach of the Congress, which did everything within its power to avoid being seen as a Hindu organisation. Unfortunately for the Congress, despite its best efforts to be seen otherwise, it would continue to be labelled Hindu by the Muslim League, primarily because of its Hindu-majority membership. This distinction between the Muslim League and the

Congress was fundamental to their respective founding DNAs and would remain so, with the exception of transient and convenient departures. It would help to bear in mind that an exception does not point to the absence of a rule; on the contrary, it underscores the existence of one. Therefore, neither the Congress nor the League must be assessed based on their transient aberrations. By and large, the former shunned an exclusively Hindu identity in exchange for a secular DNA, whereas the latter unabashedly embraced its Muslim identity while keeping its options for collaboration open to protect and advance Muslim interests. As we shall see, this reflected even in the choice of locations for their annual sessions.

The Congress chose Karachi for its 1913 session, which was its twenty-eighth, to expand its base among Muslims, while the League chose Agra, a place associated with the Mughals, for its seventh session. The Congress session, whose president was Nawab Syed Muhammad, saw a repeat of its past resolutions and demands for the most part. What is of relevance to the discussion at hand is resolution IV, which showed the attempts by the Congress and the League to mend fences with each other:[71]

> That this Congress places on record its warm appreciation of the adoption by the All India Moslem League of the ideal of self-Government for India within the British Empire and expresses its complete accord with the belief that the League has so emphatically declared at its last sessions that the political future of the country depends on the harmonious working and co-operation of the various Communities in the country which has been the cherished ideal of the Congress. This Congress most heartily welcomes the hope expressed by the League that, the leaders of the different communities will make every endeavour to find a modus operandi for joint and concerted action on all questions of national good and earnestly appeals to all the sections of the people to help the object we all have at heart.

This resolution was passed since several delegates, including the president, welcomed the League's resolution on self-government and its spirit of rapprochement with the Congress. Further, on the same lines as in the 1912 Bankipur session, the position of Islam outside Bharat was addressed. Here are a few relevant extracts from the presidential speech:[72]

> Before I conclude, I desire to refer however briefly, to the troubles and misfortunes that the Muslim world outside India has endured during the past few years. The period has been fraught with fateful changes in the recent history of Islam, changes materially affecting the importance of Muslim countries as independent countries which stirred Muslim feeling throughout the world to a degree seldom witnessed before. *The Mussalmans who have seen the subversion of the Ottoman power in Europe, and the strangling of Persia, cannot find the same comfort as before in their past achievements or present temporal power, when they*

have to think of the future of Islam. The progress of the unfortunate Balkan War was anxiously watched by Mussalmans of India, its disastrous results caused the greatest concern and disappointment the dismemberment of Turkey by depriving her of her European Provinces evoked wide-spread regret, in which non-Muslims also shared, and the fate of Muslim States and their treatment by Europe made the deepest and most painful impression.

I do not consider it necessary to go at any length into the subject as abler men have fully dealt with it on other occasions. I trust that it will not be construed as a desire on my part to underrate in any way the supreme importance which the question has in the eyes of the Muslim. *European critics in estimating the effect of the Turkish reverses in the Balkans on the Muslim world have generally failed to take into account the Muslim opinion itself. But M. Mijatovich who has represented Servia both at Constantinople and at the Court of St. James's is very conciliatory when he says that 'Political interest made us, the Balkan nations, paint the Turks as cruel Asiatic tyrants incapable of European civilisation. An impartial history would prove that the Turks are rather Europeans than Asiatics, and that they are not cruel tyrants, but a nation loving justice and fairness and possessing qualities and virtues which deserve to be acknowledged and respected. The martial era of the Turkish history having been, not ingloriously, closed, historical Providence seems to have in store a high mission for the Turks.'* Gentlemen, the defeat of Turkey, while it has caused intense grief and depression to the Islamic world, has also brought Muslims closer together in a way that nothing else was capable of doing. The worst adversity has—its lessons to teach him who has a mind to profit by it. The Mussalmans have realised the full import of the grave crisis in their history, which has roused in them a feeling of brotherhood. They never before felt the strength of Islam as a unifying force so keenly as they do at present. They had great faith in the essential beneficence of modern civilisation. But it is greatly to be deplored that that faith has been rudely shaken; and they rightly feel that their future lies in their own hands. I look upon the desire for unity and self-reliance manifested by my co-religionists as an awakening pregnant with great possibilities for the future. – Cheers. [Emphases added]

The Congress was making the right overtures to woo the Muslim League. As for the League's session, the Kanpur mosque incident featured prominently in its deliberations. Since Hardinge had personally visited Kanpur to make amends, the reference to the incident was in measured tones. The most critical aspect of this session consisted of the observations of Ibrahim Rahimtulla, president of the session, on the Balkan War, the foreign policy of the British and its impact on Muslims in Bharat. This speech was perhaps the clearest indication of the coming of a Khilafat Movement—i.e., a movement in support of the Islamic Caliphate whose seat was then the Ottoman empire. That pan-Islamism had become an important component of the Indian political reality would become evident from the following extract from Rahimtulla's speech:[73]

Balkan War

It must be with a feeling of relief that you will have seen the end of the Balkan War. Turkey has not been turned out bag and baggage from Europe. Though its European dominions have been curtailed, it still has a strong footing on the Continent of Europe. Adrianople, round which a strong Muslim sentiment has concentrated, again flies the Turkish flag. Turkish reverses have this redeeming feature, that they brought to the surface the fact that however much Musalmans may be divided amongst themselves, the religious sentiment of Muslim brotherhood is a living force throughout the entire Muslim world. Musalmans in different parts of the world have all proved their readiness to come forward in a spirit of self-sacrifice and devotion to stand by their co-religionists in their hour of trial and trouble. It is the living miracle of Islam that the sentiments of Islamic brotherhood are seated deep down in the hearts of the followers of our revered Prophet, and that the lapse of centuries has in no way blunted the effects of his noble mission.

Foreign Policy of Great Britain and Indian Musalmans

During the time of stress and strain, charges were made against the Musalmans of India that they wanted to dictate the foreign policy of Great Britain, that they desired that England should go to war to protect the Muslim States in Europe and Asia. Can anything be further removed from the truth? The Indian Musalmans fully recognize the danger to England, with all its interests spread over the face of the whole world, to hint that she should thoughtlessly involve herself in a bloody war. It is doing the Muslims of India a grave injustice to suggest that they had the remotest notion of dictating what foreign policy England should pursue. And as a matter of fact they have never dreamt of doing so. All that they have urged—and I think they had ample justification in doing so—was that England, as the sovereign power of millions of Musalman subjects, should, out of regard for their sentiments, endeavour to see that Turkey obtained fair and just treatment in the councils of Europe. I do not think anyone could venture to assert that the request, nay even the demand, that England should do its best in the councils of Europe to ensure fair, just and equitable treatment to Turkey can possibly be regarded as being in any way unreasonable. It is because the utterances of responsible British Ministers appeared to them to indicate that England's sympathies were against the Turks that Indian Muslim feelings were naturally hurt and that they felt aggrieved. Can any fault be found with them under the circumstances?

At the time of the declaration of war between Turkey and the Balkan Allies, Sir Edward Grey said in the House of Commons that 'the great powers are taking what steps they can to prevent a breach of the peace; definite proposals were made yesterday for collective steps to be taken by or on behalf of the

Great Powers to overcome these difficulties by representations to the Balkan States and at Constantinople and we agreed to them.' The steps indicated by Sir Edward Grey were the declaration that 'if nevertheless war breaks out between the Balkan States and the Ottoman Empire they will not admit as the result of the conflict any modifications of the territorial status quo in European Turkey.' This was at the time of the commencement of the war. We may reasonably draw the inference from this declaration that if Turkey had been victorious it would not have been allowed to retain any portion of the conquered territory. At the time war was declared, it was generally felt in the Chancelleries of Europe that the Turkish soldiers would sweep over the surrounding territory belonging to the Allies; and if these expectations had been realized, the might of Europe, including the power of England, would have been asserted to deprive Turkey of any territorial expansion as the result of its victories. But the tide of victory went the other way, and the Balkan Allies proved victorious immediately after the conflict had begun in earnest. This completely upset the preconceptions of the Chancelleries of Europe; and they felt that the declaration of the maintenance of the status quo in European Turkey would be prejudicial to the Balkan Allies. Mr. Asquith, the Prime Minister of Great Britain, took an early opportunity of then declaring that whatever may be the result of the war, the Concert of Europe could not possibly deprive the victorious party from securing the fruits of their victories. Are the Musalmans of India to be blamed if they feel that England was associated with the other European Powers in laying down and enforcing a policy that if the Turks had proved victorious in the combat, they would not have been allowed to obtain any territory belonging to any of the Balkan Allies, but that if the Balkan Allies proved victorious, they would be permitted to annex important portions of the European dominions of Turkey? Is it unreasonable that the Musalmans of India should feel that fair and equitable treatment was not being meted out to their co-religionists beyond the seas, and that England was taking a prominent part in such treatment?

Mr. Asquith and the Peace of London

Well, as you are aware, after the Peace of London was signed and the Balkan Allies fell out amongst themselves, resulting in a redistribution of the conquered territory, Turkey, availing itself of the opportunity which became so providentially available, recaptured the town of Adrianople and the surrounding country, with which a strong Muslim sentiment was associated. Was it wise, was it statesmanlike for Mr. Asquith to declare that so far as Turkey was concerned, it would be required to lie within the boundary line settled at the Peace of London? In the face of such and similar declarations from the highest ministers of the British Crown, no fault could be found with the Musalmans of India if they concluded that England, far from trying to be just and fair towards Turkey, far from endeavouring to secure fair play to the Muslim Khilafat, was siding against it, and was co-operating with other

European Powers who are the declared enemies of the Turkish Empire. Under all this provocation, have the Musalmans done anything which would attach any blame to them? Have they swerved in the slightest degree in their feeling of sincere loyalty towards the British Crown? However painful the episode has been to them, they have exercised full self-control and restraint, and their conduct far from being blameworthy deserves the highest commendation.

Other than the above observations on the situation in the Balkans, for the most part the substance of the League's resolutions, from those on the situation in South Africa to self-government, was similar to that of the Congress. This indicated that the Congress–League rapprochement was at work thanks to the influence of the Muslim Nationalists and pan-Islamists in the League, despite their being outnumbered by the conservatives. This was particularly evident in the case of resolution V, which dealt with extension of communal electorates to self-governing bodies. The resolution was proposed by Maulvi Rafi-ud-Din and seconded by Mujib-ur-Rahman with an amendment, while two other members, Maulana Muhammad Ali and Muhammad Ali Jinnah, suggested that this issue be postponed until the next session to demonstrate the League's commitment to collaborating with the Congress. To be clear, Jinnah's suggestion was not motivated by any altruistic need to maintain communal harmony because he himself added that his suggestion for the postponement was in the interest of political expediency and that he did not want to spell out in public the reasons for his position.[74] When the issue was put to vote, the original resolution proposed by Maulvi Rafi-ud-Din and seconded by Mujib-ur-Rahman won eighty-nine votes whereas Jinnah's position secured forty votes.[75] That Jinnah's pragmatic position on such an important subject for the Muslim community got forty votes itself demonstrated that Muslim Nationalists and pan-Islamists were not negligible in number, although the conservatives had the last word.

The year 1914 would prove to be a crucial one for all the entities under discussion. In the Congress, Gandhi and Lala Lajpat Rai were proposed as the presidential candidates for the twenty-ninth session which was to be held in Madras in December 1914.[76] Although Gandhi returned to Bharat in December 1914, he stayed on the sidelines of the political scene for a year. As for Rai, he turned down the offer saying that his differences with the Congress's moderate position, with its unswerving loyalty to the British and its policy of appeasing the Muslims, remained.[77] Further, he made no bones of the fact that he saw Congressmen such as Surendranath Banerjea, who had been elected to the Legislative Councils, as careerists. Rai was right in turning down the offer, since his candidature was opposed by Dinshaw Wacha, Subramanya Iyer, G.A. Natesan, Nawab Syed Muhammad and Fazlul-Haque citing potential opposition from the government and Muslims.[78] Daniel Argov points out that the extent of the Congress's subservience to Muslim opinion and the clout of Muslims within the Congress was evident from the fact that its Muslim members threatened to boycott the Madras session if Rai presided over it. As a consequence, his candidature being both turned down by himself and rejected by Muslims, the Madras session would be presided over by Bhupendranath Basu. That the Congress was still the stronghold of the Moderates who did not want the Extremists back in their fold was demonstrated by Pherozeshah Mehta's stout refusal of Annie Besant's proposal to amend the Congress's constitution to bring back the other Extremists.[79]

In the meantime, though the Second Balkan War had ended in August 1913, its after-effects led to the First World War. On 28 June 1914, Archduke Franz Ferdinand, heir to the Austro-Hungarian throne, was assassinated by a Bosnian Serb, Gavrilo Princip, during the former's visit to Sarajevo, the capital of Bosnia and Herzegovina. This served as the immediate trigger for the First World War, which began on 28 July 1914. There were apprehensions in the British Parliament and hopes in Germany that the outbreak of the Great War would see an uprising in Bharat against the British.[80] Bharat turned out to be Germany's greatest disappointment since, instead of an uprising, the country saw the Congress pledge its wholehearted and unswerving support to the British.[81] A resolution was passed in the Imperial Legislative Council on 8 September 1914, wherein Indian members of the Council pledged unwavering loyalty and enthusiastic devotion to the King-Emperor and also offered to share the heavy financial burden of the war.[82] This was followed by further expressions of loyalty and support at the Madras session, where the Congress thanked the government for sending Indian troops as a mark of its trust in Indians, and sought self-government in return (I had briefly touched upon this in Chapter 11 of the first book). Here's resolution V from the 1914 session:[83]

V. The Indian Expeditionary Force

This Congress notes with gratitude and satisfaction the despatch of the Indian Expeditionary Force to the theatre of war, and begs to offer his Excellency the Viceroy its most heartfelt thanks, for affording the people of India an opportunity of showing that, as equal subjects of His Majesty, they are prepared to fight shoulder to shoulder, with the people of other parts of the Empire in defence of right and justice, and the cause of the Empire.

Here's resolution XIX, commending Indian troops on their valour and contribution to the British War effort:[84]

XIX. Indian Troops

This Congress rejoices to place on record its deep sense of gratification and pride at the heroic conduct of the Indian troops whose deeds of valour and conspicuous humanity and chivalry in the Great War, are winning the respect of civilised mankind for the mother country, and resolves to send a message of hearty and affectionate greetings to them and their comrades in arms, with fervent prayers for their well-being and success.

The President be requested to cable the above resolution to the Indian troops through the proper channels.

And here's resolution X, proposed by Surendranath Banerjea, requesting for self-government in lieu of the loyalty demonstrated by Indians in supporting the British war effort with men and materials:

> That, in view of the profound and avowed loyalty that the people of India have manifested in the present crisis, this Congress appeals to the Government to deepen and perpetuate it, and make it an enduring and valuable asset of the Empire, by removing all invidious distinctions, here and abroad, between His Majesty's Indian and other subjects, by redeeming the pledges of Provincial autonomy contained in the Despatch of 25th August 1911, and by taking such measures as may be necessary for the recognition of India as a component part of a federated Empire, in the full and free enjoyment of the rights belonging to that status.

Resolution XII acknowledged Gandhi's contributions in South Africa, while the rest of the resolutions were a repeat of the ones passed in past Congress sessions. Apart from the resolutions, the proceedings of the Madras session too must be read for the speech delivered by S. Subramania Iyer as the chairman of the reception committee. To me, that speech represents a textbook case of dual consciousness. Among other things, Iyer spoke of making 'our beloved Aryavarta the brightest jewel in the Imperial Crown'.[85] This was followed by the presidential speech of Bhupendranath Basu. On the meaning of self-government within the empire, the following were his views, which were echoed by Banerjea and Annie Besant:

Self-government within the Empire

> The two extremes—the one of separation, the other of subordination— are both equally impossible and must be put out of our mind. The ideal that we must pursue, and which the Congress has set before itself, is that of co-ordination and comradeship, of a joint partnership on equal terms (Hear, hear). I do not say that it must materialize to-day, but I do say that every step that we take, or ask the Government to take, must point in that direction. *India no doubt is a continent and not a country divided into small administrative areas: it is divided into communities, castes and sects: it is divided by religion, language*

and race, by different types and stages of civilization and progress, and by different methods of administration. It has within its limits princes of ancient lineage and traditions, and people great numbers of whom are still in a state of mental darkness: the educated middle classes are still a small, if no longer a microscopic, minority: there are peoples within its borders who know of nothing else but personal rule, and large classes which are ready to accept a representative government. Can any system of self-government be evolved in a country like this which will bring into coherence its heterogeneous elements, or must India from the very nature of its constitution be for ever subject to outside dominion? I hope I have stated the case for the other side fairly. Let us see how we can apply our ideal to a state of things like this: let us clearly realise what that ideal may be. From the very extent of India and the diversity of her population, we must have a system of Government modelled on the lines of the Commonwealth of Australia, or the United States of America, modified according to Indian conditions and presided over by a representative of our Sovereign. In this constitution all will find a place, the Englishman as well as the Indian, the prince as well as the peasant, and all communities, by a judicious combination of the methods of election and selection in the case of the less advanced. I am only suggesting tentative lines of development and not a scheme, and I am aware that it may be laughed at as chimerical: but I shall not complain, as criticism is the touch-stone of truth. And I do not despair, for the position is not hopeless. [Emphasis added]

Expressing unequivocal support for the British war effort, Bhupendranath Basu said:[86]

... We are in the midst of a great and devastating war, comparable only to the fearful cataclysms of nature; we are involved in a struggle for life and death, and what is more between the elemental passions and the higher ideals of humanity. The mind is absorbed in the great issues now hanging in the battlefields of Europe, where our brethren, British and Indian, are mingling their blood in the cause of honour, liberty and justice (Hear, hear). This is not the time to deal with matters upon which we may differ: all controversies must be laid to rest in the presence of the great and awe-inspiring drama of human history now being enacted before our eyes, and we must present to the world the spectacle of a united Empire, animated by the sole desire to bravely combat the dangers with which we are threatened, and to see that not only civilization, but the very soul of humanity, may not lapse into chaos and be utterly lost. We hesitated, therefore, for a long time over the holding of this session of the Congress, and though I accept the ultimate decision not to have a break in the continuity of the Congress, I confess I find my course very difficult.

India's New Horoscope[87]

... India has recognised that, at this supreme crisis in the life of the Empire, she should take a part worthy of herself and of the Empire in which she has no mean place. She is now unrolling her new horoscope, written in the blood of her sons, in the presence of the assembled nations of the Empire and claiming the fulfilment of her Destiny (Hear, hear).

No wonder that in 1914–15, Moderate stalwarts like Surendranath Banerjea spoke at over thirty public meetings, each to support the recruitment and contribution of materials towards the war effort.[88] While this was the attitude of the Moderates, even among the Extremists, Tilak (who was released from Mandalay Prison in June 1914[89]) and Bipin Chandra Pal advocated cooperation with the British war effort.[90] The most vocal opposition from the Extremists to Bharat's participation in the war effort came from Lala Lajpat Rai, who believed that Bharatiyas must not act as England's mercenaries in the war. In stark contrast to his denouncement of the 'cult of bomb' in the 1912 session, Rai praised Basanta Kumar Biswas for the Delhi bomb attack on Hardinge. He expressed regret that the Revolutionaries did not get the support they deserved from their wealthy compatriots or from the masses.[91] Since there was widespread support from the Congress for Indian participation in the war—barring a few voices such as Rai's—the British government drew heavily from Bharat for its troops as well as to meet the expenditure of the war. It is estimated that Bharat sent at least a million troops and incurred an expenditure of £146 million, in addition to contributions and gifts from princes and the wealthy class towards the war effort.[92]

The Muslim League did not hold a session in 1914 for multiple reasons. The conservatives within the League wanted to defer the session as a mark of loyalty to the British government. The other reason, which was perhaps the primary one, was that the pan-Islamists like the Ali Brothers within the League were openly voicing their views in favour of Turkey and against Britain, so much so that they were arrested.[93] This resulted in accelerating the rapprochement between the Congress and the League since the pan-Islamists and Muslim Nationalists realised that they would need the support of the Congress to carry on their advocacy of Turkey and their criticism of the British since their own conservative colleagues within the Muslim League preferred to stay away from the Congress and not be disloyal to the British. As a mark of solidarity with the Congress, Jinnah and Wazir Hasan suggested that the Congress and the League hold their annual sessions at the same place and around the same time.[94] To this end, since the Congress's annual session for 1915 was scheduled to be held in December in Bombay, Jinnah convinced quite a few members of his community from Bombay, namely the Khoja Muslims, to invite the League to hold its 1915 session in Bombay.[95] According to Hugh Owen, apart from these efforts, Annie Besant worked from the Congress's side to prepare a scheme of constitutional reforms in the direction of self-government, which could be jointly advocated by the

Congress and the League.[96] This effort was supported by Jinnah and Wazir Hasan, both of whom were Shias. Their efforts met with staunch opposition from the conservative Muslims, especially Sunnis such as Maulvi Rafi-ud-Din, as well as from a sizeable cross-section of the Khojas. However, the League's council met in Lucknow in November 1915 and accepted Jinnah's proposal to hold its annual session in Bombay.

The 1915 annual sessions of the Congress and the League in Bombay reflected the changing dynamics in both organisations. The Congress session was presided over by S.P. Sinha and was held against the backdrop of the loss of two Moderate stalwarts. Gokhale had passed away in February 1915 and Pherozeshah Mehta in November 1915, which weakened the old Moderate leadership to some extent, although Banerjea was still active and holding the fort for the Moderates.[97] However, the death of the two veteran Moderates, in particular Pherozeshah Mehta, meant that Annie Besant could once more work towards bringing back into the party fold the Extremists, especially Tilak, since his primary disagreement with the Moderates had been on the means employed to achieve the goal of self-government for Bharat.[98] As discussed earlier, of all the Extremists, Tilak's end vision came closest to that of the Moderates. Also, since his six-year imprisonment in Burma had mellowed his opposition to the Congress's methods, it allowed Besant to rope him in the preparatory efforts towards the Congress–League joint scheme for post-war constitutional reforms demanding self-government/Home Rule. As we shall see, this would lead to the Home Rule Movement.

As for the League's session, it saw a rift between those who wanted to collaborate with the Congress and those who did not. The session saw open confrontation between Jinnah and Maulana Hasrat Mohani; although a pan-Islamist, Mohani was conservative in his outlook and saw Jinnah as Westernised and detested his openness to working with the Congress.[99] Notwithstanding these tensions in the League, both the Congress and the League passed resolutions to the effect that they would appoint their respective committees to prepare a joint scheme of post-war constitutional reforms, to be jointly advocated and presented to the British government. Here's resolution XIX passed by the Congress on self-government, which was proposed by Surendranath Banerjea and seconded by Annie Besant:[100]

Self-government

That this Congress is of opinion that the time has arrived to introduce further and substantial measures of reform towards the attainment of Self-Government as defined in Article I of its Constitution, namely, reforming and liberalising the system of Government in this country so as to secure to the people an effective control over it, amongst others, by

(a) The introduction of Provincial autonomy including financial independence;

(b) Expansion and reform of the Legislative Councils so as to make them truly and adequately representative of all sections of the people and to give them an effective control over the acts of the Executive Government;

(c) The re-construction of the various existing Executive Councils and the establishment of similar Executive Councils in Provinces where they do not exist;

(d) The reform or the abolition of the Council of the Secretary of State for India;

(e) Establishment of Legislative Councils in Provinces where they do not now exist;

(f) The readjustment of the relations between the Secretary of State for India and the Government of India; and

(g) A liberal measure of Local Self-Government:

> That this Congress authorises the All-India Congress Committee to frame a scheme of reform and a programme of continuous work, educative and propagandist, having regard to the principles embodied in this Resolution and further authorises the said Committee to confer with the Committee that may be appointed by the All-India Moslem League for the same purpose and to take such further measures as may be necessary; the said Committee to submit its report on or before the 1st of September 1916 to the General Secretaries, who shall circulate it to the different Provincial Congress Committees as early as possible.

This session also marked the growing stature of Gandhi within the Congress. By now, his work in South Africa was well known and he had even been considered for the post of president for the 1914 session. In this session too, Gandhi spoke in some detail on the situation in South Africa and Canada, and a resolution was passed on the subject. Coming to the League's session, it was presided over by Mazhar-ul-Haque. The following resolution V was moved by Jinnah, which was seconded by Maulana Abul Kalam Azad, among others, and passed unanimously:[101]

> The All-India Muslim League resolves that a committee consisting of the following gentlemen be appointed to formulate and frame a scheme of reforms, and that the said Committee is authorized to confer with political and other organizations or committees if any, appointed by such organizations as they may deem fit, provided always that due regard is paid to the needs and interests of the Musalmans of India in the formation of the aforesaid scheme of reforms.

> The Committee shall submit its report and scheme to the Council of the All-India Muslim League to be presented at its next Annual Session.

When proposing this resolution, Jinnah spelled out the terms of engagement with the Congress, which would demonstrate that the proposal of joint action with the Congress was without rendering secondary or marginalising the bottom line—namely, Muslim interests. Here is the relevant portion from a record of the proceedings:[102]

> Mr. Jinnah said that in view of the present situation, when questions of the readjustment and reconstruction of the Government of India would soon to be taken up, it was desirable that a committee consisting of responsible leaders of the Mohammedans should be appointed to formulate a scheme of reforms. He did want to go into details, and would content himself by saying that the object of the resolution was to formulate a scheme of reforms. As to the second part of this resolution, it empowered this Committee, whilst formulating a scheme of reforms, to confer with other political organizations of this country, such as the Indian National Congress. The Congress and the League were the two chief representative political organizations of India; and the Committee of the League should, without the slightest prejudice to Mohammedan interests and with due regard to Mohammedan needs, formulate a scheme of reforms, and do it so far as possible in conformity with the scheme to be formulated by the Indian National Congress. After the scheme had been formulated by the League and the Congress, they could go to the authorities and say these were the reforms which they demanded in the name of United India (Loud applause).

After the Bombay annual sessions, by early 1916 the All-India Congress Committee and the League's reforms committee had to work on finding common ground with respect to (a) the steps India must take towards achieving self-government, (b) the manner of preserving separate electorates for Muslims under such government in accordance with the phrase 'system of self-government suitable to India', and (c) the actual proportion in which such separate representation to Muslims was to be given in the Central and Provincial Legislatures.[103]

In April 1916, Lord Minto was succeeded by Lord Chelmsford as the Viceroy/Governor General of India, who posed the following two questions at the first meeting of his Executive Council:[104]

1. What was the goal of British rule in India?
2. What were the steps on the road to that goal?

The answer to the first question was that *'the endowment of British India as an integral part of the British Empire with self-government was the goal of British Rule'*, which would be achieved through a three-step process—development of local self-government, increase in native presence in the administration and expansion of Provincial Legislative Councils.[105] Around the same time, on 24 April 1916, the Congress had prepared a draft scheme of reforms and shared it with the Muslim League for its inputs.[106] Meanwhile, due to tensions within the League on collaboration with the Congress, the work on preparing a draft scheme was delayed. Finally, Wazir Hasan added his inputs to the scheme shared by the Congress, and this draft was shared with the provincial Muslim Leagues for their views. Under this draft, in the central legislature consisting of 100 members, sixty-five would be elected, out of whom fifteen would be Muslims elected through separate electorates. As for the provincial legislatures, they would consist of seventy-five elected members out of a total of 100, twenty of the seventy-five being Muslims elected through separate electorates.[107] This was a tentative draft put together by Wazir Hasan and had quite a few details missing, owing to lack of participation from the provincial leagues. The Reforms Committee of the League discussed this draft on 21 August 1916 in Lucknow.[108] Several members of the Congress, including Extremists like Tilak who had re-entered the Congress by then, thanks to Besant's efforts, were of the view that in order for a joint effort for self-government to succeed, concessions would have to be given to the Muslims by way of separate electorates. Here were Tilak's views on the issue:[109]

> A considerable section of the educated Mahomedans have begun to perceive ... the necessity of political agitation on the Congress lines and it would be a fault of the Congress if it does not meet them halfway ... suitable concessions [must be] made.

Jinnah defended the concession to his fellow Congressmen as follows:[110]

> ... rightly or wrongly the Muslim community is absolutely determined for the present to insist upon separate electorates ... I would, therefore, appeal to my Hindu brethren that in the present state of [the] position they should try to win the confidence and the trust of the Muslims ... If they are determined to have separate electorates, no resistance should be shown to their demands.

Jinnah also convinced the Congress that the Muslim community's trust in the Congress would increase if the latter were to accept separate electorates for Muslims as part of the joint scheme.[111] In light of the role played by Jinnah in securing Muslim interests by retaining his dual membership of the Congress and the League, two things emerge: first, notwithstanding the claims that Jinnah was of a secular mindset owing to his Westernised bearings and his membership of the Congress, it is evident that he put his membership of the Congress to the best use of the Muslim community by softening the opposition within the Congress to separate electorates for Muslims; and second, Jinnah also elevated his profile within the League, thanks to the role he played in preparing the joint reforms. We will see later that Jinnah's primary goal behind staying in the Congress until 1920 was to advance the cause of his community. In this sense, Muslim nationalists were not 'Nationalist Muslims', i.e., their nationalism was defined by their Muslim identity and was meant to serve Muslim interests.

Coming back to the joint reforms, two developments of consequence took place by October 1916. First, Annie Besant wanted to launch the Home Rule League, given the Congress's loss of vitality and relevance, especially after the death of Gokhale and Pherozeshah Mehta. Surendranath Banerjea opposed this, as he felt the formation of a new organisation would weaken and undermine the Congress.[112] In the face of such opposition, Annie Besant founded the Home Rule League with the support of Tilak in September 1916;[113] Tilak had already launched the Indian Home Rule League in April 1916.[114] Second, on 12 October 1916—as mentioned in Chapter 11 of my first book—a six-page memorandum on self-government in India, signed by nineteen of the twenty-seven non-official elected members of the Imperial Legislative Council, was sent to Viceroy Chelmsford.[115] Naturally, the signatories included members of the Congress and the League, including Jinnah. Following were the specific measures suggested jointly by the Congress and the League:[116]

1. In all the Executive Councils, Provincial and Imperial, half the number of members should be Indians; the European element in the Executive Councils should, as far as possible, be nominated from the ranks of men trained and educated in the public life of England, so that India may have the benefit of a wider outlook and larger experience of the outside world. It is not absolutely essential that the members of the Executive Councils, Indians or Europeans, should have experience of actual administration, for, as in the case of ministers in England, the assistance of the permanent officials of the departments is always available to them. As regards Indians, we venture to say that a sufficient number of qualified Indians, who can worthily fill the office of members of the Executive Council and hold portfolios, is always available. Our short experience in this direction has shown how Indians like Sir S.P. Sinha, Sir Syed Ali Imam, the late Mr. Krishnaswami Iyer, Sir Shams-ul-Huda and Sir Sankaran Nair have maintained a high level of administrative ability in the discharge of their duties. Moreover, it is well known that the Native States, where Indians have opportunities, have produced renowned administrators like Sir Salar Jang, Sir T. Madhava Rao, Sir Seshadri Aiyar, Dewan Bahadur Raghunath Rao, not to mention the present administrators in the various Native States of India. The statutory obligation, now existing, that three of the members of the Supreme Executive Council shall be selected from the public services in India, and similar provisions with regard to Provincial Councils, should be removed. The elected representatives of the people should have a voice in the selection of the Indian members of

the Executive Councils and for that purpose a principle of election should be adopted.

2. All the Legislative Councils in India should have a substantial majority of elected representatives. These representatives, we feel sure, will watch and safeguard the interests of the masses and the agricultural population with whom they are in closer touch than any European officer, however sympathetic, can possibly be. The proceedings of the various Legislative Councils and the Indian National Congress and the Muslim League bear ample testimony to the solicitude of the educated Indians for the welfare of the masses and their acquaintance with their wants and wishes. The franchise should be broadened and extended directly to the people; Muhammadans or Hindus, wherever they are in a minority, being given proper and adequate representation, having regard to their numerical strength and position.

3. The total number of the members of the Supreme Council should be not less than 150, and of the Provincial Councils not less than 100 for the major Provinces, and not less than 60 to 75 for the minor Provinces.

4. The Budget should be passed in the shape of money bills, fiscal autonomy being conceded to India.

5. The Imperial Legislative Council should have power to legislate on, and discuss and pass resolutions relating to, all matters of Indian administration, and the Provincial Councils should have similar powers with regard to Provincial administrations, save and except that the direction of military affairs, of foreign relations, declarations of war, the making of peace, and the entering into treaties, other than commercial, should not be vested in the Government of India. As a safeguard, the Governor General in Council or the Governor in Council, as the case may be, should have the right of veto, which, however, should be exercised subject to certain conditions and limitations.

6. The Council of the Secretary of State should be abolished. The Secretary of State should, as far as possible, hold in relation to the Government of India a position similar to that which the Secretary of State for the Colonies holds in relation to the Colonies. The Secretary of State should be assisted by two permanent Under-Secretaries, one of whom should be an Indian. The salaries of the Secretary and the Under-Secretaries should be placed on the British estimates.

7. In any scheme of Imperial Federation, India should be given through her chosen representatives a place similar to that of the Self-Governing Dominions.

8. The Provincial Governments should be made autonomous, as stated in the Government of India's despatch, dated 25th August, 1911.

9. The United Provinces, as well as the other major Provinces, should have a Governor brought from the United Kingdom and should have an Executive Council.

10. A full measure of Local Self-Government should be immediately granted.
11. The right to carry arms should be granted to Indians on the same conditions as to Europeans.
12. Indians should be allowed to enlist as volunteers and units of a territorial army established in India.
13. Commissions in the army should be given to Indian youths under conditions similar to those applicable to Europeans. [Emphasis added]

The interesting aspect of point 2 of the memorandum is that it spoke of adequate representation to *both* Hindus and Muslims wherever they were in a minority. In this sense, the principle of separate electorates was being extended to Hindus too, in provinces where they were in a minority. After the dispatch of the memorandum to the Viceroy, on 16 November 1916, the League met once more to discuss the draft scheme and decided to propose that Muslim presence in the central and provincial legislatures must be one-third of the total elected members, which was higher than the percentage proposed in the draft circulated by Wazir Hasan.[17] On 17–18 November 1916, a joint conference of the Congress and the League took place in Calcutta. While the Congress accepted in principle the idea of separate electorates, the issue that neither party could agree upon was the proportion of Muslim representation in the United Provinces and Bengal. The League wanted 40 per cent of the seats in the United Provinces and 50 per cent in Bengal, which was vehemently opposed by leaders such as Malaviya and Chintamani, which meant that the issue needed further deliberations.

In the meantime, a detailed dispatch, dated 24 November 1916, was sent by the Government of India to the then Secretary of State for India, Austen Chamberlain, who had succeeded Lord Crewe in 1915 and held office until his replacement by Edwin Montagu in July 1917. This dispatch, which was issued in view of the Congress–League memorandum of October 1916, said the following on the subject of self-government in India:[18]

> The goal to which we look forward is the endowment of British India as an integral part of the Empire, with self-government, but the rate of progress towards that goal must depend upon the improvement and wide diffusion of education, the softening of racial and religious differences, and the acquisition of political experience.

> The form of self-government to which she may eventually attain must be regulated by the special circumstances of India. They differ so widely from those of any other part of the Empire that we cannot altogether look for a model in those forms of self-government which already obtain in the great Dominions. In all parts of the Empire which now enjoy self-government, it has been the result, not of any sudden inspiration of theoretical statesmanship, but of a steady process of practical evolution, substantially facilitated by the

possession of a more or less common inheritance of political traditions, social customs and religious beliefs.

British India has been built up on different lines, and under different conditions, and must work out by the same steady process of evolution a definite constitution of her own. In what form this may eventually be cast it is neither possible nor profitable for us to attempt now to determine, but we contemplate her gradual progress towards a larger and larger measure of control by her own people, the steady and conscious development of which will ultimately result in a form of self-government, differing perhaps in many ways from that enjoyed by other parts of the Empire, but evolved on lines which have taken into account India's past history, and the special circumstances and traditions of her component peoples, and her political and administrative entities.

Our most anxious desire is to see a real and immediate advance made towards this goal, and in the belief that the time has now come when the rate of progress may be accelerated on definite lines we propose:

(a) To develop urban and rural self-government in the direction of giving greater powers to the local boards and councils, and making these more predominantly non-official and elective in character, while at the same time extending the franchise in the wards or other constituencies by which the elected members are chosen.

(b) To increase the proportion of Indians in the higher branches of the public service, and thereby to enable Indians to take a more importar part in the administration of the country.

(c) To pave the way for an ultimate enlargement of the constitutional powers of the provincial legislative councils—(i) through an increase in the elected element; and (ii) through a material expansion of the constituencies by which the elected members are chosen, so as to bring about a state of things under which they will become more truly representative of the interests of the people as a whole.

Although the dispatch mentioned specific steps to be taken towards increased participation in government for Indians, its evasive approach to the eventual grant of self-government to Indians in letter and spirit failed to inspire the confidence of either the Congress or the League. This added a greater sense of urgency on their part to iron out their differences, in particular on the issue of provincial communal electorates. To bridge the gulf between the two parties, joint marathon meetings were held in Lucknow on 25, 26 and 28 December 1916 before their respective annual sessions. Also, Besant, Jinnah, Tilak, Bhupendranath Basu, Wazir Hasan, Motilal Nehru and Tej Bahadur Sapru had to intervene to get the parties to agree.[119] Finally, the League agreed to 30 per cent and 40 per cent representation for Muslims in the legislatures of the United Provinces and Bengal, respectively.[120]

Here's a table capturing the proportion of seats agreed upon for Muslims in the provincial legislatures, and their proportion in the population of the provinces:[121]

Provinces	Muslim Percentage	Muslim Percentage in Population
Bengal	40	53
United Provinces	30	14
Punjab	One-half	55
Bombay	One-third	20
Madras	15	6
Bihar and Orissa	25	10
Central Provinces	15	6

In return for concessions in the United Provinces and Bengal, a critical concession was demanded by Jinnah, which was accepted by the Congress: under the proposed reforms, any legislation that affected a particular community would be withdrawn if three-fourths of that community's legislators opposed it.[122] This was a far-sighted and smart concession that Jinnah managed to extract from the Congress, since he knew that although it was available to any community to invoke the principle, Muslim members of the Congress and the League would place the community's interests over and above any other interest. In stark contrast, the majority of the members of the Congress did not see themselves as preserving Hindu interests, and therefore Hindu interests would either have a minority voice or, worse, would be orphaned. Effectively, under the concession, anything from language policy to cow protection could be objected to by Muslim legislators, leaving the Congress with no other option but to drop such issues, owing to the Lucknow Pact. Effectively, by acceding to this demand, the Congress had bought 'Hindu–Muslim unity' at a steep price to secure 'self-government suitable to India'.

The joint reforms scheme was finally adopted by the Congress and the League at their respective annual sessions in Lucknow in December 1916 and would henceforth be known as the Lucknow Pact. The Congress session was held from 26 December to 30 December 1916 in Lucknow, with Ambika Charan Mazumdar (A.C. Mazumdar, whose book I have quoted from in the previous chapters) as its president. Welcoming the delegates, Pandit Jagat Narain, the chairman of the reception committee, had this to say about the reunion of the Moderates and the Extremists and the party's collaboration with the Muslim League:[123]

> The present year will be a memorable one in the history of our political evolution. For the first time since the unfortunate split at Surat we witness

the spectacle of a united Congress. Realizing that in union alone is strength, both the parties have laid aside their differences and resolved to work shoulder to shoulder to win for India a position compatible with her self-respect and dignity in the British Empire. They have heard the call of the country and, obliterating old divisions, rallied round her in the hour of her need.

Equally hopeful and encouraging is the patriotic spirit which inspires our Mahomedan brethren. There was a time, now happily gone for ever, when short-sighted counsels prevailed among them and they gave to their community what was meant for the country. But education and the new spirit have done their work as surely among them as among the other sections of our countrymen. They grave enlarged their vision and broadened their sympathies. Both the communities share the same aspirations to-day and realize in a larger measure than they ever did before, that united action is essential to the fulfilment of their common destiny. Some of the most important leaders of Muslim public opinion in these provinces have joined our committee. And it is a significant sign of the times that the representatives of the Congress and the Muslim League met together formally at Calcutta on the 17th and 18th of last month to formulate a scheme of reform, to be pressed, after the conclusion of the present war, on the attention of the Parliament and the people of Great Britain in the name of a united India, in order that we may have a controlling voice in the administration of our internal affairs. The conference marked a great step forward in our political evolution and disclosed a substantial identity of views between Hindus and Mahomedans. A few differences, no doubt, still remain; but I am not without hope that they will prove short-lived and that we shall soon see the two sister-communities marching hand in hand on the path of progress. (Cheers.)

On India's contributions in the First World War and its political aspirations, Narain said:[124]

Gentlemen, it will be the supreme duty of the Congress to give expression to the hopes and aspirations to which the war has given a fresh vitality. The last decade has witnessed the birth of a new nationalism in India. The efforts of the older generation to awaken the consciousness of the people have produced their inevitable result. A new generation has arisen with new thoughts and new ideas, impatient of its dependent position and claiming its rights as free citizens of the British Empire. The advent of the European war infused a new enthusiasm into the people and galvanized their aspirations into a new life. England entered into the war avowedly to champion the cause of truth and justice and to protect the rights of those who were too weak to defend themselves. Face to face with the danger of Prussian militarism and threatened with the destruction of their noblest ideals, her people saw the doctrine of physical force in a new light and turned from it in disgust to the conception of a new order which shall be built on the rock of enduring principles. This sentiment found an answering echo in every corner of the Empire. Men learnt to set a new value on justice and liberty and began to examine how far their institutions were in accord with these principles. The new tendency is exhibiting itself in India as well, and forces have been set in motion which it is the duty of statesmanship to deal with to-day.

Gentlemen, the war, besides intensifying the longing for free institutions, enabled India to demonstrate her loyalty and to realize her value to the Empire. No one with an insight into the Indian mind ever doubted that India was thoroughly loyal, and that whatever differences might exist between her and Great Britain in regard to her internal affairs, she would rally round the Imperial Banner in the hour of danger. But men were not wanting who cast unjust doubts on her loyalty and believed that England's trouble would be India's opportunity. (Shame.) Instead of trying to bind her to the Empire with the silken tie of love, they were always forging new fetters to keep her in bondage. The war has effectually silenced these croakers and some of them had the courage to avow openly during the earlier months of the war that they had never understood the Indian character. It had never occurred to them that Indian patriotism is the greatest guarantee of India's loyalty (Hear, hear), for the realization of her most cherished hopes depends upon the continuance of British rule.

The assistance rendered by India during the war has fired her imagination. She has, so to say, found herself. She has acquired a new spirit of self-reliance and dignity, and realized her own worth by coming to Britain's help at a critical juncture. The battle-fields of Europe, Africa and Asia bear witness to the fighting qualities of her sons, and their deeds of heroism, written in characters of blood, have thrilled every Indian heart. Had England been true to her traditions and followed a more enlightened policy in India, who can doubt that she would have had military of resources at her disposal such as no other nation has? (Hear, hear.) But regard being had to the disabilities that India labours under, it cannot be gainsaid that she has done the utmost that she could. His Excellency the Viceroy has shown this conclusively in his speech to the Imperial Legislative Council on the 5th September last. 'The winter of 1914–15,' said his Excellency, 'was one of the most critical periods of the war, for it was evident that the troops then available on the continent and in the United Kingdom were inadequate for the defensive role allotted to them and the only way, pending the raising and training of the new armies, in which the position could be saved was by replacing the regulars serving in the Mediterranean and Colonial garrisons with Territorials and by drawing upon India for troops to the fullest possible extent'. The demands then made on us were honoured in full and with 'the utmost promptitude.' Our contribution to the war has largely increased since 1914 ...

... Gentlemen, India now demands that after the war things shall not revert to their original condition, but that she shall occupy a position worthy of herself as a member of the Imperial family. (Hear, hear.) She is not asking for rewards in return for her loyalty, but having fought in defence of human freedom she expects that her own sons will no longer be denied their birth-right as freemen. (Applause.) It will be strange indeed if England, who is fighting to preserve the sacredness of treaties and the integrity of small nations, should turn a deaf ear to the cry of her own subjects and refuse to redeem her plighted word.

On self-government, Narain said:[125]

Gentlemen, in my opinion, statesmanship demands that Great Britain should announce to the people of this country that a self-governing India is the goal of her policy (Applause), and grant us a substantial instalment of reform after the war, as a step towards that goal. Representative government should be made a reality by the fullest control over civil affairs being given to the elected representatives of the people whose decisions should be binding on the executive. Indians should no longer be debarred from an honourable participation in the defence of their hearths and homes, but should be given every opportunity of developing their martial spirit. The slow deterioration which is taking place in the manhood of the race is one of the saddest results of British rule in India, and steps should be taken to repair the injury as early as possible. It is also essential that in any scheme of Imperial Federation India should occupy the same position as the self-governing dominions. The memorandum submitted to his Excellency the Viceroy by our elected representatives, although not a complete statement of our demands, proceeds on these lines and the same principles underlie the scheme of reform which has been prepared jointly by the All-India Congress Committee and the Muslim League Reform Committee, and which will soon come before you. But these reforms, which fall far short of colonial self-government, cannot satisfy India for all time to come and in any legislation undertaken to give effect to them, it should be provided that full responsible government shall be conferred on her within a generation. (Hear, hear.)

A.C. Mazumdar echoed the same sentiments in his presidential speech. On the Hindu–Muslim question and the Lucknow Pact, he sanguinely added:[126]

Another difficulty put forward is the eternal question of the difference between the Hindus and the Mahomedans of India. But the game has been nearly played out, and the Hindus and the Mahomedans have practically solved the question. It is more than five years ago that some of us dreamt [a] dream which appears now not to have been all a dream. The Congress and the League have come to meet at the same place and the day may not be far distant when in spite of the Siren-song which has so far diverted their course they will come to meet in the same pavilion and at the same time. The Hindus and Mahomedans are rapidly converging towards each other, and indeed it would be a miracle if they did not so converge and if they continued to fly off at a tangent despite the irresistible attraction of the great centripetal force which is drawing them towards their common centre. The stock argument based upon occasional differences and disturbances between Hindus and Mussalmans cannot have much force. These are confined mostly to lower classes of people on either side. It is neither fair nor judicious to exaggerate their importance. There are Hindus and Mahomedans side by side in every Native State. In the Mahomedan State of Hyderabad with a Hindu population of nearly 70 per cent and the Hindu State of Kashmere with 60 per cent Mahomedan subjects we do not hear of any cow-killing riots or Mohurrum disturbances or of any ill-feeling between the two communities. And one wonders why a different state of things should prevail in British territories. A nationality is now no longer either a religious or a social federation, but a political unit. Diverse races professing different forms of religion and following distinct varieties of manners, customs and traditions easily submit to a common political faith to work out their common destiny. The Picts and the Scots, the Saxons and the Normans, the Protestants and the Catholics are now all welded into the great British nation. The Teutons and the Slavs, the Prussians and the Poles have formed one of the mightiest empires which has lit up a world-wide conflagration; while in that curious Dual Monarchy of Austro-Hungary the Magyars, the Hungarians, Czecks, the Poles, the Slavs, the Serbs, the Croates and the Rumanians have formed themselves into a national federation of no ordinary solidarity and strength. The Hindus and Mussalmans are both of common Aryan stock, while Hindu anthropology traces them to a common descent within the legendary period of their ancient history. Neither the Parsis nor the Mahomedans of India owe any temporal allegiance either to the Shah of Persia or the Sultan of Turkey. They are now Indians as much as the Hindus. But why indulge in speculations against a settled fact? I think I break no secret when I announce to you that the Hindu–Moslem question has been settled and the Hindus and Mussalmans have agreed to make a united demand for Self-Government. The All-India Congress Committee and the representatives of the Moslem League who recently met in conference at Calcutta have after two days' deliberations in one voice resolved to make a joint demand for a Representative Government in India. There are little differences on one or two minor points of detail, but they count for nothing. The vital issue has been solved and the main point has been gained. The report of the Conference will shortly be placed before you and I need not enter into details. We have many historic days, but I believe the 17th November will rank among the brightest and the most notable of them all. I would now appeal to both the communities to sink all their minor domestic differences and present a solid united front for the realization of their common destiny within the Empire. Only the seeds having been sown, the seedlings have just sprouted and for God's sake let us not quarrel over the division of the crop which still demands our combined labour and attention before the harvest comes. What are special electorates and communal representations when there is really no electorate and no representation among a people? What matters it if Dinshaw Edulji Wacha or Surendra Nath Banerjee or Muzhur-ul Huque were to represent us in our National Assembly?

Resolution XII on self-government, moved by Surendranath Banerjea, read as under:[127]

1. *That having regard to the fact that the great communities of India are the inheritors of ancient civilizations and have shown great capacity for Government and administration, and to the progress in education and public spirit made by them during a century of British rule,* and further having regard to the fact that the present system of Government does not satisfy the legitimate aspirations of the people and has become unsuited to the existing conditions and requirements, this Congress is of opinion that the time has come when His Majesty the King-Emperor should be pleased to issue a proclamation announcing that it is the aim and intention of British policy to confer self-government on India at an early date.
2. That this Congress demands that a *definite step should be taken towards self-government by granting the reform contained in the scheme prepared by the All-India Congress Committee in concert with the Reform Committee appointed by the All-India Moslem League.*
3. That in the re-construction of the Empire, India shall be lifted from the position of a dependency to that of an *equal partner in the Empire with the self-governing Dominions.* [Emphases added]

After moving the resolution, Banerjea, Hirdaya Nath Kunzru, Annie Besant and Tilak spoke in support of it. Besant and Tilak, in particular, discussed Home Rule at length. Here is an extract from Besant's speech:[128]

... I want very briefly, for my time is short, to meet the objections that are made. We see at this moment much talk about the five nations who are to form a federated Empire after the war. The five nations are the United Kingdom, Australia, New Zealand, South Africa and North America. Where is India? Oh, she is not one of the five. She is a coloured people, she is not colourless, and colourless people have the right of domination over them a coloured people. Coloured people have only the duty of submission. (Cries of Shame.) But that is not the doctrine that this coloured nation at least is willing to accept. We are not uncivilized natives of Central Africa, that we should bow our neck beneath the yoke of the five white nations. Has God given liberty alone to the pale faces and not to the coloured people of the globe? It is not colour that counts, it is the clever brain and the strong heart that count, and not the coloured skin that covers them. The Lord Buddha, the Lord Mahomed and the Lord Christ were coloured men. All the founders of religions were coloured men. Have the colourless produced a single founder of a religion among the five nations? We will never bow beneath the yoke of the colonies.

We are told not to spread bitterness against the Colonies. I think the writer of that has begun at the wrong end. Have we excluded the Colonials from India because they could not talk or write some language of which they could know nothing? Was it this country or was it Australia that passed that law? Have we said that no North American or Canadian could come to India unless he comes straight from port to port when there is no line of ships that carried a passenger straight from one to other, or has Canada made that law against the Indian people? Have we said that no colonist shall have his wife and children join him, or has British Columbia said so in relation to the Sikhs? Have we put a brand of inferiority on the colourless people, and said that their trades should be licensed, that they must pay three pounds a head, and that their marriage is no marriage, or has South Africa done it to our Indian brethren? What is this talk of bitterness? Bitterness is caused by the Colonies, and not by India. Let this advice be [to] the colonists and not to India. The Indians had no share in the making of that feeling, but resent the indignity to which they, the subjects of the King-Emperor, are subjected. Oh, you are not fit to govern yourselves, you are divided! Are we? (Cries of 'No'.) We have shown some power of union during the last few years. The Congress split into half nine years ago. But we stand a united Congress today at Lucknow. Hindus and Muslims had a gulf between them, —not in Kashmir, where a Hindu prince rules, not in the Deccan, where a Muslim prince is sovereign, but only in the British Raj, and that gulf has been bridged over by Muslims and Hindus themselves, and we have linked our hands in love, trust, in mutual forbearance, in mutual respect, and we stand today a united nation, so that nothing shall hereafter break us asunder. 'Oh, you are not fit for self-government. You are ignorant.' Who has the right to cast that reproach at the masses of our people? It was Gopal Krishna Gokhale who tried to win free and compulsory education, cautiously, carefully, step by step, for he was not an impatient idealist in word, however much his heart went with impatient idealism; an Indian tried to educate his brethren. But who was it that denied it? It was the Imperial Council with its perpetual majority of Officials. Does it, then, lie in the mouth of Englishmen to reproach us, with ignorance, when the Government would not educate our people and would not help us to do it. (Cries of 'Shame'.) Then they say: 'You cannot defend yourselves.' Did we pass the Arms Act? Did we take away weapons from the hands of our people? Or has there been since 1878 a law that no pure-blooded Indian, whether Hindu or Mussalman, could possess arms without a license, to the gaining of which all sorts of difficulties are attached? Is it India's fault that it is undefended? For thirty years the Congress has asked for the repeal of the Arms Act, and for permission to volunteer and to open military colleges, and those who have treated every demand with contempt say that we are not fit to govern ourselves because we cannot defend ourselves!

It is only Home Rule that will enable us to defend ourselves. Until we have Home Rule we cannot be armed as we should be ...

Here's an excerpt from Tilak's speech in support of resolution XII:[129]

The resolution which I wish to support embodies all these principles. It is the resolution of Self-Government. It is that for which we have been fighting, for which the Congress has been fighting for thirty years. The first note of it was heard ten years ago on the banks of the Hoogly, and it was sounded by the Grand Old Man of India, that Parsee patriot of Bombay, Dadabhai Naoroji. *Since the note was sounded differences of opinion arose. Some said that the note ought to be carried on and ought to be followed by a detailed scheme at once, that it should be taken up and made to resound all over India as soon as possible. There was another party amongst us that said that it could not be done so soon, and the tune of that note required to be a little lowered, and that was the cause of dissension ten years ago, and I am glad to say that I have lived these ten years to see that we are reunited in this Congress and we are going to put our voices and shoulders together to push on this scheme of Self-Government; and not only have we lived to see these differences closed, but to see the differences of Hindus and Mahomedans closed as well.* So we have now united in every way in the United Provinces, and we have that luck in Lucknow. (Laughter.) So I consider the most auspicious session of this thirty-first Indian National Congress.

There are only one or two points on which I wish to address you. It has been said, Gentlemen, by some, that we Hindu have yielded too much to our Mahomedan brethren. I am sure I represent the sense of the Hindu community all over India, when I say that we could not have yielded too much. I would not care if the rights of Self-Government are granted to the Mahomedan community only. (Hear, hear.) I would not care if they are granted to Rajputs; I would not care if they are granted to the lowest classes of the Hindu population, provide the British Government consider them more fit than the educated classes of India for exercising those rights; I would not care if these rights are granted to any section of the Indian community. Then the fight will be between them and other sections of the community and not as at present a triangular fight. We have to gain these rights, remember, from a powerful bureaucracy, an unwilling bureaucracy, naturally unwilling because the bureaucracy now feels that these rights, these privileges, this authority will pass out of their hands. I would feel the same if I were in that position, and I am not going to blame the bureaucracy for entertaining that natural feeling; but natural as that feeling may be, it is a feeling which we have to combat against. It is a feeling that is not conducive to the growth of Self-Government in this country. We have to fight against that feeling, and when you have to fight against a third party, it is a very important thing that we stand on this platform united, united in race, united in religion and united as regards all shades of different political opinion. That is the most important event of the day.

Let us glance, as I said, ten years ago. *When Mr. Dadabhai Naoroji declared that Swaraj should be our goal, its name was Swaraj. Later on, it came to be known as Self-Government and constitutional reform, and we Nationalists style it Home Rule. It is all the same, one in three different names. There is the objection raised that Swaraj has a bad odour in India and Home Rule has a bad odour in England, and hence we ought to call it constitutional reform. I do not care for the name ... Do not think it is an easy task, nothing can be gained by passing resolutions on this platform, by the simple union of the two races, Hindus and Mahomedans, and the two parties, Moderates and Nationalists. The Union is intended to create a certain power and energy among us and unless that power and energy are exercised to the utmost you cannot hope to succeed, so great are the obstacles in your way. You must now prepare to fight out the scheme ...* [Emphases added]

After passing the resolution on self-government, the reform scheme jointly prepared by the Congress and the League was detailed as part of the proceedings and adopted as the goal to work towards. Naturally, this scheme was captured in the proceedings of the League's Lucknow session too. For the benefit of the readers, here is clause 4 of the scheme, which showcases the extent of accommodation of the League's demands by the Congress:[130]

4. Adequate provision should be made for the representation of *important minorities* by election, and the Mohamedans should be represented through special electorates on the Provincial Legislative Councils in the following proportions:

Punjab	One-half the elected members
United Provinces	30% the elected members
Bengal	40% the elected members
Bihar	25% the elected members
Central Provinces	15% the elected members
Madras	15% the elected members
Bombay	One-third the elected members

Provided that no Mohamedan shall participate in any of the other elections to the Imperial or Provincial Legislative Councils, save and except those by electorates representing special interests:

Provided that further no bill, nor any clause thereof, nor a resolution introduced by non-official members affecting one or the other community, which question is to be determined by the members of that community in the Legislative Council concerned, shall be proceeded with, if three-fourths of the members of that community in the particular Council, Imperial or Provincial, oppose the bill or any claim thereof or the resolution.

All the above makes it clear that the 1916 session of the Congress marked an important and mixed milestone for the following reasons:

1. Muslim demands of communal electorates and communal veto on legislation were accepted by the Congress, the Extremists included, in the hope that the demands were temporary, and that by conceding to them it would be possible to present a united face to the British government in the demand for self-government;

2. The session marked the re-entry of Extremists such as Tilak and Pal into the Congress, owing to the efforts of Annie Besant and the demise of Pherozeshah Mehta and Gokhale;

3. Gandhi entered Indian political life, having spent over two decades in South Africa.

Coming to the League's session of 1916 in Lucknow, whose president was Jinnah, while there were similarities with the Congress's session, the League was careful and clear enough to underscore its priorities without mincing words, notwithstanding the joint scheme it had entered into with the Congress for self-government. In his welcome speech, Syed Nabiullah said as follows on the two principal objects of the League:[131]

> The All-India Muslim League stands today for two principal objects, namely, for the safeguarding of the political situation of Musalmans and for co-operation with the other communities for the attainment of self-government or home rule. The realization of the first object is, as all fair-minded persons would be ready to admit, an essential condition of the success of the second. It would be idle to talk of co-operation if the Musalmans did not feel a complete sense of security as regards their communal future. They are a 'minority', and in all political developments tending towards a democratic form of State organization, a minority must have certain definite, statutory safeguards. The Muslim demand for such safeguards is, therefore, natural and legitimate; and the 'majority', which in any case holds the balance of power, cannot oppose this demand without laying itself open to the charge of selfishness and political insincerity. Let our Hindu brethren remember that an adequate and effective representation of Musalmans in the self-governing institutions of the country can in no case deprive them of the decisive power of the majority. When such power is guaranteed to them by their number, I fail to see why some of their communal enthusiasts should deny the Musalmans the right to secure the basis of their political existence. Opposition of this character breeds distrust, and the good faith of those who justify such opposition on the overworked pleas of 'unity' and 'nationalism' comes to be questioned by the Muslim rank and file.

Nabiullah's speech was followed by the presidential speech of Jinnah, which called for Hindu–Muslim unity, among other things. Ironically, resolution IX of the League demanded the treatment of Urdu as the sole common language of India.[132] Clearly, the League was better at pushing its primary agenda—namely, protection of Muslim interests—which was in stark contrast to the

Congress's 'secular' agenda. Therefore, notwithstanding the joint adoption of the reform scheme by the Muslim League with the Congress, the latter had revealed its willingness to accommodate almost every demand of the League to preserve 'Hindu–Muslim unity'. This willingness, as we shall see, would be exploited to the hilt to secure the Congress's support for the Khilafat Movement. In fact, the Congress too was keen to support the Movement to demonstrate its continued commitment to protection of local and global Muslim interests.

With this, the discussion of developments on the Indian political landscape until 1916 ends. In the next chapter, I will discuss the period from 1917 to 1918, which covers the Home Rule Movement, the Montford Reforms and the beginnings of active Khilafat at the end of the First World War.

From the Home Rule Movement to Rumblings of Khilafat (1917–1918)

Annie Besant (1847–1933)

In Chapter 11 of my first book, I had discussed the Montford Reforms and the enactment of the Government of India Act of 1919 primarily from the perspective of the coloniality of international law and the founding of the League of Nations. In this chapter, I will discuss the same issue from a domestic perspective, specifically in the context of the Home Rule Movement. The Lucknow sessions of the Congress and the League, it was believed, heralded a new chapter in Hindu–Muslim relations since the Congress had demonstrated its 'secular' bona fides by including communal electorates and communal veto as part of the joint reform scheme submitted to the British government. However, the British, including Viceroy Chelmsford, branded the scheme as 'catastrophic' since, according to them, it envisaged grant of self-government to Indians at a pace which was impractical.[1] To mount pressure on the government by gathering support from the masses, Annie Besant and Tilak went on an all-Bharat campaign between the Lucknow session in December 1916 and June 1917 vigorously advocating Home Rule, for which they had been laying the groundwork ever since Tilak was released from Mandalay Prison in 1914.[2] The effectiveness of the campaign can be gauged from the following remark by a home member of the government of India on 17 January 1917 in a confidential report:[3]

> The position is one of great difficulty. Moderate leaders can command no support among the vocal classes who are being led at the heel of Tilak and Besant.

Tilak even held an annual conference for the Home Rule League at Nasik in May 1917, where he showcased the primary difference between the Congress's passive and loyal approach to the British through petitions, and his own approach of involving the masses through a sustained campaign with the sole objective of securing Home Rule.[4] No wonder both Besant and Tilak were detested by the Moderates, because their work brought into sharp relief the moribund state that defined the Congress, apart from vindicating Besant's decision to re-induct Extremists like Tilak and Pal into the party.[5] However, the Moderates could not openly oppose the two because of the popularity they enjoyed among the masses as well as among the rulers of princely states such as the Maharaja of Bikaner[6]—so much so that when Besant was arrested in June 1917, the Moderates were forced to grudgingly criticise the arrest,[7] as was the League.[8] Unfortunately for the British and the Moderates, the arrest only added more vigour to the Home Rule Movement.[9]

That the Home Rule Movement had begun to make its impact even before Besant's arrest was evident from the fact that India was allowed to participate in the Imperial War Conference held in London in March 1917, which was hitherto limited only to self-governing Dominions of the British empire. Although India was not yet a self-governing Dominion, it was allowed to participate on a special basis and outside the official constitution of the Conference, despite staunch opposition from other Dominions such as Australia and Canada that felt that Bharat's inclusion meant bringing them down to its level.[10] In fact, these Dominions were particular about maintaining the 'racial purity' of the Conference. In the face of such unvarnished Christian white supremacism, Bharat's participation was made possible because of the support of the Secretary of State Austen Chamberlain who, in turn, had the support of then British Prime Minister Lloyd George. Both were of the opinion that in view of the enormous contributions made by India towards the war effort, it would be nothing short of an outrage not to include it in the Conference. Upon India's entry into the Imperial War Conference, Chamberlain then made a case for India's inclusion in the regular Imperial Conference so that it could participate *almost* at par with the self-governing dominions.[11] Effectively, this marked the beginning of India's inclusion in what is now popularly known as the 'British Commonwealth'.

What is indeed surprising is that Bharat continues to be part of this so-called Commonwealth even after attaining 'Independence' in August 1947. No self-respecting country would want to be part of a commonwealth of its former coloniser *after* political decolonisation. At the very least, it would insist on the nomenclature being changed to reflect its status as an independent sovereign nation, and not as a former colony or territory of the British empire. Surely, a state that calls itself a 'civilisational state', with aspirations of becoming a Vishwaguru, can take these baby steps towards psychological decolonisation.

Coming back to 1917, Bharat's inclusion in the Imperial Conference, both regular and war, was interpreted as a sign of things to come in the direction of self-government.[12] However, true to British policy of the past, repression and reform went hand in hand, the former being used to temper expectations with respect to the latter. Therefore, on the one hand, while giving the impression that Britain was indeed cognisant of Bharat's contributions and expectations, the police powers of the state were used to actively dissuade leaders, the educated classes and the common people from supporting the Home Rule Movement of Besant and Tilak. This was being done to nip in the bud any expectations of early grant of Home Rule. To this end, the entry of Besant, Tilak and Pal into various provinces as part of their Home Rule campaign was prohibited, and eventually Besant was arrested in June 1917, while Tilak was once again charged with sedition for his speeches as part of the campaign.[13] Both were found guilty by the trial court; however, the Bombay High Court set aside the verdict against Tilak. As for Besant, she was unsuccessful despite appeals to the Madras High Court and the Privy Council against the trial court verdict. Ultimately, to pay the sureties imposed on her, Besant had to sell two of her printing presses, after which she continued with the campaign.[14] Thanks to the commitment of these two individuals and their followers, by the time Edwin Montagu replaced Austen Chamberlain as the Secretary of State for India in July 1917, the agitation for Home Rule had intensified and had managed to unite all strands of political opinion.[15] Even

Jinnah joined Besant's Home Rule League and led its Bombay branch.[16] In fact, the Movement's impact was comparable with and was perhaps even more forceful than that of the Swadeshi Movement. This forced Chelmsford to write to Austen Chamberlain as follows:[17]

> Mrs. Besant, Tilak and others are fomenting with great vigour the agitation for immediate Home Rule, and in the absence of any definite announcement by Government of India as to their policy in the matter, it is attracting many of those who hitherto have held less advanced views. The agitation is having a mischievous effect on public feeling throughout the country.

By keeping Besant in jail, the British had given Tilak the perfect ammunition to rally the country around the Home Rule Movement, apart from demanding Besant's release. As R.C. Majumdar says, Besant fired up the campaign further, being in jail rather than free outside.[18] S.R. Mehrotra too says the effect of the Movement was felt even in the British Parliament, where the Government of India was criticised for its wooden and outdated approach to administration. Castigating the British Government of India for its handling of the situation and its reluctance to understand the impatience of Indians, Edwin Montagu said as follows, before he was appointed the Secretary of State in July 1917:[19]

> But whatever be the object of your rule in India, the universal demand of those Indians whom I have met and corresponded with is that you should state it ... The history of this War shows that you can rely upon the loyalty of the Indian people to the British Empire—if you ever doubted it! If you want to use that loyalty you must take advantage of that love of country which is a religion in India, and you must give them that bigger opportunity of controlling their own destinies, not merely by councils which cannot act, but by control, by growing control, of the Executive itself.

On 28–29 July 1917, at a joint conference organised in Bombay by the All-India Congress Committee and the Muslim League's Council, the following demands were put forth to the British government:[20]

1. To declare its policy position on the issue of grant of self-government to India within the British empire;
2. To accept the Congress–League Scheme for implementation after the war;
3. To publish the Government's proposals on reforms for public discussion;
4. To release Besant and her supporters; and
5. To release pan-Islamists such as the Ali brothers and Maulana Abul Kalam Azad, who were under internment for their activities in support of the Ottoman Caliphate/Khilafat.

Further, a recommendation was made to the Congress and the League by their respective committees to consider employing passive resistance to ensure that their demands were met.[21] Thanks to this mounting pressure, and to the fact that Britain needed all the help it could get from India for the war,[22] the new Secretary of State, Montagu, in response to a question on the issue of the government's policy on the demands for self-government in India,[23] declared in the House of Commons on 20 August 1917 as follows:[24]

> The policy of His Majesty's Government, with which the Government of India are in complete accord, is that of the increasing association of Indians in every branch of the administration and the gradual development of self-governing institutions, with a view to the progressive realisation of responsible government in India as an integral part of the British Empire.

> I would add that progress in this policy can only be achieved by successive stages. The British Government and the Government of India on whom the responsibility lies for the welfare and advancement of the Indian peoples, must be the judges of the time and measure of each advance, and they must be guided by the co-operation received from those upon whom new opportunities of service will thus be conferred, and by the extent to which it is found that confidence can be reposed in their sense of responsibility.

Although this was a significant acknowledgement from the British government that it could no longer postpone its response to the demands for greater autonomy in the administration of Bharat, Montagu used the words 'responsible government' instead of 'self-government', which raised fresh suspicions as to the import of the former. Further, there was no clarity as to the time frame the British had in mind for the grant of self-government to Bharat. According to S.R. Mehrotra, although Montagu had suggested 'self-government' in the draft of his declaration, it was Lord Curzon who altered it to 'responsible government'.[25] In fact, a day after the declaration, Montagu wrote to Chelmsford wondering as to the difference between self-government and responsible government, and Curzon's intention behind the change. It appears that Curzon's intention was to declare a policy in principle, with sufficient room for manoeuvre and without any time frame being committed to.[26] We shall see that even Montagu was not in favour of expeditious and time-bound grant of self-government to India.

Apart from this declaration of policy by Montagu, Besant and her supporters were released, but the Ali Brothers remained incarcerated.[27] To further advocate the cause of self-government, specifically the Congress–League Scheme, upon Montagu's arrival in India the joint conference of both organisations appointed a deputation which would meet him. However, before Montagu's arrival in November 1917, massive Hindu–Muslim riots broke out in September 1917, in Bihar and in the eastern United Provinces, specifically in Arrah, Gaya, Patna and Jaunpur, around the time of Baqr Id, which threatened to derail the joint efforts.[28] The trigger for the riots was the slaughter of cows by Muslims, which remained a flashpoint notwithstanding all the attempts made by representatives of the two communities to 'patch up' and show a united face to the British. Invariably, Hindus were expected to give up their objections to cow slaughter in order to preserve Hindu–Muslim unity. Also, predictably, the riots led to fresh demands by the League to alter the joint reforms Scheme to include greater protection for Muslims and their religious practices. After a few more accommodations were made by the Congress to address Muslim concerns, a joint memorandum was yet again presented by the Congress–League deputation to Montagu on 26 November 1917.[29]

While this process was under way, Tilak maintained unrelenting pressure on the government through his campaign, the effectiveness of which was evident from the fact that Montagu met Tilak alone on 27 November 1917.[30] Thanks to the intensity of the Home Rule Movement under the combined leadership of Besant and Tilak, the Congress was forced to abandon its moderate ways to a significant extent, at least temporarily, and identify itself with the Movement. In other words, the Congress was, at this point, much more amenable to pressure from the Extremists than ever before, which was attested to by an official report of the government on Tilak's activities:[31]

> The capture of the Congress organization by Mrs. Besant and Tilak is complete. The moderate Party in the Congress is extinguished. The Congress is completely identified with Home Rule.

Montagu also wrote on Tilak in his diary as follows:[32]

> Tilak is at the moment probably the most powerful leader in India, and he has it in his power, if he chooses, to help materially in the war effort. His procession to Delhi to see me was a veritable triumphant one.

Naturally, this reflected in the thirty-second annual session of the Congress held in Calcutta on 26, 28 and 29 December 1917, when Besant, Tilak's nominee for the post of president, was elected. At this session, Besant introduced the following resolution on self-government:[33]

> [Resolution XII]
>
> This Congress expresses its grateful satisfaction over pronouncement made by His Majesty's Secretary of State for India on behalf of the Imperial Government that its object is the establishment of responsible government in India.
>
> This Congress strongly urges the necessity for the immediate enactment of a Parliamentary statute providing for the establishment of responsible government in India, the full measure to be attained within a time-limit to be fixed in the statute itself at an early date.

This Congress is emphatically of opinion that the Congress–League Scheme of reforms ought to be immediately introduced by the statute as the first step in the process.

The resolution was then moved by Surendranath Banerjea and supported by Jinnah, Pal and Tilak. In this regard, Pal and Tilak made relevant observations on the possible dissolution of communal electorates at some point when the Muslim community was ready for it, and on the inconsistent use of 'responsible' and 'self-government' by the British. Here's what Pal said:[34]

I feel like an interloper for this reason: because, I could not heartily support the resolution that has been proposed and seconded, neither could I prudently oppose it (Laughter). I proposed to put in an amendment that would express not only the almost united voice and the considered opinion of all the districts of Bengal, but I take it also, of every individual Congressman present here; and that amendment would have run something like this: I wanted to propose, after the necessary grateful recognition of the pronouncement of the policy made by Mr. Montagu—after that preamble, I wanted to demand that an act should be immediately passed in Parliament and in that Act provision should be made for the progressive realisation of Responsible Government in India as an integral part of the British Empire. And I wanted to propose that in that Act it should be distinctly laid down that the functions of the Government of India must be clearly demarcated from the functions of the Provincial Governments. (The functions of the Government of India must be strictly confined to Imperial affairs and inter-provincial relations, and after the functions of the Government of India have been clearly demarcated from the functions of provincial governments, these latter should be confined to the management of strictly provincial affairs, and that they should be relieved from the present control of the Government of India in regard to all provincial affairs, including provincial finance.) ... I would demand the complete elimination of the official vote and official nomination from our provincial Legislative Councils (Hear, hear). I would demand that the executive council in the provinces must be formed by one of the members of the Legislative Council at the command of the Governor or Lieutenant-Governor, as the case may be, who represents His Imperial Majesty in the provincial administration. At the command of the Governor or Lieutenant-Governor, some member of the Legislative Council who enjoys the confidence of the House must be entrusted with the duty of forming an Executive Council and the Council thus formed must be made subject to the control of the Legislative Council. *I would further ask that in this Act provision must be made for the entire elimination of all sorts of indirect representation and provision must also be made for the representation of important minorities, important interests and the so-called backward classes who are not—I speak here from intimate experience of the submerged classes in Great*

Britain—our backward classes are no more backward in intelligence, in character, in understanding and in humanity (Cheers)—than similar classes across the seas. With regard to the so-called backward classes we shall have special representative of these classes by the special electorates. I would further demand that the percentage of Mahomedan members in all our Legislative Councils as fixed by the Congress-League scheme must be incorporated in this Act so that it shall be binding upon us and upon all, to keep our Mahomedan friends exactly in the position which they want to be kept in until they do agree to coalesce with us and all communal representation is eliminated from the Statute book, until with their help and under their leadership we are enabled to frame our new franchise ... [Emphases added]

And here were Tilak's views on Home Rule and responsible government at the session:[35]

My definition of Home Rule is a simple one; and every one, even a peasant can understand it. Home Rule is 'to be in my own country what Englishmen are in England and in the colonies.' All those bombastic phrases 'to be placed on a footing of equality', 'to be a partner in the empire' and so on,—all these mean that I must be master in my own country, in the same sense as an Englishman is master in his own. That being so, complete Home Rule is our goal. If any one is going to grant it tomorrow, I shall be very glad. I do not oppose the immediate introduction of Home Rule in India. But I do not think that it is a practical demand. Some compromise has therefore to be made with those that are in power and also with our opponents here. Even the British Government in India was introduced by a compromise, by a charter from the Delhi Government. The first step of British Rule in any province which they did not conquer was always by consent and compromise; and, in the matter of self-government, what this first step should be is explained in this resolution. *I fully sympathise with all talk of future progress, about the establishment of responsible government in the province first and afterwards in the central government. But what I am not prepared to admit is the adequacy of the suggested first step to the introduction of Home Rule in India. That is the difference between Mr. Pal and myself. We agree in principle. We do not want the whole hog at once. We demand only the first step for the present, so that the introduction of the second step will be much easier. The Government, in the pronouncement, has used the word 'Responsible Government' and not Home Rule or Self-Government; and Mr. Montagu in his reply has done the same without defining it—because, responsible government, as naturally understood, means an Executive Government responsible to the Legislature. But in one place, in Mr. Curtis's letters, I find that 'responsible government' is defined to be a government, where the Legislature is subject to the Executive (Laughter). So you will see that it is quite necessary to define responsible government,* otherwise the words may be interpreted quite contrary to our intention, and it may be said, 'we promised responsible government in which the Legislature ought to be under the control of the Executive and the more it is placed under the control of the Executive, the more responsible will be the government you get'. (Laughter) I must tell you frankly that this is not the kind of responsible government we want. *We understand by responsible government a government where the Executive is entirely responsible to the Legislature,—call it 'control' or call it by any other name—and that Legislature should be wholly elected. This is responsible government: this is the full responsible government that we want.* When I say that the Executive should be under the control of the Legislature, I go so far as to say that even the Governors and the Lieutenant-Governors should also be elected. That, however, will be the final step. But in the present circumstances, I shall be quite content, and, so I think will most of you, if the first step that we demand is granted to us immediately ...

... That pronouncement says that it will be granted to you by stages. We also agree to that. The third part of the declaration is that these stages will be determined by the Government. We demur. We want the stages to be determined by us and not by the sweet will of the Executive. Nor do we want any compromise about them. We demand and insist upon a clear statement in the Act, defining the stages and fixing the time, when full Responsible Government may be automatically obtained. This is the second part of the resolution before you and this is what we mean by fixing the time by legislation. A definite time should be named in the Statute, which we hope will be passed very soon ...

... The case of India is somewhat like that of an emasculated man, who has been made to lose his nervous power, or in the case of a nervous paralysis, or nervous emasculation of the whole body, you have to begin with the brain and not with the toe. You must, if you want to restore to health a man like that, give him a brain tonic, for the brain is the centre of the nervous system. So it is with India. If the present Government is unfit to carry on the administration of the country in the best interests of the empire, the best remedy is to begin with the brain which is at Simla. Unless you obtain some power over that brain, unless that brain is made properly sane, you cannot expect that any local remedy applied to the different parts of the body, to the hands or the feet or any other parts of the body, will be of any avail. So, the Congress–League Scheme provides, mark that, that we must have certain powers of control in the Central Government itself. If the Executive is not made removable, we must at least be placed on a footing of equality in it. Half the members of the Executive Council must be ours. Half the members of the Imperial Executive Council at least must therefore be elected; and our scheme provides for it ... [Emphases added]

Interestingly, Tilak also moved a resolution demanding release of the Ali Brothers who had been under detention for their pro-Caliphate/Khilafat activities. For all practical purposes, it could be said that the Khilafat Movement, which is typically dated to 1919, started well before that, thanks to the pro-Caliphate activities of the Ali Brothers, Maulana Abul Kalam Azad and others whose hearts bled for the Ottoman empire, then the seat of the Islamic Caliphate. The following was the resolution moved by Tilak:[36]

That this Congress urges on the Government the immediate release of Messrs. Mahommed Ali and Shaukat Ali who have remained incarcerated since October, 1914, and are now kept interned because of religious scruples which they hold in common with the whole of Islam in India and elsewhere and which are not incompatible with loyalty to the King Emperor.

Supporting the resolution, Tilak said:[37]

You all know, gentlemen, why Mr. Md. Ali was interned under the Defence of India Act of 1914. That Act is a very elastic Act. It invests the Executive Government with complete powers of despotism. All that the Act states is that if the Executive Government thinks, of itself, without any further enquiry, that can be conducted through the C.I.D.—if the Executive Government on the evidence so collected—I may say even manufactured according to their wishes (Shame)—if they think, on that evidence, that there is danger to the public safety and tranquillity, without knowing or without caring to divulge what kind of tranquillity and peace they mean thereby, if they think so they can intern a person of their own accord by an Executive order ... So it happened that Mr. Md. Ali was interned in 1914 apparently for certain articles in the 'comrade' but really because he displeased the high authorities and proved rather inconvenient to them. The best way and the only way for the despot is to say 'I throw you into jail without any trial'. That is the weapon of a despot and that weapon was used against him. He was interned without trial. We, both, Mahomedans and Hindus, requested the Government to publish the grounds on which the Executive Government entertained fears, that his very presence in the country would be detrimental to public safety and peace. No grounds were ever published. Absolutely no response was made to the public protest on this point. Gradually, the Government climbed down and they were willing to let them off, both Md. Ali and Shaukat Ali. There were negotiations going on during this year and influential Mahomedan gentlemen—I may mention the names of the Hon. Raja Saheb of Mamudabad, and the Hon. Mr. Jinnah (Applause)—both were willing to assure Government that there would be no danger in letting off the interned gentlemen. Mind, both these gentlemen have the whole Mahomedan community at their back, so you may say that the whole Mahomedan community was prepared to stand guarantee for the good conduct of these men (Applause) and to it you may also add the voice of the whole Hindu community (Cheers). Practically, the whole of India was unanimous in assuring the Government of India that there was not the least danger of the public peace broken by letting these people free. No, the Government thought otherwise at one time. But subsequently, as I said, they climbed down a bit. The C.I.D. did not like the idea (Laughter). Sometimes the C.I.D. try to control the Executive also (Laughter) ... They were entrusted with the task of finding out evidence by which the detention of these two brothers could be supported. They found none. The Government of India was on the point of releasing these two men. What happened then? A C.I.D. officer went to Chhindwara and had a talk with Md. Ali and Shaukat Ali. He had ready access to them, being a C.I.D. man, he needs no permission from the Government of India. If you or I were to go and see them, we would first have had to obtain permission, and perhaps we could not have got that permission. It is said that what happened there was that the C.I.D. man went there and had a talk and somehow or other got something from these two brothers. I do not know exactly what occurred, because all this correspondence is confidential—Government would not publish it. But it is said that what occurred was that the C.I.D. man wanted to ascertain whether they would be loyal to the Crown. It was not a new thing to the interned but then there was a condition attached—what was that condition? What they said was that they owed allegiance to two—to the God above and the Executive God below (Laughter) and that they were prepared to be loyal to the King Emperor—not only prepared, they were bound to do so and were willing to do so provided their religious scruples were observed. They could not sacrifice their religious scruples to their political allegiance: This statement was pounced upon at once by the C.I.D. and the Executive Government: They said that the men could not be released. The men were not originally detained for this but for something else. It is a post facto reason discovered after their detention, only during the negotiations that were being carried on for their release. That was caught hold of and made a ground for detaining them further at Chindwara (Shame) ...

... We need not discuss it. *During these negotiations two new grounds were disclosed—one is the religious scruples which I have pointed out to you to be entirely fallacious and erroneous. It was settled 2000 years ago by no less a personage than Jesus Christ. You have His dictum that the duty towards your King is not inconsistent with your duty towards your God. That is the maxim of all religions. I do not think that either the Mahomedan religion or the Hindu religion denies that.* Nations are not made up of people belonging to one religion only. Though Emperors and Kings used to be called in olden times 'Defenders of the faith,' when the whole nation was of one religion and owed allegiance to one God, yet, now, the maxim does not hold good in present day politics. So to say that their religious scruples are inconvenient to Government—that Government regards them with suspicion, is to a certain extent ignoring all the political progress made in the past 20 centuries. That is the point. That argument does not hold good now ... *we demand that Messrs. Mahommed Ali and Shaukat Ali should be immediately released (Applause). If the Government has to say anything in defence, let them prosecute these two men before a public tribunal. If it is not prepared to do so, there is no other course left open to the Government but to release them, if Government means to be just and loyal to the Constitution, for even Government itself has got to be loyal to the Constitution. For, what we now urge is that both these brothers should be immediately released. That is the resolution put*

into my hands. And as I said in the beginning, it is a very solemn matter. We are
passing this resolution in the presence of their mother ... [Emphases added]

What needs to be appreciated from the above extracts is that the
Congress, even under Extremists such as Besant, Tilak and Pal, supported
the pro-Caliphate activities of the Ali Brothers and others in order to
preserve 'Hindu–Muslim unity' to secure self-government for Bharat. The
reason this becomes important is that in popular discourse Gandhi is often
held responsible for supporting the Khilafat Movement, which strengthened
Muslim separatism and pan-Islamism to the detriment of Bharat. While this
is not untrue (as we shall see), it is equally important to bear in mind that
Gandhi was not influential enough to call the shots in the Congress in 1917
when the resolution was moved by Tilak for the release of pan-Islamists
such as the Ali Brothers on the ground that their pan-Islamism was not at
loggerheads with their loyalty to the British. In other words, the Congress's
support for the Khilafat Movement started even before Gandhi had the power
to influence, much less dictate, the Congress's course of action. Importantly,
the potential impact of encouraging pan-Islamism and the divided loyalties
it engendered on the social fabric of Bharat did not seem to feature much
even in the calculus of leaders like Tilak. Instead, *Christian* justifications were
invoked by Tilak to justify a pan-Islamic sentiment and to demand the release
of its proponents.

Coming to the League's session of 1917, which was its tenth, it was held in
Calcutta on 30 December 1917 and 1 January 1918.[38] Prior to the session, in
November 1917, the League wanted to send a Muslim deputation to Montagu
with the following demands:

1. The release of the Ali Brothers and other pan-Islamists;
2. Reservation of seats for Muslims in government services in every province;
3. Muslim representation on the governing bodies of public universities;
4. Maintenance of Urdu with its Persian script as the lingua franca in those
   provinces where it was in use; and
5. The freedom to practise Islam and its ceremonies on Id-ul-Azha and
   Moharram without any interference.

Montagu refused to meet the deputation as long as it sought the release of
the pan-Islamists, and since the League did not want to delete that demand,
the meeting never happened.[39] This featured heavily in the League's Calcutta
session—apart from the mandatory defence of communal electorates and the
need to preserve them as long as Muslims were a minority. In his address, the
Raja of Mahmudabad defended pan-Islamism and support for the Caliphate
by Muslims while remaining subjects of the British empire.[40] Here are certain

excerpts from his address which show that the defence of the Caliphate, namely the Khilafat Movement, was vocal even as of 1917:

> For almost three years the Government preserved a sphinx-like silence as to the reasons why Mohammad Ali and Shaukat Ali were interned. At last to the question of the Hon'ble Mr. Jinnah, the ex-President of our League, they vouchsafed the reply that they were interned because they expressed and promoted sympathy with the King's enemies. This reply has for the first time brought within the cognizance of the public reasons, unsupported by any fact, which have induced Government to restrict the liberties of the two brothers. I say deliberately and emphatically that the Musalmans of India refuse to accept this condemnation of our two friends. We refuse to believe it, and we demand that, if Government have any evidence to justify that statement, let it be produced and scrutinized and submitted publicly to those tests without which no evidence is worth the name. We know our friends. Their lives have been an open book. They have worked constitutionally and above-board in the cause of their community and of India; and this grave charge, unsubstantiated by any facts, unproved by evidence impartially sifted, has failed to shake the confidence of the public in their innocence.
>
> Is an expression of sympathy with Islam and Musalmans in their tribulations, in India and outside it, to be treated as an act of disloyalty to the State? On this point, the League, in the resolution I have quoted above, says: 'The League further puts on record its unswerving conviction that the views expressed by Mohammad Ali in his draft undertaking faithfully reflect the attitude of the Mohammedan community of India, his offence, if it is an offence, being that speaking the unvarnished truth, he has rendered a public service alike to the Government and his own people; further that in the considered opinion of the League the view expressed by Mr. Mohammad Ali and also the passive sympathies of the Musalmans in general with their co-religionists, all over the world, based on purely religious grounds is not in the least degree inconsistent with the fullest measure of sincere and reasoned loyalty to His Majesty the King Emperor. Lastly, the League desires to convey to the Government the profound disbelief in the charges and allegations which have been officially made against Mr. Mohammad Ali without any attempt at substantiation, and so long as the public is not fully put in possession of the sources and the character of the information upon which the Government based their policy, it will continue to regard such action as devoid of any justification; further that the League do resolve in response to the universal wishes of the Musalmans of India to initiate a campaign of constitutional agitation to ventilate this matter, both in this country and in Great Britain, with a view to securing the release of the two brothers.'

In spite of these emphatic declarations, which show that the sentiments expressed by Mr. Mohammad Ali and his brother are sentiments shared with them by the whole of Muslim India, though they are in no way inconsistent with deep and reasoned loyalty to the King Emperor—a loyalty which is being daily put to the proof on the battle fields on every front where Indian Mohammedans are sacrificing their lives for King and country as freely and as willingly as any other section of His Majesty's subjects—in spite, I say, of these declarations and these proofs, the Government has continued its policy of repression, of distrust and of suspicion. There need be little wonder, then, that a feeling of disquietude, depression and resentment prevails in the minds of Muslims. And in this condition of mind, we are asked to discuss, in an atmosphere of serenity and calmness, the prospective reforms in the constitution of the government. We are to preserve an attitude of peace and calm in the face of the greatest and the most persistent aggravation of our most deep-rooted grievance. The coping stone to this attitude of Government was laid when, in a spirit of unreasonableness hard to parallel, the Home Department of the Government of India refused to allow an All-India Deputation of Musalmans to wait on Mr. Montagu, unless the prayer for the release of Mohammad Ali and other internees was deleted.

I can hardly say that the section of the more impulsive amongst us is to be blamed when it refuses to be comforted by what is being dangled before it and exclaims with Khaiyam:

Oh take the cash, and let the credit go,
Nor heed the rumbling of a distant drum!

But much as I sympathize with this attitude, I appeal to my eager and bitterly tried friends not to give way to feelings of despondency and despair. Even those brave men who have lost their liberties for us would not wish that this spirit should get the better of us. They would wish us, I know, to continue the struggle, and work for the cause with that singleness of purpose which characterized them. The cause of the country is too great, too sacred to be forsaken through any misfortune. It is in the spirit of an unshakable devotion to our faith and our country that we have assembled here. In the clash of arms and the din of conflict, many of the old-world ideals have crumbled and vanished, but the apotheosis of patriotism, of love of country and of race has once again become an abiding and a consuming faith to millions of men, who, hitherto unmoved by any consideration except that of material gain, have made the supreme sacrifice on the altar of this faith. Gentlemen, to you this seemingly new phase of man's mentality, does not come in the nature either of a new discovery or even as a truth restored to its pristine purity. Your fidelity to your faith is a wonder to the world, and Hubbul-Watan (love of country) you regard as part of your faith.

I will not waste your time on the trite question of whether we are Musalmans first and Indians afterwards, or Indians first and Musalmans next; for we are both, and it does not matter in the least whether you put the one attribute first and the other afterwards or the other way about. I maintain that we are both at one and the same time, and the record of the organization to which we all are proud to belong, I mean the All-India Muslim League, is a splendid exemplification of the Indian Musalman.

To the All-India Muslim League belongs the glory of burning the great truth into the hearts of Indian Musalmans, that they must devote an equal portion of their lives for the service of the motherland as for their faith.

The Question of the Caliphate

The question of the Caliphate is, for example, one which, now when Islam is already on the qui vive, has been recently treated in a flippant manner by men in authority, who ought to know, and by influential organs of public opinion, which ought to be taught better. It is not a shuttle-cock for European diplomacy to play with. It is a question which has got its seat in the very fibre of the faith of a vast majority of the Mohammedans of the world, no less than of India. They are greatly mistaken who think that any interference or dictation in this matter will not be resented by the Musalmans.

Gentlemen, the disintegration of Mohammedan countries is going on apace. Countries, every inch of which is sacred to the Musalmans, have been made battlegrounds in consequence of this world conflagration. The announcement which the Government of His Majesty and His Majesty's representative in India made at the beginning of this war, and which has contributed to an enormous degree to the self-control of the Indian Musalmans, is not forgotten. It assured them of the inviolability and the integrity of the Muslim sacred places and of their immunity from attack—Jerusalem is one of those sacred places.

And here are a few resolutions passed by the League in this session, including the one demanding the release of the Ali Brothers, which was supported by Gandhi (who was present at the League's session), among others:[41]

VI. The All-India Muslim League enters a strong protest against the objection taken by the Government of India to the passage in the address of the All-India Muslim Deputation relating to the internment of distinguished Muslim leaders under the Defence of India Act—a question which, the League is convinced, is closely bound with the contentment of very large numbers of His Majesty's subjects, and which, in its opinion, does involve an important constitutional issue.

The League is further of opinion that the refusal by the Government of India to allow the All-India Muslim League Deputation to be received by the Secretary of State, unless the passage referred to above were deleted, constitutes an encroachment on the rights of Indian citizens to place their political grievances before His Majesty's representatives. Having regard, moreover, to the fact that other deputations were allowed to present addresses to the Secretary of State containing a number of matters not bearing on the question of constitutional reforms, and considering also that this attitude of the Government debarred the Deputation from placing before the Secretary of State and the Viceroy the views of the Musalmans of India on many important questions of constitutional reforms contained in its address, the League deplores the decision of the Government of India and deems it its duty to bring to the notice of the Secretary of State the circumstances which prevented the Deputation from placing the Muslim viewpoint regarding the political situation before the Right Hon'ble the Secretary of State and His Excellency the Viceroy. (From the Chair.)

X. (a) The All-India Muslim League views with great alarm the outburst of Hindu fanaticism on the last Baqrid and Moharram in Bihar and Chaurari in the Jaunpore district and other places, and condemns the rioters and their secret sympathizers as the enemies of the country. This meeting also expresses its deep regret at the silence of responsible Hindu leaders at the occurrences in Bihar and Chaurari.

(b) The All-India Muslim League expresses its indignation at failure of the Criminal Investigation Department to obtain timely information of the huge organization set on foot by a large section of the Hindu population in the districts of Arrah, Gaya and Patna to plunder the houses of the Musalmans, defile and destroy mosques and the Holy Quran, and commit other excesses, and refuses to believe that the stupendous anti-cow-killing movement could have been organized without the help and co-operation of a number of Hindu members of the force. This meeting also expresses its deep regret at the weakness shown by the authorities in facing the situation, and their omission to adopt drastic measures against the rioters who carried on the pillage from village to village, and is of opinion that by having recourse to strong measures at the outset the spread of the trouble could have been avoided. (Proposed by Mr. S. Riza Ali; seconded by Mr. Abul Qasim.)

XII. The All-India Muslim League deplores the fact that in spite of the expression of the overwhelming sentiment of the community, as indicated in the unanimous election of Mr. Mohammad Ali to the presidentship of this Session of the All-India Muslim League, both he and his brother, Mr. Shaukat Ali, have remained unreleased. The All-India Muslim League cannot too strongly urge upon the attention of the Government that the course followed by them is having a profoundly disquieting effect upon the community at large. The League feels it its duty to point out that, if it were not for the special appeal of His Excellency the Viceroy for co-operation in making the mission of the Secretary of State a success, the prevailing sense of the co-community would undoubtedly have restrained the Musalmans from any participation, at this juncture, in the representations to the Secretary of State. The League further puts on record its unswerving conviction that the views expressed by Mr. Mohammad Ali in his draft undertaking faithfully reflect the attitude of the Musalmans of India, his offence, if it is an offence, being that in speaking out the unvarnished truth he has rendered a public service alike to Government and his own people; further that in the considered opinion of the League, the views expressed by Mr. Mohammad Ali, and also the passive sympathies of the Musalmans in general with their co-religionists all over the world, based on purely religious grounds, are not in the least degree inconsistent with the fullest measure of sincere and reasoned loyalty to His Majesty the King Emperor. Lastly, the League desires to convey to Government its profound disbelief in the charges and allegations which have been officially made against Mr. Mohammad Ali, and the League does resolve, in response to the universal wishes of the Musalmans of India, to initiate a campaign of constitutional agitation, both in this country and in Great Britain, with a view to securing the release of the two brothers. (Proposed by Mr. Fazlul Haque; seconded by Mr. S. Zahur Ahmed; supported by Mrs. Sarojini Naidu, Mr. M.K. Gandhi, Dr. Saif-ud-Din Kitchlew, Mr. Mohammad Shafi.)

XIII. The All-India Muslim League strongly urges upon the Government to set free Maulana Mahmud-ul-Hasan, Maulana Abul Kalam Azad, Maulana Hasrat Mohani and all the other Muslim internees who have unjustly been deprived of their liberties, and to remove the great discontent prevailing in the Muslim community in consequence of such internments. (Proposed by Moulvi Mohammad Ismail; seconded by Maulvi Najm-ud-Din; supported by Syed Mohsin Shah.)

XV. In view of the strong desire of the Muslim community to have definite provisions for the protection of its interests, this League urges upon the Government that the following safeguards be adopted in the forthcoming reforms:

(a) Musalmans should be adequately represented in the public services of the country.

(b) Musalmans should have representation on Government Universities in the same proportion as the representation accorded to Musalmans on the Legislative Council of the province concerned may be.

(c) The Urdu language and Persian character should be maintained in courts and public offices in those provinces where they are in vogue, and Urdu should be employed as the medium of primary education in the aforesaid provinces.

(d) Musalmans should be afforded facilities, protection and help in the observance and performance of their religious rites, ceremonies and usages on the occasion of Baqrid, Moharram, etc., without any restriction by any official or community. (Proposed by Mr. Mohammad Yaqub; seconded by Mr. Ismail Shirazi.)

The scene that emerges from the sequence of events leading to the Lucknow Pact and thereafter is that a cross-section of the Muslim League realised that the Congress needed its support to present a 'united face' to the British to secure self-government and that the Congress was willing to make critical concessions to achieve that goal. Such concessions included agreeing to communal electorates, communal veto over legislation, and support for pan-Islamism. Every Hindu–Muslim riot, regardless of the cause, required greater assurances and accommodation from the Congress on behalf of Hindus, even though the Congress did not even see itself as a Hindu organisation. Clearly, Hindu–Muslim unity demanded unilateral concessions—with disastrous long-term ramifications for Hindus—in return for Muslim assurances of 'peace' and support for self-government. It is against this backdrop that the Congress's support under Gandhi for the Khilafat Movement must be understood, since the policy of accommodation, concession and appeasement of the Muslim League was entrenched *well before* he took centre stage and, critically, when *Extremists* such as Tilak and Pal wielded significant influence over the Congress, thanks to the Home Rule Movement.

The Montford Report and Reactions to It

After the Calcutta sessions of the Congress and the League, it was clear to the British that the Moderates did not enjoy the same influence they used to in the Congress. To counter the growing influence of the Extremists, Montagu proposed the creation of yet another organisation that would function as a safety valve, which had hitherto been the role of the Moderates:[42]

> A new organization of India is to be created, assisted in every possible way by the Government, for propaganda on behalf of our proposals, and to send a delegation to England to assist us.

To this end, Montagu held discreet and informal meetings with Bhupendranath Basu and S.P. Sinha. Commenting on the outcome of the meetings, Montagu wrote as under:[43]

> We talked about the formation of a moderate party; they were very enthusiastic; and talked about editing newspapers, and so forth. I think they mean business.

On the same lines as its Congress experiment, this time the British helped to found the National Liberation Party, populating it with Moderate leaders from the Congress who did not want to remain in it. Simultaneously, the period between January and April 1918 saw the preparation of the 256-page Montagu–Chelmsford Report on Constitutional Reforms, which was completed in Simla on 22 April 1918 and published on 8 July 1918. The

Report would form the basis of the Government of India Act of 1919 to a significant extent, with a few departures. In Chapter 11 of the first book, I had briefly discussed the Report, primarily from the perspective of underscoring its Christian colonial consciousness. Here I will discuss the Report from the perspective of understanding the gap between the expectations of the Congress and the League on the one hand, and the vision of the Montford pair on the other.

The Montford Report is an extremely educative document from the perspective of understanding the multiple factors and considerations,

Edwin Samuel Montagu, Secretary of State for India from 1917 to 1922

both international and national, which shaped British policymaking in another round of reforms after the Minto–Morley Reforms of 1909. Not just that, it captured in significant detail the evolution of the political infrastructure in Bharat after the arrival of the British. In terms of immediacy, the Report identified the growing sense of confidence on the part of Indians that they too were entitled to exercise the right of self-determination at par with other 'nations' (paragraph 24 of the Report).[44] This was further bolstered by the knowledge that India had contributed significantly in terms of 'blood and treasure' to defending the British empire, which demonstrated its loyalty and readiness (paragraph 23).[45] Critically, in paragraph 25, the Report recognised that the Home Rule Movement gave formal expression to the demand for self-government. In paragraph 26, the Report observed that the loyalty of Muslims towards the British government remained largely intact until 1911 and that it was disturbed primarily on account of British neutrality in the war between Italy and Turkey, which was then worsened by the reunification of Bengal. According to the Report, the British–Muslim estrangement was further contributed to by the Balkan War, the Kanpur mosque incident and, finally, the entry of Turkey into the Great War (the First World War). In Chapter 7 of the Report, the Congress–League scheme and its unviability from the British perspective was discussed. Specifically, British objections to the scheme related to the issue of making the government accountable to the legislature and also to the pace at which the Congress–League scheme envisaged the grant of self-government. In other words, apart from structural disagreements on the proposals contained in the scheme, the government was not on the same page as the Congress and the League on India's readiness for self-government. On the latter subject, the following was the road map envisaged by the Report, in paragraph 179:[46]

> ... Indians must be enabled, in so far as they attain responsibility, to determine for themselves what they want done. The process will begin in local affairs which we have long since intended and promised to make over to them; the time has come for advance also in some subjects of provincial concern; and it will proceed to the complete control of provincial matters and thence, in the course of time, and subject to the proper discharge of Imperial responsibilities, to the control of matters concerning all India. We make it plain that such limitations on powers as we are now proposing are due only to the obvious fact that time is necessary in order to train both representatives and electorates for the work which we desire them to undertake; and that we offer Indians opportunities at short intervals to prove the progress they are making and to make good their claim not by the method of agitation, but by positive demonstration, to the further stages in self-government which we have just indicated.

> 180. Further, we have every reason to hope that as the result of this process, India's connexion with the Empire will be confirmed by the wishes of her people. The experience of a century of experiments within the Empire goes all in one direction. As power is given to the people of a province or of a dominion to manage their own local affairs, their attachment becomes the stronger to the Empire which comprehends them all in a common bond of union. The existence of national feeling, or the love of, and pride in, a national culture need not conflict with, and may indeed strengthen, the sense of membership in a wider commonwealth. The obstacles to a growth in India of this sense of partnership in the Empire are obvious enough. Differences of race, religion, past history, and civilization have to be overcome. But the Empire, which includes the French of Canada and the Dutch of South Africa—to go no further—cannot in any case be based on ties of race alone. It must depend on a common realization of the ends for which the Empire exists, the maintenance of peace and order over wide spaces of territory, the maintenance of freedom, and the development of the culture of each national unity of which the Empire is composed. These are aims which appeal to the imagination of India and, in proportion as self-government develops patriotism in India, we may hope to see the growth of a conscious feeling of organic unity with the Empire as a whole.

Apart from using constitutional reforms as a means of civilising colonised societies (as discussed in the first book), according to the report, the self-government to be granted would start at the level of provinces before proceeding to the national level in stages and over an extended period of time, which would be determined by the British government. To this end, the Report also suggested changes to the education system in order to train people to take charge of the administration. Having thus set out this broad plan, the Report then dealt with the specifics of the proposed Reforms, starting from the provincial governments to the Government of India, the princely states, the bureaucracy and the army. I will deal with only select aspects of the proposals which convey the gist of the report and its primary recommendations.

In paragraph 188, the report makes it clear that Montagu's announcement of 20 August 1917 in the British Parliament was a statement of vision, envisaging gradual empowerment only upon satisfactory progress being made at each stage and at every level, starting with local bodies, followed by provincial governments and finally the Government of India.[47] Also, it was underscored that the pace of progress could not be the same at all levels. This effectively meant that the Imperial government's control over the Government of India would be the last to be relaxed, in order to secure British interests as well as to stave off external threats. To this end, the first formula of the Report was captured as follows:[48]

> There should be, as far as possible, complete popular control in local bodies and the largest possible independence for them of outside control.

In paragraph 189, a direct elective component was spelt out for provincial governments, in accordance with the meaning of 'responsible government'. However, this did not mean that the whole of the provincial government would be an elected body. Instead, a dual form was proposed, which has come to be known as 'dyarchy', which meant a composite body with both elected and unelected components. Here's paragraph 189:[49]

> 189. When we come to the provincial Governments the position is different. Our objective is the realization of responsible Government. We understand this to mean first that the members of the executive Government should be responsible to, because capable of being changed by, their constituents; and, secondly, that those constituents should exercise their power through the agency of their representatives in the assembly. These two conditions imply in their completeness that there exist constituencies based on a franchise broad enough to represent the interests of the general population, and capable of exercising an intelligent choice in the selection of their representatives; and, secondarily, that it is recognized as the constitutional practice that the executive Government retains office only so long as it commands the support of a majority in the assembly. But in India these conditions are as yet wanting. The provincial areas and interests involved are immense, indeed are on what would elsewhere be regarded as a national scale. The

amount of administrative experience available is small; electoral experience is almost entirely lacking. There must be a period of political education, which can only be achieved through the gradual, but expanding, exercise of responsibility. The considerations of which we took account in chapter VI forbid us immediately to hand over complete responsibility. We must proceed therefore by transferring responsibility for certain functions of government while reserving control over others. From this starting point we look for a steady approach to the transfer of complete responsibility. We may put our second formula thus:

'The provinces are the domain in which the earlier steps towards the progressive realization of responsible government should be taken. Some measure of responsibility should be given at once, and our aim is to give complete responsibility as soon as conditions permit. This involves at once giving the provinces the largest measure of independence, legislative, administrative? and financial, of the Government of India which is compatible with the due discharge by the latter of its own responsibilities'

In paragraph 190, the movement towards responsible government was spelt out as follows:

190. But, as we shall see, any attempt to establish equilibrium between the official and popular forces in government inevitably introduces additional complexity into the administration. For such hybrid arrangements precedents are wanting; their working must be experimental, and will depend on factors that are yet largely unknown. We are not prepared, without experience of their results, to effect like changes in the Government of India. Nevertheless, it is desirable to make the Indian Legislative Council more truly representative of Indian opinion, and to give that opinion greater opportunities of acting on the Government. While, therefore, we cannot commend to Parliament a similar and simultaneous advance, both in the provinces and in the Government of India, we are led to the following proposition:

'The Government of India must remain wholly responsible to Parliament, and saving such responsibility, its authority in essential matters must remain indisputable, pending experience of the effect of the changes now to be introduced in the provinces. In the meantime the Indian Legislative Council should be enlarged and made more representative and its opportunities of influencing Government increased'

Since the above proposals could not go hand in hand with the existing degree of control from and by England, reduction in interference from 'Home', namely England, was captured in paragraph 191 as follows:

191. Further, the partial control of the executive in the provinces by the legislature, and the increasing influence of the legislature upon the executive in the Government of India, will make it necessary that the superior control over all Governments in India which is now exercised by the authorities at

Home must be in corresponding measure abated; for otherwise the executive Governments in India will be subjected to pressure from different sources which will wholly paralyse their liberty of action, and also the different pressures may be exercised in opposite directions. We may put this proposition briefly as follows:

'In proportion as the foregoing changes take effect, the control of Parliament and the Secretary of State over the Government of India and provincial Governments must be relaxed'

Based on these proposals, the specifics of local self-government were elaborated upon in paragraphs 194–196. The specifics of provincial governments, including the provincial executive and provincial legislatures, were dealt with in Chapter 8 of the Report. As part of the discussion on provincial legislatures, the issue of communal electorates was discussed in paragraphs 227–232, which reveal a significant departure in thinking from the Minto–Morley Reforms:[50]

227. At this point we are brought face to face with the most difficult question which arises in connexion with elected assemblies—whether communal electorates are to be maintained. We may be told that this is a closed question, because the Muhammadans will never agree to any revision of the arrangement promised them by Lord Minto in 1906 and secured to them by the reforms of 1909. But we have felt bound to re-examine the question fully in the light of our new policy, and also because we have been pressed to extend the system of communal electorates in a variety of directions. This is no new problem. It has been discussed periodically from the time when the first steps were taken to liberalize the councils. There has hitherto been a weighty consensus of opinion that in a country like India no principle of representation other than by interests is practically possible. Lord Dufferin held this view in 1888, and in 1892 Lord Lansdowne's Government wrote that:- 'The representation of such a community upon such a scale as the Act permits can only be secured by providing that each important class shall have the opportunity of making its views known in council by the mouth of some member specially acquainted with them.' We note that in 1892 the small size of the councils was reckoned as a factor in the decision and that the contrary view was not without its exponents; but we feel no doubt that Lord Minto's Government followed the predominant opinion when in 1908 they pressed for an important extension of the communal principle. Thus we have had to reckon not only with the settled existence of the system, but with a large volume of weighty opinion that no other method is feasible.

228. The crucial test to which, as we conceive, all proposals should be brought is whether they will or will not help to carry India towards responsible government. Some persons hold that for a people, such as they deem those of India to be, so divided by race, religion and caste as to be unable to consider

the interests of any but their own section, a system of communal and class representation is not merely inevitable, but is actually best. They maintain that it evokes and applies the principle of democracy over the widest range over which it is actually alive at all by appealing to the instincts which are strongest; and that we must hope to develop the finer, which are also at present the weaker, instincts by using the forces that really count. According to this theory communal representation is an inevitable, and even a healthy, stage in the development of a non-political people. We find indeed that those who take this view are prepared to apply their principles on a scale previously unknown, and to devise elaborate systems of class or religious electorates into which all possible interests will be deftly fitted. But when we consider what responsible government implies, and how it was developed in the world, we cannot take this view. We find it in its earliest beginnings resting on an effective sense of the common interests, a bond compounded of community of race, religion and language. In the earlier form which it assumed in Europe it appeared only when the territorial principle had vanquished the tribal principle, and blood and religion had ceased to assert a rival claim with the State to a citizen's allegiance; and throughout its development in Western countries, even in cases where special reasons to the contrary were present, it has rested consistently on the same root principle. The solitary examples that we can discover of the opposing principle are those of Austria, a few of the smaller German states, and Cyprus. It is hardly necessary to explain why we dismiss these as irrelevant or unconvincing. We conclude unhesitatingly that the history of self-government among the nations who developed it, and spread it through the world, is decisively against the admission by the State of any divided allegiance; against the State's arranging its members in any way which encourages them to think of themselves primarily as citizens of any smaller unit than itself.

229. Indian lovers of their country would be the first to admit that India generally has not yet acquired the citizen spirit and if we are really to lead her to self-government we must do all that we possibly can to call it forth in her people. Division by creeds and classes means the creation of political camps organized against each other, and teaches men to think as partisans and not as citizens; and it is difficult to see how the change from this system to national representation is ever to occur. The British Government is often accused of dividing men in order to govern them. But if it unnecessarily divides them at the very moment when it professes to start them on the road to governing themselves it will find it difficult to meet the charge of being hypocritical or short-sighted.

230. There is another important point. A minority which is given special representation owing to its weak and backward state is positively encouraged to settle down into a feeling of satisfied security; it is under no inducement to educate and qualify itself to make good the ground which it has lost compared

with the stronger majority. On the other hand, the latter will be tempted to feel that they have done all they need do for their weaker fellow countrymen, and that they are free to use their power for their own purposes. The give-and-take which is the essence of political life is lacking. There is no inducement to the one side to forbear, or to the other to exert itself. The communal system stereotypes existing relations.

231. We regard any system of communal electorates, therefore, as a very serious hindrance to the development of the self-governing principle. The evils of any extension of the system are plain. Already communal representation has been actually proposed for the benefit of a majority community in Madras. At the same time we must face the hard facts. The Muhammadans were given special representation with separate electorates in 1909. The Hindus' acquiescence is embodied in the present agreement between the political leaders of the two communities. The Muhammadans regard these as settled facts, and any attempt to go back on them would rouse a storm of bitter protest and put a severe strain on the loyalty of a community which has behaved with conspicuous loyalty during a period of very great difficulty, and which we know to be feeling no small anxiety for its own welfare under a system of popular government. The Muhammadans regard separate representation and communal electorates as their only adequate safeguards. But apart from a pledge which we must honour until we are released from it, we are bound to see that the community secures proper representation in the new councils. How can we say to them that we regard the decision of 1909 as mistaken, that its retention is incompatible with progress towards responsible government, that its reversal will eventually be to their benefit; and that for these reasons we have decided to go back on it? Much as we regret the necessity, we are convinced that so far as the Muhammadans at all events are concerned the present system must be maintained until conditions alter, even at the price of slower progress towards the realization of a common citizenship. But we can see no reason to set up communal representation for Muhammadans in any province where they form a majority of the voters.

The sum and substance of the above cogitation was that communal electorates, according to the authors of the Report, went against the grain of 'single nationhood'. According to them, the only reason they had to grudgingly agree to continue with the system of communal electorates for Muslims was owing to the promises given to the Simla Deputation by Lord Minto in October 1906, whose basis was the Two-Nation Theory. In my view, given the long-standing animosity between Hindus and Muslims, it would have been ahistorical to behave as if the Two-Nation Theory was not a lived reality. Importantly, it is critical to understand that the basis of the theory was not purely racial since obviously there were a large number of Muslims who were forced converts from the Hindu fold. The basis of the

Two-Nation Theory, therefore, was and remains one of consciousness fuelled by the ethno-religious supremacism and consequent expansionism of Middle Eastern coloniality. While the Two-Nation Theory may offer some basis for separate electorates for Muslims, albeit tenuous, the converse of this is that extension of communal electorates or any other concept similar in principle to communities which subscribed to faith systems native to Bharat would have the effect of Balkanisation of the Indic civilisation and its Dharmic undergirding.

The above-mentioned point is relevant to the discussion, since in paragraph 232 of the Report the authors state that drawing inspiration from Muslims, several other communities, namely the Sikhs, the non-Brahmins in Madras (whom the Report recognised as being the overwhelming majority), Indian Christians, Anglo-Indians, Europeans and the Lingayat community in Bombay too had sought similar class representation. Grant of separate electorates to the Sikhs, the non-Brahmins of Madras or the Lingayat community would have been detrimental to the integrity of the Indic fold. Fortunately, the Report did not deem it fit to recommend separate electorates for any other community except the Sikhs. Instead, a process of nomination was recommended for them.

The demand for separate electorates for the non-Brahmins of Madras was made by the Justice Party, which had been founded in 1917 in Madras, primarily on the anti-Brahmin plank. The Justice Party was a party of wealthy, landed and 'upper-caste' non-Brahmin groups that sought the ouster of Brahmins from the government owing to the latter's disproportionate presence there. It must be clarified that these groups did not object to Brahmin presence in the British establishment on patriotic grounds, but on the ground that 'upper-caste' non-Brahmin groups of Madras were not represented enough in the British establishment. This, coupled with the social prestige conventionally bestowed upon Brahmins by Hindu society owing to their traditional learning, notwithstanding their lack of wealth, fuelled the anti-Brahminism of the Justice Party. Not surprisingly, the party was supported in its campaign by the provincial government helmed by Lord Pentland, then Governor of Madras. To counter Annie Besant's Home Rule Movement, it was mischievously characterised as a 'Brahminical movement', enabling the Justice Party to oppose the demand for Home Rule.[51] In fact, Dr T.M. Nair, who founded the Justice Party along with C. Natesa Mudaliar and Theagaraya Chetty, *demanded* the *continuance* of British rule because Home Rule, according to him, meant Brahmin rule. According to G.N. Singh, Nair personally went to England to oppose any transfer of power to Indian hands.

As for the Sikhs, their demand for separate electorates was accepted by the Montford Report, primarily owing to their importance to British rule from a military perspective. G.N. Singh sheds light on the genesis of this demand.[52] He points out that until 1919, the Sikhs did not have a separate political representation from Hindus. He traces the origins of this demand in 1919 to the creation of a 'Sikh reform' association called Khalsa Diwan in 1888, which established a network of associations, the Singh Sabhas, all over the Punjab Province. The purpose of the association was to purge Sikhism of 'Hindu rites and customs' and encourage the use of 'Sikh forms and ceremonies'. By the beginning of the twentieth century, the Khalsa Diwan was replaced by the Chief Khalsa Diwan. This organisation ultimately sent a deputation to Montagu and Chelmsford presenting a Sikh memorandum on similar lines as the Simla Deputation of 1906 by the Muslims. Highlighting the political, economic and military importance of the Sikhs, especially the fact that they constituted 20 per cent of the British Indian Army, a demand was made for one-third representation in the Punjab Council as well as in the services. Despite support for their position from the Punjab government and recognition of their demand by the Montford Report, the Punjab Council did not accept their demand on the ground that the Congress–League Scheme did not envisage separate electorates for the Sikhs. This led to the formation of a Sikh League. Thenceforth, the Sikh League and the Chief Khalsa Diwan would advocate the cause of the Sikhs as a separate community. The alienation of the Sikh identity from the Dharmic fold after the advent of the British, in particular after the 1857 Mutiny, deserves a dedicated book from the perspective of decoloniality, although there is enough literature on the subject by several scholars.

Coming back to the Report, Chapter 9 dealt with the government of India and the India Office. In this chapter, paragraphs 271–274 are important and are reproduced here:[53]

271. We have explained already how the executive council of the Governor General is constituted and how Portfolios are allotted in it. Its changed relations with provincial governments will in themselves materially affect the volume of work coming before the departments, and for this reason alone some redistribution will be necessary. We would therefore abolish such statutory restrictions as now exist in respect of the appointment of members of the Governor General's Council so as to give greater elasticity both in respect of the size of the Government and the distribution of work. If it is desired to retain parliamentary control over these matters they might be embodied in statutory orders to be laid before Parliament.

272. Further, we propose to increase the Indian element in the executive council. We do not think it necessary to argue the expediency of enabling

the wishes of India to be further represented in the Cabinet of the country. The decision of Lord Morley and Lord Minto to appoint one Indian member to the council marked an important stage in India's political development; and has proved of value in enabling the Government to have first-hand acquaintance with Indian opinion. In recommending a second appointment we are only pursuing the policy already determined upon in respect of the public services. There exists, of course at present no racial prescription in the statute, nor do we propose that any should be introduced. There is even no formal guarantee that any appointment shall be made on the grounds of race. The appointment of Indian members will be made in the future as in the past as a matter of practice by the Crown on the recommendation of the Secretary of State; and we suggest the appointment of another Indian member as soon as may be.

273. We now come to the changes required in the Indian Legislative Council. Its existing composition we have already explained. No argument is needed to show that under present conditions 27 elected members, many of them returned by small class electorates, cannot adequately represent the interests of the entire country in the supreme assembly. Indeed no council the composition of which is conditioned by the necessity of maintaining an official majority could possibly serve that purpose. We recommend therefore that the strength of the legislative council, to be known in future as the Legislative Assembly of India, should be raised to a total strength of about 100 members, so as to be far more truly representative of British India. We propose that two-thirds of this total should be returned by election; and that one third should be nominated by the Governor General of which third not less than a third again should be non-officials selected with the object of representing minority or special interests. We have decided not to present to His Majesty's Government a complete scheme for the election of the elected representatives; our discussions have shown us that we have not the data on which to arrive at any sound conclusions. Some special representation, we think, there must be, as for European and Indian commerce and also for the large landlords. *There should be also communal representation for Muhammadans in most provinces and also for Sikhs in the Punjab.* There is no difficulty about direct election in the case of special constituencies. It is in respect of the general, or residuary, electorate, including therein the communal electorates for Muhammadans and Sikhs, that complexities present themselves. Our decided preference is for a system of direct electorates, but the immensity of the country makes it difficult; it may be impossible to form constituencies of reasonable size in which candidates will be able to get into direct touch with the electorates. Moreover, there is the further difficulty (which, however, presents itself in any system of constituencies) of the inequalities of wealth existing between the different communities. If constituencies are to be approximately even in size it may be necessary to concede a special franchise to the Muhammadans, who,

taken as a whole, are poorer than the Hindus; and this means giving a vote to some Muhammadans who would not be entitled to vote if they were Hindus. That is an undesirable anomaly, to which we should prefer the anomaly of unequal constituencies; but on our present information we find it impossible to say how great the practical difficulties of variation in size might be. Similar problems will present themselves in respect of constituencies for the elections to provincial councils. It is obviously desirable to deal on uniform lines with the electoral arrangements both in the provincial and Indian councils. As regards the former we have already recommended the appointment of a special committee to investigate questions of franchises and electorates; and to that body we would therefore also commit the task of determining the electorates and constituencies for the Indian Legislative Assembly. They may find it wholly impracticable to arrange for direct election. In that case, they will consider the various possible systems of indirect election. We are fully aware of the objections attaching to all forms of indirect election; but if the difficulties of direct election compel us to have recourse to indirect, we incline to think that election by non-official members of provincial councils is likely to prove far more acceptable to Indian opinion and, in spite of the smallness of the electoral bodies, certainly not open in practice to greater objection than any of the other alternative methods which have been from time to time proposed. For reasons similar to those which we have given in the case of the provincial legislative councils we recommend that members of the Indian Legislative Assembly should not be designated 'Honourable' but should be entitled to affix the letters M.L.A. to their names.

274. The suggestion we have made for the number of elected members was based on the calculation that the three presidencies would be represented by 11 members each; the United Provinces by 10, the Punjab and Bihar and Orissa by 7 each, the Central Provinces by 5, Burma by 3, and Assam by 2. We also think that in view of the importance of the Delhi province as the Imperial enclave and the seat of the central Government it should be represented by a member. [Emphasis added]

In Paragraph 277 the Report proposed a 50-member Council of State which would enable the Government of India to pass 'essential' legislation if the lower house, namely the Indian Legislative Assembly, did not pass them. This enabled retention of power in the hands of the British government over important issues. To this end, in paragraph 278, the Report clearly stated as follows:[54]

278. Inasmuch as the Council of State will be the supreme legislative authority for India on all crucial questions, and also the revising authority upon all Indian legislation, we desire to attract to it the services of the best men available in the country. We desire that the Council of State should develop something of the experience and dignity of a body of Elder Statesmen;

Clearly, the Council, which would be presided by the Governor General, was meant to prevail over the Indian Legislative Assembly on 'crucial questions'. The Report presented the British government's overall vision of India's future as follows:[55]

Conception of India's Future

349. We may conveniently now gather up our proposals, so as to present a general picture of the progress which we intend and of the nature and order of the steps to be taken on the road. Our conception of the eventual future of India is a sisterhood of States, self-governing in all matters of purely local or provincial interest, in some cases corresponding to existing provinces, in others perhaps modified in area according to the character and economic interests of their people. Over this congeries of States would preside a central Government, increasingly representative of and responsible to the people of all of them; dealing with matters, both internal and external, of common interest to the whole of India; acting as arbiter in inter-state relations; and representing the interests of all India *on equal terms with the self-governing units of the British Empire.* In this picture there is a place also for the Native States (Princely States). It is possible that they too will wish to be associated for certain purposes with the organization of British India in such a way as to dedicate their peculiar qualities to the common service without loss of individuality.

350. But it seems to us axiomatic that there cannot be a completely representative and responsible Government of India on an equal footing with the other self-governing units of the British Commonwealth until the component States whose people it represents and to whom it is responsible, or at least the great majority of them, have themselves reached the stage of full responsible government. Nor even then can we say that the form or the degree of responsibility which will be reached in India will exactly correspond to that attained by the Dominions. The final form of India's constitution must be evolved out of the conditions of India, and must be materially affected by the need for securing Imperial responsibilities. The dominating factor in the intermediate process must be the rate at which the provinces can move towards responsible government. At the same time change obviously cannot be confined to the provinces. In proportion as they become more responsible the control which the Government of India exercises over them must diminish. But it is not merely a question of the extent of the control; the nature and manner of its exercise must in course of time be modified. We cannot think that States on the way to responsible government, which have imbibed a large element of responsibility into their constitutions, can be controlled by a purely autocratic power. So also with the duties extending over the whole of India which will be discharged by the Government of India as its special concern. It is impossible that while other duties which differ from them mainly in being

local in scope or subject to provincial differentiation are being administered by responsible governments, those which fall to the Government of India should be administered autocratically. It follows, therefore, that change in the provinces implies change in the Government of India, but it does not imply that the change should be simultaneous or in equal proportion. On the contrary the change need simply be so much as to render the Government of India a suitable instrument for controlling the provinces at the stage at which they have for the time being arrived.

351. Similarly all movement towards responsible government in India implies a corresponding change in the constitution of the controlling agency in England. We cannot predict what kind of agency India will wish to maintain in London once she has attained the status of full partnership in the Empire; but it must be very different from the existing arrangements. These are based upon complete control by Parliament through the Secretary of State over every phase of administration in India. The Secretary of State is advised, and to some extent controlled, in the exercise of his functions by a Council designed to supply defects of direct knowledge and experience of India in himself and his subordinates in the India Office; and also to watch the interests of India in cases where these may be threatened by competing British interests. Both Secretary of State and Council, however, are in almost complete subordination to Parliament which may, if it chooses, exercise its authority over every detail of administration in India. Now in relation to India Parliament will, we imagine, observe the principles long adopted towards the British self-governing colonies, and will contract its interference and control in direct proportion to the expansion of self-government. As this grows, the volume of business in which Parliament will interfere will steadily shrink, and the occasions will be rarer on which the Secretary of State will have to exercise control and will need to be advised regarding its exercise. This points to a diminution in the establishment of the India Office and possibly to a modification in the Council of India. But here, again, it is a question not merely of the volume of work but also of the spirit in which it is conducted. In dealing with organizations which have become largely representative and in some degree responsible, the need for mutual understanding and action strengthened by consent will be continually enhanced.

352. Again, while the growth of responsibility in India will lead to decreased intervention by the Secretary of State and Parliament in day-to-day administration, the fact that India's further political progress is to be determined by Parliament makes it imperative that Parliament should be better informed about and more keenly interested in Indian conditions. The decisions to be taken in the future must to some extent be controversial; different advice about them will be offered from different sources; and Parliament which is the final arbiter of India's destiny should be in a position to form a wise

and independent judgment. For these reasons we have suggested means of improving its opportunities of exercising a well-informed control.

353. We conclude therefore that change in any one portion of the Indian polity will involve changes on parallel lines but by no means at an equal pace in the other portions: and we claim that our proposals satisfy this fundamental principle. We begin with a great extension of local self-government so as to train the electorates in the matters which they will best understand. Simultaneously we provide for a substantial measure of self-government in the provinces and for better representation and more criticism in the Government of India and for fuller knowledge in Parliament. And we suggest machinery by means of which at regular stages the element of responsibility can be continuously enlarged and that of official control continuously diminished, in a way that will guarantee ordered progress and afford an answer to intermediate representations and agitation.

From these excerpts of the Montford Report it could be said that while the reforms proposed by the Montagu–Chelmsford pair were certainly a significant forward movement from the Minto–Morley Reforms, self-government for Bharat even in the manner enjoyed by other Dominions of the British empire and as demanded by the Congress–League Scheme was still a good distance away according to the British. Upon publication of the Report, the Extremists in the Congress were disappointed with its recommendations, calling them 'grudging, half-hearted, meagre, inadequate, and hence disappointing and abortive'.[56] Not surprisingly, Moderates such as Surendranath Banerjea were in favour of accepting the recommendations.[57] As for the League, its reactions were measured and mixed, given the acceptance of communal electorates in the Report, which took forward the policy of the Minto–Morley Reforms. Special sessions were organised both by the Congress and the League in Bombay between 29 August and 1 September 1918 to discuss the Report.

At its special session, whose president was Syed Hasan Imam, the Congress felt that the non-essential aspects of the Congress–League Scheme had been accepted by the Montford Report while the essentials had been rejected.[58] V.J. Patel, brother of Vallabhbhai Patel, who headed the reception committee for the session, suggested the following modifications to the Report:[59]

Modifications

Passed through the alembic of public opinion the proposed reform scheme will have to shed several ingredients if it is to form a basis of mutual trust and co-operation between the Government and the people. Full responsible government must be given to advanced provinces at the outset; (hear, hear), in other provinces reserved subjects should be as few as possible and provision must be made for their automatic transfer within a period of, say, five years. A substantial beginning of responsible government must be made in the Government of India at once, (hear, hear), and that Government should come within the purview of the periodic commissions appointed by the approval of Parliament, at intervals of less than ten years. A time limit must be fixed for granting full responsible government to India and that limit should not exceed fifteen to twenty years. Full fiscal freedom must be given to India at once. If these and other alterations that will doubtless be suggested by the Congress are accepted by the Government a substantial step will have been taken towards the progressive realization of responsible government in India. (Loud and continued applause).

The following was the resolution passed on self-government:[60]

Resolution On Self-Government.

The President: The second resolution is also to be put from the Chair and it runs as follows:

Resolution II. 'That this Congress re-affirms the principles of reform contained in the Resolutions relating to self-government adopted in the Indian National Congress and the All-India Muslim League held at Lucknow in December 1916 and at Calcutta in December 1917 and declares that nothing less than self-government within the Empire can satisfy the Indian people and by enabling it to take its rightful place as a free and self-governing nation in the British Commonwealth strengthen the connection between Great Britain and India.'

I take it, gentlemen, that this resolution is also passed. (Loud cries, of 'Passed, passed.') I declare that this resolution is passed.

Here is the two-part resolution moved by Annie Besant on India's readiness for 'responsible government':[61]

Resolution III. (a) That this Congress declares that the people of India are fit for Responsible Government and repudiates the assumption to the contrary contained in the Report on Indian Constitutional Reforms.

(b) That this Congress entirely disagrees with the formula contained in the said Report that the Provinces are the domain in which the earlier steps should be taken towards the progressive realisation of Responsible Government and that the authority of the Government of India in essential matters must remain indisputable pending experience of the effect of the changes proposed to be introduced in the Provinces and this Congress is of opinion that simultaneous advance is indispensable both in the Provinces and the Government of India.

Here's an interesting resolution moved by Pandit Gokaran Nath Mishra, titled 'Declaration of Indian Rights', which included the right to bear arms.[62]

Declaration of Indian Rights

That the Statute to be passed by Parliament should include the Declaration of the Rights of the People of India as British Citizens:

(a) That all Indian subjects of His Majesty and all the subjects naturalised or resident in India are equal before the law, and there shall be no penal or administrative law in force in the Dominions, whether substantive or procedural, of a discriminative nature;

(b) That no Indian subject of His Majesty shall be liable to suffer in liberty, of life, property, or of association, free speech or in respect of writing, except under sentence by an ordinary Court of Justice, and as a result of lawful and open trial;

(c) That every Indian subject shall be entitled to bear arms, subject to the purchase of a license, as in Great Britain, and that the right shall not be taken away save by a sentence of an ordinary Court of Justice;

(d) That the Press shall be free, and that no license or security shall be demanded on the registration of a press or a newspaper;

(e) That corporal punishment shall not be inflicted on any Indian subject of His Majesty, save under conditions applying equally to all other British subjects.

Resolution VII was on 'Mahomedan representation', which was passed unanimously as follows:[63]

Resolution VII. The proportion of Mahomedans in the Legislative Councils and the Legislative Assembly as laid down in the Congress League Scheme must be maintained.

On women's franchise, the following resolution was moved by Sarojini Naidu, which was passed by a majority vote:[64]

Resolution VIII. Women, possessing the same qualifications as are laid down for men in any part of the scheme shall not be disqualified on account of sex.

Moderates such as Banerjea who were satisfied with the recommendations of the Montford Report and unhappy with the sway enjoyed by Extremists such as Tilak and Pal over the Congress, seceded from the Congress to found the All-India Moderates Conference, which convened on 1 November 1918. Here were Banerjea's words of anguish on the tables being turned compared to the Surat session, which led to the ouster of the Extremists:[65]

We had contributed to build up the great National Institution with our life-blood. We had raised it up from infancy to adolescence, from adolescence to maturity, and now, in full view of the crowning reward of our lifelong labours, we found the sacred temple of national unity swayed by divided counsels, resounding with the voice of conflict and controversy, and divorced from the healing accents of moderation and prudence. We could not but secede; for the difference between those who captured the machinery of the Congress and ourselves was fundamental.

R.C. Majumdar was of the view that the founding of the All-India Moderates Conference was the handiwork of Montagu, who had also facilitated the setting up of the National Liberation Party.[66] While the Congress once again saw an open rift between the Moderates and the Extremists, the League's position in the Montford Report was similar to that of the Extremists, although much more reserved to avoid giving the impression of disloyalty, especially after the Allied victory in the war. After all, the League was more interested in negotiating with the British on the issue of preservation of the Ottoman Caliphate. In the special session of the League organised at around the same time as the Congress's special session, the chairman of the reception committee, Sir Fazulbhoy Currimbhoy, expressed his gratitude on behalf of the League for the recommendations of the Report and proposed a few modifications.[67] He clarified that although securing self-government was a goal the League was committed to, its primary goal was to protect and defend Muslim interests.[68]

In his presidential speech, the Raja of Mahmudabad said that the Report fell short of natural and legitimate expectations which had arisen as a consequence of Montagu's declaration of 20 August 1917. The Raja then proceeded to share his three-point counter-proposal to the recommendations of the Report, which were similar to the recommendations of the Congress. Resolutions II, III and VII were expressions of disappointment with the Report and sought adoption of the proposals contained in the Congress–League Scheme.[69]

Similar resolutions were passed at the respective annual sessions of the Congress and the League in December 1918. Since the subject of the discussions and the resolutions passed at these annual sessions were broadly the same as at the special sessions, I will discuss only those aspects of the annual sessions which were additionally noteworthy. It bears noting that the 1918 annual sessions of the Congress and the League were being held after the conclusion of the First World War and before the commencement of the Paris Peace Conference which would result in the creation of the League of Nations and the Treaty of Versailles being signed between the Allied Powers and Germany. Importantly, the Ottoman empire had been defeated and was in a shambles, which, naturally, was a matter of great concern for Muslims in Bharat. It is against this backdrop that the deliberations on the right to self-determination, self-government and support for the Khilafat Movement at the Congress's session must be understood. As part of his welcome speech, the chairman of the reception committee, Ajmal Khan, spoke of Gandhi's support for the Khilafat Movement as follows:[70]

Closely connected with the War and its results is the question of Muslim Holy places, the Khilafat and Muslim States. I think it necessary to give expression to Muslim feeling on these questions from this Platform, for, I feel that no assembly which claims to represent the whole of India can ignore questions so profoundly affecting 70 millions of her population. To show the vital relations of these questions with Indian politics and the safety of the Empire, *I cannot do better than quote the acknowledged and revered leader of the country Mahatma Gandhi,* to whom I take this public opportunity to offer the grateful thanks of my co-religionists for his sincere and brotherly sympathy in their troubles and for his brave and outspoken championship of their cause. Need I assure him that my co-religionists fully and cordially reciprocate the brotherly feeling expressed by him? In this sympathy and good-will lies the secret of true unity.

In his letter to the Viceroy, dated Delhi, the 29th April, 1918, Mahatma Gandhi writes:

'*Lastly I would like to request His Majesty's Ministers to give definite assurances about Mahomedan States. I am sure you know that every Mahomedan is deeply interested in them. As a Hindu I cannot be indifferent to their cause. Their sorrows must be our sorrows. In the most scrupulous regard for the rights of these States and for the Muslim sentiment as to the places of worship and in your just and timely treatment of Indian claim to Home Rule lies the safety of the Empire.*'

No better exposition of the case could be made.

Mussulmans in India occupied a peculiarly difficult and delicate position during this War and it does not need my statement to show with what commendable restraint they conducted themselves. The Government was engaged in a war with their brothers in faith and most painful and provoking news about their Holy Places incessantly poured in. They were not deficient in courage to give expression to their feelings during the continuance of the War but they preferred to wait till after the great conflict was over.

Mahatma Gandhi has said that for the safety of the Empire it is necessary to regard most scrupulously the right of Muslim States and Muslim sentiment about their places of worship. I would like to add that it is necessary to do so for the ordered and peaceful progress of the world. Islam is not a fraternity which is confined to India alone. Its more than 300 million members are scattered all over the globe. As Mussulmans, they take the keenest brotherly interest in each other's welfare and desire to see their States in the world free and independent. They want to live honourably and let others live honourably. I need not point out the feeling of resentment and the sense of wrong that it will create throughout the Muslim world in general and among the Mussulmans of India in particular if, in the contemplated reconstruction of the world, the integrity and independence of Muslim States suffer at the hand of the Allies who to-day stand forth as champions of freedom and liberators of the human race. This general sense of wrong, it is needless for me to say, cannot promote that feeling of sympathy and willing co-operation which can never become dispensable. Ladies and Gentlemen, it has been our painful duty to observe the disastrous results of ignoring this great fact. But for the entry of Turkey on the side of Germany this war would have ended long before now. Is it wise to repeat that mistake? No reconstruction of the world which is not based on an equal and impartial application of the principles of freedom and liberty to all nationalities of the world can be permanent. What is more, it can never be just and honest and will never bring true peace to this world of ours.

The safety and independence of the Holy places is another question which touches Mussulmans deeply. These places are sanctified by the pious memories of their great prophets and sacred injunctions of their Holy Book, and are in fact a very considerable phenomenon in their social, political and religious life. Their present condition is causing them great anxiety and profound pain. They want to see them in truly independent Muslim hands and I urge upon the Government the recognition of their most cherished and deep-seated religious sentiment.

Closely associated with this is the question of Khilafat. It is a purely religious question whose decision rests entirely with Mussulmans. It is a part and parcel of the Muslim faith and no kind of outside interference with its settlement will be tolerated by the Mussulmans. If all the powers of the world combine to force a Khalifa on Mussulmans the humblest of them will not follow him. If any one can have a right to choose a new religion for Mussulmans he can also appoint a Khalifa for them. It is not for me to point out that when the meanest nationalities and the smallest countries are being given the fullest liberty in temporal matters it will be highly detrimental to the great principles of true statesmanship which are the very basis of every civilised and good government, if Mussulmans are made to feel that it is proposed to interfere with their religious questions. [Emphases added]

Pandit Madan Mohan Malaviya, who was the president of the session, threw his weight behind the Khilafat Movement as follows:[71]

... More proud are we of the fact that throughout all these four years of trial and tribulation, in the face of the extreme suffering which the war inflicted upon our people, and even when the sky seemed to be much overcast, India remained unshaken equally in her loyalty to the King-Emperor and in her resolve to do her utmost to help the Empire till the end. This is particularly noteworthy in the case of our Mussulman brethren. Every one knows how deep are their religious sentiments towards Turkey, and how profound their concern in everything that affects her. When, therefore, unfortunately, Turkey was persuaded by the Central Powers to join them against our King-Emperor and his Allies, the feelings of our Mahomedan brethren were put to the sorest test. No thoughtful Mahomedan could be indifferent to the fate which might overtake Turkey. But it must to-day be a source of the sincerest satisfaction to every Indian Mahomedan who loves his country and community, that the community did not at any time allow its religious sentiments to overpower its sense of duty to the King and to the motherland, and that it remained firm in its support of the cause of the Empire. This is a fact of great moment in the history of our country. It is a matter for sincere thankfulness and congratulations to all our fellow-subjects and ourselves.

On the subject of the right to self-determination by 'nations', which featured prominently at the Paris Peace Conference (as discussed in the first book), Malaviya said as follows:[72]

The Principle of Self-determination

Ladies and Gentlemen, let us make it clear what we mean when we talk of self-determination. There are two aspects of self-determination, as it has been spoken of in the Peace proposals. One is that the people of certain colonies and other places should have the right to say whether they will live under the suzerainty of one power or of another. So far as we Indians are concerned we have no need to that we do not desire to exercise that election. Since India passed directly under the British Crown, we have owed allegiance to the Sovereign of England. We stand unshaken in that allegiance. We gladly renewed our allegiance to His Majesty the King-Emperor in person when he was pleased to visit India in 1911 after his Coronation in England. We still desire to remain subjects of the British Crown. There is, however, the second and no less important, aspect of self-determination, namely, that being under the British Crown, we should be allowed complete responsible government on the lines of the Dominions, in the administration of all our domestic affairs. *We are not yet asking for this either. We are asking for a measure of self-government which we have indicated by our Congress–League Scheme of 1916. We urge that the measure of self-government, i.e. of responsible government, to be given to us should be judged and determined in the light of the principle of self-determination which has emerged triumphant out of this devastating war. In order that this should be done it is not necessary that the proposals of reform which have been elaborated by Mr. Montagu and Lord Chelmsford should be laid aside and a brand new scheme be prepared. The Special Congress and the Moslem League have expressed their willingness to accept those proposals with the modifications and improvements which they have advocated.* This great Congress representing the people of all classes and creeds—Hindus, Mussulmans, Parsis and Christians—representing all interests, landholders and tenants, merchants and businessmen, educationists, publicists and representatives of other sections of the people, is assembled here to-day to express the mind of the people on this question. *One special and particularly happy feature of this Congress is the presence at it of nearly nine hundred delegates of the tenant class who have come at great sacrifice, from far and near, to join their voice with the rest of their countrymen in asking for a substantial* measure of self-government. *This representative Congress of the people of India will determine and declare what in its opinion should be the measure of reform which should be introduced into the country. Let the British Government give effect to the principle of self-determination in India by accepting the proposals so put forward by the representatives of the people of India. Let the preamble to the Statute which is under preparation incorporate the principle of self-determination and provide that the representatives of the people of India shall have an effective voice in determining the future steps of progress towards complete responsible government. This will produce contentment and gratitude among the people of India and strengthen their attachment to the British Empire.*

Ladies and Gentlemen, I think I have said enough to show how strong is our case on the ground of justice for a substantial measure of Responsible Government. *While we have noted with thankfulness the attitude of British statesmen towards the cause of Indian Reform, while we have noted with satisfaction that in their election manifestoes Mr. Lloyd George, Mr. Bonar Law, Mr. Asquith, in short, leaders of all parties in the United Kingdom, have pledged themselves to the introduction of Responsible Government in India, we regret to find that a Limited Liability Company of businessmen known as the Indo-British Association have organised themselves in London with the distinct object of opposing the cause of Indian Reform (Cries of shame, shame).* This Indo-British Association and other narrow-minded European and Anglo-Indian bodies in India and in England, who are opposed to any power being transferred to Indians *have been misusing the Rowlatt Committee Report to create a wrong impression in the minds of the British public that the people of India are disaffected towards the British Crown. This is a wicked attempt. One should have thought that with the overwhelming evidence of the loyalty of the people of India to the British Crown, fresh in the minds of the English people and of the Allied world, not even the worst detractors of Indians would venture to make such a dastardly attempt at this juncture. The Rowlatt Committee itself has brought the fact of that loyalty into great prominence. The Committee have summed up their conclusions as follows:*

'We have now investigated all the conspiracies connected with the revolutionary movement. *In Bombay they have been purely Brahmin and mostly Chitpavan. (I am quoting from the Report and not expressing my own opinion.) In Bengal the conspirators have been young men belonging to the educated classes. Their propaganda has been elaborate, persistent and ingenious. In their own province it has produced a long series of murders and robberies. In Bihar and Orissa, the United Provinces, the Central Provinces and Madras it took no root but occasionally led to crime or disorder. In the Punjab the return of emigrants from America bent on revolution and bloodshed produced numerous outrages and the Ghadr Conspiracy of 1915. In Burma too the Ghadr movement was active but was arrested. Finally came a Muhammadan conspiracy confined to a small clique of fanatics and designed to overthrow British rule with foreign aid. All these plots were directed towards one and the same objective the overthrow by force of*

British rule in India. Sometimes they have been isolated, sometimes they have been interconnected, sometimes they have been encouraged and supported by German influence.'

Now, ladies and gentlemen, assuming that the whole of this statement is correct, let us see what the Committee say further about these plots. They say: 'All have been successfully encountered with the support of Indian loyalty.' (Hear, hear.) This should be enough to silence the calumniators of India. *Mr. Montagu and Lord Chelmsford observed in their report on Indian Constitutional Reforms: 'Whatever qualifications may be needed in the case of particular classes, the people of India as a whole are in genuine sympathy with the cause which the Allies represent. However much they may find fault with the Government, they are true in their loyalty to the British Crown.' In another place they truly observed: 'The loyalty of the country generally was emphasised by the attempts made by a very small section of the population to create trouble.'* I most sincerely deplore, as I am sure every thoughtful Indian does, that any of our youths should have been misled into what the Rowlatt Committee have described as a movement of perverted religion and equally perverted patriotism. I deplore that even a few of our young men should have been misled into criminal organisation or conspiracy against the Government. I equally deplore that they should have committed any acts of violence against any of their fellowmen. But let not the misdeeds of a small number of unfortunately misguided youths be pitted against the unswerving loyalty of 320 millions of the people of India. It is not fair. [Emphases added]

Apart from the resolutions on self-government, the application of the principle of self-determination to Bharat and the release of the Ali Brothers, resolution X, which denounced the recommendations of the Rowlatt Committee Report on the grounds that they would interfere with the fundamental rights of Indians and impede the growth of public opinion, was also passed. It was argued that this would defeat the very object of the constitutional reforms being sought—namely, public participation in the political process.

Coming to the League's session of December 1918, it too was held in Delhi. The presidential speech of Fazlul Haque was dominated by Muslim apprehensions over the fate of Turkey, the demand for the release of the Ali Brothers and Maulana Abul Kalam Azad, and objections to the Montford Report, which were jointly prepared with the Congress at the special session held in Bombay. The following is a critical excerpt from Haque's speech, which remains relevant even today:[73]

Questions Relating to the Khilafat and Muslim Holy Places

Brethren, I fully realize that I have already trespassed too much on your time and patience, but I cannot resume my seat without a brief reference to the questions relating to the Khilafat and the protection of our holy places. You have heard the speech of Dr. M.A. Ansari on both these points. He has dealt with all questions relating to both these vital affairs so thoroughly that there is hardly anything for me to say. In my opinion, the question of the Khilafat should be dealt with by Muslims themselves without interference from non-Muslims, and our holy places should also be immune from non-Muslim influences. We should object to having anything to do with political mummers who outwardly profess Islam and claim some amount of influence in public. The revolt of the Sherif of Mecca has endangered the future of our holy places, and the world of Islam is watching with sorrow and anxiety the effects of the Sherif's declaration of Independence. I wish to leave these questions to be dealt with by the revered Ulema whom I see present here; but I cannot but say a few words on one point which is likely to escape the notice of officials. All questions relating to the Khilafat and the protection of our holy places are intimately bound up with the vital articles of our faith. Our rulers are in the habit of distorting political problems by setting up their tools and sycophants to defend official points of view; but however entertaining this pastime may be in the case of political affairs, it is fraught with danger if the experiment is tried with reference to questions relating to our religious views. *We are loyal subjects of the rulers, and are prepared to prove our loyalty in actual practice by making sacrifices. But this temporal loyalty is subject to the limitation imposed by our undoubted loyalty to our faith. We wish to warn our rulers that in making sacrifices one after another, the dividing line may soon be reached; and we need hardly emphasize that in case there is a conflict between Divine Laws and the mandates of our rulers, every true Musalman will allow the Divine Commandments to prevail over human laws, even at the risk of laying down his life.* [Emphasis added]

While resolutions were passed on each of the topics discussed in the presidential speech, here's the one on the subject of the Caliphate/Khilafat wherein the nexus between the position of Muslim powers outside Bharat and the political position of Muslims in Bharat was spelt out with clarity:[74]

Having regard to the fact that the Indian Musalmans take a deep interest in the fate of their co-religionists outside India, and that the collapse of the Muslim Powers of the world is bound to have an adverse influence on the political importance of the Musalmans in the country, and the annihilation of the military powers of Islam in the world cannot but have a far-reaching effect on the minds of even the loyal Musalmans of India, the All-India Muslim League considers it to be its duty to place before the Government of India and His Majesty's Government the true sentiments of the Muslim community, and requests that the British Representatives at the Peace Conference will use their influence and see that in the territorial and political redistribution to be made, the fullest consideration should be paid to the requirements of the Islamic law with regard to full and independent control by the Sultan of Turkey,

Khalifa of the Prophet, over the holy places and over the Jazirat-ul-Arab as delimited in the Muslim books. The League further hopes that in determining the political relations of the Empire, for the future, His Majesty's Ministers shall pay the fullest consideration to the universal and deep sentiment of the Musalmans of India, and that resolute attempts should be made to effect a complete reconciliation and lasting concord between the Empire and Muslim states, based on equity and justice, in the interests alike of the British Empire and the Muslim world.

The global and interconnected nature of the ummah, which both Shah Waliullah Dehlawi and Syed Jamal al-Din al-Afghani were keen to impress upon the Muslims in Bharat, found unequivocal and clear expression in the above-extracted resolution of the Muslim League. Importantly, the divided loyalties of the Muslim community, or perhaps the Muslims' *overriding* loyalty to the community, owing to their religious obligations, too was captured pithily in the resolution. This sentiment, which spoke of a Muslim community without or notwithstanding political boundaries ('the Muslim world'), coupled with Gandhi's support for it, would effectively shape the events of 1919 and thereafter. In the next chapter, the momentous events of the period between 1919 and 1924, which cemented the road to Pakistan through further entrenchment of pan-Islamism and Muslim separatism, shall be discussed.

Gandhi, Rowlatt, Government of India Act of 1919, Khilafat and Non-Cooperation (1919–1924)

This card, with the handwritten title 'Mr Mahamad Ali and Mr Shaukat Ali, Homerule leaders' was sent by B. Bhorey from Baroda to Mrs A.G. Strong, Esq., Professor of Household Arts, Olaga University, New Zealand.

The period from 1919 to 1924 was peppered with multiple major developments, not all of which can be covered here. For the purposes of the discussion at hand, I will limit myself to the ones relevant to the theme and scope of this book, and take the narrative forward. To this end, the title of this chapter reflects the specific developments I intend to focus on to connect the dots. In particular, this period witnessed a series of major Hindu–Muslim riots, the Moplah Riots being just one of them. Given the importance of this event and the grotesque 'secular' distortion it has been subjected to, I have consciously chosen to dedicate the final chapter to briefly examining four major riots—those of Malegaon, Malabar, Gulbarga and Kohat—in order to connect them with Middle Eastern consciousness and the Wahhabi Movement dealt with in the first section of the book.

In the previous chapter, I drew attention to the fact that Gandhi's support for the Khilafat Movement was acknowledged by Ajmal Khan in his welcome speech at the Congress's thirty-third annual session in 1918 in Delhi. It is noteworthy that only a year before, at the 1917 annual session, Gandhi was referred to as M.K. Gandhi and not as 'Mahatma Gandhi'. Also, this much is clear from the annual resolutions of the Congress and the scholarly literature—that support for the Khilafat did *not* start with Gandhi and was certainly *not* limited to him. It bears noting that thanks to the Home Rule Movement, the period from 1916 to 1918 saw Annie Besant and Tilak occupy centre stage and gather the support of the masses for the cause. Therefore, it could be said that despite recognition for his fight against racial discrimination in South Africa and for his abilities as a thinker, Gandhi was not exactly a force to reckon with at least until 1917. By this, I mean that he was not in a position to influence mass opinion either within the Congress or outside of it. What, then, explains the sudden showering of attention on Gandhi at the 1918 session with the use of the honorific 'Mahatma' and the later association of Gandhi with support for the Khilafat Movement in the popular discourse? To understand this, a brief primer on Gandhi's rise after his return to Bharat from South Africa in late 1914 becomes important. Given the surfeit of literature on him, the scope of this primer is again limited to the discussion at hand.

From 1894 to 1914, Gandhi fought against apartheid and racism in South Africa. His use of Satyagraha between 1906 and 1914 resulted in the enactment of the Indian Relief Act of 1914, which addressed some of the grievances of the Indian community in South Africa.[1] During this period, he attended the Congress's annual sessions on and off, starting at least from 1901. As stated in the previous chapter, according to Daniel Argov, Gandhi stayed out of active politics for a year after his return to Bharat in late 1914, and even turned down the post of president of the Congress for its annual session that year.[2] In 1915, he founded the Sabarmati Ashram in Ahmedabad.[3] Despite his first-hand experience with colonial ethno-religious supremacism for two decades, Gandhi remained a British loyalist in the same mould as the Moderates, which was evident from the views he expressed in his *Hind Swaraj* published in 1909. His endorsement of the vision and methods of the Moderates was not a surprise, given his mentorship by Gokhale.[4] For all his pacifism, Gandhi actively recruited men on behalf of the British to support its War efforts (for the First World War or the Great War). To be fair, it could be argued that the leaders of this period, including Gandhi, were forced to choose between a known devil and a known and perhaps worse devil of that period—namely Germany.

Importantly, what needs to be highlighted is Gandhi's opposition to the Home Rule Movement. S.R. Mehrotra points out that when Annie Besant invited Gandhi to join the Movement, he refused to, on the grounds that he did *not* share her distrust of the British and did not want to take advantage of the War to secure Home Rule for Bharat.[5] He went to the extent of saying that Congress ought to withdraw all resolutions with even a whisper of Home Rule or 'responsible government' during the War. Mehrotra underscores the fact that even Montagu recorded in his diary that Gandhi wanted India's millions to leap to the assistance of the British throne and inspire loyalty for Britain in every Indian. When Jinnah supported Home Rule, even he was exhorted by Gandhi to support recruitment for the War if he wanted to secure Home Rule[6]—such was Gandhi's undying faith in the British sense of justice and fair play. Clearly, in his formative years in Indian politics, Gandhi was more Moderate than the staunchest of Moderates.

The years 1917 and 1918 were important for Gandhi. In 1917, he launched a Satyagraha, his first in Bharat, in Champaran, Bihar, on behalf of the peasants working on the indigo plantations owned by Europeans.[7] This incident gave Gandhi traction, because his Satyagraha did force the government to take notice of the condition of the indigo peasants. In 1918, Gandhi took up two issues, both of which put him on the national map: first, the publishing of the report of the Sedition Committee headed by Justice Sidney Rowlatt, also known as the Rowlatt Report; and second, the end of the First World War with the defeat of the Central Powers, including the Ottoman empire, lending a greater sense of urgency to the growing Khilafat Movement in Bharat. It is not possible to deal with these two developments in watertight compartments and in a linear fashion, since in 1919 the controversy surrounding the Rowlatt Bills, the massacre in Jallianwalla Bagh, the Khilafat Movement and the discontent with respect to the Government of India Act of 1919 based on the Montford Report went hand in hand to create an explosive mix. Therefore, I will do my best to present a panoramic overview which allows for understanding the big picture.

The Rowlatt Act and the Jallianwalla Bagh Massacre

In Chapter 5, I had recommended a book by James Campbell Ker on the Revolutionary Movement in Bharat between 1907 and 1917, apart from Volume 2 of R.C. Majumdar's *History of the Freedom Movement in India* which also contains a detailed look at the revolutionary activity in Bharat. The third document which I would strongly urge readers to read, to understand the extent and seriousness of the Revolutionary Movement, especially from an official British perspective, is the 286-page Report of the six-member Sedition Committee prepared under Justice Sidney Rowlatt as its president. The Report was commissioned by Chelmsford with the approval of Montagu on 10 December 1917, and was submitted by the committee to the British government on 15 April 1918.[8] The following was the mandate of the Rowlatt Committee:

1. To investigate and report on the nature and extent of the criminal conspiracies connected with the Revolutionary Movement in India;

Indians were forced to crawl up Kucha Kurrichhan street on their hands and knees as punishment by orders from General Dyer as revenge for assault on Ms Sherwood, a Christian missionary, 1919.

2. To examine and consider the difficulties that have arisen in dealing with such conspiracies and to advise as to the legislation, if any, necessary to enable Government to deal effectively with them.

The introduction to the Report makes for an interesting read since it sought to give the impression that the Revolutionary Movement was effectively the attempt of the Chitpavan Brahmins to regain their lost power, which they had wielded as Peshwas under the Maratha empire. Therefore, the British government zeroed in on the Brahmins of Poona for indications of revolutionary activity.[9] To this end, the first chapter of the Report examined 'Revolutionary Conspiracies in Bombay' and pinned the blame for them on the public Ganapati festivals organised by Tilak. The assassination of the Poona Plague Commissioner, Rand, by the Chapekar Brothers was attributed to Tilak's articles in his *Kesari*. Tilak himself was referred to as '*Bal Gangadhar Tilak, a Chitpavan Brahmin*'. In the subsequent twelve chapters, the Report dealt with the revolutionary activities in Bengal, including the rise of the samitis, followed by such activities in Bihar, Orissa, the United Provinces, the Central Provinces, Punjab, Madras and Burma. In paragraph 131, the Report specifically noted as follows:[10]

> So far all the trouble had been Hindu but the war between Turkey and Italy and the apparent indifference of Great Britain throughout the Balkan War bitterly annoyed some Muhammadans of the Punjab ...

Chapter XIV was exclusively dedicated to Muslim activity and was titled 'A Muhammadan Current', and contained a brief discussion on the continued existence of the Wahhabi sect in the NWFP *even as of 1918*. Tucked into paragraph 175 was perhaps the true apprehension that led to the formation of the Rowlatt Committee and the need for a new legislation: a suitable substitute for the Defence of India Act of 1915 upon its lapsation. This legislation was enacted to deal with both nationalist and revolutionary activities during the First World War, in particular to deter collaboration between the Revolutionaries and foreign powers to destabilise British power in India. After all, Bharat had made tremendous contributions in terms of men and material to the British War effort. So, apart from the 'dangerous convicts' interned under the Defence of India Act, who were to be released at the end of their terms, the soldiers returning from the Great War were another concern for the British Indian government. There was a fear that they could stir up discontent in view of their heightened sense of political awareness as well as their enhanced self-esteem. After having served the British empire with their blood, they would not be happy to come back home only to be treated once again as second-grade human beings and third-rate citizens of the empire. The British-made famines in Punjab would only add to their sense of frustration, which in turn would strengthen revolutionary activity in Punjab and Bengal, the two major flashpoints for the empire in Bharat.[11] The third development that added a sense of urgency to the need for strengthening legislative measures was the growing chorus in support of the Khilafat in Bharat in view of the feared dismemberment of the Ottoman empire to add to the humiliation of its resounding defeat.

In paragraph 177 of Chapter XVII, the Report suggested two kinds of measures, punitive and preventive, to contain extremist, revolutionary and anti-British activities of any hue. The measures included a prohibition on persons convicted of offences against the state from addressing public meetings for a period of two years after their release, apart from restrictions on their movements. Paragraph 178 of the Report recommended emergency measures of two kinds, again punitive and preventive. This envisaged emergency measures coming into force through a mere notification by the Governor General, although subject to safeguards. In paragraph 181, the Report suggested emergency provisions for speedy trials, which allowed for dispensing with juries since they could be affected by public opinion. The same paragraph also contained a suggestion to do away with the right to appeal, which would apply equally, at least in theory, to convictions and acquittals. These and a few other such proposals, including restrictions on inter-provincial movements, were suggested.

Naturally, this Report was discussed with great concern and resolutions were passed both by the Congress and the League in their special sessions in Bombay[12,13] in August–September 1918 as well as in their annual sessions in Delhi in December 1918.[14] Two bills were introduced in the Imperial Legislative Council on 6 February 1919 pursuant to the Rowlatt Report. One was a temporary measure, a stopgap arrangement upon lapsation of the Defence of India Act, and the other a permanent one. The former resulted in the Anarchical and Revolutionary Crimes Act in mid-March 1919,[15] which would be infamously known as the Rowlatt Act or the Black Act.[16] Illustrating the nature of this Act, its part I provided for speedy trials with no right of appeal, and for the trial court to convene at any place in-camera, meaning the proceeding would not be a public one, which is one of the expectations of a fair trial. Under part II, the movement of a suspect could be severely restricted by the local government, and under part III, the local government could arrest a person without a warrant. The fact that such provisions could be pressed into service at the discretion of the Governor General exacerbated their already capricious and draconian nature.

When the Bill for this Act was introduced in the Legislative Council, it was justified by the government on the ground that normal laws were inadequate to deal with Revolutionaries and their activities, which was borne out by the poor rate of convictions. Leaders of the Congress and the League protested, saying the proposed law could be misused against legitimate political expression and dissent, in the process defeating the very object of constitutional reforms even to the unsatisfactory extent proposed by the Montford Report.[17] In other words, they saw it as a continuation of the Minto–Morley policy of 'repression and reform', where one hand would take away what the other hand gave. To be fair to Montagu, he agreed with the protesters that the Black Act would only create more trouble for his successors and those of Chelmsford.[18] Advocates of Home Rule pointed out that the best way to curb revolutionary activity was to grant self-government. On this, even Surendranath Banerjea agreed, citing the example of Sinn Fein in Ireland and the positive effect of the grant of self-government to that country.[19] Despite these protestations and suggestions, the government chose to bulldoze its way through them, which only added fuel to the protests.

In the meantime, Gandhi formed the Satyagraha Sabha in Bombay in February 1919 along with leaders such as Vallabhbhai Patel and Sarojini Naidu, to protest against the Rowlatt Bills.[20] On 24 February 1919, the following Satyagraha Pledge was signed by members of the Sabha:[21]

> Being conscientiously of opinion that the Bills known as the Indian Criminal Law (Amendment) Bill No. I of 1919 and the Criminal Law (Emergency Powers) Bill No. II of 1919 are unjust, subversive of the principle of liberty and justice and destructive of the elementary rights of individual on which the safety of the country as a whole and the State itself is based. we solemnly affirm that in the event of these Bills becoming law and until they are withdrawn, we shall refuse civilly to obey those laws and such other laws as a Committee to be hereafter appointed may think fit and we further affirm that in this struggle we will faithfully follow the truth and refrain from violence to life, person or property.

The seeds of the Non-Cooperation Movement as well as the idea of Civil Disobedience were captured in this Pledge. In fact, Banerjea called the Rowlatt Act and the opposition to it that followed, the parent of the Non-Cooperation Movement.[22] A good number of Moderates in the Congress as well as Annie Besant were opposed to the idea of Satyagraha or passive resistance because they apprehended anarchy, given the mood of the country.[23] While this may have been a fair assessment of the situation, this was, in fact, a turning point for Besant as well since she was gradually moving towards the side of the Moderates which, as we shall see, would also translate to a change in her attitude towards the Montford Reforms. To once again paraphrase Tilak, labels such as Moderates and Extremists were fairly fluid and kept changing with time, circumstance and issue.[24]

Coming back to Gandhi's Satyagraha Sabha, the Pledge was made public on 1 March 1919.[25] On 21 March 1919, the first Rowlatt Bill became an Act, at which time Gandhi was in Madras.[26] He informed Chakravarti Rajagopalachari ('Rajaji') that he *had a dream the night before* that the country should observe a general hartal or strike and observe a day of 'self-purification' through fasting and prayer to express its opposition to the Act.[27] The date of the hartal was originally fixed for 30 March 1919 but subsequently pushed to 6 April 1919. As a result, some parts of the country, including Delhi, observed hartal on the former date and the rest on the latter date. On 30 March, trouble broke out between the protesters, including Swami Shraddhananda, and the police in Delhi, resulting in eight deaths and multiple wounded due to police firing.[28] The local leaders in Delhi called upon Gandhi to visit them. However, Gandhi's entry into Punjab and Delhi was prohibited, and he was sent to Bombay with police escort. His arrest led to riots in Ahmedabad and the death of twenty-eight protesters, and the unrest there did not abate until 13 April 1919, when Gandhi was allowed to enter the city to restore peace and order.[29] Thanks to the countrywide public response to Gandhi's Satyagraha, he was now seen as a national leader who commanded the following of the masses. In view of the riots in Delhi, Ahmedabad and other parts of the country, perhaps Gandhi saw sense in Besant's opposition to his passive resistance and called off the Satyagraha until he could raise a corps of 'true Satyagrahis' who could conduct themselves peacefully.[30] Without being insensitive to the loss of lives, it is indeed surprising to note that the leaders of the time, in particular the Moderates, believed that it was possible to achieve Home Rule, let alone independence, without shedding blood, and that too from a coloniser who had enough incentive to hold on to Bharat. After all, at the end of the First World War, Britain had more reasons to keep Bharat within its imperial fold than before, given the cash cow it represented and the supply of men it provided to fight the empire's wars.

While Gandhi was busy drawing up the rules of an ideal Satyagraha and the virtues of an ideal Satyagrahi, Punjab was on the boil under Lieutenant Governor Michael O'Dwyer, who was keen on stamping out all political activity, peaceful or otherwise, which in his opinion undermined British rule. He did not want the Congress to 'contaminate' Punjab with its agitation for self-government and its opposition to the Rowlatt Act. The arrest of two Congress organisers, Dr S. Kitchlew and Dr Satyapal, on 10 April 1919 for deportation to Dharamshala under the Defence of India Act led to widespread protests and destruction of public property, resulting in the army being called in to control the situation.[31] In particular, Lahore, Kasur and Gujranwala witnessed violent confrontations between the protesters and authorities. With reports of violence from Delhi and Calcutta also coming in, Dwyer was convinced that a nationwide conspiracy was afoot to overthrow the British government.[32] To understand the British government's version of the events preceding the Jallianwalla Bagh Massacre and those that led to it, one must read the 362-page Disorders Inquiry Committee Report of 1919–1920, better known as the Hunter Committee Report, a comprehensive document.[33] Named after the president of the committee, Lord William Hunter (not to be confused with W.W. Hunter referred to earlier in this book), this document reveals the colonial consciousness of the British establishment, for it sought to *justify* the Jallianwalla Bagh Massacre, as we shall see shortly.

In his speech delivered before the Punjab Legislative Council on 7 April 1919 on the need for martial law in Punjab, which was de facto in force from 10 April 1919,[34] Dwyer expressed his position publicly as follows:[35]

> The Government of this Province is and will remain determined that public order, which was maintained so successfully during the time of war, shall not be disturbed in times of peace. Action has, therefore, already been taken under the Defence of India Act against certain individuals at Lahore and Amritsar, who, whatever their motives, were openly endeavouring to rouse public feeling against the Government. The British Government which has crushed foreign foes and quelled internal rebellion, could afford to despise these agitators, but it has a duty of protection to the young and the ignorant, whom they may incite to mischief and crime, while themselves standing aside. I, therefore, take this opportunity of warning all, who are connected with political movements in the province, that they will be held responsible for the proper conduct of meetings, which they organise, for the language used at and consequences that follow such meetings.

He then referred to the demonstrations of 6 April:

> The recent puerile demonstrations against the Rowlatt Act in both Lahore and Amritsar would be ludicrous, if they did not indicate, how easily the ignorant and the credulous people, not one in a thousand knows anything of the measure, can be misled. Those who want only to mislead them incur a serious responsibility. I would remind them of President Lincoln's famous saying: 'you can, if you are very clever and very unscrupulous, mislead all people for sometime and some people for all time, but you cannot mislead all people for all time. Those who appeal to ignorance rather than to reason have a day of reckoning in store for them.'

Dwyer could not have been clearer that he meant business. After the mayhem caused by the arrest of Dr Kitchlew and Dr Satyapal, Brigadier General Dyer arrived in Amritsar on 11 April. All public meetings were prohibited from 12 April onwards. However, the Hunter Committee Report itself observed that adequate steps were not undertaken to make proclamation of the prohibition known to the public. On the evening of 12 April, it was peacefully announced by the organisers that a public meeting would be held the next day at 4.30 p.m. at Jallianwalla Bagh. Despite this announcement, no measures were taken by the authorities to inform the public of the prohibition on public meetings and to dissuade them from holding it. Even on the fateful day of 13 April 1919, which happened to be Baisakhi, no attempt was made to prevent entry of the public into the venue of the meeting.[36] By all accounts, including British, which were not particularly sympathetic to the cause of Bharatiyas, Dyer arrived at the venue with fifty troops within minutes of commencement of the meeting. The access points to and from the Bagh were blocked. Without any warning being issued to the crowd to disperse, Dyer ordered his troops to open fire at the densest sections of the crowd which numbered anywhere between 10,000 and 20,000, including women, children, infants and the elderly. The firing went on for ten minutes until the ammunition was exhausted, by which time 1,650 rounds had been fired into the crowd. More would have been killed but for the fact that the passageway leading to the Bagh was too narrow for the two armoured cars containing machine guns that Dyer had brought for the operation. Dyer had no compunction in stating before the Hunter Committee that he was limited only by the paucity of ammunition and inability to take the machine guns through the narrow passageway of the Bagh.[37]

While British government accounts pegged the number of dead at 400, the Congress inquiry committee's estimate was at least 1,000.[38] Dyer made no bones of the fact that his intention was *not* to seek dispersal of the crowd but to instil terror in the heart of Punjab in order to restore law and order there.[39] Apart from the people who were killed on 13 April, several others died for want of water and medical attention at the Bagh owing to a curfew order imposed by Dyer on the very day of the massacre, with instructions to shoot at sight anyone found on the streets after 8 p.m.[40] This prevented anguished relatives from even stepping outside their homes to help their wounded loved ones and cremate or bury the dead. The curfew order remained in force for weeks, contributing to more deaths, and martial law was formally imposed only on 15 April 1919.[41] During this period, water and electricity supplies to Amritsar were cut off.[42] To add to it, a 'crawling order' was issued to teach the 'natives' a lesson, at the complaint of an English missionary, Marcella Sherwood.[43] During the riots that erupted after the arrest of Satyapal and Kitchlew, Europeans, including Marcella Sherwood, were attacked. Although Sherwood was rescued by a Hindu family, Dyer issued a crawling order which required the 'natives' to crawl past the spot where she was attacked. He justified the order, saying that since the 'natives' anyway crawled to see their gods, they must crawl before a British woman too since she was as sacred as their gods.

Lieutenant Governor Dwyer competed with Brigadier General Dyer in ordering acts of terror against the civilian population. Bombs and machine guns were frequently used to terrorise the peasant population of Punjab. In fact, planes were used to drop bombs indiscriminately on the population.[44] Given that Dwyer and Dyer led by example, they had worthy subordinates, such as Captain Deveton at Kasur, who ordered people to touch their foreheads to the ground to acknowledge British authority; peasants were made to draw lines in the sand with their noses; people were lime-washed and made to stand in the sun, and there were some cases of Indians being shut in public cages in lots of over 100 and left out in the burning sun.[45] So much for the Christian tolerance of the British and their claim of being an enlightened civilisation.

Only after the withdrawal of martial law did the rest of the country become aware of the tragedy and the reign of terror in Punjab. There were vehement demands for recall of the Viceroy and impeachment of the Lieutenant Governor of Punjab. This time around even the Moderates could not defend the indefensible. Rabindranath Tagore's renouncement of his knighthood in protest and Pandit Madan Mohan Malaviya's relentless efforts to bring facts to light worried the government and pushed it harder to work on the Montford Reforms.[46] However, before doing so, the British government revealed its fundamentally unreliable character through two things—it appointed the Hunter Committee to inquire into the events of Punjab and simultaneously passed the Indemnity Bill to protect the officers whose conduct would be looked into by the Committee.[47]

The report of the Committee, published on 26 May 1920, was not unanimous. There were thus two reports—the majority view of five Europeans and the minority view of three Indians. Both reports generally agreed that the police and the army were justified in firing upon the mobs in Punjab and that the unrest was caused by Gandhi's Satyagraha.[48] As for the Jallianwalla Bagh incident, while the majority view let Dyer off the hook by terming his inhuman conduct as a mere 'error of judgement', the minority view condemned it as inhuman and un-British. That said, both views exonerated the Government of India of all blame. Although Dyer was removed from active service by the government, Dwyer and Chelmsford were absolved of all guilt. Pertinently, Dyer's removal was *condemned* by the majority in the House of Lords. He was hailed as the saviour of Punjab by his compatriots in India and England, barring a few dissenting voices, and demands were made for his reinstatement in service. A Dyer Appreciation Fund was set up in India by his compatriots and he was presented with a sword and £20,000, apart from being rewarded with good commercial prospects in India. Even in the British Parliament, the predominant opinion was that the situation was 'ably handled' by Lieutenant Governor Dwyer.[49] The ethno-religious supremacism of the British establishment was writ large on the Amritsar tragedy.

As for the 'Mahatma', for whose Satyagraha people had laid down their lives, he made the following announcement on 21 July 1919 after being 'cautioned' by the government about the risk to public security caused by his agitation:[50]

> *The Government of India had given me, through His Excellency the Governor of Bombay, a grave warning that the resumption of civil disobedience is likely to be attended with serious consequences to public security. This warning has been reinforced by His Excellency the Governor himself at the interviews to which I was summoned. In response to these warnings and to the urgent desire publicly expressed by Dewan Bahadur L.A. Govinda Raghava Aiyar, Sir Narayan Chandavarkar and several Editors, I have, after deep consideration, decided not to resume civil resistance for the time being. I may add that several prominent friends belonging to what is called the Extremist Party have given me the same advice on the sole ground of their fear of a recrudescence of violence on the part of those who might not have understood the doctrine of civil resistance.* When, in common with most other Satyagrahis, I came to the conclusion that the time was ripe for the resumption of civil resistance as part of Satyagraha, I sent a respectful letter to H.E. the Viceroy, advising him of my intention so to do and urging that the Rowlatt Legislation should be withdrawn, that an early declaration be made as to the appointment of a strong and impartial Committee to investigate the Punjab disturbances, with power to revise the sentences passed, and that Babu Kalinath Roy, who was, as could be proved from the record of the case, unjustly convicted, should be released. The Government of India deserve thanks for the decision in Mr. Roy's Case (Mr. Roy was the Editor of The Tribune). Though it does not do full justice to Mr. Roy, the very material reduction in the sentence is a substantial measure of justice. I have been assured that the committee of enquiry, such as I have urged for, is in the process of being appointed. *With these indications of good will, it would be unwise on my part not to listen to the warning given by the Government. Indeed, my acceptance of the Government's advice is a further demonstration of the nature of civil resistance. A civil resister never seeks to embarrass the Government.* I feel that I shall better serve the country and the Government and those Punjabi leaders who, in my opinion, have been so unjustly convicted and so cruelly sentenced, by the suspension of civil resistance for the time being. (I have been accused of

throwing a lighted match. If my occasional resistance be a lighted match, the Rowlatt Legislation and the persistence in retaining it on the Statute Book is a thousand matches scattered throughout India. The only way to avoid civil resistance altogether is to withdraw that legislation.) Nothing that the Government have published in justification of that Bill has moved the Indian Public to change their attitude of opposition to it. [Emphases added]

Gandhi ended this announcement with an exhortation to his fellow Satyagrahis to seek the cooperation of all to propagate use of pure Swadeshi goods and promote Hindu–Muslim unity. Notwithstanding the suspension of the Satyagraha, the net result of these developments was that Gandhi had arrived on the national scene. It must be appreciated that while the events in Punjab demanded the country's attention, the Montford Reforms and the Government of India Bill kept the Congress and the League occupied.

The Government of India Act of 1919

Citing Dr Ambedkar in my first book, I had called the Government of India Act of 1919 the first British-made Constitution for Bharat, despite the fact that the Indian Councils Act of 1861 and its subsequent avatars, including the Indian Councils Act of 1909, served as constitutional frameworks for Bharat until the 1919 Act. I called it so because it was through the 1919 Act that a comprehensive constitutional framework, as we understand it now, was first introduced. This was done as part of the internationalisation of the template of Westphalian constitutional nation-states through the League of Nations, as discussed in the first book. Apart from globalisation of the Westphalian worldview, which the Government of India Act of 1919 represented, it is clear that it was also the product of domestic circumstances and expectations.

Having discussed the Montford Report and its salient recommendations in the previous chapter and Gandhi's arrival on the national scene through his Satyagraha against the Rowlatt Act, I will now share with the readers select extracts from the debates held in the British Parliament during the passing of the Government of India Act of

Frederic John Napier Thesiger (1868–1933), 1st Viscount Chelmsford, was the Viceroy and Governor General of India from 1916 to 1921.

1919. The purpose is to understand the colonial establishment's reading of the situation in Bharat and the need for the Montford Reforms.

The Government of India Bill—based significantly, if not entirely, on the Montford Report—was introduced in the House of Commons on 22 May 1919.[51] In the run-up to the introduction of the Bill and thereafter, deputations of the Congress, the Home Rule Leagues, the All-India Moderates Conference and the Muslim League visited England for representation of their views. In particular, these deputations presented their views before the Joint Select Committee appointed by the British Parliament after the second reading of the Government of India Bill on 5 June 1919.[52] The Committee consisted of seven members each from the House of Commons and the House of Lords. The deputation of the All-India Moderates Conference, which had seceded from the Congress, was, of course, led by Surendranath Banerjea and comprised C.Y. Chintamani, Srinivasa Sastri and Tej Bahadur Sapru.[53] On behalf of the Home Rule Leagues and the Congress under the Extremists, Tilak, Besant and V.J. Patel were present, and on behalf of the Muslim League a five-member deputation headed by Jinnah attended the proceedings before the Committee.[54] Interestingly, Banerjea, according to Daniel Argov, was of the view that Annie Besant was a tower of strength to the deputation of the Moderates, which indicated her gradual movement in that direction from the Extremist side, which was, ironically, now led by Gandhi, the protege of Gokhale who was the textbook Moderate.[55] The inputs from the various deputations were captured in the report of the Joint Select Committee, along with the proposed amendments. After consideration of the report by the House of Commons, the amended Bill was passed by the House on 5 December 1919.[56] Subsequently, the Bill was passed in the House of Lords on 18 December 1919 and finally received Royal Assent on 23 December 1919.[57] I will now present a few relevant excerpts from the proceedings in the British Parliament on the Bill.

Before the Government of India Bill was introduced by Montagu on 22 May 1919 in the House of Commons, a query was put to him on 12 May 1919 by a member, which was recorded thus:[58]

> Sir J.D. REES asked the Secretary of State for India whether since the signature of the Armistice there has been any change in the policy or attitude of the Government of India or of His Majesty's Government in respect of constitutional reforms in India, or in respect of any other important matter arising out of or connected with the pronouncement he made on behalf of His Majesty's Government on 20th August, 1917?

To this, Montagu replied, 'None whatever.' On 22 May, the Government of India Bill was taken up as part of the discussion on 'East India Revenue

Accounts'. Montagu began his summary on the state of affairs in India as follows, underscoring India's contribution to the Allied victory in the Great War:[59]

... I would like the House to be good enough to listen to me while I try to sketch the position in India to-day. If we are considering only the position of India vis-à-vis the great nations of the world, the situation is a bright one. After having taken up the challenge which Germany and her Allies presented to the civilised world, after having devoted her invaluable troops and her limited resources to the Allied cause, India has won for herself a place in international discussion equal to that of the British Dominions, and greater than the position occupied by any Power in the world, except, of course, those who are colloquially known as the Big Five. Not only has she separate access to the Peace Conference, not only have her representatives received from the King power to sign on his behalf peace with His Majesty's enemies, but as members of the British Empire Delegation they share in the task of concerting the policy of the British Empire. I can only say on behalf of my colleagues, His Highness the Maharajah of Bikanir, and Lord Sinha, and myself, that we have devoted ourselves in Paris with all the more concentration to the interests of the Indian Empire, because we realise we are the representatives of a people not yet unfortunately self-governing. It must have been a satisfaction to the House of Commons to learn that India was to be an original Member of the League of Nations, and that Indian representatives are to sit in the far-reaching and important international labour organisation which is to result from the Peace Treaty. I can only repeat that these things, together with the place occupied by my friend and colleague, Lord Sinha in the House of Lords, commit this House and Parliament to the view that this position is only justified if you can raise India to the position of a sister nation in the British Empire, and it is wholly inconsistent with a position of subordination. And I must go one step further. I would say to our colleagues who have sat with us round the Conference Table representing the great Dominions of this Empire, that the position of equality which they have given to the representatives of India is wholly inconsistent, in my humble opinion, with the treatment of the citizens of India in British Dominions.

A member, Colonel Wedgewood, asked if he was referring to South Africa. Montagu replied:[60]

Yes, in South Africa or anywhere, in the position which puts them lower than the citizens of any other parts of the British Empire. I turn to India herself. There the position is not so satisfactory. Having come through the War with a record which will compare with the record of any other country in the world, we find now a country in mourning. Rebellion and revolution have appeared internally. War has broken out afresh on her frontiers. It is to this subject that I would invite the attention of the House this afternoon, to an analysis of the causes, to a description of the state of affairs, and to a suggestion as to the remedies. I am not going to say very much about Afghanistan. It is now quite clear that the new Amir, having achieved the throne, has, in a moment of almost suicidal folly, authorised an unprovoked attack upon the territories for which we are responsible. His motives are doubtful. They must be partly attributed to the unrest which exists throughout the Mahomedan world—on which I shall have something to say in a minute—partly to a pathetic effort, by the worst possible means, to consolidate his position on a shaky throne, partly to the emissaries of that dark and murderous doctrine which battens upon unrest, feeds on discontent, spreads disorder wherever it shows its head—Bolshevism, and the Bolshevist emissaries of Russia. [AN HON. MEMBER: 'And Germany, too!'] All these have played their part, and the result was inevitable. I shall publish daily as I receive the reports on the military situation. It is not necessary for me to say that we desire nothing in Afghanistan but the friendly relations with a neighbouring country which we had when Afghanistan was ruled by that wise statesman, Habibullah, who was so recently and treacherously done to death. We desire peace and no interference, but we do intend to exact stern and just punishment for the raids and invasions perpetrated by unscrupulous forces on the peoples under our protection, and explanations and withdrawals of the strange messages we have received from the present Amir. As to the internal situation in India, I propose to deal frankly with the trouble in India, but I do so with this word of preface: The danger is not past, it exists, it is not something that is finished, it threatens. I shall charge myself with the task of saying nothing that will fan the flames or increase the grievous responsibility of those whose first duty it is to restore order. Those who govern India, those who wish her well, those who desire for her peace and progress, speak in a critical time in her history. I feel sure I can appeal to all those hon. Members who will take a part in this Debate to recognise, as I think the whole of India has recognised, that the first duty of the Government to-day is to restore order. It is not necessary to exaggerate the situation. Riots involving the destruction of life and of property have occurred in certain parts of the Presidency of Bombay, in the province of the Punjab, extending over one-tenth of the area and involving one-third of the population, on one occasion in the city of Delhi, and to a minor extent in the streets of Calcutta. There has been no trouble in Madras, no trouble in the Central Provinces, no trouble in the United Provinces, no trouble in Bihar, Orissa, or Burma. In Calcutta, the Bengali had little or no share in the trouble at all. Throughout India, generally speaking, the country districts remained quiet, and the trouble was confined to the towns. I would ask this House to join with me in an expression of sincere sympathy to all those who have suffered in these disturbances. There has been the loss of much property, there has been the loss of many innocent lives, there have been, as doubtless will be revealed when the whole story is told, many stirring deeds of heroism.

I say again that these events have shown the unshakeable, undismayed loyalty of India as a whole. There have been striking incidents of the co-operation of Indians in localising the trouble and in using efforts to restore order. That does not detract from the fact that Englishmen in no way connected with the Government and in no way responsible for the deeds—misdeeds or good deeds—of the Government, have lost their lives and have been foully murdered. Official Indians and non-official Indians have been done to death, yes, and even many of the rioters deserve our sympathy, for when these things occur the man who loses his life as a result of a soldier's bullet is as much the victim of those who promoted the riots as those who are killed by the rioters themselves.

In these circumstances the Indian Army to a man, and the Indian Police, despite attempts to promote insubordination and indiscipline, remained without a single stain upon their reputation or a single unpleasant incident. This is a tribute to the men who have won renown on all the fields of war, who played so conspicuous, indeed the main and predominant, part in the defeat of one of our enemies, Turkey ...

Commenting on the trouble brewing in India owing to the Rowlatt Act and to Gandhi and the Revolutionaries, Montagu said:

I now come to two other political causes—causes more indirect because they only affect the politically-minded part of the population, but causes which must be reckoned with. One is a fear, based upon the ceaseless activities of the Indo-British Association, that the reforms promised on the 20th of August, 1917, will not be carried out in an acceptable form. This is an association formed with the most laudable motives, which has carried on a ceaseless campaign against those reforms ever since the announcement was made. They have slandered and libelled whole sections of the Indian population. They have very often hardly paid to the facts the respect to which facts are entitled, and they have provoked the suspicion that the British Parliament intends to go back upon that pronouncement, or at least not to carry it out in an adequate way. Lastly, there is the Rowlatt Act, which has caused widespread, I would almost say universal opposition throughout India: although the disturbances I have just described are so local, and although this shows that they are not directly due to opposition to the Rowlatt Act, let the House make no mistake, the Rowlatt Act was throughout Indiaa very unpopular Act. I have read from end to end all the Debates which took place upon the Rowlatt Act, and I am not here to apologise for it. I am still convinced that in the circumstances, as passed, as it is now on the Statute Book, for it has been left to it operation, the Rowlatt Act was necessary, ought to have been passed and could not have been avoided. Evidence accumulates every day that there is in India a small body of men who are the enemies of government, men whom any Government, bureaucratic or democratic, alien or indigenous, if it was worthy the name of Government, must deal with. I cannot do better, in describing this body of men, than quote the words of a very great and distinguished Indian, Mr. Gandhi. There is no man who offers such perplexity to a Government as Mr. Gandhi, a man of the highest motives and of the finest character, a man whom his worst enemy, if he has any enemies, would agree is of the most disinterested ambitions that it is possible to conceive, a man who has deserved well of his country by the services he has rendered, both in India and outside it, and yet a man who his friends, and I would count myself as one of them, would wish would exercise his great powers with a greater sense of responsibility and would realise in time that there are forces beyond his control and outside his influence who use the opportunities afforded by his name and reputation. My hon. and gallant Friend (Colonel Wedgewood) will realise that Mr. Gandhi is not the only man who, despite the most laudable motives, sometimes shows a lack of political wisdom.

At this juncture Colonel Wedgewood remarked that he should be quite content if he had Mr Gandhi's virtues and powers. This was followed by a response of Montagu:

Gandhi has himself said about these things—he was deploring, as, of course, he would do, the acts of violence which have occurred—He realised that there were clever men behind it all and some organisation beyond his ken. That is the real revolutionary, the man who lurks in dark corners, whom nothing can locate or convert, who is subject to the influences of an organisation ramifying throughout the world with its secret emissaries and influences, men who are a danger to any country, and against whom the Government of India are determined to do unceasing battle until they have been extirpated. The Defence of India Act has helped us to do much with regard to these men. No one in this House will accuse Lord Carmichael of being a stern, unbending bureaucrat. These are his words: The Defence of India Act is what has helped us. I am only saying what I believe to be absolutely true when I say that, the Defence of India Act has helped to defend the young educated men of Bengal as nothing else has defended them, not their own fathers, not their teachers, for they were ignorant, not their associates nor they themselves, for they were blind to the danger. Under the Defence of India Act a certain number of these people have been dealt with. The greater number of the persons were mainly required to live in their own homes and not to move without permission. The Act is comparable to our own Defence of the Realm Act and was passed for the duration of the War only. Under it some 1,600 people alone have been dealt with, of whom nearly two-thirds have subsequently been released, leaving at present about 464 subjects to restraint. All the cases in Bengal have been investigated by a Commission of Inquiry consisting of Mr. Justice Beechcroft and Sir Narayan Chandavarkar, and in all the cases which they have investigated they have found the Government was justified in the action they took except in six cases.

The problem before the Government of India was this. Were we, when peace was restored, to rely on the ordinary law as it existed before the Defence of India Act was passed, or was it necessary to take any new steps? We did not decide that by correspondence between the Secretary of State and the Government of India, but we appointed a Committee of Inquiry into the facts. It was presided over by an English judge, Mr. Justice Rowlatt, whom I asked [to] go out there. His associates were two Indian judges, one an Indian and one an Englishman, an Indian Civil servant and an Indian lawyer in a large way of practice. They presented, after a full investigation, a unanimous Report, and the facts which they brought to light have never been challenged. It is their recommendation which has been carried out in the Rowlatt Act. Does the House mean to suggest to me that, confronted with this evil, having considered the situation arising out of the end of the Defence of India Act, having appointed a Committee for this purpose, thus constituted, having got from it a unanimous report of this authority, we were to say we would disregard their advice and do nothing? It has been objected that this Commission was entirely legal, that they were all lawyers, and that a different result might have been obtained if some other element had been upon the tribunal. Our anxiety was to try to rely entirely upon legal processes rather than upon executive action. What better tribunal can you have to advocate the great advantages of the law than lawyers? This fact added to my mind the importance of their findings.

Let me shortly describe the Act which is based upon their recommendations. First of all it is not in force anywhere. Does the House realise that? It will never be in force unless the circumstances which justify it occur, and then it would be unflinchingly used. It is divided into parts, and the application of each part depends upon a declaration of the Government of India that in different degrees anarchical or revolutionary crime exists.

A member, Sir Donald Maclean, asked:

Do I understand that the Indian Defence of the Realm Act is considered to be sufficient to cover the Indian difficulties until the War ends, and then, that the Rowlatt Act or Acts would, if necessary, being on the Statute Book, be put into operation?

To this Montagu responded:

That is absolutely accurate. It was stated several times in the Debate by members of the Government of India that they had no intention of using the Rowlatt Act until the end of the War. Under the first part of the Bill when the results of anarchical or revolutionary movement are comparatively mild, nothing is suggested but the speeding up of the ordinary legal processes. I think I am right in saying that I need not waste time with that particular part of the Act, because it has met with very little opposition. Under the other two parts of the Act, where anarchical or revolutionary movements are giving cause for grave anxiety—I am not quoting the exact words—or are prevailing to such an extent as to endanger the public safety, then the local Government may deprive a man of his liberty, not as a punishment but as a preventative, and intern him for a prolonged period. But in that case, the local Government first of all has to submit the case to a judicial officer to advise them upon it. It is not until they have received his report that they take action, and when they have taken action, within a month of having taken action they must submit the whole case to what is called an investigating authority, consisting of three individuals, of whom one shall be a non-official, to go into the whole case afresh and see that the Act has not been misapplied. That is, roughly speaking, the machinery.

On the need for speedy introduction of the Government of India Bill, Montagu said:

Lastly, I am more than ever convinced that we must now proceed without delay to the introduction of the promised Bill for the alteration of the Government of India. The pronouncement of the 20th of August must be made to live. I am authorised to say this afternoon that the Cabinet has consented to my introduction on their behalf of a Bill which will be introduced, I hope, at the beginning of June. There is now no longer any reason for delay. Lord Southborough's Committee has reported and has shown that we can get an electorate in India one hundred and fifty seven times as big as the present one, which is good for a beginning. Mr. Feetham's Committee has reported and shown that you can divide the functions of the Government of India from those of the local Government and thus admit of the long-desired decentralisation, and that of the functions of the local Government there are many and substantial functions that can be entrusted at once to the charge of representatives of the peoples of India, bring home better to this House what I start of that kind has been made the rest of the local functions of the local Governments will follow. The Bill which I will introduce, therefore, is only awaiting two events—the recommendations of Lord Crewe's Committee as to those changes in the India Office which will require statutory enactment, and the publication, which I hope to have next week, of the dispatches of the Government in India and of the local Governments upon the Report. When these documents are published it will be found—I do not want to anticipate debate on this question—that the majority of the local Governments do not like that portion of the Montagu–Chelmsford form of government which is known as 'diarchy'; and they have said so very forcibly. After they had written their letters of dissent the heads of the local Governments went to Delhi and conferred with the Viceroy. As a result they produced an alternative scheme which will be published next week and it is endorsed by the Governments of the United Provinces, Punjab, Central Provinces, and Assam. The Governor of Bengal and the Lieutenant Governor of Behar and Orissa prefer the original scheme. The Governments of Madras and Bombay were not represented. The dispatch of the Government of India seems to me to be a striking defence of the original scheme and invites Parliament to reject the alternative scheme proposed by a majority of the local Governments. I do not want to anticipate the Second Reading Debate upon the Bill which, after it has been introduced, according to promise, is to be referred to a Joint Committee of both Houses that will hear evidence, discuss the alternative and upon whose recommendations I presume the House will ultimately form judgment.

To a question from Lieutenant Colonel A. Murray as to whether the whole bill would be referred to the joint committee, Montagu replied in the affirmative. In reply to a query from another member, Colonel Wedgewood, about the Regulations, Montagu said:

I am coming to that in a moment. The keystone, the whole basis, the vital point of Indian reform today is the transference of power from the bureaucracy to the people, gradual if you like, but real at every stage. I cannot bring home better to this House what I mean by the essence of that than to ask them to consider the situation in this country. During the War Parliamentary government has been diminished and Executive control has been substituted. I read in the papers every day a demand that our lives, our occupations, our businesses, should be freed from Executive control. The only differences between the complaint here and in India are that in India nobody suggests that Executive control is exercised by too many officials—it is done by a singularly few—whereas the complaint here is as to the number. But nobody questions the single-mindedness, the ability, the devotion to duty of the officials to whose power we in this country, now that peace is restored, so much object. What we demand in this country is that officials should govern, not merely for our good, but on our behalf, carry out the orders of Parliament, be responsible to Parliament, Parliament alone deciding upon them. That is where the grievance in India is. There is, believe me, a passion for self-government. Nobody questions that it must come gradually, but I say at every stage the transference of power must be real and substantial. It must be definite and concrete; it must be beyond the reach of the personal generosity of character or the suspicious nature, or the autocratic temper, or the easy-going disposition of the particular incumbent of any governorship or lieutenant governorship. You must transfer the power from the officials to the people. You must make a beginning, and you must go on doing it. That is what is meant by the progressive realisation of responsible government. There is a great part to play for the Civil servant, English and Indian in India today, greater almost than the great part he has played in the past. But so far as responsibility for policy goes the pronouncement of 20th August meant nothing if it did not mean that the power of directing policy should first in some things and then in others, until finally in all, be transferred to the elected representatives of the people of India. Therefore, I am going to oppose, and I shall ask the House to oppose any colourable programme which leaves an irresponsible executive confronted with a majority which they have to oppose or defer to at their will on all or any subjects as they choose. That is not responsible government, and if that is the only alternative to diarchy, diarchy holds the field. Therefore it will be seen that the Bill I shall introduce, I hope, shortly, will in substance carry out the proposals which the Viceroy and I submitted to Parliament a year ago. It will be seen in the dispatch of the Government of India that certain Amendments have been suggested. Of those Amendments some have been incorporated in the Bill, others I shall invite the Joint Committee to decide against.

After reading all the criticisms to which I could gain access, after considering all the Amendments for improvement which have come to my notice, I have this to observe. The scheme which the Viceroy submitted to the people was elaborated after discussion with all the local Governments, with many officials and non-officials and after prolonged discussion with the Government of India. I remain now of the opinion that I expressed last year in this House, that we require all the assistance that the Joint Committee of Parliament can give us, to improve our suggestion, to find a better way even yet of carrying out the policy of His Majesty's Government, to make Amendments of our Bill. But I did not sign my name to that document in the belief that it was either a minimum or maximum. I believe it embodied the extent to which Parliament ought to go. Do it differently if you like, find other methods if it please you, but I beg of you, do not do less. You cannot put before the world a scheme which is elaborated over the signature of the Viceroy and the Secretary of State, and then do what is called in India, whittle down the scheme. Amend it, alter it, turn it inside out, start on a new route, but I beg of you to go as far, and as long as I hold the office with which I am now entrusted, so long as I remain a Member of this House, I will ask the House not to pull bricks out of, but to build on the foundation recommended to the extent of the scheme in the Report which the Viceroy and I laid before Parliament.

I must once again apologise for the length of my remarks. I think I have said all that I desire to say in this stage of the Debate. The policy which I have attempted to advocate is that which many of, I think all, my predecessors have advocated. It can be summed up in a sentence. I would put first the maintenance of order. Secondly, a searching and tireless effort to investigate the causes of disorder and discontent, to remove those which are removable, to eradicate the sources of disturbance and disorder, and to go on with a determination, courageous, unhesitating, zealous, to make of India what may be very loosely described as a union of great self-governing countries, entrusted with the custody of their own well-being, partners in the great freedom-loving British Commonwealth. That is a task in every way worthy of this Parliament, to my mind the only conceivable outcome of the unexampled and magnificent work that has been done by British effort and enterprise in India in the past.

In the same discussion, the issue of rallying the Moderates to the side of the government was also brought up. Adding to the need for expedition to enact the Montford Reforms in view of the Revolutionary Movement, one of the members, D. Maclean, said:

> I only add this one point with regard to that, and it is this. I must sincerely trust that the relegation of that matter, after Second Reading, to a Joint Committee of both Houses will not result in a long hanging-up of that measure. One knows very often of Joint Committees what cold storage chambers of warm sympathetic reformers they have been in the past. I trust that will not be the fate of this measure, because on that measure lies the real hope not only of maintaining India as a real part of the Empire, but the only hope of bringing her fully into the sisterhood of the nations which comprise that great association of the British commonwealth—the only hope. A great deal of interest and apprehension has been manifested at the position which obtains in India today, but I do not wonder at it. As my right hon. Friend spoke I began to put myself, as far as I could, in the place of an educated intelligent Indian of the moderate classes. It is the only way really to judge political or other problems, the extent to which you can put yourself in the other man's place, and then form a judgment. To that extent I think you approach to some degree comparatively to the formation of a reasonable judgment. Let us suppose he was not in the secrets of the Indian Government. What are the facts which are present to his mind? As far as I recollect them, they are these. In 1911 the visit of the King and Queen to India, and that splendid gesture in which they removed the capital from Calcutta, the sea base where it was in close touch with all the resources of the British Empire, to the sacred city in the centre of India, a gesture of trust and confidence in the Indian people, and from then, with all the difficulties quite inherent to Indian Government, we progressed until the outbreak of the great War. And what a response was theirs; how it shattered the hopes, nay, the confident anticipations, of our enemies! Instead of the signs of breaking away from the British Raj, there was an extraordinary rally to the British arms. He sees that, and he hears from time to time of the great appreciation expressed in and through the Houses of Parliament, not by formal votes, but in the course of Debate, of the part which India was then playing and still plays. In January, 1918, the Imperial War Cabinet sent a message of glowing appreciation to India of her services, and in March, 1918, in our dark days on the Western Front, a War Conference was called in India, to which the Indian Princes came, the Viceroy presiding, and again pledges were given of Indian help and coherence to the Allied cause.

> At that very time, while that was going on, the Rowlatt Commission was sitting. In due time it issues its Report, and with a haste—I am taking the position of an Indian—which must be to his mind only commensurate with a state almost bordering upon active revolution, the Report is transformed into a Bill, comes before the appropriate tribunal in India, and I do not say it is rushed through, but there is no delay in that proceeding, at any rate, and it is carried by the

vote of the official members against the unofficial members. Intelligent India knows that, and from then we know what has happened. *The great message which was given by a great Indian—I think it was Mr. Gokhale—'Whatever you do, rally the moderates to your side,' comes to my mind, but what has happened? Instead of the rally of the moderates to our side, the rally of the moderates has been to the extremists, and most extraordinary things have happened. For the first time in India Moslems and Hindus have met in a joint ceremony. No wonder the Government is alarmed, and no wonder we at home were wondering what was happening. All the forces in India to which we had been accustomed to look for steadiness were drifting towards what seemed to us the extreme revolutionary side. Looking at it as well as I can from my standpoint, I can understand well how young, intelligent India was seriously disturbed and began to lose confidence in the good faith of the central authorities. That is the danger, and that is the position in which at present we find ourselves.* [Emphasis added]

Defending the loyalty of the Moderates to the British empire and emphasising the need to work with them, Thomas Bennett said:

If in India we on the one hand firmly assert the law, as the right hon. Gentleman assured us he means to do, and on the other hand meet the legitimate aspirations of the people and show them that we are in sympathy with their progressive ideas, then I believe that the problem will be solved. But we must bear this in mind, that we have to encourage our friends in India and not to countenance efforts which are being made in this country, which I think will make it difficult if they succeed for us to keep the friends that the Government have got. We are being told that the Moderates in India have no real loyalty towards the Government. To my mind the most harmful thing that has been done lately is the attempt to discredit the loyalty of the Moderates in India. I read the other day in a publication which is intended to check the reform movement this: In regard to the paramount duty of maintaining law and order and of preventing sedition, murder and anarchy, the views of both Moderates and Extremists coincide to such an extent as to be prejudicial to the claims of Indian politicians to manage their own affairs, and fraught with great danger to the stability of the Government which the Reform scheme proposes to establish in India. That, in my opinion, is as harmful, unjust, and as unfair a thing as could possibly have been written. I have the happiness to count amongst the Moderates of India a number of personal friends, whose loyalty and high character I can attest by many years of close friendship and association. On their behalf I resent this. It is not only untrue; it is a cruel libel, and it is harmful. Unless we know where to find our friends, and unless we satisfy the Moderates of India that we trust them and wish to work with them and they with us, our day in India is done.

On 12 November 1919, in the House of Lords, in the following words Lord Sydenham posed a question to Under-Secretary of State for India Lord

Sinha regarding the next Congress session scheduled to be held at Amritsar in December of that year in view of the recent disturbances:[61]

... My Lords, in 1907 the National Congress shed its extreme elements, led by Mr. Tilak, after a free fight at Surat. Subsequently Congress became much more moderate in tone, and the noble Lord will probably remember this, as he presided over one of the meetings at Bombay himself. Unfortunately the extremists, with the assistance of Mrs. Besant, captured the Congress completely during the war, and it remains now entirely in their hands, though there has been a schism which has led to the formation of a new party. The effect of the domination of the extremists in the Congress has naturally been to increase the bitterness and kind of language which is calculated to create race hatred in India.

There was a special Congress meeting in Bombay in August, 1918, at which very strong language was used—language which undoubtedly helped to intensify an agitation that has been such a painful feature in India since 1916. In December, 1918, another Congress met at Delhi at which also some inflammatory language was used. This meeting was described at the time as 'a triumph of mobocracy and extremism.' Three months later there was a dangerous rising in the Punjab and elsewhere, which was shown to have been precipitated (although well organised in advance) by the passing of the Rowlatt Act, and which was not unconnected with the Afghan invasion.

In spite of all these circumstances it is now arranged that there should be another meeting at Amritsar, and it is difficult to believe that this meeting is being held without a purpose. In June last the Amritsar branch of the Congress, which had taken alarm, cancelled the invitation to the Congress which it had previously given. Then followed what so often happens in India. Strong influences were brought to bear on the branch, and it changed its mind again and cancelled its former resolution. Agricultural classes in the Punjab have rendered magnificent service during the war. They provided more than half of the total combatants which India brought to bear on the war.

But, unfortunately, there has been another side to the picture. During the war the Punjab has passed through two distinct and very dangerous crises. In 1915 there was the most serious conspiracy that has ever been known since the Mutiny. That was discovered and very ably handled by Sir Michael O'Dwyer, and this year there was another most serious rising in many places which, if it had not been promptly suppressed, might have paralysed the campaign on the Frontier and led to a really great disaster. Amritsar was one of the scenes of violence; where the mob shouted 'Kill the English'; where they destroyed Government buildings and mission buildings, and where several murders were perpetrated. The steps taken by Sir Michael O'Dwyer to restore order have been attacked in unmeasured language both here and in India, and his impeachment and that of the Viceroy has been demanded. The result of that has only been to create an atmosphere of unrest and hostility to Government and to British residents almost all over India.

In these circumstances, therefore, to allow another meeting to be held at Amritsar does seem likely to have a very disturbing effect at a time when calm is wanted for the introduction of the new reforms into India. On the third of this month the Viceroy appealed to the Princes and Chiefs, who, he said—could lend valuable assistance by guarding their States against a lawless and malicious spirit, and by refusing to tolerate the lying stories as to the motives of the British Government.

That is significant, because these things have not taken place in the Native States where the Chiefs have taken steps to prevent them. I understand that sober opinion in the Punjab is opposed to this meeting being held—and well it may be. I think myself it is never wise to take risks in a country so inflammable as India, and I submit that in allowing this meeting to take place a risk will be run which is not justified in the circumstances I have described.

The debates make it clear that the British government continued to see loyal allies in the Moderates even in 1919. Further, the so-called rapprochement between the Moderates and the Extremists achieved in the 1916 session had reverted to its broken status of 1907. Also, what is evident is that the Extremists and the Revolutionaries were more successful in securing the interests of Bharat in their own respective ways, while the Moderates seemed keener to preserve their cosy equations with the colonial establishment. That said, as stated earlier, it needs to be reiterated that these labels were transient and issue-specific, since the Extremists, under pressure from Gandhi, would end up supporting the Khilafat Movement more than ever before, and the Moderates were now being led by a former Extremist Annie Besant.

As for the Government of India Act of 1919, it had forty-seven sections and five schedules in its final form. For all the claims made by the Montford pair that the 1919 Act represented a significant evolution from the Indian Councils Act of 1909, some aspects remained the same. For instance, section 44 of the 1919 Act was similar to section 6 of the 1909 Act, which empowered the Governor General to frame rules with the approval of the Secretary of State. This effectively meant that despite expanding the elective component both at the level of the province and the Government of India, a significant degree of power and prerogative remained in the hands of the Governor General and the Secretary of State through rule-making power, in addition to the Council of State as discussed in the previous chapter. Pertinently, although the Act received Royal Assent in December 1919, the rules under the Act, which were meant to give effect to its provisions, were published only on 20 July 1920. By the time elections were held under the new framework and the new 'reformed' legislatures came into existence, it was January 1921.[62]

The annual sessions of the Congress and the League for 1919 were naturally dominated by three major developments of that year—the enactment of the Rowlatt Act; the events in Punjab, especially the Jallianwalla Bagh Massacre; and the Government of India Act of 1919—apart from the Khilafat Movement. Both sessions were held in Amritsar. At the Congress session, its thirty-fourth, Tilak, Gandhi, Malaviya, Bipin Chandra Pal, Jinnah, Dr Kitchlew, Dr Satyapal were some of the prominent names present. The chairman of the reception committee of the session was Swami Shraddhananda Saraswati of the Arya Samaj (who would be assassinated seven years later by Abdul Rashid for his attempts to reconvert Muslims to the Hindu fold), and the president of the session was Motilal Nehru.

Capturing the split between the Moderates and the Extremists on the Montford Reforms and proposing a settlement between the two factions, Swami Shraddhananda said:[63]

THE POLITICAL SPLIT

Mr. Montagu's Reform Scheme is pointed out as the main source of this present political split. The Moderates urged that they would join the others if the latter were prepared to accept the Reform Scheme. Here one naturally asked them if they would be satisfied with only this change. They answered and said 'No. It is one thing to accept what is given to us, and then to ask for more, and quite another to reject as unacceptable even what is given'. This was a legitimate reply from the Moderates, but even the extremists now subscribe to this view. Now even Lokmanya Tilak says, 'accept what is given now, and keep up an agitation for getting more'. Then where lies the difference? Both appear to say the same thing. The Moderates affirm, 'we have not receded from our position, the Extremists have changed their views. They have come up to us, so it should be acknowledged that we have scored a victory.' The Extremists say, 'The Moderates were for accepting whatever was offered, without any question. Now they are rising up to our position, and so must acknowledge defeat'. The reasons of either side have been published in newspapers and I need not repeat them here. The plain fact is that neither of them is ready to admit defeat. Both stand firm in their respective positions. The Moderates contend that the Secretary of State for India was impressed with the moderation of their proposals, and has therefore conferred some extended rights on us. The Extremists can well answer this contention saying, 'Had we not agitated for full swaraj even this much could not have been granted to us'. They can urge the following Panjabi proverb in their support:

'Condemn a man to death and he will willingly accept suffering.' But Mr. Montagu is putting forward quite a distinct view. In the course of his speech on the Reforms Scheme in the House of Commons he said in answer to a question by Mr. Spoor, 'Neither the commons are introducing these changes in the system of Indian Government on account of the agitation in India, nor do they believe that this agitation would continue'. He further added, 'Agitation will not hasten the transference of power, but it might delay it.'

There are three parties, and their views go against one another. The view of every party is true in its own estimation. If the Moderates had supported the proposals of Mr. Montagu, they would have found it difficult to refute the arguments of the opposers of the Reform Scheme. But did not Mr. Bonar Law advance it as an argument for the speedy adoption of the Reforms Bill, that this one grievance of the Indian National Congress be removed before its next session. Mr. Montagu is also true, for it is with the help of his firm resolve that he has been able to move the British parliament to confer these extended rights on the Indians. The Moderates and the Extremists served him merely as pawns for his moves on the political chessboard.

A Settlement

How can this baneful conflict be got rid of? Reform Scheme is no longer open to dispute. Its acceptance by the Moderates and rejection by the Extremists are both worthless boasts. Good or bad, complete or incomplete, the Reform Scheme is now a law for us. Of course, the Moderates would accept it, but I ask the Extremists what they mean by rejecting it. Are you prepared to boycott it completely? Would you not make an effort that such representatives be returned to the Legislative Councils, as may fully voice your views on those assemblies? There might have been some sense in Government rejection of the Scheme had the entire country joined hands in doing, so. This is, however, an impossibility now. But how is this controversy to end? In reality the dispute has already been settled, for Lokmanya Tilak Maharaj has pronounced his verdict saying, 'accept what has been given to you, and keep up a constitutional agitation for a full measure of self-Government'.

Maharaj Tilak occupies an exalted position among the pioneers of political work, who were the first to preach the doctrine of political unity. What other here has suffered so much in the service of the motherland as this illustrious person has done? Will not the soldiers constituting the army for the service of the motherland bow down before the mandate of this old weather-beaten General?

That clears the way. Both the Moderates and the Extremists agree that the reforms should be accepted. They differ only in ascribing the credit of these reforms. I put forward a suggestion before that numerically strong party, which at present holds the reins of this National assembly. You are very powerful. Some of your Moderate friends might have a monopoly of wisdom and policy, but for the time being you are the stronger both in numbers and in influence. In front of you stand no enemies, they are the sons of the same Motherland. Among them there are some old warriors who have suffered innumerable hardships in the service of the Motherland. Can you forget Mr.

Gokhale who forgot himself in the service of the Motherland and laid down his life at the same altar. Can you ignore that political Sannayasi, the noble Srinivasa Shastri, who has taken the place of Mr. Gokhale? Or could you look down upon that foremost political fighter Sri Surendra Nath Bandopadhaya, whatever change the present times might have brought on him ...

After condemning the Amritsar tragedy, Motilal Nehru in his presidential speech commented on the broad powers the Viceroy and the Secretary of State had reserved for themselves through the rule-making power under section 44 of the 1919 Act:

Coming to the provisions of the new Act, we find that a considerable part of this measure is in the nature of a blank cheque. The filling up of this cheque is left to the Executive Government of India, subject to the supervision of the Secretary of State. This process may make or mar whatever benefits are intended to be conferred by the very large number of proposals which are subject to the extensive rule-making powers provided under the Act. There are yet further commissions or committees to come, and further investigations to be made in order to settle details. It is on the completion of this work that the Act will be fully put in operation.

On the Khilafat question, Nehru said:[64]

The Khilafat Question.—I now turn to a question of supreme importance to our Mohammadan brothers and, for that reason, of equal importance to all Indians. I mean the Khilafat question. It is impossible for one part of the nation to stand aloof while the other part is suffering from a serious grievance. This was clearly shown when the vast majority of non-Muslims made common cause with the Muslims and abstained from participating in the recent peace celebrations in India. No words of mine are necessary to emphasize the obvious duty of this Congress to give the question its best consideration.

The entry of Turkey in the war was a most momentous event from the Indian Muslims' point of view. They felt no inconsiderable misgivings about their attitude when they saw that an issue had arisen, which seemed to involve a conflict between their loyalty to their King and country and duty to the religious head of the Islamic world. But these doubts were happily shortlived and the Indian Mohammadans cheerfully cast in their lot with the British Empire when the memorable announcement of the 2nd November, 1914, was made by Lord Hardinge, securing to the Mohammadans complete immunity from any interference with their religious feelings. This announcement was followed by similar assurances from other British statesmen. Mr. Lloyd George in his famous speech of the 5th January, 1914, said, 'Nor are we fighting to deprive Turkey of its capital or of the rich and renowned lands of Asia Minor and Thrace which are Predominantly Turkish in race'.

The war has ended in complete victory for the allied arms. Moslem India, nay United India, demands that full effect be given to these assurances.

Apart from the promises and pledges given to His Majesty's Muslim subjects they have the right to demand the application of the principle of self-determination to the component parts of the Turkish Empire in the same way as it has been applied to Poland and the Yugo-Slav. What reason is there for a different treatment of Mesopotamia and Syria, where the population is almost entirely Muslim in faith, or of Palestine and Armenia, where Muslims are more numerous than the followers of any other religion?

As to who is the rightful Khalifat-ul-Islam, it is unnecessary for me to enter into historical or religious considerations. Lord Robert Cecil has admitted in the House of Commons that 'His Majesty's Government have never departed from the attitude that the question of Khilafat is one for Muslim opinion alone to decide.' Muslim opinion has now decided it, in a manner which leaves no possible doubt, in favour of the Sultan of Turkey. With Arabia independent, with foreign powers governing Mesopotamia, Syria and Armenia in the guise of mandatories, with Palestine restored to the Jews, with the Greeks securely lodged in Smyrna and the hinterland, with Constantinople itself internationalized, what I ask is the position of the Khalifat-ul-Islam? Fellow delegates, it is a serious question demanding your most earnest attention.

Here's resolution XV which was passed in relation to the Khilafat issue:[65]

This Congress respectfully protests against the hostile attitude of some of the British Ministers towards the Turkish and Khilafat question as disclosed by their utterances and most earnestly appeals to and urges upon His Majesty's Government to settle the Turkish question in accordance with the just and legitimate sentiments of Indian Mussalmans and the solemn pledges of the Prime Minister without which there will be no real contentment among the people of India.

Motilal Nehru's speech, as well as the resolution on Khilafat, shows that the Congress saw support to the Khilafat Movement as a necessary concomitant of Hindu–Muslim concord. The other reason for this was contained in resolution XXVI on the issue of cow slaughter:[66]

This Congress gratefully welcomes the resolution of the All-India Moslem League recommending the discontinuance of the slaughter of cows in India on the Bakr-id festival removing as it does a cause of great offence to the universal Hindu sentiment and recognises the resolution as one of the greatest steps on the part of Indian Musulmans towards complete unity between Hindus and Mahommedans and trusts that the Hindus will fully reciprocate the good feelings of their Mahommedan brethren indicated by their generous resolution.

This resolution was passed unanimously with cries of '*Hindu Mussalman ki jai*'. The other important resolutions passed at this session were as follows:

1. Resolution II, moved by Gandhi, was on the condition of Indians in South Africa;
2. Resolution VI sought removal of Dyer and Resolution VII sought removal of Dwyer from their respective positions. The Ali Brothers, Muhammad Ali and Shaukat Ali, who had been released from jail, supported the latter resolution;
3. Resolutions IX, X and XI dealt with Jallianwalla Bagh, the Rowlatt Act and the Indemnity Act respectively;
4. Resolution XXIII acknowledged Lala Lajpat Rai's efforts towards the cause of self-government by undertaking a constitutional agitation in the United States and requested him to continue his efforts.

From 1916 until his return to Bharat in February 1920, Lajpat Rai was in the United States actively advocating the cause of self-government for Bharat and its right to self-determination. When the 1919 Act was passed, he denounced the grateful attitude of the Moderates towards the Montford Reforms and castigated them for seeking to ostracise the Extremists as careless demagogues.[67] Notably, by this time Rai seemed to have moved from his previous Hindu Nationalist position to becoming an advocate for Hindu–Muslim unity.[68] This change may be attributed to the Lucknow Pact and the accommodation of the Khilafat Movement by the Congress, even under Extremists such as Tilak.

The 1919 session of the Congress saw another noteworthy development—this was perhaps the first session in which Gandhi participated prominently in the discussions on issues other than discrimination in South Africa, specifically on the subject of self-government. Resolution XIV on self-government, which was moved by C.R. Das, originally read as follows:[69]

1. That this Congress reiterates its declaration of last year that India is fit for full Responsible Government and repudiates all assumptions and assertions to the contrary wherever made. (Hear, Hear).
2. That this Congress adheres to the resolutions passed at the Delhi Congress regarding Constitutional Reforms and is of opinion that the Reforms Act is inadequate, unsatisfactory and disappointing. (Hear, Hear).
3. That this Congress further urges that Parliament should take early steps to establish full Responsible Government in India in accordance with the principle of self-determination. (Hear, Hear).

Gandhi proposed an amendment by way of addition of the following clause to the resolution:[70]

(d) Pending such introduction, this Congress begs loyally to respond to the sentiments expressed in the Royal Proclamation, namely, 'Let the new era begin with a common determination among my people and my officers to work together for a common purpose, and trust that both the authorities and the people will co-operate so to work the reforms as to secure the early establishment of full Responsible Government,' and this Congress offers its warmest thanks to the Right Hon. E.S. Montagu for his labours in connection with them.

He sought inclusion of this clause to express conditional gratitude for Montagu's efforts in securing incremental reforms despite opposition in the British Parliament. Jinnah supported this amendment, which was finally accepted as part of resolution XIV.[71]

Coming to the All-India Moderates Conference under Surendranath Banerjea, a session was held on 30 December 1919 wherein the reforms were welcomed as a substantial step towards responsible government and Indians were urged to wholeheartedly cooperate with it.[72] Unlike in the previous chapters where I discussed the League's annual sessions along with the Congress', I will discuss its 1919 annual Amritsar session as part of the larger discussion on the Khilafat Movement, given that the issue featured heavily in the League's deliberations at the session.

The Khilafat Movement until December 1918: A Summary

In the previous chapters, I discussed in some detail the thought behind and the history of pan-Islamism in Bharat, citing the views of Shah Waliullah Dehlawi, as well as global pan-Islamic thought, citing the views of Syed Jamal al-Din al-Afghani. I have placed material showing the exalted position of the Ottoman Sultan as the Khalifa of Islam among Muslims in India at least since the mid-1800s, and the correspondence exchanged between Shah Muhammad Ishaq Dehlawi, the great-grandson of Shah Waliullah Dehlawi, and the Ottoman empire after Syed Ahmad Barelvi's death.[73] I have also juxtaposed the views of Jamal al-Din al-Afghani alongside those of Syed Ahmed Khan to bring out the overlaps and conflicts between the former's pan-Islamism and the latter's Two-Nation Theory–driven Muslim Nationalism. Importantly, I have described the gradual merger of both schools of thought to evolve into an Islamic federal framework, wherein attempts were made to harmonise the disagreements between Afghani's global pan-Islamism and Syed Ahmed Khan's Two-Nation Theory in the Bharatiya context, in order to secure the position of the global ummah as well as the position of Muslims in a Hindu-majority Bharat under British rule. After all, Muslim leaders such as Syed Ameer Ali, Nawab Abdul Latif and Syed Ahmed Khan, saw British rule both as the will of Allah, owing to the profligacy of Muslim rulers in Bharat, and as

Abul Kalam Azad became the first education minister of independent India.

a necessary counterweight to the Congress, which they saw as a Hindu party, despite the Congress's efforts to prove its 'secular' character.

It is against the above backdrop that the predicament of Muslims in Bharat upon the outbreak of Anglo-Egyptian and Anglo-Turkish hostilities before, during and especially *after* the First World War must be understood, to appreciate the crux and the nuances of the Khilafat Movement. In other words, while the Khilafat Movement is typically assigned the period between 1919 and 1921 in the popular discourse, for all practical purposes it had started well before 1919 and continued well after 1921. To understand the Movement and its impact on Bharatiya history, I have drawn from a number of scholarly sources as well as primary literature, including but not limited to the following:

1. 'The Khilafat Movement in India 1919–1924' by Muhammad Naeem Qureshi, a doctoral thesis submitted to the University of London in 1973
2. *The Muslim League: Its History, Activities and Achievements,* by Lal Bahadur (1954)
3. *A History of the All-India Muslim League 1906–1947,* by M. Rafique Afzal (2013)
4. 'Foundations of Pakistan', *All-India Muslim League Documents: 1906–1947,* Volumes 1 and 2 (1969 and 1970), by Syed Sharfuddin Pirzada
5. *The Political Aspirations of Indian Muslims and the Ottoman Nexus,* by Syed Tanvir Wasti (2006)

6. *History of the Freedom Movement in India* (Volume 3), by R.C. Majumdar (1963)

7. *The Ulama and Khilafat Movement*, by Mushirul Hasan (1981)

8. *Nationalism and Communal Politics in India*, by Mushirul Hasan (1979)

9. *Pathway to Pakistan*, by Choudhry Khaliquzzaman (1961)

10. *Evolution of Muslim Political Thought in India (Volume 2): Sectarian Nationalism and Khilafat*, by A.M. Zaidi (1975)

11. *Gandhi and Anarchy*, by C. Sankaran Nair (1922)

12. Proceedings of the annual sessions of the Congress and the League; and

13. Debates in the British Parliament and the Imperial Legislative Council

While readers may refer to these sources on their own should they wish to go deeper into the topic, in the interest of the narrative flow I will present only the key aspects of the Movement that are relevant to one of the central themes at hand—the nature, role and impact of Middle Eastern coloniality on the Indic civilisational consciousness and the emergence of its contemporary politico-constitutional thought. Specifically, the Movement's contribution to the reality of the Two-Nation Theory and the consequent solidification of the idea of Pakistan define the metes and bounds of my discussion. At the end of this discussion, I will leave it to the readers to draw parallels, if any, between the Congress's accommodation of pan-Islamism during this period, citing 'Hindu–Muslim unity' as a requirement for securing self-government, and the current state of affairs in Bharat.

Before I delve into the specifics of the Movement, a politico-theological foregrounding of the concept of Khilafat becomes necessary. In the first chapter, citing the views of Shah Waliullah Dehlawi on the concept of an Islamic Caliphate/Khilafat, I said the following:

> On the political front, Dehlawi was of the view that Muslims all over the world *needed* a central leadership in the form of a caliphate which would serve two purposes—the first to provide permanent spiritual and temporal guidance, and the second to keep Muslim rulers under some form of unified umbrella command.[74] He was of the view that there were two caliphates, the outward and the inward, the former being the preserve of the State and the latter being the preserve of the ulema. He held that the corruption of the latter ultimately manifested as corruption in the former, and that it fell upon the ulema to set the Islamic house in order so as to preserve the unity of the community. Given that both Islam and Christianity belong to the family of Abrahamic faiths, it is hardly surprising that the doctrine of two caliphates is similar, if not identical, to the Theory of Two Kingdoms, Spiritual and Temporal, which formed the basis of the Protestant Reformation. [Emphasis added]

This requires some elaboration to understand the logic that animated the Khilafat Movement and the role of the ulema in driving the Movement in accordance with Dehlawi's views. Unlike the Pope, the Khalifa or the Caliph who heads the Khilafat or the Caliphate is the custodian of all religious *and temporal* power on earth for *all* Sunni Muslims.[75] The equal emphasis on temporal power must be understood well, because, as Maulana Mawdudi said, one of the central goals of Islam is complete destruction of the existing social order and its replacment with an Islamic social order. To achieve this objective, both political power and jihad are necessary and indispensable means. Therefore, the political position of the Khalifa, along with the territory under his control, cannot be altered since that upsets the power balance and achievement of the ultimate goal. Consequently, it becomes the duty of the ummah to strive for restoration of balance in favour of the Khalifa, and hence Islam. Since the Ottoman empire held the position of the Caliphate until the end of the First World War in 1918 and even thereafter until 1924, its defeat and consequent dismemberment scripturally mandated, and not just led to, the Khilafat Movement by Sunni Muslims, although Shias too participated in the Movement.

At the cost of repetition, the nuance that needs to be borne in mind is this—it is evident from the resolutions of the Muslim League that the emphasis was as much on preservation of the Caliphate/Khilafat as it was on protection of Muslim holy places and suzerainty of the Caliphate over the 'Jazirat-ul-Arab'—namely Arabia, Syria, Iraq and Palestine. In other words, notwithstanding the defeat of the Ottoman empire at the hands of the Allied Forces, it was not sufficient for Muslims all over the world to merely secure the safety of their holy places and Muslim control over the territories in which they were located; it was equally important that the outcome of the War did not result in the redrawing of territories under the Caliphate since the Caliphate represented Islam's temporal or earthly/political power. This reflects the totalising worldview of Islam, which does not make a distinction between the secular and the religious the way the Christian worldview does. This would mean that it would be theologically, or at least historically, incorrect to compare the position of the Pope in Catholic Christendom with that of the Khalifa in Islam, since the Pope was meant to be—or at least has become—merely a religious figure, whereas the Khalifa wields power over *both* religious and 'non-religious' aspects of the Muslim community. Again, this distinction between religious and non-religious is not entirely accurate because, given the all-encompassing nature of Islam, no aspect of Islamic life is untouched by the faith. Ram Swarup demonstrated this rigorously in his work *Understanding Islam through Hadis,*[76] and so did Arun Shourie in his seminal work *The World of Fatwas, or The Shariah in Action.*[77]

It must also be understood that the expectation that all Sunni Muslims must swear allegiance to the Caliphate directly leads to a case of dual or divided loyalties, or more accurately, a *hierarchy* of loyalties. To support this postulation, I have reproduced below an extract from Fazlul Haque's presidential speech at the 1918 session of the Muslim League in Delhi, wherein he said thus, under the head 'Questions Relating to the Khilafat and Muslim Holy Places':[78]

> We are loyal subjects of the rulers, and are prepared to prove our loyalty in actual practice by making sacrifices. But this temporal loyalty is subject to the limitation imposed by our undoubted loyalty to our faith. We wish to warn our rulers that in making sacrifices one after another, the dividing line may soon be reached; and we need hardly emphasize that in case there is a conflict between Divine Laws and the mandates of our rulers, every true Musalman will allow the Divine Commandments to prevail over human laws, even at the risk of laying down his life.

Bearing this politico-theological framework in mind, and the consequent hierarchy of loyalties it creates, I will now proceed to discuss the specifics of the Khilafat Movement with a brief recapitulation of the position until December 1918 before dealing with the crucial developments of 1919 and thereafter.

As stated in Chapter 2, the Ottoman empire acquired the Caliphal mantle in 1517 after its conquest of the Mamluk Sultanate–ruled Egypt, its previous bearer.[79] Around the same time, in 1526, after the First Battle of Panipat, the Mughal dynasty was established in Bharat with the defeat of the Lodhi dynasty. Despite exchange of correspondence between the Ottomans and the Mughals in later years, the Caliphal claim of the Ottomans did not find much purchase in Bharat owing to the rival power of the Mughals. However, the situation changed after the decline of the Mughal empire during Aurangzeb's lifetime under the onslaught of the Marathas, followed by that of the British. By the mid-1700s, the Ottoman empire was the last surviving hope of Islam, including for Muslims in Bharat.[80] The recognition in Bharat of the Caliphal status of the Ottoman empire around this period is evident from Tipu Sultan's letter to the Ottoman Caliph Abdul Hamid I in 1789 seeking the latter's endorsement of his position as an independent ruler.[81]

By the mid-1800s, ulema such as Shah Muhammad Ishaq Dehlawi had established contact with the Caliph. The extent of proximity between Muslims in Bharat and the Ottoman empire that existed in the 1850s can be gauged from the fact that during the Crimean War (1854–1856) which saw

France, the United Kingdom and the Ottoman empire ally against Russia, Muslims here were invested in Ottoman victory. During this period, after the 1857 Mutiny, the British reliance on endorsement of their rule in Bharat from the Ottoman Caliph underscored the importance of the Caliphate for Muslims of the subcontinent. On its part, the Ottoman empire too counted on global Muslim support in its constant disputes with Europe, in particular Russia. By the 1870s, the Friday khutba in mosques in Bharat was read in the name of the Ottoman Sultan.[82] From an Indian perspective, as long as the British and the Ottomans were on the same side, Muslims here were saved the trouble of choosing between the two, having already pragmatically committed themselves to pro-British loyalism under the influence of leaders such as Nawab Abdul Latif, Syed Ameer Ali and Syed Ahmed Khan to keep Hindus in check.

When war broke out between Russia and Turkey in 1877, Muslims in Bharat put together a Turkish Fund. This development reflected the gradual disregard for Syed Ahmed Khan's policy of treating the Ottoman Caliph as merely a religious head and the Ottoman empire as a model of Islamic modernity but with no political significance for Muslims of the subcontinent. It was around this time that Syed Jamal al-Din al-Afghani's visit to Bharat strengthened latent, pre-existing pan-Islamic notions, despite opposition from Syed Ahmed Khan.

In the first decade of the twentieth century, Russian confrontation with Persia, Italy's invasion of Ottoman Tripoli and the Balkan War that followed between Turkey and the Balkan states (Greece, Bulgaria, and Serbia and Montenegro) had contributed significantly to the weakening of loyalty towards the British among Muslims in this part of the world insofar as Anglo-Turkish relations were concerned. Further, Britain's non-interference or participation in or tacit support to the adversaries of Ottoman empire in these wars, despite the exhortations of Muslims here to press into service Britain's position to help Turkey, did not go down well with the Muslim community. As in 1877, a fund collection drive was initiated by Muslims to support Turkey in the Balkan War and a volunteer corps was organised to help it with fighting men. Even Shias like Syed Ameer Ali rushed to the aid of the Caliphate with medical missions in the form of his Red Crescent from London, and M.A. Ansari with medical missions from India.[83] After all, the Shias too were interested in preserving the position of the sole surviving Muslim power. These gestures brought the Muslims of the Bharatiya subcontinent considerably closer to the Ottoman Caliphate.[84] From a domestic perspective, the annulment of the Partition of Bengal in 1911 added to the distance between the British and Muslims.

It was this period that threw up prominent pan-Islamic and pro-Khilafat voices, such as Maulana Abul Kalam Azad, who had been mentored by Shibli Nomani (one-time colleague of Syed Ahmed Khan at Aligarh, who later co-founded the Darul Uloom Nadwatul Ulama in Lucknow) and the brothers Maulana Muhammad Ali Jauhar and Maulana Shaukat Ali.

In May 1913, a year before the First World War broke out, the Anjuman-i-Khuddam-i-Kaaba (Society of the Servants of Kaaba) was founded in Delhi with the support of the Ali Brothers. The base of the Anjuman was later shifted to Firangi Mahal in Lucknow, with Maulana Qayyam-ud-din Mohammed Abdul Bari of the Mahal as the president. Firangi Mahal was an influential seminary established during Aurangzeb's reign and remains a force to reckon with till date. The ostensible object of the Anjuman was to campaign for the protection of Muslim holy places from the effects of the wars being fought.[85] Although the Anjuman-i-Islam had been founded in Bombay in 1876 for the very same purpose,[86] the Anjuman-i-Khuddam-i-Kaaba's work was much more effective. This was because the true purpose of the Anjuman, according to Muhammad Naeem Qureshi, was to strengthen Turkey as the sole surviving Muslim power which could retain suzerainty over the territories in which Muslim holy places were located—namely the Jazirat-ul-Arab. To this end, its members were required to take an oath freeing them from any allegiance to the Indian government.[87] This marked a significant departure from the policy of loyalty to the British Government in Bharat by a significant cross-section of the Muslim society. As discussed earlier, this development created three camps within the Muslim League— the Muslim conservatives, the Muslim nationalists and the pan-Islamists, who were defined by their respective attitudes towards collaboration with the Congress and their positions in relation to the colonial establishment. That said, the common goal of all three groups lay in securing Muslim interest above all, the limited divergence being on the means to be employed to achieve that goal.

The primary contribution of the Anjuman was to bring together the Western-educated Muslim political leadership and the traditional ulema, which combination would prove to be formidable.[88] In light of the history of Muslim revivalist movements, which was discussed in the first two chapters of this book, this was a remarkable breaking of walls within the Muslim community, allowing them to combine the best of both worlds. It meant a coming together of those who knew how to navigate the 'modern' colonial establishment and those who held sway over the Muslim masses.[89] Given the deep roots in the Muslim community of the ulema of the various Dehlawite movements through their network of mosques and seminaries, they were able to provide the Khilafat Movement with the muscle needed to grab the attention of the British establishment.[90] Thanks to this far-sighted collaboration, the Anjuman quickly established branches in London, Constantinople, Cairo and even Singapore.[91] Keeping with the pan-Islamic spirit of the Anjuman, the members of these branches too were expected to give up their allegiance to their respective national governments.[92] The rallying cry of the pan-Islamic movement was 'Islam is in danger. Save Islam' (*Islam khatre mein hai. Islam ko bachao).*[93]

In the very year of the Anjuman's founding, two specific incidents strengthened the anti-colonial sentiment, which in turn bolstered the pan-Islamic movement. The first was the British government's rejection of the Aligarh College's request for power of affiliation. The college wanted to reshape itself as a Muslim university to which colleges outside the province may seek affiliation. Montagu opposed the use of 'Muslim' in its nomenclature, as that would vindicate the allegation that the government continued to employ the divide and rule policy.[94] This was followed by the Kanpur Mosque incident in September 1913, which was discussed in Chapter 6. This incident was a tipping point of sorts, since the ulema and Muslim political leadership chose to agitate aggressively—to the extent that Viceroy Hardinge had to visit Kanpur in October 1913 and assure the community of reconstruction of the demolished portion of the mosque at government expense.

By 1914, the rapprochement between the Congress and the League had begun, with pressure being exerted on the League from within by Muslim nationalists and pan-Islamists to collaborate with the Congress for self-government in return for reciprocal support on issues of Muslim interest, such as the safety of the Khilafat. Since the Congress was keen on securing self-government and was in the throes of the Home Rule Movement under Tilak and Besant, it conceded to Muslim expectations in the form of communal electorates and communal veto. In early 1914, even before the beginning of the First World War, Turkey had sent its emissaries to thank and reward pan-Islamists in Bharat for their efforts during the Tripolitan and Balkan Wars. Critically, Turkey had engaged a German firm from Hamburg to arm Muslims in Bharat with rifles.[95] That said, even after the Great War broke out, Muslim attitudes in the early months of the War ranged from indifference to prayers for British victory. Until Turkey's involvement in the War, the hope among Muslims was that European Christendom would fight within itself and weaken, leaving Turkey better off. In fact, the Great War was seen as a punishment from Allah for the Balkan Wars.[96] That apart, it must be appreciated that the educated elite among Muslims, who were largely products of the Aligarh establishment, were still loyal to the British to a significant extent, notwithstanding the growing estrangement since 1911.[97] To this end, the Muslim League repeatedly assured the British government of the deep-rooted loyalty of Muslims in Bharat.[98] However, as stated earlier, this loyalty was conditional or hierarchical, since it was contingent on the safety of the Khilafat, the Ottoman Caliphate.

This conditional loyalty of the Muslim community was put to the test in August 1914, when information began coming in from their co-religionists in Turkey as well as from pilgrims returning from the Haj in Mecca that there was evidence of mobilisation of troops by Turkey in favour of the Central Powers.[99] Efforts were made by the pan-Islamists in Bharat to counsel Turkey to remain neutral in the war or support the British, to make life easier for Muslims in Bharat. To this effect, a telegram was sent on 31 August 1914 by Maulana Abdul Bari of Firangi Mahal, president of the Anjuman. It read as follows:[100]

> Placing our faith and confidence, which we the Indian Muslims have in the Khilafat, we respectfully urge upon your Majesty either to support Britain or to keep neutral in this war.

To convince the British government of continued Muslim loyalty, the medical stores and instruments used for the Turkish mission during the Balkan Wars were handed over to the British government in its 'righteous' war for the cause of justice and liberty against Germany.[101,102] The Red Crescent organised a volunteer corps to assist British troops and significant contributions were made to the British War Relief Fund. As late as September 1914, the following was the position of Mazhar-ul-Haque, a leading member of the Congress:[103]

> We are Musalmans and we are Indians and we have to perform our duty in this double capacity. I am happy to believe that these two interests do not clash, but are entirely identical.

Apart from urging Turkey to remain neutral or support Britain, Muslim leaders also urged Viceroy Hardinge to enable Turkey's continued neutrality. The government, to err on the side of caution, decided to invoke the Press Act to clamp down on pan-Islamic literature being published by Maulana Abul Kalam Azad in his *Al-Hilal*. Azad, on his part, also wrote a book, *Masla-i-khilafat-wa-Jazirat-ul-Arab*, to provide a theological justification for the Khilafat as an institution for the security and welfare of the Muslim community.[104] Importantly, Azad gave a theological precedent for Muslim collaboration with Hindus against the British, which explains the pressure exerted by the pan-Islamists on the Muslim League to collaborate with the

Congress to secure self-government for Bharat. Citing the Islamic Prophet's pact with the Jews in 622 CE, Azad made the case that it was Quranic to collaborate with one group of non-Muslims, namely the Hindus, to act against another group of non-Muslims, namely the British.[105] Until then, readers may recollect, the British, being Christians, were seen as Ahl-i-Kitab or People of the Book by Muslim leaders to provide an Islamic justification for their support to the British establishment.

Clearly, the League's collaboration with the Congress at the behest of the pan-Islamists to secure self-government for India was strategic, because it would mean loosening of the British government's hold over Muslims in Bharat. This would, in turn, allow the Muslims to freely support the Caliphate without being bogged down by their loyalty to the British. Citing Ayesha Jalal, I had stated in Chapter 2 that Azad was a student of Afghani's school of pan-Islamism which endorsed the use of jihad as a scriptural mandate to give effect to the will of Allah. This is pertinent to the discussion at hand because Mushirul Hasan corroborates this fact and says that Azad called for the revival of jihad to secure freedom from the British.[106] Contrary to the secular, humanist and rational hue with which Azad, the first education minster of Independent Bharat, is painted in the popular discourse, Hasan categorically states as follows:[107]

> Religion was the fundamental cause which brought Mohamed Ali, Azad, and Zafar Ali into the forefront of agitational politics. They were devout Muslims with an abiding faith in Islam which, in their opinion, embodied a complete set of rules for human success and happiness. Above all, they saw themselves as part of the larger Islamic community (umma) and sought tenaciously to preserve and strengthen it against the forces of nationalism and imperialism. In their attempt to achieve this object, they developed a wide network of connections ranging from educational institutions to political parties. They had close links with the seminaries at Deoband, Nadwa and Firangi Mahal which were the traditional centres of Islamic education. No less important was their influence on the M.A.O. College, Aligarh, where, despite the legacy of Sir Syed's opposition to pan-Islamism, they evoked a favourable response.

> Students flocked to the meetings addressed by Mohamed Ali and Zafar Ali and were swayed by the pan-Islamic ideology. Aligarh soon became one of the important centres of Khilafat activity.

While all this explains the League's motivations for collaborating with the Congress, the latter, on the other hand, chose to support the Khilafat Movement since it meant gaining the confidence of Muslims and their support for the cause of self-government. When Turkey joined the War on the side of the Central Powers on 1 November 1914, the Viceroy issued a notification assuring Muslims of the safety of their holy places in Arabia, Syria, Iraq and Palestine (the Jazirat-ul-Arab)[108] in order to prevent hostile reactions from the Muslims of the subcontinent. This was to assure them that the War did not have a religious character. At the instance of the British empire, France and Russia too gave similar assurances to Muslims the world over.[109] Thanks to these assurances, Nawab Salimullah, Fazl-ul-Haq, the Raja of Mahmudabad, Nizam Mir Osman Ali Khan of Hyderabad, the Begum of Bhopal, Nawab Syed Hamid Ali Khan of Rampur, the Muslim League in general, and the ulema of Nadwa and Deoband came forward to reaffirm their loyalty to the British despite Turkish participation in the War against the British. Since the pan-Islamists (the extremists within the League) were outnumbered, they too chose to toe this line, but without condemning Turkey for allying with the Central Powers.[110] However, through their mouthpieces—namely the *Al-Hilal, Comrade, Islamic Mail* and *Musalman*—the pan-Islamists made a suggestion that would become the basis of the Khilafat Movement. The suggestion was that in order to allay Muslim apprehensions, the British must not only assure them protection of their holy places but *also* that the territorial integrity of the Ottoman Caliphate would remain unaffected by the outcome of the War. After all, the Muslim perspective was that the concept of Caliphate extended to both religious authority and temporal powers.

It was around this period that hijrat, or emigration, was also considered by those Muslims who wanted to fight for Turkey. Like Barelvi's hijrat to the then NWF to fight the British, and the current-day emigration of a section of Muslims to fight for the ISIS given its Caliphal claims, in February 1915, a group of students from Lahore crossed over into Afghanistan to proceed to Turkey. During this period, a section of the pan-Islamists also allied with the Revolutionaries who had the support of Germany to fight the British empire. The combined propaganda of the pan-Islamists and the Revolutionaries resulted in defections and mutiny in those British Indian Army regiments that had significant numbers of Muslim soldiers.[111] In May 1915, Maulana Muhammad Ali Jauhar wrote a piece titled 'Choice of the Turks' defending Turkey's decision to ally with the Central Powers, which resulted in the internment of the Ali Brothers by the British.

This period also witnessed the establishment of a short-lived provisional Government of India in Kabul by the ulema from Deoband, such as Mahmud-al Hasan and Obeidullah Sindhi, along with the Revolutionaries, with the support of the Afghan government and the Turko-German Mission in Kabul.[112] A plot was hatched to launch a jihad against the British for which an army called 'Junud Allah' (Army of Allah) was established. To secure Caliphal approval for the jihad, for circulation among Muslims in Bharat, a declaration titled 'Ghalib Nama' was obtained from the Ottoman governor of Hejaz, Ghalib Pasha. However, the entire correspondence in this regard, which would be known as the 'Silk Letters', was accidentally discovered by the Punjab CID, which resulted in the plot being revealed and a wave of arrests and internments of pan-Islamists, including Azad.[113]

Prior to the internment of the Ali Brothers in May 1915, Gandhi, who had returned from South Africa in December 1914, had established communication with them. Here are his words, from his autobiography:[114]

PASSION FOR UNITY

The Kheda campaign was launched while the deadly war in Europe was still going on. Now a crisis had arrived, and the Viceroy had invited various leaders to a war conference in Delhi. I had also been urged to attend the conference. I have already referred to the cordial relations between Lord Chelmsford, the Viceroy, and myself.

In response to the invitation I went to Delhi. I had, however, objections to taking part in the conference, the principal one being the exclusion from it of leaders like the Ali Brothers. They were then in jail. I had met them only once or twice, though I had heard much about them. Everyone had spoken highly of their services and their courage. I had not then come in close touch with Hakim Saheb, but Principal Rudra and Dinabandhu Andrews had told me a deal in his praise. I had met Mr. Shuaib Qureshi and Mr. Khwaja at the Muslim League in Calcutta. I had also come in contact with Drs. Ansari and Abdur Rahman. I was seeking the friendship of good Musalmans, and was eager to understand the Musalman mind through contact with their purest and most patriotic representatives. I therefore never needed any pressure to go with them, wherever they took me, in order to get into intimate touch with them.

I had realized early enough in South Africa that there was no genuine friendship between the Hindus and the Musalmans. I never missed a single opportunity to remove obstacles in the way of unity. It was not in my nature to placate anyone by adulation, or at the cost of self-respect. But my South African experiences had convinced me that it would be on the question of Hindu–Muslim unity that my ahimsa would be put to its severest test, and that the question presented the widest field for my experiments in ahimsa. The conviction is still there. Every moment of my life I realize that God is putting me on my trial.

Having such strong convictions on the question when I returned from South Africa, I prized the contact with the Brothers. But before closer touch could be established they were isolated. Maulana Mahomed Ali used to write long letters to me from Betul and Chhindwada whenever his jailers allowed him to do so. I applied for permission to visit the Brothers, but to no purpose.

It was after the imprisonment of the Ali Brothers that I was invited by Muslim friends to attend the session of the Muslim League at Calcutta. Being requested to speak, I addressed them on the duty of the Muslims to secure the Brothers' release. A little while after this I was taken by these friends to the Muslim College at Aligarh. There I invited the young men to be fakirs for the service of the motherland.

Next I opened correspondence with the Government for the release of the Brothers. In that connection I studied the Brothers' views and activities about the Khilafat. I had discussions with Musalman friends. I felt that, if I would become a true friend of the Muslims, I must render all possible help in securing the release of the Brothers, and a just settlement of the Khilafat question. It was not for me to enter into the absolute merits of the question, provided there was nothing immoral in their demands. In matters of religion beliefs differ, and each one's is supreme for himself. If all had the same belief about all matters of religion, there would be only one religion in the world. As time progressed I found that the Muslim demand about the Khilafat was not only not against any ethical principle, but that the British Prime Minister had admitted the justice of the Muslim demand. I felt, therefore, bound to render what help I could in securing a due fulfillment of the Prime Minister's pledge. The pledge had been given in such clear terms that the examination of the Muslim demand on the merits was needed only to satisfy my own conscience.

Friends and critics have criticized my attitude regarding the Khilafat question. In spite of the criticism I feel that I have no reason to revise it or to regret my co-operation with the Muslims. I should adopt the same attitude, should a similar occasion arise.

When, therefore, I went to Delhi, I had fully intended to submit the Muslim case to the Viceroy. The Khilafat question had not then assumed the shape it did subsequently.

But on my reaching Delhi another difficulty in the way of my attending the conference arose.

The 'difficulty' Gandhi was referring to was the rumour that in 1915, Britain, France, Russia and Italy had concluded secret treaties among themselves, under which, in the event of Allied victory in the War, the Ottoman empire would be partitioned into four spheres of influence, in addition to Turkish territories being annexed by each of the Allied states, which included Russia, the United States and Japan.[115] The stated object of the treaties was to 'set free populations' from the 'bloody tyranny of the Turks' and to evict the Ottoman empire out of Europe since it was 'decidedly foreign to Western Civilization'.[116] This was *after* assuring Muslim populations in Bharat and elsewhere that the War was not religious. However, it must be equally stressed here that the Ottoman Caliphate had a long history of massacring non-Muslim populations, the Greek and Armenian genocides (both of which accounted for at least 2.5 million non-Muslim deaths) being stark testaments to the same.[117] Therefore, there was more than an element of truth in the West's attempt to free the subjugated populations of Turkey. This much is clear, that at least for the West, the First World War was a clash of civilisations insofar as the Ottoman empire was concerned, while it may have been political in relation to the other Central Powers, which were European. As for the Ottoman empire, they saw the war as a continuum of the clash between the Cross and the Crescent. After all, the Ottoman empire was built on the Eastern Roman empire, also known as the Byzantine empire, whose capital had been Constantinople, named after the Roman Emperor Constantine 'the Great'. In many ways, the clash between the Allied Powers and the Ottoman empire was indeed a clash between European and Middle Eastern colonialities.

To add to the rumours about the secret treaties, the Arab Revolt against the Ottoman empire in June 1916 seriously undermined the cause of pan-Islamism since the epicentre of the revolt was the holiest of places for Muslims—Mecca.[118] The revolt was led by Hussein bin Ali al-Hashimi, the Sharif of Mecca, which resulted in the capture of Mecca, Jeddah and Taif by the Arab rebels.[119] On 26 June 1916, the council of the Muslim League met in Lucknow and passed a resolution condemning Hussein for his 'outrageous conduct' which had jeopardised the safety of the holy places. Maulana Abdul Bari called him an enemy of Islam.[120] Although Muslims in Bharat accused the British of stabbing them in the back by sponsoring the revolt, scholar Naeem Qureshi holds that the Revolt was indigenous, with the British having merely supported it to weaken the Ottoman empire on the eastern front of the War. Thomas Edward Lawrence, who would later be famously known as 'Lawrence of Arabia', was the British officer instrumental in supporting Hussein against the Ottomans.[121]

However, the British were clear that they would not involve themselves in the 'Khilafat Question', i.e., whether the mantle of the Khilafat/Caliphate had passed on from the Ottoman empire to the newly independent Kingdom of Hejaz under Hussein or not. The British assured the Muslims in Bharat and other countries that the issue of Khilafat would be settled by the ummah, without non-Muslim interference.[122] The British gave the further assurance to them that no non-Muslim power would be allowed to control the Jazirat-ul-Arab. These assurances were given because, despite desertions and defections, a good number of Muslim soldiers from Bharat were fighting the Ottoman empire on behalf of the British, even while the Friday khutba was being offered in the name of the Ottoman Caliph in mosques here.

Meanwhile, back in Bharat, Tilak, Annie Besant and Gandhi supported the League's demand for release of the Ali Brothers. As mentioned in the previous chapter, at the joint conference organised by the Congress and the League in Bombay in July 1917, one of the demands put forth to the British government was for release of the Ali Brothers and Maulana Azad. A resolution to the same effect was moved by Tilak at the 1917 annual session of the Congress, where he had delivered a speech in support of it. At the League's annual session of 1917, apart from demanding the release of the Ali Brothers, the Raja of Mahmudabad warned against non-Muslim interference in the Khilafat question. Gandhi, who attended the League's session, supported the resolution demanding the release of the Ali Brothers.

The year 1917 was a turning point in the War for another reason. Thanks to the Bolshevik Revolution in Russia and the conclusion of a separate peace treaty between Germany and Russia, the burden on the rest of the Allied Powers increased. The British had to depend more on Commonwealth support, in particular India's, for supply of men and materials. To make matters worse for the British, the Bolsheviks disclosed and confirmed to the world the existence and contents of the secret treaties, which only added to Muslim distrust of the British. Further, the First Imperial War Conference, which was held in London for the British Commonwealth from 21 March to 27 April 1917, had no Muslim representation from Bharat despite the Muslim League's requests for it. As discussed in the previous chapter, only the Secretary of State, along with S.P. Sinha and the Maharaja of Bikaner, represented Bharat at the Conference.[123] Critically, on 2 November 1917, the foreign secretary of the United Kingdom, Arthur James Balfour, wrote to Lord Rothschild, a leader of the British Jewish community, a letter that contained the Balfour Declaration (a misnomer, given that it was the British Crown's Declaration, which Balfour merely relayed):[124]

Dear Lord Rothschild,

I have much pleasure in conveying to you, on behalf of his Majesty's Government, the following declaration of sympathy with Jewish Zionist aspirations which has been submitted to, and approved by, the Cabinet.

'His Majesty's Government view with favour the establishment in Palestine of a national home for the Jewish people, and will use their best endeavours to facilitate the achievement of this object, it being clearly understood that nothing shall be done which may prejudice the civil and religious rights of existing non-Jewish communities in Palestine, or the rights and political status enjoyed by Jews in any other country.'

I should be grateful if you would bring this declaration to the knowledge of the Zionist Federation.

Yours,

Arthur James Balfour

The Federation referred to in the letter was the Zionist Federation of Great Britain and Ireland.

Realising that these developments—coming as they did at a crucial juncture in the War—could cumulatively lead to massive and adverse reactions from Muslims all over the world, and in particular India, the British prime minister Llyod George gave a speech, which had the unanimous support of all political parties in the UK, defining the aims of the War.[125] In this speech made on 5 January 1918, he declared that the British and the Allied Powers were not fighting '*to deprive Turkey of its capital, or of the rich and renowned lands of Asia Minor and Thrace, which are predominantly Turkish in race*'. He added that '*the passage between the Mediterranean and the Black Sea (was) being internationalised and neutralised*'. Critically, he added that '*Arabia, Armenia, Mesopotamia, Syria, and Palestine are, in our judgment, entitled to a recognition of their separate national conditions*', and that '*it would be impossible to restore [them] to their former sovereignty*'. This view was endorsed by the US president Woodrow Wilson in his message to the US Congress on 8 January 1918.[126] This effectively meant that the Jazirat-ul-Arab, the land where lay the holy places of Muslims, would no more be under the control of the Ottoman empire. This, in turn, meant that its Caliphal status was seriously undermined. This also effectively meant that the British promise of non-interference on the question of the Khilafat stood reneged.

Back in Bharat, in January 1918, Gandhi urged the Viceroy to release the Ali Brothers, but was rebuffed.[127] From March 1918, Gandhi frequently met Maulana Abdul Bari in connection with the Ali Brothers. In one of his letters to Maulana Muhammad Ali, he confessed that his 'selfish' interest in securing their release was to strengthen Hindu–Muslim relations in the interest of Swaraj or self-government. In April 1918, Gandhi once again wrote to the Viceroy against the backdrop of the Delhi Imperial War Conference. An extract from his letter is reproduced below:[128]

> Lastly I would like to request His Majesty's Ministers to give definite assurances about Mahomedan States. I am sure you know that every Mahomedan is deeply interested in them. As a Hindu I cannot be indifferent to their cause. Their sorrows must be our sorrows. In the most scrupulous regard for the rights of these States and for the Muslim sentiment as to the places of worship and in your just and timely treatment of Indian claim to Home Rule lies the safety of the Empire.

In July 1918, Gandhi declared his intention to 'engage the Government in a duel' to secure the release of the Ali Brothers.[129] His efforts in this direction made him popular among the Muslim community. This reflected in Ajmal Khan's welcome speech at the Congress's 1918 annual session in Delhi, wherein he referred to Gandhi as 'Mahatma Gandhi', the 'acknowledged and revered leader of the country'. It is this popularity that enabled Gandhi to take up the agitation against the Rowlatt Act with support from across the country, especially from the Muslim community.[130] The other practical reason for Muslim support to Gandhi's anti-Rowlatt agitation was the fact that the Rowlatt Act could severely restrict the activities of the pan-Islamists. Therefore, the Muslim community had a specific incentive to support Gandhi on this front.

Meanwhile, the War was drawing to a close and the Second Imperial War Conference for the British Commonwealth was held in London from 12 June to 26 July 1918. Once again, S.P. Sinha represented Bharat, and again there was no Muslim representation. The curtains were drawn on armed hostilities in the War when an armistice was entered into by the Allied Powers and Turkey on 30 October 1918, followed by an armistice with Germany on 11 November 1918. Under the terms of the armistice with Turkey, the issue of territorial readjustment was left to the Paris Peace Conference; however, the armistice ruled out restoration of Turkish sovereignty over the 'liberated' territories. The UK, France and Italy quickly moved to give effect to the secret treaties—which were no more secret, thanks to the Bolsheviks—by way of creating their respective spheres of influence. Accordingly, the Straits, Arabia and Iraq would come under British influence, Syria under French, and the Dodencanese Islands and Adalia under Italian influence.[131] Coupled with the establishment of Hussein's kingdom of Hejaz, the creation of the Palestine Mandate and the promise of an independent homeland for Jews in Palestine, Turkey would lose complete control over the Jazirat-ul-Arab.[132]

From the perspective of Muslims in Bharat, loss of global Muslim political importance translated to loss of political importance in Bharat.[133] This sentiment was not helped by the Montford Report's reservations on the principle of communal electorates, despite the Report retaining the position under the Minto–Morley Reforms. The continued internment of the Ali Brothers and of Azad and Maulana Hasrat Mohani did not help either, although the Ali Brothers were given a three-week parole in December 1918 to visit their sick relatives in Rampur. The Ali Brothers visited Maulana Abdul Bari and decided to launch a systematic agitation for the Khilafat along with other leaders of the Khilafat, such as Moshir Hossain Kidwai, *before* the commencement of the Paris Peace Conference in January 1919, where the issue of territorial readjustment would be decided. The December 1918 session of the League, to be held in Delhi, was chosen as the platform for the launch of the agitation in collaboration with members of the Congress.[134]

It is for this reason that the annual sessions of 1918 of the Congress and the League assume significance, since extensive deliberations were held at both sessions on the question of the Khilafat, the future of Turkey, the safety of Muslim holy places and the continued detention of the Ali Brothers, Maulana Abul Kalam Azad and Maulana Hasrat Mohani. In the previous chapter, I had shared extracts from Ajmal Khan's welcome speech and Malaviya's presidential speech at the Congress session in Delhi which dealt with the issue of the Khilafat. The League's session saw a huge presence of ulema, who put their stamp of religious approval on the League's Khilafat demands. The chairman of the reception committee, Dr M.A. Ansari, reminded the British Crown of its wartime pledges to the Muslim community regarding saving the temporal power of Islam, namely the Ottoman Caliphate, from further dismemberment.[135] He demanded that all non-Muslim control be removed from the Jazirat-ul-Arab and that the suzerainty of the Ottoman Sultan over those territories be restored. Lashing out at Hussein bin Ali for staking a claim to the position of Caliph, he accused him of being driven by personal ambition and selfish interests, saying he thus deserved to be *killed*. Interestingly, this portion was omitted in the English summary of Ansari's speech, owing to objections from the government because of its incendiary nature.[136]

Coming to Fazlul Haque's presidential speech at the League's session, I had included an extract from it in the previous chapter. Here is a more comprehensive portion from his speech, which can now be better understood in light of the foregoing discussion on the Khilafat:[137]

Presidential Address of Mr. A.K. Fazlul Haque

You have been pleased to summon me, a mere commoner from a corner of the Indian Continent, to preside over the deliberations of a body whose activities, based on the noble principles of Islam, have been moulding into shape the nascent aspirations of the Muslim nationhood in India. The honour which you have thus conferred upon me is unique and invokes my heartfelt gratitude; but the responsibility which this position carries with it is also unquestionable and immense, specially at a time when dark clouds are louring over the political horizon of the country, big with the possibilities of a political devastation which may engulf civilization all over the globe. My remarks apply with special force to the Musalmans of India, who are being hemmed in on all sides by enemies bent on the destruction, not merely of Islamic Empires, but also of Islamic civilization and culture. The great World War, which seems to be coming to an end, has brought problems relating to Islam to the forefront all over the world. These problems call for solution, not only to protect the temporal power of Islam, but also those spiritual forces which for the last 13 centuries have illumined the path of material and moral progress all over the civilized world. I feel confident that having conferred such a unique honour upon me, you will also come forward to render me all help and assistance in carrying on the duties of such an exalted office. I also feel sure that with your help and assistance we will be able to guide the deliberations of this session of the League in a way which will lead to the successful attainment of all those aims and aspirations, which we have always kept in view as the guiding principles of the great organization to which we all have the honour to belong.

Muslim Apprehension about the Fate of Turkey

Brethren, we have met to-day under circumstances entirely different from those that prevailed in this Sub-Continent during the last four years. The Great World War seems to be coming to an end. The thunders of cannon balls and the clash of arms are becoming fainter and fainter, and we are all on the tiptoe of expectation for the peace which alone can bring relief from the awful conditions through which we have passed during the War. Anything that was good and noble in the civilized world has been practically shattered to pieces, and when the long-wished-for peace will come, we will have to rebuild a new order of things out of the ruins of the old. But even this peace is still far off, and we will have to wait anxiously for the opportunity which peace will bring in its train. There are many difficulties in the way of real peace. The innate and inborn envy and jealousies of the nations of Europe will raise insurmountable difficulties in the way of peace, and unless some unforeseen event happens, all our cherished hopes for peace will end in disappointment.

The present age is full of anxieties for Muslims all over the world. The Great World War, which appears to be ending so happily and triumphantly for the Allies, has unfortunately brought deep and gloomy forebodings to Muslim minds. Muslim countries are now the prey of the land-grabbing propensities of the Christian nations, in spite of the solemn pledges given by these very nations that the World War was being fought for the protection of the rights of small and defenceless minorities. Morocco, Tunis, Algiers, Egypt have all their tales of woe to tell about the unabashed greed of Christain Powers, and hardly do we get a little breathing time to deal with one unfortunate Muslim state, when cries of distress come from other quarters.

Only yesterday, the attempts made by the Christian Powers to throttle Iran raised loud protests from all over the Muslim world, and today we find the same powers seriously bent on the dismemberment of Turkey. To us, the Muslims all over the World, the fate of Turkey is bound with problems of deep concern. We cannot forget that Turkey raises, for all Muslims, the questions of the Khilafat and the protections of our holy places. We are often told that England has under its sway more Muslims than any other power in the world.

But alas, is it not within the memory of even the present generation that the ministers of the British Crown have seldom had any scruples in casting to the winds their obligations to the Muslims, specially of India, and even trampled under foot, solemn pledges given time and again to the Muslim world? Over the past misdeeds of British statesmen, we may draw a veil, but we feel that the time has come when we should warn these statesmen that it is against all rules of prudence to draw ceaseless drafts on the bank of loyalty. It is a trite saying, but nevertheless true, that it is the last straw that often breaks the camel's back. It will be a miracle if it is otherwise with Indian Muslims.

From a consideration of the prospects of a speedy peace, let us turn to the efforts that are being made by the victorious Allies to discuss the terms of Peace. It is a matter of great regret that in these deliberations of the various Powers, no Muslim Power will be allowed to take any part. Muslim cases will thus go by default. It is obvious that we cannot depend on British statesmen to represent the Muslim cause. Only the other day, a prominent British statesman, Lord Robert Cecil, declared that Turkey has shown an utter incapacity for ruling subject races. Fortunately, no detailed discussion on this point is necessary, because it will suffice if we refer the noble lord to the pages of Gibbon, Froude and Arnold, and of Orientalists like Margouleith and Pickthall for an authentic testimony to the manner in which Turkey has discharged her obligations to subject races. Even the most hostile critic of Turkey will admit that history abounds with instances not merely of the liberal administrative policy of the Turks, but also of the manner in which Turkey has often given shelter to small Christian nations, who but for Turkish help, would have been wiped out of existence by bigger Christian Powers. I would have treated the remarks of the British minister with supreme contempt had it not been for the fact that these words of the British minister clearly indicate that a case is being made out to throttle Turkey. I will therefore venture to take up a little of your time to discuss this question briefly before I pass on to other matters.

Turkish Treatment of Subject People

Eminent historians have borne testimony to the magnanimity with which Turkey has often treated its Christian subjects, even in cases of proved treason and disloyalty, and how the much maligned Turks have given practical demonstrations of that toleration which Christians often preach in theory but never show in practice. Everyone knows that for centuries past, Russia has been the biggest enemy of Turkey. The internal dissensions in Russia have often given Turkey opportunities of bringing about a dismemberment of the Russian Empire. But Turkey never played a mean part by hitting Russia below the belt. Only the other day thousands of Russian Jews were turned out of Russia in the most inhuman manner. They were homeless and resourceless in a foreign land, and would have succumbed to the privations with which they were faced, had not the hospitality of the Turks saved them from the dismal fate that awaited them. In this respect, the history of Europe has been repeating itself for centuries. Not once or twice but times without number, the Jews have been turned out, bag and baggage, from Christian countries only to get shelter in the domains of the very Turks whom Christian statesmen have denounced as incapable of dealing with subject races. The phrase 'Wandering Jew' has passed into a proverb to represent the sad plight of Jews all over Europe, knocking at every Christian door but getting a response from none. It is the Turks who have invariably given them shelter, and at the present moment it is well known that the Middle East and Near East have become colonies of these wandering Jews, who have concentrated in Salonica as their final abode to live peacefully and happily under Turkish rule...

Questions Relating to the Khilafat and Muslim Holy Places

Brethren, I fully realize that I have already trespassed too much on your time and patience, but I cannot resume my seat without a brief reference to the questions relating to the Khilafat and the protection of our holy places. You have heard the speech of Dr. M.A. Ansari on both these points. He has dealt with all questions relating to both these vital affairs so thoroughly that there is hardly anything for me to say. *In my opinion, the question of the Khilafat should be dealt with by Muslims themselves without interference from non-Muslims, and our holy places should also be immune from non-Muslim influences.* We should object to having anything to do with political mummers who outwardly profess Islam and claim some amount of influence in public. *The revolt of the Sherif of Mecca has endangered the future of our holy places, and the world of Islam is watching with sorrow and anxiety the effects of the Sherif's declaration of Independence. I wish to leave these questions to be dealt with by the revered Ulema whom I see present here; but I cannot but say a few words on one point which is likely to escape the notice of officials. All questions relating to the Khilafat and the protection of our holy places are intimately bound up with the vital articles of our faith. Our rulers are in the habit of distorting political problems by setting up their tools and sycophants to defend official points of view; but however entertaining this pastime may be in the case of political affairs, it is fraught with danger if the experiment is tried with reference to questions relating to our religious views. We are loyal subjects of the rulers, and are prepared to prove our loyalty in actual practice by making sacrifices. But this temporal loyalty is subject to the limitation imposed by our undoubted loyalty to our faith. We wish to warn our rulers that in making sacrifices one after another, the dividing line may soon be reached; and we need hardly emphasize that in case there is a conflict between Divine Laws and the mandates of our rulers, every true Musalman will allow the Divine Commandments to prevail over human laws, even at the risk of laying down his life.* [Emphases added]

Importantly, in view of the weakened position of the global ummah, thanks to the defeat of the Caliphate, Fazlul Haque urged Muslims in Bharat to establish good relations with non-Muslims to safeguard their own future.[138] Although this was a well-meaning exhortation, it also shows that the health of the relationship of Muslims in Bharat with non-Muslims was (and perhaps remains) a function of the strength of the global ummah and certainly not independent of it. This is to be expected, given the hierarchy of loyalties that is inherent to the worldview of Middle Eastern consciousness. After Fazlul Haque, in his turn, Maulana Abdul Bari objected to the display of the Union Jack at the venue; and this objection too is absent from the English translation of the proceedings of the session. The anger against the British establishment was clearly simmering, although others such as Jinnah and Nabiullah cautioned against the use of intemperate language and display of aggressive behaviour on the League's platform since it could jeopardise the position of the League in the eyes of the British.[139]

The following were the League's resolutions at this session:[140]

Having regard to the fact that the Indian Musalmans take a deep interest in the fate of their co-religionists outside India, and that the collapse of the Muslim Powers of the world is bound to have an adverse influence on the political importance of the Musalmans in the country, and the annihilation of the military powers of Islam in the world cannot but have a far-reaching effect on the minds of even the loyal Musalmans of India, the All-India Muslim League considers it to be its duty to place before the Government of India and His Majesty's Government the true sentiments of the Muslim community, and requests that the British Representatives at the Peace Conference will use their influence and see that in the territorial and political redistribution to be made, the fullest consideration should be paid to the requirements of the Islamic law with regard to full and independent control by the Sultan of Turkey, Khalifa of the Prophet, over the holy places and over the Jazirat-ul-Arab as delimited in the Muslim books. The League further hopes that in determining the political relations of the Empire, for the future, His Majesty's Ministers shall pay the fullest consideration to the universal and deep sentiment of the Musalmans of India, and that resolute attempts should be made to effect a complete reconciliation and lasting concord between the Empire and Muslim states, based on equity and justice, in the interests alike of the British Empire and the Muslim world.

The All-India Muslim League views with great dissatisfaction the unreasonable attitude of the Government in not releasing Maulana Mohammad Ali and other Musim internees, even after the signing of the Armistice, and urges their immediate release in order to ally [sic] Muslim feelings. In view of the vague nature of the charges framed against them by the Committee of Enquiry appointed by the Government to investigate their case, the League strongly protests against the continuation of internment of Messrs. Shaukat Ali and Mohammad Ali.

Mr. Wazir Hussein, who spoke on the resolution, said that in the case of the two Ali Brothers it was not only injustice but oppression.

It must be appreciated that the government was apprehensive about releasing the pan-Islamist internees in view of the impending Paris Peace Conference where the issue of territorial readjustment and distribution would be discussed and decided. However, by not releasing them, the government was adding to Muslim anger; effectively, the government was between a rock and a hard place. As regards the Khilafat agitators ('Khilafatists'), they wanted the release of the internees *precisely* because they would add strength to their agitation and put greater pressure on the government to restore the territorial integrity of Turkey, in particular over the Jazirat-ul-Arab. The stage was set for the Khilafat Movement to mature into the Khilafat Agitation.

Thus ended the League's session of 1918, *without* the customary cheers for the King-Emperor, marking an open estrangement between the League and the government.[141] Old-timers like the Raja of Mahmudabad and Wazir Hasan, who were seen as Moderates in the League, resigned from the League in March 1919.

With this summary of events until December 1918, I shall now proceed to discuss the momentous course of the Khilafat Agitation and Non-Cooperation Movement from January 1919 up to the time of the Nagpur sessions of the Congress and the League in December 1920.

The Khilafat Agitation and the Non-Cooperation Movement from 1919 to 1920

The significance of the League's 1918 session, its tone, and the import of its resolutions, were not lost on the British Indian government. The government realised that it may have trouble on its hands, both on account of soldiers returning home from the War, who included Muslims, and the reactions from the Khilafatists to developments at the Paris Peace Conference where the fate of Turkey hung in the balance. The ante was upped by the ulema by way of formalisation of their Khilafat demands in typical Islamic fashion. Upon commencement of the Peace Conference in January 1919, Maulana Abdul Bari issued a fatwa to the effect that all Muslims were duty-bound to contribute to the restoration of the Khilafat in Ottoman hands.[142] This fatwa was signed by sixty ulema, although there were notable politically correct abstentions. The result of this was that the Viceroy as well as the government in the UK were deluged with representations and telegrams from educated

Staff and students of the National College, Lahore, founded in 1921 by Lala Lajpat Rai with a view to train students for the Non-Cooperation Movement. Standing fourth from the right is Bhagat Singh, later executed by the British for his revolutionary activities.

Muslims urging the British to prevent the dismemberment of Turkey. The government's reaction to this may be discerned from Chelmsford's Report to Montagu on 31 January 1919:[143]

> That Muslim feeling in India and also on the Frontier is much disturbed over prospect of dismemberment of the Turkish Empire there is no doubt. This feeling is most marked with regard to the Holy Places, but is also strong regarding Constantinople as the seat of the Khalifate and the capital of last great Islamic power ... Failure to voice her [i.e. Muslim India's] views would exacerbate feelings already sore ...

To prepare for any eventuality, the government decided to equip itself with emergency powers through the Rowlatt Bills, which, as stated earlier, were introduced in the Imperial Legislative Council on 6 February 1919 and resulted in the Rowlatt Act in mid-March. Jinnah resigned from the Council in protest,[144] while Gandhi launched his Satyagraha. At this point, Gandhi and Maulana Abdul Bari reached out to each other; the former needed the support of the Muslim community for his Satyagraha while the latter sensed an opportunity to widen the scope of the Khilafat Agitation by partnering with Gandhi. Further, a barter of sorts was made, which is best captured in the following report of a government informer:[145]

> It was agreed (reported a Government informer) that when the agitation was at its height there would be a large meeting of Ulemas (sic) Maulvis and Mahommadans generally, at which Abdul Bari should be elected Shaikh-ul-

Islam and the Muslim demands regarding the Khilafat, the holy places, etc., should be formulated. *The Hindus would support these demands which should be submitted to His Excellency the Viceroy with the warning that nonacceptance of them would mean jehad.* In return for the assistance of the Hindus, Abdul Bari, in his capacity as Shaikh-ul-Islam, was to issue a fatwa declaring that the animal originally sacrificed by Ibrahim was a sheep and not a cow and that cow-sacrifice was prohibited in future. [Emphasis added]

Thanks to the Maulana's support, Syed Hasan Imam and Mazhar-ul-Haque helped to mobilise thousands of Muslims for Gandhi's agitation in Patna;[146] in Lahore, Dr. Saifuddin Kitchlew, Pir Tajuddin, Mohsin Shah, Fazl-i-Hussain and Mohammad Iqbal mobilised the crowds for Gandhi;[147] and in Delhi, an address by Swami Shraddhananda at the Jama Masjid was organised by Dr M.A. Ansari, Arif Hussain Haswi, editor of the *Congress* and the *Inquilab*, and Barrister Asaf Ali. Apart from the Khilafat Agitation and the anti-Rowlatt agitation, the economic downturn caused by the War too contributed to the massive numbers at Gandhi's meetings. After all, Bharat had bled for the British Crown in more ways than one. In this sense, a variety of grievances found ventilation through the anti-Rowlatt agitation. The convergence of interests between Gandhi and Maulana Bari no doubt led to a powerful countrywide mobilisation of the masses.

Alongside the agitation, in the middle of March 1919, the Bombay Khilafat Committee was established under Seth Mian Muhammad Hajee Jan Muhammad Chotani[148] with the help of wealthy followers of Bari's seminary, Firangi Mahal. This committee would play a huge role in the agitation. Importantly, on 24 April 1919, the Ali Brothers wrote a memorandum to the Viceroy from Chhindwara prison spelling out the specific demands of the Khilafat Agitation:[149]

Moslem loyalty and support had so often been assured to Government in our gene ration, and even Moslem contentment was so often unduly taken for granted, that other communities had with some justice made our attitude towards Government almost a matter of reproach. It was a strange return for all this loyalty and support, that, without any effective protest, and often with the concurrence of His Majesty's Government, blow after blow was aimed at the temporal power of Islam ... If Britain decided to retain the goodwill of the Mussalmans, a hundred millions of whom were members of her composite Empire, she must befriend and keep the Caliphate on her side, and deal more fairly and equitably with Moslem Kingdoms and countries such as Persia, Afghanistan and Morocco.

...There should be no attempt by non-Muslim[s] to interfere in the free choice by the Muslims of the Khalifa, the sovereignty of the Khalifa over the Holy Places should not be dismembered 'even among Moslem Governments for it would weaken the temporal power of Islam'; Egypt and the other territories of the former Turkish Empire should be restored to the Khalifa; Muslim religious places should not be occupied or controlled by non-Muslims. The Muslim should not be asked to assist in the prosecution of war against the Khalifa; no Muslim should be punished for promoting sympathy with his brother Muslims in any part of the world; the British Government should pay more respect to the sentiments of Muslims in India and should cultivate friendly relations with the Muslim governments of Turkey, Persia, Afghanistan and Morocco.

The government realised that although Gandhi's agitation was primarily aimed at the Rowlatt Act on the face of it, the support of the Khilafatists was contributing significantly to the agitation. This realisation was captured in a telegram dated 18 May 1919 from Chelmsford to Montagu wherein the former shared his views as follows:[150]

Muslim feeling is already deeply stirred ... If the fate of Turkey approximates to worst anticipations, we warn you results may be very grave ... Already Hindu intrigue has successfully exploited Muslim soreness, and results are to be seen in the Punjab, Calcutta and Bombay disorders. Now we have war on the frontier waged by a Mahomedan Kingdom and proclaimed by Amir as Jihad (holy war) ... Spectacle of Turkey completely dismembered by Christian powers may conceivably make Muslims turn to Amir as waging Jihad on behalf of Islam. A Mahomedan religious rising is a contingency not to be ruled out of account.

Despite this realisation, there was no attempt to include Muslim representation from Bharat as part of the Bharatiya delegation at the Paris Peace Conference, which comprised Montagu, S.P. Sinha and the Maharaja of Bikaner.[151] This was because the British government in the UK and the British Indian government saw the Turkish problem differently. While the former was pro-Greek, anti-Turk and in favour of implementing the Balfour Declaration, the latter was concerned about the growing Muslim discontent and feared a repeat of 1857.[152] To add to it, the Bharatiya delegation in Paris could not hope to make any headway, thanks to the secret treaties between the Allied Powers that were being given effect to. Also, apart from the formal beneficiaries of the secret treaties—and contrary to the assurance given by Lloyd George in his declaration of 5 January 1918—in May 1919, Greece was invited to occupy Smyrna and later even Eastern Thrace, which was specifically mentioned in the Declaration, as belonging to Turkey.[153] Around this time, the League's delegation led by Jinnah, which had come to London to give evidence on the Montford Reforms to the Joint Select Committee of the British Parliament, sought an appointment with the British prime minister to present the perspective of Muslims in Bharat on Turkey.[154] However, Jinnah failed to secure an appointment.

In June 1919, the Turkish National Movement, which had its origins in the Young Turks Movement, had started under the leadership of Mustafa Kemal Pasha, popularly known as Kemal Ataturk. The irony was that while the Muslims in Bharat and other parts of the world were agitating for restoration of the Ottoman Caliphate, the home-grown Young Turks Movement, which was followed by the Turkish National Movement, wanted to replace Ottoman monarchy with a constitutional democracy. This development would prove to be extremely significant for the Khilafat Agitation in Bharat, as we shall see.

Coming back to Bharat, with no attempt on the part of the government to address Muslim concerns regarding the dismemberment of Turkey, the tone and tenor of the Khilafat Agitation became more desperate and aggressive, especially in Punjab and the NWFP, which was also worsened by the anger in Punjab post the Amritsar tragedy. This exposed a fundamental problem at the heart of the Gandhi–Bari pact; Gandhi's Satyagraha was non-violent by definition, whereas Bari's religious beliefs allowed and *required* the waging of jihad to secure the goal of the Khilafat. This was not an easy alliance, because both parties had to cut ideological and religious corners, which divergence was bound to surface at some point. The incidents of violence in Punjab and other places, which ultimately culminated in the Amritsar tragedy, led Gandhi to call off his Satyagraha on 21 July 1919. Naturally, the Khilafatists were not happy about his decision. In August 1919, when Bari sought Gandhi's support for more concerted action, the latter insisted that any such action would have to be non-violent in the interests of the future of Islam in Bharat and the future of Bharat itself.[155] In the very same month, reports surfaced that the British government had approved the internationalisation of Constantinople (Istanbul) and cession of Thrace to Greece.

To respond to this, the Central Council of the League convened on 29 August 1919 and resolved to create a broader platform so that even non-League Muslims could present their views.[156] Accordingly, it was resolved that an All-India Muslim Conference would be held on 21 September 1919 under the stewardship of Maulana Bari. The Conference demanded preservation of the Ottoman Sultan's position as the Caliph and opposed the dismemberment of the empire and its distribution to Christian powers as their mandatories or protectorates. The internationalisation of Istanbul and the cession of Thrace and Smyrna to Greece were condemned. Further, it was resolved to form a central body for coordination, and 17 October 1919 (a Friday) was fixed as Khilafat Day, a day of prayer and fasting. Gandhi asked Hindus to join Muslims in observing Khilafat Day in solidarity with them and in the interest of Hindu–Muslim unity.[157] Pursuant to this, the

Khilafat Committee of Bombay was tasked with acting as the central body which would oversee the establishment of branches all over the country. Accordingly, on 11 November 1919, the Bombay Committee was renamed 'The Central Khilafat Committee of India, Bombay'—hereinafter referred to as the CKC[158]—whereas the entire group of Khilafat organisations would be known as the Jamiat-i-Khilafat-i-Hind, which would grow larger than the Muslim League.[159]

This was followed by a joint All-India Khilafat Conference, which was held in Delhi on 23 and 24 November 1919 at the behest of the Muslim League's president, Fazlul Haque. Gandhi was elected the president of the Conference. It was resolved at this Conference that the British celebrations of the Allied victory in the War and British goods would both be boycotted (despite Gandhi's reservations on the practicality of the boycott of goods[160,161]). It was also resolved that in the event the Turkish question was not satisfactorily settled, all cooperation with the British Indian government would be withheld. As we shall see, the Non-Cooperation Movement, which is typically traced to 1920, would build on the resolutions of this Conference.

As pointed out in the first chapter, another important organisation of long-term consequence was founded in November 1919—the Jamiat ulema-i-hind, hereinafter referred to as JUH. This was founded under the leadership of Maulana Mahmud-ul-Hasan of the Deoband seminary (of Dehlawite persuasion) with the support of Maulana Bari, who represented Firangi Mahal. The stated object of the JUH was as follows:[162]

> to protect Islam and Islamic centres (Hijaz and the Jazirat-ul-Arab), to defend Islamic customs and way of life, to propagate Islam through missionary activities in India and abroad; to provide a common platform for the Ulama, to organise the Muslim community and launch a programme for its moral and social reform, to guide it in political and non-political matters from a religious point of view, to protect Muslim religious and civic rights and to establish religious courts; to work for the complete independence of India, to establish religious courts; to work for the complete independence of India, to establish good relations with other communities and promote their rights and interests.

Notwithstanding the inclusion of complete independence of India and good relations with other communities, the Dehlawite Muslim revivalist worldview and vision were written all over the goals of the JUH. This underscores the fact that the Khilafat Agitation facilitated the mainstreaming of the ulema, thanks to their collaboration with Western-educated pan-Islamic voices. The long-term effects of this collaboration are being felt till date across the subcontinent and outside of it. Even the references to the complete independence of Bharat and good relations with other communities must be understood from the strategic need of the Khilafatists to secure Hindu support for the Khilafat and to dangle over the British empire the prospect of losing Bharat should it fail to protect Turkish and, hence, Muslim interests. From December 1919, the JUH would start holding its annual sessions. Along with the sessions of the Congress, the League and the CKC, the annual sessions of the JUH too will henceforth be discussed here.

In December 1919, Amritsar was the venue for four important events— the thirty-fourth annual session of the Congress (which was discussed earlier in this chapter), the twelfth annual session of the Muslim League, the second All-India Khilafat Conference and the first session of the JUH. At the Congress session, which was held from 27 December 1919 to 1 January 1920, Gandhi, Motilal Nehru and Bipin Chandra Pal were more vocal in their support for the Khilafat than before, while Tilak was more measured in his position.[163] Importantly, on the second day of the Congress session, Pandit Gokarn Nath Misra informed the delegates that he had received a telegram from the Ali Brothers that they had been released on 28 December 1919 and that they would reach Amritsar on 30 December 1919.[164] On 30 December, the Ali Brothers attended and spoke at the sessions of both the Congress and the League. Maulana Azad was released in January 1920.

At the Muslim League's annual session, which was held from 29 December to 31 December 1919, quite a few Congressmen were present, including Gandhi, Malaviya, Motilal Nehru and Annie Besant. In his presidential speech on 29 December 1919, Ajmal Khan touched upon the events in Punjab, including the Jallianwalla Bagh Massacre, and welcomed the Montford Reforms though they fell short of the minimum demands made by the Congress–League Scheme. He went to the extent of saying that notwithstanding the continuing issue of the Khilafat, the Reforms must be welcomed while pursuing the struggle for self-government.[165]

On the subject of Hindu–Muslim relations, he echoed the Gandhi– Bari pact on cow slaughter in view of the Hindu support for the Khilafat Agitation.[166] This was followed by a detailed exposition on the Khilafat and Muslim holy places in the Jazirat-ul-Arab.[167] On the Paris Peace Conference, he regretted that the Bharatiya delegation did not have a single Muslim representative who could articulate the Muslim position. Emphasising that non-Muslim interference on the question of Khilafat would not be tolerated and making a distinction between the position of the Pope in Christendom and the Khalifa in Islam, Ajmal Khan captured the League's position on what would be an acceptable outcome of the Peace Conference:[168]

> The Muslims will be satisfied only when independence (in the true sense of the term) is secured to the Arabs and other Turkish subjects by assigning Turkey

the mandate to administer their provinces, subject to the supervision of a League of Nations not swayed by more than one vote of each country. The Muslims know that the right to hold a mandate (if mandatory government is at all necessary) in any of the lands previously under Ottoman rule primarily belongs to Turkey, because the people inhabiting these lands are predominantly Muslim in faith, and no non-Muslim Power can under any pretext have the right to hold sway over them. The Musalmans cannot be expected to forget that these lands have been the cradle of Islam, where the holy places are situated, and where no non-Muslim can ever have even the semblance of mandatory or any other rule. Trampling upon Muslim sentiments in this respect would mean creating not transitory but perennial unrest in the entire Muslim world, which would otherwise mean the deliberate awakening of unfriendly feelings in an otherwise unobtrusive people.

Towards the conclusion of his speech, Ajmal Khan expressed gratitude to the Hindus and to 'Mahatma' Gandhi, and demanded the release of the Ali Brothers, Azad and Mohani (since his speech was delivered a day before the news of their release was received). The resolutions passed at the session were significantly based on the subject of Khan's speech.

The second Khilafat Conference was held in Amritsar in December 1919 under Shaukat Ali's presidency, wherein a draft constitution framed by the CKC was circulated for inputs from the provincial Khilafat committees.[169] Importantly, it was also resolved that a deputation comprising both Hindus and Muslims would be sent to the Viceroy and a joint memorandum signed by Hindu and Muslim leaders submitted.[170]

At the first session of the JUH, which was held in Amritsar from 28 December to 1 January 1919 under Maulana Abdul Bari and Mufti Kifayatullah, a resolution was passed underscoring the JUH's position that the Sultan of Turkey was the Khalifa of Muslims and that the Friday khutba would continue to be read in his name.[171] Another resolution urged the King-Emperor to allow a delegation of Hindus and Muslims to attend the Paris Peace Conference so that the Turkish issue may be resolved in accordance with the tenets of Islam, failing which it could disturb and *agitate* the minds of millions of Muslims.

From December 1919, the Ali Brothers would take charge of the CKC and the Movement would be guided by the CKC along with the JUH, with the League playing a secondary role. The memorandum prepared by Maulana Muhammad Ali, as resolved at the second Khilafat Conference, was presented to the Viceroy on 19 January 1920. It stated that both communities, Hindus and Muslims, were *'now happily reunited and standing shoulder to shoulder will be equally aggrieved if the just demands of the Muslims were not accepted'.*[172]

This deputation represented a brief honeymoon period between the two communities, which would unravel soon, given that it was an arrangement of convenience based on an *assumption* of convergence of interests and visions. However, the Viceroy politely dashed the hopes of the deputation by stating clearly that Britain alone could not decide the future of Turkey even if it wanted to, and that having allied with Germany, Turkey could not hope to be treated better and differently merely because there were underlying religious sentiments. The day following this meeting, a statement was issued by the CKC that if the peace terms were not favourable to Turkey, the Viceroy must not hope for continued Muslim loyalty.[173] Further, deputations were put together for dispatch to England, Syria, Mesopotamia (Iraq), Palestine, Yemen and Hejaz.

The third Khilafat Conference was held in Bombay in February 1920. Here was finalised the constitution of the CKC, according to which the core object of the CKC was:[174]

> To secure for Turkey a just and honourable peace; to obtain the settlement of the Khilafat question; also of the holy places of Islam and the Jazirat-ul-Arab in strict accordance with the requirements of the Shariat; to secure the fulfilment of the pledges of Rt. Hon. Mr. Lloyd George, given on 5th January, 1918 and of Lord Hardinge, regarding the preservation of the integrity of the Turkish Empire; for the above purpose to approach the British Ministers, the Viceroy of India and the British public; to carry on propaganda work in and out of India; to take such further steps as may be deemed necessary.

Once again, the issues of Non-Cooperation with the government, boycott of British goods, along with the sensitive aspect of encouraging desertion in the army was brought up by the hardline faction led by Maulana Bari. However, the Moderates in the CKC proposed that the issues be shelved until the result of the delegation to Britain was known. Reports started emerging that Turkey would lose Istanbul as well as the Hagia Sophia, which would revert to being a church. This invited sharp reactions at the Bengal Provincial Khilafat Conference held in Calcutta on 28 and 29 February 1920 and presided over by Maulana Azad, who had been released from jail by then. At this Conference, Maulana Bari gave expression to Muslim anger and brought up the issues of Non-Cooperation and boycott of British goods yet again. He threatened to 'cease all relations of loyalty' with Britain and to 'assist the Caliph *by all possible means*'.[175] Further, given the aggressive mood, Gandhi's reservations on boycott were brushed aside by the majority and it was resolved that 19 March 1920 would be observed as Khilafat Day along with a hartal or general strike.[176] Naturally, this alarmed the Moderate stakeholders across the board as well as members of the British community in Bharat. Gandhi himself was taken aback and conveyed that his support and the support of Hindus would cease '*the moment there was violence actually done, advised or countenanced*'.[177] Informing Montagu as to the state of affairs on 7 March 1920, Chelmsford wrote as under:[178]

> ... the open expression of disloyalty although conditional is danger signal and may at any rate lead to local disorder. Bengal and other Local Governments have been consulted by us as to the measures to be adopted to deal with the situation and to check further extension of campaign of violence recognising on the one hand the danger that fanaticism of masses may be excited to disorder point by unchecked agitation, and on the other hand the danger that action against individuals may precipitate trouble.

Concerned about the loss of support of Gandhi and the Hindus for the agitation, the CKC issued a statement that the hartal of 19 March 1920 would be observed peacefully.[179] However, Shaukat Ali made it clear that in case the Khilafat demands were not met, the steps proposed at the Calcutta session would be implemented. Meanwhile, the deputation to the UK was received by the British Prime Minister Lloyd George on 9 March 1920.[180] He categorically informed the deputation that the principle of self-determination which was applied to the Austro-Hungarian empire was equally applicable to the Arabs, who had the right to choose to not live under the Ottoman Sultan; as regards Asia Minor, due to the Sultan's poor governance, a degree of Allied supervision was called for, and finally, that Smyrna and Thrace belonged to Greece.[181] The meetings with the French and Italian prime ministers too yielded no result. Consequently, the hartal as planned for 19 March was observed, but mostly by Muslims, with nominal Hindu participation.

According to Maulana Abul Kalam Azad, 'methods of begging' were of no consequence and it was time to exert 'direct pressure'.[182] As a devout student of Afghani, who advocated jihad as both necessary and Islamic, Azad's reference to 'direct pressure', twenty-six years before Jinnah's call for 'direct action', meant jihad. On 22 March 1920, a meeting was convened to discuss the implementation of the Calcutta resolutions. Gandhi too was present at the meeting. His suggestion to consider only non-violent ways of implementing Non-Cooperation did not meet with the approval of Bari and other attendees. However, given the support Gandhi commanded, his suggestion was accepted, albeit with much reluctance. By now, Gandhi realised that he was being treated as a mascot whose presence was necessary to gather the masses but who equally stood in the way of 'direct pressure'. After all, Gandhi was the only prominent Hindu on the CKC. To reassure Gandhi that violence would be *avoided as much as possible*, the CKC resolved between 11 and 14 April 1920 that the Non-Cooperation would be implemented in a phased manner after the publication of the peace terms between the Allied Powers and Turkey, which were expected in May.[183]

On 11 May 1920, the peace terms were announced under the Treaty of Sevres between the Allied Powers and the Ottomans. Under this, Thrace was ceded to Greece, and Asia Minor (including Smyrna) would remain under Turkish suzerainty but with Greek administration, its fate to be decided through a plebiscite after five years. Also, for all practical purposes, Turkey lost control over the Jazirat-ul-Arab. Its rights over the Suez Canal were renounced in favour of Britain; the size of the Turkish Army was significantly reduced while its navy was abolished and its air force disbanded.[184] In addition to its dismemberment, financial terms were imposed on Turkey. Barring the retention of Istanbul, the terms had a similar effect on Turkey as did the Treaty of Versailles on Germany.

As expected, when the peace terms were published in Bharat on 15 May 1920, Muslims found them 'outrageous'. Realising that Non-Cooperation was the only alternative for ventilation of Muslim anger, the CKC released its manifesto for Non-Cooperation on 28 May 1920 in Bombay. It was based on the following four stages outlined by Gandhi:[185]

> We may therefore begin at the top as well as the bottom. Those who are holding offices of honour or emoluments ought to give them up. Those who belong to the menial services under Government should do likewise. Non-co-operation does not apply to service under private individuals. I cannot approve of the threat of ostracism against those who do not adopt the remedy of Non-co-operation. It is a voluntary withdrawal alone that is a test of popular feeling and dissatisfaction. Advice to the soldiers to refuse to serve is premature. It is the last, not the first step. We should be entitled to take that step when the Viceroy, the Secretary of State and the Premier leave us. Moreover, every step withdrawing co-operation has to be taken with the greatest deliberation. We must proceed slowly so as to ensure retention of self-control under the fiercest heat.

The manifesto also said that should the Non-Cooperation fail, Muslims reserved the *right to take other steps in accordance with their religion.*[186] However, the manifesto made no one happy, least of all Azad, who found it too passive.[187] Under pressure from Gandhi and Shaukat Ali, the CKC decided to give the steps proposed by the former a chance before considering 'other' options. This much was clear, that while Gandhi's presence managed to contain Muslim anger as and when it threatened to erupt, he was progressively losing ground, and in the process both pan-Islamic vision and methods were being entrenched in Bharat's body politic. The larger implication of the Khilafat Movement and Agitation was the recognition of the extraterritorial loyalties of Muslims as an acceptable part and parcel of Bharatiya social and political life, which would have far-reaching consequences.

By this time, quite a few Congressmen had second thoughts about the extent of the Congress's involvement in the Khilafat Agitation and the adoption of Non-Cooperation, regarding which sentiments were voiced in the CKC meeting of 1–3 June 1920 held in Allahabad. Among the sceptics were Besant, Rai, Malaviya and Motilal Nehru.[188] What disturbed Rai and Malaviya deeply was the suggestion of Maulana Hasrat Mohani that the Khilafatists could join the Afghan army and invade Bharat to drive out the British. Both Rai and Malaviya made it clear that Hindus would actively oppose any such move.[189] Naturally, there were growing concerns about the direction the Agitation was taking. This matter was scheduled to be taken up for discussion at the special session of the Congress which was to be held in September in Calcutta. It was decided by Muslims that they would proceed with Non-Cooperation without awaiting the decision of the Congress.

However, before they did so, on 22 June 1920, a memorial on behalf of Sunni Muslims was presented to the Viceroy and he was informed of commencement of Non-Cooperation in August should the demands of the Khilafatists not be met.[190] The month of July was spent by Khilafatists trying to explain the aims and methods of Non-Cooperation extensively in northern Bharat. This period also witnessed hijrat, or emigration, to Afghanistan, in significant numbers by Muslims from Bharat to wage war against the British.[191] Even this did not stop Gandhi from continuing to support the Agitation. Fortunately, the hijrat came to an abrupt end when Afghanistan refused further admission of '*muhajirins*' from Bharat.[192]

As conveyed to the Viceroy by the CKC in June, since there was no sign of revision of the peace terms, on 1 August 1920, which was observed as Khilafat Day, the CKC formally launched the Non-Cooperation campaign. Despite the advice of leaders like Malaviya urging Gandhi not to support launch of the campaign until the Congress's special session in September where the advisability and practicality of Non-Cooperation was to be taken up, Gandhi went ahead since he did not want his 'Mussalman brethren' to doubt his commitment to their cause;[193] after all, it was on the strength of their support that he had become a national figure. Importantly, on the very day the Non-Cooperation campaign was launched, Tilak passed away. Apart from his death being a monumental loss to the country, it also meant that Gandhi had a freer hand in steering the future of the Congress.

In accordance with Gandhi's four-stage process, the campaign started with the return of British-bestowed honours and medals by both Muslims and Hindus. Fortunately for the Khilafatists, since the Hunter Committee report on the events in Punjab was released in May, they could combine both causes and convert the campaign into a powerful movement.[194] Under Shaukat Ali's guidance, the CKC instructed the various Khilafat organisations across the country to conduct the campaign peacefully.

In September 1920, both the Congress and the League held special sessions in Calcutta. The special session of the Congress, presided over by Lala Lajpat Rai, was being held pursuant to a resolution by the All-India Congress Committee passed at its meeting in Benares on 30 and 31 May 1920 asking for the views of the provincial Congress committees on the principle and programme of Non-Cooperation.[195] At the session held from 4 September to 9 September 1920, the Congress passed a resolution to the effect that in view of the government's non-response to the Khilafat Agitation and its lack of remorse over the events in Punjab, as reflected in the Hunter Committee report, the people of India had no other option but to approve of and adopt the policy of progressive, non-violent Non-Cooperation inaugurated by Mr Gandhi, until the said wrongs were righted and Swaraj was established. Apart from outlining the stages of the Non-Cooperation campaign, promotion of Swadeshi goods and boycott of British goods were also resolved. Two facts explain these resolutions. First, Gandhi's launch of the campaign in August, even before the Congress's special session, forced the Congress to adopt the campaign; and second, Gandhi, along with the Khilafatists, attended the session and took charge of the proceedings.

Further, this session saw Gandhi, Shaukat Ali and their Khilafatists on one side, whereas Motilal Nehru, Annie Besant,[196] Bipin Chandra Pal, Jinnah, Malaviya and C.R. Das were on the opposite side.[197] Motilal Nehru was subsequently persuaded by his son Jawaharlal Nehru to support Gandhi.[198] As for the Moderates under Surendranath Banerjea, they refused to participate in the session.[199]

The League's session was held on 7 September 1920, with Jinnah as its president. In his speech, Jinnah touched upon the Rowlatt Act, the atrocities in Punjab and the Khilafat;[200] however, and notably, he did not voice support for the Non-Cooperation Movement. By October 1920, the Sikh League and the Home Rule League were on board the Non-Cooperation campaign.[201] Maulana Muhammad Ali, who returned to Bharat in October 1920 after the failure of the foreign deputations, joined his brother Shaukat Ali to share the responsibility of the Khilafat Agitation and the Non-Cooperation campaign.

The Brothers, along with Gandhi, visited the M.A.O. College in Aligarh in October to convince the trustees and students of the institution to do away with government interference and demand the establishment of a national

Muslim university. This led to a confrontation between the students and the 'non-cooperators' on one side, and the trustees and the government on the other. Ultimately, the police were called to eject the non-cooperators and over a hundred students who supported them. This culminated in the establishment of the 'National University' or 'Jamia Millia Islamia' on 30 October 1920 with the support of the Ali Brothers, Maulana Mahmud Hasan of Deoband (who co-founded the JUH) and Ajmal Khan.[202] Thanks to the agitation of the non-cooperators, the government hastened the grant of university status to M.A.O. College with effect from 1 December 1920, with the Raja of Mahmudabad as the vice chancellor and the Begum of Bhopal as the chancellor.[203] Thus was set up the Aligarh University.

The Non-Cooperation campaign also impacted the first elections to be conducted under the Government of India Act of 1919, whose rules were published in June 1920. The boycott of the elections by the non-cooperators saw a significant number of vacancies in several constituencies, in particular Muslim.[204] By November 1920, the JUH had been roped in by the CKC to intensify the religious fervour of the campaign. This resulted in a fatwa, which would come to be known as the 'Muttafiqqa Fatwa', being prepared by the JUH justifying the Non-Cooperation Quranically. However, this development was temporarily kept under wraps by the CKC to prevent Hindu supporters of the campaign from being deterred by its Islamisation.[205]

In December 1920, the thirty-fifth annual session of the Congress and the thirteenth annual session of the League were held in Nagpur. The Congress session, which was presided over by C. Vijayaraghavachariar, would turn out to be important for multiple reasons, as we shall see. For starters, Annie Besant stayed away from this session along with the majority of the Moderates, who had a separate session of their own in Madras under the 'National Liberation Federation of India', which categorically disapproved of the policy of Non-Cooperation.[206,207] Second, Lala Lajpat Rai, along with C.R. Das and Malaviya, wanted to oppose Gandhi at the session owing to his unrestrained support of the Khilafat Agitation and its Non-Cooperation campaign. However, Rai was forced by the delegates of Punjab to either stand by Gandhi fully or vacate his position as their leader from Punjab. As we shall see, Rai ended up supporting Gandhi at the session. Third, the Ali Brothers enabled Gandhi's dominance of the session, underscoring the fact that Gandhi's rise as a national leader was significantly owed to the Khilafat Movement, and the support of the Ali Brothers and their co-religionists. In fact, his agitation against the Rowlatt Act too was made possible due to the support of the Khilafatists, especially Maulana Bari, as stated earlier. Clearly, the convergence of the anti-Rowlatt agitation with the Khilafat Movement was deliberate and the product of give and take between Gandhi and the Khilaftists, in particular Maulana Bari and the Ali Brothers.

Coming to the Congress session, the president, Vijayaraghavachariar, placed a draft constitution proposed by him for the 'dominion of India' at the end of his speech. Following this, the first resolution of the session, titled 'Change of Creed', was moved by Gandhi, and read as follows:[208]

> The object of the Indian National Congress is the attainment of Swarajya by the people of India by all legitimate and peaceful means.

The importance of this resolution was that it was a radical departure from the Congress's constitution of 1907, which resulted in the exit of the Extremists at the Surat session. In his speech justifying and explaining the proposed resolution, Gandhi stated that the continuation of a connection between Britain and India was *contingent* on the former acknowledging its mistakes and that it was the duty of every Indian to seek justice from the empire for its mistakes.[209] By 'mistakes', Gandhi was primarily referring to the Khilafat issue and the reign of terror in Punjab under Dwyer. This would become evident from the language of resolution II on Non-Cooperation. Gandhi was also clear in stating that should the empire fail to right its wrongs, it was the bounden duty of every Indian to destroy the empire. This 'Change of Creed' resolution was seconded by Lala Lajpat Rai who, apart from detailing the history of the split between the Moderates and the Extremists, stated that India's decision to remain within the British Commonwealth must be its own and not at the dictation of the empire.

After Rai, Jinnah spoke in opposition to the resolution moved by Gandhi. He pointed out that the language of the proposed resolution, when read as it was, implied complete independence, and there was no hint of any conditional connection with the British. He also objected to the practicality of the 'peaceful and legitimate' means proposed by Gandhi. The following were Jinnah's views on the issue and his exchange with other delegates, including Maulana Muhammad Ali:[210]

> Mr. President, Ladies and Gentlemen, the Resolution which has been placed before you by Mr. Gandhi is divided into two parts. The first part of the Resolution aims at the attainment of Swaraj by India. Reading that Resolution by itself, in my opinion, I feel this that there is no doubt that it makes a declaration of complete independence. The word Swaraj I venture to say does not mean in this Resolution that there is any possibility of British Connection. Therefore, in my opinion the first part of the Resolution declares complete independence for India (cries of no, no). Does it mean that we retain British Connection? (cries of no). I venture to say that it does not. (A voice it is left to us). But Mahatma Gandhi and Lala Lajpat Rai explained that it means with

or without British Connection. Now, Ladies and Gentlemen, I entirely agree with Lala Lajpat Rai in most part of the indictment that he placed before you against the Government ...

The question before you is this, as Lalji put it, that in 1907 we who adopted the present Creed of the Indian National Congress felt that there was neither the will nor the means of making that declaration. To-day we have accomplished one thing and that is the majority have the will to make this declaration and I entirely agree that the majority have the will to make this declaration. But the second proposition is, have we got the means of making this declaration? (A voice—Yes, decidedly). I say the means which are placed before you by Mr. Gandhi are 'legitimate and peaceful' not 'legitimate or peaceful' but 'legitimate and peaceful'. Therefore Mr. Gandhi thinks (cries of Mahatma Gandhi)—Yes, Mahatma Gandhi thinks that by peaceful methods, having declared complete Independence for India, he will achieve it. With very great respect for Mahatma Gandhi and those who think with him I make bold to say in this Assembly that you will never get your Independence without blood-shed (cries of no, no). If you think that you are going to get your Independence without bloodshed I say that you are making the greatest blunder (cries of, no no—a voice Nonsense) Therefore I say that at this moment you are making a declaration which you have not the means to carry out. On the other hand you are exposing your hand to your enemies.

... Lala Lajpat Rai has said that this is intended to give notice to the British Government. With very great respect I really fail to understand that argument. No organization, much less a National organization, adopts for its object a creed which can be considered a notice. If that is your intention, if that is your object, you should pass a Resolution and not change the creed. By all means pass a Resolution. Say to the world—to the British Government that it is a sine qua non that unless you redress our chief grievances we give you notice that we shall sever from you altogether. That is a very different story. But what we are undertaking to-day is the replacing of this Article I as the creed of the Indian National Congress. But it is said that it is open to you. You can take it any way you like and tell the people that (cries of no, no) I want to keep the British Connection. It is open for us to say that we do not want to keep the British Connection. Gentlemen, I appeal to your reason. What is the good of this camouflage (cries of no, no) ...

... Mahatma Gandhi says that, if the British Government are willing to give us what we want, then we shall have the Connection; if not, we shall not have the Connection. Therefore it is quite clear according to Mahatma Gandhi's speech that he has not as yet made up his mind notwithstanding what Lala Lajpat Rai describes the British Government and the British Statesmen to be namely that, there is no one whose words can be considered any better than that of a grocer, that no British statesman is to be trusted, that the British Government is absolutely a wicked Government.

(A voice—Quite so, hopeless.)

Then may I know whether you still say that you will keep the Connection if possible?

(Voice—Give them a chance and when they mend.)

... Mr. Jinnah continuing said—I say if you want to give notice to the British Government I have no objection at all. I say by all means give a notice, but you are not doing that. You are going to tell your people the moment this resolution is passed that the Indian National Congress has made a bid for Complete Independence, that our Indian National Congress, as Mr. Gandhi (Cries of Mahatma Gandhi)—as Mahatma Gandhi said, that you want to destroy the British Empire. Then you may have that feeling, you may have that wish. But I ask you in the name of reason, have you considered how you are going to destroy the British Empire? ... If I am right in my opinion that for the moment to day it is a mere dream to say that you will destroy the British Empire notwithstanding the fact that we are thirty crores and more—if I am right then I say you are making a declaration and you are committing the Indian National Congress to a programme which you will not be able to carry out. (A voice—We will) What is the reasoning? The only reason that I have been able to get beyond mere sentimental feeling and expression of anger and desperation, and I assure you, I don't feel anything but desperate myself but I may be able to control myself more than others—(A voice—Slave mentality). But what is the reason that is given to us ?—The only reason that I have been able to get from the speakers on the Creed was given to me in the Subjects Committee by Mr. Mahammad Ali (Cries of Maulana). Mr. Mahammad Ali told me (Loud cries of Maulana Mohammad Ali). If you will not allow me the liberty to address you and speak of a man in the language in which I think it is right, I say you are denying me the liberty which you are asking for. I am entitled to say Mr Mahammed Ali (cries of Moulana and cries of 'go on') I say the only reason that Mr. Mahammad Ali gave me was that there are some people who find it impossible to sign the Congress Creed, and therefore the congress Creed must be changed.

(Mr. Mahammad Ali—That was not the only reason I gave you.)

Mr. Jinnah—That is the only reason that I gathered; that is the only reason which I understood. I do not say that Mr. Mahammad Ali did not give other reasons, but the only reason that I understood after he had made a long speech was this—that in order to enable certain people who are not willing to sign the present Congress Creed, it is necessary to change the Creed. Do you think that is a sufficient reason ? (A voice—No). You will hear from Mr. Mahammad Ali when he comes here what his reasons are beyond mere sentimental talk. I do not say that we should not believe in sentiments nor do I say that sentiment does not play an important part. But remember that you are changing your constitution. Remember this constitution which you change is going to take place in the books of your constitution as a firm, permanent thing which it is not easy to change. You cannot pass a constitution this year and change it next year. The constitution must be sacred to us. The constitution if it is changed, must be changed at least with this object in view that you see at least quarter of a century ahead of, you ... Is the constitution of the Indian National Congress to be changed because there are some people who say, 'we will not sign the Creed'?

(A voice—All, all.)

Then I have nothing more to say ...

Therefore my objection is this. To summarise it in a few words—first of all, I object to this Creed because as I read it, it means nothing else but a declaration for complete independence. The word 'Swarajya' is not qualified and the word means nothing else but own Complete Independence. It does not at all provide for any kind of Connection which may or may not be retained. You find that only in the speeches. Therefore, that is my first objection. I say if that is your intention why don't you make it clear.

My second objection is that Non-co-operation on peaceful methods, legitimate, but peaceful methods, may be an excellent weapon for the purpose of bringing pressure upon the Government. But let me tell you once more that the weapon will not succeed in destroying the British Empire (A voice—Will succeed) I therefore object to the methods; because if you want complete independence let us not be limited to methods, Why should you be limited to methods? Who is to decide as we go on, what will be the effective methods to achieve the complete Swarajya which you are asking for? ... I have given you my opinion, gentlemen. Don't for a single moment believe from what I have been saying (A voice—It is your weakness) I am told it is weakness. I was told in the Subjects Committee it is want of courage. I don't wish to stoop to say that a particular man is weak or dishonest or wanting in courage. If I wish to retort I can say in return that it is your foolhardiness; but these words do not help us (Cries of shame).

I have said what I have to say. In conclusion, to quote the words of our President who is sitting here, he said at the moment the destinies of the country are in the hands of two men and among those two he mentioned Mahatma Gandhi. Therefore standing on this platform, knowing as I do know that he commands the majority in this Assembly, I appeal to him to pause, to cry halt before it is too late (Cries of shame and hear hear and cries of Mahatma Gandhi-ki-jay. A voice—a political imposter.)

It is important to make sense of the dynamics at play here between Gandhi and Jinnah and the multiple grey areas in it. Gandhi proposed an open-ended resolution, which hinted at complete independence from the British or at best conditional dependence. However, he was doing so on the strength of a pan-Islamic Agitation which was open to inviting the Amir of Afghanistan to invade Bharat to evict the British. Had it not been for opposition from leaders like Rai and Malaviya, this would have meant eviction of the Christian European coloniser, only to be replaced by the Islamic invader. After Tilak's death, Besant's transition to the side of the Moderates along with Surendranath Banerjea, and the subjugation of Rai and Malaviya within the party owing to Gandhi's clout, Gandhi's path had been cleared. Here is an accurate summary of Gandhi's domination of the Nagpur session by the Chief Commissioner of the Central Provinces:[211]

> The outstanding feature of the Congress has been the personal domination of Gandhi over all political leaders and followers alike. He has carried through the policy that he had decided for this Congress without any material modification ... The moderates of Nagpur were not heard; the extremist opponents under Khaparde and Moonje were brushed aside; Pandit Madan Mohan Malaviya's efforts were negatory; Jinnah carried no influence; Lajpat Rai wobbled and then became silent.

Although Gandhi's goals were similar to those of the Extremists, which was independence from the British or autonomy at the very least, his decision to encourage pan-Islamic sentiments and vision had awakened a creature which was waiting for the right opportunity to reassert itself in Bharat, namely Middle Eastern coloniality. This was evident from the massive participation of the ulema in the Khilafat Movement and Agitation, and in the setting up of the JUH with its clear goals of spreading Middle Eastern consciousness on the back of the Khilafat Agitation. In a way, Gandhi provided the Dehlawites with the perfect and politically correct facade to revive and mainstream their vision.

Coming to Jinnah, despite his support for the Khilafat, for the most part he was a Muslim nationalist of the Aligarh mould during this period, as distinguished from hardcore pan-Islamists like Maulana Azad and conservatives like Nawab Salimullah. He was supportive of the idea of self-government, albeit *within* the British empire, which is why he supported Tilak's and Besant's Home Rule Movement and was in charge of the Bombay branch of the Home Rule League. Jinnah was clear that even if the goal identified by Gandhi was indeed complete independence, to hope to achieve it through 'peaceful and legitimate means' was impractical and strategically unsound, since it limited the scope of options that may be employed to achieve the end. Given his difference of opinion with Gandhi on the ends and the means, coupled with the fact that the Congress under Gandhi and the Ali

Brothers did not have much patience for dissenting voices, Jinnah quit the Congress as well as the Home Rule League after the Nagpur session.

While Gandhi's hope of keeping the agitation peaceful and legitimate was idealistic to a fault and certainly impractical in light of the atrocities the British were open to committing in Punjab, which they had justified through the Hunter Committee report, Jinnah made it clear that he was open to non-peaceful means to attain a goal if he was convinced of it. No wonder he would make the call to 'direct action' in 1946 to secure Pakistan for Muslims in Bharat. Perhaps the ideal approach to deal with the coloniser may have been to aim for complete independence from the start and not limiting oneself to a specific basket of impractical and ineffective options in the face of an adversary who did not hesitate to resort to violence through state machinery.

As for the Moderates, as stated earlier, they were now led by Besant and Banerjea, who remained loyal to the British and whose aim was to secure self-government within the empire. Effectively, the difference between Gandhi's open-ended declaration of Swaraj and the Moderate position was that Gandhi was open to severing the connection with the empire if it did not make up for its 'mistakes', whereas the latter's position was consistent with the vision of the Home Rule Movement. Argov points out that during the Non-Cooperation Movement after the Nagpur session, when the Non-Cooperators were returning their honours and titles to the government in January 1921, Banerjea was knighted and appointed minister of local self-government. His acceptance of the title and position was heavily condemned and criticised. Apart from being sidelined from the national movement, hartals were observed wherever he went.[212]

Coming back to the Nagpur session, Gandhi's resolution was passed unanimously on the second day. This became the new article 1 of the Congress. The second resolution which was moved was on Non-Cooperation. Until the special session at Calcutta in September 1920, the Non-Cooperation campaign was primarily a product of the Khilafat Agitation, as stated earlier. It was being undertaken under the stewardship of the CKC, with Shaukat Ali overseeing its implementation in accordance with Gandhi's expectation of non-violence. The Congress's participation as an organisation in the campaign was mixed, ranging from aloofness to wariness to support under pressure from Gandhi. The Nagpur session was meant to formalise its participation in the Movement as an organisation to a greater degree. The resolution as passed finally reads as follows:[213]

II. The Non-co-operation Resolution

Whereas in the opinion of the Congress the existing Government of India has forfeited the confidence of the country;

And Whereas the people of India are now determined to establish Swaraj;

and Whereas all methods adopted by the people of India prior to the last Special Session of the Indian National Congress have failed to secure due recognition of their rights and liberties and the redress of their many and grievous wrongs, more specially in reference to the Khilafat and the Punjab;

Now this Congress while reaffirming the resolution on Non-violent Non-co-operation passed at the Special Session of the Congress at Calcutta declares that the entire or any part or parts of the scheme of Non-violent Non-co-operation, with the renunciation of voluntary association with the present Government at one end and the refusal to pay taxes at the other, should be put in force at a time to be determined by either the Indian National Congress or the All-India Congress Committee and that in the meanwhile, to prepare the country for it, effective steps should continue to be taken in that behalf:

(a) Boycotting schools—by calling upon the parents and guardians of school children (and not the children themselves) under the age of 16 years to make greater efforts for the purpose of withdrawing them from such schools as are owned, aided or in any way controlled by Government, and concurrently to provide for their training in national schools or by such other means as may be within their power in the absence of such schools;

(b) by calling upon students of the age of 16 and over to withdraw without delay, irrespective of consequences, from institutions owned, aided or in any way controlled by Government, if they feel that it is against their conscience to continue in institutions which are dominated by a system of government which the nation has solemnly resolved to bring to an end, and advising such students either to devote themselves to some special service in connection with the non-cooperation movement or to continue their education in national institutions;

(c) Nationalizing educational institutions—by calling upon trustees, managers and teachers of Government, affiliated or aided schools and municipalities and local boards to help to nationalise them;

(d) Courts—by calling upon lawyers to make greater efforts to suspend their practice and to devote their attention to national service including boycott of law courts by litigants and fellow lawyers and the settlement of disputes by private arbitration;

(e) Hand spinning and Hand weaving—in order to make India economically independent and self-contained, by calling upon merchants and traders to carry out a gradual boycott of foreign trade relations, to encourage hand-spinning and hand-weaving, and, in that behalf, by having a scheme of economic boycott planned and formulated by a committee of experts to be nominated by the All-India Congress Committee;

(f) Call for sacrifice—and inasmuch as self-sacrifice is essential to the success of non-co-operation, by calling upon every section and every man and woman in the country to make the utmost possible contribution of self sacrifice to the national movement;

(g) Organising Congress Committees—by organising Committees in each village or group of villages with a provincial central organisation in the principal cities of each province for the purpose of accelerating the progress of non-co-operation;

(h) Workers—by organising a band of national workers for a service to be called the Indian National Service; and

(i) Tilak Memorial Swarajya Fund—by taking effective steps to raise a national fund to be called the ALL-INDIA TILAK MEMORIAL SWARAJYA FUND for the purpose of financing the foregoing National Service and the non-co-operation movement in general.

The Councils—This Congress congratulates the nation upon the progress made so far in working the programme of non-co-operation, specially with regard to the boycott of Councils by the voters, and claims, in the circumstances in which they have been brought into existence, that the new Councils do not represent the country, and trusts that those, who have allowed themselves to be elected in spite of the deliberate abstention from the polls of an overwhelming majority of their constituents, will see their way to resign their seats in the Councils, and that if they retain their seats in spite of the declared wish of their respective constituencies in direct negation of the principle of democracy, the electors will studiously refrain from asking for any political service from such councillors.

The Police—This Congress recognises the growing friendliness between the Police and the Soldiery and the people, and hopes that the former will refuse to subordinate their creed and country to the fulfilment of orders of their officers, and, by courteous and considerate behaviour towards the people, will remove the reproach hitherto levelled against them that they are devoid of any regard for the feelings and sentiments of their own people.

Govt. Servants—And this Congress appeals to all people in Government employment, pending the call of the nation for resignation of their service, to help the national cause by importing greater kindness and stricter honesty in their dealings with their people and fearlessly and openly to attend all popular gatherings whilst refraining from taking any active part therein and, more specially, by openly rendering financial assistance to the national movement.

Non-violence—This Congress desires to lay special emphasis on Non-violence being the integral part of the non-co-operation resolution and invites the attention of the people to the fact that Non-violence in word and deed is as essential between people themselves, as in respect of the Government, and this Congress is of opinion that the spirit of violence is not only contrary to the growth of a true spirit of democracy, but actually retards the enforcement (if necessary) of the other stages of non-co-operation.

Finally, in order that the Khilafat and the Intercommunal Punjab wrongs may be redressed and Swarajya established within one year, this Congress urges upon all public bodies, whether affiliated to the Congress or otherwise, to devote their exclusive attention to the promotion of non-violence and non-co-operation with the Government and, inasmuch as the movement of non co-operation can only succeed by complete co-operation amongst the people themselves, this Congress calls upon public associations to advance Hindu–Muslim unity and the Hindu delegates of this Congress call upon the leading Hindus to settle all disputes between Brahmins and Non-Brahmins, wherever they may be existing, and to make a special effort to rid Hinduism of the reproach of untouchability, and respectfully urges the religious heads to help the growing desire to reform Hinduism in the matter of its treatment of the suppressed classes.

The resolution was moved by C.R. Das and seconded by Gandhi. In his opening speech, Das reiterated that the 'wrongs' which must be addressed by the British immediately were the ones relating to the Khilafat and Punjab. He repeated Gandhi's position that the nature of the wrongs was such that Bharat must attain Swaraj immediately. Among the other resolutions passed, the one which was noteworthy, resolution XVI, related to cow slaughter, and read as follows:[214]

(The President) There is one more resolution which I am charged to place before you. It relates to the protection of agricultural and milch cattle. Firstly we thank our Mosulman brethren for their endeavours to co-operate with us in protecting them, and secondly we urge upon all the great economic necessity for the protection of cattle. The resolution runs in these terms:

1. This Congress tenders its thanks to the Muslim Associations for their resolutions against cow slaughter.
2. This Congress recognises the great economic necessity for the protection of cattle and urges upon the people of India to do their best to achieve this object, particularly by refusing to sell cattle or hides for export trade.

Those who are for the resolution will say aye. (Cries of Aye). Those who are against it will say No. (Cries of None). The resolution is carried.

Later, in March 1921, when a resolution was moved to the above effect by Lala Sukhbir Sinha in the newly formed Council of States seeking a legislation to ban cow slaughter, other members such as Umar Hayat Khan and Nawab Abdul Majid opposed it, on the ground that it should be resolved through the society instead of by legislation.[215] Both were of the view that since Muslims and Christians too lived in Bharat, they could not be expected to give up cow meat to respect Hindu sentiments. In other words, Gandhi and his followers delivered support for the Khilafat at the expense of alienating a sizeable cross-section of the Congress, hoping, among other things, that there would be reciprocity at least on the issue of cow slaughter. Instead, what they got was prevarication, as reflected by the subsequent developments.

Apart from the various resolutions passed by the Congress in Nagpur, there was one moved by Gandhi with the support of Motilal Nehru for a new and more comprehensive constitution for the Congress.[216] This constitution divided the country into twenty-one provinces on linguistic basis, each headed by a provincial congress committee. Further, the organisation itself was divided into various committees, with the All-India Congress Committee at the top. Primary membership of the Congress was open to anyone over twenty-one years of age who accepted in writing the objectives and methods of the Congress and paid an annual subscription of 4 annas.

On the overall significance and effect of the Nagpur session, while it could be said that the session marked a much deeper and wider estrangement between the Moderates and the Extremists in the Congress than the Surat session of 1907, it was equally true that the distinctions between the two camps were blurred in a much more complicated way. This was due in large part to Gandhi's support for the Khilafat, which strengthened a pre-existing pan-Islamist undercurrent. This, in turn, strengthened the Two-Nation Theory even more than did the constitutional acceptance of communal electorates, first by the Minto–Morley Reforms in 1909 and then by the Montford Reforms in 1919. Importantly, this time the British could not be accused of adopting a divide and rule policy because, obviously, support for the Khilafat was not induced by the British. It was encouraged, mainstreamed and legitimised by Gandhi, thereby strengthening the pre-existing extraterritorial loyalties of the Muslim community, which, ironically, even Syed Ahmed Khan could not. The founding of the JUH in 1919, with its goals bluntly identified and spelt out, is proof of this.

To this extent, Gandhi had helped advance Syed Jamal al-Din al-Afghani's vision more than Syed Ahmed Khan did. Had Afghani been alive around the time of the Khilafat Movement and Agitation, he would have been proud of Gandhi for furthering the former's vision and cause, and prouder of Maulana Abdul Bari, Maulana Muhammad Ali, Maulana Shaukat Ali, Maulana Abul Kalam Azad and Maulana Hasrat Mohani for getting a 'Hindu leader' to support the cause of pan-Islamism in such a big way. After all, it may be said that the Non-Cooperation campaign, hitherto spearheaded by the CKC and largely observed by Muslims with only mixed support from the Congress, would come to take the shape of the more sweeping Non-Cooperation Movement, with the Congress under Gandhi throwing its full weight behind it. What ought to have been led by the League for the CKC was being led by the Congress under the 'Mahatma'. This would also create a 'secular' facade for what was essentially a Sharia-compliant pan-Islamic movement (excluding the non-violent component) based fully and solely on Islamic beliefs and sentiments. This fact was best captured and explained with Quranic support by Dr M.A. Ansari in his presidential speech at the League's annual session of 1920 in Nagpur. Here's the relevant portion from his speech under the head 'Non-Co-operation':[217]

> So far as the Musalmans are concerned the principle of non-co-operation is not a new idea; rather it is a clear and definite injunction of the divine Shariat which the Musalmans of India had in their forgetfulness consigned to oblivion. At the commencement, some members of the Khilafat Committee and some of the leading Muslim divines brought this matter before the public; and when the question was carefully discussed, as regards the application of this principle, it was decided that the present times furnish all the circumstances and the conditions laid down in the Muslim Shariat. It has therefore become binding that we should practise non-co-operation against the opponents of Islam.

> Mahatma Gandhi's far-sighted mind saw, in this Muslim religious principle, an effective method of wide application, well suited to the present requirements of the country and entirely in conformity with the principle of Satyagraha. His whole-hearted and single-minded advocacy of this principle resulted in its adoption by all the great political organizations representing the views of the overwhelming majority of the inhabitants of this country. Non-co-operation is based on the obvious truth that no Government can carry on administration of a country without the active co-operation or passive acquiescence of the people inhabiting that country. And if the Government of the country be unjust and heedless of the rights and liberties of the people, the only peaceful way of reforming the recalcitrant Government is to cease co-operation with it.

> The consideration of this principle from the ethical point of view need not detain us very long. In order to have any wrong done to a people redressed, it is not enough that a few individuals should be cognizant of the wrong: the entire people, or at least a larger majority of them, must feel the wrong. Then again the mere fact of feeling a wrong does not absolve you from your moral duty; you must refuse to help the wrong-doer in perpetuating the wrong, and by creating a very strong public opinion, you must make the repetition of that wrong impossible.

> As regards the religious aspect of this principle, I shall only discuss it briefly from the Muslim point of view. The Muslim Shariat enjoins tark-i-mawalat, or the abandonment of friendship (which means no connection of love, service or help), with those non-Muslims who are enemies at war with Islam and Muslim countries. Again the Holy Quran imperatively demands that Musalmans should behave righteously, affectionately and in a friendly manner

towards all those non-Muslims who are neither at war with Muslims nor are they assailants intending to invade or occupy their territories. 'Allah does not forbid you respecting those who have not made war against you on account of (your) religion, and have not driven you forth from your homes, that you show them kindness and deal with them justly; surely, Allah loves the doers of justice. Allah only forbids you respecting those who made war upon you on account of (your) religion, and drove you forth from your homes and backed up (others) in your expulsion, that you make friends with them and whoever makes friends with them: these are unjust.' (Quran: Sura-i-Mumtahanah 60:8–9) And Allah says: 'Oh you who believe! Do not take my enemy and your enemy for friends. Would you offer them love while they deny what has come to you of the truth?' (Quran: Sura-i-Mumtahanah 60:1).

It is not necessary to lay stress on the fact that non-co-operation is not only a political or moral necessity to a Musalman, it is a religious obligation and hence graver responsibility attached to him in carrying it out.

Accordingly, resolution III of the League's session reaffirmed its commitment to non-violent non-cooperation.[218] Resolution V amended rule 2 of the League's constitution to reflect that one of the objects of the League was to attain Swaraj through all peaceful and legitimate means.[219] Around the same time as the Congress and League sessions, on 29 December 1920, another All-India Khilafat Conference was held, with Maulana Azad presiding.[220] The tone of the session was expectedly more belligerent than the sessions of the Congress and the League, which reflected the true intent and character of the Khilafat Agitation when the façade of the Congress was lifted. Importantly, it was a clear sign of things to come—the Congress would thenceforth provide the secular cover for the goals of the CKC and the JUH, while the Muslim League would play second fiddle to this troika.

The JUH's second session was held in Delhi from 17 to 19 December 1920, with Maulana Mahmudul Hasan of Deoband as its president. The session was attended by over 500 delegates from across the country, among whom were Maulana Abdul Bari, Maulana Abul Kalam Azad, Maulana Abdul Majid Badauni, Maulana Abdul Kafi Allahabadi, Maulana Abdul Wafa Sanaullah, Maulana Daud Ghaznavi, Maulana Fazlullah and Maulana Shabbir Ahmed Usmani.[221] Readers may recollect that in Chapter 6 of the first book of this trilogy, I had pointed out—citing Venkat Dhulipala's book *Creating a New Medina*—that Maulana Shabbir Usmani was one of the founding members of Jamia Millia Islamia University and founder of the pro-Pakistan political party Jamiat Ulema-e-Islam. In 1946, Usmani would furnish a Quranic basis for the establishment of Pakistan by citing the distinction between *momin* (believer) and *kafir* (infidel).

Among the resolutions passed by the JUH at the Delhi session, the first exhorted Muslims to live in accordance with the Shariat in every manner possible. It read as follows:

Commandments of Shariat

This meeting of the Jamiatul Ulema-e-Hind calls upon the Muslims to sincerely try to honour and *observe the commandments of Shariat.* It is essential that our manners, dress, morals and conduct, specially our duties should conform to it. (Emphasis added)

This was followed by the following resolutions:

Relations with Britain

This session of the Jamiatul Ulema-e-Hind after deep deliberation (sic), makes this announcement *according to the dictates of religious commandments* that it was a cardinal sin to cooperate or have dealings with the British Government and in furtherance of that, the following points have to be taken into account.

1. Surrender of the titles and honorary offices.
2. Resigning from the membership of the councils and refusing to vote for the candidates for membership.
3. Depriving the enemies of Muslim Faith of Commercial benefits.
4. Refusal to accept financial aid from the government for schools and colleges and disassociation from the government universities.
5. Refusal to enlist in the army of the enemies of Muslim Faith and refusal to extend any kind of military aid to them.
6. Refusal to take cases to the courts and refusal by the lawyers to plead the cases there.

Students

This session of Jamiatul Ulema-e-Hind considers it essential *from the points of view of Shariat* that as a measure of non-cooperation the students should boycott schools and colleges which are affiliated to Government Universities that receive grants from the Government and considers the conduct of those scholars who have left such schools and colleges *as compliance of the behests of Islam.*

Non-Muslim Support to Khilafat

This session of Jamiatul Ulema-e-Hind appreciates the co-operation of our fellow countrymen to the cause of Khilafat and hopes that the Muslims of India would try to cultivate more cordial relations with fellow countrymen *within the limits prescribed by Shariat.*

Ulema and the Non-Cooperation

This session of Jamiat regretfully expresses its disagreement and disassociation with the conduct of some of the Ulema of the time, who have denied the legality and enforcement of such *an express religious commandment as Non-Cooperation* and have put forth doubts and suspicions regarding it, and announces that the Ulema-e-Hind are not responsible for this conduct and warns the Muslims in general that they should not regard the words and conduct of these persons as emanating from the Ulema in general.

Educational Institutions

This session of Jamiat declares that all those persons who are managers or members of the executives of national educational institutions and have refused to give up Government aid and the affiliation with Government Universities, *have betrayed Muslims and have sided with the enemies of Islam* and so, as long as they do not desist from their present conduct, all the Muslims should withdraw their support from them, and the students and parents should have nothing to do with those schools and colleges. (Emphases added)

It needs to be understood in light of Ansari's unambiguous Quranic justification for the Non-Cooperation Movement and the JUH's Sharia-compliant resolutions that it is both factually incorrect and embarrassingly ignorant to treat the Non-Cooperation Movement as a secular anti-colonial movement whose intention was to free Bharat from the clutches of the British. Swaraj, from the perspective of the Khilafatists, was a Quran-sanctioned Islamic means to a purely Islamic end—namely to get the British government to undo the Treaty of Sevres and restore the position of the Ottoman Caliphate. Or pay the price for it with the loss of its most prized possession, Bharat. In other words, the Non-Cooperation Movement must necessarily be understood as a platform for the wider dissemination of the Khilafat Agitation, with Swaraj being merely an *incidental* goal as it was *not* the trigger for the Agitation; dismemberment of the Caliphate was the real trigger. By hoping to secure Swaraj with the help of pan-Islamism, Gandhi had struck a Faustian bargain, the ultimate price being paid with the blood of millions of people and the dismemberment of Indic civilisation's only sacred geography—Bharat. On a more current note, in view of the history of the Khilafat Movement and its ultimate effect, the present-day tendency to include and celebrate this manifestly pan-Islamic movement as part of the 'Indian Freedom Movement' reflects the continuing effect of that gift of European coloniality—secularism—which keeps on giving, and which also continues to eat into the very foundations of Indic civilisational consciousness.

With this, I will now proceed to discuss the period from January 1921 to December 1922.

Hindu–Mussalman ki Jai: An Uneasy and Short-lived Bonhomie, 1921–1922

With the full support of the Congress, its organisational prowess and Tilak Memorial Swarajya Fund at its disposal, in the early months of January 1921, the CKC was able to spread the Khilafat Agitation far and wide through the Non-Cooperation Movement. Schools, colleges, factories, farmers, police and even the armed forces were within reach. Naturally, the British Indian government was deeply concerned. As early as on 23 January 1921, Chelmsford informed Montagu that the situation had 'undoubtedly worsened' in many parts of Bharat.[222] Therefore, once again, the search for a 'safety valve' began, both within and outside

Gandhi and Sarojini Naidu with Aga Khan III, 1931

Bharat. From an internal perspective, it was clear that the ulema were not happy being led by Gandhi; not only was he non-Muslim, but he also forbade the use of violence, which impeded jihad. As for an external safety valve, the possibility of bestowing the mantle of Caliph on King Hussein of the kingdom of Hejaz was toyed with.[223] The other external development that had a direct bearing on the issue of Khilafat was the Turkish National Movement under Kemal Ataturk, as mentioned earlier.[224] After all, if Turkey was reshaped as a 'modern' constitutional democracy, it would result in either abolition of the monarchy, and therefore the Caliphate; or reduction of the monarchy to a titular position, along the same lines as the British monarchy, which would effectively kill the substance and spirit of the Caliphal position. After all, a Khalifa without temporal/political powers was not really a Khalifa. The period from 1921 until 1924 would be animated by each of these developments.

Since the Treaty of Sevres had not yet been ratified, the Turkish nationalists were afforded an opportunity by the Allied Powers in February 1921 to revisit the Turkish issue. Sensing an opportunity to pacify the Khilafatists in Bharat, Chelmsford, through Montagu, obtained British Prime Minister Lloyd

George's permission to secure a place for an Indian delegation at the table.[225] The idea was to show that the British government had done everything it could to ensure that the Khilafatists were at least heard. Accordingly, a six-member delegation comprising the Aga Khan, Syed Hasan Imam, Chotani (who founded the Bombay Khilafat Committee), M.A. Ansari, Abdul Ghaffar and M.H. Kidwai arrived in London on 7 March 1921, almost at the fag end of the Peace Conference, and was given an audience with Lloyd George on 12 March 1921. That this was merely an exercise in optics was clear from the fact that the proposals for modification of the Treaty had already been approved on 10 March 1921, rendering the presence of the Indian delegation moot.[226] While there were concessions made to Turkey, they did not cover the central demands of the Khilafatists. The delegation was given another audience on 24 March, again in vain.

Back in Bharat, the failure of the delegation added fuel to the fire, and the promise of a non-violent campaign seemed to be tottering on the edge. In the third week of March, the JUH spoke of severing Bharat completely from the British empire and punishing those who opposed this through Sharia tribunals. The government had to crack down in the form of arrests, press gags and army marches in several parts of the country.[227] Against this backdrop, Chelmsford left Bharat on 2 April 2021 as one of the most unpopular Viceroys and was succeeded by Lord Reading. Reading's reading of the situation was that Maulana Muhammad Ali was the live wire of the Khilafat Agitation, and that Gandhi was more amenable to reason.[228] Fortunately for Reading, the Khilafatists themselves would contribute to the growing unease between the Maulana Abdul Bari group and the Gandhian faction on the question of use of violence.

First, Maulana Muhammad Ali's speech in Erode, Madras, on 2 April 1921 gave the impression that he would assist the Afghans if they invaded Bharat.[229] This effectively alienated a sizeable cross-section of Hindu supporters of the Khilafat Agitation, apart from giving reasons for critics within the Congress such as Rai, Pal and Malaviya to urge Gandhi to reconsider his support for the Khilafat.[230] This also led the British government to consider prosecuting Muhammad Ali for his statement. However, Gandhi was told by the Viceroy in Simla that if he could get the Maulana to apologise and retract his statement, he would not be prosecuted. While Gandhi managed to convince him to issue an apology in writing, the apology was projected in the press as surrender by the Ali Brothers. This incident embarrassed Gandhi as well as the Ali Brothers, for they were seen as having buckled under fear of prosecution while urging the rest of the country to not cooperate with the government.[231] Although this did not lead to an immediate parting of ways between Gandhi and the Ali Brothers, a formidable fault line had indeed emerged, which would only deepen.

At the All-India Khilafat Conference organised in Meerut from 7 to 10 April 1921, the ulema were vocal and vociferous in their objections to the Khilafat Agitation being led by Gandhi, a Hindu.[232] Further, they wanted the scope and methods of the Agitation defined in Sharia-compliant terms. Abdul Bari himself threatened that Muslims were prepared to desert Gandhi and employ means more *consistent* with their religious beliefs, namely jihad. To add to this, in April 1921, riots broke out in Muslim-majority Malegaon which exposed the uneasy nature of 'Hindu–Mussalman ki Jai'. By May 1921, the ulema proceeded to set up Sharia tribunals as threatened. Called 'Dar-ul-Qaza', they were to punish those who opposed Non-Cooperation. At the Bombay Khilafat Conference in June, a motion was proposed to the effect that Gandhi and the Hindus should no longer take part in the Khilafat Agitation. At the Karachi Khilafat Conference in July, the JUH's Muttafiqqa Fatwa of November 1920 stating that it was haram for a Muslim to serve in the British Indian Army was introduced by Maulana Hussain Ahmad Madani and endorsed by the Ali Brothers and the ulema from Deoband.[233] The commencement of Civil Disobedience was also threatened. By August 1921, the Moplah Riots (not 'Rebellion') had broken out in the Malabar under the leadership of Ali Musaliar and V.K. Haji with the support of the communists. (Given the 'secularisation' of the Moplah Riots over the years, as stated earlier, the final chapter will discuss the Moplah Riots along with riots in Malegaon, Gulbarga and Kohat.) The sheer scale and brutality of the violence—in particular sexual violence—that was meted out to the Hindus of Malabar by the Moplah Muslims shook Hindus as well as Congressmen. Gandhi still failed to part ways with the Khilafatists. In the very same month that the riots broke out, leaflets bearing the JUH's Muttafiqqa Fatwa were found with army units that had Muslim soldiers; there was also evidence of attempts to bribe soldiers to desert the army using the money collected in the Khilafat Fund.[234] This led to raids at the Delhi offices of the JUH and confiscation of copies of the Fatwa.

The British Indian government decided to step in. Muhammad Ali was arrested on 14 September 1921 while he was on his way to Malabar with Gandhi to pacify the Moplah rioters. The others, namely Shaukat Ali, Dr Kitchlew, Pir Ghulam Mujaddid, Hussain Ahmad Madani and Nisar Ahmad, were arrested at different places and kept in custody in Karachi.[235] Interestingly, the Shankaracharya of Sharda Peeth, who too supported the Khilafat Movement, in particular the resolutions of the Karachi Khilafat Conference, was also arrested. As for the Ali Brothers, here is a stellar extract from Maulana Muhammad Ali's statement before the magistrate of Karachi where he pleaded not guilty to the charges framed against him:[236]

> After all what is the meaning of this precious prosecution. By whose convictions are we to be guided, we the Musalmans and the Hindus of India? Speaking as a Musalman, if I am supposed to err from the right path, the only way to convince me of my error is to refer me to the Holy Koran or to the authentic traditions of the last Prophet—on whom be peace and God's benediction—or the religious pronouncements of recognized Muslim divines, past and present, which purport to be based on these two original sources of Islamic authority demands from me in the present circumstances, the precise action for which a Government, that does not like to be called satanic, is prosecuting me to-day. If that which I neglect, becomes by my neglect a deadly sin, and is yet a crime when I do not neglect it, how am I to consider myself safe in this country?
>
> I must either be a sinner or a criminal ... *Islam recognizes one sovereignty alone, the sovereignty of God, which is supreme and unconditional, indivisible and inalienable ... The only allegiance a Musalman, whether civilian or soldier, whether living under a Muslim or under a non-Muslim administration, is commanded by the Koran to acknowledge is his allegiance to God, to his Prophet and to those in authority from among the Musalmans chief among the last mentioned being of course that Prophet's successor or commander of the faithful ... This doctrine of unity is not a mathematical formula elaborated by abstruse thinkers but a work-a-day belief of every Musalman learned or unlettered ...* Musalmans have before this also and elsewhere too, lived in peaceful subjection to non-Muslim administrations. *But the unalterable rule is and has always been that as Musalmans they can obey only such laws and orders issued by their secular rulers as do not involve disobedience to the commandments of God who in the expressive language of the Holy Koran is 'the all-ruling ruler'. These very clear and rigidly definite limits of obedience are not laid down with regard to the authority of non-Muslim administration only. On the contrary they are of universal application and can neither be enlarged nor reduced in any case.* [Emphases added]

On 1 November 1921, all of the accused barring the Shankaracharya were convicted and sentenced to two years' rigorous punishment.[237] Those of the Khilafatists who were not apprehended, such as Maulana Hasrat Mohani, angrily called for the immediate adoption of Civil Disobedience. Fortunately for Gandhi, who was reluctant to initiate Civil Disobedience, the pandemonium created by the Khilafatists in Bombay upon the arrival of the Prince of Wales (later King-Emperor Edward VIII) gave him the reason he needed to postpone its launch.[238] Notwithstanding this, even within the Congress, leaders such as C.R. Das and others were severely unhappy with Gandhi's leadership and were hoping that Gandhi would either retire or get arrested.[239]

The embarrassment caused by the Khilafatists at the arrival of the Prince of Wales in Bombay gave the government reason to effect a further crackdown, which, it understood, would not be objected to by the Moderates. From mid-November, the government began mass arrests of agitators in several parts of the country. This was followed by arrests of prominent leaders such as Maulana Azad, Lala Lajpat Rai, the Nehrus (father and son) and several others. Unfortunately for the government, the public outcry against such arrests, especially during the visit of the Prince of Wales, was huge. At this juncture, the Moderates under Besant came to the government's rescue to ensure that the visit of the Prince of Wales was not a disaster.[240] Against this volatile backdrop, the annual session of the JUH was held in November 1921, whereas the annual sessions of the Congress, the League and the CKC were held in December 1921 in Ahmedabad.

The JUH's third session was held in Lahore with Maulana Azad as the president.[241] The first resolution was on the confiscation of the Muttafiqqa Fatwa, which read as follows:

Confiscation of 'Fatwa'

This conference of the Jamiat confirms the decision of the meeting of the Executive of Jamiat held at Delhi on 21st September 1921, which it had given unanimously about the confiscation of the Fatwa (religious mandate). The decision was as follows;

This meeting of the Executive of Jamiatul Ulema-e-Hind declares that the religious mandate (Fatwa) which has been confiscated by the order of Chief Commissioner of Delhi dated July 12 in Delhi and some other provinces too is based on the Commandments of the Islamic Shariat which are in force for the last thirteen hundred years in all their finality without any change and it is the duty and obligation of every Muslim to have faith in them, to practice them and to propagate them. Therefore the Ulema of Islam cannot tolerate any situation which interferes in the preaching and propagation of these commandments. The Ulema of Islam, in accordance with these commandments, declare it to be the duty of Muslims to continue printing and publishing the mandate disregarding the interference of the confiscation order, and remain engaged in preaching and propagation. The members of the Executive of the Jamiat too shall continue to publish and propagate.

On the arrest of the Khilafatists, the following resolution was passed:

Khilafat Resolution

This session of Jamiatul Ulema-e-Hind confirms the decision of the meeting of the Executive of the Jamiat held at Delhi on 21st September, 1921 about the Karachi Resolution. The decision was as follows:

This meeting of the Executive of the Jamiat declares that the resolution of the Khilafat Conference held on 8–10 July 1921 for which the Government has arrested, Maulana Shaukat Ali, Maulana Mohammed AH, Maulana Husain Ahmed, Pir Ghulam Mujaddid, Dr. Kitchlew and Maulana Nisar Ahmad, is one of the explicit and final commandments of Islam in force for the last thirteen hundred years and have been duly propagated in India too. Under no circumstances, can Muslims be prevented from propagating them and their propagation shall continue as long as Islam is there. Jamiat-ul Ulema calls upon all the Muslims to get ready for the trial of their sense of duty and in every way possible engage in the publication and propagation of this Commandment of the Shariat and thus strive to propagate the word of God.

On the propaganda for the cause of the Khilafat and Kemal Ataturk's rise in Turkey, the following resolutions were passed:

Khilafat

This conference of Jamiatul Ulema-e-Hind proposes that as soon as possible delegations for the purpose of propaganda be arranged which may go to various provinces inside India and carry on propaganda in favour of Khilafat-e-Islamia and Ghazi Mustafa Kemal Pasha and other Islamic matters and authorises the President and Secretary of the Jamiat to arrange such delegates and send them off.

Kemal Pasha

This conference of Jamiatul Ulema-e-Hind sincerely acknowledges the services of Ghazi Kemal Pasha and offers him felicitations on behalf of the Jamiat and reminds Muslims of their Islamic duty, that at this time, the highest form of piety and striving in cause of Islam is to help this great fighter for the cause of Islam.

On the Moplah Riots, the following was the resolution passed:

Mopla Unrest

This conference of Jamiat does not make bold to confirm the rumours published in the papers about the Moplas, that they have harassed their Hindu neighbours and have forcibly converted some Hindus to Islam, unless they are verified by trustworthy sources, and declares that if these rumours are proved true, the conduct of Moplas is against Islamic teachings and therefore condemnable.

Coming to the thirty-sixth annual session of the Congress, it was held on 27 and 28 December 1921 in Ahmedabad. The chairman of the reception committee was Vallabhbhai Patel and the president of the session Ajmal Khan. Once again, Non-Cooperation and Khilafat were extensively discussed. At the end of his presidential speech, here is how Ajmal Khan, the 'moderate Muslim' and a follower of Gandhi, dealt with the grave situation in the Malabar where thousands of Hindus had been killed or converted, and several women raped:[242]

> I cannot close without referring to the tragic events that are daily taking place in Malabar and the prolonged agonies of our unfortunate Moplah brethren. And here I must make it quite clear that this question has two aspects: one with reference to the Government in the country and the other with reference to the treatment by the Moplahs of their Hindu brethren. As to the first, judging from the evidence before the public, one cannot help coming to the conclusion that the responsibility of provoking these disturbances rests entirely on the shoulders of the Government. While as to the method adopted in suppressing these, there will be no thinking person in the country who·will not condemn them. All of us who have had the experience of Amritsar know the horrible nature of this 'pacification'. It was only accidently [sic] that the terrible train-tragedy was revealed to the public the other day. But how many other tragedies there are that have not come to light?

> As to our Hindu brethren who have been forcibly converted or have otherwise suffered at the hands of some of the Moplahs, I fully sympathise with them and there will be no Muslim worthy of the name who will not condemn this entirely un-Islamic act in the strongest possible terms. I feel sure that these stray incidents are the acts of a few misguided individuals and that the rest of the Moplahs are as ready and strong in condemning them as any of us here. Still I should not like the fair name of Islam to be tarnished in the slightest degree and I sincerely regret these deplorable incidents.

Importantly, it was resolved that the Non-Cooperation Movement would continue until the 'wrongs of Punjab and Khilafat are redressed and Swaraj is established'.[243] Here is the resolution passed on the situation in Malabar:[244]

> This Congress expresses its firm conviction that the Moplah disturbance was not due to the Non-co-operation or the Khilafat movement, especially as the non-co-operators and the Khilafat preachers were denied opportunity of carrying on effective propaganda of non-violence in the affected parts by the district authorities for six months before the disturbance, but is due to causes wholly unconnected with the two movements and that the outbreak would not have occurred had the message of non-violence been allowed to reach them. Nevertheless, this Congress deplores the acts done by certain Moplahs by way of forcible conversions and destruction of life and property and is of opinion that the prolongation of the disturbance in Malabar could have been prevented by the Government of Madras accepting the proffered assistance of Maulana Yakub Hassan and other non-co-operators and allowing Mahatma Gandhi to proceed to Malabar and is further of opinion that the treatment of Moplah prisoners as evidenced by the asphyxiation incident was an act of inhumanity unheard of in modern times and unworthy of a Government that calls itself civilised.

A resolution was passed congratulating '*Ghazi Mustafa Kemal Pasha and the Turks upon their successes and assures the Turkish nation of India's sympathy and support in its struggle to retain its status and independence*'.[245] And here is Maulana Hasrat Mohani's proposed resolution, which was opposed by Gandhi and his followers:[246]

Ladies and gentlemen, you know it, in connection with the Khilafat question, that the Musalmans have accepted Swaraj as their goal for two reasons: first, because they are Indians and secondly, as Musalmans, for the solution of the Khilafat question. So far as India alone is concerned, the Colonial form of self-government may suffice but so far as the Khilafat is concerned Swaraj can have only one meaning and that is complete independence. The Khilafat question is not possible of solution so long as British Imperialism is not broken. The British will not retrace their steps from Iraq, Arabia, and the Jazirat-ul-Arab and the whole world will not be free from their domination so long as their Imperialism is not broken. For this reason Swaraj can have only one meaning when applied to the Khilafat and that is complete independence. The Colonial form of self-government would not solve the Khilafat question but it would, on the other hand, go against the Khilafat for this reason that it will strengthen British Imperialism. Mahatma Gandhi's claim that we shall be able to solve the Punjab and the Khilafat problems is incapable of realisation so long as India is not completely independent. So far as my Mussalman brothers are concerned, the majority of them have begun to take Swaraj to mean complete independence. This question could not be brought before the Khilafat Conference yesterday by chance; yet in the public meeting held after the Conference the Mussalmans unanimously passed a resolution to the effect that Swaraj meant complete independence. If you accept this view, and if you want to stand by the great leaders who have been sent to the gaol, please adopt this resolution without a division ...

That Swaraj was the Khilafatists' way of punishing the British for their Turkish dismemberment could not have been stated in clearer terms.

Coming to the League's session, its fourteenth, held on 30 December 1921, it was presided over by Maulana Hasrat Mohani. On the check-and-balance dynamic between Hindus and Muslims, Mohani said:[247]

Hindus and Muslims

The generality of Musalmans, with few exceptions, are afraid of the numerical superiority of the Hindus, and are absolutely opposed to an ordinary reform scheme as a substitute for complete independence. The primary reason for this is that in a merely reformed, as contrasted with an independent government, they will be under a double suspicion: first, a subjection to the Government of India, which will be common to Hindus and Musalmans; secondly, a rejection by a Hindu majority, which they will have to face in every department of Government. On the other hand, if the danger of the English power is removed, the Musalmans will only have the Hindu majority to fear. Fortunately this fear is such that it will be automatically removed with the establishment of the Indian Republic; for while the Musalmans, as a whole, are in a minority in India, yet nature has provided a compensation in the fact that the Musalmans are not in a minority in all provinces. In some provinces, such as Kashmir, the Punjab, Sind, Bengal and Assam, the Musalmans are more numerous than the Hindus. This Muslim majority will be an assurance that in the United States of India, the Hindu majority in Madras, Bombay and the United Provinces will not be allowed to overstep the limits of moderation against the Musalmans. Similarly, so long as a completely liberated India does not come into the hands of the Hindus and Musalmans themselves, the Hindus will always be suspicious that, in case of a foreign invasion, the Musalmans would aid their co-religionist invaders; but on the establishment of the Indian Republic, which will be shared in common by Musalmans and Hindus, there will be no possibility of such a suspicion, for no Musalman would desire that the power of even a Muslim foreigner should be established over his country.

Here were his views on the Moplah Riots and his justification of them on behalf of the rioters:[248]

The Mopla Rebellion

Gentlemen, I have just stated it as a necessary condition of the Hindu–Muslim compromise that the third party, the English, should not be allowed to step in between us. Otherwise, all our affairs will fall into disorder. Its best example is before you in the shape of the Mopla incident. You are probably aware that Hindu India has an open and direct complaint against the Moplas, and an indirect complaint against all of us, that the Moplas are plundering and spoiling their innocent Hindu neighbours; but possibly you are not aware that the Moplas justify their action on the ground that, at such a critical juncture, when they are engaged in a war against the English, their neighbours not only do not help them or observe neutrality, but aid and assist the English in every possible way. They can, no doubt, contend that, while they are fighting a defensive war for the sake of their religion and have left their homes, property and belongings, and taken refuge in hills and jungles, it is unfair to characterize as plunder their commandeering of money, provisions and other necessaries for their troops from the English or their supporters. Both are right in their complaints; but so far as my investigation goes, the cause of this mutual recrimination can be traced to the interference of the third party. It happens thus: whenever any English detachment suddenly appears in a locality and kills or captures the Mopla inhabitants of the place, rumour somehow spreads in the neighbourhood that the Hindu inhabitants of the place had invited the English army for their protection, with the result that after the departure of the English troops, the neighbouring Moplas do not hesitate to retaliate, and consider the money and other belongings of the Hindus as lawful spoils of war taken from those who have aided and abetted the enemy. Where no such events have occurred, the Moplas and Hindus even now live peacefully side by side; Moplas do not commit any excesses against the Hindus, while the Hindus do not hesitate in helping the Moplas to the best of their ability.

Mohani's defence of the Moplah rioters at the League's session was not a one-off occurrence. At a meeting of the Congress Subjects Committee, he was consistent in his defence, saying that since the Moplahs suspected their Hindu neighbours of colluding with the government, they were justified in *presenting the Quran to the Hindus. And if the Hindus became Mussalmans to save themselves from death it was a voluntary change of faith and not forcible conversion.*[249]

On whether Muslims must limit their methods to non-violent cooperation and the effect, if any, of Turkish national developments on the Khilafat Agitation, Mohani said as follows:[250]

The Duty of Muslims

At this stage, some people would like to ask how it is that, while the Hindus are content to adopt non-violent non-co-operation as the means for attaining independence, the Musalmans are anxious to go a step further. The answer is that the liberation of Hindustan is as much a political duty of a Musalman as that of a Hindu. Owing to the question of the Khilafat, it has become a Musalman's religious duty as well.

In this connection, I should like to say just one word. The glories of Ghazi Mustapha Kemal Pasha and the conclusion of the recent Franco-Turkish Treaty might create an idea in some people's minds that the evacuation of Smyrna by the Greeks is certain, and the restoration of Thrace to the Turks, if not certain, is within the bounds of possibility. Consequently, they might entertain the hope that the struggle in the Near East is coming to a close. I want to warn all such people that the claims of the Musalmans of India are founded more on religious than political principles. So long as the Jazirat-ul Arab (including Palestine and Mesopotamia) are not absolutely freed from non-Muslim influence, and so long as the political and military power of the Khilafat is not fully restored, the Musalmans of India cannot suspend their activities and efforts.

Finally, Mohani summarised Muslim demands thus:[251]

Muslim Demands

As regards the Khilafat, the Muslim demands are these: (1) that in the pursuance of the promise of Mr. Llyod George, Thrace and Smyrna, along with the city of Smyrna (Izmir), should remain under purely Turkish control, so that the political status of the Khilafat-ul-Muslimeen which is essential for the Khilafat, should suffer no diminution; (2) all non-Turkish control should be removed from Constantinople, the shores of Marmora and the Dardanelles, in order that the Khilafat at Constantinople may not be under non-Muslim control, which is essential for the Khilafat; (3) all naval and military restrictions imposed on the Khilafat should be removed, as otherwise, the Khalifa would have no power to enforce his orders; (4) the Jazirat-ul-Arab, including the Hedjaz, Palestine, and Mesopotamia, should be free from all non-Muslim influence, and not be under British mandate: as it was the death-bed injunction of the Prophet. It should be noted that in the fourth demand, we wish the English to give up their mandate over Mesopotamia and Palestine, and to remove their influence from the Hedjaz. As to the questions of whether the Arabs will acknowledge the Sherif of Mecca or the Sultan of Turkey as their Khalifa, or whether the Arab Government of Hedjaz, Mespotamia and Palestine will be independent or under the suzerainty of the Khalifa, these will be decided by the Musalmans. We do not want non-Muslim advice and assistance.

The following were some of the key resolutions passed at this session:[252]

II. This Session of the All-India Muslim League humbly tenders the assurance of its unshakable earnest faith to the Porte of the Khalifa, His Majesty Ghazi Sultan Mohammad Wahiduddin VI, the Khalifat-ul-Muslimeen and Khadim-ul-Harmain-ish-Shareefain and resolves that this loyal assurance be communicated to His Majesty the Khalifa.

III. This Session of the All-India Muslim League heartily congratulates Ghazi Mustafa Kemal Pasha upon the success which he has won in the Greco-Turkish war, in recognition of the magnificent service rendered by him to Islam, and prays that the Almighty God may grant him a long life and may continue to make his activities more and more fruitful in the interests of the Islamic world.

V. Having regard to the fact that no independent and impartial statements relating to the Mopla troubles have yet been published, that the Muslim public, not being prepared to accept the accuracy of the accounts issued from Government sources, look with horror and resentment upon the severe sentences, including sentences of death, passed upon the Moplas by the Military Courts, in spite of the fact that thousands of them were killed and wounded in the military operations directed against them, and that particular horror and dismay have been created by the railway train incident that resulted in the death of 70 Mopla prisoners by suffocation, among Muslim circles that regard the Government officers in Malabar responsible, for such barbarous conduct, with contempt, this Session of the All-India Muslim League appoints a committee of the following members, viz. M. Mushir Husain Kidwai (Barabanki), G.M. Bhurgri (Sindh), Hon. Syed Raza Ali (Allahabad), Abbas S. Tyabji (Gujrat), and Moulvi Syed Murtaza (Trichinopoly), with power to add to their number, for the purpose of making an enquiry into the causes and incidents of the Mopla troubles by investigations on the spot in Malabar. This Session of the League also expresses its regret at the misconduct of Moplas who may have caused any trouble to the Hindus without just cause. (Proposed by Khawaja Abdul Rahman Ghazi and seconded by Sardar Ali Saheb, Maulana Azad Subhani, S. Abbas Tyabji, Moulvi Syed Murtaza.)

Mohani also dominated the Khilafat Conference which was held on 26 December 1921. His resolution for complete independence was opposed by Ajmal Khan and accepted by half of the delegates after angry scenes on stage, which forced Ajmal Khan to leave the stage.[253] The net result was that—barring hardline Khilafatists such as Maulana Abdul Bari, Maulana Hasrat Mohani and ulema from Deoband and other seminaries—complete independence was not fully endorsed, either by the Congress or the League, although they wanted Swaraj. As stated earlier, the ulema demanded Swaraj only as a way of punishing the British for their dismantling of the Caliphate. And Gandhi's presence in the CKC prevented that organisation too from calling for complete independence.

As for Civil Disobedience, a heavily caveated position was taken—namely that it could be initiated if both central and provincial organisations were convinced that it would be conducted peacefully.[254] Thus ended 1921, which marked the peak of the Khilafat Agitation and the Non-Cooperation Movement. From here on, with several of the Khilafatists, especially the Ali Brothers, in jail, the Agitation would flag; the bonhomie of convenience between Hindus and Muslims, already marred severely by the Moplah Riots, would unravel, thanks to frequent riots in different parts of the country. And to add to this, the revolutionary developments in Turkey would raise serious questions on the need for Muslims in Bharat to continue with the Khilafat Agitation.

As more facts relating to the Moplah Riots began to emerge, the attempts of the Khilafatists to brush them under the carpet incensed leaders like Malaviya, Rai, B.S. Moonje and Swami Shraddhananda. The Moplah experience led these leaders to conclude that Hindus must unite and consolidate to protect themselves against such genocidal attacks in the future.[255] This sentiment, which gave birth to the Sangathan Movement, had already taken root after the experience of the anti-Hindu riots in Eastern Bengal post the Partition of Bengal in 1905. The introduction of communal electorates in 1909 under the Minto–Morley Reforms further solidified the need for an umbrella Hindu organisation which could protect and defend Hindu interests. Under the leadership of Rai and Malaviya, this Movement would culminate in the establishment of the Hindu Sabha in April 1915 at the Kumbh Mela in Haridwar. This would later become, in April 1921, the Akhil Bharat Hindu Mahasabha, of which Swami Shraddhananda, B.S. Moonje and Veer Savarkar too were members.[256] The brutality suffered by Hindus in large numbers in the Moplah Riots in August 1921 only vindicated the need for organisations like the Mahasabha. While multiple riots had occurred both before and after the Lucknow Pact of 1916, for instance, the riots in Arrah and Jaunpur, what shook the conscience of Hindu leaders about the Moplah Riots was not only their scale and staggering brutality, but also the consistent denial of the atrocities committed in the name of the Khilafat. This, coupled with Maulana Muhammad Ali's earlier statement in April 1921 expressing support for an Afghan invasion of Bharat, ostensibly to evict the British, brought to a jarring halt the short-lived honeymoon of '*Hindu–Mussalman ki Jai*'.

Further, barring the Khilafat committees which were under the immediate control of Gandhi, it was clear that non-violence was the exception and not the norm. Perhaps to channel this Muslim rage, in January 1922, Gandhi decided to get the preparations for Civil Disobedience going, for which Bardoli in Surat was chosen as the venue for launch.[257] To this end, non-payment of taxes was encouraged. Attempts at bringing Gandhi and the government to the negotiation table were made by Jinnah and others; however, Viceroy Reading had no incentive to engage with Gandhi since he was already assured of the support of the Moderates led by Besant and Banerjea.[258] With no further bargaining chips left in Gandhi's favour, the All-India Congress Committee under Gandhi reluctantly greenlit the launch of Civil Disobedience at its meeting in Surat at the end of January 1922. The reluctance was evident from the fact that on 1 February 1922, in the hope of getting the government to the table, Gandhi shared the manifesto of the Civil Disobedience Movement with Reading, giving the government a week from the date of publication of the manifesto to change its position. The government responded on 6 February 1922, saying that the proposed Civil Disobedience was a call to lawlessness.

However, before the week elapsed, there was a violent clash on 4 February 1922 at Chauri Chaura in Gorakhpur between non-cooperators and the police, which resulted in fatalities on both sides. This was followed by riots in Bareilly on 5 February 1922. Reports of both incidents were telegraphed to Gandhi by Congressmen, who urged him to postpone the launch of mass Civil Disobedience. On 5 February 1922, Gandhi suspended the decision to launch the Movement, which was confirmed at the meeting of the All-India Congress Committee at Bardoli on 12 February 1922.[259] As an alternative to mass Civil Disobedience, Gandhi proposed *mass spinning of the charkha to make khadi*, and other 'social work'.[260] Having already forbidden the option of jihad, the downgrading of Civil Disobedience to mass spinning of charkha to make khadi surely did not go down well with Sharia-observant Khilafatists.

Whether one likes to admit it or not, as of 1922 Jinnah's objections to Gandhi's resolution in 1920 at the Nagpur session, proclaiming an intentionally ambiguous Swaraj as the goal to be attained through all peaceful and legitimate means, stood vindicated. Jinnah's differences with Gandhi on the ambivalence of the end goal aside, he understood that to hope to achieve Swaraj with absolutely no bloodshed smacked of political naïveté. Interestingly, Gandhi did not equate legitimate means with 'lawful', since that would have rendered the Civil Disobedience Movement unlawful. Further, the irony was that while the Khilafatists were ready to embrace jihad to secure the goals of the Khilafat and use Swaraj to hurt the British empire by calling for complete independence, Gandhi did not categorically call for complete independence and had further limited the means to non-violent methods. Despite being repeatedly let down after his recruitment drive for the British during the First World War, and despite the lack of remorse or contrition on the part of the British for the Amritsar tragedy, Gandhi continued to believe that his non-violent methods would somehow yield a different outcome. Critically, he assumed that it was possible to conduct a mass movement peacefully in a country the size of undivided Bharat, and that too with the involvement of the Khilafatists, who did not share his views on non-violence. Perhaps this was 'the Mahatma Complex' at work. By postponing the launch of mass Civil Disobedience indefinitely, Gandhi had revealed the limitations of being a Mahatma, which did not go unnoticed.

The first to react were, of course, the Khilafatists, who were already unhappy with Gandhi's insistence on non-violence. His inability to now launch Civil Disobedience gave them enough reason to revisit the need for Gandhi and their association with him for the achievement of their goals. With the Ali Brothers in jail, Gandhi did not have anyone to rein them in or speak to them on his behalf. After all, he was always dependent on Shaukat Ali to get the Khilafatists to do his bidding. Accordingly, on 17 February 1922, the Kanpur Khilafat Committee resolved to proceed with Non-Cooperation as originally planned, with or without Gandhi and the Congress.[261] Gandhi was also heavily criticised for his lack of nerves by Lala Lajpat Rai and Motilal Nehru. Gandhi's response to the criticism was a summary dismissal of it and a fast of five days. Once again, the Ali Brothers came to his rescue from inside jail by issuing a statement of support for Gandhi's decision.[262] While the Congress formally adopted Gandhi's Bardoli resolution to postpone Civil Disobedience sine die, hardline Khilafatists such as Maulana Abdul Bari and Maulana Hasrat Mohani were scathing in their criticism of Gandhi, despite the support of the Ali Brothers for the latter's decision.[263]

On the government front, Gandhi, who could not be touched hitherto owing to his immense popularity, was now vulnerable. This, coupled with the growing clamour in Britain and in the English establishment in Bharat for action to be taken against him, led to his arrest for sedition on 10 March 1922 in Ahmedabad. On 18 March 1922, he was sentenced to six years' imprisonment. While he was released in February 1924, well before completion of the term, his two-year absence gave the government the freedom it needed to arrest the other leaders of the Non-Cooperation Movement.[264] However, the government realised that the Muslim sentiment in India was still strongly pro-Khilafat and that this was responsible for the frequent confrontation between the government and the agitators, most of whom were Muslim. Since a meeting between the Allied Powers was scheduled to be held in Paris in March, Chelmsford issued a dispatch to Montagu requesting the British government to reconsider the Treaty of Sevres in order to pacify the Muslims in India. This dispatch was prematurely published in Bharat on 8 March 1922, primarily due to a series of communication mishaps.[265] While the contents of the dispatch gave hope to Muslims, it led to Montagu's resignation as he was held responsible for its indiscreet publication.

The overall effect of the publication was that the Khilafatists, including the likes of Abdul Bari and Hasrat Mohani, felt that there was more to be gained from supporting the government than from continuing with the Non-Cooperation Movement.[266] The agitation gradually began losing its vigour, despite some within the CKC who wanted to continue with it until May 1922.[267]

However, on 29 March 1922, when the revised Paris Peace Proposals were published in Bharat, they fell short of the expectations of the Khilafatists despite an improvement in the terms. The impasse continued until June 1922, when at the Khilafat Conference in Lucknow the hardliners demanded the immediate launch of Civil Disobedience.[268] This was easier said than done, since all the stalwarts of the Movement who could galvanise the masses were in jail and Hindu support for the agitation had dwindled.

In August 1922, Ataturk-led Turkey managed to defeat Greece and recapture Smyrna and Asia Minor, which lifted the Muslim spirit in Bharat.[269] The celebration was, however, short-lived, since Turkey's recapture of Smyrna and Asia Minor brought it directly into conflict with Britain as the 'neutral zone', which included Istanbul, was held by British troops. When the CKC and Muslims in Bharat decided to volunteer support to Turkey, the British Indian government invoked the Foreign Enlistment Act of 1870 which empowered the government to regulate and control the mercenary activities of subjects of the British empire. Before matters could precipitate further, an armistice was signed between Turkey, led by the Turkish nationalists, and the Allied Powers in October 1922. Under this agreement, Greece would evacuate Thrace.[270] Further, both parties agreed to renegotiate the terms of the Treaty of Sevres in November 1922 at Lausanne. Mischievously, the Allied Powers extended invitations to Ottoman Sultan Vahideddin Mehmed VI as well as to the Turkish nationalist government under Ataturk to attend the Lausanne Conference.[271] This gave Ataturk an opportunity to cut the monarchy to size by vesting the power of government in the Grand National Assembly *and* also the power to *select a Caliph* from the house of Osman/Ottoman. The Sultan chose to flee with *British* help on a *British* battleship, which allowed the Grand National Assembly of Turkey to formally declare the deposition of the Sultan from the position of Khalifa.[272] In his place, Abdul Mejid, a son of the late Sultan Abdul Aziz, was 'elected' as the Khalifa, whose powers were now restricted to the spiritual and not temporal.

With this, the concept of the Caliphate had been altered—despite being impermissible in Islam—and all that Muslims in Bharat were fighting for was brought to naught. It certainly did not help their cause to know that the Ottoman Caliph had used a British battleship to flee Turkey. To add to the embarrassment of the Khilafatists, the Ataturk-led government (known as the 'Angora/Ankara government') relinquished claims over the Jazirat-ul-Arab and the Muslim holy places located therein.[273] As a face-saving measure, the Khilafatists argued that the institution of the Khilafat had been restored to its pristine glory, since the process of election of the Caliph was prevalent in the golden age of Islam under the first four Caliphs of Islam. As for the distinction between the temporal and the spiritual powers of the Caliph made by Turkish nationalists, the Khilafatists claimed that since the Grand National Assembly was now the defender of the Khilafat as well as its elector, the principle of Khilafat remained intact.[274] Thenceforth, the Khilafatists declared, the khutba in mosques in Bharat would be read in the name of Abdul Mejid, the new Khalifa.[275] Although the Lausanne Conference was still pending, for all practical purposes the core demands of the Khilafatists had either been addressed or rendered moot. But they still decided to continue their agitation until Turkey's interests had been secured at the Lausanne Conference.

The League, which had been sidelined during this period, did not hold an annual session in 1922, and neither did the JUH. The thirty-seventh session of the Indian National Congress was held in Gaya with C.R. Das as the president. In his speech, where he compared Gandhi to Jesus, Das spoke thus on the 'declaration of rights of different communities' under a Swaraj government:[276]

> It (the Congress) should commence its work for the year by a clearer declaration of the rights of the different communities in India under the Swaraj Government. So far as the Hindus and the Mahomedans are concerned there should be a clear and emphatic confirmation of what is known as the Lucknow

Compact, and along with that there should be an emphatic recognition of each other's rights, and each should be prepared to undergo some kind of sacrifice in favour of the other. Let me give an instance to make my meaning clear. Every devout Musalman objects to any music in front of a mosque, and every devout and orthodox Hindu objects to cows being slaughtered. May not the Hindus and the Musalmans of India enter into a solemn compact so that there may not be any music before any mosque and that no cows may be slaughtered? Other instances may be quoted. There should be a scheme of a series of sacrifices to be suffered by each community so that they may advance shoulder to shoulder in the path of Swaraj. As regards the other Communities such as Sikhs, Christians and Parsees, the Hindus and the Mahomedans who constitute the bulk of the people should be prepared to give them even more than their proportional share in the Swaraj administration. I suggest that the Congress should bring about real agreement between all these communities by which the rights of every minority should be clearly recognised in order to remove all doubts which may arise and all apprehensions which probably exist. I need hardly add that I include among Christians not only pure Indians, but also Anglo-Indians and other people who have chosen to make India their home. Such an agreement as I have indicated was always necessary but such an agreement is specially necessary in view of the work which faces us to-day.

The following were the resolutions passed on the Khilafat and the Turkish situation:

This Congress congratulates Ghazi Mustafa Kamal Pasha and the Turkish Nation on their recent successes and further records the determination of the people of India to carry on the struggle till the British Government has done all in its power and removed all its own obstacles to the restoration of the Turkish Nation to free and independent status and the conditions necessary for unhampered national life and effective guardianship of Islam and the Jazirat ul-Arab freed from all non-Muslim control.

In view of the serious situation in the Near East which threatens the integrity of the Khilafat and the Turkish Government and in view of the determination of the Hindus, Mussalmans and all other peoples of India to prevent any such injury, this Congress resolves that the Working Committee do take steps in consultation with the Khilafat Working Committee in order to secure united action by the Hindus, Mussalmans and others, to prevent exploitation of India for any such unjust cause and to deal with the situation.

The Last Gasps of the Khilafat Agitation and of Hindu– Mussalman ki Jai (January 1923–December 1924)

While the Khilafat Conference of December 1922 was being held in Gaya, around the same time as the annual session of the Congress, news arrived on 30 December that the negotiations at Lausanne, which started on 30

Sultan Vahideddin Mehmed VI departing from the back door of the Dolmabahçe Palace in Istanbul. A few days after this picture was taken, the Sultan was deposed and exiled (along with his son) on a British warship to Malta (17 November 1922), then to San Remo, Italy, where he eventually died in 1926.

November 1922, had reached a stalemate. This led to the following resolution being passed by the Conference on 1 January 1923:[277]

> That in the event of war with Turkey due to the unjust attitude of the Allies, particularly British, the Muslims of India would immediately launch civil disobedience with a programme which would include spreading their propaganda among the Police and Army, stoppage of fresh recruitment, refusal to subscribe to war loans, recruitment to the Angora legion, picketing of foreign cloth and liquor shops and preventing export of food grains.

By this time, the cause of the Khilafat had become largely academic because a nationalist Turkey, and not the Ottoman Caliphate, was fighting on the issue of territory, sans the religious aspects. Also, several members of the Congress felt that it was better to discard Non-Cooperation and revert to Tilak's policy of active Non-Cooperation, which meant becoming a part of the lawmaking bodies and voicing concerns while staying within the government. This group, comprising C.R. Das, Motilal Nehru and Khaliquzzaman, formed the Congress–Khilafat Swaraj Party, or the Swaraj Party, in January 1923.[278]

Critically, with the Khilafat issue being rendered academic for all practical purposes, the 'Hindu–Muslim unity' that was needed to keep the Khilafat Agitation going unravelled rapidly under the pressure of the pre-existing long-standing differences between the communities, which were now widened on account of the legitimate apprehensions about the increased Islamisation caused by the Agitation. The assurances given on behalf of the Khilafat committees to encourage Muslims to avoid cow slaughter did not stand the test of time and the issue came to the fore again. By June 1923, Punjab, Bengal and United Provinces saw multiple riots with instances of murder, arson, looting and desecration of places of worship and prayer.[279,280]

With the signing of the Treaty of Peace on 24 July 1923 by the Allies and Turkey, under which Turkey regained Istanbul and Thrace along with control over the Straits, there was no further reason for the Khilafatists to put stock in Hindu–Muslim unity or even Swaraj for that matter. The old policy of loyalty to the British to counteract the 'Hindu Congress' was back in force. However, the unexpected blow to the Khilafatists once again came from Turkish nationalists, who declared Turkey a republic helmed by Kemal Ataturk as the president. This effectively reinforced the purely spiritual nature of the Caliph. The only reason now for continuing the Khilafat Movement was the fate of the Jazirat-ul-Arab, which had to be freed from non-Muslim powers.

In 1923—after having held their sessions in the same cities every year following the Lucknow Pact of 1916—the Congress and the League would once again start holding their sessions in different cities. The 1923 annual session of the Congress, its thirty-eighth, held in Cocanada (present-day Kakinada) was a lacklustre event. The League's fifteenth session was held in Lucknow on 31 March and 1 April 1923.[281] The primary subject was, of course, the decision taken by Turkey to declare itself a republic. However, this session of the League came to an abrupt end and was adjourned sine die as a result of a confrontation between Dr M.A. Ansari and Jinnah. Jinnah wanted Muslims to enter Legislative Councils and work for Dominion Status for India, whereas Ansari was opposed to this as a leading member of the Non-Cooperation Movement. While Jinnah's position was defeated twelve to nine, the session was indefinitely postponed.

As for the JUH, its fourth annual session was held in Gaya on 24 December 1923, with Maulana Habibur Rahman of Deoband as its president and Maulana Abdul Rauf as the chairman of the reception committee.[282] The deliberations at this session naturally focused on the developments in Turkey regarding the position of the Khalifa/Caliph. In his welcome address, Maulana Rauf was of the view that while the Caliph could be elected or nominated, and deposed, he must possess *both* spiritual and temporal authority. He categorically objected to Ataturk's decision to strip the Caliph of his temporal powers. This point was repeated in the presidential speech of Maulana Rahman.

The year 1924 brought with it the ultimate disappointment and embarrassment for the Khilafatists—not from the British but from Turkish nationalists, who legally *abolished* the Caliphate on 1 March 1924, *deposed* the Caliph, Abdul Mejid, and asked him to *leave* Turkey for Switzerland.[283] One of the reasons for this decision taken by Republican Turkey was to allay Allied fears of the revival of pan-Islamism which used the Caliph as the central rallying point.[284] Expectedly, the Khilafatists could not contain their anguish because Turkey had decided all this on behalf of the ummah, and without consulting the ummah. Representations were sent by the Khilafatists to Ataturk urging him to reconsider his decision and even requesting him to assume the Caliphal mantle, but in vain.[285] On 5 March 1924, King Hussein of Hejaz proclaimed himself the Khalifa, which invited the scorn of Muslims in Bharat who continued to see him as an opportunist and a traitor.[286]

With the Khilafat Movement all but dead, the attention of the Muslim community in Bharat moved back to the Muslim League, which had been playing second fiddle to the Congress and the CKC all this while. Jinnah assumed its presidency at the Lahore session in May 1924, which was a continuation of the adjourned fifteenth session.[287] In his presidential speech, Jinnah recounted the events that had happened on the national scene from March 1919 onwards and concluded that each of the movements initiated by Gandhi had *failed* to achieve its goal and that it was now time to refocus on Swaraj and achievement of Dominion Status for Bharat. Although he added that Hindu–Muslim unity was essential for Swaraj, unity here meant preserving the Muslim-majority status of specific provinces and preserving communal electorates in those provinces where Muslims were not in the majority. The following six points were identified as the basic and fundamental principles of Swaraj, which were included in resolution II of the session:[288]

Whereas the speedy attainment of Swaraj is one of the declared objects of the All-India Muslim League, whereas it is now generally felt that the conception of Swaraj should be translated into the realm of concrete politics and become a factor in the daily life of the Indian people, the All-India Muslim League hereby resolves that in any scheme of a constitution for India, the following shall constitute its basic and fundamental principles:

(a) The existing provinces of India shall all be united under a common government on a federal basis so that each province shall have full and complete provincial autonomy, the functions of the central government being confined to such matters only as are of general and common concern.

(b) Any territorial redistribution that might at any time become necessary shall not in any way affect the Muslim majority population in the Punjab, Bengal and N.W.F. Province.

(c) The basis of representation in the Legislature and in all other elected bodies shall be population, except that very small minorities may be given representation in excess of their numerical proportion in those cases in which they would remain entirely unrepresented in the absence of such exceptional treatment, however to the essential proviso that no majority shall be reduced to a minority or even to an equality.

(d) Full religious liberty, i.e. liberty of belief, worship, observances, propaganda, association, and education shall be guaranteed to all communities.

(e) The idea of joint electorates with a specified number of seats being unacceptable to Indian Muslims, on the ground of its being a fruitful source of discord and disunion and also of being wholly inadequate to achieve the object of effective representation of various communal groups, the representation of the latter shall continue to be by means of separate electorates as at present, provided that it shall be open to any community at any time to abandon its separate electorates in favour of joint electorates;

(f) No bill or resolution or any part thereof affecting any community, which question is to be determined by the members of that community in the elected body concerned, shall be passed in any legislature or in any other elected body, if three-fourths of the members of that community in that particular body oppose such bill or resolution or part thereof.

With this session, the League had made a comeback while the Congress was a divided house, although the Swaraj Party had captured a good number of seats in the Councils. As for the CKC, in June 1924 it decided to reinvent itself by focusing on reorganising the Muslim community, now that the issue of the Khilafat was no more central. Between July and September 1924, once again riots broke out in several parts of the country. The breaking point was the mass killing of Hindus and Sikhs and their ultimate exodus from Kohat in the NWFP in September 1924.[289] The riots also led to strained equations between Gandhi and the Ali Brothers because Gandhi realised that a genocide and a consequent exodus of Hindus had taken place in Kohat, for which he would categorically hold the Muslims of Kohat responsible at the Congress's annual session in December that year. Although a Unity Conference was organised in Delhi in September to appeal for harmony between Hindus and Muslims, it had very little impact on the overall situation in the country.

By the end of September 1924, King Hussein of Hejaz was defeated by Ibn Saud, Sultan of Nejd. Now the Khilafat issue revolved around Arabia, the home of Islam, and it managed to divide the Muslim community owing to the iconoclasm of Saud, who directed the removal of domed structures from the graves of Muslims who were held in high regard by the community.[290]

Although Indian Khilafatists tried to mediate between Hussein and Saud, it yielded no result. While the issue of Hejaz would keep the Khilafat organisations afloat at least until 1926 and the CKC would continue to exist until 1938—until the death of Shaukat Ali—for all practical purposes, and from the Indian perspective, it had ceased to be relevant as an organisation or a movement in December 1924.[291] However, the heightened sense of Islamic consciousness and the hierarchy of loyalties that came with it remained.

The thirty-ninth annual session of the Congress was held in Belgaum in December 1924, where an agreement was signed between the Congress and the Swaraj Party, with Gandhi representing the former as its president and Motilal Nehru and C.R. Das representing the latter.[292] The agreement recognised the need for both factions to work together. Among other things, it was agreed that Non-Cooperation as a national programme would be suspended except for boycott of foreign cloth, and the 'Spinning Franchise', also known as the Khadi Movement, was launched.[293] This Movement was aimed at making Bharat self-sufficient and at promoting 'spinning' as a means to forge national unity. In his presidential speech, Gandhi admitted that the Non-Cooperation Movement had not resulted in attainment of Swaraj but had brought deplorable results.[294] Importantly, he recognised that Hindus had to flee from Muslim-majority Kohat and that it was for the Muslims of Kohat to demonstrate that Hindus could return safely.[295] He also urged the Hindus of Kohat not to return until the Muslims of the region guaranteed their lives and property. Pertinently, Hindus were 7 per cent of the population in Kohat in 1924, today they are close to 0.1 per cent and Kohat is in Pakistan.

After having spelt out a twelve-point Swaraj Scheme, Gandhi turned to the question of 'independence'; he clarified that his vision of Swaraj presupposed *retention* of the British connection, preferably on honourable and equal terms.[296] Despite voices within the Congress asking for complete independence, Gandhi's position was still one of conditional and honourable dependence. It would be fair to state that even as of 1924, the Congress did not embrace complete independence as the goal to be achieved.

Among the resolutions passed, resolution V related to the agitation in Burma. It was moved by S.A.S. Tyabji. Ironically, having accepted the principle of communal electorates for Muslims in Bharat, the resolution, while supporting the agitation in Burma, deprecated the demand for communal representation by Indian settlers in Burma as being bad in principle. Resolution VI related to the riots in Kohat and Gulbarga, and read as follows:

> The Congress deplores the Hindu–Moslem tension and the riots that have taken place in various parts of India. The Congress deplores the riots that recently took place in Kohat, resulting in loss of life and destruction of

property including temples and is of opinion that the local authority failed to perform the primary duty of protection of life and property. The Congress further deplores the enforced exodus of the Hindu population from Kohat and strongly urges the Mussalmans of Kohat to assure their Hindu brethren of full protection of their lives and property and to invite them to return as their honoured friends and neighbours. The Congress advises the refugees not to return to Kohat except upon an honourable invitation from the Kohat Mussalmans and upon the advice of Hindu and Mussalman leaders. The Congress advises the public, whether Hindus or Mussalmans, not to accept the finding of the Government of India, as also of others, in the Kohat tragedy and to suspend judgment till the Board appointed by the Unity Conference or some other equally representative body has inquired into the unfortunate event and come to a decision upon it.

The Congress expresses its heart-felt sympathy for the sufferers in the Gulbarga riots and condemns the desecration committed on the places of worship in that town.

Resolutions VII and IX related to removal of untouchability and support for the Akali Movement, respectively. In the former resolution, the support of the princely state of Travancore for removal of untouchability as part of the Vaikom Movement was specifically recognised.

The sixteenth session of the League was held in Bombay in December 1924 and was presided over by Syed Riza Ali.[297] This was attended by Besant and the Nehrus, among others. On the constitutional front, Riza Ali drew attention in his presidential speech to the setting up of a reforms inquiry committee by Viceroy Reading to look into the difficulties arising out of the Government of India Act of 1919 and the Rules thereof. The committee, headed by Alexander Muddiman, had Jinnah and Tej Bahadur Sapru among its members. Although the Swaraj Party, which was represented in the Indian Legislative Assembly, was invited to take part in the deliberations of the committee, it refused to do so. By 3 December 1924, the committee had submitted its 212-page report—which would be known as the Muddiman Report—to the government, along with its recommendations. Given that the Report was made public in 1925, and given its consequential developments fall beyond the timeline of this book, I will discuss it in detail in the third book of the trilogy.

Coming back to the League's session, the party placed the blame on Hindus for their exodus from Kohat although they were in the minority (7 per cent or less) there.[298] In fact, a specific resolution, resolution X, held the minority Hindu population of Kohat responsible for the outbreak of the riots.[299] The overall tone and tenor of the session was back to one of loyalism to the British, Muslim exceptionalism and demand for special and separate treatment. Effectively, the short period of Hindu–Muslim entente, which began in 1916 with the Lucknow Pact, was over by December 1924 along with the loss of the Khilafat steam.

The fifth session of the JUH was held on 29 December 1924 in Coconada.[300] Citing the treatment of Islam and Turkey at the hands of Europe in his presidential speech, Maulvi Syed Hussain Ahmad said that it was the first and foremost duty of Muslims to stand against the British Indian government and free India from British control to prevent further degeneration of Islam under the British. Freeing the Jazirat-ul-Arab from the control of non-Muslim powers was the other issue he focused on. One of the resolutions passed at this session related to building a *memorial* for 'Mopla martyrs'.

The period after December 1924 would witness the gradual movement of the pan-Islamist Muslim leaders thrown up by the Khilafat Movement in three different directions. The first group, led by the Ali Brothers, Maulana Abdul Bari and Maulana Hasrat Mohani, would continue to work with the CKC and JUH for resolution of the Hejaz issue as well as for the cause of Muslims in Bharat; the second group, which included Choudhry Khaliquzzaman, would move to the League, owing to its revival by and under Jinnah. This group too would work for the cause of Muslims in Bharat; and the third group, who called themselves 'Nationalist Muslims' as opposed to 'Muslim Nationalists', namely Mukhtar Ahmad Ansari, Maulana Abul Kalam Azad, Ajmal Khan, Asaf Ali, A.M. Khwaja, T.A.K. Sherwani and Syed Mahmud, would move into or back to the Congress and claimed to work for the cause of 'Indian nationalism', 'secularism' and India's 'composite culture'.[301] Leaders like B.S. Moonje, Malaviya and Rai, however, were concerned that the role of these 'Nationalist Muslims' in the Congress was to exert pressure from within the party and that the role of the other two groups was to exert pressure from outside it. Whether their concerns were validated with time or not, and whether there was any difference at all between the goals of Muslim Nationalists and Nationalist Muslims, we shall see in the third book of the trilogy.

With this the scope of discussions outlined for this book stands covered. Only the discussion of the four riots—namely Malegaon, Malabar, Gulbarga and Kohat—remains, which will be taken up in the final chapter of this book, I will share my concluding remarks for this book at the end of the discussion on the riots because they are better understood against the backdrop of the riots and the brazen denials, following the riots, of the massacre of Hindus in the Malabar and Kohat.

9

Malegaon, Malabar, Gulbarga and Kohat: The Two-Nation Theory in Action

'Secular' historians have often characterised some of the Hindu–Muslim riots which took place during the Khilafat years as 'peasant rebellions against Hindu landlords or attacks on Hindu collaborators of the British', or have held that the attacks on Hindus were incidental to the attacks on the colonial establishment. However, this is a patently inaccurate representation of facts, given the long history of riots between the two communities for a variety of reasons, including cow slaughter and processions before mosques, much before the riots of the Khilafat years. In the previous chapter, I had mentioned the unravelling of an already uneasy and short-lived Hindu–Muslim compact by mid-1921 on account of frequent riots between the two communities, the most prominent of them being the Moplah Riots in the Malabar, whose beginnings are typically traced to August 1921. However, Malabar was not the only flashpoint.

As C. Sankaran Nair points out in his book *Gandhi and Anarchy*,[1] thanks to Gandhi's encouragement of the Khilafat Agitation and its pan-Islamic vision, there were riots in Malegaon, Malabar, Multan, Lahore, Saharanpur, Amritsar, Allahabad, Calcutta, Delhi, Gulbarga, Kohat, Lucknow, Shahjahanpur and Nagpur during the core Khilafat period, i.e., from 1919 to 1924. This is attested to by Gopal Krishna too in his study of communal violence in Bharat,[2] as well as by Dr Ambedkar in his book *Pakistan or the Partition of India*.[3] Of these, I have chosen four riots to discuss, in order to demonstrate the position that 'Hindu–Muslim unity' that began with the Lucknow Pact of 1916 until 1921 was the exception and not the norm and, importantly, simply a product of political necessity on both sides. There was no 'Ganga–Jamuni tehzeeb' foundation to begin with, for the unity to last. Therefore, it was bound to come undone, especially once the Khilafatists no longer needed Hindu support

Wikimedia Commons

A typical Mapilla war knife

any more for their Agitation in view of the developments in Turkey which robbed them of their purpose.

It must be understood that even before Turkish nationalists under Kemal Ataturk began dismantling the edifice of the Khilafat brick by brick, and *on their own* in 1923, riots were a regular feature. Once the Turkish nationalist government, known as the Angora/Ankara government, began the process of dismemberment of the Ottoman Caliphate, whatever little reason or need had existed for the inherently brittle Hindu–Muslim entente ceased to exist. Further, in view of the long history of Middle Eastern coloniality in Bharat, in particular the rise of Islamic revivalism and reformation (discussed in the first section of this book), it could be said that things were bound to revert to square one sooner or later. After all, if the unity had an inherently strong foundation, the Two-Nation Theory would have never found acceptance; nor would it have entrenched itself in the body politic of this country and in its constitutional apparatus by way of communal electorates. It is important to bear these fundamental causal realities in mind instead of latching on to comfortable myths that an otherwise perfectly healthy and sunny relationship between the two communities was destroyed by the politics of self-interest of careerist politicians, or by that ever-handy punching bag—the divide and rule policy of the British. The bloody history of the relationship between the two communities *much before* the arrival of the European coloniser and *after* his exit should put an end to such idle, wishful and historically inaccurate 'secular' theorisation.

Critically, it is important to understand the demographic status of Muslims in Bharat as of 1921. The following is a table from Mushirul Hasan's book *Nationalism and Communal Politics in India, 1916–1928,* capturing the proportion of Muslim population in the provinces based on the census of 1921:[4]

Province	Muslim Population	Percentage of Muslim Population
Madras	2,840,488	6.71
Bombay	3,820,153	19.74
Bengal	25,210,802	54.00
United Provinces	6,481,032	14.28
Punjab	11,444,321	55.33
Bihar and Orissa	3,690,182	10.85
Central Provinces and Berar	563,574	4.05
Assam	2,202,460	28.96
North-West Frontier Province	2,062,786	91.62

In light of these figures in 1921, perhaps the frequent riots in Bengal, Punjab and NWFP were to be expected to the point of exodus of Hindus in places like Kohat in the NWFP. In hindsight, it is not surprising that the demography of these provinces contributed significantly to the solidification of Pakistan by 1946, both politically and territorially, in the matter of just a quarter of a century.

With these prefatory thoughts for this chapter, I will proceed to discuss the riots of Malegaon (April 1921), Malabar (August 1921), Gulbarga (August 1924) and Kohat (September 1924). Given the already voluminous nature of this book, the discussions on Malegaon, Gulbarga and Kohat shall be brief and factual, citing debates from the British Parliament and a few scholarly sources, to the extent that they demonstrate that the Two-Nation Theory was, and perhaps remains, a lived and living reality. The Moplah Riots will be discussed in some detail at the end.

Malegaon, Gulbarga and Kohat

In the previous chapter, I had extracted portions of Maulana Muhammad Ali's statement before the magistrate in Karachi in 1921 in which he defiantly expressed that the Khilafatists were governed only by the law of the Quran. Citing this, Sankaran Nair had the following to say on Gandhi's deliberate ignoration of this statement and its implications:[5]

> It is impossible to believe that Gandhi and his adherents are not aware that this claim of the Mahomedans to be judged only by the law of the Koran, is a claim which is the fons et origo of all Khilafat claims of whatever kind. It is as well to be clear about this, for not only does the acceptance of the claim mean the death knell of the British Empire or Indo-British commonwealth, whatever name we may care to give to the great fraternity of nations to which we belong, but specifically as regards India it means a real denial of Swaraj. For it involves Mahomedan rule and Hindu subjection or Hindu Rule and Mahomedan subjection. Let there be no mistake about this, no camouflage. Whatever the Hindus may mean by the Hindu Muslim entente, and I believe they mean a true equality, and whatever the more enlightened Mussalmans may mean, Mohamad Ali, Shaukat Ali, and those of their persuasion, mean a Mussalman dominion pure and simple, though they are of course clever enough to keep the cat in the bag so long as the time for its emergence is yet unripe. They protest, it need hardly be said, that they are animated by no arriere pensee, no sectarian spirit, only by the most loving goodwill towards the Hindu brethren. But there are some of us who are too experienced to be caught by this mischievous and pernicious chaff and must sound the warning to those less experienced and more gullible. Considering the high character of some of the men who follow Gandhi, I can only

Kohat Tehsil gate, 1919

believe that this realization came to them so late that it was difficult for them to withdraw.

As pointed out in the Karachi trial, these movements at first appear innocuous, then grow dangerous.

Nair points out that on 15 March 1920, a Khilafat Committee was formed in Malegaon with a body of volunteers. The Committee would deliver regular lectures and religious sermons, largely attended by members of the Muslim community in Malegaon. In January 1921, Shaukat Ali visited Malegaon, and this led to an increase in political activity there. As part of the Non-Cooperation Movement, two Muslim schools in Malegaon decided to refuse the government's grant-in-aid and instead chose to raise money from the local community, which largely comprised weavers, mostly Muslim. To this end, a 'paisa fund' was created, and it was decided that for every sari sold by the weavers, one paisa or a quarter of an anna would go to the fund. The problem with the idea was that it did not allow people the choice of non-participation. On 27 February 1921, the Committee and its volunteers decided that those who did not contribute to the paisa fund would be commercially boycotted. To give effect to the boycott, pickets were established by the Khilafatists outside those shops that did not fall in line with the Khilafat Committee's diktat, which were mostly Hindu. Despite appeals to the authorities by those who were affected by this boycott, no action was taken.

Further, in view of the volatile atmosphere, on 30 March 1921, the district magistrate issued orders prohibiting the carrying of swords and cudgels to the lectures and sermons organised by the Khilafat Committee. To defuse the situation in a more constructive way, at a meeting called by the subdivisional officer on 13 March 1921, the officer proposed collection boxes to collect voluntary contributions instead of forcing them. However, the Khilafat Committee did not agree to the suggestion. On 15 April, the local authorities decided to initiate legal proceedings against two-dozen Khilafat volunteers who had violated the proclamation against the carrying of swords and cudgels. Here's Nair's description of the events that followed:[6]

On the 24th April, the day before the hearing of these cases, a meeting was again called at night at which a leading Mahomedan is reported to have used the following words:—

'They must not be afraid of Government or of the police and that the volunteers would see about the cases brought against them and may God give the volunteers strength to promote their religion.' The next day April 25th twelve of these cases came on for hearing before Mr. Thakar the resident magistrate. They ended in the conviction of the 6 volunteers and their being fined Rs. 50 each with the alternative of 4 weeks' simple imprisonment. The fines were not paid.

On the result being known the mob that had collected gave vent to their feelings by loud cries of 'Alla-ho-akbar,' the war cry used by the mob throughout the riot, assaulted all the police to be found in the town of Malegoan, burned a temple, killed the sub-inspector of police, not the only one killed and threw his body into the fire and looted the houses of all who were opposed to the Khilafat movement, the owners themselves having fled in the meantime.

This illustrates the 'non-violent' methods followed by the Khilafat committees and volunteers. I give another instance in full for illustration Barabanki (App. XI) which shows perhaps more forcibly the violent fanaticism supporting the movement. More instances can be easily given.

On 4 May 1921, the Malegaon Riots were mentioned in the House of Lords by Lord Sydenham in his question to the Under-Secretary of State for India.[7] More specifically, given the situation on the Afghan border, his question was on the potential impact of any reduction in the army's size on its ability to defend India against an Afghan invasion as well as to control the internal situation, thanks to the Khilafat-fuelled Muslim fanaticism in Bharat. Here's the relevant extract:

The danger to the peace of India, internally and externally, was never so great as it is now. The Dobbs mission has been in Cabul for four months and apparently has accomplished nothing. That is a humiliating fact which must tell against our prestige throughout the whole of the East. It is admitted. It has been admitted in this House that the Afghans, while negotiating with our Mission, concluded a Treaty with the Bolsheviks. Since then, according to the Manchester Guardian, a supplementary clause has been added to that Treaty providing for a subsidy of one million gold or silver roubles, and also the construction of a telegraph line from Kustk through Herat and Kandahar to Cabul, with any technical assistance which may be required. The object of that telegraph line is obvious. But it is also reported now that another Treaty has been made with the Nationalist Turks by the Afghans. *So it seems that the Afghans are rapidly falling under the influence either of the Bolsheviks, or of Pan-Islam, or possibly of both.*

Besides that, fighting is now constantly taking place on the frontier, as we read almost every day. With a hostile Afghanistan, or even an unfriendly Afghanistan, frontier warfare would be far more serious and more continuous than it was in the past. In 1897 we employed 120,000 troops on the frontier, though the Afghans at that time were quite friendly to us. *In the spring of 1919 when the Afghans invaded India, we required over 200,000 troops on the frontier, or, with non-combatants, about 300,000 men, though only part of the tribes rose at that time.* Is the Government sure that when the Army is reduced as proposed it will be able to deal with the much greater troubles that may at any time arise on the frontier and at the same time be sufficient to preserve order in India?

The internal situation, in my opinion, was never so menacing as it is to-day. I am most anxious not to seem to exaggerate the situation, but I must say that some of the reports we receive are really most fallacious. *Latterly, I have seen it said that Mr. Gandhi is rapidly losing his influence with the educated classes and that his non-cooperation movement is breaking down.* That may be true to some extent, but what is forgotten is that his appeal to the ignorant and fanatical masses has aroused a feeling of race hatred which may take years before it subsides, if, indeed, it ever does subside. He has followed Mrs. Besant's earlier efforts but with much greater effect, working upon the masses and upon the boys and students, to imbue them with dislike and contempt not only of the British Government, but of all British officials in India, and the strength of that appeal lies in its religious aspects. Mr. Gandhi and his myrmidons teach that British rule is satanic, that it is the duty of all religious Indians to get rid of it. No one who has not lived in India can quite understand how dangerous such teaching is, especially when the teacher claims, and is conceded, supernatural powers and supernatural sanction.

The Moslem extremists are even more violent in their language than Mr. Gandhi himself, and the wildest falsehoods about our treatment of the holy places of Islam have been widely circulated amongst the fanatical classes in India. During the last month we have seen two shocking outbreaks of violence, one at Malegaon in the Bombay Presidency, and the other on the Bengal coalfield. The police were easily overpowered, and loss of life and destruction occurred because troops were not available in time to deal with these disturbances. Then the forces of Bolshevism are certainly being brought to bear upon parts of India at the present time. The objects of the Bolsheviks, of course, differ from those of Mr. Gandhi and his associates, but they reinforce each other, because they both agree in the determination to turn us out of India. [Emphases added]

As for the Gulbarga Riots of 1924, here's an account of them by R.C. Majumdar:[8]

The Muhammadan mobs attacked all the Hindu Temples in the city, numbering about fifteen, and broke the idols. They also raided the Sharan Vishveshwar Temple and attempted to set fire to the Temple car. The Police were eventually obliged to fire, with the result that three Muhammadans, including the Police Superintendent Mr. Azizullah, were killed and about a dozen persons injured. Next morning the streets were again in the hands of Muhammadan mobs and considerable damage was done to Hindu houses and shops. On the arrival of Police Reinforcement, order was restored. On the 14th August the Muslim mob fury was at its height and almost all the temples within the range of the mob, some fifty in number, were desecrated, their sanctum sanctorum entered into, their idols broken and their buildings damaged.

It is pertinent to note that Gulbarga fell within the dominion of the Nizam of Hyderabad.

Coming to the Kohat Riots in the NWFP, the resolutions passed on the Kohat Hindu exodus by the Congress, the League and the JUH at their respective annual sessions of 1924 were discussed in the previous chapter. I will now draw from the proceedings of the Congress session, in particular Lala Lajpat Rai's narration of events in the Kohat exodus to place the facts before the reader. Resolution VI, which dealt with both the Gulbarga and Kohat Riots, was moved by Motilal Nehru, who acknowledged in his speech in support of the resolution that the Hindu population of Kohat was indeed a 'very small minority' which had 'suffered very greatly and grievously'.[9] He further said that such a tragedy had never taken place in his lifetime. He conveniently added that he did not propose to delve into the question as to who was responsible for inciting the trouble. This was followed by a speech in Urdu by Shaukat Ali, who vaguely appealed for Hindu–Muslim unity, followed by Lala Lajpat Rai's speech.

Rai's speech, which was based on the undisputed facts contained in a government report,[10] inform us that in mid-August 1921, on the eve of Janmashtami, a publication that denigrated the Hindu faith was authored by a Muslim and circulated in Kohat, where 93 per cent of the population was Muslim and 7 per cent Hindu. In response to the anti-Hindu publication, Jewan Das, the secretary of the local Sanatana Dharma Sabha, responded in kind with a poem. Expectedly, the poem offended the sentiments of the Muslims of Kohat. Given that the Hindus were vastly outnumbered, on 2 September 1924, the elders of the community chose to apologise on behalf of Jewan Das and went to the extent of passing a resolution expressing their apology and sought the forgiveness of the Muslim community.

However, copies of the so-called blasphemous poem were sent by the local Muslims to the local Khilafat Committee, the government authorities and to the border Muslim tribes. In the meantime, Jewan Das was arrested and released on bail with a bond of Rs 10,000, which angered the Muslims. On 8 September 1924, the Muslims of Kohat reportedly took a 'vow of divorce' at a local mosque—that if their demands were not fulfilled by the authorities and Jewan Das was not punished to their satisfaction, they would take the law in their own hands and do what was expected of them by their faith, or divorce their wives. As we shall see later in the context of the Moplah Riots, this is a common practice among Muslims before they seek 'martyrdom'.

Early in the morning of 9 September 1924, the attack on the Hindus and Sikhs of Kohat began with the looting of their shops. Frantic messages were sent by the Hindu community to the local authorities, but to no avail. The attacks continued on 10 September, with Hindu and Sikh houses being set on fire. Finally, apprehending mass slaughter of Hindus and Sikhs, they were evacuated to the cantonment and then to Rawalpindi.[11] Commenting on the entire episode and the frequency of communal riots across the country, following is an extract from Ambedkar's book *Pakistan or the Partition of India*:[12]

> Though the year 1922–23 was a peaceful year the relations between the two communities were strained throughout 1923–24. But in no locality did this tension produce such tragic consequences as in the city of Kohat. The immediate cause of the trouble was the publication and circulation of a pamphlet containing a virulently anti-Islamic poem. Terrible riots broke out on the 9th and 10th of September 1924, the total casualties being about 155 killed and wounded. House property to the estimated value of Rs. 9 lakhs was destroyed, and a large quantity of goods were looted. As a result of this reign of terror the whole Hindu population evacuated the city of Kohat. After protracted negotiations an agreement of reconciliation was concluded between the two communities. Government giving an assurance that, subject to certain reservations, the prosecution pending against persons concerned in rioting should be dropped. With the object of enabling the sufferers to restart their businesses and rebuild their houses, Government sanctioned advances, free of interest in certain instances, amounting to Rs. 5 lakhs. But even after the settlement had been reached and evacuees had returned to Kohat there was no peace, and throughout 1924–25 the tension between the Hindu and

Musalman masses in various parts of the country increased to a lamentable extent. In the summer months, there was a distressing number of riots. In July, severe fighting broke out between Hindus and Musalmans in Delhi, which was accompanied by serious casualties. In the same month, there was a bad outbreak at Nagpur. August was even worse. There were riots at Lahore, at Lucknow, at Moradabad, at Bhagalpur and Nagpur in British India; while a severe affray took place at Gulbarga in the Nizam's Dominions. September–October saw severe fighting at Lucknow, Shahjahanpur, Kankinarah and at Allahabad. The most terrible outbreak of the year being the one that took place at Kohat which was accompanied by murder, arson and loot.

Without adding any further comment on the above, I will proceed to place the facts before the reader with respect to the Moplah Riots of 1921 in the Malabar, which are often misrepresented as the 'Moplah Rebellion'.

The Moplah Outrage of 1921–1922: Peasant Rebellion or Hindu Genocide?

Thus far, I have used the generic word 'Riots' in the context of the disturbance witnessed in the Malabar in 1921–1922. Perhaps the more accurate term, which has been used in British records, would be 'Outrage', given the sheer ferocity and one-sided barbarity of the episode.[13] Accordingly, I shall use the word 'Outrage' for the remainder of this discussion.

Brahmin family in Malabar, 1902

The Moplah Outrage of 1921–1922 was not an aberration. In view of the near-unbroken violent communal history of the place, which dates back, at the very least, to Tipu Sultan's invasion of the Malabar,[14] and earlier by his father Hyder Ali, it would be factually incorrect to pin the blame for the Outrage entirely on the Khilafat Movement and Agitation. At best, the Khilafat Agitation provided an opportunity or façade that enabled yet another round of ethnic cleansing of the Hindus of the region, this time the difference being only in scale and brutality, and the fact that the atrocities were chronicled in multiple sources, making denial of the occurrence impossible. It is for this reason that 'secular' approach to history in Bharat is: what cannot be denied must be justified. This explains the typically Marxist treatment of the Hindu Genocide in Malabar as a rebellion by Moplah peasants against the British establishment and Hindu landlords. In Chapter 1, if one might recall, it was pointed out that a similar Marxist trope was employed to justify the anti-Hindu campaign of the Wahhabi Titu Mir in Baraset in Bengal, to call it the 'Baraset Uprising' of 1831. Terms like 'Rebellion' and 'Uprising' do not change facts that speak for themselves.

Since a detailed examination of the history of the region as well as the Moplah Outrage is beyond the scope of this book and has already been undertaken in several works, I will enumerate these sources for the interested reader:

1. *Correspondence on Moplah Outrages in Malabar for the Years 1849–53* (Volumes 1 and 2), (1863)
2. *Malabar Manual* (Volumes 1 and 2), by William Logan (1887)
3. *Gandhi and Anarchy*, by C. Sankaran Nair (1922)
4. *The Mapilla Rebellion, 1921–1922*, a 456-page report, known as the Knapp Report prepared by Arthur Rowland Knapp and published by the Madras Provincial Government (1922)
5. *The Moplah Rebellion, 1921*, by Diwan Bahadur C. Gopalan Nair (1923)
6. *The Moplah Rebellion of 1921–22 and Its Genesis*, by Conrad Wood (1975)
7. Debates in the Central Legislative Assembly, Council of States and the House of Lords

In this chapter, I will limit myself to drawing from these sources and other scholarly articles to present the facts relating to the Moplah Outrage against the specific backdrop of the Khilafat Agitation. Given the 'secular' attempt to obfuscate the facts regarding this subject, I have consciously chosen to quote extensively from various sources to present a more objective basis from which to draw conclusions.

A Short History of Fanaticism in the Malabar until 1921

It is said that the Moplahs or the Mapillas are those Muslims of the Malabar who trace their roots to Arab traders who married the locals, which made them the sons-in-law ('*mapillai*', son-in-law) of the Malabar.[15] According to scholars, the Moplahs enjoyed the patronage of the Samoothiri (Zamorin) of Calicut and settled along the coast, where they lived until the arrival of the Portuguese (Vasco da Gama) in 1498, who challenged the commercial interests of the Mapillas and pushed them further inland.[16] Gradually, there seems to have emerged a distinction between the Mapillas of north Malabar (where Kannur is located) and south Malabar (comprising the Ernad and Walluvanad taluks), based on the communities the converts came from. The former group was seen as relatively more upwardly mobile whereas the latter group, according to Robert Hardgrave, was:[17]

> ... entirely separate from those of the rest of Malabar ... The low state of their intelligence, the subservience in which they had hitherto lived, and the absence of any men of learning to instruct them in their new religion, even were they capable of understanding, all tended to provide a race which would prove an easy prey to fanaticism and lawlessness.

Hardgrave adds that the Ernad and Walluvanad taluks (the focii of the 1921 Outrage) populated by the latter group of Mapillas became hotbeds for continual communal conflict even before the invasions of Malabar by Hyder Ali and his son Tipu Sultan.[18] Subsequently, during the invasions of Hyder Ali and Tipu Sultan, the region witnessed religious atrocities on Hindus and Christians on a scale hitherto unknown, which is attested to by several sources. Citing William Logan's *Malabar Manual*, Gopalan Nair says:[19]

> In March, 1789, a Mysorean force of 19000 men with 46 field-pieces, surrounded 2000 Nayars with their families in an old fort at Kuttipuram, the head-quarters of the Kadathanad Raja's family which the besieged defended for several days. *'At last, finding it untenable. they submitted to Tippu's terms which were a voluntary profession of the Muhammadan faith or a forcible, conversion with deportation from their native land. The unhappy captives gave a forced assent and on the next day the rite of circumcision was performed on all the males, every individual of both sexes being compelled to close the ceremony by eating beef. This achievement was held out as an example to the other detachments of the army. Christian and Pagan women were forcibly married to Muhammadans.'*
>
> *Tippu had made repeated vows to honour the whole of the people of Malabar with Islam and would have carried out the vow, and Malabar would have been a Moslem country, but for the treaty dated 18th March, 1792, under which Tippu was forced to yield Malabar to the East India Company.* [Emphases added]

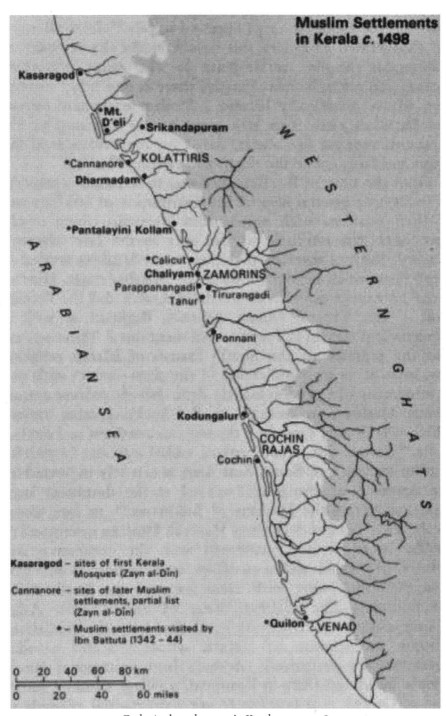

Early Arab settlements in Kerala up to 1498

According to Dhanagare:[20]

Tipu Sultan, who was both more ruthless and more ambitious than his father, Hyder Ali, resumed the invasion of Malabar in the 1780s, persecuting and forcibly converting the Hindus. Moplahs seized this opportunity to further their economic interests, as well as improve their numerical strength.

After Tipu's death, those who had sought refuge in the kingdom of Travancore returned to their homes in south Malabar and their lands were restored to a large extent to them by the British in 1792. This created three different groups of people in the region, based on the sharecropping pattern—*jenmis* or landlords (mostly Namboodiri Brahmins), *kanamdars* or tenants/leaseholders (mostly Nairs), and *verumpattamdars* (mostly the southern Mapillas) or sub-lessees, who actually cultivated the crop or were hired for cultivation by the kanamdars.[21] In a sense, the verumpattamdars of the Malabar were similar to the *bargadars* who were sharecroppers in the northern parts of Bharat. Naturally, the restoration of the lands to the jenmis and the kanamdars was resented by the Mapillas, who were now back to being verumpattamdars. This would result in frequent attacks on the Namboodiris and Nairs by the Moplahs in the form of violence, including sexual violence, forced conversions through force-feeding of beef, and desecration of temples.[22,23]

Both William Logan and Conrad Wood record the existence of continual communal conflict starting from at least 1836 (after the end of the Coorg War of 1834) in the region. In the interests of brevity and authenticity, I would draw the reader's attention to the enumeration of instances of Moplah fanaticism from 1836 to 1885 by William Logan, contained on pages 557 to 598 of Volume 1 of the *Malabar Manual*;[24] Conrad Wood's thesis on the subject lists at least twenty-nine instances from 1836 to 1919.[25] That at least for a hundred years before the Moplah Outrage of 1921 the region witnessed frequent acts of fanaticism by the Moplahs was observed as follows by a three-judge special tribunal constituted in Calicut to prosecute the offenders of the Moplah Outrage of 1921:[26]

> For the last hundred years at least, the Moplah community has been disgraced from time to time by murderous outrages. In the past these have been due to fanaticism. They generally blazed out in the Ernad Taluk (county), where the Moplahs were, for the most part, proselytes drawn from the dregs of the Hindu population. These men were miserably poor and hopelessly ignorant, and their untutored minds were particularly susceptible to the inflammatory teaching that Paradise was to be gained by killing Kufirs. They would go out on the warpath, killing Hindus, no matter whom, and seek death in hand-to-hand conflict with the troops. In some cases they may have been inspired by

hatred of a particular landlord, but no grievance seems to have been really necessary to start them on their wild careers.

In his 1923 article titled 'The Moplah Rebellion of 1921', John J. Banninga observed that for a century before the Moplah Outrage of 1921, there were at least *fifty-one* outbreaks of Moplah fanaticism.[27] In light of this history, to blame tenancy issues alone for the Outrage of 1921 is to cut the head, pun intended, to fit the Marxist hat. In fact, Banninga, while noting that were indeed serious agrarian and tenancy difficulties and tensions in the Malabar, remarked:[28]

... I would say that the Hindu coolies of the Mohammedan tenants of the Brahmin and Nair landlords are worse off than their employers. I have nowhere seen such abject servility as in the Cherma of Malabar.

Deflating the peasant rebellion theory, Wood too says:[29]

Almost without exception, every British official concerned with interpreting the Moplah outbreak was prepared to concede that all was not well with landlord–tenant relations in Malabar, and the grievance over insecurity of tenure was repeatedly stressed by them. *However, explaining outbreaks as anti-jenmi (anti-landlord) manifestations posed difficult problems with which those Malabar Collectors most responsive to tenant grievance grappled with only very partial success. In particular, since Hindu tenants and labourers admittedly suffered quite as much, if not more, from the great power of the big jenmi, why were outbreaks confined to the Muslim community? Moreover, why should some of the assaults have been directed against Hindus who were not only not landlords, but members of the slave caste at least as vulnerable to the exercise of jenmi power as many of the assailants themselves? Failure by those who stressed the agrarian explanation for outbreaks adequately to answer such questions undermined their case for legislation to grant occupancy rights to tenants, a measure they urged as essential if the Moplah problem were to be solved.* [Emphasis added]

The extent of fanaticism that drove the Moplahs can be gathered from the fact that the British had to enact two legislations, namely the Moplah Outrages Act and Moplah War Knives Act of 1855, which resulted in a significant reduction in, if not elimination of, the outrages. Here are a few excerpts from the introductory remarks of H. Forbes when he moved the Bill in the Imperial Legislative Assembly on 30 April 1859 to continue the Moplah legislations of 1855:[30]

The Moplas of Malabar were a race of Mahomedans active in their worldly calling, energetic in the pursuit of gain, thriving, and increasing in wealth and number; but they had always been over-bearing and intolerant, had hesitated at no violence in endeavouring to obtain their ends, and for many years past had been but too notorious for the perpetration of outrages of the most atrocious character. Prior to 1841 these outrages were the work of single fanatics, without open aid or sympathy from others; but since that year, bodies of Moplas had, in open day, attacked Hindoos of wealth and respectability, murdered them under circumstances the most horrible, burnt their houses or given them up to pillage, desecrated Hindoo temples, and had wound up their crimes by throwing away their lives in desperate resistance to the Police and the Military. These outrages had gradually become more sanguinary and more difficult of repression; greater numbers had joined in them; it had become necessary to employ larger bodies of troops, and to call in the aid of European Soldiers, when in the beginning of 1852, an outrage occurred in all respects more deplorable and formidable than any that had preceded it: men, women, and children were indiscriminately slaughtered, and the Government determined, at the recommendation of the Magistrate, the late Mr. Conolly, to appoint a Commissioner to investigate and report upon the causes of these outbreaks, and to advise the Government upon the means to be adopted for their repression.

Before he proceeded to state the result of the enquiry then held, he would give a short abstract of one or two cases of outrage, in order that the Council might clearly know the kind of crime with which they were now requested to deal.

In 1849 a party of Moplas attacked the residence of a Hindoo of high rank and importance, and seized possession of his temple situated on a commanding Hill; they numbered in all sixty-six, and held out for a period of nine days. Troops at an early period sent against them, but the few who ventured into action were repulsed with the loss of an officer and five men. They killed several persons with cold-blooded atrocity, and holding out to the last in the hope of winning the crown to martyrdom by dying in action against those whom they considered unbelievers, were finally destroyed by a Company of European Soldiers.

In 1851 a case occurred in which the victims were mostly men of note. Four, with a servant, fell in one neighborhood, after which the criminals walked off about eight miles, and invaded the house of a man of eighty years of age, of large possessions and much consideration. He was brutally dragged out, and his body cut to pieces in the presence of his affrighted tenants. The criminals eventually amounted to nineteen; they held out for three days, repulsed a detachment of Native infantry, but were destroyed by a party of Europeans, four of whom were killed.

In 1852 fifteen Moplas forced their way into the house of an influential landlord, butchered the whole of the inmates, consisting of fifteen persons, including women and children, and then plundered and burnt the house, an unusually large and substantial one; they then went from place to place, burning, killing, and wounding, and finally attacked the house of another large proprietor, by whose retainers, after a contest sustained for three quarters of an hour, they were despatched.

Such was the nature of the outbreaks, into the cause of which the Government, in 1852, ordered that special enquiry should be made. The result of that enquiry was a report, which it was stated that in about ten years prior to 1852 there had been sixteen actual outbreaks, by Moplas, in which murder had been committed or attempted. In these sixteen outbreaks forty victims were killed and sixteen wounded, most of them desperately, and always with intent to kill; sixteen others were sought for but escaped; seventeen of those killed were Brahmins, of whom twelve perished in one house; eleven houses were burnt down, six pagodas partially destroyed, and six others injured and desecrated. The Commissioner made an elaborate enquiry, with the view of ascertaining what had led to these disastrous occurrences, and after avowing his entire disbelief of the existence of an oppression or wrong or injustice suffered by the Moplas at the hands of the Hindoos, he declared his opinion that the true incentive to them had been the most decided fanaticism. The victims or intended victims had all been Hindoos and their slayers or intended slayers all Moplas, who had carried out their purposes with the avowed object of seeking death in arms against those whom they considered unbelievers, with the view of including the joys of their fancied Paradise.

The close unity of the Moplas in all that concerned their religion, and the jealousy and hatred of the Hindoos, which were common to them, led to the greatest sympathy when any fanatical outrage was committed. One Mopla would not betray another in matters wherein the honor or advantage of his caste was concerned, and the destruction of the criminals engaged in outrage had no deterring effect, because their crime, in lieu of causing shame, brought only glory.

These were the circumstances under which Act XXIII of 1854 was passed by the Council ...

Since that Act was passed there had been but one crime such as those against which the law was pointed, and that was the murder, in 1855, of the Collector and Magistrate, Mr. Conolly, in revenge for his having been instrumental in deporting the Mopla High Priest, who had been found strongly to incite his disciples to outrage, to encourage them in crimes, and to give his sanction to and blessing on their perpetration.

On the occurrence of this murder, the Act was at once enforced. The murderers, who, as usual would not be taken alive, were shot, their bodies were burnt in Jail, their property was confiscated, and heavy fines were collected from the inhabitants of their villages, and, although there was nothing in all this to compensate for the death of a public servant, one who, when still a Collector and Magistrate in the Provinces, had been nominated to a seat in the Government, the last of a band of brothers who all but one met a violent death—and nearly all met death in the service of their country—still it was some consolation to Mr. Conolly's many friends, and he (Mr. Forbes) for one should always be proud to have been among their number, to eel (sic) that sudden death could have come to no one better prepared to meet it; it was also some satisfaction to know that the law once energetically enforced, had not again been broken, and that means had been found to crush the spirit of fanaticism which so long filled the Province of Malabar with dread.

... These Acts would expire with the present year, and it was the object of the Bill which he had now to introduce to continue them in force. The spirit of fanaticism which called them forth had not died out, it was but suppressed by the stringency of these laws, which were now, and which would be for many years to come, as essential to the peace of society as they were when first passed. All the local Officers were agreed upon the absolute necessity for the continuance of the present law, and he thought that in the few remarks that he had made, and in the papers which he should print with the Bill, the Council would find sufficient to warrant the measures which he proposed.

Critically, in his detailed thesis on the Moplah 'Rebellion', Conrad Wood narrates the manner of preparation for an outrage by the Moplahs as follows:[31]

Characteristically, the preparations for an outbreak involved the intending participants donning the white clothes of the martyr, *divorcing their wives*, asking those they felt they had wronged for forgiveness, and *receiving the blessing of a Tangal, as the Sayyids or descendants of the Prophet are called in Malabar*, for the success of their great undertaking.

Once the outbreak had been initiated openly, by the murder of their Hindu victim, the participants would await the arrival of Government forces by ranging the countryside paying off scores against Hindus they felt had ill-used them or other Moplahs, burning and defiling Hindu temples, taking what food they needed, and collecting arms and recruits.

Finally, as the Government forces closed in on them, a sturdy building was chosen for their last stand. Often the mansion of some Hindu landlord (frequently the residence of one of their victims) was selected, but Hindu temples, mosques, and other buildings were also used, the main criterion being, apparently, to avoid being captured alive. As a Moplah captured at Payyanad temple in 1898 put it, it was decided to die there 'as it was a good building and we were afraid lest we would be shot in the legs and so caught alive'.

By the time the Government forces had surrounded them, the outbreak participants had worked themselves into a frenzy by frequent prayers, shouting the creed as a war-cry and singing songs commemorating the events of past outbreaks, especially that of October 1843 in which 7 Moplahs armed mainly with 'war knives' scattered a heavily-armed detachment of sepoys with their charge. The climax of the drama came when they emerged from their 'post' to be killed as they tried to engage in hand-to-hand combat.

Divergences from this ideal pattern were frequent, but the essence of the Moplah outbreak, demarcating it from other forms of violence, resided in the belief that participation was the act of a shahid or martyr and would be rewarded accordingly. As one outbreak participant (who receded at the last moment and was captured) said in explanation of why he and his associates 'went out' (i.e. participated in the outbreak):

'I have heard people sing that those who ... fight and die after killing their oppressors, become shahids and get their reward. I have heard that the reward is "Swargam" (Paradise).'

The pattern of the Moplah outbreak was dictated by the fact that participants had no intention of evading the heavy hand of justice. On the contrary, their objective was to compass their own destruction by hurling themselves in a suicidal charge against the forces sent to deal with them.

In the words of a wounded Moplah captured at Manjeri temple in 1896:

'We came to the temple intending to fight with the troops and die. That is what we meant to do when we started.'

The defining characteristic of the Moplah outbreak was devotion to death. (Emphasis added)

The Sayyids/Syeds in Malabar, referred to locally as 'Tangals', were of Arab descent and provided the Mapillas/Moplahs with the necessary religious inspiration to undertake their near-suicidal outrages. The Tangals/Sayyids of the Mambram or the Mampuram Mosque in Tirurangadi (in current-day Malappuram district in Kerala) played a crucial role in the indoctrination of the Moplahs.[32] Here's a relevant observation from William Logan's *Malabar Manual*:

Tirurangadi, the adhikari of which was killed, lay close to the residence of the Arab Tangal or High Priest who was generally credited with having incited the Mapillas to commit these outrages. The Tangal died shortly afterwards and was buried at the Mabram mosque situated on the river bank opposite Tirurangadi. Fanatics who intend to commit outrages, and those who committed them do, as a rule even now, proceed to this mosque to pray at the Tangal's Shrine.

The Tangals/Syeds of the Mambram Mosque, along with the Tangals of the Ponnani Juma Masjid (again in current-day Malappuram district in Kerala), featured heavily in the Outrage of 1921. On the role of the Tangals/Syeds in fomenting hatred against the Hindus even before 1921, Dhanagare says:[33]

How did the Thangals and the other religions leaders maintain the solidarity of the Moplah community? What idiom and language did they use in arousing a collective awareness? Did they provoke and incite their illiterate followers into hostility against the landed upper classes between 1830 and 1880? These are very important questions but difficult to answer in the absence of adequate source material. *It is, however, certain that some Thangals did provoke some of their followers into physical violence and, in their own interests, tried to turn the anti-jenmi sentiments of the poor Moplah peasants into anti-Hindu sentiment.* [Emphasis added]

In this regard, readers may also recollect Chapter 1, wherein I dealt with the spread of Wahhabism under Syed Shahid Barelvi to all parts of the country, including Madras, of which Malabar was a part. The spread of the Wahhabi sentiment to the Malabar was made easier by the fact that the Tangals and the Moplahs traced their origins to Arabs and took pride in their Arab lineage. Therefore, this heady blend of ethnic separatism and supremacism, coupled with religious indoctrination that promised Paradise with the ever-virgin houris to the community, inspired the Moplahs to commit their outrages. Tenancy issues only added fuel to a pre-existing religious fire. As Hardgrave points out, the Malabar Tenants' Association formed in 1916 was predominantly composed of Nairs and Mapillas. However, the activities of the Association did not gain momentum or traction until the arrival of the Khilafat Agitation in Malabar in 1920, which led to the linking of tenancy-related resentment with the Sharia-compliant Agitation for a pan-Islamic cause.[34]

It is against the above backdrop that the Moplah Outrage of 1921 must be understood before it is reduced to the simplistic Marxist template of a 'peasant rebellion', which is nothing but a restatement of the Marxist existential need to find a class war in every situation and to reduce it to one. It shall be seen from the following discussion that the Khilafat Agitation presented the Mapillas in Malabar as well as the Khilafatists elsewhere with the perfect excuse to vent their medieval fanaticism by branding Hindus as British collaborators. Ironically, when the Swadeshi and Boycott Movements began in Bengal in 1905 to protest against the Partition of Bengal, the Muslims of Bengal did not want to be coerced into participating in those movements against the British. However, during the Khilafat Agitation, the very same choice and freedom were not available to Hindus, especially for a cause that was manifestly Muslim, pan-Islamic and extraterritorial, to which the Hindus owed no allegiance or obligation. After all, the Ottoman Caliphate was of no consequence to Hindus. This coerced and enforced participation of Hindus for a non-Bharatiya cause was the reason for the Malegaon Riots, as we saw earlier, and contributed significantly to the Outrage in Malabar as well.

The Khilafat and the Moplah Outrage of 1921

In April 1920, a conference was held by the Congress in Manjeri in Ernad taluk (in present-day Malappuram district) wherein the central issues were the Montford Reforms and support for the Khilafat. The conference was attended by a large number of Moplahs. On the issue of the Reforms, the national rift between the Moderates and the Extremists manifested itself in Malabar as well. Annie Besant, who attended the conference, opposed the call for Non-Cooperation. However, with the support of the Moplahs, the non-cooperators who opposed the Reforms prevailed.[35] The resolution on the Khilafat too was passed with the support of the Moplahs, which would result in Khilafat committees being established in the Malabar. Pertinently, in May

Ali Musaliar, the rebel leader of the Mapilla Outrage (1921–1922), shortly before his execution in Coimbatore (March 1922)

1920, Variankunnath Kunhamad Haji (V.K. Haji) from Ernad, whose family had a tradition of taking part in outrages,[36] was appointed to collect funds for the Khilafat Movement.[37] Later known as 'Khilafat King', Haji was one of the prominent Moplah leaders who led gangs of Moplahs in the Outrage of 1921.

On 18 August 1920, Gandhi and Shaukat Ali visited Calicut as part of the Khilafat Agitation and the consequent Non-Cooperation, which had already been initiated by the CKC.[38] In his speech, Gandhi, as usual, exhorted Hindus to stand by Muslims in their fight against the British for the protection of the Khilafat. After the Nagpur session of the Congress in December 1920 when the Non-Cooperation Movement was formally adopted, the Malabar Khilafat Committee became even more active.[39]

Before I proceed to narrate the events of 1921, it may help to know that in 1921, the Moplahs were the largest and fastest growing community in the Malabar.[40] They numbered a million and constituted 32 per cent of the population of Malabar. In Ernad taluk, which was the epicentre of the Outrage, they made up 60 per cent of the population.

In January 1921, at a Khilafat Committee meeting in Calicut under the Tangal/Syed of the Ponnani Juma Masjid, who was then the highest religious authority for the Moplahs, it was decided to extend complete support to the Nagpur resolution of the Congress.[41] Accordingly, a number of Moplahs (northern and southern) resigned from government posts, returned their titles and honours, and boycotted courts and schools. The local Khilafat Committee of Cannanore (present-day Kannur) was extremely active in coordinating the Non-Cooperation. At this juncture, it needs to be pointed out that although Gandhi's call for Non-Cooperation was accepted, the Gandhian tenet of non-violence was not, a distinction which is underscored by Conrad Wood.[42]

Around the same time, the agitation of the Malabar Tenants' Association intensified and merged with calls for Non-Cooperation with the Khilafat Agitation, which resulted in the landlords, predominantly the Namboodiris, being painted as collaborators of the British. Unfortunately for the Nairs of the Tenants' Association, it would matter little to the Moplahs/Khilafatists whether the Nairs too were members of the tenancy agitation or not. Ultimately, *both* the Namboodiris and the Nairs would be at the receiving end of the Moplah Outrage.

In February 1921, the Congress leaders of Calicut and V.K. Haji invited Maulana Yakub Hassan, a Muslim leader from Madras, to address meetings in Malabar. Given Haji's involvement in inviting Yakub Hassan, the district magistrate banned the latter from holding meetings in the region, apprehending that the feelings of the southern Moplahs would be incited by Hassan not just against the British but also against the Hindus, in particular the Hindu jenmis/landlords.[43] Hassan and the Malabar Congress leaders chose to defy the ban, for which they were arrested and sentenced to six months' imprisonment. This resulted in a confrontation between 12,000 Moplahs armed with sticks and knives and the district authorities, which, fortunately, did not lead to violence.[44] Congress leaders, including C. Rajagopalachari, chose to highlight this incident in the Madras Legislative Council and called Hassan and others 'Kerala Patriots',[45] which resulted in giving greater impetus to the Khilafat-Non-Cooperation Agitation; 230 Congress Sabhas were formed in the region and the Congress's membership increased.[46] Gradually, the Moplah Khilafatists increased their aggression and hostility towards the authorities as well as towards the Hindu jenmis, resulting in frequent arrests. Non-violence had been thrown to the wind.

In April 1921, the conference for which Gandhi, along with the Ali Brothers, visited Erode in Madras was attended in large numbers by Moplahs.[47] Readers may recollect that it was at this conference that Maulana Muhammad Ali had made the statement that if the Afghans invaded Bharat to evict the British, he would support them and fight the British and *anyone else* who opposed the Afghan invasion. Naturally, this made an impact on the Moplahs in the audience. To add to this, in the same month, Dhanagare points out, Majlis-ul-Ulema too held a conference in Erode and called upon the Moplahs to launch a jihad.[48]

By June 1921, according to Gopalan Nair, '*every Moplah centre had a Khilafat association, with a Moplah president, a Moplah secretary and a majority of Moplah members. The number of such Khilafat committees is not known, but in Case No. 128 of 1922, on the file of the Special Judge, Calicut, it has been mentioned that ... there may have been as many as 100 Khilafat committees formed in the two taluks of Ernad and Ponnani*'.[49] This period witnessed the rise of the Imam of the Mambram Mosque in Tirurangadi, Ali Musaliar. Nair says:[50]

> On 8th June, Ramzan Day, Ali Musaliar headed a procession of 300 to 400 Khilafat Volunteers, who were mostly dressed in Khaki and had swords, and went from Kizhekkepalli Mosque to the compound next to the public offices at Tirurangadi, where Moplahs killed in one of the outbreaks of the last century were buried. There they offered prayers. These graves were a prohibited place of meeting and such prayers were only offered before an outbreak and, in the present instance, it was done for the success of the Khilafat cause (Judgement in Case No. 7/21).

On 18 June 1921, when the deputy superintendent of police visited Tirurangadi to interview Ali Musaliar, the meeting happened in the presence of 600 Moplahs, of whom fifty were Khilafat volunteers carrying knives in sheaths. From 24 July onwards, knife-wielding Khilafat volunteers in their khaki uniforms would march frequently on the streets with their leaders, in groups of fifty to hundred, to attend Khilafat meetings.[51] Around 31 July, a dispute arose in the village of Pokkottur in Ernad taluk between the Nilambur Raja (a Namboodiri landlord) and V. Mohammad, a Moplah Khilafatist, over the theft of a gun from the residence of the Raja. It bears noting that in July 1921, the number of Hindus in the village was 437 and the number of Moplahs 852.[52] When the police arrived to search the residence of the Moplah Khilafatist, drums began to be beaten in the mosques in the area, and with 'astounding rapidity', hundreds of Moplahs from nearby villages, including Khilafatists in their khaki uniforms, converged on the area with war knives, country swords, long spears, formidable bludgeons, other weapons and guns.[53] The mob marched to the residence of the Raja, but police dispersed it with the intervention of the president of the Khilafat Committee of Malappuram.[54]

Realising that a storm was brewing, the district collector, E.F. Thomas, wrote to the government as follows, pleading for reinforcements of British troops:[55]

> We are in for a bad time in Ernad ... I feel powerless with my present force ... We have peace now on a precarious tenure only if we make no move ... It is with full sense of responsibility, as it is with the deepest regret, that I inform

Government that the situation is beyond the District officials ... We cannot go on as we are—with peace only so long as we remain inert ... Crime has been committed and remains unpunished.

In his fortnightly report, the Governor of Madras wrote to the Viceroy as follows:[56]

It seems difficult to arrive at an exact appreciation of the situation at present, but there seems to be no doubt that continued provocative speeches on the Khilafat question combined with the resolutions of the recent All-India Khilafat Conference at Karachi have produced an impression on the mind of the Mappilla that the end of the British Raj is at hand. It is certainly true that as a result of Khilafat propaganda the Mappillas are better organized than they used to be and also better informed as to the strength of their own position and the difficulty of taking military action against them.

Once the reinforcements arrived, District Collector Thomas directed those responsible for the Pukkottur incident, including Ali Musaliar, to appear before the authorities. They refused to appear, which led to warrants for their arrest being issued. On 14 August 1921, after consultations between the district authorities and the Special Commissioner for Malabar Affairs, Arthur Rowland Knapp (who would later prepare the Knapp Report on the Outrage), it was decided that a message needed to be sent to the Moplahs that the British Raj was still in place. Accordingly, the British government decided to take action at the epicentre, Tirurangadi.[57] A regiment of the Gurkhas arrived in the early hours of 20 August 1921 for arrest of the twenty-four accused and to search houses in Tirurangadi. Reinforcements were also kept ready in Bangalore should the need arise. Although the Mambram Mosque was not searched, rumours were spread by the Moplahs that the mosque had been attacked and razed to the ground.

Between 11.30 a.m. and 2 p.m. on 20 August 1921, a mob of 2,000 Moplahs armed to the teeth with weapons and flying Khilafat flags attacked the police and the Gurkha regiment from the east and west. While the mob was dispersed with gunfire, one officer and a constable were brutally hacked and mutilated to death in true Moplah fashion. By evening, railway lines had been destroyed to prevent the possibility of additional reinforcements arriving and also to block civilian escape to Calicut. By night, the district civil authorities had left for Calicut by train from Feroke and had handed over charge of the area and the situation to the commanding officer of the troops. The following was the communique issued on the situation in the area:[58]

... This attempt to make searches and arrests under legal warrants in due conformity with the law has been a signal for an outburst of fanaticism throughout Ernad, Walluvanad and Ponnani directed first against European

Officials and Non-officials and latterly against Hindu Jenmis and others. Public Offices have been looted everywhere, Manas (Namboodri residence) and Kovilagams pillaged, Hindus murdered or forcibly converted, and the line cut to an extent, regarding which there is no information.

On the devastation that followed at the hands of the Moplahs, here's an extract from Gopalan Nair's account:[59]

The storm had burst with a vengeance. Civil administration came to a standstill: the sub-treasuries in the rebellion area were looted and lakhs of rupees carried away: public buildings and records were burnt: Munsiffs, Magistrates, and Police Officers had to seek refuge elsewhere: Police Officials were overwhelmed by rebel hordes and had to surrender their arms: Hindu Village Officials had left their villages: and, eventually, the train traffic stopped for a week between Shoranur and Calicut. Murders, dacoities, forced conversions and outrages on Hindu women became the order of the day. Hindu refugees in thousands poured into Calicut, Palghat, the Cochin State and other places wending their weary way over hills and through jungles for safety from the lust and savagery of the Moplahs.

On 21 August, the troops returned to Calicut since the city was surrounded on three sides by the Moplahs. Martial law was declared temporarily by the commanding officer in Calicut. On 22 August, Ali Musaliar declared himself 'King' of Tirurangadi. Reinforcements from Madras, Bangalore and Colombo arrived by 25 August. On 26 August, there was another round of confrontation of these forces with a huge mob of Moplahs, which resulted in 400 Moplahs being killed. By 28 August, communication was restored, and on 29 August, martial law was imposed in Ernad, Ponnani, Walluvanad, Calicut, Kurumbranad and Wayanad. Despite martial law having been declared, and given that the Amritsar Tragedy of 1919 was still fresh in the public memory, the government was wary of being accused of repeating Jallianwalla Bagh. As expected, District Collector Thomas was called the 'Dyer of Malabar' by the local press.[60] Cashing in on the government's cautious approach, the local vernacular press, which was sympathetic to the Moplahs and Khilafatists, reported as follows:[61]

If Government officials had acted with prudence, there would have been no riot at all ... The actions of the authorities have so far only fanned the flame of trouble ... In short the principal parties in the riots now are the Police and the Military. It need no longer be called 'Moplah riots'.

On 30 August, troops marched to the Kizhekkepalli Mosque, which was opposite the Mambram Mosque, as the Moplahs had assembled in the former. However, the troops did not enter the mosque, to avoid being accused of desecrating it and inflaming passions further. On the morning of 31 August, both sides clashed when the Moplahs opened fire. This left twenty-four Moplahs dead; thirty-eight surrendered, including the 'King', Ali Musaliar. Describing the atrocities committed on Hindus between 20 August and 31 August by Ali Musaliar and his followers, Gopalan Nair says:[62]

> With the capture of Ali Musaliar on 31st August ends the first act of the drama. During these ten days, 20th to 31st, Hindu Malabar lay helpless at the feet of the Mopla rebels: it was a tale of woe to every Hindu family: it was destruction of every public building and of every temple: it was murder of Europeans, whenever possible and sufficient Government forces were not available until the 28th to cope with the situation. The one bright light was the Pookotur battle, the effect of which was the salvation of the Ernad Hindus. It had been arranged that on 26th August, Friday, after the Jama prayer, all the Hindus in Manjeri and the neighbouring villages should be brought into the Mosques and converted to the Moslem faith: caps, dresses, and jackets were all ready for distribution among the converts, but the idea of wholesale conversion had to be given up at the time, in consequence of the Pookotur Battle.

The second phase of the Outrage, which was its peak, was from September to November 1921. During this phase, the battle between the troops and the Moplahs was waged in the jungles and hills. Given the unfamiliarity of the terrain for the troops, the Moplahs resorted to guerrilla tactics and by 9 December 1921, Moplah surrenders were more frequent and in significant numbers. By 25 December 1921, the chief Tangals/Syeds, including Chembrasseri Imbichi Koya Tangal, who were instructing the Moplahs, surrendered, and the affected areas were deemed fit for the refugees to return to. On the extent of involvement of the Tangals/Syeds in the Outrage, here is an extract from Nair's book on the personal role of Chembrasseri Imbichi Koya Tangal:[63]

> 6. Another Tangal who acquired notoriety was Chembrasseri Imbichi Koya Tangal. He held his court about midway between Tuvoor and Karuvarakundu on the slope of a bare hillock with about 4,000 followers from the neighbouring villages. More than 40 Hindus were taken to the Tangal with their hands tied behind their back, charged with the crime of helping the Military by supplying them with milk, tender cocoanuts etc., and 38 of these Hindus were condemned to death. He superintended the work of murder in person and seated on a rock near a well witnessed his men cutting at the neck of his victims and pushing the bodies into the well. Thirty-eight men were murdered, one of whom a pensioned Head Constable to whom he owed a grudge had his head neatly divided into two halves. The Tangal surrendered at Melattur, was tried by court martial and ordered to be shot. He was shot accordingly on 20th January 1922.

Meanwhile, on 2 November 1921, the special tribunal in Calicut found 'King' Ali Musaliar guilty of waging war against the King-Emperor and sentenced him to death.[64] On 7 January 1921, V.K. Haji, self-styled 'Colonel of the Khilafat Army', was captured, along with twenty-one of his followers. He was tried by a military court and shot dead on 20 January 1922.[65] Although two bands of Moplahs under Moideen Kutty Haji and Konnara Tangal still evaded capture, by 23 January 1922, 2,266 Moplahs had been killed, 1,615 wounded and 5,688 captured; there were also 38,256 surrenders.[66] In other words, conservatively speaking, close to 48,000 Moplahs were involved in the Outrage of 1921. I leave it to the readers to understand the implications of such a large number for the Hindus of Malabar. By February 1922, most of the remaining leaders and their followers were either killed or captured, while one of the Syeds, Konnara Mohammad Koya Tangal, who remained elusive, was arrested only on 25 August 1922.[67] On paper at least, this brought an end to the Moplah Outrage of 1921.

I will now excerpt a few of the legislative debates on the Outrage and end the discussion on this subject with reactions to it in the public domain. I would urge a careful reading of the extracts to truly understand and internalise their implications.

Legislative Debates on the Moplah Outrage

The Moplah outrage was discussed in legislative debates from at least from 5 September 1921 until 11 July 1923. Given the length of these debates, I will reproduce here only a few excerpts from them, on an illustrative basis. On 5 September 1921, in the Council of States, Sir Maneckji Dadabhoy moved an adjournment to detail the 'State of affairs in Malabar' and the Moplah Outbreak. Here are important extracts from his speech wherein he questioned the government's preparedness and response:[68]

Freeman Freeman-Thomas (1866–1941), 1st Marquess of Willingdon, Governor of Madras during the Malabar Rebellions and later Viceroy and Governor General of India during 1931–1936

> Sir, we have all read in the newspapers the accounts of the terrible atrocities which are now going on in Malabar with poignant grief. I am representing the sentiments of the Indian nation when I say that the catastrophe which has taken place in Malabar is now pre-eminently occupying the attention of the general public and every news in connection therewith is waited by the general public with great interest and anxiety. It is unfortunate that the

Government of the Madras Presidency is having a very anxious time. We have all read the harrowing accounts; we have also seen the fragmentary official and unofficial news and notices; we have read the Madras Government's Communiqué on the subject; *but the Council will agree with me when I say that the whole history of the outbreak has not been presented by the Madras Government in a connected narrative form, and we, therefore, await to-day a most exhaustive statement from the Government of India on the subject. We have read the Chapter of crimes committed in Malabar, of the destruction of public and private property, the looting of Government Treasuries and Sub-Treasuries, the defiling of Hindu temples and also of the forcible conversion of Hindus to Islam, with great horror and real grief. We want to know who is responsible for these acts and atrocities, and was it not within the power of Government to have avoided this catastrophe or minimised the severity of this catastrophe to a certain extent? It is true that the state of affairs in Malabar has been bad for the last six months. It is well known that the preachings of seditionists, that the poisonous doctrines which these seditionists and anarchists were daily pouring into that highly fanatical soil of Malabar was gaining ground.* Government was aware of it. Government knew of the danger that was coming. And in this connection I will draw the attention of the House to a statement made by my friend the Honourable Sir William Vincent in February last in the Legislative Assembly. He said:

'We are now faced in this country with the frequent prospects of disorders here and there. I myself think that we shall be very fortunate if we escape in the next six months without serious outbreaks of sporadic disorder in different places.'

I have made it perfectly clear that the Government anticipated danger, *and I cannot therefore understand why Government did not take precautionary measures for the suppression of these atrocities in Malabar. As Government knew that the people of Malabar were collecting swords, spears, fire-arms and other instruments, it is difficult to understand why stringent measures of a precautionary character were not adopted* in the right time. It might have averted a great deal of bloodshed, it might have averted the sanguinary battles that have taken place there and the loss of innocent lives that has unfortunately occurred. I, therefore, think that in this connection an explanation is due to the country from the Government, which cannot be altogether exonerated from a certain measure of responsibility in this matter. Further, *Sir, it is perfectly clear that the Moplahs were prepared for the occasion and that there was a wide-spread organisation behind them; all these pitched battles with three and four thousand people which recently took place clearly demonstrate the existence of a well-conducted and nefarious organisation behind the back of these revolts. It is therefore necessary that the Government should make a complete statement on the point and place before the country any information that may exist on the subject,* as I consider the time has now arrived when there is no longer any necessity for keeping the matter secret. I make bold to say in this connection, and I feel I echo the sentiments of all of us here, official and non-official Members, whether they be Europeans or Indians, that in any measures which Government may decide to adopt for the suppression of the revolts, for the promotion of order and the maintenance of peace, this Council will whole-heartedly give its support. Things are going from bad to worse; innocent lives are being lost; the country is almost in a state of consternation; *riots are taking place not only in Malabar, but in all parts of India; every where there are seen forces of disruption and disorganisation; law-abiding citizens are not in a position to do their ordinary work; there is a state of havoc and intense anxiety. I think the time has arrived when the Government should adopt strict measures for the suppression of these riots and for the maintenance of peace and order.* I would also like the Honourable the Home Member to enlighten the Council, as fully as possible, as to the origin and cause of these disturbances; a history of the genesis of these disturbances will be extremely valuable. I would also like the Honourable the Home Member to distinctly state the total number of casualties, both European and Indian. I would also like the Honourable the Home Member to assure this Council that Government have now taken precautionary measures immediately in the troubled parts of Madras, and within what period he expects peace and order to be fully restored in that troubled country. *Government have promulgated the Martial Law Ordinance; a Martial Law Ordinance is always distasteful and unpalatable to the people. It can only be justified in case of absolute necessity, and I have no doubt that the Government was satisfied before the promulgation of the Ordinance in substituting martial law for the common law of the country …* Further, I am very pleased, and the country has noticed with great satisfaction, that in the preparation of this Martial Law Ordinance the blunders that were committed at the time of the Punjab affair have been studiously avoided. The power and authority of the civil law has been to a certain extent maintained. Consultations by the military officers with the Civil Department have been rendered obligatory, and prior to the issue of notices and regulations, and the rules for summary trial of cases the necessity of following the provisions of the Code of Criminal Procedure has been indicated and enforced. [Emphases added]

To Maneckji's question, the following was the detailed response of Sir William Vincent, the Member for Home Affairs on the Governor General's Council:[69]

It would perhaps interest Honourable Members if I were to preface my remarks with a brief reference as to the origin and cause of this rising in Malabar. *The fact is that these Moplahs are an ignorant people, many of them poor and nearly all of them fanatical and entirely under the influence—as I learn from the information before me—of a bigoted priesthood. As I think all Honourable Members know they are descendants of Arab traders and soldiers who first came to the Malabar coast some time, I think, about 800 AD, and we are told that they later established themselves by intermarriage and conversion, or perversion, whichever term appeals to different Honourable Members of this Council, of the local residents to Muhammadanism. There have been many outbreaks of these people who now number about a million in the past, indeed during a period of about 20 years— between 1836 and 1853, there were 22 outbreaks, but the biggest one about which I have any information occurred in 1885 after which 20,000 arms including 9,000 guns were collected from the insurgents.*

The present rising in itself appears to be purely religious, though, no doubt, it has been accentuated by economic distress. In the past agrarian trouble has frequently been at the bottom of risings, but I have no information before me which leads me to think that Hindu landlords are responsible for the present outbreak. It is, however, known that certain Extremist Muhammadan agitators—I do not wish to use any word that will cause resentment, because many gentlemen feel very strongly about the Khilafat who are not really Extremists in the sense I mean—have been at work for two years in this locality working up the people over the Khilafat. *There is on the information before us no sympathy for the non-co-operation movement as such, and indeed there is little regard for Mr. Gandhi's personality. There is certainly no sympathy for a movement of purely non-violent, non-co-operation as the results show.* At the beginning of this year, Honourable Members will remember *certain inflammatory speeches were delivered at Erode, Mangalore and in Madras, and there is no doubt according to the reports we have had that those speeches had considerable effect on this fanatical population of Malabar which is singularly prone to violence; the situation in April and May was in consequence somewhat dangerous. It subsequently, as we thought, or as the Local Government thought, improved, and we were told that the Ramẓan had been the quietest known for years in the Malabar District. In June, there were reports that volunteer associations were being formed, but later again we were told that these associations had ceased as the leaders had realised the danger of continuing them. That information, I am afraid, was incorrect, and these associations were being secretly organised all the time. The Government and local authorities were apparently misled in this matter, but there was nothing to show this till the end of July when the situation suddenly deteriorated largely as the result, as has been reported to us, of the Karachi Conference.* Now I should like to cite here a passage from the Madras letter on this point. I have the leave of the Madras Government to cite it. This is what it says:

'It is difficult to arrive at an exact appreciation of the situation at present, but there seems to be no doubt that continual provocative speeches on the Khilafat question, combined with the resolutions of the recent All-India Khilafat Conference at Karachi, have produced an impression on the mind of the Mappilla that the end of the British Raj is at hand. It is certainly true that, as the result of Khilafat propaganda, the Mappillas are better organised than they used to be and also better informed as to the strength of their own position and the difficulty of taking military action against them.'

The *first actual signs of lawlessness occurred on the 31st July when some Police-officers went to arrest a man who was accused in a criminal case. I think there had been a case of housebreaking in the residence of a Nambadri Brahmin. Armed Moplahs collected in large numbers to prevent the arrest, and there was grave danger of a serious riot.* That was happily averted, and the police apparently, though this is not clear from the reports before me, went home without arresting any one. In any case, the police were powerless to face the mob, and the incident was significant because it was regarded by the Moplahs as a victory and a defeat for the Government. The District Magistrate then applied for extra troops to be sent to Calicut, and they were sent. Finally, on the 20th, the District Magistrate determined to *arrest certain persons who were in the possession of arms, under the Moplah Outrages Act,* at Tirurangala, with the aid of a military force. Three men were arrested without any trouble, and a party of police were left behind to search for others. In the course of this search a mosque was entered by the Moplah Police-officers who, however, removed their shoes before entering. I may say that in times past rebellious Moplahs have frequently taken refuge in mosques. While these occurrences were taking place, news had quickly spread round as to what was happening and a large mob of Moplahs collected, some coming by train and some on foot. This mob first attacked the party of police and later on in the day attacked the military forces to which I have referred. The attack was beaten off, but I regret to say with the loss of two British Officers, one being Lieutenant Johnstone of the Leinster Regiment and the other a Police-officer named Rowley. By this time railway communications had been cut and the telegraph wires destroyed, and the troops had to remain where they were. Subsequently the outbreak of violence in this single area of Tirurangadu developed into a general rising throughout a large part of the Malabar District of a definitely anti-Government character: Swaraj was proclaimed and a green flag hoisted. I have here rather an interesting account of the reasons for this outbreak from an officer who has had considerable experience of this locality. He has given me leave to use it. This is an extract of a letter received by him:

'The Moplah believes that the Sirkar is nearing its end, and the day is looming when he will not have to pay either taxes to the Government or rent to the Hindu landholders. Economic distress is another factor not to be left out of account. Then he goes on to speak of the failure of the monsoon.'

This is not an official account. Here is another extract:

'At first all the violence shown was anti-official and anti-European, but now the mob of five thousand and ten thousand are seen to be disintegrating into small gangs who having no telegraph lines to cut or culverts to destroy are devoting their scheme to harrying the Hindus, especially the high caste Hindus—Nambudris and Nayars whom they lost of their grain and riches and occasionally murder.'

I think I have now told the Council all I can in the time available as to how this rising originated. As to the casualties our information is that up to the present one British Officer and three British of other ranks have been killed, one British Officer and a number of other ranks have been wounded; two Assistant Superintendents of Police, one Inspector and two Head-Constables have been killed, a planter has been murdered, and others have narrowly escaped. We cannot be sure now that this death roll is complete. *Many Hindus have been murdered. Numbers are missing, but we hope that some of them may escape and turn up later on. Some have been forcibly converted, as I understand, under threat of death. I dare say Honourable Members have read the account of the maltreatment by the Moplahs of an old lady of over 84 at Calicut, the mother of a Mr. Menon, who is a member of the local municipality. They have also probably heard of the murder of a retired Indian Inspector of Police whose head was cut off and carried about on the top of a spear. There has also been very great damage to property of all kinds. Temples, I regret to say, have been desecrated and numerous acts of arson and pillage committed. As regards Moplah Casualties, I can give no figures except that I am informed that in an engagement 400 men were killed. The press reports indicate about a thousand deaths, but this is purely a matter of surmise, though I expect it is by no means an excessive estimate.* We know that at Pudokottur these Moplahs who are exceedingly courageous and fearless of death, fought desperately for many hours. In fact their attacks on the troops were only repelled after five hours of heavy fighting. They were armed with carbines looted from the police, sporting rifles taken from various places and with swords and knives. This is all the information I can give on the second portion of the Honourable Member's motion.

I have explained that it is doubtful how far this movement or rising can be ascribed clearly to non-co-operation–non-violent non-co-operation, i.e., Mr. Gandhi's movement, but it certainly seems on the information before us to be connected very definitely with the Khilafat. The policy of Government towards the non-co-operation movement has been very fully explained to this Council on previous occasions, but the *Honourable Member now attacks me and says, 'why did not Government do more? Why did you not take more vigorous action and prosecute these people, and arrest them.'* Now what I want to put to Honourable Members is that this Council cannot have it both ways. *Last Session, when I stood up in this Council, and stood up in the Legislative Assembly, was there a single man here— except perhaps one or two—who asked Government to take any more strenuous measures than they were taking?* I do not remember the Honourable Sir M. Dadabhoy standing up then and saying: 'You must take more drastic action; you must strengthen your military forces, prosecute here, and prosecute there,' and I think it is rather hard on us that we should be challenged therefore in this Council on that account. On the merits I would put it in this way. The question when to undertake and when to forbear from general repressive measures against a movement of this character is always one of difficulty for any Government to decide, and very much more difficult in present political circumstances in India. I think every one will admit that. The Government have been very much exercised over this situation, but we had no reason to believe that it was going to develop in such a speedy manner in this area.

There is also another aspect of this question. You cannot say because there has been a rising in Malabar among a notoriously turbulent people that the Government of India should embark upon a general campaign of repression throughout India ...

... There are however two facts which I omitted to mention. The first is that there were in July certain very violent speeches made in Malabar, and the Government of Madras were considering the question of prosecuting the speakers when these outrages occurred. *The second is one to which I ought in justice to the Madras Government to refer. In May the Local Government were about to prosecute Mahomed Ali for speeches delivered down in Madras and Erode. Council are aware that after that there were meetings between His Excellency the Viceroy and Mr. Gandhi, and rightly or wrongly, the Government of India thought that it was only fair to give this gentleman Mahomed Ali a locus poenitentia after his apology in the hope that he would abstain from preaching violence in future.*

As to precautionary measures, troops were sent down to Calicut immediately the demand was made by the local authorities. That, I think, was between the 11th and the 14th. The numbers were not large. But unless the Members of the Legislative Assembly are prepared to vote considerably larger sums of money than they do at present for internal defence and other military expenditure, we must take certain risks of being able to check disturbances of this kind with small forces.

As to the situation, at present, I can only say that all possible measures to suppress the rising have been taken, but the situation is far from satisfactory. An appreciation of the present situation from Madras runs as follows:

'*Your telegram. Political, dated 28th August 1921. Appreciation general situation. Malabar Railway to Calicut has been temporarily restored for running by day and is being held by troop. Garrison Malappuram having been brought back to Calicut the whole interior of South Malabar except Palghat Taluk is in the hands of the rebels. Probable that the troops will again have to meet and overcome determined resistance by the rebels in fore. Subsequent operations will take the form of locating and dealing with numerous small and mobile parties of Moplahs in extremely difficult country. Active assistance by local inhabitants cannot be counted on. Situation from point of view of civil administration is that local machinery of Government has broken down. Throughout the affected area Government offices have been wrecked and looted and record, destroyed. Communications have been obstructed. Those officials who have not escaped are, as far as known, either captives or in hiding. All Government officers and Courts have ceased to function and ordinary business is at a stand-still. Famine conditions imminent in portions of affected area. Europeans and numerous Hindu refugees of all classes now concentrated at Calicut.*'

I do not propose to tell the Council, and I think they will not expect me to tell them, the exact military force available, because any information that is published will undoubtedly get to the Moplahs themselves and indeed to others who perhaps are hostile to Government. *I may say, however, that the Madras Government asked for further reinforcements recently, but the last I have heard is that they are satisfied with the number of troops they have now in Malabar.* The situation is now in hand. We shall, however, probably hear of at least one more serious attack by these Moplahs, and then I hope that the thing may dwindle down to more or less desultory disorders ...

... No one can however altogether avoid action which may affect religious sentiments if a number of armed Moplahs collect in mosques in furtherance of their criminal purpose.

I think I have now given the Council all the information I have, but I should like to convey to the people, in Malabar, some expression of sympathy, some expression of regret from the Government of India and from this Council for the lives lost, temples desecrated, injuries caused, and property destroyed, and I am sure I am voicing the sentiments of everybody in this Council in this matter. I should like also to convey to them, Military and Auxiliary Forces, and indeed to all servants of the Crown in Malabar, our gratitude for their services. I should like also, if I may, to express our sympathy with the Madras Government and to convey to them an expression of our recognition of the manner in which all concerned have performed duties, both arduous and distasteful ... [Emphases added]

Another member, Annamalai Chettiyar (founder of Annamalai University and one of the founders of Indian Bank), commented on the atrocities as follows:[70]

... With Koran in one hand and the sword in the other these lawless bands marched through rich villages forcing conversion or death on the unwilling Hindu population of the locality. *The houses of those Hindus and other non-Muslims have been broken into and properties, valued at several lakhs of rupees, have been looted and carried away. Inmates of houses were tortured. Men, women and children were murdered in cold blood. Age and sex mattered not to then. Hindu temples were destroyed; the images were broken; the temple jewels were carried away. The landed aristocracy of the place were subjected to a most cruel treatment.* People in large numbers have been forced to leave off their belongings and flee for life to the town of Calicut where they have now taken refuge. The European community also have suffered much at the hands of the rioters, and it is miraculous that some of them have been able to make good their escape across the troubled area into Calicut. Such is the nature of the tragedy enacted in Malabar.

Mr. Yakub Hasan, the President of the Madras Provincial Conference, who says that he knows these Moplahs rather intimately has some fine things to say of them. In his Presidential address at Tanjore, he says, 'Once the blood of the Moplah is up, there is no knowing what it will lead to. Leaders of the community who have influence with the Moplahs, alone can pacify them.' The blood of the Moplah is up, Sir, and we know to our cost what it has led to.

While events are thus moving so rapidly in Malabar, *it is a matter for very great regret that responsible Muslim leaders in different parts of the country have not yet come forward with their condemnation of this dastardly rising. It may be suggested that an immediate expression of their opinion will not carry weight with the Moplahs now that they are in the full swing of their fury. It is my humble opinion, however, that such an expression of their opinion will go far to pacify the rioters, to allay public feeling and restore peace which we all so much desire.*

It may not be out of place here to refer to the attempts made in recent years by the leaders of the two great communities, the Hindu and the Muhammadan, for the promotion of good feeling and for the establishment of a Hindu Moslem unity. That, Sir, is a consummation devoutly to be wished. I for one am a firm believer in the growth of such a feeling. *But, for the unity to be harmonious, it must be spontaneous and when such a unity does establish itself, we shall have no more of these regrettable occurrences. I appeal to you, Sir, whether actions of this kind, such as the wholesale destruction of life, the looting of property, the desecration of sacred temples, the cold-blooded murders of men, women and children and the trampling under foot of the cherished sentiments of the Hindus, whether there are calculated to secure that unity which we have so much at heart.* I am sure a decided 'no' will be the answer from the responsible leaders of the Muhammadan community. Having regard to the present outbreak it is imperative therefore that responsible Muslim leaders should come forward boldly to denounce and condemn the action of these unruly Moplahs, take the initiative in the matter of giving relief to the sufferers and thus pave the way for a real unity among the two great communities ...

... In conclusion, I appeal to the Honourable Members of this Council, more especially to the Muhammadan Members, to support in unambiguous and unequivocal terms any action seeking to give the innocent victims adequate relief for all the losses they have sustained through no fault of their own, irrespective of any consideration other than the extent of their losses and the demands of justice. [Emphases added]

Unsurprisingly, another member, Syed Raza Ali of the Muslim League, said that the Moplah Outrage had nothing to do with religion and that similar riots had been started by Hindus. Here is the relevant extract from his speech where the blame was predictably laid at the doors of the government for entering a mosque and on the Hindu landlords for tenancy issues, apart from calls for waiting for the law to take its own course:[71]

... Now, we are very sorry indeed that excesses have been committed by the Moplahs who belong to the religion to which I have the honour to belong, and that they have acted in a manner which cannot be said to be anything but mad and insane. All the same since the discussion has come up before this Council, I would just, with the permission of my Honourable Colleagues, make a few suggestions which, I hope, would be helpful to Government, on the one hand, and my Hindu friends on the other. *As a matter of fact there is no Hindu–Muhammadan question involved in the unfortunate disturbances, with this exception that the Moplahs happen to be Mussalmans. Well, excesses have not been unknown in the past, though I would not like to refer to them, in which perhaps the boot has been on the other leg; but I feel convinced that whether in the past in some places excesses have been committed by the Hindus or at present excesses on a larger scale, a much larger scale, are being committed by the Moplahs who are Mussalmans, that will not and that cannot affect the question of Indian nationality in any way. That is how I feel.* No doubt these disturbances will give a set-back to the movement for the time being, but there is not the least doubt that in course of time we will be able to see these disturbances in their true perspective, and after that there will be an inclination on the part of my Hindu friends to forgive these ignorant and highly excitable Moplahs who have enacted, and are enacting, a very sad Chapter in the history of India ...

I think I would rather wait and see what shape matters take and what inquiries are held and what opinions are pronounced by the Courts of Law, *but it does seem to me rather strange that all of a sudden the Moplahs should have started on a wholesale campaign of destruction of life and property, and should they have gone insane and mad, I can say no word in justification of their conduct, but as was pointed out in a nationalist paper the other day, the gunpowder was there but who lighted the match? This is a question which I would ask my Honourable Colleagues to consider carefully. The Honourable the Home Member referred to the events which took place on the 31st July and subsequently he went on to say that an attempt was made towards the end of the third week of August to arrest certain persons, and certain members of the police entered the mosque after taking off their shoes.* In the statement that has been officially issued by the Madras Government, I notice that that has been stated to be the main cause of the trouble, and, if that is so, *are we not entitled to ask ourselves and ask the Government to hold an inquiry into the whole question as to how it is that knowing, as the District Magistrate did, the excitable nature of the Moplahs and the religious fanaticism with which they have always been fired, whether it was discreet, whether it was right and proper, whether it was expedient to order a Moplah police force to enter the mosque?* I do not say that this action was a sufficient justification, or any justification at all, for the Moplahs starting on their murderous campaign. I do not say that at all, but the incident is not unconnected with the subsequent events, and, if so, is not the District Magistrate responsible for that order? It seems to me that, while we condemn the men and ask the Government to take all reasonable steps, and that as expeditiously as possible, to restore law and order, it is the bounden duty of this House to approach the Government with the request that they do appoint a Committee to go into the whole question.

The Honourable the Home Member referred to the economic distress and I have seen it stated in the Press that to a certain extent the present *rioting is not unconnected with the treatment of the Zemindars most of whom are Hindus.* I do not for one moment say that that allegation is correct, but all the same it is high time that an inquiry should be made into the relations between the Moplah peasants, on the one hand, and the Zemindars, on the other. That is another important question which has got to be gone into.

It is *stated in official documents that the Moplahs had proclaimed 'swaraj' and it is also stated that they were forcibly converting Hindus to Islam. I am not prepared to say whether this is correct or not. But if I know the word correctly and if I know its proper meaning, it means not only the rule of the Muslim, not only the rule of the Hindu, nor of the Christian, of the Jew, of the Sikh, and of the Parsi, but the rule of all those nationalities and creeds united together. If the Moplahs are such great patriots as to declare 'swaraj' then I entirely fail to see how they can possibly convert by force Hindus to Islam.* That is another question which has got to be inquired into. Whichever way we may look at it, we come to the conclusion that the disturbances which have occurred in the Malabar District are of sufficient importance to justify us in asking the Government to appoint a small Committee: to inquire into these questions at an early date and to submit its report. which in the fulness of time, I have no doubt will be laid on the table of this Council ... [Emphases added]

Reactions in the Public Domain to the Moplah Outrage

Here is an extract from an article written in the *Times of India* by Sankaran Nair, titled 'Diabolical Atrocities' on the Outrage in Malabar:[72]

Calicut, Sept. 7—In my first article I dealt with the prime causes of the present outbreak, the dangerous game played by the leaders of the Khilafat and Non-Co-operation movements in Malabar which set the whole of Ernad and Walluvanad ablaze, and the extent of plunders, murders and forcible conversions committed by the Mopla rebels. In this article I intend to confine myself to the nature of the atrocities committed by them and other details.

'Malabar Rebellion. Moplah Atrocities', World (Hobart, Tas.: 1918–1924), Friday, 7 Oct, 1921

The experiences I am about to relate will satisfy every Hindu endowed with ordinary common sense that the Moplas resorted to most repugnant fanaticism, which may be ascribed to nothing but selfishness, love of money and love of power, which are the prominent features of the present outbreak. *Refugees narrate that, after forcibly removing young and fair Nair and other high caste girls from their parents and husbands, the Mopla rebels stripped them of their clothing and made them march in their presence naked, and finally they committed rape upon them. In certain instances, devoid of human feelings and blinded by animal passion, the Moplas are alleged to have utilised a single woman for the gratification of the carnal pleasures of a dozen or more men. The rebels also seem to have captured beautiful Hindu women, forcibly converted them, pierced holes in their ears in the typical Mopla fashion, dressed them as Mopla women and utilised them as their temporary partners in life. Hindu women were threatened, molested and compelled to run half-naked for shelter to forests abounding in wild animals. Respectable Hindu gentlemen were forcibly converted and the circumcision ceremony performed with the help of certain Musaliars and Thangals. Hindu houses were looted and set fire to, will not all these atrocities remain as a shameful image of the Hindu Muslim 'unity', of which we have heard much from the Non-Co-operation Party and Khilafat-wallahs? The ghastly spectacle of a number of Hindu damsels being forced to march naked in the midst of a number of licentious Moplas cannot be forgotten by any self respecting Hindu, nor can it be erased from their minds. On the other hand, I have never heard of the modesty of a Mopla woman being outraged by a Mopla rebel.* [Emphasis added]

The true nature and extent of depravity that the Hindus of the Malabar were subjected to was captured in Annie Besant's stinging open letter to Gandhi, titled 'Malabar's Agony', in *New India*. Here are a few extracts from this letter dated 29 November 1921:[73]

It would be well if Mr. Gandhi could be taken into Malabar to see with his own eyes the ghastly horrors which have been created by the preaching of himself and his 'loved brothers,' Muhommad and Shaukat Ali. The Khilafat Raj is established there; on August 1, 1921, sharp to the date first announced by Mr. Gandhi for the beginning of Swaraj and the vanishing of British Rule, a Police Inspector was surrounded by Moplas, revolting against that Rule. From that date onwards thousands of the forbidden war-knives ware secretly made and hidden away, and on August 20, the rebellion broke out, Khilafat flags were hoisted on Police Stations and Government offices. Strangely enough it was on August 25th 825 A.D. that Cherman Perumal ascended the throne of Malabar, the first Zamorin, and from that day the Malayalam Era is dated that is still in use; thus for 1096 years a Zamorin has ruled in Calicut, and the Rajas are mostly Chiefs who for long centuries have looked to a Zamorin as their feudatory Head. These are the men on whom the true pacification of Malabar must ultimately depend. The crowded refugees will only return to their devastated homes when they see those once more in safety in their ancestral places. Their lands, which they keep under their own control, are largely cultivated by Moplas, who are normally hardy, industrious agricultural labourers.

Our correspondent has sent accounts of the public functions connected with my hurried visit to Calicut and Palghat, and that which I wish to put on record here is the ghastly misery which prevails, the heart-breaking wretchedness which has been caused by the Mopla outbreak, directly due to the violent and unscrupulous attacks on the Government made by the Non-Co-operators and the Khilafatists and the statements scattered broadcast, predicting the speedy disappearance of British Rule, and the establishment of Swaraj, as proclaimed by the N.C.O. and Khilafat Raj as understood by the Moplas from the declarations of the Khilafatists. On that, there is no doubt whatever, so far as Malabar is concerned. The message of the Khilafats, of England as the enemy of Islam, of her coming downfall, and the triumph of the Muslims, had spread, to every Mopla home. The harangues in the Mosques spread it everywhere, and Muslim hearts were glad. They saw the N.C.O. preachers appealing for help to their religious leaders, naturally identified the two. The Government was Satanic, and Eblis, to the good Muslim, is to be fought to the death. Mr. Gandhi may talk as he pleases about N.C.O.s accepting no responsibility. It is not what they accept; it is what facts demonstrate. He accepted responsibility for the trifling bloodshed of Bombay. The slaughter in Malabar cries out his responsibility. N.C.O. is dead in Malabar. But bitter hatred has arisen there, as fighting men from the dragon's teeth of Theseus. That is the ghastly result of the preaching of Gandhism, of N.C.O. of Khilafatism. Every one speaks of the Khilafat Raj, and the one hope of the masses is in its crushing by the strong arm of the Government. Mr. Gandhi asks the Moderates to compel the Government to suspend hostilities, i.e., to let loose the wolves to destroy what lives are left. The sympathy of the Moderates is not, I make bold to say, with the murderers, the looters, the ravishers, who have put into practice the teachings of paralysing the Government of the N.C.O.'s, who have made 'war on the Government' in their own way. How does Mr. Gandhi like the Mopla spirit, as shown by one of the prisoners in the Hospital, who was dying from the results of asphyxiation? He asked the surgeon, if he was going to die, and surgeon answered that he feared he would not recover. 'Well, I'm glad I killed fourteen infidels,' said the Brave, God-fearing Mopla, whom Mr. Gandhi so much admires, who 'are fighting for what they consider as religion, and in a manner they consider as religious.' Men who consider it 'religious' to murder, rape, loot, to kill women and little children, cutting down whole families, have to be put under restraint in any civilised society.

Mr. Gandhi was shocked when some Parsi ladies had their saries torn off, and very properly, yet the God-fearing hooligans had been taught that it was sinful to wear foreign cloth, and doubtless felt they were doing a religious act; can he not feel a little sympathy for thousands of women left with only rags, driven from home, for little children born of the flying mothers on roads in refuge camps? The misery is beyond description. Girl wives, pretty and sweet, with eyes half blind with weeping, distraught with terror; women who have seen their husbands hacked to pieces before their eye, in the way 'Moplas consider as religious'; old women tottering, whose faces become written with anguish and who cry at a gentle touch and a kind look waking out of a stupor of misery only to weep, men who have lost all, hopeless, crushed, desperate. I have walked among thousands of them in the refugee camps, and some times heavy eyes would lift as a cloth was laid gently on the bare shoulder, and a faint watery smile of surprise would make the face even more piteous than the stupor. Eyes full of appeal, of agonised despair, of hopeless entreaty of helpless anguish, thousands of them camp after camp. 'Shameful inhumanity proceeding in Malabar,' says Mr. Gandhi. Shameful inhumanity indeed, wrought by the Moplas, and these are the victims, saved from extermination by British and Indian swords. For be it remembered the Moplas began the whole horrible business; the Government intervened to save their victims and these thousands have been saved. Mr. Gandhi would have hostilities suspended—so that the Moplas may sweep down on the refugee camps, and finish their work?

I visited in Calicut three huge Committee camps, two Christian, and the Congress building and compound where doles of rice are given daily from 7 A.M. to noon. In all, the arrangements were good. Big thatched sheds, and some buildings shelter the women and children, the men sleep outside. They are all managed by Indians, the Zamorini's Committee distributing cloths and money to all, except the Congress committee, which works independently and gives food from its own resource. At Palghat, similar arrangements are made by the Zamorini's Committee, and the order and care in feeding are good to see.

Let me finish with a beautiful story told to me. Two Pulayas, the lowest of the submerged classes, were captured with others, and given the choice between Islam and Death. These, the outcaste of Hinduism, the untouchables, so loved the Hinduism which had been so unkind a step-mother to them, that they chose to die Hindus rather than to live Muslim. May the God of both, Muslim and Hindus send His messengers to these heroic souls, and give them rebirth into the Faith for which they died. [Emphasis added]

Here's an extract from another piece in *New India* dated 6 December 1921:[74]

Wilful murders of Hindus and arson were first begun in my own place by Chembrasseri Thangal and his Lieutenant, another Thangal. You might have read accounts written by me in the Malabar journal which was sent to you last time. This contagion began to spread like wild fire and we began to hear of murders daily. Within a fortnight cold-blooded murders of Hindus became very common. From within the borders of Calicut and Ernad taluks refugees come in large numbers with tales of murders and atrocities committed by the rebels. At Puthur Amson in Ernad only 12 miles northeast of Calicut—One day in broad daylight twenty-five persons who refused to embrace Islam were butchered and put into a well. One out of these who narrowly escaped death got out of the well when the rebels left the place and ran to Calicut for life. He is now in the hospital. So the accounts must be true as he himself was one of the victims.

During the last week news of numerous murders and forcible conversions came from another quarter also, Mannur near Aniyallur and Kadalundi railway station in Ernad taluk. This place also is only 14 miles away from Calicut. Every train to Calicut was carrying with it daily hundreds of refugees during the last week. If there were ten thousand refugees fed by the Relief Committee last week, it must have fed fifteen thousand this week. According to the statements given by them there must be at least fifty murders and numerous cases of conversions and house-burning. Can you conceive of a more ghastly and inhuman crime than the murders of babies and pregnant women? Two days back I had occasion to read a report given by a refugee in Calicut. A pregnant woman carrying 7 months was cut through the abdomen by a rebel and she was seen lying dead on the way with the dead child projecting out of the womb. How horrible! Another: a baby of six months was snatched away from the breast of his own mother and cut into two pieces. How heart-rending! Are these rebels human beings or monsters? From the same quarters numerous forcible conversions are also reported. One refugee has given statement that he had seen with his own eyes that the heads of a dozen people were being shaved by the rebels and afterwards they were asked to recite some passages from the Quran. This he witnessed from a tree. I wonder what is the authority of some people who contradict the news of murders, and forcible conversions of Hindus. Let them come here and test the veracity of these statements for themselves.

Yesterday another report of murders came from a place very near Kottakal. The report says that eleven Hindus (males and females), were murdered by the rebels.

A fortnight ago fifteen dead bodies of Hindus were seen under culvert on the road between Perinialmanna and Melatur.

Will you not be sick of these stories of murders? All these reports are, as far as possible, proved also to be correct.

Words fail to express my feelings of indignation and abhorrence which I experienced when I came to know of an instance of rape, committed by the rebels under Chembrasseri Thangal. A respectable Nayar Lady at Melatur was stripped naked by the rebels in the presence of her husband and brothers, who were made to stand close by with their hands tied behind. When they shut their eyes in abhorrence they were compelled at the point of sword to open their eyes and witness the rape committed by the brute in their presence. I loathe even to write of such a mean action. I thank God that my family and relatives reached safe at Calicut without being dishonoured by these brutes, though we sustained serious loss of property and the loss of four lives (two servants and two relatives—More afterwards). This instance of rape was communicated to me by one of her brothers confidentially. There are several instances of such mean atrocities which are not revealed by people.

Here are a few extracts from a joint letter sent by the members of the Kerala Congress to Gandhi:[75]

Truth is infinitely of more paramount importance than Hindu–Muslim unity or Swaraj, and therefore, we tell the Maulana Sahib and his co-religionists and India's revered leader Mahatma Gandhi—if he too is unaware of the events here—that atrocities committed by the Moplahs on the Hindus are unfortunately too true and that there is nothing in the deeds of Moplah rebels which a true non-violent non-co-operator can congratulate them for. What is it for which they deserve congratulation? Their wanton and unprovoked attack on the Hindus, the all but wholesale looting at their houses in Ernad, and parts of Valluvanad, Ponnani, and Calicut Taliques; the forcible conversion of Hindus in a few places in the beginning of the rebellion and the wholesale conversion of those who stick to their homes in its later stages, the brutal murder of inoffensive Hindus, men, women, and children in cold blood, without the slightest reason except that they are 'Kaffirs' or belong to the same race as the Policemen, who insulted their Tangals or entered their Mosques, the desecration and burning of Hindu Temples, the outrage on Hindu women and their forcible conversion and marriage by Moplahs; do these and similar atrocities proved beyond the shadow of a doubt by the statements recorded by us from the actual sufferers who have survived, deserve any congratulation? On the other hand should they not call forth the strongest condemnation from all right-minded men and more especially from a representative body of Mohamedans like the Khilafat Conference pledged to non-violence under all provocation? Did the Moplahs, who committed such atrocities, sacrifice their lives in the cause of their religion?

(Sd.) K.P. Kesahava Menon,
Sec. Kerala Pro. Cong. Comit.

(Sd.) K. Madhavan Nair,
Sec. Calicut Dis. Cong. Comit.

(Sd.) T.V. Mohamad,
Sec. Ernad Khilafat Comit.

(Sd.) K. Karunakara Menon,
Treas. Kerala Pro. Comit.

(Sd.) K.V. Gopal Menon.

Despite the overwhelming evidence of the atrocities having been unprovoked and one-sided, Khilafatists like Maulana Hasrat Mohani attempted to justify them. I will once again reproduce Maulana Mohani's statement on the Moplah Outrage at the Muslim League's annual session of 1922, which I had quoted in the previous chapter too:

The Mopla Rebellion

Gentlemen, I have just stated it as a necessary condition of the Hindu–Muslim compromise that the third party, the English, should not be allowed to step in between us. Otherwise, all our affairs will fall into disorder. Its best example is before you in the shape of the Mopla incident. You are probably aware that Hindu India has an open and direct complaint against the Moplas, and an indirect complaint against all of us, that the Moplas are plundering and spoiling their innocent Hindu neighbours; but possibly you are not aware that the Moplas justify their action on the ground that, at such a critical juncture, when they are engaged in a war against the English, their neighbours not only do not help them or observe neutrality, but aid and assist the English in every possible way. They can, no doubt, contend that, while they are fighting a defensive war for the sake of their religion and have left their homes, property and belongings, and taken refuge in hills and jungles, it is unfair to characterize as plunder their commandeering of money, provisions and other necessaries for their troops from the English or their supporters. Both are right in their complaints; but so far as my investigation goes, the cause of this mutual recrimination can be traced to the interference of the third party. It happens thus: whenever any English detachment suddenly appears in a locality and kills or captures the Mopla inhabitants of the place, rumour somehow spreads in the neighbourhood that the Hindu inhabitants of the place had invited the English army for their protection, with the result that after the departure of the English troops, the neighbouring Moplas do not hesitate to retaliate, and consider the money and other belongings of the Hindus as lawful spoils of war taken from those who have aided and abetted the enemy. Where no such events have occurred, the Moplas and Hindus even now live peacefully side by side; Moplas do not commit any excesses against the Hindus, while the Hindus do not hesitate in helping the Moplas to the best of their ability.

To this justification of the Moplah attacks on Hindus, Madhavan Nair of the Congress from Calicut responded thus:[76]

Maulana Mohani justifies the looting of Hindus by Moplahs as lawful by way of commandeering in a war between the latter and the Government or as a matter of necessity when the Moplahs were forced to live in jungles. Maulana perhaps does not know that in the majority of cases, the almost wholesale looting of Hindu houses in portions of Ernad, Valluvanad and Ponani Taluques was perpetrated on the 21st, 22nd, and 23rd of August before the military had arrived in the affected area to arrest or fight the rebels even before Martial law had been declared. The Moplahs had not betaken themselves to jungles at the time as Moulana supposes nor had the Hindus as a class done anything to them to deserve their hostility. The out-break commenced on the 20th of August, the police and the District Magistrate withdrew from Tirunangadi to Calicut on the 21st and the policemen throughout the affected area had taken to their heels. There was no adversary to the Moplahs at the time whom the Hindus could possibly have helped or invited, and the attack on them was most wanton and unprovoked.

Condemning the denial of the atrocities committed by the Moplahs on the Hindus and Christians of Malabar, the following resolution was passed in February 1922 at a conference organised by the Zamorin of Calicut:[77]

VI. That the conference views with indignation and sorrow the attempts made in various quarters by interested parties to ignore or minimise the crimes committed by the rebels such as

(a) Brutally dishonouring women;
(b) Flaying people alive;
(c) Wholesale slaughter of men, women and children;
(d) Burning alive entire families;
(e) Forcibly converting people in thousands and slaying those who refused to get converted;
(f) Throwing half dead people into wells and leaving the victims for hours to struggle for escape till finally released from their sufferings by death;
(g) Burning a great many and looting practically all Hindu and Christian houses in the disturbed area in which even Moplah women and children took part, and robbing women of even the garments on their bodies, in short reducing the whole non-Muslim population to abject destitution;
(h) Cruelly insulting the religious sentiments of the Hindus by desecrating and destroying numerous temples in the disturbed area, killing cows within the temple precincts—putting their entrails on the holy image and hanging the skulls on the walls and roofs.

The following petition was written by the women of Malabar to the wife of the Viceroy, Lord Reading:[78]

To
Her Gracious Excellency
The Countess of Reading,
Delhi.

The humble memorial of the bereaved and sorrow-stricken women of Malabar.

May it please your gracious and compassionate Ladyship.

We, the Hindu women of Malabar of varying ranks and stations in life who have recently been overwhelmed by the tremendous catastrophe known as the Moplah rebellion, take the liberty to supplicate your Ladyship for sympathy and succour.

2. Your Ladyship is doubtless aware that though our unhappy district has witnessed many Moplah outbreaks in the course of the last one hundred years, the present rebellion is unexampled in its magnitude as well as unprecedented in its ferocity. But it is possible that your Ladyship is not fully appraised of all the horrors and atrocities perpetrated by the fiendish rebels; of the many wells and tanks filled up with the mutilated, but often only half dead bodies of our nearest and dearest ones who refused to abandon the faith of our fathers; of pregnant women cut to pieces and left on the roadsides and in the jungles, with the unborn babe protruding from the mangled corpse; of our innocent and helpless children torn from our arms and done to death before our eyes and of our husbands and fathers tortured, flayed and burnt alive; of our hapless sisters forcibly carried away from the midst of kith and kin and subjected to every shame and outrage which the vile and brutal imagination of these inhuman hell-hounds could conceive of; of thousands of our homesteads reduced to cinder-mounds out of sheer savagery and a wanton spirit of destruction; of our places of worship desecrated and destroyed and of the images of the deity shamefully insulted by putting the entrails of slaughtered cows where flower garlands used to lie, or else smashed to pieces; of the wholesale looting of hard earned wealth of generations reducing many who were formerly rich and prosperous to publicly beg for a piece or two in the streets of Calicut, to buy salt or chilly or betel-leaf—rice being mercifully provided by the various relief agencies. These are not fables.

The wells full of rotting skeletons, the ruins which once were our dear homes, the heaps of stones which once were our places of worship—these are still here to attest to the truth. The cries of our murdered children in their death agonies are still ringing in our ears and will continue to haunt our memory till death brings us peace. We remember how driven out of our native hamlets we wandered starving and naked in the jungles and forests; we remember how we choked and stifled our babies' cries lest the sound should betray our hiding places to our relentless pursuers. We still vividly realise the moral and spiritual agony that thousand[s] of us passed through when we were forcibly converted into the faith professed by these blood thirsty miscreants; we still have before us the sight of the unendurable and life long misery of those— fortunately few—of our most unhappy sisters who born and brought up in respectable families have been forcibly converted and then married to convict coolies. For five long months not a day has passed without its dread tale of horror to unfold.

3. Your gracious Ladyship's distracted memorialists have endeavoured without exaggeration, without setting down aught in malice to convey at least some idea of the indescribably terrible agonies which they and thousands more of their sisters have been enduring for over five months now through this reign of inhuman frightfulness inaugurated and carried on in the name

of the Khilafhat. We have briefly referred without going into their harrowing details to our heartrending tale of dishonour, outrage, rapine, and desolation. But if the past has been one of pain and anguish, the future is full of dread and gloom. We have to return to a ruined and desolated land. Our houses have been burnt or destroyed; may of our breadwinners killed; all our property looted; our cattle slaughtered. Repatriation without compensation means for us ruin, beggary, starvation. Will not the benign Government come to our aid and give us something to help us to begin life anew? We are now asked to settle down as paupers in the midst of the execrable fiends who robbed, insulted and murdered our loved ones—veritable demons such as hell itself could not let loose. Many of us shrink from the idea of going back to what there is left of our homes; for though the armed bands and rebels have been dispersed the rebellion cannot be said to be entirely quelled. It is like a venomous serpent whose spine has been partly broken, but whose poison fangs are still intact and whose striking power, if diminished, has not been destroyed. A few thousands of rebels have been killed and a few more thousands have been imprisoned, but as the Government are only too well aware many more thousands of rebels, looters, savagely militant evangelists and other inhuman monsters yet remain at large, a few in concealment, but most, moving about with arrogance openly threatening reprisals on all non-Moslims who dare to return and resume possession of their property. Many refugees who went back have paid for their temerity with their lives. In fact, repatriation, if it is not to be a leap from the frying pan into the fire, must mean for the vast bulk of your Ladyship's impoverished and helpless memorialists and their families a hard inexorable problem of financial help, and adequate protection against renewed hellish outrages from which immunity would be utterly impossible as long as thousands of men and even women and children of this semi-savage and fanatical race in whom the worst instinct of earth hunger, blood-lust and rapine have been awakened to fierce activity are free to prey upon their peaceable and inoffensive neighbours who—let it be most respectfully emphasised—because of their implicit trust in the power and the will of a just and benign Government to protect them, had suffered their own art and capacity for self defence to emasculate and decay.

4. We, Your Ladyship's humble and sorrow-stricken memorialists do not seek vengeance. Our misery will not be rendered less by inflicting similar misery upon this barbarous and savage race; our dead will not return to us if their slayers are slaughtered. We would not be human, however, if we could ever forget the cruel and shameful outrages and indignities perpetrated upon us by a race to whom we have always endeavoured to be friendly and neighbourly; we would be hypocritical if, robbed of all our possessions we did not plead for some measure of compensation to help us out of the pauperism now forced upon us; we would be imbecile, if knowing the ungovernable, anti-social propensities and the deadly religious fanaticism of the moplah race

we did not entreat the just and powerful government to protect the lives and honour of your humble sisters who have to live in the rebel-ravaged zone. Our ambition after all is low enough; sufficient compensation to save us and our children from starvation, and enough military protection against massacre and outrage are all that we want. We beseech Your Compassionate Ladyship to exercise all the benevolent influence that you possess with the government to see that our humble prayers are granted. But if the benign Government does not consider it possible to compensate us and to protect us in our native land we would most fervently pray that free grants of land may be assigned to us in some neighbouring region which though less blessed with the lavish gifts of nature may also be less cursed by the cruelty and brutality of man.

We beg to remain,
Your Ladyship's most humble
and obedient servants

And here is an extract on the subject from Ambedkar's *Pakistan or the Partition of India*:[79]

Beginning with the year 1920 (sic) there occurred in that year in Malabar what is known as the Mopla Rebellion. It was the result of the agitation carried out by two Muslim organizations, the Khuddam-i-Kaba (servants of the Mecca Shrine) and the Central Khilafat Committee. Agitators actually preached the doctrine that India under the British Government was Dar-ul-Harab and that the Muslims must fight against it and if they could not, they must carry out the alternative principle of Hijrat. The Moplas were suddenly carried off their feet by this agitation. The outbreak was essentially a rebellion against the British Government. The aim was to establish the kingdom of Islam by overthrowing the British Government. Knives, swords and spears were secretly manufactured, bands of desperadoes collected for an attack on British authority. On 20th August a severe encounter took place between the Moplas and the British forces at Pinmangdi Roads were blocked, telegraph lines cut, and the railway destroyed in a number of places. As soon as the administration had been paralysed, the Moplas declared that Swaraj had been established. A certain Ali Mudaliar was proclaimed Raja, Khilafat flags were flown, and Ernad and Wallurana were declared Khilafat Kingdoms. As a rebellion against the British Government it was quite understandable. But what baffled most was the treatment accorded by the Moplas to the Hindus of Malabar. The Hindus were visited by a dire fate at the hands of the Moplas. Massacres, forcible conversions, desecration of temples, foul outrages upon women, such as ripping open pregnant women, pillage, arson and destruction—in short, all the accompaniments of brutal and unrestrained barbarism, were perpetrated freely by the Moplas upon the Hindus until such time as troops could be hurried to the task of restoring order through a difficult and extensive tract of the country. This was not a Hindu–Moslem riot. This was just a Bartholomew. The number of Hindus who were killed, wounded or converted, is not known. But the number must have been enormous.

Based on all the factual material produced here above from multiple sources, I leave it to the reader to decide whether the Moplah Outrage was indeed driven by tenancy-related grievances or religious fanaticism or patriotic anti-colonial sentiments or a combination of these, and if it is the latter, which sentiment was most predominant. Here is one final extract on the subject by way of an epilogue to the Outrage:[80]

> In 1969, in response to the demands of the Muslim League in Kerala and as a reward for its political support, the United Front ministry of E.M.S. Namboodiripad redrew the boundaries of Kozhikode and Palghat districts so as to carve out the new, predominantly Muslim district of Malappuram. Denounced by its opponents as 'the illegitimate child of the old Two Nation theory,' Malappuram—'Moplastan' to its critics—combined within a single district those taluks which forty-eight years before, in 1921, had been the scene of the Mappilla rebellion.

In 1957, E.M.S. Namboodiripad had the distinction of heading the first democratically elected Communist government in Bharat and the second-ever Communist government to be democratically elected in the world after the 1945 election of a Communist government in the Republic of San Marino in Europe. In his second term as the chief minister of Kerala from 1967 to 1969, Namboodiripad created the Muslim-majority Malappuram district by combining those taluks which were the centres of the Moplah Outrage in 1921. According to the 2011 census, Muslims constituted 70.24 per cent of the total population of 4,112,920 in the district, whereas Hindus constituted 27.6 per cent and Christians 1.98 per cent.[81]

Conclusion

With this, the discussion sought to be undertaken in this book comes to an end. This much is clear—by the end of 1924, Bharat's indigeneity may have found a way, although not ideal, to live with a dual consciousness, namely the Bharatiya and the European. However, it was once again confronted with an earlier form of coloniality, namely Middle Eastern, which had managed to revive, reinvent and organise itself after the decline of the Mughal empire and was once again on the march. This time around, Bharat was ill-prepared to deal with this challenge owing to its dual consciousness, which severely limited its ability to call a spade a spade. Consequently, Bharat had embarked on the fatal path of accommodation and compromise under the burden of 'values' inherited from the Christian European coloniser, which muddled its sense of self, in the process leaving it woefully ill-equipped to weather the storm, which was no more brewing but had already announced its bloody arrival—or, more accurately, re-arrival—by the end of 1924. Accordingly, in the next book, I will resume this civilisational–constitutional discussion from 1925 and continue with the examination of undivided Bharat's fateful journey towards Pakistan, or the partition of this sacred geography—Bharat.

Finally, my experience of writing this book has left me all the more convinced that any reading or interpretation of the Constitution which is oblivious to the history of this land is bound to further the cause of either or both forms of colonialities, European and Middle Eastern, much to the detriment of Indic civilisational consciousness. To paraphrase writer and philosopher George Santayana, those who do not learn from history are doomed, and dare I say, cursed and condemned to repeat it.

मातर्मे मधुकैटभघ्नि महिषप्राणापहारोद्यमे
हेलानिर्जितधूम्रलोचनवधे चण्डमुण्डार्दिनि।
निश्शेषीकृतरक्तबीजदनुजे नित्ये निशुम्भापहे
शुम्भध्वंसिनि संहराशु दुरितं दुर्गे मस्तेऽम्बिके।।

−दाक्षायणीस्तोत्रम् 23 श्लोक:
−Dākṣāyaṇī stotra 23rd Śloka

O my Mother! slayer of Madhu and Kaitabha,
One who took the effort to slay Mahishāsura

One who effortlessly slayed Dhumralochana,
Destroyer of Chaṇḍa and Muṇḍa!

The One who crushed the dānava Raktabeeja, leaving not a trace,
the One who is ever-present, the slayer of Shumbha

The destroyer of Nishumbha; O Durge! Annihilate all my troubles
this instant; my namaskāra to You O Ambike!

सर्वाबाधाप्रशमनं त्रैलोक्यस्याखिलेश्वरि।
एवमेव त्वया कार्यमस्मद्वैरि विनाशनम्।।

−मार्कण्डेयपुराणम् − सावर्णिकमन्वन्तरं −
देवीमाहात्म्यं − 11 अध्याय: − 37 श्लोक:
−Mārkaṇḍeya Purāṇa − Sāvarnika Manvatara −
Devīmāhatmya − 11th Adhyāya − 37th Śloka

O Akhileshvari, Goddess of all three worlds! May You remove all the
obstacles in our path
And in this manner, destroy all our enemies!

Appendix

Presidential Address of Syed Ali Imam, Amritsar Session, All-India Muslim League, 1908

Gentlemen, I thank you heartily for the great honour you have conferred upon me by asking me to preside at your deliberations on the occasion of this the first Annual Session of the All-India Muslim League held after its constitution was passed last March. To occupy the position with which you have favoured me to-day, is, to my mind, a proud privilege and, however unworthily I may possess it, I wish to assure you that the present moment is the proudest in my life. The political conditions that affect the Musalmans of India bristle with problems of much gravity; it is, therefore, greatly to be regretted that unforeseen circumstances have deprived this gathering of the presence amongst us of a leader of such exceptional ability as Syed Amir Ali, C.I.E. His vast learning, mature views and ardent love of Islam and Muslims entitle him to rank as one of the foremost Indian Musalmans of the day, eminently fitted to give the right direction to the political energy of our community.

You will miss in your deliberations on the present occasion the masterly guidance of a savant, an erudite scholar and a profound thinker. Under the circumstances, I keenly feel the weight of the responsibility placed on my shoulders for having been called upon to preside in this assembly. Political deliberations require much clearness of vision, foresight, temperate and dispassionate language, exactness of expression, sagacity, judgement, a genuine regard for the view of the opponent and no less an appreciation of the points of his case. Overwhelmed with the conviction of my own shortcomings, I am buoyed up with the confidence that the assembly in which I have the honour to preside to-day represents the intense earnestness, the high aspirations, and the elevating ideals of a community that, for all its numerical inferiority, is rich in quality of race and traditions of political perception and administrative ability. I feel assured that on the task that you have set to yourselves, the political development of your community, you will bring to bear in our proceedings the sobriety, the patience and the wisdom which are the forerunners of the success of any undertaking.

Politically speaking, the Mohammedans of India occupy a unique position. I believe it is without a parallel in the history of the world. Close upon a thousand years ago, the Arab Mohammedan scented the desert air of Sind and found its sand-mounds and date-groves reminding him of Hejaz, of Arabia Felix. Since then wave upon wave of Muslim conquest has rolled over the entire length and breadth of India. In serried ranks, Musalman Royal Houses rose and fell, but Muslim domination of the country remained more or less an unbroken chain, till in comparatively more recent times supremacy hung in the balance between the Mahratta spear and the British bayonet. Islam, in its world-wide career of conquest and conversion, met on Indian soil with a resistance which had little of the admirable military prowess of the Hindus. What Hindu chivalry was powerless to protect, Hindu ethics, Hindu philosophy and Hindu social system had made impregnable. Centuries rolled by but the conqueror and the conquered in point of nationality, character and creed suffered not from their political association. Characteristics of race and religion and political and social ideals of the two presented irreconcilabilities. Quranic teaching throws open wide the door of conversion with equal right and liberty, social and political, to the new-comer. His entrance into the brotherhood of Islam is a passport to all that is the highest and the best in that community. Islam is expansive, has the capacity to hold all nations in its embrace. Hinduism inculcates a tenacious adherence to a faith that is not proselytizing, that has encased itself within the rigidity of the caste-system and that has no catholicity. To be a Hindu one has to be born one. Birth imposes no limitations on the Muslim. The methods of theological thought of the two communities are totally different. The Muslim's severely puritanical unitarian idea of the Godhead stands in violent contrast with the beautiful but crowded mythology of the Hindu. In the East, religion enters into the very life of the people. It permeates the fabric of society, supplies the spring of individual action in everyday life, and dominates habits of thought in a measure unknown to the West. The social relations of the Indian Muslim and the Hindu have not yet received the geniality of a common dinner-table nor the sacrament or legal sanction of matrimony. The two communities, from the truly social point of view, are as far apart to-day as they were a thousand years ago. Time has not worn out any of the angularities that characterized their social systems when they first came face to face. Similarly some of their political methods have been distinct. The two communities have different notions of sovereignty. The Musalman sovereign presides in the council chamber, leads at prayer and commands in the battlefield. He is at once the head of the state and the church. The Hindu monarch considered it a privilege, under religious obligation, to kiss the Brahmin's toe. The Hindu

Rajah has an overlord in the authority of the hierarchy. Papal Bulls had not the same terror for the crowned heads of Christian Europe as the frown of the Brahmin for a Hindu chief.

It is clear, therefore, that, apart from ethnic diversity of character, the two communities have nothing in common in their traditional, religious, social and political conceptions. There must be something imperishable in the cherished beliefs of both. Each has so far passionately clung to its own. Indeed there is much in Hinduism that evokes admiration. It is indestructible. It is perfect and complete in itself. Its foundation is laid in the innermost recesses of the sentiments and emotions of its people. It is a magnificently organized system, each part in faultless co-ordination with the rest. Hidebound, it has lived down the influence of ages of alien rule. On the other hand, the vitality and robustness of Islamic principles made it impossible for the conqueror to be absorbed in the civilization of the land where he had come to stay. The soul-stirring preaching that followed the descent of the Great Prophet from Mount Hera has given mankind the essence of a rational and living faith. The trumpet call of Mohammad to duty, to righteousness, to Islam have left undying echoes. Under such conditions the fusion of the two, Hinduism and Islam, could not be predicated. The verdict of history is that, in holding India under subjection for centuries, the Mohammedan held only her body and not her soul. For political ends, for the happiness of the country as a whole and the formation of a flourishing commonwealth, the relation of the two communities was anomalous and out of joint. The keen sighted statesmanship of the great Akbar saw this and aimed at unification by conciliation, compromise and concession in religious, social and political directions. A long and tolerant reign of about 50 years proved the failure of the experiment. Unification demands absorption and obliteration of the old landmarks of differences and divergences. The imperial reformer at best achieved a friendly understanding with his Hindu subjects, which resulted more from the consciousness of a just liberal government than any acceptance of the ethics of Islam or its religious, social and political principles. The innate difference of creed and character, of race and tradition and of social and political ideas remained ready to spring into active hostility as soon as a favourable opportunity presented itself. Aurangzeb saw, no less than his great-grandfather, the political necessity of unification. He adopted, however, the desperate and hazardous method of religious intolerance and forcible conversion. The experiment failed again. Prejudices and practices of both the communities, sanctified by the observance of ages, defied cohesion. Persuasion and persecution equally proved futile. With the weakening of administrative control, the Musalman found himself isolated. New Hindu powers rose in rebellion round the tottering throne of the Mogul. The strife had all the character of a crusade, and the disruption was but the reflexion of the irreconcilability of Hinduistic with Islamic conceptions.

It was at this period when the country was torn and bleeding, when sectarian passions and prejudices had leapt up from their hidden lairs, and when Islam, whatever of it that was in India, was on the brink of an inglorious annihilation, that an inscrutable providence ordained the advent of a power that gave the country peace and religious toleration, that vanquished the forces of anarchy and disorder, and that introduced a form of government that paralysed the hand of fanaticism. The coming of the British into the country was the signal for Hinduism and Islam to retire, each within its own limits. It gave the land a strong and well-ordered form of administration that respects the personal law and religious principles and prejudices of all communities so long as they do not interfere with the general peace of the country. It is idle to deny that, however fortuitously, one immediate manifestation of British rule in India was the complete immunity the Indian Musalmans received from the not unnatural but fierce resentment of the Hindu. A new era dawned on the destinies of the vast continent of India, a morning full of promise and hope, of intellectual advancement and material prosperity. The impact of the Western methods of administration, the characteristically generous desire to govern in deference to popular views and the inauguration of a high-souled policy of public instruction, have created in the last 50 years aspirations and political perceptions which the people of India had never felt before. A free press, and till very recently an irresponsible press, public speaking, and similarly till very recently an unrestrained public speaking, have engendered indefinite and vague ideas of home rule, self-government, autonomy and *Swaraj* among many other political conundrums that have brought about an unrest which has in the present day occupied the anxious thoughts of many friends of India, both among the rulers and the ruled. It is impossible for a thoughtful man to approach the subject without regard to the pathetic side of the present situation. It is the liberalism of the great British nation that has taught Indians, through the medium of English education, to admire democratic institutions, to hold the rights of the people sacred above all rights, and to claim for their voice first place in the government of the country. The mind of close upon three generations of the educated classes in the land has been fed on the ideas of John Stewart Mill, Milton, Burke, Sheridan and Shelley, has been filled with the great lessons obtainable from chapters of the constitutional history of England, and has been influenced by inexpressible considerations arising out of the American War of Independence, the relation of Great Britain with her colonies, and last, though not least, the grant of autonomy to the

Boers after their subjugation at an enormous sacrifice of men and money. The bitterest critic of the educated Indian will not hold him to blame for his present state of mind.

It is the English who have carefully prepared the ground and sown the seed that has germinated into what some of them are now disposed to consider to be noxious weed. It will be a dwarfed imagination, however, that will condemn the educational policy of the large-hearted and liberal-minded Englishmen who laid its foundation in this country. Those who inaugurated it aimed at raising the people to the level where co-operation and good understanding between the rulers and the ruled is possible. Under the circumstances, the desire of the educated Indian to take a prominent part in the administration of his country is neither unnatural nor unexpected. The gracious proclamation of Her Late Majesty Queen Victoria, our loved and revered Malaka Moazzama, issued in 1858, contributed in no small measure to give shape to Indian aspirations. Among other messages of hope and peace not the least luminous was that her subjects of 'whatever race or creed should be freely and impartially admitted to offices in her service, the duties of which they may be qualified by their education, ability and integrity duly to discharge.' Since the promulgation of this Proclamation the country has enjoyed the inestimable blessings of internal peace. Education has taken long strides, commercial enterprise has shown enormous activity, industrial, agricultural and economic resources have developed, sanitation has improved, free medical aid has been brought within the reach of all, and the administration of the Public Works Department has been a monumental success. Railways and canals, roads and bridges and postal and telegraphic facilities have annihilated distance and brought distant provinces of the country within intelligent touch of each other. High offices of the state, both administrative and judicial, have been filled by Indians. Bengal has seen the highest Executive Office next to the Lieutenant-Governor and the highest Judicial Office next to no one held by Indians. A liberal Secretary of State has reserved two seats on his Council for Indians, and the selection of the Honourable Syed Husain Bilgrami, C.S.I., to represent our community in that august assembly is a recognition of his towering personality among the Musalmans of India. It is a selection of which we are justly proud. There are expectations in the near future of the appointment of an Indian to the membership of the Executive Council of the Viceroy, and I have no doubt the country can furnish men of the necessary education, ability and integrity duly to discharge the duties of the Viceregal colleague. As long as there are men of the necessary accomplishment amongst us, our community need not despair of seeing its representative occupy the proposed place. Recent appointments of Indian Musalmans to high judicial posts in different provinces of the country is indicative of the desire of the Government to co-operate with the Indian Musalmans in the work of administration with as much willingness and cordiality as with other communities. Given the necessary qualification of education, ability and integrity, the protection of the special interests of the Mohammedans demands their admission to high offices of the state. Where the requisite efficiency is forthcoming, it is but the adjustment of political balance to admit Indians of all races and creeds to the public service. His Excellency the Viceroy very rightly emphasized the wisdom of this principle when in his speech in the Council on the occasion of the passing of the Sedition Bill he gave expression to these words: 'I repudiate once for all the insinuation that has sometimes reached me that the Government of India has for political reasons favoured the interests of one community against those of another. It has been the pride of the British Raj to balance without prejudice the claims of nationalities, of religions and of castes. It will continue to do so.' It is clear therefore that, while developing the material resources of the country, the Government has not been regardless of its duty to invite and to admit the people of the country to share the responsibilities of administration. The grant of local self-government, the concession of the right of interpellation, the recognition of popular associations and corporations to send their representatives to the Legislative Chambers of the country, the tendency to encourage useful discussion in budget speeches, and the keen desire to take the natural leaders of the people into the confidence of Government before a measure is passed into law, are but emphatic expressions of appreciation of the popular element in the transaction of the affairs of the state. With fostering care, for years the Government has from time to time introduced institutions and encouraged methods that have abundantly furnished opportunity for political training.

Above all, one not the least remarkable development of the results of British occupation of the country is that India has come to acquire a common language. English is now a common medium of exchange of ideas from one end of the country to the other. It has drawn the myriad races and communities of India closer together than ever before. Material, intellectual and political activities have brought about conditions of which the educated Indian is the embodiment. Hindu or Mohammedan, Parsee or Christian, intellectually the educated Indians have drawn nourishment from one and the same feeding-bottle, the great liberalizing influence of the great British race. With all the theological, social and ethnic differences between communities in India, it is futile to question the fact that the educated Indians, of whatever race they may be, have acquired a common attitude of thought relating to the land of their birth. There seems to be unanimity in the sentiment of love for the mother country. The passion to serve her, to advance her material and moral prosperity and to ameliorate her general condition, has taken firm root in the breast of the educated Indians. We, the educated Musalmans of India, have no less love for the land of our birth than the members of the other communities inhabiting the country. India is not only the land of our birth, we are tied to her by the sacred association of ages. We yield to none in veneration of and affection for our motherland. All our hopes and all our aspirations are wrapped up in the general advancement of our country, an advancement all along the line, giving protection and preferment to all her children alike without any invidious distinction. England may well be congratulated on the success of the result of her undertaking.

It was a proud moment when last June at the Indian Civil Service dinner in London, Lord Morley made reference to the awakening in India. Addressing his hosts, His Lordship said: 'It would be idle to deny that there is at this moment, and there has been for some little time past, and very likely there will be for some time to come, a living movement in the mind of those people for whom you are responsible. A living movement and a movement for what? A movement for objects which we ourselves have all taught them to think desirable objects.' It has gratefully to be acknowledged that British rule has given the peoples of India a common platform where they can come together, and from where it is possible for them to proclaim a broad-based patriotism that will hold in loving solicitude the interests of all the races and creeds that inhabit our vast country.

From the point of view of race and creed, two communities only stand forth most prominently out of the large group that forms the Indian population. These two are the great Hindu community, embracing nearly four-fifths of the inhabitants of British India, and the no less important community, the Musalmans of India, that make up between one fifth and one fourth of the entire population. True, the significance of the Indian Musalmans in point of number, though over 62 millions, is not very large when compared with the number of their Hindu countrymen. But the uncivilized portions of the country classified as Hindu take away in no small measure from the strength of the Hindu community as a numerical majority, and thereby accord the Musalmans a larger proportion to the real Hindu majority. The importance of the Musalmans of India, however, if not based in their comparative numerical strength, is incalculably great on grounds of political considerations, as was pointed out in the Address presented by the famous Mohammedan Deputation at Simla two years ago to His Excellency the Viceroy, Lord Minto. That Address, in urging the claims of the Mohammedan community, drew attention to 'the value of the contribution which they make to the defence of the Empire', as also to 'the position which they occupied in India a little more than a hundred years ago, and of which the traditions have naturally not faded from their minds'. His Excellency's reply dealing with the position taken in the Address recognized its validity in these words: 'You justly claim that your position should be estimated not merely on your numerical strength but in respect to the political importance of your community and the service it has rendered to the Empire. I am entirely in accord with you.' But, gentlemen, it is not necessary that the political importance of the Indian Musalmans should be, as it has been, ratified by Viceregal utterances. Our Hindu countrymen have paid us the just compliment, time after time, to say that their great organization, the Indian National Congress, remains incomplete as a political agency without the Musalmans freely participating in its activities. In the last 23 years, leaders of that assembly have been at great pains to draw the Musalmans of India to their annual deliberations. Indeed, from about September when the sittings of the Congress are about to be held, the political importance of Musalman co-operation is openly preached. Exhortations from the platform rend the air and publications from the press carry far and wide to Musalmans the invitation to join. The reasons why the Musalmans of India have not responded to the appeal of the Congress leaders, I will dwell upon later.

I am at this stage of my discourse concerned with impressing upon you the consideration that you are a great community, that in the political affairs of the country you hold a place of unique importance, and it is your duty to realize fully the responsibility attaching to the position you occupy. Indifference to the political developments of the country and disregard of the phase through which these developments are passing are not possible any more. Side by side with the political activities of the Indian National Congress, the educational activity of the Musalmans has proceeded at no ordinary pace. It was stimulated thanks to the efforts of the Mohammedan Association by the well-known Government Resolution of 1885, which secures state encouragement to education among the Mohammedans and their employment in the Public Service. Consecration of lifelong devotion to the cause by private individuals was not wanting. The genius of our Grand Old Man, the Late Sir Syed, the burning eloquence of his late coadjutor, our Mehdi, the untiring energy of our Mushtaq, the inspiring songs of Hali, the thoughtful writings of Nazir Ahmad, and the learned disquisitions of Shibli have done their work. They spurred on the Mohammedans to take to Western learning and their efforts have been crowned with success, and the inevitable result is that the younger generation of Indian Musalmans is not in a frame of mind to eschew politics.

It may be, it is not yet, in the words of Lord Morley, 'intoxicated with the ideas of freedom, of nationality and self-government', but, I say, it has sipped the strong wine of the intellectual vintage of Mill and Burke. It was some consideration of this sort that prompted a significant statement in the Simla Deputation Address: 'Recent events have stirred up feelings, specially among the younger generation of Mohammedans, which might, in certain circumstances and under certain contingencies, easily pass beyond the control of temperate counsel and sober guidance.' The Mohammedan community, I feel persuaded, is confronted with problems of great political import.

One of the questions that the community had before it was whether its political requirements in relation to Government and to its countrymen of other races and creeds called for a separate political organization. The answer to this has been the founding of the All-India Muslim League. It is nearly a decade since Nawab Viqar-ul-Mulk Bahadur called an informal meeting of leading Mohammedans of India at the house of my esteemed friend Mr. Hamid Ali Khan of Lucknow. I was present in that meeting. After the necessary deliberations, the gathering broke up and all of us who had taken part in it felt the absolute necessity of a political organization of our own. Two years ago that necessity became an urgent call which terminated in the Simla Deputation. On the occasion of the Deputation, advantage was taken of such a representative gathering, and the 35 signatories to the Address formed a band for the political organization of their people. A few months later, under the hospitality of that generous nobleman, the noble Premier of East Bengal, the Nawab Bahadur of Dacca, the foundation was laid. Last year Karachi saw that prince of merchants, Sir Adamji Peerbhoy, deliver the inaugural address. It was there that the constitution was framed, which an Extraordinary Sitting of the League passed last March at Aligarh; thereafter the acceptance of the presidential chair of the League by His Highness the Aga Khan was universally acclaimed by Indian Musalmans as the pledge of the stability of the organization. The presence of representative Musalmans from all the different parts of India in our gathering to-day is an assurance that the community has realized its political responsibility and that it is answerable for stewardship to the younger generation both within itself and without. We identify ourselves with all that aims at the general advancement of the true interests of the country. We have a rooted conviction that the true interests of the country lie in the maintenance of cordial relations among the Indian communities, and that the true political ideal is the one that aims at peaceful progress of such a national character as subserves the protection and advancement of the interests of all denominations.

Gentlemen, I claim for the League responsibility for working out political amelioration not only for the Musalmans but for all races that inhabit our beloved country, India. I assert that ours is not a mission narrowed down to self-seeking and sectarian aggression. I repudiate the suggestion that the League is in opposition to other political organizations of the country and that it has given a blank cheque to Government. We reserve the right of frankly, fearlessly and boldly criticizing the measures of Government; we reserve the right to protest, howsoever respectfully, against the continuance of certain of its methods; we reserve the right to refuse to believe in the soundness of a particular policy of it; and we also reserve the right of standing shoulder to shoulder with our brethren of other denominations when we find our country suffering under a real grievance. But at the same time we declare that in our relations with Government we will not permit malice to cross our path, warp our judgement and create disaffection.

Gentlemen, in these days of political tribulation and unrest, professions of loyalty stand on slippery ground. But this I will say that, apart from ethical aspects of loyalty to the British Crown, the best sense of the country recognizes the fact that the progress of India rests on the maintenance of order and internal peace, and that order and internal peace, in view of the conditions obtaining in our country at present and for a very long time to come, immeasureably long time to come, spell British occupation. British occupation not in the thin and diluted form in which Canada, Australia and South Africa stand in relation to England, but British occupation in the sense in which our country has enjoyed internal peace during the last 50 years. Believe me that as long as we have not learnt to overcome sectarian aggressiveness, to rise above prejudices based on diversity of races, religions and languages, and to alter the alarming conditions of violent intellectual disparity among the peoples of India, so long British occupation is the principal element in the progress of the country. The need of India is to recognize that true patriotism lies in taking measure of the conditions existing in fact and devoting oneself to amelioration. Idealism may be enchanting but has little place in practical politics.

The idealistic *Swaraj*, as understood in the light of a Calcutta High Court ruling, is a fascinating picture, but their Lordships who delivered that judgement were not concerned with the political inadaptability of the moral it teaches; they were concerned only with the question whether it teaches anything unlawful. Now, no one can claim that to advocate the grant of *Swaraj* to India as understood by their Lordships is unlawful or treasonable, but I do think that there are strong and valid reasons to hold that it will be the biggest political blunder for the peoples of India to ask, and the British

Parliament to grant, it in the near or even the measurably remote future. I admit it is difficult to detect treason if the self-government of the idealist is, as put by that eminent countryman of ours, Dr. Rash Behari Ghose, 'autonomy within the Empire and not absolute independence'. But, gentlemen, the entire population of India is not made up of lawyers nor is it concerned with legal subtleties. What disastrous consequences may not flow by the lay public acquiring notions of *Swaraj* without the capacity to understand the technicalities on which their Lordship's decision is based. *Swaraj* or self-government, autonomy or a self-governing Member of the Empire, in other words, home rule under the aegis of the British Crown in India, is possible only when racial, religious, social and intellectual disparities are removed, and a fusion has levelled down characteristics of separate denominations to a plane where the pulsations of a common national life are the most prominent features.

I cannot say what you think, but when I find the most advanced province of India put forward the sectarian cry of 'Bande Mataram' as the national cry, and the sectarian *Rakhibandhan* as a national observance, my heart is filled with despair and disappointment; and the suspicion that, under the cloak of nationalism, Hindu nationalism is preached in India becomes a conviction. Has the experiment tried by Akbar and Aurangzeb failed again? Has 50 years of the peaceful spread of English education given the country only a revival of denominationalism? Gentlemen, do not misunderstand me. I believe that the establishment of conferences, associations and corporate bodies in different communities on denominational lines are necessary to give expression to denominational views, so that the builders of a truly national life in the country may have before them the crystallized needs and aspirations of all sects. In this connection, every lover of India will welcome such institutions as the Kayestha Conference, the Bhuinhar Conference, the Rajput Conference, Mohammedan *anjumans* and conferences, the associations of the domiciled community, and all such denominational institutions. Such activities help to bring into focus the thoughts of all sections of the population of India. Regard for the feelings and sentiments, needs and requirements of all is the key-note to true Indian nationalization. It is far more imperative where the susceptibilities of the two great communities, Hindus and Musalmans, are involved. Unreconciled, one will be as great a drag on the wheel of national progress as the other. I ask the architects of Indian nationalism, both in Calcutta and Poona, do they expect the Musalmans of India to accept *'Bande Mataram'* and the Sivaji Celebration? The Mohammedans may be weak in anything you please, but they are not weak in cherishing the traditions of their glorious past. I pray the Congress leaders to put before the country such a programme of political advancement as does not demand the sacrifice of the feelings of the Hindu or the Mohammedan, the Parsee or the Christian.

The preparation for self-government does not consist in merely insisting on it year after year in language that fires the imagination of the educated classes of the country into uncontrollable and fatal excesses, as is too painfully manifested in what is happening in Bengal. It does not consist in launching forth on the troubled waters of Indian politics the frail bark of *Swaraj* without care of its seaworthiness. Does *Swaraj* mean transfer of control, from the British to the peoples of India, of all internal affairs of the country, legislation, finance, administration of civil and criminal justice, police, state education, military service? I suppose this is what is contemplated by Article I of the Allahabad Convention Committee. That Article sums up the object of the Indian National Congress to be 'the attainment by the people of India of a system of government similar to that enjoyed by the Self-Governing Members of the British Empire'. As a mere ideal without any reference to the conditions prevailing in India it is unexceptionable. Utopia is not unimaginable. But that it should furnish a basis in practical politics to divide off into moderates and extremists is incomprehensible. Have politicians of these two cults considered the futility of a schism that is engaged in laying down irreconcilable lines of policy for conditions that are not likely to be possible even in any measurably remote future? Is it wise to weaken the solidarity of political unity? Have we Indians put our own house in order? Have the Hindu and Mohammedan sunk their many differences? What has kept the Mohammedans as a people away from the Indian National Congress? It was, I say, this very demand for the transfer of legislative and administrative control from the rulers to the ruled; in other words, that the ruling authority should vest in the party that commands a majority of votes in the Council Chambers of the Indian Autonomy. It did not require much imagination to see that such a majority would be the Hindu majority. What did the suggested change of masters signify? Twenty-one years ago Sir Syed answered the question in his memorable Lucknow speech, and that answer has been for over two decades the rule of conduct for the Mohammedans of India in relation to the Congress. The All-India Muslim League has to answer that very question again. Should the Mohammedans of India accept the views of what was the Indian National Congress before the fateful and abortive Surat Sitting? It seems to me that there are many questions of practical politics where the interests of the two communities are identical, and that in so far as these questions go, there is no earthly reason why the League should not hold out its hand in loving and patriotic grasp to the Congress.

The separation of the judicial from the executive, the repeal of degrading Colonial Ordinances, the extension of primary education, the adoption of measures of sanitation, the admission of Indians of all races in larger numbers into the higher branches of the public service, discontinuance of official interference in matters of local self-government, reasonable reduction of military expenditure without endangering efficiency, recognition of the legitimate and patriotic desire of the warlike races of India to render military service as volunteers, the grant of commissions in the army to Indians, equitable adjustment of Home Charges, limitation of revenue on land belonging to the state, establishment and development of village unions for the disposal of petty civil and criminal cases, encouragement and protection of indigenous arts and industries, the eradication of insolence, on one hand, and feeling of inferiority and mortification, on the other, between the rulers and the ruled, are some of the many grave questions of practical politics in India that equally affect all classes of our countrymen. I deny the accusation that the Mohammedans of India have not either the capacity to understand the value of co-operation for the accomplishment of reforms or the courage to face official disapprobation. Gentlemen, Mohammedan political foresight and Mohammedan courage do not require any advocacy. The world has seen enough of both to judge that they are wanting in neither. Why is it then that we have held aloof from the Indian National Congress? Not because we do not want co-operation, not because we do not feel the urgency and wisdom of the reforms mentioned above and others of their kind, and not because we suffer from any nervous or morbid fear of the rulers, but because the Indian National Congress does not only seek reforms such as are described above. It wants far more. To ask our rulers for specific measures of reform is to admit and recognize the necessity of their control, but to ask them to hand over that control is to ask them, however politely, to take to their ships and return from India. To ask for the latter is to ask for a change of government, and to press for the former would be, as put in Article I of the Allahabad Convention, 'a steady reform of the existing system of administration'. It is obvious that the existing system of administration is not 'a system of government similar to that enjoyed by the Self-Governing Members of the British Empire'. That article puts the latter as the object of the Congress and the reform of the former as the method of attainment.

It seems to me therefore that to attain the object, the method suggested would not be 'reform', however steady, of the 'existing system', but its extinction. The article does not seem to seek reform but revolution, though bloodless. Surely the Indian public has a right to have more light thrown on the meaning of that article. A shrewd suspicion may read between the lines and find the genesis of the inconsistency in the desire to pull together men of different shades of political views, loyalists, ultra-moderates, moderates and those verging on extremism. The desire is laudable, but the *modus operandi* questionable. It is possible to hide in dialectic obscurity the differences of basic principles for a time, but it will be blind folly to hope they will remain there. I wonder how those who have gone to Madras interpret 'steady reform of the existing system of administration'. If it really means extinction, the language of the Convention may serve to capture the unwary but not to captivate him. It resolves itself into the ideal put forward by the Indian National Congress year after year. The moderate wants autonomy or representative government under the aegis of the British Crown, and the extremist wants the same but without the fiction of the aegis. They both desire the extinction and not the reform of the present system of administration. Canada and Australia are tied to England by sentiments of race, character and creed, and their continuance as such under the aegis of the British Crown, as long as they are not treated with unpolitic interference, has an intelligent basis. The grant of autonomy to the Boers is of too recent a date to prognosticate that the aegis will be respected. In the case of America the aegis proved too brittle to survive the effects of the Boston Port Bill. In the light of the differences of social, moral and religious standards of England and India, and the diversity of race, character and creed between the ruler and the ruled, one may be pardoned for thinking that of the two ideals, however impracticable both, the one of the extremist, though steeped in treason, is not disingenuous. It definitely sets before the country the honest version that if self-government is attained by India, the British may not flatter themselves with the belief that they will have even the slender thread of the aegis to connect them with this country. The moderate hopes to hasten self-government by giving assurances of profound loyalty to the aegis, and with such assurances asks for autonomy. But gentlemen is this all that is needed for India? The ideal of the one or of the other? Is the present need of India contemplation of ideals? Has the good sense of the country run away with the notion that self-government is to be built in the land from the apex and not the base?

I crave your indulgence to quote from a speech that I delivered when I had the honour to preside at the first session of the Bihar Provincial Conference. 'To my mind the greater problem is how to equip ourselves for receiving and assimilating the amenities and advantages of self-government, than an insistence on the right to enjoy a privilege which, once we have reached the requisite efficiency, can no more be denied than the truth that water finds its own level. I consider that in the development of national life in India there is far less danger from without than from within.' Have the apostles of Indian autonomy given us, up to this time, any indication how their great ideal will maintain internal peace, what will be its relation to the ruling chiefs, what will be the features of its military administration, how will it adjust the difference of standards of morality in its scheme of national education, how will it conduct itself in the devious and difficult paths of foreign policy, what guarantee will it give to capitalists of other countries who have their millions vested in India, what protection will it accord to the domiciled European, how will it get over the dangers of intellectual disparity between races and sexes in India, and how will it reconcile religious, social and racial antipathies? Are religion, society and politics watertight compartments? Can you separate politics from the other two? If a religious procession, the slaughter of a particular animal, the moral of Bunkim's plot in *Anund Muth*, the preachings of fanatics in East Bengal or any other part of India, and numerous other subjects connected with religion, inflame the mind, it is insanity to dissociate Indian politics from them. Surely gentlemen, the mere elevation of an ideal is no title to its serious acceptance. True statesmanship is to work for the highest public good realizable. Before self-government, our ideal should be 'United India'—united in a patriotism that leaves distant and visionary ideals to moulder in the vagueness and impracticability of their conception, and that addresses itself to working on non-controversial lines. How true are the words of the president of the unfortunate Surat Sitting of the Congress in his undelivered speech. He said: 'hasty maxims drawn from the history of other nations and other times are extremely dangerous, as the conditions are never the same, and action which produces certain results in one country at one time may lead to a directly opposite result in another country and at another time.' Has not this ideal of self-government, however elevated, caused impatience on account of its impracticability, and has not the impatience carried the idealist off his feet, and has not this loss of equipoise created extremism, and has not extremism given birth to anarchism, bombs, secret societies and assassination, and is not all this the greatest menace to the peaceful progress of the country?

Gentlemen, does the contemplation of an almost impossible ideal compensate for all the repressive measures that have been passed in the last two years? Resurrection of Regulation 3 of 1818, the Ordinance of May 1907, the Seditious Meetings Act, the Newspaper (Incitement to Offences) Act, and the Indian Criminal Law Amendment Act are the bitter fruits of the misspent labour of the idealist in the last two decades. These Acts may be a reproach to the Statute Book, but who is responsible for the reproach? The responsibility lies with those who, infatuated with the seductions of an idealistic but impractical autonomy, have caused widespread intellectual distemper among the educated Indians, a distemper utterly regardless of surroundings, of expediency and of the best interests of the country. The gospel of representative government in India has been preached with reckless carelessness, and the energy of the educated intellect of the country has been employed for the creation of longings the fulfilment of which within any measurable distance of time is impossible. The result is a sullen, disappointed, demoralized and morbid disposition in the best portion of the national asset of the country—the educated Indians.

Is this not sufficiently deplorable a state of affairs to serve as a warning to us, Musalmans? Has not the League a right to beseech the Congress leaders not to prolong the agony any more, imperil the safety of the country any further and jeopardize peaceful progress by a profitless devotion to a chimera? Let the Indian National Congress shake itself free from the baneful blandishments of 'Self-Governing member of the British Empire'; and let it announce that in our practical politics, loyalty to the British administration of the country is loyalty to India, and that the reform of the 'existing system' is possible only with the maintenance of British control. Gentlemen, I am not putting this supplication forward in any spirit of cavil, but solely with a view to bringing about an entente cordiale between the Indian National Congress and the great community that you represent—and also with a view that in the great work of the regeneration of India, the firm but guiding hand of our rulers may be in comradeship with our own. As long as the leaders of the Indian National Congress will not give us a workable policy like the one indicated above, so long the All-India Muslim League has a sacred duty to perform. That duty is to save the community it represents, and specially the youth of that community, from the political error of joining an organization that in the main, as put by Lord Morley, cries for the moon.

There is another matter not of principle but of procedure that influences the question of the participation of the Musalmans in the deliberations of the Congress. The Allahabad Convention with the best of motives has adopted the conciliatory measure contained in its Article XXVI. That article lays down the procedure that in the Subject Committee or in the Congress no subject shall be introduced to which the Hindu or Mohammedan delegates may object as a body by a majority of three-fourths of their number. I have read much in papers, as also in a contribution to the *Hindustan Review* by Mr. Abbas Tyabji, of the soundness of the safeguard this Article provides for the protection of minorities. It is with the greatest deference to the framers of that Article and its admirers that I venture to point out that this safeguard does not count for much as long as the number of delegates to the Congress is not fixed, and as long as the minorities do not have their own denominational electoral colleges. For it is quite obvious that when an unlimited number of delegates are permitted to attend the Congress, the few simple souls of our community who may join the Congress with the genuine desire of serving Indian Musalmans in that body may find themselves swamped by their own co-religionists, no doubt, but mandatories of non-Muslim electorates. For the principle of the protection of minorities, it is necessary that a minority should feel and enjoy absolute security in its own solidarity, which is impossible without a denominational basis. I believe this was recognized in the scheme of the reform of Councils, and therefore a separate electorate for the Musalmans was considered necessary. Once the Congress Convention has recognized the wisdom of the unqualified protection of the minorities, I have no doubt it will see the necessity of carrying Article XXVI to its logical conclusion.

It seems to me therefore, gentlemen, that should the Indian National Congress in the two particulars mentioned above, the one of the policy underlying the abandonment of an unrealizable ideal and the other of the procedure affecting the protection of minorities, be pleased to reconsider its position, there is every hope that the aspiration of the All-India Muslim League—United India—may be realized in the near future. It is then alone that Mohammedans can work with Hindus on non-controversial lines. I may take the liberty of mentioning that we have made a beginning in this direction in Bihar, and that the Bihar Provincial Conference held last April at Patna brought Hindus and Mohammedans together because it resolved to work on a non-controversial and practical basis. Gentlemen, should my feeble voice ever reach the ears of such stalwart leaders of the Indian National Congress as Sir Pherozeshah Mehta, Mr. Gokhale and Dr. Rash Behari Ghose, I pray them to believe in the earnestness of my appeal. The creed of the All-India Muslim League is co-operation with the rulers, co-operation with our non-Muslim countrymen and solidarity amongst ourselves. This is our idea of United India.

Gentlemen, I fear I have already trespassed too long on your patience, but I cannot close my address without an appeal to all my Musalman brethren of India, of whatever persuasion they may be, that the one paramount duty they owe to their king, country and themselves is the maintenance of a strong and powerful solidarity within their own community. We must not forget that division amongst ourselves means sacrifice and surrender of our political position. Gentlemen, if you desire your voice to be heard in the land, you must strive for and maintain unity amongst yourselves. The Government and your non-Muslim countrymen have equal need of your services. It is your duty to support and uphold the Government in the measures it has adopted to stamp out lawlessness, sedition and anarchism. It is your duty equally to co-operate with your non-Muslim countrymen in praying Government to inaugurate a policy of steady reform and courageous conciliation consistent with the dignity and integrity of British control. Gentlemen, the country is passing through the throes of a political convulsion. Of all times, this is the one when, in serving the best interests of the country, you should stand together and make your presence felt in the proper and happy adjustment of the relations between the rulers and the ruled. Can you do so without unity amongst yourselves? Without an absolute political solidarity your position is full of peril, and I implore you to unite to exist.

Gentlemen, the last Despatch of Lord Morley to His Excellency the Viceroy on the scheme of the Reform of Councils, seems to overlook the principle that representation to minorities must have its origin in a denominational basis from the very start to finish, from the first voting unit to the elected representative. Without this the Musalmans cannot hope to secure the true protection which their interests demand. Hasty expression to my views on this Despatch, received last week, I hesitate to give; but the principle involved is of vital consequences to our community, and a united expression of our views alone can save us from the perils of imperfection contained in the Despatch. Gentlemen, I again call upon you to unite. It is a solemn and sacred duty you owe to yourself and to your posterity.

Notes

Chapter 1: The Seeds of Pakistan

1. Qeyamuddin Ahmad, *The Wahabi Movement in India*, 3rd edition, Firma K.L. Mukhopadhyay, Calcutta, 1966.
2. Barbara D. Metcalf, *Islamic Revival in British India: Deoband, 1860–1900*, Princeton University Press, 1982, p. 25.
3. Qeyamuddin Ahmad, *The Wahabi Movement in India*, 3rd edition, Firma K.L. Mukhopadhyay, Calcutta, 1966, p. 13.
4. Ibid., p. 17.
5. Ahmad Dallal, 'The Origins and Objectives of Islamic Revivalist Thought, 1750–1850', *Journal of the American Oriental Society*, July–September 1993, vol. 113, no. 3, pp. 341–359, p. 341.
6. Charles Allen, 'The Hidden Roots of Wahhabism in British India', *World Policy Journal*, Summer 2005, vol. 22, no. 2, Duke University Press, pp. 87–93.
7. Saiyid Athar Abbas Rizvi, *Shah Wali Ullah and His Times*, Ma'rifat Publishing House, Australia, 1980, p. 215.
8. Noor Mohammad, 'The Doctrine of Jihad: An Introduction', *Journal of Law and Religion*, 1985, vol. 3, no. 2, Cambridge University Press, pp. 381–397, p. 393.
9. Ahmad Dallal, 'The Origins and Objectives of Islamic Revivalist Thought, 1750–1850', *Journal of the American Oriental Society*, July–September 1993, vol. 113, no. 3, pp. 341–359, p. 341.
10. Ibn Taymiyya, 'Rulings of Fighting the Mongols', *Fatawa*, 28/524, as quoted in 'Understanding History's Seven Stages of Jihad', Sebastian Gorka, *CTC Sentinel*, October 2009, vol. 2, no. 10. https://Ctc.Usma.Edu/Understanding-Historys-Seven-Stages-Of-Jihad/
11. Ira M. Lapidus, 'Islamic Revival and Modernity: The Contemporary Movements and the Historical Paradigms', *Journal of the Economic and Social History of the Orient*, 1997, vol. 40, no. 4, pp. 444–460.
12. S.A.A. Rizvi, *Shah Wali-Allah and His Times: A Study of Eighteenth Century Islam, Polities and Society in India*, Ma'rifat Publishing House, Australia, 1980.
13. Ayesha Jalal, *Partisans of Allah: Jihad in South Asia*, Harvard University Press, London, 2008.
14. Barbara D. Metcalf, *Islamic Revival in British India: Deoband, 1860–1900*, Princeton University Press, 1982.

15. A.J. Halepota, 'Shāh Waliyullāh and Iqbāl, The Philosophers of Modern Age', *Islamic Studies*, December 1974, vol. 13, no. 4, Islamic Research Institute, International Islamic University, Islamabad, pp. 225–233.

16. Vasileios Syros, 'An Early Modern South Asian Thinker on the Rise and Decline of Empires: Shah Wali Allah of Delhi, the Mughals, and the Byzantines', *Journal of World History*, December 2012, vol. 23, no. 4, pp. 793–840.

17. Alan M. Guenther, 'Hanafi Fiqh in Mughal India: The Fatāwā-I Ālamgīrī', in *India's Islamic Traditions 711–1750*, ed. Richard Eaton, Oxford University Press of India, New Delhi, 2003, pp. 209–233.

18. Saiyid Athar Abbas Rizvi, *Shah Wali Ullah and His Times*, Ma'rifat Publishing House, Australia, 1980, pp. 294–295.

19. Ibid., p. 299.

20. M.A. Karandikar, *Islam in India's Transition to Modernity*, Orient Longmans Limited, Bombay, 1968, p. 127.

21. J.M.S. Baljon, *Religion and Thought of Shah Wali Allah Dihlawi: 1703–1762*, Leiden, Brill, 1986, pp. 1–2.

22. Barbara D. Metcalf, *Islamic Revival in British India: Deoband, 1860–1900*, Princeton University Press, 1982, p. 55.

23. R. Upadhyay, 'Shah Wali Ullah's Political Thought. Still a Major Obstacle against Modernisation of Indian Muslims', 2003. *Source:* http://Www.Saag. Org/Papers7/Paper629.Html >

24. T.G. Percival Spear, *A History of India. Vol. 2: From the Sixteenth Century to the Twentieth Century*, Harmondsworth: Penguin Books, 1990, p. 224.

25. Arshad Islam, 'Shah Wali Allah Dehlavi: Some Aspects of His Life and Works (1703–1762)', *Journal of the Pakistan Historical Society*, 2004, vol. 52, no. 3, pp. 81–110, p. 91.

26. M.A. Karandikar, *Islam in India's Transition to Modernity*, Orient Longmans Limited, Bombay, 1968, p. 127.

27. Ayesha Jalal, *Partisans of Allah: Jihad in South Asia*, Harvard University Press, London, 2008, pp. 40–41.

28. Shah Waliullah, *Hujjut Allah Al-Baligha*, Urdu, trans. Maulana Mohammed Manzur Al-Wajaidi, Lahore: Sheikh Ghulam Ali and Sons, N.D., pp. 895–896. Henceforth Waliullah, Hujjat (Urdu), as quoted in *Partisans of Allah: Jihad in South Asia*, by Ayesha Jalal.

29. Qeyamuddin Ahmad, *The Wahabi Movement in India*, 3rd edition, Firma K.L. Mukhopadhyay, Calcutta, 1966, p. 12.

30. Ira M. Lapidus, 'Islamic Revival and Modernity: The Contemporary Movements and the Historical Paradigms', *Journal of the Economic and Social History of the Orient*, 1997, vol. 40, no. 4, pp. 444–460, p. 455.

31. Saiyid Athar Abbas Rizvi, *Shah Wali Ullah and His Times*, Ma'rifat Publishing House, Australia, 1980, p. 293.

32. Ibid., p. 294.

33. Ibid., p. 295.

34. Ibid., p. 294.

35. Ibid., p. 295.

36. Ibid., p. 296.

37. Ibid., p. 302.

38. *Shāh Valī Dihlavī ke Siyāsī Maktūbāt*, ed. Khalid A. Nizami, Nadvat Al-Musannifin, Delhi, pp. 15, 52.

39. Saiyid Athar Abbas Rizvi, *Shah Wali Ullah and His Times*, Ma'rifat Publishing House, Australia, 1980, pp. 303–304.

40. Ibid., p. 305.

41. Ibid.

42. Ibid., p. 306.

43. Ibid., p. 307.

44. Govind Sakharam Sardesai, *New History of the Marathas*, Volume 2, Pheonix Publications, Bombay, 1948, pp. 447–448.

45. Barbara D. Metcalf, *Islamic Revival in British India: Deoband, 1860–1900*, Princeton University Press, 1982, p. 46.

46. Syed Tanvir Wasti, 'The Political Aspirations of Indian Muslims and the Ottoman Nexus', *Middle Eastern Studies*, September 2006, Taylor and Francis, vol. 42, no. 5, pp. 709–722, p. 709.

47. Bashir Ahmad Khan, 'The Forgotten Soul of the Resistance Movement: Maulana Syed Mohammad Nazir Hussain Muhaddith Dehlavi', (1220/1805–1320/1902), *Proceedings of the Indian History Congress*, Diamond Jubilee, 1999, Page Publishing, vol. 60, pp. 507–520, p. 507.

48. Qeyamuddin Ahmad, *The Wahabi Movement in India*, 3rd edition, Firma K.L. Mukhopadhyay, Calcutta, 1966, p. 68.

49. R.C. Majumdar, *History of the Freedom Movement in India*, Volume 1, 2nd edition, Firma K.L. Mukhopadhyay, Calcutta, 1971, p. 116.

50. Ibid., p. 117.

51. Ayesha Jalal, *Partisans of Allah: Jihad in South Asia*, Harvard University Press, London, 2008, p. 138.

52. Ibid.

53. R.C. Majumdar, *History of the Freedom Movement in India*, Volume 1, 2nd edition, Firma K.L. Mukhopadhyay, Calcutta, 1971, p. 117.

54. Qeyamuddin Ahmad, *The Wahabi Movement in India*, 3rd edition, Firma K.L. Mukhopadhyay, Calcutta, 1966, p. 94.

55. R.C. Majumdar, *History of the Freedom Movement in India*, Volume 1, 2nd edition, Firma K.L. Mukhopadhyay, Calcutta, 1971, p. 118.

56. Ibid.

57. Tara Chand, *History of the Freedom Movement in India*, Volume 2, Ministry of Education, Government of India, 1967, p. 12.

58. Qeyamuddin Ahmad, *The Wahabi Movement in India*, 3rd edition, Firma K.L. Mukhopadhyay, Calcutta, 1966, p. 94.

59. Ibid., pp. 88–89.

60. Sana Haroon, 'Reformism and Orthodox Practice in Early Nineteenth-Century Muslim North India: Sayyid Ahmed Shaheed Reconsidered', *Journal of the Royal Asiatic Society*, April 2011, Third Series, vol. 21, no. 2, Cambridge University Press on Behalf of the Royal Asiatic Society of Great Britain and Ireland, pp. 177–199, p. 180.

61. Abdullah Khan, *The Religious Thought of Shah Ismail Dihlawi*, MA dissertation, Institute of Islamic Studies, McGill University, Montreal, 1984, p. 2.

62. Maulana Syed Abul Hasan Ali Nadwi, *Life Sketch of Syed Ahmed Shahid*, Board of Islamic Studies, Indore, 1974.

63. Abdullah Khan, *The Religious Thought of Shah Ismail Dihlawi*, MA dissertation, Institute of Islamic Studies, McGill University, Montreal, 1984, p. 4.

64. Qeyamuddin Ahmad, *The Wahabi Movement in India*, 3rd edition, Firma K.L. Mukhopadhyay, Calcutta, 1966, pp. 25–26.

65. Maulana Syed Abul Hasan Ali Nadwi, *Life Sketch of Syed Ahmed Shahid*, Board of Islamic Studies, Indore, 1974, p. 7.

66. Abdullah Khan, *The Religious Thought of Shah Ismail Dihlawi*, MA dissertation, Institute of Islamic Studies, McGill University, Montreal, 1984, p. 5.

67. W.W. Hunter, *The Indian Musalmans*, 3rd edition, Trubner and Company, London, 1976, p. 12.

68. Qeyamuddin Ahmad, *The Wahabi Movement in India*, 3rd edition, Firma K.L. Mukhopadhyay, Calcutta, 1966, p. 25.

69. Ibid., p. 27.

70. Barbara D. Metcalf, *Islamic Revival in British India: Deoband, 1860–1900*, Princeton University Press, 1982, p. 52.

71. Altaf Qadir and Naseem Khattak, 'Roving Preachers, Fund Raising and Jihad: Organization of the Mujahidin Movement in Northern India (1830s–1858)', *Journal of the Research Society of Pakistan*, 2015, vol. 52, no. 1, pp. 211–223.

72. Barbara D. Metcalf, *Islamic Revival in British India: Deoband, 1860–1900*, Princeton University Press, 1982, p. 55.

73. H.V. Seshadri, *The Tragic Story of Partition*, 2nd edition, Jagarana Prakashana, Bangalore, 1982, p. 22.

74. Hafeez Malik, *Sir Sayyid Ahmed Khan and Muslim Modernization in India and Pakistan*, Columbia University Press, New York, 1980, p. 261.

75. Sana Haroon, 'The Rise of Deobandi Islam in the North-West Frontier Province and Its Implications in Colonial India and Pakistan 1914–1996', *Journal of the Royal Asiatic Society*, January 2008, Third Series, vol. 18, no. 1, Cambridge University Press on behalf of the Royal Asiatic Society of Great Britain and Ireland, pp. 47–70, p. 48.

76. Barbara D. Metcalf, *Islamic Revival in British India: Deoband, 1860–1900*, Princeton University Press, 1982, p. 59.

77. Qeyamuddin Ahmad, *The Wahabi Movement in India*, 3rd edition, Firma K.L. Mukhopadhyay, Calcutta, 1966, p. 28.

78. Azimabad, which was named after Aurangzeb's favourite grandson, Azim, who was the Subahdar of the region, is now known as Patna.

79. Maulana Syed Abul Hasan Ali Nadwi, *Life Sketch of Syed Ahmed Shahid*, Board of Islamic Studies, Indore, 1974, p. 9.

80. W.W. Hunter, *The Indian Musalmans*, 3rd edition, Trubner and Company, London, 1976, p. 12.

81. Maulana Syed Abul Hasan Ali Nadwi, *Life Sketch of Syed Ahmed Shahid*, Board of Islamic Studies, Indore, 1974, p. 10.

82. Qeyamuddin Ahmad, *The Wahabi Movement in India*, 3rd edition, Firma K.L. Mukhopadhyay, Calcutta, 1966, p. 30.

83. Ibid., p. 31.

84. W.W. Hunter, *The Indian Musalmans*, 3rd edition, Trubner and Company, London, 1976, p. 13.

85. Altaf Qadir and Naseem Khattak, 'Roving Preachers, Fund Raising and Jihad: Organization of the Mujahidin Movement in Northern India (1830s–1858)', *Journal of the Research Society of Pakistan*, 2015, vol. 52, no. 1, pp. 211–223.

86. Maulana Syed Abul Hasan Ali Nadwi, *Life Sketch of Syed Ahmed Shahid*, Board of Islamic Studies, Indore, 1974, p. 11.

87. Ibid., p. 12.

88. Qeyamuddin Ahmad, *The Wahabi Movement in India*, 3rd edition, Firma K.L. Mukhopadhyay, Calcutta, 1966, p. 43.

89. Maulana Syed Abul Hasan Ali Nadwi, *Life Sketch of Syed Ahmed Shahid*, Board of Islamic Studies, Indore, 1974, p. 12.

90. Ibid., p. 13.

91. Shan Muhammad, *Muslims and India's Freedom Movement*, Institute of Objective Studies, University of Michigan, 2002, p. 11.

92. C. Mallampalli, *A Muslim Conspiracy in British India? Politics and Paranoia in the Early Nineteenth-Century Deccan*, Cambridge University Press, 2017, p. 66.

93. Qeyamuddin Ahmad, *The Wahabi Movement in India*, 3rd edition, Firma K.L. Mukhopadhyay, Calcutta, 1966, p. 124,

94. Girish Chandra Pandey, 'Revisiting the History and Nature of the Wahabi Movement (1826–1861)', *Proceedings of the Indian History Congress*, vol. 76, 2015, pp. 488–99.

95. Maulana Syed Abul Hasan Ali Nadwi, *Life Sketch of Syed Ahmed Shahid*, Board of Islamic Studies, Indore, 1974, p. 13.

96. Qeyamuddin Ahmad, *The Wahabi Movement in India*, 3rd edition, Firma K.L. Mukhopadhyay, Calcutta, 1966, pp. 31, 38,

97. Maulana Syed Abul Hasan Ali Nadwi, *Life Sketch of Syed Ahmed Shahid*, Board of Islamic Studies, Indore, 1974, p. 15.

98. Ibid., p. 5.

99. Qeyamuddin Ahmad, *The Wahabi Movement in India*, 3rd edition, Firma K.L. Mukhopadhyay, Calcutta, 1966, p. 46.

100. W.W. Hunter, *The Indian Musalmans*, 3rd edition, Trubner and Company, London, 1976, pp. 14–15.
101. Qeyamuddin Ahmad, *The Wahabi Movement in India*, 3rd edition, Firma K.L. Mukhopadhyay, Calcutta, 1966, p. 53.
102. Ibid.
103. W.W. Hunter, *The Indian Musalmans*, 3rd edition, Trubner and Company, London, 1976, p. 17.
104. Dr Sultan Mahmood, Hafiz Nasiruddin, Dr Muhammad Rizwan, 'Struggle for Islamic State and Society: An Analysis of Syed Ahmad Shaheed's Jihad Movement', *Pakistan Annual Research Journal*, 2014, vol. 50, p. 182.
105. W.W. Hunter, *The Indian Musalmans*, 3rd edition, Trubner and Company, London, 1976, p. 17.
106. Ibid., p. 18.
107. Qeyamuddin Ahmad, *The Wahabi Movement in India*, 3rd edition, Firma K.L. Mukhopadhyay, Calcutta, 1966, p. 56.
108. Ibid., p. 65.
109. Ayesha Jalal, *Partisans of Allah: Jihad in South Asia*, Harvard University Press, London, 2008, p. 1.
110. Qeyamuddin Ahmad, *The Wahabi Movement in India*, 3rd edition, Firma K.L. Mukhopadhyay, Calcutta, 1966, p. 79.
111. Ibid., p. 78.
112. W.W. Hunter, *The Indian Musalmans*, 3rd edition, Trubner and Company, London, 1976, p. 20.
113. Qeyamuddin Ahmad, *The Wahabi Movement in India*, 3rd edition, Firma K.L. Mukhopadhyay, Calcutta, 1966, p. 87.
114. Altaf Qadir and Naseem Khattak, 'Roving Preachers, Fund Raising and Jihad: Organization of the Mujahidin Movement in Northern India (1830s–1858)', *Journal of the Research Society of Pakistan*, 2015, vol. 52, no. 1, pp. 211–223, p. 212.
115. Qeyamuddin Ahmad, *The Wahabi Movement in India*, 3rd edition, Firma K.L. Mukhopadhyay, Calcutta, 1966, p. 105.
116. Altaf Qadir and Naseem Khattak, 'Roving Preachers, Fund Raising and Jihad: Organization of the Mujahidin Movement in Northern India (1830s–1858)', *Journal of the Research Society of Pakistan*, 2015, vol. 52, no. 1, pp. 211–223, pp. 212–213.
117. Ibid., pp. 216–218.
118. Qeyamuddin Ahmad, *The Wahabi Movement in India*, 3rd edition, Firma K.L. Mukhopadhyay, Calcutta, 1966, p. 107.
119. Ibid.
120. Ibid., p. 108.
121. Ibid., p. 109–110.
122. Ibid., p. 112.
123. Ibid., p. 113.

124. Ibid., p. 114.
125. W.W. Hunter, *The Indian Musalmans*, 3rd edition, Trubner and Company, London, 1976, p. 22.
126. Ibid.
127. Qeyamuddin Ahmad, *The Wahabi Movement in India*, 3rd edition, Firma K.L. Mukhopadhyay, Calcutta, 1966, p. 119.
128. Ibid., pp. 119–120.
129. Rajendra Prasad, *India Divided*, 3rd edition, Hind Kitabs Publisher, Bombay, 1947, p. 91.
130. Qeyamuddin Ahmad, *The Wahabi Movement in India*, 3rd edition, Firma K.L. Mukhopadhyay, Calcutta, 1966, pp. 228–229.
131. W.W. Hunter, *The Indian Musalmans*, 3rd edition, Trubner and Company, London, 1976, pp. 22–23.
132. Ibid., p. 23.
133. Qeyamuddin Ahmad, *The Wahabi Movement in India*, 3rd edition, Firma K.L. Mukhopadhyay, Calcutta, 1966, p. 121.
134. Ibid., p. 124.
135. R.C. Majumdar, *History of the Freedom Movement in India*, Volume 1, 2nd edition, Firma K.L. Mukhopadhyay, Calcutta, 1971, p. 249.
136. Qeyamuddin Ahmad, *The Wahabi Movement in India*, 3rd edition, Firma K.L. Mukhopadhyay, Calcutta, 1966, p. 226.
137. R.C. Majumdar, *History of the Freedom Movement in India*, Volume 1, 2nd edition, Firma K.L. Mukhopadhyay, Calcutta, 1971, p. 252.
138. Qeyamuddin Ahmad, *The Wahabi Movement in India*, 3rd edition, Firma K.L. Mukhopadhyay, Calcutta, 1966, p. 188.
139. W.W. Hunter, *The Indian Musalmans*, 3rd edition, Trubner and Company, London, 1976, p. 24.
140. Qeyamuddin Ahmad, *The Wahabi Movement in India*, 3rd edition, Firma K.L. Mukhopadhyay, Calcutta, 1966, p. 189.
141. W.W. Hunter, *The Indian Musalmans*, 3rd edition, Trubner and Company, London, 1976, p. 26.
142. Ibid., p. 27.
143. Qeyamuddin Ahmad, *The Wahabi Movement in India*, 3rd edition, Firma K.L. Mukhopadhyay, Calcutta, 1966, p. 208.
144. Ibid., p. 209.
145. Ibid., pp. 238–239.
146. W.W. Hunter, *The Indian Musalmans*, 3rd edition, Trubner and Company, London, 1976, p. 85.
147. Qeyamuddin Ahmad, *The Wahabi Movement in India*, 3rd edition, Firma K.L. Mukhopadhyay, Calcutta, 1966, p. 232.
148. Ibid., pp. 234–235.
149. Ibid., p. 243.

150. W.W. Hunter, *The Indian Musalmans*, 3rd edition, Trubner and Company, London, 1976, p. 105.

151. Ibid., p. 106.

152. Qeyamuddin Ahmad, *The Wahabi Movement in India*, 3rd edition, Firma K.L. Mukhopadhyay, Calcutta, 1966, p. 256.

153. Ibid., p. 273.

154. Ibid., p. 317.

155. Ibid., p. 318.

156. Lal Baha, 'The Activities of the Mujāhidīn 1900–1936', *Islamic Studies*, Summer 1979, vol. 18, no. 2, Islamic Research Institute, International Islamic University, Islamabad, pp. 97–168.

157. Aravind Ganachari, *Nationalism and Social Reform in Colonial Situation* (quoting Maharashtra State Archives, Judicial Department, 24 March 1869, vol. 14/767; no. A-52), Kalpaz Publications, Delhi, 2005, p. 56.

158. https://Eparlib.Nic.In/Bitstream/123456789/785236/1/Ilcd_25-11-1870. Pdf#Search=Null%20[1870%20TO%201879]

159. https://Eparlib.Nic.In/Bitstream/123456789/784022/1/Ilcd_18-February-1898.Pdf#Search=Null%20[1870%20TO%201898]

160. https://Eparlib.Nic.In/Bitstream/123456789/784962/1/Ilcd_5-March-1913.Pdf#Search=Wahabi%20[1913%20TO%201914]

161. https://www.constitutionofindia.net/constitution_assembly_debates/volume/7/1948-12-01

162. Qeyamuddin Ahmad, *The Wahabi Movement in India*, 3rd edition, Firma K.L. Mukhopadhyay, Calcutta, 1966, pp. 305–309.

163. R.C. Majumdar, *The History and Culture of the Indian People*, Volume X, *The British Paramountcy and the Indian Rennaisance*, Part II, 4th edition, Bharatiya Vidya Bhavan, 2007, p. 141.

164. Yusuf Abbasi, *Muslim Politics and Leadership in the South Asian Sub-continent 1876–1892*, 2nd edition, National Institute of Historical and Cultural Research, Islamabad, 2018, p. 6.

165. Barbara D. Metcalf, *Islamic Revival in British India: Deoband, 1860–1900*, Princeton University Press, 1982, p. 72.

166. Ayesha Jalal, *Partisans of Allah: Jihad in South Asia*, Harvard University Press, London, 2008, p. 123.

167. Ibid., p. 146.

168. Barbara D. Metcalf, *Islamic Revival in British India: Deoband, 1860–1900*, Princeton University Press, 1982, p. 72.

169. Bashir Ahmad Khan, 'The Forgotten Soul of the Resistance Movement: Maulana Syed Mohammad Nazir Hussain Muhaddith Dehlavi', (1220/1805–1320/1902), *Proceedings of the Indian History Congress*, 1999, vol. 60, Diamond Jubilee, 1999, pp. 507–520.

170. Bashir Ahmad Khan, '"Wahabi" to "Ahl-I-Hadith": A Historical Analysis', *Proceedings of the Indian History Congress, 2000–2001*, vol. 61, Part One: Millennium (2000–2001), pp. 747–760.

171. Ayesha Jalal, *Partisans of Allah: Jihad in South Asia*, Harvard University Press, London, 2008, p. 145.

172. Ibid., p. 116.

173. Ibid., p. 145.

174. Ibid., p. 146.

175. Charles Allen, 'The Hidden Roots of Wahhabism in British India', *World Policy Journal*, Summer 2005, vol. 22, no. 2, Duke University Press, pp. 87–93, p. 92.

176. Ayesha Jalal, *Partisans of Allah: Jihad in South Asia*, Harvard University Press, London, 2008, p. 280.

177. Sayyid Mahboob Rizvi, *History of the Dar al-Ulum Deoband*, Maulana Abdul Haq, Idara-e-Ihtemam, Dar Al-Ulum, Deoband, Uttar Pradesh, 1980.

178. Sana Haroon, 'The Rise of Deobandi Islam in the North-West Frontier Province and Its Implications in Colonial India and Pakistan 1914–1996', *Journal of the Royal Asiatic Society*, January 2008, Third Series, vol. 18, no. 1, Cambridge University Press on behalf of the Royal Asiatic Society of Great Britain and Ireland, pp. 47–70, pp. 47–50.

179. Ibid.

180. Ibid., p. 49.

181. Ibid., p. 51.

182. Ibid., p. 52.

183. Ibid., p. 55.

184. Ibid.

185. Ibid., p. 57.

186. Ayesha Jalal, *Partisans of Allah: Jihad in South Asia*, Harvard University Press, London, 2008, p. 276.

187. Ibid.

188. Ibid., p. 274.

189. Ibid., p. 279.

190. Ibid., p. 267.

191. Ibid., p. 268.

192. Ibid., p. 242.

193. Ibid., p. 248.

194. Ibid., p. 247.

195. Ibid., p. 249.

196. Ibid., p. 252.

197. Ibid., p. 260.

198. Ibid., p. 274.

199. Charles Allen, 'The Hidden Roots of Wahhabism in British India', *World Policy Journal*, Summer, 2005, vol. 22, no. 2, Duke University Press, pp. 87–93, p. 93.

200. R.C. Majumdar, *The History and Culture of the Indian People*, Volume X, *British Paramountcy and the Indian Rennaisance*, Part II, 4th edition, Bharatiya Vidya Bhavan, 2007, p. 142.

201. Ayesha Jalal, *Partisans of Allah: Jihad in South Asia*, Harvard University Press, London, 2008, p. 146.

202. Ibid.

203. Barbara D. Metcalf, *Islamic Revival in British India: Deoband, 1860–1900*, Princeton University Press, 1982, p. 297.

204. Ibid., pp. 335–36.

205. Ibid., p. 337.

206. Ibid., pp. 338–39.

207. Ibid., p. 339.

208. Ibid., p. 344.

209. Ibid., p. 352.

210. Ayesha Jalal, *Partisans of Allah: Jihad in South Asia*, Harvard University Press, London, 2008, p. 162, pp. 308–309.

211. Ibid., p. 166.

212. Ibid., p. 164.

213. Ibid., p. 163.

214. Barbara D. Metcalf, *Islamic Revival in British India: Deoband, 1860–1900*, Princeton University Press, 1982, pp. 313–314.

Chapter 2: Syed Ahmed Khan, the Aligarh Movement and the Two-Nation Theory

1. Aziz Ahmad, 'Sayyid Aḥmad Khān, Jamāl al-dīn al-Afghānī and Muslim India', *Studia Islamica*, 1960, no. 13, pp. 55–78, p. 57.

2. Barbara D. Metcalf, *Islamic Revival in British India: Deoband, 1860–1900*, Princeton University Press, 1982, p. 315.

3. R.C. Majumdar, *The History and Culture of the Indian People*, Volume X, *British Paramountcy and Indian Renaissance*, Part II, 4th edition, Bharatiya Vidya Bhavan, 2007, p. 297–98.

4. Ibid., p. 298

5. Yusuf Abbasi, *Muslim Politics and Leadership in the South Asian Sub-continent 1876–1892*, National Institute of Historical and Cultural Research, Islamabad, 2018, p. 14.

6. Barbara D. Metcalf, *Islamic Revival in British India: Deoband, 1860–1900*, Princeton University Press, 1982, p. 70.

7. Yusuf Abbasi, *Muslim Politics and Leadership in the South Asian Sub-continent 1876–1892*, National Institute of Historical and Cultural Research, Islamabad, 2018, p. 15–18.

8. Syed Tanvir Wasti, 'Sir Syed Ahmad Khan and the Turks', *Middle Eastern Studies*, July 2010, vol. 46, no. 4, pp. 529–542.

9. Barbara D. Metcalf, *Islamic Revival in British India: Deoband, 1860–1900*, Princeton University Press, 1982, p. 317.

10. Aziz Ahmad, 'Sayyid Aḥmad Khān, Jamāl al-dīn al-Afghānī and Muslim India', *Studia Islamica*, 1960, no. 13, pp. 55–78, p. 57.

11. Ibid., footnote 1.

12. G.F.I. Graham, *The Life and Work of Syed Ahmed Khan*, William Blackwood and Sons, 1885, p. 1.

13. Barbara D. Metcalf, *Islamic Revival in British India: Deoband, 1860–1900*, Princeton University Press, 1982, p. 318.

14. G.F.I. Graham, *The Life and Work of Syed Ahmed Khan*, William Blackwood and Sons, 1885, p. 7.

15. Barbara D. Metcalf, *Islamic Revival in British India: Deoband, 1860–1900*, Princeton University Press, 1982, p. 318.

16. Shamim Akhtar, 'Evolution of Syed Ahmad Khan's Religious Thought: A Note', *Proceedings of the Indian History Congress*, 2012, vol. 73, pp. 1012–1015.

17. Ibid., p. 1013.

18. Ibid., p. 1012.

19. Barbara D. Metcalf, *Islamic Revival in British India: Deoband, 1860–1900*, Princeton University Press, 1982, p. 318.

20. Ayesha Jalal, *Partisans of Allah: Jihad in South Asia*, Harvard University Press, London, 2008, p. 167.

21. M.S. Jain, *The Aligarh Movement, Its Origin and Development (1858–1906)*, Shri Ram Mehra & Co. Publishers, Agra, 1965, p. 10.

22. Barbara D. Metcalf, *Islamic Revival in British India: Deoband, 1860–1900*, Princeton University Press, 1982, p. 318.

23. G.F.I. Graham, *The Life and Work of Syed Ahmed Khan*, William Blackwood and Sons, 1885, p. 36.

24. Yusuf Abbasi, *Muslim Politics and Leadership in the South Asian Sub-continent 1876–1892*, National Institute of Historical and Cultural Research, Islamabad, 2018, p. 6.

25. Ayesha Jalal, *Partisans of Allah: Jihad in South Asia*, Harvard University Press, London, 2008, p. 132.

26. G.F.I. Graham, *The Life and Work of Syed Ahmed Khan*, William Blackwood and Sons, 1885, p. 35.

27. Ibid., p. 39.

28. Ayesha Jalal, *Partisans of Allah: Jihad in South Asia*, Harvard University Press, London, 2008, p. 134.

29. M.S. Jain, *The Aligarh Movement, Its Origin and Development (1858–1906)*, Shri Ram Mehra & Co. Publishers, Agra, 1965, p. 12.

30. Peter Hardy, *The Muslims of British India*, Cambridge University Press, 1972, p. 67.

31. G.F.I. Graham, *The Life and Work of Syed Ahmed Khan*, William Blackwood and Sons, 1885, p. 19.

32. Ayesha Jalal, *Partisans of Allah: Jihad in South Asia*, Harvard University Press, London, 2008, p. 133.

33. M.S. Jain, *The Aligarh Movement, Its Origin and Development (1858–1906)*, Shri Ram Mehra & Co. Publishers, Agra, 1965, p. 9.

34. G.F.I. Graham, *The Life and Work of Syed Ahmed Khan*, William Blackwood and Sons, 1885, p. 59.

35. M.S. Jain, *The Aligarh Movement, Its Origin and Development (1858–1906)*, Shri Ram Mehra & Co. Publishers, Agra, 1965, p. 18.

36. Barbara D. Metcalf, *Islamic Revival in British India: Deoband, 1860–1900*, Princeton University Press, 1982, p. 319.

37. Ayesha Jalal, *Partisans of Allah: Jihad in South Asia*, Harvard University Press, London, 2008, p. 151.

38. Yusuf Abbasi, *Muslim Politics and Leadership in the South Asian Sub-continent 1876–1892*, National Institute of Historical and Cultural Research, Islamabad, 2018, p. 19.

39. Ibid.

40. Barbara D. Metcalf, *Islamic Revival in British India: Deoband, 1860–1900*, Princeton University Press, 1982, p. 321.

41. Ibid., p. 322.

42. Ibid.

43. Ibid., 323.

44. M.S. Jain, *The Aligarh Movement, Its Origin and Development (1858–1906)*, Shri Ram Mehra & Co. Publishers, Agra, 1965, pp. 16–17.

45. Arun Shourie, Harsh Narain, Jay Dubashi, Ram Swarup, and Sita Ram Goel, *Hindu Temples: What Happened to Them? A Preliminary Survey*, Volume 1, Voice of India, New Delhi, 1990, p. 1.

46. Ayesha Jalal, *Partisans of Allah: Jihad in South Asia*, Harvard University Press, London, 2008, p. 168.

47. M.S. Jain, *The Aligarh Movement, Its Origin and Development (1858–1906)*, Shri Ram Mehra & Co. Publishers, Agra, 1965, p. 27.

48. Barbara D. Metcalf, *Islamic Revival in British India: Deoband, 1860–1900*, Princeton University Press, 1982, p. 325.

49. M.S. Jain, *The Aligarh Movement, Its Origin and Development (1858–1906)*, Shri Ram Mehra & Co. Publishers, Agra, 1965, p. 37.

50. G.F.I. Graham, *The Life and Work of Syed Ahmed Khan*, William Blackwood and Sons, 1885, p. 252.

51. Ibid., p. 326,

52. Yusuf Abbasi, *Muslim Politics and Leadership in the South Asian Sub-continent 1876–1892*, National Institute of Historical and Cultural Research, Islamabad, 2018, p. 42.

53. M.S. Jain, *The Aligarh Movement, Its Origin and Development (1858–1906)*, Shri Ram Mehra & Co. Publishers, Agra, 1965, p. 37.

54. R.C. Majumdar, *The History and Culture of the Indian People*, Volume X, *British Paramountcy and Indian Renaissance*, Part II, 4th edition, Bharatiya Vidya Bhavan, 2007, p. 306.

55. Ibid., p. 312.

56. Ibid.

57. Ibid., p. 313.

58. Ibid.

59. Yusuf Abbasi, *Muslim Politics and Leadership in the South Asian Sub-continent 1876–1892*, National Institute of Historical and Cultural Research, Islamabad, 2018, p. 59.

60. M.S. Jain, *The Aligarh Movement, Its Origin and Development (1858–1906)*, Shri Ram Mehra & Co. Publishers, Agra, 1965, p. 50.

61. Ibid., p. 26.

62. Yusuf Abbasi, *Muslim Politics and Leadership in the South Asian Sub-continent 1876–1892*, National Institute of Historical and Cultural Research, Islamabad, 2018, p. 45.

63. Barbara D. Metcalf, *Islamic Revival in British India: Deoband, 1860–1900*, Princeton University Press, 1982, pp. 333–334.

64. G.F.I. Graham, *The Life and Work of Syed Ahmed Khan*, William Blackwood and Sons, 1885, pp. 54–55.

65. Sharif Al Mujahid, 'Sir Syed Ahmad Khan and Muslim Nationalism in India', *Islamic Studies*, Spring 1999, vol. 38, no. 1, Islamic Research Institute, International Islamic University, Islamabad, pp. 87–101.

66. Arshi Siddiqui and Ismail Siddiqui, 'Usage of Urdu as the Language of Elitism among the Muslims of the Northern and the Deccan Parts of India: A Socio-Cultural Review', *Middle Eastern Journal of Research in Education and Social Sciences (MEJRESS)*, vol. 1, no. 2, 2020, p. 110.

67. Ibid.

68. M.S. Jain, *The Aligarh Movement, Its Origin and Development (1858-1906)*, Shri Ram Mehra & Co. Publishers, Agra, 1965, p. 50.

69. R.C. Majumdar, *The History and Culture of the Indian People*, Volume X, *British Paramountcy and Indian Renaissance*, Part II, 4th edition, Bharatiya Vidya Bhavan, 2007, p. 305.

70. Ibid., p. 311.

71. Ibid., p. 310.

72. Ibid., pp. 310–311.

73. Ibid., p. 317.

74. Ibid., p. 314.

75. http://www.columbia.edu/itc/mealac/pritchett/00islamlinks/txt_sir_sayyid_lucknow_1887.html

76. R.C. Majumdar, *The History and Culture of the Indian People*, Volume X, *British Paramountcy and Indian Renaissance*, Part II, 4th edition, Bharatiya Vidya Bhavan, 2007, p. 309

77. http://www.columbia.edu/itc/mealac/pritchett/00islamlinks/txt_sir_sayyid_meerut_1888.html

78. R.C. Majumdar, *The History and Culture of the Indian People*, Volume X, *British Paramountcy and Indian Renaissance*, Part II, 4th edition, Bharatiya Vidya Bhavan, 2007, p. 314.

79. Sharif Al Mujahid, 'Sir Syed Ahmad Khan and Muslim Nationalism in India', *Islamic Studies*, Spring 1999, vol. 38, no. 1, Islamic Research Institute, International Islamic University, Islamabad, p. 89.

80. *The Indian National Congress*, G.A. Natesan & Co. Madras, 1910, pp. 32–33.

81. R.C. Majumdar, *The History and Culture of the Indian People*, Volume X, *British Paramountcy and Indian Renaissance*, Part II, 4th edition, Bharatiya Vidya Bhavan, 2007, p. 316.

82. Ibid., pp. 316–317.

83. Ibid., p. 309.

84. Syed Tanvir Wasti, 'Sir Syed Ahmad Khan and the Turks', *Middle Eastern Studies*, July 2010, vol. 46, no. 4, pp. 529–542, p. 533.

85. Aziz Ahmad, 'Sayyid Aḥmad Khān, Jamāl al-dīn al-Afghānī and Muslim India', *Studia Islamica*, 1960, no. 13, pp. 55–78, p. 65.

86. Syed Tanvir Wasti, 'Sir Syed Ahmad Khan and the Turks', *Middle Eastern Studies*, July 2010, vol. 46, no. 4, pp. 529–542, p. 531.

87. Ibid., p. 532.

88. Ibid., p. 536.

89. Ibid., p. 533.

90. Ibid., p. 534.

91. A. Ahmad, *Islamic Modernism in India and Pakistan 1857–1964*, Oxford University Press, Oxford, 1967, p. 126.

92. R.C. Majumdar, *The History and Culture of the Indian People*, Volume X, *British Paramountcy and Indian Renaissance*, Part II, 4th edition, Bharatiya Vidya Bhavan, 2007, p. 304.

93. Aziz Ahmad, 'Sayyid Aḥmad Khān, Jamāl al-dīn al-Afghānī and Muslim India', *Studia Islamica*, 1960, no. 13, pp. 55–78.

94. Nikki R. Keddie, *Sayyid Jamal al-Din al-Afghani, A Political Biography*, University of California Press, 1972, pp. 10–11.

95. Ibid., pp. 23–24.

96. Aziz Ahmad, 'Afghani's Indian Contacts', *Journal of the American Oriental Society*, July–September 1969, vol. 89, no. 3, pp. 476–504.

97. Nikki R. Keddie, *Sayyid Jamal al-Din al-Afghani, A Political Biography*, University of California Press, 1972, pp. 26–28.

98. Sharif al-Mujahid, *Sayyid Jamal al-Din al-Afghani: His Role in the Nineteenth Century Muslim Awakening*, McGill University, 1954, p. 50.

99. Ibid., pp. 57–58.

100. Nikki R. Keddie, *Sayyid Jamal al-Din al-Afghani, A Political Biography*, University of California Press, 1972, p. 39.

101. Ibid., p. 40.

102. Ibid., p. 58.

103. Ayesha Jalal, *Partisans of Allah: Jihad in South Asia*, Harvard University Press, London, 2008, p. 184.

104. Ibid., p. 185.
105. Nikki R. Keddie, *Sayyid Jamal al-Din al-Afghani, A Political Biography*, University of California Press, 1972, p. 59.
106. Ibid., pp. 68–70.
107. Ibid., p. 17.
108. Andrew C. Hess, 'The Ottoman Conquest of Egypt (1517) and the Beginning of the Sixteenth-Century World War', *International Journal of Middle East Studies*, 1973, vol. 4, no. 1, pp. 55–76.
109. Nikki R. Keddie, *Sayyid Jamal al-Din al-Afghani, A Political Biography*, University of California Press, 1972, p. 19.
110. Ibid., p. 20.
111. Aziz Ahmad, 'Sayyid Aḥmad Khān, Jamāl al-dīn al-Afghānī and Muslim India', *Studia Islamica*, 1960, no. 13, pp. 55–78, p. 55.
112. Nikki R. Keddie, *An Islamic Response to Imperialism: Political and Religious Writings of Sayyid Jamal al-Din al-Afghani*, University of California Press, 1968, p. 21.
113. Ibid., p. 21.
114. Ibid., p. 53.
115. Ayesha Jalal, *Partisans of Allah: Jihad in South Asia*, Harvard University Press, London, 2008, p. 186.
116. Aziz Ahmad, 'Sayyid Aḥmad Khān, Jamāl al-dīn al-Afghānī and Muslim India', *Studia Islamica*, 1960, no. 13, pp. 55–78, p. 65.
117. Ibid., p. 71.
118. Nikki R. Keddie, *Sayyid Jamal al-Din al-Afghani, A Political Biography*, University of California Press, 1972, pp. 148–152.
119. Nikki R. Keddie, *An Islamic Response to Imperialism: Political and Religious Writings of Sayyid Jamal al-Din al-Afghani*, University of California Press, 1968, p. 101.
120. Ayesha Jalal, *Partisans of Allah: Jihad in South Asia*, Harvard University Press, London, 2008, p. 189.
121. Nikki R. Keddie, 'The Pan-Islamic Appeal: Afghani and Abdülhamid II', *Middle Eastern Studies*, October 1966, vol. 3, no. 1, pp. 46–67, p. 54.
122. Ibid., p. 65.
123. Ayesha Jalal, *Partisans of Allah: Jihad in South Asia*, Harvard University Press, London, 2008, p. 189.
124. Aziz Ahmad, 'Sayyid Aḥmad Khān, Jamāl al-dīn al-Afghānī and Muslim India', *Studia Islamica*, 1960, no. 13, pp. 55–78, p. 69.
125. Ibid.
126. Ayesha Jalal, *Partisans of Allah: Jihad in South Asia*, Harvard University Press, London, 2008, pp. 191–192.
127. Aziz Ahmad, 'Sayyid Aḥmad Khān, Jamāl al-dīn al-Afghānī and Muslim India', *Studia Islamica*, 1960, no. 13, pp. 55–78, pp. 69–70.

Chapter 3: The Partition of Bengal (1899–1905)

1. Amalendu De, *Roots of Separatism in Nineteenth Century Bengal*, Ratna Prakashan, Calcutta, 1974, p. 21.
2. Ibid., p. 22.
3. Ibid., p. 23.
4. Ibid.
5. Ibid.
6. Ibid., p. 24.
7. Ibid., p. 25.
8. Ibid.
9. Ibid., p. 26.
10. Ibid., p. 27.
11. Ibid., p. 31.
12. Ibid., p. 32.
13. Ibid.
14. Ibid., p. 33.
15. Amalendu De, 'The Social Thoughts and Consciousness of the Bengali Muslims in the Colonial Period', *Social Scientist*, April –June 1995, vol. 23, no. 4/6, pp. 16–37, p. 21.
16. Ibid.
17. Nilanjana Paul, *Muslim Education and Communal Conflict in Colonial Bengal: British Policies and Muslim Responses from 1854 to 1947*, PhD disertation, West Virginia University, 2016, p. 85.
18. Ibid., pp. 77–78.
19. Ibid., p. 78.
20. *Report of the Indian Education Commission*, Calcutta, 1882, pp. 483, 505.
21. Amalendu De, *Roots of Separatism in Nineteenth Century Bengal*, Ratna Prakashan, Calcutta, 1970, p. 38.
22. Ibid., p. 33.
23. Abdul Karim, *Muhammadan Education in Bengal*, Metcalfe Press, Calcutta, 1900, pp. 2–3.
24. *Political History of Assam*, Volume 1, 1826–1919, Government of Assam, Gauhati, 1980, p. 176.
25. Nilanjana Paul, *Muslim Education and Communal Conflict in Colonial Bengal: British Policies and Muslim Responses from 1854 to 1947*, PhD dissertation, West Virginia University, 2016, p. 92.
26. Vinod Kumar Saxena, *The Partition of Bengal (1905–1911)*, Kanishka Publishing House, Delhi, 1987, p. 1.
27. R.C. Majumdar, *History of the Freedom Movement in India*, Volume 2, 2nd edition, Firma K.L. Mukhopadhyay, Calcutta, 1975, p. 3.
28. *Political History of Assam*, Volume 1, 1826–1919, Government of Assam, Gauhati, 1980, p. 177.

29. Peter Hardy, *The Muslims of British India*, Cambridge University Press, 1972, p. 149.
30. Gopal Krishan, 'Demography of the Punjab (1849–1947)', *Journal of Punjab Studies*, 2004, vol. 11, no. 1, pp. 77–89, p. 89.
31. Peter Hardy, *The Muslims of British India*, Cambridge University Press, 1972, p. 147.
32. G.N. Singh, *Landmarks in Indian Constitutional and National Development (1600–1919)*, The Indian Bookshop, 1933, p. 241.
33. Ibid., p. 243.
34. Peter Hardy, *The Muslims of British India*, Cambridge University Press, 1972, p. 147.
35. https://www.nationalarchives.gov.uk/education/empire/usefulnotes/g2cs4s6u.htm
36. G.N. Singh, *Landmarks in Indian Constitutional and National Development (1600–1919)*, The Indian Bookshop, 1933, p. 219.
37. Ibid., p. 220.
38. Ibid., p. 223.
39. Ibid.
40. Syed Sharfuddin Pirzada, 'Foundations of Pakistan', *All-India Muslim League Documents: 1906–1947*, Volume 1 (1906–1924), National Publishing House Limited, Karachi, p. xxix.
41. Ibid., pp. xxx–xxxi.
42. Ibid., p. xxxi.
43. M.R.A. Baig, 'The Partition of Bengal and Its Aftermath', *The Indian Journal of Political Science*, April–June 1969, vol. 30, no. 2, pp. 103–129, p. 109.
44. G.N. Singh, *Landmarks in Indian Constitutional and National Development (1600–1919)*, The Indian Bookshop, 1933, p. 311.
45. Ibid., p. 312.
46. *Political History of Assam*, Volume 1, 1826–1919, Government of Assam, Gauhati, 1980, p. 177.
47. Ibid.
48. Ibid., p. 178.
49. Vinod Kumar Saxena, *The Partition of Bengal (1905–1911)*, Kanishka Publishing House, Delhi, 1987, p. 2.
50. Ibid., p. 3.
51. Daniel Argov, 'The Ideological Differences between Moderates and Extremists in the Indian National Movement with Special Reference to Surendranath Banerjea and Lajpat Rai 1885–1919', PhD dissertation, School of Oriental and African Studies, University of London, 1964, p. 176.
52. *Political History of Assam*, Volume 1, 1826–1919, Government of Assam, Gauhati, 1980, p. 178.
53. Vinod Kumar Saxena, *The Partition of Bengal (1905–1911)*, Kanishka Publishing House, Delhi, 1987, p. 3.

54. R.C. Majumdar, *History of the Freedom Movement in India*, Volume 2, 2nd edition, Firma K.L. Mukhopadhyay, Calcutta, 1975, p. 4.

55. A.C. Mazumdar, *Indian National Evolution*, G.A. Natesan & Co., Madras, 1917, p. 205.

56. *Political History of Assam*, Volume 1, 1826–1919, Government of Assam, Gauhati, 1980, p. 179.

57. A.C. Mazumdar, *Indian National Evolution*, G.A. Natesan & Co., Madras, 1917, p. 205.

58. Vinod Kumar Saxena, *The Partition of Bengal (1905-1911)*, Kanishka Publishing House, Delhi, 1987, p. 10.

59. Nilanjana Paul, *Muslim Education and Communal Conflict in Colonial Bengal: British Policies and Muslim Responses from 1854 to 1947*, PhD dissertation, West Virginia University, 2016, p. 98.

60. Peter Hardy, *The Muslims of British India*, Cambridge University Press, 1972, p. 150.

61. Vinod Kumar Saxena, *The Partition of Bengal (1905–1911)*, Kanishka Publishing House, Delhi, 1987, p. 6.

62. G.N. Singh, *Landmarks in Indian Constitutional and National Development (1600–1919)*, The Indian Bookshop, 1933, p. 312.

63. M.R.A. Baig, 'The Partition of Bengal and Its Aftermath', *The Indian Journal of Political Science*, April–June 1969, vol. 30, no. 2, pp. 103–129, p. 112.

64. Ibid., pp. 111–113.

65. Nilanjana Paul, *Muslim Education and Communal Conflict in Colonial Bengal: British Policies and Muslim Responses from 1854 to 1947*, PhD dissertation, West Virginia University, 2016, p. 92.

66. R.C. Majumdar, *History of the Freedom Movement in India*, Volume 2, 2nd edition, Firma K.L. Mukhopadhyay, Calcutta, 1975, p. 28.

67. Vinod Kumar Saxena, *The Partition of Bengal (1905–1911)*, Kanishka Publishing House, Delhi, 1987, p. 7.

68. H.V. Seshadri, *The Tragic Story of Partition*, Jagrana Prakashana, Bangalore, 1982, p. 31.

69. R.C. Majumdar, *History of the Freedom Movement in India*, Volume 2, 2nd edition, Firma K.L. Mukhopadhyay, Calcutta, 1975, pp. 4–5.

70. A.C. Mazumdar, *Indian National Evolution*, G.A. Natesan & Co., Madras, 1917, p. 207.

71. Muin-ud-Dun Ahmad Khan, *Muslim Struggle for Freedom in Bengal (A.D. 1757–1947)*, East Pakistan Government Press, 1960, p. 50.

72. Earl of Ronaldshay, *The Life of Lord Curzon*, Volume II, Ernest Benn, London, 1928, p. 329.

73. M.R.A. Baig, 'The Partition of Bengal and Its Aftermath', *The Indian Journal of Political Science*, April–June 1969, vol. 30, no. 2, pp. 103–129, p. 115.

74. https://api.parliament.uk/historic-hansard/commons/1905/jun/05/the-province-of-bengal

75. https://api.parliament.uk/historic-hansard/commons/1905/jul/04/contemplated-partition-of-bengal

76. G.N. Singh, *Landmarks in Indian Constitutional and National Development (1600–1919)*, The Indian Bookshop, 1933, p. 313.

77. R.C. Majumdar, *History of the Freedom Movement in India*, Volume 2, 2nd edition, Firma K.L. Mukhopadhyay, Calcutta, 1975, p. 6.

78. https://api.parliament.uk/historic-hansard/commons/1905/aug/01/proposed-partition-of-bengal

79. G.N. Singh, *Landmarks in Indian Constitutional and National Development (1600–1919)*, The Indian Bookshop, 1933, p. 314.

80. Peter Hardy, *The Muslims of British India*, Cambridge University Press, 1972, p. 150.

81. https://api.parliament.uk/historic-hansard/commons/1905/aug/08/proposed-partition-of-bengal

82. https://api.parliament.uk/historic-hansard/commons/1905/aug/09/east-india-province-of-bengal

83. https://api.parliament.uk/historic-hansard/commons/1905/aug/10/east-india-province-of-bengal

84. A.C. Mazumdar, *Indian National Evolution*, G.A. Natesan & Co., Madras, 1917, p. 212.

85. G.N. Singh, *Landmarks in Indian Constitutional and National Development (1600–1919)*, The Indian Bookshop, 1933, p. 314.

86. A.C. Mazumdar, *Indian National Evolution*, G.A. Natesan & Co., Madras, 1917, p. 213.

87. G.N. Singh, *Landmarks in Indian Constitutional and National Development (1600–1919)*, The Indian Bookshop, 1933, p. 315.

88. Vinod Kumar Saxena, *The Partition of Bengal (1905–1911)*, Kanishka Publishing House, Delhi, 1987, pp. 145, 146.

Chapter 4: The Story of Moderate Nationalism, Muslim Nationalism and Electoral Separatism (1905–1909)

1. Goutam Neogi, 'The First National Revolutionary Secret Society of Colonial Bengal: The Atmonnoti Samiti (1897–1902)', *Proceedings of the Indian History Congress*, vol. 63, 2002, pp. 596–603, p. 596.

2. G.N. Singh, *Landmarks in Indian Constitutional and National Development (1600–1919)*, The Indian Bookshop, 1933, p. 330.

3. Ibid.

4. R.C. Majumdar, *History of the Freedom Movement in India*, Volume 2, 2nd edition, Firma K.L. Mukhopadhyay, Calcutta, 1975, p. 282.

5. *Political History of Assam*, Volume 1, 1826–1919, Government of Assam, Gauhati, 1980, p. 193.

6. G.N. Singh, *Landmarks in Indian Constitutional and National Development (1600–1919)*, The Indian Bookshop, 1933, p. 315.

7. *Political History of Assam*, Volume 1, 1826–1919, Government of Assam, Gauhati, 1980, p. 187.

8. G.N. Singh, *Landmarks in Indian Constitutional and National Development (1600–1919)*, The Indian Bookshop, 1933, p. 316.

9. Ibid., p. 318.

10. Ibid.

11. *Political History of Assam*, Volume 1, 1826–1919, Government of Assam, Gauhati, 1980, p. 192.

12. Ibid.

13. G.N. Singh, *Landmarks in Indian Constitutional and National Development (1600–1919)*, The Indian Bookshop, 1933, p. 322.

14. R.C. Majumdar, *History of the Freedom Movement in India*, Volume 2, 2nd edition, Firma K.L. Mukhopadhyay, Calcutta, 1975, p. 171.

15. G.N. Singh, *Landmarks in Indian Constitutional and National Development (1600–1919)*, The Indian Bookshop, 1933, pp. 325–326.

16. Daniel Argov, 'The Ideological Differences between Moderates and Extremists in the Indian National Movement with Special Reference to Surendranath Banerjea and Lajpat Rai 1885–1919', PhD dissertation, School of Oriental and African Studies, University of London, 1964, pp. 7–10.

17. M.N. Das, *India under Morley and Minto: Politics Behind Revolution, Repression and Reforms*, George Allen and Unwin Ltd, 1964, p. 13.

18. A.C. Mazumdar, *Indian National Evolution*, G.A. Natesan & Co., Madras, 1917, p. 3.

19. Ibid., p. 4.

20. Briton Martin, Jr, 'Lord Dufferin and the Indian National Congress, 1885–1888', *Journal of British Studies*, November 1967, vol. 7, no. 1, Cambridge University Press, pp. 68–96.

21. A.C. Mazumdar, *Indian National Evolution*, G.A. Natesan & Co., Madras, 1917, p. 5.

22. R.C. Majumdar, *History of the Freedom Movement in India*, Volume 1, 2nd edition, Firma K.L. Mukhopadhyay, Calcutta, 1971, pp. 324–325.

23. A.C. Mazumdar, *Indian National Evolution*, G.A. Natesan and Co., Madras, 1917, p. 10.

24. Briton Martin, Jr, 'Lord Dufferin and the Indian National Congress, 1885–1888', *Journal of British Studies*, November 1967, vol. 7, no. 1, Cambridge University Press, pp. 68–96, p. 70.

25. R. Palme Dutt, *India Today and Tomorrow*, People's Publishing House, Delhi, 1955, p. 115.

26. A.C. Mazumdar, *Indian National Evolution*, G.A. Natesan & Co., Madras, 1917, pp. 29–30.

27. Ibid., p. 31.

28. Daniel Argov, 'The Ideological Differences between Moderates and Extremists in the Indian National Movement with Special Reference to Surendranath Banerjea and Lajpat Rai 1885-1919', PhD dissertation, School of Oriental and African Studies, University of London, 1964, p. 14.

29. Ibid., pp. 13–14.

30. R. Palme Dutt, *India Today and Tomorrow*, People's Publishing House, Delhi, 1955, p. 116.

31. R.C. Majumdar, *History of the Freedom Movement in India*, Volume 1, 2nd edition, Firma K.L. Mukhopadhyay, Calcutta, 1971, pp. 344–345.

32. Sir William Wedderburn, *Allan Octavian Hume, C.B. 'Father of the Indian National Congress' 1829–1912*, T. Fisher Unwin, London, 1913, p. 50.

33. Briton Martin, Jr, 'Lord Dufferin and the Indian National Congress, 1885–1888', *Journal of British Studies*, November 1967, vol. 7, no. 1, Cambridge University Press, pp. 68 –96, p. 71.

34. Ibid.

35. Ibid., p. 74.

36. Ibid.

37. Sir William Wedderburn, *Allan Octavian Hume, C.B. 'Father of the Indian National Congress' 1829–1912*, T. Fisher Unwin, London, 1913, pp. 50–53.

38. Ibid., p. 53.

39. R. Palme Dutt, *India Today and Tomorrow*, People's Publishing House, Delhi, 1955, pp. 115–116.

40. Ibid., p. 117.

41. A.C. Mazumdar, *Indian National Evolution*, G.A. Natesan & Co., Madras, 1917, pp. 36–37.

42. Daniel Argov, 'The Ideological Differences between Moderates and Extremists in the Indian National Movement with Special Reference to Surendranath Banerjea and Lajpat Rai 1885–1919', PhD dissertation, School of Oriental and African Studies, University of London, 1964, p. 25.

43. Ibid.

44. Ibid, p. 27.

45. Ibid., p. 26.

46. Ibid., p. 27.

47. Ibid.

48. Sir Surendranath Banerjea, *A Nation in Making, Being the Reminiscences of Fifty Years of Public Life*, Oxford University Press, 1925, p. 74.

49. R.C. Majumdar, *History of the Freedom Movement in India*, Volume 1, 2nd edition, Firma K.L. Mukhopadhyay, Calcutta, 1971, p. 332.

50. Briton Martin, Jr, 'Lord Dufferin and the Indian National Congress, 1885–1888', *Journal of British Studies*, November 1967, vol. 7, no. 1, Cambridge University Press, pp. 68–96, p. 72.

51. Daniel Argov, 'The Ideological Differences between Moderates and Extremists in the Indian National Movement with Special Reference to Surendranath

Banerjea and Lajpat Rai 1885–1919', PhD dissertation, School of Oriental and African Studies, University of London, 1964, pp. 46–48.

52. Ibid., p. 48.

53. Ibid., p. 49.

54. Briton Martin, Jr, 'Lord Dufferin and the Indian National Congress, 1885–1888', *Journal of British Studies*, November 1967, vol. 7, no. 1, Cambridge University Press, pp. 68–96, p. 68.

55. Ibid., p. 76.

56. Ibid., pp. 76–77.

57. R. Palme Dutt, *India Today and Tomorrow*, People's Publishing House, Delhi, 1955, p. 117.

58. Sir William Wedderburn, *Allan Octavian Hume, C.B. 'Father of the Indian National Congress' 1829–1912*, T. Fisher Unwin, London, 1913, pp. 59–60.

59. R.C. Majumdar, *History of the Freedom Movement in India*, Volume 1, 2nd edition, Firma K.L. Mukhopadhyay, Calcutta, 1971, p. 346.

60. Ibid., pp. 347–348.

61. S.R. Mehrotra, *India and the Commonwealth 1885–1929*, Routledge, New York, 2022, pp. 15–16.

62. Sanjay Seth, 'Rewriting Histories of Nationalism: The Politics of "Moderate Nationalism" in India, 1870–1905', *The American Historical Review*, February 1999, vol. 104, no. 1, pp. 95–116, pp. 97–98.

63. Daniel Argov, 'The Ideological Differences between Moderates and Extremists in the Indian National Movement with Special Reference to Surendranath Banerjea and Lajpat Rai 1885–1919', PhD dissertation, School of Oriental and African Studies, University of London, 1964, pp. 8–9.

64. A.C. Mazumdar, *Indian National Evolution*, G.A. Natesan & Co., Madras, 1917, p. 48.

65. Sir Surendranath Banerjea, *A Nation in Making, Being the Reminiscences of Fifty Years of Public Life*, Oxford University Press, 1925, pp. 98–99.

66. Daniel Argov, 'The Ideological Differences between Moderates and Extremists in the Indian National Movement with Special Reference to Surendranath Banerjea and Lajpat Rai 1885–1919', PhD dissertation, School of Oriental and African Studies, University of London, 1964, p. 59.

67. Sir William Wedderburn, *Allan Octavian Hume, C.B. 'Father of the Indian National Congress' 1829–1912*, T. Fisher Unwin, London, 1913, p. 58.

68. Briton Martin, Jr, 'Lord Dufferin and the Indian National Congress, 1885–1888', *Journal of British Studies*, November 1967, vol. 7, no. 1, Cambridge University Press, pp. 68–96, p. 82.

69. *Proceedings of the First Indian National Congress* held at Bombay on 28th, 29th, 30th December 1885, p. 3.

70. Ibid., p. 9.

71. Ibid.

72. Ibid., p. 76.

73. Jogesh Chandra Bagal, *History of the Indian Association 1876–1951*, published by Indian Association, Calcutta, 1953, pp. 93–96.

74. Ibid., p. 96.

75. Briton Martin, Jr, 'Lord Dufferin and the Indian National Congress, 1885–1888', *Journal of British Studies*, November 1967, vol. 7, no. 1, Cambridge University Press, pp. 68–96, p. 90.

76. S.R. Mehrotra, *India and the Commonwealth 1885–1929*, Routledge, New York, 2022, p. 17.

77. Daniel Argov, 'The Ideological Differences between Moderates and Extremists in the Indian National Movement with Special Reference to Surendranath Banerjea and Lajpat Rai 1885–1919', PhD dissertation, School of Oriental and African Studies, University of London, 1964, p. 62.

78. Ibid.

79. Ibid., p. 65.

80. Ibid., pp. 66–67.

81. Ibid., p. 67.

82. R.C. Majumdar, *History of the Freedom Movement in India*, Volume 1, 2nd edition, Firma K.L. Mukhopadhyay, Calcutta, 1971, p. 356.

83. S.R. Mehrotra, *India and the Commonwealth 1885–1929*, Routledge, New York, 2022, p. 18.

84. Daniel Argov, 'The Ideological Differences between Moderates and Extremists in the Indian National Movement with Special Reference to Surendranath Banerjea and Lajpat Rai 1885–1919', PhD dissertation, School of Oriental and African Studies, University of London, 1964, p. 69.

85. B. Shiva Rao, *The Framing of India's Constitution, Select Documents*, Volume 1, Indian Institute of Public Administration, New Delhi, 1966, pp. 3–4.

86. R.C. Majumdar, *History of the Freedom Movement in India*, Volume 1, 2nd edition, Firma K.L. Mukhopadhyay, Calcutta, 1971, p. 358.

87. Daniel Argov, 'The Ideological Differences between Moderates and Extremists in the Indian National Movement with Special Reference to Surendranath Banerjea and Lajpat Rai 1885–1919', PhD dissertation, School of Oriental and African Studies, University of London, 1964, p. 87.

88. B. Pattabhi Sitaramayya, *History of the Indian National Congress Volume I (1885–1935)*, S. Chand & Co., 1969, p. 25.

89. Daniel Argov, 'The Ideological Differences between Moderates and Extremists in the Indian National Movement with Special Reference to Surendranath Banerjea and Lajpat Rai 1885–1919', PhD dissertation, School of Oriental and African Studies, University of London, 1964, pp. 92–93.

90. Ibid., p. 99.

91. Ibid., p. 102.

92. Ibid.

93. Ibid.

94. R.C. Majumdar, *History of the Freedom Movement in India*, Volume 1, 2nd edition, Firma K.L. Mukhopadhyay, Calcutta, 1971, pp. 372–373.

95. Daniel Argov, 'The Ideological Differences between Moderates and Extremists in the Indian National Movement with Special Reference to Surendranath Banerjea and Lajpat Rai 1885–1919', PhD dissertation, School of Oriental and African Studies, University of London, 1964, p. 114.

96. Ibid., p. 115.

97. Ibid., p. 126.

98. B. Shiva Rao, *The Framing of India's Constitution, Select Documents*, Volume 1, Indian Institute of Public Administration, New Delhi, 1966, p. 5.

99. R.C. Majumdar, *History of the Freedom Movement in India*, Volume 1, 2nd edition, Firma K.L. Mukhopadhyay, Calcutta, 1971, pp. 376–377.

100. Daniel Argov, 'The Ideological Differences between Moderates and Extremists in the Indian National Movement with Special Reference to Surendranath Banerjea and Lajpat Rai 1885–1919', PhD dissertation, School of Oriental and African Studies, University of London, 1964, pp. 130–131.

101. Ibid., p. 137.

102. Ibid., p. 138.

103. R.C. Majumdar, *History of the Freedom Movement in India*, Volume 1, 2nd edition, Firma K.L. Mukhopadhyay, Calcutta, 1971, p. 378.

104. Ibid., pp. 378–379.

105. Daniel Argov, 'The Ideological Differences between Moderates and Extremists in the Indian National Movement with Special Reference to Surendranath Banerjea and Lajpat Rai 1885–1919', PhD dissertation, School of Oriental and African Studies, University of London, 1964, p. 145.

106. Ibid., p. 147.

107. S.R. Mehrotra, *India and the Commonwealth 1885–1929*, Routledge, New York, 2022, p. 19.

108. Daniel Argov, 'The Ideological Differences between Moderates and Extremists in the Indian National Movement with Special Reference to Surendranath Banerjea and Lajpat Rai 1885–1919', PhD dissertation, School of Oriental and African Studies, University of London, 1964, pp. 151–153.

109. S.R. Mehrotra, *A History of the Indian National Congress*, Volume I, 1885–1918, Vikas Publishing House, New Delhi, 1995, p. 201.

110. Daniel Argov, 'The Ideological Differences between Moderates and Extremists in the Indian National Movement with Special Reference to Surendranath Banerjea and Lajpat Rai 1885–1919', PhD dissertation, School of Oriental and African Studies, University of London, 1964, pp. 156–157.

111. Ibid., p. 165.

112. *The Indian National Congress*, Part 3, G.A. Natesan & Co., Madras, 1910, p. 118.

113. Daniel Argov, 'The Ideological Differences between Moderates and Extremists in the Indian National Movement with Special Reference to Surendranath

Banerjea and Lajpat Rai 1885–1919', PhD dissertation, School of Oriental and African Studies, University of London, 1964, p. 159.

114. Ibid., p. 160.
115. Ibid., p. 171.
116. Ibid., p. 175.
117. Ibid., p. 178.
118. Ibid., p. 182.
119. Ibid., p. 184.
120. Ibid., p. 188.
121. Ibid., p. 189.
122. Ibid., p. 190.
123. Ibid.
124. Ibid., pp. 190–191.
125. Vinod Kumar Saxena, *The Partition of Bengal (1905–1911)*, Kanishka Publishing House, Delhi, 1987, p. 145.
126. Ibid., p. 146.
127. Syed Sharfuddin Pirzada, 'Foundations of Pakistan', *All-India Muslim League Documents: 1906–1947*, Volume 1 (1906–1924), National Publishing House Limited, Karachi, 1969, p. xxxii.
128. *Political History of Assam*, Volume 1, 1826–1919, Government of Assam, Gauhati, 1980, p. 190.
129. Henry W. Nevinson, *The New Spirit in India*, Harper & Bros, London, 1908, p. 193, as cited in Vinod Kumar Saxena, *The Partition of Bengal (1905–1911)*, Kanishka Publishing House, Delhi, 1987, p. 15.
130. Vinod Kumar Saxena, *The Partition of Bengal (1905–1911)*, Kanishka Publishing House, Delhi, 1987, p. 92.
131. Ibid., p. 11.
132. *Political History of Assam*, Volume 1, 1826–1919, Government of Assam, Gauhati, 1980, p. 190.
133. Henry W. Nevinson, *The New Spirit in India*, Harper & Bros, London, 1908, p. 193, as cited in Vinod Kumar Saxena, *The Partition of Bengal (1905–1911)*, Kanishka Publishing House, Delhi, 1987, pp. 11–12.
134. Syed Razi Wasti, 'Lord Minto and the Indian Nationalist Movement, with Special Reference to the Political Activities of Indian Muslims, 1905–1910', PhD dissertation, School of Oriental and African Studies, University of London, 1962, p. 54.
135. Syed Sharfuddin Pirzada, 'Foundations of Pakistan', *All-India Muslim League Documents: 1906–1947*, Volume 1 (1906–1924), National Publishing House Limited, Karachi, 1969, pp. xxxii–xxxiii.
136. Syed Razi Wasti, 'Lord Minto and the Indian Nationalist Movement, with Special Reference to the Political Activities of Indian Muslims, 1905–1910', PhD dissertation, School of Oriental and African Studies, University of London, 1962, p. 32.

137. Ibid., p. 33.

138. Ibid., p. 34.

139. Ibid.

140. Daniel Argov, 'The Ideological Differences between Moderates and Extremists in the Indian National Movement with Special Reference to Surendranath Banerjea and Lajpat Rai 1885–1919', PhD dissertation, School of Oriental and African Studies, University of London, 1964, p. 200.

141. Ibid., pp. 200–201.

142. Ibid., p. 201.

143. Syed Razi Wasti, 'Lord Minto and the Indian Nationalist Movement, with Special Reference to the Political Activities of Indian Muslims, 1905–1910', PhD dissertation, School of Oriental and African Studies, University of London, 1962, p. 36.

144. Syed Sharfuddin Pirzada, 'Foundations of Pakistan', *All-India Muslim League Documents: 1906–1947*, Volume 1 (1906–1924), National Publishing House Limited, Karachi, 1969, p. xxxiv.

145. Ibid.

146. Ibid., p. xxxvi.

147. Ibid.

148. Syed Razi Wasti, 'Lord Minto and the Indian Nationalist Movement, with Special Reference to the Political Activities of Indian Muslims, 1905–1910', PhD dissertation, School of Oriental and African Studies, University of London, 1962, p. 36.

149. Ibid., p. 38.

150. Ibid., p. 39.

151. Syed Sharfuddin Pirzada, 'Foundations of Pakistan', *All-India Muslim League Documents: 1906–1947*, Volume 1 (1906–1924), National Publishing House Limited, Karachi, 1969, pp. xxxvi–xxxvii.

152. Ibid., p. xxxvii.

153. Ibid., pp. xlii–xliii.

154. Syed Sharfuddin Pirzada, 'Foundations of Pakistan', *All-India Muslim League Documents: 1906–1947*, Volume 3 (1906–1947), Royal Book Company, Karachi, 1990, pp. 7–8.

155. Ibid., p. iii.

156. Syed Razi Wasti, *Memoirs and Other Writings of Syed Ameer Ali*, Renaissance Publishing House, New Delhi, 1920, pp. 150–177.

157. Syed Sharfuddin Pirzada, 'Foundations of Pakistan', *All-India Muslim League Documents: 1906–1947*, Volume 3, Royal Book Company, Karachi, 1990, pp. 2–7.

158. Ibid., pp. 10–11.

159. Ibid., p. xxxviii.

160. M.S. Jain, *The Aligarh Movement, Its Origin and Development (1858–1906)*, Shri Ram Mehra & Co. Publishers, Agra, 1965, pp. 153–154.

161. Syed Sharifuddin Pirzada, 'Foundations of Pakistan', *All-India Muslim League Documents: 1906–1947*, Volume 1 (1906–1924), National Publishing House Limited, Karachi, 1969, p. xliv.

162. *Political History of Assam*, Volume 1, 1826–1919, Government of Assam, Gauhati, 1980, p. 191.

163. Syed Sharifuddin Pirzada, 'Foundations of Pakistan', *All-India Muslim League Documents: 1906–1947*, Volume 1 (1906–1924), National Publishing House Limited, Karachi, 1969, p. xlv.

164. Ibid., pp. xlv–xlix.

165. Syed Razi Wasti, 'Lord Minto and the Indian Nationalist Movement, with Special Reference to the Political Activities of Indian Muslims, 1905–1910', PhD dissertation, School of Oriental and African Studies, University of London, 1962, pp. 73–74.

166. S.R. Mehrotra, *India and the Commonwealth 1885–1929*, Routledge, New York, 2022, p. 41.

167. Ibid., pp. 41–42.

168. Ibid., p. 42.

169. Daniel Argov, 'The Ideological Differences between Moderates and Extremists in the Indian National Movement with Special Reference to Surendranath Banerjea and Lajpat Rai 1885–1919', PhD dissertation, School of Oriental and African Studies, University of London, 1964, pp. 202–203.

170. Ibid., p. 204.

171. Syed Razi Wasti, 'Lord Minto and the Indian Nationalist Movement, with Special Reference to the Political Activities of Indian Muslims, 1905–1910', PhD dissertation, School of Oriental and African Studies, University of London, 1962, p. 75.

172. Ibid., p. 76.

173. Syed Sharifuddin Pirzada, 'Foundations of Pakistan', *All-India Muslim League Documents: 1906–1947*, Volume 1 (1906–1924), National Publishing House Limited, Karachi, 1969, p. 1.

174. R.C. Majumdar, *History of the Freedom Movement in India*, Volume 2, 2nd edition, Firma K.L. Mukhopadhyay, Calcutta, 1975, p. 109.

175. Ibid., p. 108.

176. Ibid., p. 104.

177. Henry W. Nevinson, *The New Spirit in India*, Harper & Bros, London, 1908, p. 202.

178. https://api.parliament.uk/historic-hansard/commons/1907/mar/19/comilla-riots#S4V0171P0_19070319_HOC_84

179. Sir Courtenay Ilbert, *The Government of India Supplementary Chapter, Indian Councils Act, 1909*, Oxford at the Clarendon Press, London, 1910, p. 410.

Chapter 5: The Indian Councils Act of 1909: Yet Another Ad Hoc Safety Valve (1907–1909)

1. Daniel Argov, 'The Ideological Differences between Moderates and Extremists in the Indian National Movement with Special Reference to Surendranath Banerjea and Lajpat Rai 1885–1919', PhD dissertation, School of Oriental and African Studies, University of London, 1964, pp. 205–206.

2. Ibid., p. 207.

3. Ibid., p. 208.

4. Ibid., pp. 209–213.

5. Ibid., p. 213.

6. N. Gerald Barrier, 'The Punjab Disturbances of 1907: The Response of the British Government in India to Agrarian Unrest', *Modern Asian Studies*, 1967, vol. 1, no. 4, pp. 353–383, p. 367.

7. Daniel Argov, 'The Ideological Differences between Moderates and Extremists in the Indian National Movement with Special Reference to Surendranath Banerjea and Lajpat Rai 1885–1919', PhD dissertation, School of Oriental and African Studies, University of London, 1964, p. 217.

8. Ibid., p. 218.

9. Syed Razi Wasti, 'Lord Minto and the Indian Nationalist Movement, with Special Reference to the Political Activities of Indian Muslims, 1905–1910', PhD dissertation, School of Oriental and African Studies, University of London, 1962, p. 161.

10. S.R. Mehrotra, *India and the Commonwealth 1885–1929*, Routledge, New York, 2022, pp. 42–43.

11. Ibid., pp. 43–44.

12. Daniel Argov, 'The Ideological Differences between Moderates and Extremists in the Indian National Movement with Special Reference to Surendranath Banerjea and Lajpat Rai 1885–1919', PhD dissertation, School of Oriental and African Studies, University of London, 1964, p. 222.

13. S.R. Mehrotra, *India and the Commonwealth 1885–1929*, Routledge, New York, 2022, p. 44.

14. Daniel Argov, 'The Ideological Differences between Moderates and Extremists in the Indian National Movement with Special Reference to Surendranath Banerjea and Lajpat Rai 1885–1919', PhD dissertation, School of Oriental and African Studies, University of London, 1964, p. 223.

15. Ibid., p. 224.

16. Syed Razi Wasti, 'Lord Minto and the Indian Nationalist Movement, with Special Reference to the Political Activities of Indian Muslims, 1905–1910', PhD dissertation, School of Oriental and African Studies, University of London, 1962, p. 81.

17. Daniel Argov, 'The Ideological Differences between Moderates and Extremists in the Indian National Movement with Special Reference to Surendranath

Banerjea and Lajpat Rai 1885–1919', PhD dissertation, School of Oriental and African Studies, University of London, 1964, pp. 224–225.

18. S.R. Mehrotra, *India and the Commonwealth 1885–1929*, Routledge, New York, 2022, p. 45.

19. Daniel Argov, 'The Ideological Differences between Moderates and Extremists in the Indian National Movement with Special Reference to Surendranath Banerjea and Lajpat Rai 1885–1919', PhD dissertation, School of Oriental and African Studies, University of London, 1964, p. 227.

20. Stanley A. Wolpert, *Tilak and Gokhale: Revolution and Reform in the Making of Modern India*, University of California, Berkeley, 1977, p. 215.

21. Syed Razi Wasti, 'Lord Minto and the Indian Nationalist Movement, with Special Reference to the Political Activities of Indian Muslims, 1905–1910', PhD dissertation, School of Oriental and African Studies, University of London, 1962, p. 82.

22. S.R. Mehrotra, *India and the Commonwealth 1885–1929*, Routledge, New York, 2022, p. 45.

23. Ibid., p. 46.

24. Daniel Argov, 'The Ideological Differences between Moderates and Extremists in the Indian National Movement with Special Reference to Surendranath Banerjea and Lajpat Rai 1885–1919', PhD dissertation, School of Oriental and African Studies, University of London, 1964, p. 228.

25. Ibid.

26. Ibid.

27. Lal Bahadur, *The Muslim League: Its History, Activities and Achievements*, Agra Book Store, Agra, 1954, p. 70.

28. Ibid., p. 71.

29. Ibid., pp. 71–72.

30. Syed Razi Wasti, 'Lord Minto and the Indian Nationalist Movement, with Special Reference to the Political Activities of Indian Muslims, 1905–1910', PhD dissertation, School of Oriental and African Studies, University of London, 1962, p. 122.

31. Syed Sharfuddin Pirzada, 'Foundations of Pakistan', *All-India Muslim League Documents: 1906–1947*, Volume 1 (1906–1924), National Publishing House Limited, Karachi, 1969, p. 26.

32. Lal Bahadur, *The Muslim League: Its History, Activities and Achievements*, Agra Book Store, Agra, 1954, pp. 75–76.

33. Syed Razi Wasti, 'Lord Minto and the Indian Nationalist Movement, with Special Reference to the Political Activities of Indian Muslims, 1905–1910', PhD dissertation, School of Oriental and African Studies, University of London, 1962, p. 135.

34. James Campbell Ker, *Political Trouble in India 1907–1917*, Oriental Publishers, Delhi, 1917.

35. Syed Razi Wasti, 'Lord Minto and the Indian Nationalist Movement, with Special Reference to the Political Activities of Indian Muslims, 1905–1910', PhD dissertation, School of Oriental and African Studies, University of London, 1962, p. 136.

36. Ibid., pp. 136–137.

37. Ibid., p. 140.

38. Ibid.

39. Ibid., p. 171.

40. Ibid.

41. Ibid., p. 172.

42. Ibid., p. 174.

43. Ibid., p. 178.

44. Ibid., p. 179.

45. Ibid., pp. 182–183.

46. Ibid., p. 185.

47. Ibid., p. 183.

48. Ibid., p. 177.

49. Ibid., pp. 186–187.

50. Ibid., pp. 191–192.

51. Mary, Countess of Minto, *India: Minto and Morley 1905–1910*, Macmillan and Co. Ltd, London, 1934.

52. Syed Razi Wasti, 'Lord Minto and the Indian Nationalist Movement, with Special Reference to the Political Activities of Indian Muslims, 1905–1910', PhD dissertation, School of Oriental and African Studies, University of London, 1962, p. 191.

53. Ibid., p. 246.

54. Ibid., p. 200.

55. Ibid., pp. 203–204.

56. Ibid., p. 220.

57. Ibid., p. 221.

58. Ibid., pp. 228–229.

59. Ibid., p. 230.

60. Ibid., pp. 232–233.

61. Ibid., pp. 255–256.

62. Ibid., pp. 257–258.

63. Ibid., pp. 261–263.

64. Ibid., p. 261.

65. Dietmar Rothermund, 'Reform and Repression, 1907–1910: An Analysis of British Indian Policy', *Proceedings of the Indian History Congress, 1961*, vol. 24, 1961, pp. 253–262, pp. 255–256.

66. Syed Sharfuddin Pirzada, 'Foundations of Pakistan', *All-India Muslim League Documents: 1906–1947*, Volume 1 (1906–1924), National Publishing House Limited, Karachi, 1969, pp. 42–58.

67. Daniel Argov, 'The Ideological Differences between Moderates and Extremists in the Indian National Movement with Special Reference to Surendranath Banerjea and Lajpat Rai 1885–1919', PhD dissertation, School of Oriental and African Studies, University of London, 1964, pp. 229–230.

68. Ibid., p. 230.

69. Ibid., pp. 230–231.

70. Ibid., p. 231.

71. Ibid.

72. S.R. Mehrotra, *India and the Commonwealth 1885–1929*, Routledge, New York, 2022, p. 53.

73. Ibid.

74. Daniel Argov, 'The Ideological Differences between Moderates and Extremists in the Indian National Movement with Special Reference to Surendranath Banerjea and Lajpat Rai 1885–1919', PhD dissertation, School of Oriental and African Studies, University of London, 1964, p. 232.

75. Ibid., p. 237.

76. Syed Razi Wasti, 'Lord Minto and the Indian Nationalist Movement, with Special Reference to the Political Activities of Indian Muslims, 1905–1910', PhD dissertation, School of Oriental and African Studies, University of London, 1962, p. 262.

77. Ibid., p. 264.

78. Ibid., p. 270.

79. Ibid.

80. Ibid., pp. 279–280.

81. Ibid., p. 281.

82. Ibid., p. 282.

83. Ibid., p. 283.

84. Ibid., p. 284.

85. Daniel Argov, 'The Ideological Differences between Moderates and Extremists in the Indian National Movement with Special Reference to Surendranath Banerjea and Lajpat Rai 1885–1919', PhD dissertation, School of Oriental and African Studies, University of London, 1964, p. 230.

86. Ibid., pp. 236–237.

87. Syed Razi Wasti, 'Lord Minto and the Indian Nationalist Movement, with Special Reference to the Political Activities of Indian Muslims, 1905–1910', PhD dissertation, School of Oriental and African Studies, University of London, 1962, p. 285.

88. *Report of the Proceedings of the Twenty-Fourth Indian National Congress* held at Lahore on the 27th, 28th and 29th December 1909.

89. https://api.parliament.uk/historic-hansard/commons/1907/jun/06/east-india-revenue-accounts#column_884

90. https://www.eparlib.nic.in/bitstream/123456789/763363/1/ilcd_21-12-1866.pdf, pp. 244–247.

91. https://www.eparlib.nic.in/bitstream/123456789/763366/1/ilcd_04-01-1867.pdf, pp. 7–8.

92. Ibid., pp. 8–9.

93. https://eparlib.nic.in/bitstream/123456789/784463/1/ilcd_27-march-1908.pdf, pp. 184–185.

94. https://eparlib.nic.in/bitstream/123456789/784463/1/ilcd_27-march-1908.pdf

95. https://api.parliament.uk/historic-hansard/commons/1908/dec/17/reforms-in-india#column_2158

96. https://api.parliament.uk/historic-hansard/lords/1909/feb/23/second-reading#column_125

97. https://eparlib.nic.in/bitstream/123456789/785209/1/ilcd_29-march-1909.pdf, pp. 175–177.

98. https://eparlib.nic.in/bitstream/123456789/785209/1/ilcd_29-march-1909.pdf, pp. 211–213.

99. https://eparlib.nic.in/bitstream/123456789/785209/1/ilcd_29-march-1909.pdf, pp. 290–291.

100. https://api.parliament.uk/historic-hansard/commons/1909/apr/01/indian-councils-bill-lords

101. https://api.parliament.uk/historic-hansard/commons/1909/apr/26/indian-councils-bill-lords

Chapter 6: Reunification of Bengal, the First World War and the Lucknow Pact: Murmurings of Khilafat (1910–1916)

1. Lal Bahadur, *The Muslim League: Its History, Activities and Achievements*, Agra Book Store, Agra, 1954, p. 78.

2. Syed Sharfuddin Pirzada, 'Foundations of Pakistan', *All-India Muslim League Documents: 1906–1947*, Volume 1 (1906–1924), National Publishing House Limited, Karachi, 1969, pp. 87–88.

3   Ibid.

4. Ibid.

5. Ibid., p. 94.

6. Ibid., p. 100.

7. Daniel Argov, 'The Ideological Differences between Moderates and Extremists in the Indian National Movement with Special Reference to Surendranath Banerjea and Lajpat Rai 1885–1919', PhD dissertation, School of Oriental and African Studies, University of London, 1964, p. 239.

8. R.C. Majumdar, *History of the Freedom Movement in India*, Volume 2, 2nd edition, Firma K.L. Mukhopadhyay, Calcutta, 1975, pp. 360–361.

9. Daniel Argov, 'The Ideological Differences between Moderates and Extremists in the Indian National Movement with Special Reference to Surendranath Banerjea and Lajpat Rai 1885–1919', PhD dissertation, School of Oriental and African Studies, University of London, 1964, p. 240.

10. Ibid., p. 241.

11. Ibid., pp. 246–247.

12. Ibid., p. 247.

13. F.A. Eustis II and Z.H. Zaidi, 'King, Viceroy and Cabinet: The Modification of the Partition of Bengal, 1911', *History*, 1964, vol. 49, no. 166, pp. 171–184, p. 171.

14. Lord Hardinge of Penhurst, *My Indian Years 1910–1916*, John Murray, London, 1948.

15. Ibid., p. 11.

16. Ibid., p. 14.

17. Ibid., p. 11.

18. Lal Bahadur, *The Muslim League: Its History, Activities and Achievements*, Agra Book Store, Agra, 1954, pp. 83–84.

19. *Report of the Proceedings of the Twenty-Fifth Indian National Congress* held at Allahabad on the 26th, 27th, 28th and 29th December 1910, Indian Press, Allahabad, 1911, pp. 1–14.

20. Ibid., p. 31.

21. Syed Sharfuddin Pirzada, 'Foundations of Pakistan', *All-India Muslim League Documents: 1906–1947*, Volume 1 (1906–1924), National Publishing House Limited, Karachi, 1969, pp. 163–164.

22. Ibid., p. 194.

23. Lal Bahadur, *The Muslim League: Its History, Activities and Achievements*, Agra Book Store, Agra, 1954, p. 84.

24. Ibid., p. 86.

25. F.A. Eustis II and Z.H. Zaidi, 'King, Viceroy and Cabinet: The Modification of the Partition of Bengal, 1911', *History*, 1964, vol. 49, no. 166, pp. 171–184, p. 172.

26. Ibid.

27. Ibid., pp. 172–173.

28. Ibid., p. 173.

29. Ibid.

30. Ibid., p. 175.

31. Ibid., p. 172.

32. Ibid., p. 174.

33. Ibid., pp. 173–174.

34. Ibid., p. 176.

35. Ibid., p. 175.

36. Lord Hardinge of Penhurst, *My Indian Years 1910–1916*, John Murray, London, 1948, pp. 36–40.

37. F.A. Eustis II and Z.H. Zaidi, 'King, Viceroy and Cabinet: The Modification of the Partition of Bengal, 1911', *History*, 1964, vol. 49, no. 166, pp. 171–184, p. 177.

38. Ibid., pp. 177–178.

39. Ibid., p. 178.
40. Ibid., p. 180.
41. Ibid., p. 181.
42. Ibid.
43. Ibid., p. 182.
44. https://api.parliament.uk/historic-hansard/lords/1912/feb/22/india
45. Ibid.
46. Daniel Argov, 'The Ideological Differences between Moderates and Extremists in the Indian National Movement with Special Reference to Surendranath Banerjea and Lajpat Rai 1885–1919', PhD dissertation, School of Oriental and African Studies, University of London, 1964, p. 251.
47. *Report of the Proceedings of the Twenty-Sixth Indian National Congress* held at Calcutta on 26–28 December 1911.
48. Daniel Argov, 'The Ideological Differences between Moderates and Extremists in the Indian National Movement with Special Reference to Surendranath Banerjea and Lajpat Rai 1885–1919', PhD dissertation, School of Oriental and African Studies, University of London, 1964, p. 251.
49. Lal Bahadur, *The Muslim League: Its History, Activities and Achievements*, Agra Book Store, Agra, 1954, p. 87.
50. M. Rafique Afzal, *A History of the All-India Muslim League 1906–1947*, Oxford University Press, Karachi, 2013, pp. 116–117.
51. Ibid., p. 118.
52. Syed Sharfuddin Pirzada, 'Foundations of Pakistan', *All-India Muslim League Documents: 1906–1947*, Volume 1 (1906–1924), National Publishing House Limited, Karachi, 1969, pp. 225–226.
53. Ibid., pp. 234–236.
54. Ibid., pp. 250, 255.
55. M. Rafique Afzal, *A History of the All-India Muslim League 1906–1947*, Oxford University Press, Karachi, 2013, pp. 118–119.
56. Lal Bahadur, *The Muslim League: Its History, Activities and Achievements*, Agra Book Store, Agra, 1954, pp. 88–89.
57. Hugh F. Owen, 'Negotiating the Lucknow Pact', *Journal of Asian Studies*, May 1972, vol. 31, no. 3, pp. 561–587, p. 567.
58. James Campbel Ker, *Political Trouble in India 1907–1917*, Oriental Publishers, Delhi, 1917, p. 354.
59. Ibid., pp. 362–363.
60. *Report of the Proceedings of the Twenty-Sixth Indian National Congress* held at Bankipur on 26–28 December 1912, pp. 4–5.
61. Ibid., pp. 9–10.
62. Ibid., pp. 40, 64.
63. M. Rafique Afzal, *A History of the All-India Muslim League 1906–1947*, Oxford University Press, Karachi, 2013, p. 119.

64. Syed Sharfuddin Pirzada, 'Foundations of Pakistan', *All-India Muslim League Documents: 1906–1947*, Volume 1 (1906–1924), National Publishing House Limited, Karachi, 1969, p. 260.

65. Ibid., pp. 258–259.

66. Ibid., p. 260.

67. M. Rafique Afzal, *A History of the All-India Muslim League 1906–1947*, Oxford University Press, Karachi, 2013, pp. 120–121.

68. Ibid., pp. 115–116.

69. Ibid., p. 116.

70. Hugh F. Owen, 'Negotiating the Lucknow Pact', *The Journal of Asian Studies*, May 1972, vol. 31, no. 3, pp. 561–587, pp. 568–569.

71. *Report of the Proceedings of the Twenty-Eighth Indian National Congress* held at Karachi on the 26th, 27th and 28th December, 1913, p. 10.

72. Ibid.

73. Syed Sharfuddin Pirzada, 'Foundations of Pakistan', *All-India Muslim League Documents: 1906–1947*, Volume 1 (1906–1924), National Publishing House Limited, Karachi, 1969, pp. 293–295.

74. Ibid., pp. 315–316.

75. Ibid., p. 317.

76. Daniel Argov, 'The Ideological Differences between Moderates and Extremists in the Indian National Movement with Special Reference to Surendranath Banerjea and Lajpat Rai 1885–1919', PhD dissertation, School of Oriental and African Studies, University of London, 1964, p. 256.

77. Ibid.

78. Ibid., pp. 256–257.

79. Ibid., p. 257.

80. S.R. Mehrotra, *India and the Commonwealth 1885–1929*, Routledge, New York, 2022, pp. 64–65.

81. Daniel Argov, 'The Ideological Differences between Moderates and Extremists in the Indian National Movement with Special Reference to Surendranath Banerjea and Lajpat Rai 1885–1919', PhD dissertation, School of Oriental and African Studies, University of London, 1964, p. 257.

82. https://eparlib.nic.in/bitstream/123456789/799658/1/ilcd_08_09_1914.pdf

83. *Report of the Proceedings of the Twenty-Ninth Indian National Congress* held at Madras on 28–30 December 1914, p. 2.

84. Ibid.

85. Ibid., p. 13.

86. Ibid., p. 23.

87. Ibid., p. 25.

88. Daniel Argov, 'The Ideological Differences between Moderates and Extremists in the Indian National Movement with Special Reference to Surendranath

Banerjea and Lajpat Rai 1885–1919', PhD dissertation, School of Oriental and African Studies, University of London, 1964, p. 257.

89. R.C. Majumdar, *History of the Freedom Movement in India*, Volume 2, 2nd edition, Firma K.L. Mukhopadhyay, Calcutta, 1975, p. 331.

90. S.R. Mehrotra, *India and the Commonwealth 1885–1929*, Routledge, New York, 2022, p. 65.

91. Daniel Argov, 'The Ideological Differences between Moderates and Extremists in the Indian National Movement with Special Reference to Surendranath Banerjea and Lajpat Rai 1885–1919', PhD dissertation, School of Oriental and African Studies, University of London, 1964, p. 258.

92. S.R. Mehrotra, *India and the Commonwealth 1885–1929*, Routledge, New York, 2022, p. 65.

93. Hugh F. Owen, 'Negotiating the Lucknow Pact', *The Journal of Asian Studies*, May 1972, vol. 31, no. 3, pp. 561–587, p. 570.

94. G.N. Singh, *Landmarks in Indian Constitutional and National Development (1600–1919)*, The Indian Bookshop, 1933, p. 493.

95. Hugh F. Owen, 'Negotiating the Lucknow Pact', *The Journal of Asian Studies*, May 1972, vol. 31, no. 3, pp. 561–587, p. 570.

96. Ibid.

97. Daniel Argov, 'The Ideological Differences between Moderates and Extremists in the Indian National Movement with Special Reference to Surendranath Banerjea and Lajpat Rai 1885–1919', PhD dissertation, School of Oriental and African Studies, University of London, 1964, p. 263.

98. S.R. Mehrotra, *India and the Commonwealth 1885–1929*, Routledge, New York, 2022, p. 70.

99. Lal Bahadur, *The Muslim League: Its History, Activities and Achievements*, Agra Book Store, Agra, 1954, p. 94.

100. *Report of the Proceedings of the Thirtieth Indian National Congress* held at Bombay on the 27th, 28th and 29th December 1915.

101. Syed Sharfuddin Pirzada, 'Foundations of Pakistan', *All-India Muslim League Documents: 1906–1947*, Volume 1 (1906–1924), National Publishing House Limited, Karachi, 1969, pp. 353–354.

102. Ibid., p. 354.

103. Hugh F. Owen, 'Negotiating the Lucknow Pact', *The Journal of Asian Studies*, May 1972, vol. 31, no. 3, pp. 561–587, pp. 573–574.

104. S.R. Mehrotra, *India and the Commonwealth 1885–1929*, Routledge, New York, 2022, p. 74.

105. Ibid.

106. Hugh F. Owen, 'Negotiating the Lucknow Pact', *The Journal of Asian Studies*, May 1972, vol. 31, no. 3, pp. 561–587, p. 574.

107. M. Rafique Afzal, *A History of the All-India Muslim League 1906–1947*, Oxford University Press, 2013, Karachi, p. 122.

108. Hugh F. Owen, 'Negotiating the Lucknow Pact', *The Journal of Asian Studies*, May 1972, vol. 31, no. 3, pp. 561–587, p. 575.

109. Ibid.

110. Ibid., p. 576.

111. Ibid.

112. Daniel Argov, 'The Ideological Differences between Moderates and Extremists in the Indian National Movement with Special Reference to Surendranath Banerjea and Lajpat Rai 1885–1919', PhD dissertation, School of Oriental and African Studies, University of London, 1964, p. 264.

113. Ibid.

114. R.C. Majumdar, *History of the Freedom Movement in India*, Volume 2, 2nd edition, Firma K.L. Mukhopadhyay, Calcutta, 1975, p. 340.

115. B. Shiva Rao, *The Framing of India's Constitution: Select Documents* (Volume I), Indian Institute of Public Administration, New Delhi, 1966, pp. 19–24.

116. Ibid.

117. M. Rafique Afzal, *A History of the All-India Muslim League 1906–1947*, Oxford University Press, Karachi, 2013, pp. 122–123.

118. Government of India Dispatch, Home Department, Political, no. 17, 24 November 1916, p. 16; Austen Chamberlain Papers, A.C. 22/9 as cited in S.R. Mehrotra, *India and the Commonwealth 1885–1929*, Routledge, New York, 2022, pp. 75–76.

119. Hugh F. Owen, 'Negotiating the Lucknow Pact', *The Journal of Asian Studies*, May 1972, vol. 31, no. 3, pp. 561–587, pp. 577–578.

120. Ibid., p. 578.

121. M. Rafique Afzal, *A History of the All-India Muslim League 1906–1947*, Oxford University Press, Karachi, 2013, p. 123.

122. Hugh F. Owen, 'Negotiating the Lucknow Pact', *The Journal of Asian Studies*, May 1972, vol. 31, no. 3, pp. 561–587, p. 578.

123. *Report of the Proceedings of the Thirty-First Indian National Congress* held at Lucknow on the 26th, 28th , 29th and 30th December 1916, p. 2.

124. Ibid., p. 3.

125. Ibid., p. 12.

126. Ibid., p. 37.

127. Ibid., pp. 70–71.

128. Ibid., p. 81.

129. Ibid., p. 84.

130. Ibid., p. 77.

131. Syed Sharfuddin Pirzada, 'Foundations of Pakistan', *All-India Muslim League Documents: 1906–1947*, Volume 1 (1906–1924), National Publishing House Limited, Karachi, 1969, p. 367.

132. Ibid., p. 384.

Chapter 7: From the Home Rule Movement to Rumblings of Khilafat (1917–1918)

1. M. Rafique Afzal, *A History of the All-India Muslim League 1906–1947*, Oxford University Press, Karachi, 2013, p. 125.

2. Daniel Argov, 'The Ideological Differences between Moderates and Extremists in the Indian National Movement with Special Reference to Surendranath Banerjea and Lajpat Rai 1885–1919', PhD dissertation, School of Oriental and African Studies, University of London, 1964, p. 265.

3. R.C. Majumdar, *History of the Freedom Movement in India*, Volume 2, 2nd edition, Firma K.L. Mukhopadhyay, Calcutta, 1975, p. 345.

4. Ibid., p. 347.

5. Ibid., p. 339.

6. S.R. Mehrotra, *India and the Commonwealth 1885–1929*, Routledge, New York, 2022, p. 77.

7. R.C. Majumdar, *History of the Freedom Movement in India*, Volume 2, 2nd edition, Firma K.L. Mukhopadhyay, Calcutta, 1975, pp. 346–347.

8. M. Rafique Afzal, *A History of the All-India Muslim League 1906–1947*, Oxford University Press, Karachi, 2013, p. 125.

9. R.C. Majumdar, *History of the Freedom Movement in India*, Volume 2, 2nd edition, Firma K.L. Mukhopadhyay, Calcutta, 1975, p. 347.

10. S.R. Mehrotra, *India and the Commonwealth 1885–1929*, Routledge, New York, 2022, pp. 96–97.

11. Ibid., p. 97.

12. Ibid., p. 98.

13. R.C. Majumdar, *History of the Freedom Movement in India*, Volume 2, 2nd edition, Firma K.L. Mukhopadhyay, Calcutta, 1975, p. 344.

14. Ibid.

15. S.R. Mehrotra, *India and the Commonwealth 1885–1929*, Routledge, New York, 2022, p. 77.

16. M. Rafique Afzal, *A History of the All-India Muslim League 1906–1947*, Oxford University Press, Karachi, 2013, p. 125.

17. R.C. Majumdar, *History of the Freedom Movement in India*, Volume 2, 2nd edition, Firma K.L. Mukhopadhyay, Calcutta, 1975, p. 348.

18. Ibid., p. 347.

19. S.R. Mehrotra, *India and the Commonwealth 1885–1929*, Routledge, New York, 2022, p. 101.

20. M. Rafique Afzal, *A History of the All-India Muslim League 1906–1947*, Oxford University Press, Karachi, 2013, p. 125.

21. Ibid., pp. 125–126.

22. G.N. Singh, *Landmarks in Indian Constitutional and National Development (1600–1919)*, The Indian Bookshop, 1933, p. 519.

23. S.R. Mehrotra, *India and the Commonwealth 1885–1929*, Routledge, New York, 2022, p. 103.

24. Daniel Argov, 'The Ideological Differences between Moderates and Extremists in the Indian National Movement with Special Reference to Surendranath Banerjea and Lajpat Rai 1885–1919', PhD dissertation, School of Oriental and African Studies, University of London, 1964, p. 266.

25. S.R. Mehrotra, *India and the Commonwealth 1885–1929*, Routledge, New York, 2022, p. 103.

26. Ibid., p. 104.

27. M. Rafique Afzal, *A History of the All-India Muslim League 1906–1947*, Oxford University Press, Karachi, 2013, p. 126.

28. Ibid., p. 127.

29. Ibid., p. 128.

30. R.C. Majumdar, *History of the Freedom Movement in India*, Volume 2, 2nd edition, Firma K.L. Mukhopadhyay, Calcutta, 1975, p. 350.

31. Ibid.

32. Ibid.

33. *Report of the Proceedings of the Thirty-Second Indian National Congress* held at Calcutta on the 26th, 28th and 29th December, 1917, p. 90.

34. Ibid., p. 97.

35. Ibid., p. 101.

36. Ibid., p. 61.

37. Ibid., pp. 61–64.

38. Syed Sharfuddin Pirzada, 'Foundations of Pakistan', *All-India Muslim League Documents: 1906–1947*, Volume 1 (1906–1924), National Publishing House Limited, Karachi, 1969, p. 398.

39. M. Rafique Afzal, *A History of the All-India Muslim League 1906–1947*, Oxford University Press, Karachi, 2013, p. 128.

40. Syed Sharfuddin Pirzada, 'Foundations of Pakistan', *All-India Muslim League Documents: 1906–1947*, Volume 1 (1906–1924), National Publishing House Limited, Karachi, 1969, p. 427.

41. Ibid, p. 436.

42. R.C. Majumdar, *History of the Freedom Movement in India*, Volume 2, 2nd edition, Firma K.L. Mukhopadhyay, Calcutta, 1975, p. 475.

43. Ibid., p. 476.

44. *Report on Indian Constitutional Reforms* (1918), Superintendent Government Printing, India. https://upload.wikimedia.org/wikipedia/commons/8/84/Report_on_Indian_Constitutional_Reforms_%28 Montagu-Chelmsford_Report%29.pdf, p. 14.

45. Ibid., 13.

46. Ibid, p. 113.

47. Ibid., 123.

48. Ibid., 123.

49. Ibid.

50. Ibid, p. 147.

51. G.N. Singh, *Landmarks in Indian Constitutional and National Development (1600–1919)*, The Indian Bookshop, 1933, p. 625.

52. Ibid., pp. 626–628.

53. Ibid., p. 174.

54. Ibid., p. 179.

55. Ibid., p. 220.

56. R.C. Majumdar, *History of the Freedom Movement in India*, Volume 2, 2nd edition, Firma K.L. Mukhopadhyay, Calcutta, 1975, p. 478.

57. Daniel Argov, 'The Ideological Differences between Moderates and Extremists in the Indian National Movement with Special Reference to Surendranath Banerjea and Lajpat Rai 1885–1919', PhD dissertation, School of Oriental and African Studies, University of London, 1964, p. 267.

58. *Proceedings of the Special Session of the Indian National Congress* held at Bombay on August 29th to September 1, 1918, p. 8.

59. Ibid., p. 12.

60. Ibid., p. 42.

61. Ibid., p. 43.

62. Ibid., pp. 57–58.

63. Ibid., p. 108.

64. Syed Sharfuddin Pirzada, 'Foundations of Pakistan', *All-India Muslim League Documents: 1906–1947*, Volume 1 (1906–1924), National Publishing House Limited, Karachi, 1969, p. 109.

65. Daniel Argov, 'The Ideological Differences between Moderates and Extremists in the Indian National Movement with Special Reference to Surendranath Banerjea and Lajpat Rai 1885–1919', PhD dissertation, School of Oriental and African Studies, University of London, 1964, pp. 267–268.

66. R.C. Majumdar, *History of the Freedom Movement in India*, Volume 2, 2nd edition, Firma K.L. Mukhopadhyay, Calcutta, 1975, pp. 479–482.

67. Syed Sharfuddin Pirzada, 'Foundations of Pakistan', *All-India Muslim League Documents: 1906–1947*, Volume 1 (1906–1924), National Publishing House Limited, Karachi, 1969, p. 447.

68. Ibid., p. 449.

69. Ibid., p. 467.

70. *Report of the Proceedings of the Thirty-Third Indian National Congress* held at Delhi on the 26th, 28th, 29th, 30th and 31st December 1918, p. 12.

71. Ibid., p. 20.

72. Ibid., pp. 32–34.

73. Syed Sharfuddin Pirzada, 'Foundations of Pakistan', *All-India Muslim League Documents: 1906–1947*, Volume 1 (1906–1924), National Publishing House Limited, Karachi, 1969, pp. 497–498.

74. Ibid., p. 500.

Chapter 8: Gandhi, Rowlatt, Government of India Act of 1919, Khilafat and Non-Cooperation (1919–1924)

1. R.C. Majumdar, *History of the Freedom Movement in India*, Volume 3, 1st edition, Firma K.L. Mukhopadhyay, Calcutta, 1963, p. 7.

2. Daniel Argov, 'The Ideological Differences between Moderates and Extremists in the Indian National Movement with Special Reference to Surendranath Banerjea and Lajpat Rai 1885–1919', PhD dissertation, School of Oriental and African Studies, University of London, 1964, p. 256.

3. R.C. Majumdar, *History of the Freedom Movement in India*, Volume 3, 1st edition, Firma K.L. Mukhopadhyay, Calcutta, 1963, p. 12.

4. S.R. Mehrotra, *India and the Commonwealth 1885–1929*, Routledge, New York, 2022, pp. 112–113.

5. Ibid., p. 113.

6. Ibid.

7. N. Niaz Ahmed, *History of Indian National Congress 1885–1950*, Aligarh Muslim University, Aligarh, 1987, p. 9.

8. Report of the Sedition Committee, 1918, published by the Superintendent of Government Printing, Calcutta. https://indianculture.gov.in/reports-sedition-committee-1918

9. Ibid., p. xv.

10. Ibid., p. 145.

11. G.N. Singh, *Landmarks in Indian Constitutional and National Development (1600–1919)*, The Indian Bookshop, 1933, p. 659.

12. Syed Sharfuddin Pirzada, 'Foundations of Pakistan', *All-India Muslim League Documents: 1906–1947*, Volume 1 (1906–1924), National Publishing House Limited, Karachi, 1969, p. 472.

13. *Proceedings of the Special Session of the Indian National Congress* held at Bombay on 29th August–1st September 1918, pp. 115–117.

14. *Report of the Proceedings of the Thirty-Third Indian National Congress* held at Delhi on the 26th, 28th, 29th, 30th and 31st December 1918, pp. 100–104.

15. B. Pattabhi Sitaramayya, *The Indian National Congress*, Volume 1 (1885–1935), S. Chand & Co., Delhi, 1969, p. 160.

16. R.C. Majumdar, *History of the Freedom Movement in India*, Volume 3, 1st edition, Firma K.L. Mukhopadhyay, Calcutta, 1963, p. 4.

17. G.N. Singh, *Landmarks in Indian Constitutional and National Development (1600–1919)*, The Indian Bookshop, 1933, pp. 671–672.

18. Ibid., p. 672.

19. Ibid.

20. Ibid., p. 673.

21. R.C. Majumdar, *History of the Freedom Movement in India*, Volume 3, 1st edition, Firma K.L. Mukhopadhyay, Calcutta, 1963, p. 5.

22. Daniel Argov, 'The Ideological Differences between Moderates and Extremists in the Indian National Movement with Special Reference to Surendranath Banerjea and Lajpat Rai 1885–1919', PhD dissertation, School of Oriental and African Studies, University of London, 1964, p. 270.

23. B. Pattabhi Sitaramayya, *The Indian National Congress*, Volume 1 (1885–1935), S. Chand & Co., Delhi, 1969, p. 161.

24. Daniel Argov, 'The Ideological Differences between Moderates and Extremists in the Indian National Movement with Special Reference to Surendranath Banerjea and Lajpat Rai 1885–1919', PhD dissertation, School of Oriental and African Studies, University of London, 1964, pp. 269–270.

25. G.N. Singh, *Landmarks in Indian Constitutional and National Development (1600–1919)*, The Indian Bookshop, 1933, p. 673.

26. Ibid., p. 674.

27. Ibid.

28. B. Pattabhi Sitaramayya, *The Indian National Congress*, Volume 1 (1885–1935), S. Chand & Co., Delhi, 1969, p. 162.

29. G.N. Singh, *Landmarks in Indian Constitutional and National Development (1600–1919)*, The Indian Bookshop, 1933, p. 676.

30. R.C. Majumdar, *History of the Freedom Movement in India*, Volume 3, 1st edition, Firma K.L. Mukhopadhyay, Calcutta, 1963, pp. 20–21.

31. B. Pattabhi Sitaramayya, *The Indian National Congress*, Volume 1 (1885–1935), S. Chand & Co., Delhi, 1969, p. 163.

32. G.N. Singh, *Landmarks in Indian Constitutional and National Development (1600–1919)*, The Indian Bookshop, 1933, p. 678.

33. Report of the Disorders Inquiry Committee, 1920, published by the Superintendent of Government Printing, Calcutta. https://indianculture.gov.in/report-disorders-inquiry-committee-1919-1920

34. B. Pattabhi Sitaramayya, *The Indian National Congress*, Volume 1 (1885–1935), S. Chand & Co., Delhi, 1969, p. 164.

35. G.N. Singh, *Landmarks in Indian Constitutional and National Development (1600–1919)*, The Indian Bookshop, 1933, p. 678.

36. Ibid., p. 680.

37. B. Pattabhi Sitaramayya, *The Indian National Congress*, Volume 1 (1885–1935), S. Chand & Co., Delhi, 1969, pp. 164–165.

38. R.C. Majumdar, *History of the Freedom Movement in India*, Volume 3, Firma K.L. Mukhopadhyay, Calcutta, 1963, p. 28.

39. Ibid., pp. 28, 29.

40. Ibid., p. 30.

41. Ibid., p. 29.

42. Ibid., p. 30.

43. B. Pattabhi Sitaramayya, *The Indian National Congress*, Volume 1 (1885–1935), S. Chand & Co., Delhi, 1969, p. 165.

44. R.C. Majumdar, *History of the Freedom Movement in India*, Volume 3, 1st edition, Firma K.L. Mukhopadhyay, Calcutta, 1963, pp. 34–35.

45. Ibid., p. 31.

46. G.N. Singh, *Landmarks in Indian Constitutional and National Development (1600–1919)*, The Indian Bookshop, 1933, p. 689.

47. Ibid., p. 690.

48. R.C. Majumdar, *History of the Freedom Movement in India*, Volume 3, 1st edition, Firma K.L. Mukhopadhyay, Calcutta, 1963, pp. 39–42.

49. https://api.parliament.uk/historic-hansard/lords/1919/nov/12/indian-national-congress

50. B. Pattabhi Sitaramayya, *The Indian National Congress*, Volume 1 (1885–1935), S. Chand & Co., Delhi, 1969, p. 173.

51. https://api.parliament.uk/historic-hansard/commons/1919/may/22/east-india-revenue-accounts#column_639. In Chapter 11 of the first book, I had mentioned the date of introduction of the Government of India Bill in the House of Commons as 29 May. However, it appears to have been introduced by Montagu on 22 May 1919. On 29 May, he wanted it to be taken up for the second reading, but that was pushed to 5 June 1919.

52. https://api.parliament.uk/historic-hansard/commons/1919/jun/05/government-of-india-bill

53. Daniel Argov, 'The Ideological Differences between Moderates and Extremists in the Indian National Movement with Special Reference to Surendranath Banerjea and Lajpat Rai 1885–1919', PhD dissertation, School of Oriental and African Studies, University of London, 1964, p. 269.

54. M. Rafique Afzal, *A History of the All-India Muslim League 1906–1947*, Oxford University Press, Karachi, 2013, p. 130.

55. Daniel Argov, 'The Ideological Differences between Moderates and Extremists in the Indian National Movement with Special Reference to Surendranath Banerjea and Lajpat Rai 1885–1919', PhD dissertation, School of Oriental and African Studies, University of London, 1964, p. 269.

56. G.N. Singh, *Landmarks in Indian Constitutional and National Development (1600–1919)*, The Indian Bookshop, 1933, p. 557.

57. The House of Commons was informed of the grant of Royal Assent to the Government of India Act of 1919 on 28 December 1919. https://api.parliament.uk/historic-hansard/commons/1919/dec/28/royal-assent

58. https://api.parliament.uk/historic-hansard/commons/1919/may/12/constitutional-reforms

59. https://api.parliament.uk/historic-hansard/commons/1919/may/22/east-india-revenue-accounts#column_622

60. Ibid.

61. https://api.parliament.uk/historic-hansard/lords/1919/nov/12/indian-national-congress

62. G.N. Singh, *Landmarks in Indian Constitutional and National Development (1600–1919)*, The Indian Bookshop, 1933, p. 558.

63. *Report of the Proceedings of the Thirty-Fourth Indian National Congress* held at Amritsar on the 27th, 29th, 30th and 31st December 1919 and 1st January 1920, pp. 4–7.

64. Ibid., pp. 43–44.

65. Ibid., p. 157.

66. Ibid., p. 162.

67. Daniel Argov, 'The Ideological Differences between Moderates and Extremists in the Indian National Movement with Special Reference to Surendranath Banerjea and Lajpat Rai 1885–1919', PhD dissertation, School of Oriental and African Studies, University of London, 1964, p. 273.

68. Ibid., p. 276.

69. *Report of the Proceedings of the Thirty-Fourth Indian National Congress* held at Amritsar on the 27th, 29th, 30th and 31st December 1919 and 1st January 1920, p. 115.

70. Ibid., p. 124.

71. Ibid.

72. R.C. Majumdar, *History of the Freedom Movement in India*, Volume 3, 1st edition, Firma K.L. Mukhopadhyay, Calcutta, 1963, p. 50.

73. Muhammad Naeem Qureshi, 'The Khilafat Movement in India 1919–1924', PhD dissertation, School of Oriental and African Studies, University of London, 1973, pp. 9, 10.

74. M.A. Karandikar, *Islam in India's Transition to Modernity*, Eastern Publishers, Karachi, 1968, p. 127.

75. Mushirul Hasan, *Nationalism and Communal Politics in India, 1916–1928*, Manohar Publications, Delhi, 1979, p. 54.

76. Ram Swarup, *Understanding Islam Through Hadis: Religious Faith or Fanaticism?*, Voice of India, New Delhi, 1984.

77. Arun Shourie, *The World of Fatwas or the Shariah in Action*, ASA Publications, New Delhi, 1995.

78. Syed Sharfuddin Pirzada, 'Foundations of Pakistan', *All-India Muslim League Documents: 1906–1947*, Volume 1 (1906–1924), National Publishing House Limited, Karachi, 1969, pp. 497–498.

79. Andrew C. Hess, 'The Ottoman Conquest of Egypt (1517) and the Beginning of the Sixteenth-Century World War', *International Journal of Middle East Studies*, 1973, vol. 4, no. 1, pp. 55–76.

80. Muhammad Naeem Qureshi, 'The Khilafat Movement in India 1919–1924', PhD dissertation, School of Oriental and African Studies, University of London, 1973, p. 5.

81. Ibid., p. 9.

82. Syed Tanvir Wasti, 'The Political Aspirations of Indian Muslims and the Ottoman Nexus', *Middle Eastern Studies*, September 2006, vol. 42, no. 5, pp. 709–722, p. 709.

83. Choudhry Khaliquzzaman, *Pathway to Pakistan*, Longmans, Green & Co., Lahore, 1961, p. 20.

84. Muhammad Naeem Qureshi, 'The Khilafat Movement in India 1919–1924', PhD dissertation, School of Oriental and African Studies, University of London, 1973, p. 25.

85. Ibid., p. 26.

86. Syed Tanvir Wasti, 'The Political Aspirations of Indian Muslims and the Ottoman Nexus', *Middle Eastern Studies*, September 2006, vol. 42, no. 5, pp. 709–722, p. 710.

87. Muhammad Naeem Qureshi, 'The Khilafat Movement in India 1919–1924', PhD dissertation, School of Oriental and African Studies, University of London, 1973, p. 26.

88. Ibid.

89. Mushirul Hasan, 'The Ulama and Khilafat Movement', *Economic and Political Weekly*, 16 May 1981, vol. 16, no. 20, pp. 903–905, 907–912, p. 907.

90. Ibid.

91. Mushirul Hasan, *Nationalism and Communal Politics in India, 1916–1928*, Manohar Publications, Delhi, 1979, p. 56.

92. Muhammad Naeem Qureshi, 'The Khilafat Movement in India 1919–1924', PhD dissertation, School of Oriental and African Studies, University of London, 1973, p. 26.

93. Ibid.

94. Mushirul Hasan, *Nationalism and Communal Politics in India, 1916–1928*, Manohar Publications, Delhi, 1979, p. 59.

95. Muhammad Naeem Qureshi, 'The Khilafat Movement in India 1919–1924', PhD dissertation, School of Oriental and African Studies, University of London, 1973, p. 29.

96. Ibid., p. 30.

97. Ibid., p. 31.

98. M. Rafique Afzal, *A History of the All-India Muslim League 1906–1947*, Oxford University Press, Karachi, 2013, p. 132.

99. Muhammad Naeem Qureshi, 'The Khilafat Movement in India 1919–1924', PhD dissertation, School of Oriental and African Studies, University of London, 1973, pp. 31–32.

100. Choudhry Khaliquzzaman, *Pathway to Pakistan*, Longmans, Green & Co., Lahore, 1961, p. 28.

101. Ibid.

102. Muhammad Naeem Qureshi, 'The Khilafat Movement in India 1919–1924', PhD dissertation, School of Oriental and African Studies, University of London, 1973, pp. 30–31.

103. Ibid., p. 32.
104. Mushirul Hasan, *Nationalism and Communal Politics in India, 1916–1928*, Manohar Publications, Delhi, 1979, p. 110.
105. Ibid.
106. Ibid., p. 111.
107. Ibid., p. 111–112.
108. Choudhry Khaliquzzaman, *Pathway to Pakistan*, Longmans, Green & Co., Lahore, 1961, p. 28.
109. Ibid., p. 29.
110. Muhammad Naeem Qureshi, 'The Khilafat Movement in India 1919–1924', PhD dissertation, School of Oriental and African Studies, University of London, 1973, pp. 34–35.
111. Ibid., p. 39.
112. Ibid., p. 41.
113. Ibid.
114. M.K. Gandhi, *An Autobiography or the Story of My Experiments with Truth*, translated from the original in Gujarati by Mahadev Desai, Navjivan Publishing House, pp. 489–492.
115. Gopal Krishna, 'The Khilafat Movement in India: The First Phase (September 1919–August 1920)', *The Journal of the Royal Asiatic Society of Great Britain and Ireland*, April 1968, no. 1–2, pp. 37–53, p. 37.
116. Ibid., p. 37.
117. Vasileios Th. Meichanetsidis, 'The Genocide of the Greeks of the Ottoman Empire, 1913–1923', *Genocide Studies International*, Spring 2015, vol. 9, no. 1, pp. 104-173.
118. M. Rafique Afzal, *A History of the All-India Muslim League 1906–1947*, Oxford University Press, Karachi, 2013, p. 132.
119. Muhammad Naeem Qureshi, 'The Khilafat Movement in India 1919–1924', PhD dissertation, School of Oriental and African Studies, University of London, 1973, p. 42.
120. Ibid., p. 43.
121. Ibid., p. 44.
122. M. Rafique Afzal, *A History of the All-India Muslim League 1906–1947*, Oxford University Press, Karachi, 2013, p. 132.
123. Ibid., p. 133.
124. https://www.jewishvirtuallibrary.org/text-of-the-balfour-declaration
125. Gopal Krishna, 'The Khilafat Movement in India: The First Phase (September 1919–August 1920)', *The Journal of the Royal Asiatic Society of Great Britain and Ireland*, April 1968, no. 1–2, pp. 37–53, p. 38.
126. R.C. Majumdar, *History of the Freedom Movement in India*, Volume 3, Firma K.L. Mukhopadhyay, Calcutta, 1963, p. 53.
127. Mushirul Hasan, *Nationalism and Communal Politics in India, 1916–1928*, Manohar Publications, Delhi, 1979, pp. 113–114.

128. M.K. Gandhi, *An Autobiography or the Story of My Experiments With Truth*, translated from the original in Gujarati by Mahadev Desai, Navjivan Publishing House, pp. 489–492.

129. Mushirul Hasan, *Nationalism and Communal Politics in India, 1916–1928*, Manohar Publications, Delhi, 1979, pp. 113.

130. Ibid., pp. 114–115.

131. Muhammad Naeem Qureshi, 'The Khilafat Movement in India 1919–1924', PhD dissertation, School of Oriental and African Studies, University of London, 1973, pp. 48–49.

132. Ibid., p. 50.

133. Ibid.

134. Ibid., pp. 53–54.

135. Ibid., p. 55.

136. Syed Sharfuddin Pirzada, 'Foundations of Pakistan', *All-India Muslim League Documents: 1906–1947*, Volume 1, National Publishing House Limited, Karachi, 1969, pp. 473–474.

137. Ibid., pp. 475–477, 498.

138. Gopal Krishna, 'The Khilafat Movement in India: The First Phase (September 1919–August 1920)', *The Journal of the Royal Asiatic Society of Great Britain and Ireland*, April 1968, no. 1–2, pp. 37–53, p. 38.

139. Muhammad Naeem Qureshi, 'The Khilafat Movement in India 1919–1924', PhD dissertation, School of Oriental and African Studies, University of London, 1973, p. 56.

140. Syed Sharfuddin Pirzada, 'Foundations of Pakistan', *All-India Muslim League Documents: 1906–1947*, Volume 1 (1906–1924), National Publishing House Limited, Karachi, pp 500-501

141. Ibid., p. 57.

142. Ibid., p. 58.

143. Gopal Krishna, 'The Khilafat Movement in India: The First Phase (September 1919–August 1920)', *The Journal of the Royal Asiatic Society of Great Britain and Ireland*, April 1968, no. 1–2, pp. 37 –53, p. 39.

144. M. Rafique Afzal, *A History of the All-India Muslim League 1906–1947*, Oxford University Press, Karachi, 2013, p. 134.

145. Government of Bombay, *Source Material for a History of the Freedom Movement in India*, Volume 3, Part I, Bombay, 1958–1965, p. 139, as cited by Muhammad Naeem Qureshi in 'The Khilafat Movement in India 1919–1924', PhD dissertation, School of Oriental and African Studies, University of London, 1973, p. 59.

146. Mushirul Hasan, *Nationalism and Communal Politics in India, 1916–1928*, Manohar Publications, Delhi, 1979, p. 115.

147. Ibid., pp. 116–117.

148. Muhammad Naeem Qureshi, 'The Khilafat Movement in India 1919–1924', PhD dissertation, School of Oriental and African Studies, University of London, 1973, p. 60.

149. Gopal Krishna, 'The Khilafat Movement in India: The First Phase (September 1919–August 1920)', *The Journal of the Royal Asiatic Society of Great Britain and Ireland*, April 1968, no. 1–2, pp. 37–53, p. 40.

150. Ibid., p. 39.

151. Ibid.

152. Muhammad Naeem Qureshi, 'The Khilafat Movement in India 1919–1924', PhD dissertation, School of Oriental and African Studies, University of London, 1973, p. 65.

153. Gopal Krishna, 'The Khilafat Movement in India: The First Phase (September 1919–August 1920)', *The Journal of the Royal Asiatic Society of Great Britain and Ireland*, April 1968, no. 1–2, pp. 37–53, p. 40.

154. Muhammad Naeem Qureshi, 'The Khilafat Movement in India 1919–1924', PhD dissertation, School of Oriental and African Studies, University of London, 1973, p. 69.

155. Ibid., p. 70.

156. M. Rafique Afzal, *A History of the All-India Muslim League 1906–1947*, Oxford University Press, Karachi, 2013, p. 136.

157. Gopal Krishna, 'The Khilafat Movement in India: The First Phase (September 1919–August 1920)', *The Journal of the Royal Asiatic Society of Great Britain and Ireland*, April 1968, no. 1–2, pp. 37–53, p. 41.

158. Muhammad Naeem Qureshi, 'The Khilafat Movement in India 1919–1924', PhD dissertation, School of Oriental and African Studies, University of London, 1973, p. 71.

159. Ibid., p. 73.

160. Ibid., p. 79.

161. Mushirul Hasan, *Nationalism and Communal Politics in India, 1916–1928*, Manohar Publications, Delhi, 1979, p. 155.

162. Gopal Krishna, 'The Khilafat Movement in India: The First Phase (September 1919–August 1920)', *The Journal of the Royal Asiatic Society of Great Britain and Ireland*, April 1968, no. 1–2, pp. 37–53, p. 44.

163. Ibid., p. 42.

164. *Report of the Proceedings of the Thirty-Fourth Indian National Congress* held at Amritsar on the 27th, 29th, 30th and 31st December 1919 and 1st January 1920, p. 48.

165. Syed Sharfuddin Pirzada, 'Foundations of Pakistan', *All-India Muslim League Documents: 1906–1947*, Volume 1 (1906–1924), National Publishing House Limited, Karachi, 1969, pp. 502–534.

166. Ibid., pp. 518–520.

167. Ibid., pp. 520–526.

168. Ibid., pp. 527–528.

169. Muhammad Naeem Qureshi, 'The Khilafat Movement in India 1919–1924', PhD dissertation, School of Oriental and African Studies, University of London, 1973, p. 72.

170. R.C. Majumdar, *History of the Freedom Movement in India*, Volume 3, 1st edition, Firma K.L. Mukhopadhyay, Calcutta, 1963, p. 56.

171. A.M. Zaidi, *Evolution of Muslim Political Thought in India (Volume Two): Sectarian Nationalism and Khilafat*, Michiko and Panjathan, New Delhi, 1975, pp. 513–514.

172. R.C. Majumdar, *History of the Freedom Movement in India*, Volume 3, 1st edition, Firma K.L. Mukhopadhyay, Calcutta, 1963, pp. 56–57.

173. Muhammad Naeem Qureshi, 'The Khilafat Movement in India 1919–1924', PhD dissertation, School of Oriental and African Studies, University of London, 1973, p. 84.

174. Ibid., p. 72.

175. Ibid., p. 89.

176. Mushirul Hasan, *Nationalism and Communal Politics in India, 1916–1928*, Manohar Publications, Delhi, 1979, p. 162.

177. Muhammad Naeem Qureshi, 'The Khilafat Movement in India 1919–1924', PhD dissertation, School of Oriental and African Studies, University of London, 1973, p. 90.

178. Ibid.

179. Ibid., pp. 90–91.

180. According to Majumdar, the date was 17 March 1920; however, there is no footnote in Majumdar's book to corroborate his version.

181. Gopal Krishna, 'The Khilafat Movement in India: The First Phase (September 1919–August 1920)', *The Journal of the Royal Asiatic Society of Great Britain and Ireland*, April 1968, no. 1–2, pp. 37–53, p. 46.

182. Muhammad Naeem Qureshi, 'The Khilafat Movement in India 1919–1924', PhD dissertation, School of Oriental and African Studies, University of London, 1973, p. 95.

183. M. Rafique Afzal, *A History of the All-India Muslim League 1906–1947*, Oxford University Press, Karachi, 2013, p. 139.

184. Muhammad Naeem Qureshi, 'The Khilafat Movement in India 1919–1924', PhD dissertation, School of Oriental and African Studies, University of London, 1973, p. 102.

185. R.C. Majumdar, *History of the Freedom Movement in India*, Volume 3, 1st edition, Firma K.L. Mukhopadhyay, Calcutta, 1963, p. 59.

186. Gopal Krishna, 'The Khilafat Movement in India: The First Phase (September 1919–August 1920)', *The Journal of the Royal Asiatic Society of Great Britain and Ireland*, April 1968, no. 1–2, pp. 37–53, p. 50.

187. Muhammad Naeem Qureshi, 'The Khilafat Movement in India 1919–1924', PhD dissertation, School of Oriental and African Studies, University of London, 1973, pp. 104–105.

188. Mushirul Hasan, *Nationalism and Communal Politics in India, 1916–1928*, Manohar Publications, Delhi, 1979, p. 170.

189. Muhammad Naeem Qureshi, 'The Khilafat Movement in India 1919–1924', PhD dissertation, School of Oriental and African Studies, University of London, 1973, p. 108.

190. Gopal Krishna, 'The Khilafat Movement in India: The First Phase (September 1919–August 1920)', *The Journal of the Royal Asiatic Society of Great Britain and Ireland*, April 1968, no. 1–2, pp. 37–53, p. 52.

191. R.C. Majumdar, *History of the Freedom Movement in India*, Volume 3, 1st edition, Firma K.L. Mukhopadhyay, Calcutta, 1963, pp. 62–63.

192. Ibid., p. 63.

193. Muhammad Naeem Qureshi, 'The Khilafat Movement in India 1919–1924', PhD dissertation, School of Oriental and African Studies, University of London, 1973, p. 151.

194. Ibid., p. 150.

195. *The Indian National Congress, 1920–1923*, Allahabad, 1924, p. 3.

196. Ibid., p. 153.

197. Ibid., p. 158.

198. Ibid., p. 157.

199. Ibid., p. 154.

200. Syed Sharfuddin Pirzada, 'Foundations of Pakistan', *All-India Muslim League Documents: 1906–1947*, Volume 1 (1906–1924), National Publishing House Limited, Karachi, 1969, pp. 541–544.

201. Muhammad Naeem Qureshi, 'The Khilafat Movement in India 1919–1924', PhD dissertation, School of Oriental and African Studies, University of London, 1973, p. 159.

202. Ibid., p. 169.

203. Ibid., p. 171.

204. Ibid., p. 173.

205. Ibid., p. 165.

206. Ibid., p. 176.

207. Daniel Argov, 'The Ideological Differences between Moderates and Extremists in the Indian National Movement with Special Reference to Surendranath Banerjea and Lajpat Rai 1885–1919', PhD dissertation, School of Oriental and African Studies, University of London, 1964, p. 278.

208. *Report of the Proceedings of the Thirty-Fifth Indian National Congress* held at Nagpur on the 26th, 28th, 30th and 31st December, 1920, p. 46.

209. Ibid., pp. 47–49.

210. Ibid., pp. 54–57.

211. Mushirul Hasan, *Nationalism and Communal Politics in India, 1916–1928*, Manohar Publications', Delhi, 1979, p. 172.

212. Daniel Argov, 'The Ideological Differences between Moderates and Extremists in the Indian National Movement with Special Reference to Surendranath Banerjea and Lajpat Rai 1885–1919', PhD dissertation, School of Oriental and African Studies, University of London, 1964, pp. 279–280.

213. *The Indian National Congress, 1920–1923*, Allahabad, 1924, pp. 27–32.

214. *Report of the Proceedings of the Thirty-Fifth Indian National Congress* held at Nagpur on the 26th, 28th, 30th and 31st December 1920, p. 106.

215. https://eparlib.nic.in/bitstream/123456789/760548/1/cosd_01_01_03-03-1921.pdf, pp. 349–356.

216. *Report of the Proceedings of the Thirty-Fifth Indian National Congress* held at Nagpur on the 26th, 28th, 30th and 31st December 1920, pp. 108–115.

217. Syed Sharfuddin Pirzada, 'Foundations of Pakistan', *All-India Muslim League Documents: 1906–1947*, Volume 1 (1906–1924), National Publishing House Limited, Karachi, 1969, pp. 546–547.

218. Ibid., p. 553.

219. Ibid., p. 554.

220. Muhammad Naeem Qureshi, 'The Khilafat Movement in India 1919–1924', PhD dissertation, School of Oriental and African Studies, University of London, 1973, p. 178.

221. A.M. Zaidi, *Evolution of Muslim Political Thought in India (Volume 2): Sectarian Nationalism and Khilafat*, Michiko and Panjathan, New Delhi, 1975, pp. 515–518.

222. Muhammad Naeem Qureshi, 'The Khilafat Movement in India 1919–1924', PhD dissertation, School of Oriental and African Studies, University of London, 1973, pp. 178–179.

223. Ibid., p. 186.

224. Ibid., p. 185.

225. Ibid., p. 187.

226. Ibid., p. 189.

227. Ibid., p. 191.

228. Ibid., pp. 193–194.

229. R.C. Majumdar, *History of the Freedom Movement in India*, Volume 3, 1st edition, Firma K.L. Mukhopadhyay, Calcutta, 1963, p. 64.

230. Muhammad Naeem Qureshi, 'The Khilafat Movement in India 1919–1924', PhD dissertation, School of Oriental and African Studies, University of London, 1973, p. 195.

231. Ibid., pp. 196–198.

232. Mushirul Hasan, *Nationalism and Communal Politics in India, 1916–1928*, Manohar Publications, Delhi, 1979, p. 187.

233. Ibid., p. 188.

234. Ibid., p. 205.

235. Ibid., pp. 206–207.

236. R.V. Thadani, *The Historic State Trial of the Ali Brothers and Five Others*, R.V. Thadani, Karachi, 1921, pp. 69–71.

237. Muhammad Naeem Qureshi, 'The Khilafat Movement in India 1919–1924', PhD dissertation, School of Oriental and African Studies, University of London, 1973, p. 209.

238. Ibid., p. 211.

239. Ibid., p. 212.

240. Ibid., p. 217.

241. A.M. Zaidi, *Evolution of Muslim Political Thought in India (Volume 2): Sectarian Nationalism and Khilafat*, Michiko and Panjathan, New Delhi, 1975, pp. 519–523.

242. *Report of the Proceedings of the Thirty-Sixth Indian National Congress* held at Ahmedabad on the 27th and 28th, December 1921, p. 17.

243. Ibid., p. 30.

244. Ibid., p. 48.

245. Ibid.

246. Ibid., p. 53.

247. Syed Sharfuddin Pirzada, 'Foundations of Pakistan', *All-India Muslim League Documents: 1906–1947*, Volume 1 (1906–1924), National Publishing House Limited, Karachi, 1969, p. 559.

248. Ibid., pp. 559–560.

249. Mushirul Hasan, *Nationalism and Communal Politics in India, 1916–1928*, Manohar Publications, Delhi, 1979, p. 192.

250. Syed Sharfuddin Pirzada, 'Foundations of Pakistan', *All-India Muslim League Documents: 1906–1947*, Volume 1 (1906–1924), National Publishing House Limited, Karachi, 1969, p. 562.

251. Ibid., pp. 562–563.

252. Ibid., pp. 564–565.

253. Muhammad Naeem Qureshi, 'The Khilafat Movement in India 1919–1924', PhD dissertation, School of Oriental and African Studies, University of London, 1973, p. 218.

254. Ibid., p. 219.

255. Mushirul Hasan, *Nationalism and Communal Politics in India, 1916–1928*, Manohar Publications, Delhi, 1979, p. 192.

256. Bhuwan Kumar Jha, 'Forging "Unity": Hindu Mahasabha and the Quest for "Sangathan"', *Proceedings of the Indian History Congress*, vol. 68, 2007, pp. 1069–1088.

257. Muhammad Naeem Qureshi, 'The Khilafat Movement in India 1919–1924', PhD dissertation, School of Oriental and African Studies, University of London, 1973, p. 221.

258. Ibid., p. 222.

259. Mushirul Hasan, *Nationalism and Communal Politics in India, 1916–1928*, Manohar Publications, Delhi, 1979, p. 192.

260. Ibid., p. 224.

261. Ibid., p. 225.

262. Ibid., pp. 225–226.

263. Mushirul Hasan, *Nationalism and Communal Politics in India, 1916–1928*, Manohar Publications, Delhi, 1979, p. 193.

264. Ibid., p. 193.
265. Muhammad Naeem Qureshi, 'The Khilafat Movement in India 1919–1924', PhD dissertation, School of Oriental and African Studies, University of London, 1973, p. 231.
266. Ibid., p. 232.
267. Ibid., p. 233.
268. Ibid., p. 234.
269. Ibid., p. 238.
270. Ibid., p. 241.
271. Ibid., p. 244.
272. Ibid., p. 245.
273. Ibid., p. 246.
274. Ibid., p. 247.
275. Ibid., p. 248.
276. *Report of the Proceedings of the Thirty-Seventh Indian National Congress* held at Gaya on the 26th, 27th, 29th, 30th and 31st December 1922, p. 31.
277. Muhammad Naeem Qureshi, 'The Khilafat Movement in India 1919–1924', PhD dissertation, School of Oriental and African Studies, University of London, 1973, p. 250.
278. Ibid., p. 251.
279. Ibid., pp. 253–254.
280. Lal Bahadur, *The Muslim League: Its History, Activities and Achievements*, Agra Book Store, 1954, p. 145.
281. Syed Sharfuddin Pirzada, 'Foundations of Pakistan', *All-India Muslim League Documents: 1906–1947*, Volume 1 (1906–1924), National Publishing House Limited, Karachi, 1969, pp. 566–574.
282. A.M. Zaidi, *Evolution of Muslim Political Thought in India (Volume Two): Sectarian Nationalism and Khilafat*, Michiko and Panjathan, New Delhi, 1975, pp. 524–532.
283. Muhammad Naeem Qureshi, 'The Khilafat Movement in India 1919–1924', PhD dissertation, School of Oriental and African Studies, University of London, 1973, pp. 271–272.
284. Ibid., p. 270.
285. Ibid., p. 274.
286. Ibid., pp. 278–279.
287. Syed Sharfuddin Pirzada, 'Foundations of Pakistan', *All-India Muslim League Documents: 1906–1947*, Volume 1 (1906–1924), National Publishing House Limited, Karachi, 1969, pp. 575–582.
288. Ibid., p. 578.
289. Muhammad Naeem Qureshi, 'The Khilafat Movement in India 1919–1924', PhD dissertation, School of Oriental and African Studies, University of London (1973), p. 288.
290. Ibid., p. 290.

291. Ibid., p. 293.

292. *Report of the Proceedings of the Thirty-Ninth Indian National Congress* held at Belgaum on the 26th and 27th December 1924.

293. Ibid., p. 2.

294. Ibid., p. 17.

295. Ibid., p. 22.

296. Ibid., pp. 24–26.

297. Syed Sharfuddin Pirzada, 'Foundations of Pakistan', *All-India Muslim League Documents: 1906–1947*, Volume 2 (1924–1947), National Publishing House Limited, Karachi, 1990, pp. 1–30.

298. Ibid., p. 20.

299. Ibid., p. 28.

300. A.M. Zaidi, *Evolution of Muslim Political Thought in India (Volume 2): Sectarian Nationalism and Khilafat*, Michiko and Panjathan, New Delhi, 1975, pp. 533–539.

301. Mushirul Hasan, *Nationalism and Communal Politics in India, 1916–1928*, Manohar Publications, Delhi, 1979, pp. 198–201.

Chapter 9: Malegaon, Malabar, Gulbarga and Kohat: The Two-Nation Theory in Action

1. Sir C. Sankaran Nair, *Gandhi and Anarchy*, Tagore & Co., Madras, 1922.

2. Gopal Krishna, 'Communal Violence in India: A Study of Communal Disturbance in Delhi', *Economic and Political Weekly*, 12 January 1985, vol. 20, no. 2, pp. 61–74, p. 62.

3. http://www.columbia.edu/itc/mealac/pritchett/00ambedkar/ambedkar_partition/307c.html#m01

4. Mushirul Hasan, *Nationalism and Communal Politics in India, 1916–1928*, Manohar Publications, Delhi, 1979, p. 10.

5. Sir C. Sankaran Nair, *Gandhi and Anarchy*, Tagore & Co., Madras, 1922, pp. 36–37.

6. Ibid., pp. 41–42.

7. https://api.parliament.uk/historic-hansard/lords/1921/may/04/the-armyin-india#column_183

8. R.C. Majumdar, *History of the Freedom Movement in India*, Volume 3, 1st edition, Firma K.L. Mukhopadhyay, Calcutta, 1963, p. 278.

9. *Report of the Proceedings of the Thirty-Ninth Indian National Congress* held at Belgaum on the 26th and 27th December 1924, pp. 80–81.

10. Ibid., p. 86.

11. R.C. Majumdar, *History of the Freedom Movement in India*, Volume 3, 1st edition, Firma K.L. Mukhopadhyay, Calcutta, 1963, pp. 278–279.

12. http://www.columbia.edu/itc/mealac/pritchett/00ambedkar/ambedkar_partition/307c.html#m01

13. Conrad Wood, 'The Moplah Rebellion of 1921–22 and Its Genesis', PhD dissertation, University of London, 1975, p. 12.

14. Diwan Bahadur C. Gopalan Nair, *The Moplah Rebellion, 1921*, Norman Printing Bureau, Calicut, 1923, p. 4.

15. Robert L. Hardgrave, Jr, 'The Mappilla Rebellion, 1921: Peasant Revolt in Malabar', *Modern Asian Studies*, 1977, vol. 11, no. 1, pp. 57–99, p. 58.

16. D.N. Dhanagare, 'Agrarian Conflict, Religion and Politics: The Moplah Rebellions in Malabar in the Nineteenth and Early Twentieth Centuries', *Past & Present*, February 1977, no. 74, pp. 112–141, p. 114.

17. Robert L. Hardgrave, Jr, 'The Mappilla Rebellion, 1921: Peasant Revolt in Malabar', *Modern Asian Studies*, 1977, vol. 11, no. 1, pp. 57–99, p. 60.

18. Ibid., p. 61.

19. Diwan Bahadur C. Gopalan Nair, *The Moplah Rebellion, 1921*, Norman Printing Bureau, Calicut, 1923, p. 4.

20. D.N. Dhanagare, 'Agrarian Conflict, Religion and Politics: The Moplah Rebellions in Malabar in the Nineteenth and Early Twentieth Centuries', *Past & Present*, February 1977, no. 74, pp. 112–141, p. 115.

21. Ibid., pp. 116–117.

22. Robert L. Hardgrave, Jr, 'The Mappilla Rebellion, 1921: Peasant Revolt in Malabar', *Modern Asian Studies*, 1977, vol. 11, no. 1, pp. 57–99, p. 61.

23. Diwan Bahadur C. Gopalan Nair, *The Moplah Rebellion, 1921*, Norman Printing Bureau, Calicut, 1923, p. 5.

24. William Logan, *Malabar Manual* (Volume 1), Government Press, Madras, 1887.

25. Conrad Wood, 'The Moplah Rebellion of 1921–22 and Its Genesis', PhD dissertation, University of London, 1975, pp. 16–19.

26. John J. Banninga, 'The Moplah Rebellion of 1921', *The Muslim World*, October 1923, vol. 13, no. 4, pp. 379–387, p. 380.

27. Ibid., p. 379.

28. Ibid., p. 380.

29. Conrad Wood, 'The Moplah Rebellion of 1921–22 and Its Genesis', PhD dissertation, University of London, 1975, pp. 32–33.

30. https://www.eparlib.nic.in/bitstream/123456789/782948/1/ilcd_30-04-1859.pdf, pp. 322–328.

31. Conrad Wood, 'The Moplah Rebellion of 1921–22 and Its Genesis', PhD dissertation, University of London, 1975, pp. 12–14.

32. William Logan, *Malabar Manual* (Volume 1), Government Press, Madras, 1887, pp. 560–561.

33. D.N. Dhanagare, 'Agrarian Conflict, Religion and Politics: The Moplah Rebellions in Malabar in the Nineteenth and Early Twentieth Centuries', *Past & Present*, February 1977, no. 74, pp. 112–141, p. 122.

34. Robert L. Hardgrave, Jr, 'The Mappilla Rebellion, 1921: Peasant Revolt in Malabar', *Modern Asian Studies*, 1977, vol. 11, no. 1, pp. 57–99, p. 66.

35. Diwan Bahadur C. Gopalan Nair, *The Moplah Rebellion, 1921*, Norman Printing Bureau, Calicut, 1923, p. 8.

36. Robert L. Hardgrave, Jr, 'The Mappilla Rebellion, 1921: Peasant Revolt in Malabar', *Modern Asian Studies*, 1977, vol. 11, no. 1, pp. 57–99, p. 68.

37. Conrad Wood, 'The Moplah Rebellion of 1921–22 and Its Genesis', PhD dissertation, University of London, 1975, p. 230.

38. Robert L. Hardgrave, Jr, 'The Mappilla Rebellion, 1921: Peasant Revolt in Malabar', *Modern Asian Studies*, 1977, vol. 11, no. 1, pp. 57–99, p. 66.

39. Ibid., p. 67.

40. Ibid., p. 58.

41. Ibid., p. 67.

42. Conrad Wood, 'The Moplah Rebellion of 1921–22 and Its Genesis', PhD dissertation, University of London, 1975, p. 229.

43. Robert L. Hardgrave, Jr, 'The Mappilla Rebellion, 1921: Peasant Revolt in Malabar', *Modern Asian Studies*, 1977, vol. 11, no. 1, pp. 57–99, p. 68.

44. Ibid., p. 69.

45. Diwan Bahadur C. Gopalan Nair, *The Moplah Rebellion, 1921*, Norman Printing Bureau, Calicut, 1923, p. 13.

46. Ibid., pp. 13–14.

47. Robert L. Hardgrave, Jr, 'The Mappilla Rebellion, 1921: Peasant Revolt in Malabar', *Modern Asian Studies*, 1977, vol. 11, no. 1, pp. 57–99, p. 71.

48. D.N. Dhanagare, 'Agrarian Conflict, Religion and Politics: The Moplah Rebellions in Malabar in the Nineteenth and Early Twentieth Centuries', *Past & Present*, February 1977, no. 74, pp. 112–141, p. 137.

49. Diwan Bahadur C. Gopalan Nair, *The Moplah Rebellion, 1921*, Norman Printing Bureau, Calicut, 1923, p. 18.

50. Ibid., p. 19.

51. Ibid., p. 20.

52. Ibid., p. 23.

53. Robert L. Hardgrave, Jr, 'The Mappilla Rebellion, 1921: Peasant Revolt in Malabar', *Modern Asian Studies*, 1977, vol. 11, no. 1, pp. 57–99, p. 74.

54. Diwan Bahadur C. Gopalan Nair, *The Moplah Rebellion, 1921*, Norman Printing Bureau, Calicut, 1923, p. 22.

55. Robert L. Hardgrave, Jr, 'The Mappilla Rebellion, 1921: Peasant Revolt in Malabar', *Modern Asian Studies*, 1977, vol. 11, no. 1, pp. 57–99, p. 75.

56. Ibid.

57. Ibid., p. 76.

58. Diwan Bahadur C. Gopalan Nair, *The Moplah Rebellion, 1921*, Norman Printing Bureau, Calicut, 1923, p. 28.

59. Ibid., pp. 28–29.

60. Robert L. Hardgrave, Jr, 'The Mappilla Rebellion, 1921: Peasant Revolt in Malabar', *Modern Asian Studies*, 1977, vol. 11, no. 1, pp. 57–99, p. 81.

61. Ibid., p. 80.

62. Diwan Bahadur C. Gopalan Nair, *The Moplah Rebellion, 1921*, Norman Printing Bureau, Calicut, 1923, p. 37.
63. Ibid., pp. 79–80.
64. Ibid., p. 76.
65. Ibid., p. 57.
66. Ibid.
67. Ibid., p. 58.
68. https://eparlib.nic.in/bitstream/123456789/762645/1/cosd_01_02_05-09-1921.pdf#search=null%20[1921%20TO%201929], p. 88.
69. Ibid., p. 91.
70. Ibid., p. 96.
71. Ibid., p. 100.
72. Sir C. Sankaran Nair, *Gandhi and Anarchy*, Tagore & Co., Madras, 1922, pp. 130–131.
73. Ibid., pp. 132–135.
74. Ibid., pp. 135–137.
75. Ibid., p. 137.
76. Ibid., p. 138.
77. Ibid., p. 138–139.
78. Ibid., pp. 139–142.
79. http://www.columbia.edu/itc/mealac/pritchett/00ambedkar/ambedkar_partition/307c.html#m01
80. Robert L. Hardgrave, Jr, 'The Mappilla Rebellion, 1921: Peasant Revolt in Malabar', *Modern Asian Studies*, 1977, vol. 11, no. 1, pp. 57–99, p. 57.
81. https://www.censusindia.co.in/district/malappuram-district-kerala-592.

Index